# Microsoft® Office
# FrontPage® 2003:
# The Complete Reference

## About the Authors

**Martin S. Matthews** is the best-selling author of over 50 books, including *Windows Server 2003: A Beginners Guide, Windows XP: A Beginners Guide, FrontPage 2002: The Complete Reference, Windows 2000: A Beginners Guide,* and *Office 2000 Answers: Certified Tech Support.* Martin, who has more than 40 years of computer experience, also does consulting and training on a wide variety of computer topics with a number of firms nationwide.

**Carole B. Matthews** is the best-selling author of over 30 books, including *Office 2000 Answers: Certified Tech Support, Outlook 98 Made Easy,* and *Windows 98 Answers: Certified Tech Support.* Carole, who has more than 30 years of computer experience, has been a programmer, system analyst, and vice president of software development and customer support. Carole has both written books on her own and co-authored others with Marty.

**Erik B. Poulsen** is the Senior Web Developer with Sherman Software Solutions. Erik has more than 16 years of computer experience and works with corporations developing ASP.Net and database-driven web applications. He has also collaborated with Marty on a number of book projects, including *FrontPage 2002: The Complete Reference.*

# Microsoft® Office
# FrontPage® 2003:
# The Complete Reference

Martin S. Matthews
Carole B. Matthews
Erik B. Poulsen

**McGraw-Hill**/Osborne

New York  Chicago  San Francisco
Lisbon  London  Madrid  Mexico City
Milan  New Delhi  San Juan
Seoul  Singapore  Sydney  Toronto

The **McGraw·Hill** Companies

**McGraw-Hill**/Osborne
2100 Powell Street, 10^th Floor
Emeryville, California 94608
U.S.A.

To arrange bulk purchase discounts for sales promotions, premiums, or fund-raisers, please contact **McGraw-Hill/Osborne** at the above address. For information on translations or book distributors outside the U.S.A., please see the International Contact Information page immediately following the index of this book.

**Microsoft® Office FrontPage® 2003: The Complete Reference**

1234567890 DOC DOC 019876543

ISBN 0-07-222940-3

**Publisher**
  Brandon A. Nordin

**Vice President & Associate Publisher**
  Scott Rogers

**Acquisitions Editor**
  Megg Morin

**Project Editor**
  Jennifer Malnick

**Acquisitions Coordinator**
  Athena Honore

**Technical Editor**
  John Cronan

**Copy Editor**
  Janice Jue

**Proofreader**
  Susie Elkind

**Indexer**
  Claire Splan

**Composition**
  Carie Abrew,
  George Toma Charbak

**Illustrators**
  Melinda Moore Lytle, Kathleen Fay
  Edwards, Lyssa Wald, Michael Mueller

**Series Design**
  Peter F. Hancik, Lyssa Wald

This book was composed with Corel VENTURA™ Publisher.

For John Cronan, who for many years and over many books
has maintained a careful, critical eye on their technical accuracy
while being a very good friend.

—Martin Matthews


For David and Joyce, whether messing about in boats
or dancing the night away, you'll always tell me exactly what you think.
Your friendship is my great fortune.

—Erik Poulsen

# Contents at a Glance

## Part V  Appendices

# Contents

## Part II  Creating Web Sites

---

**Part III    Working Behind the Scenes**

# Acknowledgments

The great crew at Osborne who can take a mediocre manuscript and turn it into a great book has our sincere appreciation for working so patiently and expertly with us. Megg Morin, acquisitions editor; Jenny Malnick, project editor (a particular joy to work with!); and Jan Jue, copy editor, are just a few of the many who made this book a success.

John Cronan, technical editor and friend, corrected many errors, added many tips and notes, and otherwise significantly improved the book while always being there for us. Thanks, John!

Greg Sherman, database programmer and musician extraordinaire, has provided much guidance over the years. Greg's understanding of the hidden nature of data and how to reveal its secrets constantly expands my horizons. His music accompanied much of the writing of this book and has enriched my life beyond words. Thanks, Greg!

George Henny and Jeff Wallace of WhidbeyNet, Marty's Internet service provider, have been great help over this series of books, not to mention providing a very good service. Thanks, George and Jeff!

# Introduction

Unfortunately, FrontPage comes with a slim manual that gives only the briefest of instructions. Fortunately, *Microsoft Office FrontPage 2003: The Complete Reference* fills this void by giving you a clear, concise, hands-on guide to this extremely powerful product.

## About This Book

*Microsoft Office FrontPage 2003: The Complete Reference* leads you through the planning, creation, testing, deployment, and maintenance of both intranet and Internet web sites with FrontPage. It does this using substantial real-world examples and clear, step-by-step instructions. All of the major features of FrontPage are explained and demonstrated in such a way that you can follow along and see for yourself how each is used, including database connectivity, the addition of multimedia, the creation of an e-commerce site, and the incorporation of Active Server Pages (ASP).NET, JavaScript, and Visual Basic Script. In addition, this book takes you beyond basic FrontPage web site creation and introduces you to HTML, DHTML, and XML and how to use them with FrontPage, as well as how to set up an intranet site, with and without SharePoint, how to manage Internet and intranet security, and how to publish and promote your web site. *Microsoft Office FrontPage 2003: The Complete Reference* provides the one complete reference on how to make the most of FrontPage. If you are going to purchase FrontPage, or if you already use it, you need this book!

## How This Book Is Organized

*Microsoft Office FrontPage 2003: The Complete Reference* is written the way most people learn: It starts by reviewing the basic concepts and then uses a learn-by-doing method to demonstrate the major features of the product. Throughout, the book uses detailed examples and clear explanations to give you the insight needed to make the fullest use of FrontPage.

**Part I, Getting Started**    Introduces you to web sites and FrontPage; it includes Chapters 1 through 4.

- **Chapter 1, Designing Quality Web Applications**, explores the world of the Internet and intranets and looks at what makes good web pages.

- **Chapter 2, Exploring FrontPage**, takes you on a tour of the major FrontPage features, giving you a taste of the power inherent in this product.

- **Chapter 3, Using Wizards**, shows you how to create sites and web pages with these powerful tools.

- **Chapter 4, Using Templates**, demonstrates not only the use of templates in creating both sites and web pages, but also how to create templates themselves.

**Part II, Creating Web Sites**    Demonstrates each of the major features of FrontPage by leading you through examples of their implementation; it includes Chapters 5 through 11.

- **Chapter 5, Creating and Formatting a Web Page from Scratch**, sets aside the wizards and templates and looks at the steps necessary to create a full-featured site on your own.

- **Chapter 6, Adding and Managing Hyperlinks and Hotspots**, explores how to add interactivity and interconnectedness to your site.

- **Chapter 7, Using Tables and Frames**, describes two completely different methods of segmenting a page and shows how you can make the best use of these tools.

- **Chapter 8, Working with Forms**, explains ways to let the site user communicate back to you, the site creator.

- **Chapter 9, Using Web Components**, describes how to automate some of the site creation process and extend a site's interactive features.

- **Chapter 10, Advanced Formatting Techniques**, covers customizing themes, creating and using style sheets, positioning and wrapping text, and choosing web-safe colors.

- **Chapter 11, Importing and Integrating Office and Other Files**, shows you how to use existing (or *legacy*) files in your intranet and Internet sites.

**Part III, Working Behind the Scenes**    Delves into the inner workings of a web site by exploring the languages behind and the ways of activating a site; it includes Chapters 12 through 18.

- **Chapter 12, Working with HTML**, provides an extensive introduction to the HTML language and how to use it with FrontPage.

- **Chapter 13, Using Dynamic HTML**, demonstrates how you can easily add motion and animation to your web site.

- **Chapter 14, Extensible Markup Language (XML)**, provides a thorough and usable introduction to this very powerful addition to the programming used in web sites.

- **Chapter 15, Web Scripting Languages**, describes and shows you how to use JavaScript and Visual Basic Script with your FrontPage sites.

- **Chapter 16, Active Server Pages.NET**, looks at Microsoft's newest site creation tool, ASP.NET, which uses complied programming languages in place of scripts to enhance the functionality of Active Server Pages

- **Chapter 17, Working with Databases**, introduces you to interactive databases and shows you how to incorporate them in your own FrontPage sites to dynamically change the sites' contents.
- **Chapter 18, Activating Your Webs**, describes how Java and ActiveX can be used to activate web sites and then shows you how to incorporate them in your own sites.

**Part IV, Extending Your Web Site**   Covers ways of extending and enhancing what you can do with FrontPage; it includes Chapters 19 through 23.

- **Chapter 19, Adding Multimedia to Your Webs**, shows you how to add regular and streaming audio files, both prerecorded and live, to your web site.
- **Chapter 20, Security on the Web**, looks at what the Internet and intranet security issues are and explains what you can do to minimize the risks.
- **Chapter 21, Doing E-Commerce**, explores the issues behind doing business on the Web and then explains how to build a web store.
- **Chapter 22, Setting Up an Intranet Web Site**, leads you through the steps to create an intranet in your organization and how to set up a SharePoint team collaboration site within an intranet.
- **Chapter 23, Publishing and Promoting Webs on the Internet**, looks at how to locate an Internet service provider, how to transfer your completed sites to its servers, and how to promote your sites once they're online.

**Part V, Appendices**   Concludes *Microsoft Office FrontPage 2003: The Complete Reference* with information we couldn't fit into the book.

- **Appendix A, FrontPage 2003 Installation**, provides a detailed set of instructions on how to install the FrontPage 2003, both SharePoint Team Services (SharePoint 1) and Windows SharePoint Services (SharePoint 2), and Internet Information Services (IIS).
- **Appendix B, FrontPage's Shortcut Keystrokes**, lists the shortcut keystrokes that can be used to perform many of the functions in FrontPage.
- **Appendix C, Constructing Web Templates**, shows you a thorough example of how to create a web template.

## Note on SharePoint

FrontPage 2003 can be used with either, but not both at the same time, SharePoint Team Services (STS or SharePoint 1) or Windows SharePoint Services (WSS or SharePoint 2), and you can use FrontPage 2003 without either of them. In this book we talk about using them both to give a complete coverage of the product, but you need to make a decision on which is correct for you and then pick and use one or no version of SharePoint.

If you are primarily interested in building one or more intranet sites (sites internal and unique to an organization), then you definitely want to use one of the versions of SharePoint because they add many features that enhance team collaboration. If you are building a new site that does not have a FrontPage Legacy, then you probably want to use SharePoint 2 because of the many enhancements over SharePoint 1.

If your site does have much of a FrontPage legacy—in other words, older versions of FrontPage have been used to build parts of the site—you might want to use SharePoint 1 because most of the older Web Components are still available with SharePoint 1, but not with SharePoint 2.

If you are primarily interested in building one or more Internet sites, then you are likely not very interested in either version of SharePoint. In that case, you will probably want to have the FrontPage Server Extensions (FPSE) 2002 available on the server you are using both locally to develop the site and on the server you are using to deliver the site.

Both versions of SharePoint and FPSE are discussed at length in a number of chapters in this book. Principally among these are Appendix A, which discusses the installation of both SharePoints and FPSE; Chapter 4, which talks about setting up a SharePoint site; Chapter 9, which discusses the differences in Web Components in the two SharePoints and FPSE; and Chapter 22, which discusses using both SharePoints in intranet sites.

## Conventions Used in This Book

*Microsoft Office FrontPage 2003: The Complete Reference* uses several conventions designed to make the book easier for you to follow. Among these are

- **Bold type** is used for text that you are to type from the keyboard.
- *Italic type* is used for a word or phrase that is being defined or otherwise deserves special emphasis.
- The `Courier typeface` is used for the HTML and other code that is either produced by FrontPage or entered by the user.
- SMALL CAPITAL LETTERS are used for keys on the keyboard such as ENTER and SHIFT.

When you are expected to enter a command, you are told to press the key(s). If you are to enter text or numbers, you are told to type them.

# Getting Started

In this book, you will learn how you can be part of the Internet or intranet revolution. You will learn how to use FrontPage to create and maintain a presence on the Web for your business, your organization, or for yourself. This book will take you through all the steps necessary to create your own web application—from initial design to placing your content on a web server where it can be accessed by anyone on the Web.

In the first of the four chapters of Part I, you will be introduced to the Internet and intranet, learn what makes a quality web site, and see how such a web site is designed. In Chapter 2, you will explore FrontPage 2003, looking at its components and seeing how they are used to create a web site. In Chapters 3 and 4, you will learn how to use FrontPage's wizards, themes, and templates to build a web site.

# CHAPTER

# Designing Quality Web Applications

Communication, whether it be within a small group, throughout a large organization, or among many organizations, can almost always be improved—made faster, easier to receive, and easier to respond to. The *web application,* a multimedia form of communication including text, graphics, audio, video, and scripts transmitted by computers, is the latest improvement. While computers sit on the sending and receiving ends of web communication, it is what links the computers that gives web applications one of their most important features. The link means that senders and receivers can operate independently—senders can put the web content up according to their schedule, and receivers can get it anytime thereafter. The link used for the transmission of web content is one of two forms of networking, either the public *Internet,* which uses public and private networks, including phone lines, or a private *intranet,* which uses a *local area network (LAN),* generally within an organization.

The Internet is at the foundation of a global communications revolution that has changed the way people communicate, work, and conduct business. It has made it easier and cheaper to exchange information, ideas, and products around the globe. Accessing a web site halfway around the world is as easy as accessing one across the street.

## The Internet

The Internet is a network infrastructure of computers, communications lines, and switches (really other computers) that uses a set of computer hardware and software standards, or *protocols,* which allow computers to exchange data with other computers. The computers can be in the same room, or they can be located around the world from each other. They can use the same operating system software, such as Windows Server 2003, or each can use a different computer operating system, such as the Macintosh operating system, Linux, or UNIX. The standards that make up the Internet have become a modern *lingua franca*—a language enabling any computer connected to the Internet to exchange information with any other computer also connected to the Internet, regardless of the operating systems the computers use.

The birth of the Internet can be traced back to the late 1960s, when the use of computers by the Department of Defense Advanced Research Projects Agency (ARPA) and other government agencies had expanded so much that a way for the computer systems to share data was needed. ARPANET, the predecessor to what we now know as the Internet, was created to meet this need.

Another milestone in the history of the Internet came in the mid-1980s, when the National Science Foundation (NSF) added its five supercomputing centers (NSFNET) to the Internet. This gave educational centers, the military, and other NSF grantees access to the power of these supercomputers and, more importantly, created the backbone of today's information superhighway. This backbone is made up of all the high-capacity (or wide-bandwidth) phone lines and data links needed to effectively transfer all the information now on the Internet. Until this wide-bandwidth infrastructure existed, the potential of ARPANET, NSFNET, and now the Internet couldn't be realized. As a result, by the end of the 1980s, almost all the pieces were in place for a global telecommunications revolution.

## The World Wide Web

By 1990, the Internet had grown to be a highway linking computers across the United States and around the world, but it was still a character-based system. That is, what appeared on computer screens connected to the Internet was simply text. There were no graphics or hyperlinks. A *graphical user interface (GUI)* to the Internet needed to be developed. Tim Berners-Lee, a scientist working at the European Laboratory for Particle Physics (CERN) in Geneva, Switzerland, proposed a set of protocols for the transfer of graphical information over the Internet in 1989. Other groups adopted Berners-Lee's proposals, and thus the World Wide Web was born.

The Internet is a *wide area network (WAN)*, as compared with a local area network (LAN), among computers in proximity. For computers to share information over a WAN, there must be a physical connection (the communications infrastructure created by ARPA and the NSF, and now maintained by private industry) and a common software standard that the computers use to transfer data. The physical connection depends on whether you use a modem to access the Internet, or whether your computer is part of a LAN with an Internet connection. The physical layer includes the modem or network interface card in your computer. You also need a phone or dedicated network line that connects you to the Internet backbone. In either case, your computer, connected to the Internet either with a dial-up or network connection, is capable of sharing information with any other computer connected to the Internet anywhere in the world.

**NOTE** *The term "modem," as used here, includes DSL, cable, and ISDN "adapters." Such devices provide the means to use ordinary phone lines to connect to the Internet.*

## LANs and an Intranet

As important as the Internet has become to society, local area networks have become even more important to the exchange of information and communication within organizations. LANs started out as a way to share programs and data files among several people in an organization. This was then augmented by electronic mail (e-mail) for sending and receiving messages over the LAN. Intranets were added to LANs to provide a miniature version of the World Wide Web within an organization—a place for people to post and read text and graphics documents whenever they choose.

A good example of how an intranet can be put to use is a project report. Instead of e-mailing a weekly update to a long list of potentially uninterested people (and filling up everybody's inbox in the process), you could post a web page on the intranet that would give not only the current status, but also other, more static information, such as the people working on the project, its goals, and its funding. In this way, those people who are truly interested can get the information.

With Active Server Pages (ASP, which are included with Microsoft's Internet Information Services) and Microsoft Office, even more intranet interactivity is possible. Users can send commands to a web site, which with ASP become a web application, and receive customized responses. Any Microsoft Office document can be included in a web page. Databases can be queried, and custom web pages can automatically be generated to display query results. Integrating Office and other files with your FrontPage web sites is covered in Chapter 11, Active Server Pages is covered in Chapter 16, and working with databases is covered in Chapter 17.

---

**NOTE**   *Internet Information Services (IIS) is included with Microsoft's Windows Server 2003, Windows 2000 Server, Windows NT, as well as Windows XP and 2000 Professional (limited versions). IIS and FrontPage provide all the software tools you need to set up a full-scale intranet or World Wide Web site.*

---

Except for possibly the content, there is no difference between a web site on the World Wide Web and a web site on an intranet. They are created the same way and can have the same features and components. The discussion and instructions throughout this book are aimed equally at both the World Wide Web and an intranet, and there are examples included of each. So, in learning to create a web application, you can apply that knowledge to either form of dissemination.

---

**TIP**   *Think of the Internet and a LAN as equivalent means of information transmission—one public, the other private. And think of the World Wide Web and an intranet as equivalent means of posting and reading information being transmitted over the Internet or a LAN, respectively. The World Wide Web and an intranet are just advanced electronic bulletin boards, while a web page is an electronic document posted on that bulletin board.*

---

**NOTE**   *In a unique blending of two concepts, intranets can be extended to outside users, creating an "extranet." For example, a corporation may provide other businesses, such as vendors or customers, access to a select subset of corporate data as well as a way to exchange the information.*

---

## Internet Protocols

The Internet and the Web are built upon several protocols, which can also be used in LANs and intranets:

- **Transmission Control Protocol/Internet Protocol (TCP/IP)**   The language that controls how information is packaged before being transferred between computers connected through the Internet or a LAN.

- **Hypertext Transfer Protocol (HTTP)**   The language the computers use to exchange information on the Web or an intranet.

- **Hypertext Markup Language (HTML)**   The programming language used to create the documents that are distributed on the Web or an intranet and displayed on your monitor. Chapter 12 discusses HTML in depth.

- **Extensible Markup Language (XML)**   The second-generation programming language used to create and display Internet and intranet documents. XML is discussed in Chapter 14.

## TCP/IP

To transfer information over the Internet or within a LAN, several requirements must be met. These include a way to assign each computer or site on the network a unique address (just like having a unique postal address), as well as a means of "packaging" the information for transmission. The Transmission Control Protocol and the Internet Protocol handle these functions.

### Internet Protocol

The foundation of the system is the Internet Protocol (IP). The IP converts data into packets and provides an address for each site on the Internet. *Packets* are like the pages of a book. An entire book contains too much information to be printed on one page, so it is divided into multiple pages. This makes the information in the book much more manageable. The Internet Protocol does the same thing with the information in a file slated to be transmitted over the Internet or a LAN. It divides the information into packets that can be handled more easily by the network.

The other primary function of the IP is to provide addresses for the computers connected to the Internet. Each computer needs its own *IP address*—a group of four decimal numbers that provides a unique address for the computer. Examples of IP addresses are 198.68.191.10 and 204.250.144.70. These IP addresses are actually decimal representations of single 32-bit binary numbers. While a computer may be comfortable with 11000110 01000100 10111111 00001010 or 11001100 11111010 10010000 01000110 as an address, most people find decimal numbers easier to work with. This system of numbering allows for about 4.3 billion ($2^{32}$) possible combinations. If you are setting up a web server, you will need to get an IP address. You may also need a domain name. A *domain name* is a unique name that identifies a computer or network, much like the name of a city in a postal address, and is matched to a unique IP address. Examples of domain names are "microsoft.com" and "whidbey.net." The ".com" extension identifies the domain as commercial, while ".net" identifies an Internet service provider or ISP. Other domain extensions include ".org" for organizations, ".edu" for educational networks, and ".gov" for government agencies. These extensions are assigned by Internet registrars, a list of which can be found at the Internet Network Information Center (InterNIC, **http://www.internic.net**). Your Internet service provider (ISP) can help you get an IP address and domain name. You can also have a new web site located in an existing domain. If you will be using an existing web server, the network administrator or webmaster will be able to tell you what the domain name and IP addresses are.

*TIP*   *If the name you want is already used with a .com, .edu, .gov, .org, or .net extension, you can register a name with such extensions as .aero, .arpa, .biz, .coop, .info, .int, .museum, .name, or .us. Some foreign registrations, such as .cc, .to, .co.uk, and .org.uk can be registered at **http://www.register.to**. These are foreign registrations, but they are still legitimate domain names that you can use. The extension ".cc" is for the Cocos (Keeling) Islands, and ".to" is for Trinidad and Tobago. Domainit.com (**http://www.domainit.com**) provides a registration site for a number of extensions including .com, .org, .net, .cc, .to, .ac, and .sh and provides a means for listing other extensions.*

## Transmission Control Protocol

While the Internet Protocol provides the basics for sharing information over the Internet, it leaves some things to be desired. The two most important objectives are ensuring that all the packets reach their destination and that they arrive in the proper order. This is where the Transmission Control Protocol (TCP) steps in. To understand how it works, assume you want to send a book to someone, and you have to mail it one page (or packet) at a time. Also assume that there are no page numbers in the book.

How will recipients know that they have received all the pages, and how will they know the proper order of the pages? TCP solves these problems by creating an "envelope" for each packet generated by the IP. Each envelope has a serialized number that identifies the packet inside it. As each packet is sent, the TCP assigns it a number that increases by one for each packet. When the packets are received, the numbers are checked for continuity and sequence. If any numbers are missing, the receiving computer requests that the missing packet be re-sent. If the packets are out of sequence, the receiving computer puts them back in order. TCP also makes sure the information arrives in the same condition it was sent (in other words, that the data was not corrupted in transit).

TCP/IP provides the basic tools for transferring information over the Internet. The next layer up the ladder is the Hypertext Transfer Protocol, the traffic director for the Web.

*NOTE*   *To set up an intranet on a LAN, you must add the TCP/IP protocols to the existing networking protocols—possibly either IPX/SPX (Integrated Packet Exchange/ Sequenced Packet Exchange) or NetBEUI (NetBIOS Extended User Interface)—on both the server and all clients. Chapter 22 tells you how to do this.*

## Hypertext Transfer Protocol

The Hypertext Transfer Protocol (HTTP) is the heart of the World Wide Web and is also used with an intranet. HTTP composes the messages and handles the information that is sent between computers on the Internet using TCP/IP. To understand how HTTP works, you first need to understand the nature of client/server relationships.

### Client/Server Relationships

The basic function of the Internet or a LAN is to provide a means for transferring information between computers. To do this, one computer (the *server*) will contain information, and another (the *client*) will request it. The server will receive and process a client's request and transfer the information. The server may be required to process the request before it can be filled. For example, if the request is for information contained in a database, such as a request submitted to a web search engine, the server would first have to extract the information from the database before it could be sent to the client.

The passing of information between a client and a server has six basic steps:

1. A connection is made between the client and the server. TCP/IP handles this.

2. The client creates a request to the server in the form of an HTTP message.

3. The request is sent to the server using TCP/IP.

4. The server processes the request and creates a response to the client, again in the form of an HTTP message.

5. The response is sent to the client using TCP/IP.

6. TCP/IP terminates the connection between the client and the server.

TCP/IP creates the connection between the client and the server, and HTTP composes the request for information and the response from the server. This is how HTTP is used to transfer information over a TCP/IP connection.

To access information on the Web or an intranet, you need an application that can send requests to a server as well as process and display the server's response. This is the function of web browsers. The two most common web browsers are Microsoft's Internet Explorer and Netscape's Navigator/Communicator.

---

**NOTE**   *Recent releases of both Microsoft's browser, Internet Explorer, and Netscape's browser, Navigator, have grown into integrated suites of applications. Microsoft has kept the name "Internet Explorer" for their browser suite while Netscape renamed theirs "Communicator." Netscape Navigator is available both as a stand-alone browser and as part of Communicator. The term "Netscape Navigator," or just "Netscape," is used to refer both to the stand-alone Navigator and the browser component of Communicator.*

## Hypertext Markup Language

The parts of the Web or an intranet covered so far, TCP/IP and HTTP, control how information is transferred over the network. Hypertext Markup Language (HTML) is the component that controls how the information is displayed. The information sent from a web server is an HTML document. Here's what a simple HTML document looks like:

```
<HTML>
<HEAD>
<TITLE>A Simple HTML Document</TITLE>
</HEAD>
<BODY>
<H1>A Simple HTML Document</H1>
<P><B>This text is bold</B> and <I>this text is italic</I>.</P>
</BODY>
</HTML>
```

Figure 1-1 shows how a web browser displays this HTML document. Web browsers interpret the HTML document and display the results on your monitor. HTML files are simple ASCII text files that contain formatting tags controlling how information (text and graphics) is displayed and how other file types are executed (audio and video files, for example).

HTML tags are usually used in pairs. An HTML document must begin with the <HTML> opening tag and end with the </HTML> closing tag. The <HEAD></HEAD> tags enclose

**FIGURE 1-1**
A browser
displaying the
Simple HTML
document

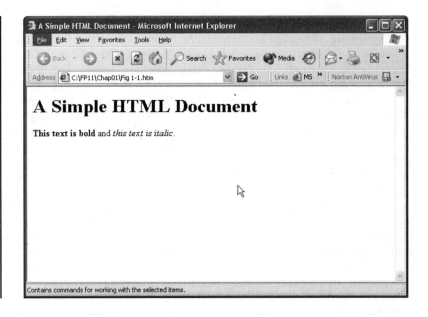

information about the beginning of a web page, such as the title, which is defined by the
<TITLE></TITLE> tags and displayed in the title bar of the web browser. The body of the web
page is enclosed by the <BODY></BODY> tags. The <H1></H1> tags define the enclosed text
as a level-1 heading. The <B></B> and <I></I> tags, respectively, define text as bold or italic, as
you saw in the preceding listing. Each paragraph is usually enclosed in the <P></P> tags.

**NOTE**    *HTML tags are not case-sensitive. They can be upper- or lowercase, or mixed case, such
as <Body>.*

In the early days of the Web, these tags were typed in using a simple text editor to create
web pages. This was time-consuming and not much fun. Today, you can use FrontPage,
a true WYSIWYG (what you see is what you get) HTML editor, to create your web pages.
Gone are the days when you had to learn all the HTML tags and proper syntax. With
FrontPage, you design a page, and the proper HTML is created automatically. It's never
been easier to create your own web site.

# What Is a Web Page?

A web application consists of one or more web pages that are interconnected. Since the focus
of this book is how to create web applications that are collections of web pages, here is a more
detailed definition of what a web page is. A good way to think of it is that a *web page* is a text
file containing Hypertext Markup Language (HTML) formatting tags, and links to graphics
files and other web pages. The text file is stored on a *web server* and can be accessed by other
computers connected to the server, via the Internet or a LAN. The file can be accessed by the
use of *web browsers*—programs that download the file to your computer, interpret the HTML
tags and links, and display the results on your monitor. Another definition is that a web page
is an interactive form of communication that uses a computer network.

There are two properties of web pages that make them unique: they are interactive and they can use multimedia. The term *multimedia* is used to describe text, audio, animation, and video files that are combined to present information—for example, in an interactive encyclopedia or a game. When those same types of files are distributed over the Internet or a LAN, you can use the term *hypermedia* to describe them. With the World Wide Web, it is now possible to have true multimedia over the Internet. However, unless your clients have a high-speed service, such as the Integrated Services Digital Network's (ISDN's) 128-Kbps service or Digital Subscriber Line (DSL) from 56 Kbps to over 1 Mbps, downloading the large hypermedia files can take too long to routinely use them. On most LANs, which are considerably faster, this is much more feasible, but there are still limitations and a potential need to keep the LAN open for high-volume data traffic.

Web pages are interactive to allow the reader or user to send information or commands back to the web site that hosts the web application. For example, the popular Google web search engine searches the Google database (over 3 billion web pages) of web sites. You can use this and other search engines to locate sites on the Web. From this web page, you can simply enter text to be searched for, or with Advanced Search, you can select which part of the Internet to search, which languages, specific dates, security filtering of adult sites, and finer definition of the keywords that the search will be based on, plus more. When you click the Google Search button, the information you've entered is sent to the Google web server. The database is then searched, and the results are used to create a new web page, which is displayed by your web browser. Figure 1-2 shows the results of a search using the keyword "FrontPage."

Each web page has an address called the *uniform resource locator (URL)*, which is displayed in the Address *combo box* (a combination of a text box and a drop-down list) at the top of the screen (below the toolbar). A URL is the path on the Internet to a specific web page (for instance, the URL for Google's home page is **http://www.google.com**) and is used the same way you use a pathname to locate files on your computer. In this case, the URL tells you that the web page is located on a web server with the domain name "google.com" connected to

**FIGURE 1-2**

Google web page created to display results of search

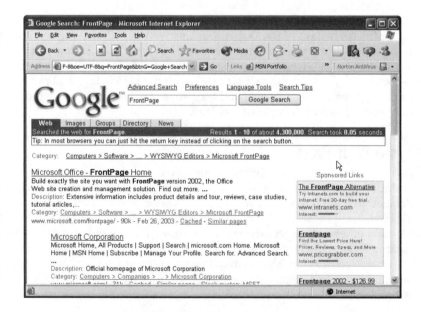

the World Wide Web ("www"). While a *domain* is two or more networked computers, the *domain name* provides a single address to access the network from the Internet. The network's domain server, meanwhile, routes the request to the correct place within the network. The actual filename of the *home page* (the top-level page of the web, which usually serves as a table of contents for the web) is usually either Default.htm or Index.htm (or Default.asp or Index.asp when using Active Server Pages, see Chapter 16). The default web page filename is set on a web server. This is the page that will be displayed if no web page filename is specified. On a LAN, the URL is similar; it uses the server name in a format like **http://*servername/folder/ homepage filename*.** The *servername* is the functional equivalent of the domain name in this case. The *homepage filename* can also be left off if it is the default filename since it is implied by being unstated.

---

**NOTE**   *Web pages located on web servers using the UNIX operating system generally have an .html extension, while web pages located on Windows web servers generally have an .htm extension. Active Server web pages have an .asp extension. Also, not all URLs include the "www." This is determined by how the URL is programmed into the network routers. Routers perform the task of matching IP (Internet Protocol) addresses to domain names. It's a good idea to have your Internet service provider (ISP) program your domain name both with and without the "www" in their routers. IP addresses and domain names were covered in the "TCP/IP" section earlier in this chapter.*

---

Google found about 4,300,000 web pages containing the keyword "FrontPage." The web page created by the Google server displays the title of each web page, an excerpt from the text on the page, and the URL for the page. The title of the page is displayed in a different color than the other text and is underlined. This indicates it is a *hyperlink*. Clicking a hyperlink will cause your browser to load the location (web page) specified in the hyperlink. The hyperlink may take you to an actual location, or *bookmark*, within the same document, the way a bookmark works in a word processor file, or it may link you to a web site anywhere in the world. In fact, if a web page doesn't have an obvious identifier to its location, you may not even be aware of what country the web server you are connected to is in. You may start "surfing" the Web by clicking hyperlinks on various pages to follow a train of thought and end up "traveling" around the world.

---

**TIP**   *With the Microsoft Internet Explorer (3.0 or later) and Netscape Navigator (3.0 or later) browsers, it is not necessary to enter* **http://** *in the Address box. With Microsoft's Internet Explorer(IE) 3.0 or later, you can also access a search engine by typing* **go***, followed by the keywords in the Address box—for example,* **go FrontPage** *(without the "http://" prefix). In IE 5.0 and later, you need only type* **FrontPage** *and click Go on the right of the Address box. In Netscape 6.0 or later, you can type* **FrontPage** *and click Search to access a search engine and see sites that relate to the word "FrontPage."*

---

**NOTE**   *Hyperlinks do not have to be underlined, although they should be displayed in a color different from the body text. With Microsoft Internet Explorer, you can use the Internet Options option in the View menu (IE 4.0) or Tools menu Internet Options Advanced tab (IE 5.0 and later) to control whether hyperlinks will be underlined, as well as what color they should be displayed in (Internet Options | General tab | Colors button).*

When you submit keywords or other information to a web site, such as Google, you are actually running an application on the web server. Web servers can also download applications—for example, a Java applet or an ActiveX control—to your computer. *Java* is a programming language that extends the flexibility and functions of the Web. *Applets* are small programs that are downloaded to your computer and then executed. *ActiveX controls* are similar in use and function to Java applets, but are written in programming languages such as Visual Basic. Java applets and ActiveX controls are used to add games, chat, menus, and other interactive components to web pages. You do not have to know how to program in Java or Visual Basic to use a Java applet or ActiveX control—a growing library of applets and controls is already available on the Web. A good place to start looking for Java applets is the Java home page, **http://www.java.sun.com**, or the Gamelan home page, **http://www.gamelan.com**. For ActiveX controls, Microsoft's web site, **http://www.microsoft.com**, is the place to start. Java and ActiveX are described in Chapters 15 and 18, as are Visual Basic Scripting Edition (VBScript) and JavaScript.

---

**TIP** *You can turn support for Java applets on or off in Internet Explorer by opening the Internet Options dialog box from the View menu (IE 4.0) or Tools menu (IE 5.0 and later), selecting the Advanced tab, and clicking the Java JIT Compiler Enabled check box. With IE 6 and later, these are off by default. In Netscape Navigator 4.5, you can turn support for Java applets and JavaScript on or off by opening the Network Preferences dialog box from the Options menu, selecting the Languages tab, and then clicking the Enable Java and Enable JavaScript check boxes. In Netscape Communicator and Navigator 4.0 or later, Java and JavaScript support are turned on or off by opening the Preferences dialog box from the Edit menu, selecting Advanced in the Category list box, and then clicking the Enable Java and Enable JavaScript (Native Object Scripting) check boxes.*

---

**NOTE** *In later releases of Internet Explorer 6, Microsoft no longer includes its JIT compiler. But you can enable/disable Active Scripting and Scripting of Java Applets in Internet Options | Security | Custom Level | Scripting.*

As you can see, the World Wide Web is a flexible and powerful means of communication. Next, look at how you can design and create a web application to use this powerful medium.

## Designing Quality Web Applications

To many, web application design is limited to what is often called the look-and-feel of the web pages—things like where you put the navigation bar or buttons, what kind of graphics you should use, and how they should be arranged on the web page. Good web design, though, also means having a clear understanding of the goals of the web application and a good feeling for the information's organization in the web application.

A lot of decisions about the design of the page are based on general design practices seen in the print media. The Web is its own medium with its own peculiarities. How it is different is partially based on the nature of the Internet and the World Wide Web. The differences are also caused by the medium with which you view the Web: the computer and its monitor. Understanding these differences is important because some things that work in print just do not translate well to the Web. But the Web can also do things that print cannot do. On the Web, you can read about a performer, see and hear the performer live, even interact with that performer in real time. Try that in a magazine!

Designing for a web application is also a process. You just don't decide that you are going to design a web application and start laying out a web page, expecting to end up with a usable product without going back and filling in the details numerous times. Good design, in addition to knowing your media and tools, has four major components:

- Gathering requirements
- Organizing information
- Structuring the web application
- Developing a navigation scheme

This chapter outlines a process that will take you from an initial concept to a completed web application with which you, your customer, and most importantly, the end user of the web application, can all be happy.

So where do you start? The best place is at the beginning. Ask yourself: Just why are you creating a web application?

## Gathering Requirements

Start by posing these questions to yourself:

- What is the purpose of this web application? That is, what is it supposed to do?
- What are the goals of the web application? Is it to amuse, amaze, educate, or sell a product? Is it to show off your web development skills, record a family event, or cybercast a live event?

It could be one or several of these, but the fundamental reason is to communicate, and you need to be clear on what it is you are communicating.

Most often, you are creating the web application for up to three groups of people. The first group, although often considered last, is end users. These people will not only use the web application, but also are your audience. The second group is the person or party who wants the web application built—your customer, the party for whom you, the web designer, are working. And last, and usually least, you are doing it for yourself, to create something that will be a good example of what you can do. What do all three of these groups want? What do all three need? The answers to these questions will provide the requirements for the web application. The answers, unfortunately, can also produce three *different*, often conflicting, sets of requirements.

The web developer needs to integrate these requirements and satisfy as many of them as possible before communicating effectively with the customer, so both have the same understanding of what the web application is supposed to do, what data and concepts it will communicate, and where it is taking the user. Everything that comes after this needs to be compared against these requirements. If it supports the requirements, it is the right thing to do. If it doesn't, it shouldn't be done unless you want to go back and revise the requirements.

The requirements stage will determine the content and functionality. Once this is understood, you can start gathering and organizing the contents of your web application.

## Organizing Information

Once you have defined the requirements, you have the job of collecting and organizing the contents. This means locating the images and articles that will make up the site, and then sorting them into logical groups of information. This stage, and the previous one of figuring out why you are doing the web application in the first place, are not glamorous and often are not nearly as fun as making impressive graphics, but your customer and audience will certainly appreciate it when they try to use your web application. It is here that you set the stage for the structure of your web application. Every web application presents a different problem, but there are some general approaches. Keep the end user in mind when organizing information. Does the display of information make sense? Will it enable the user to develop a mental map of the web application? And most important, can users easily find and use what they're looking for?

Following are some common ways of organizing information. They are meant to get you thinking about different ways of organizing your material, but they are not the only ways to do so. The following may not work for your project. If they don't, see if you can come up with another scheme. Again, keep the end user in mind.

There are two general classes of schemes. The first are those that rely on an obvious order such as the alphabetical order of the phone book's white pages—a place where the organization of its contents is clear. The second class are those schemes that are arranged in an order that is not so obvious—such as the phone book's yellow pages, which uses topics that may or may not be well understood.

### Obvious Order

Schemes with an obvious order are the easy ones to use. Once you decide to use one of them, organizing the material becomes a no-brainer. They do have their limitations, however, since they require that the users know what they are looking for. Three obvious orders are alphabetical, chronological, and geographical.

**Alphabetical**    The white pages of the phone book are a good example of alphabetical organization. The names are arranged in the order of the letters of the alphabet. It is easy to find a person if you know his or her name.

The drawback is that a person can be difficult to find if you don't know how to spell the name, or if you are not sure of the name, or if all you know about the person is that he or she is a web developer. Alphabetical organization can be used for arranging any list of things, from departments of a company to a list of recipes.

**Chronological**    Events, or anything that is associated with a date, lend themselves to a chronological organization. A list of concert dates is often arranged chronologically. Press releases, because they are dated, can be organized similarly. Chronological organization is useful as long as there is a clear date or time attached to what you are organizing. Figure 1-3 shows the schedule of the Seattle Mariners baseball team, arranged in chronological order.

You also need to ask yourself: Does your user want to look for a game by date? A list like this puts the priority on *when* rather than *whom*. People may find the date more important when they are looking for a specific game, but some may prefer to search by the name of the opposing team or a specific pitcher rather than by date. In this case, an additional alphabetical listing of opponents or pitchers would be more helpful.

**Geographical**    Some things are tied to a geographic location. For instance, a business may want to organize the information on its different sites according to the location of each office. Weather is also tied to this system of arrangement. When you look at a weather report, you typically want to check a specific location. The sizes of the areas may range widely—for instance, a city like Duluth as opposed to the whole continent of

**FIGURE 1-3**
A baseball team schedule arranged in chronological order

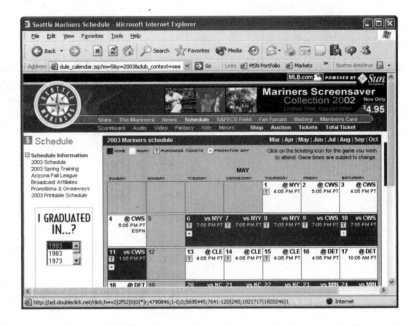

Asia—nevertheless both are geographical locations. A similar system is shown in Figure 1-4, which shows a map used to select airfares by clicking a part of the world.

### Not-So-Obvious Order
These less-obvious schemes are more difficult to set up and more open to interpretation, but people often don't know exactly what they are looking for when they begin searching.

**FIGURE 1-4**
Geographically selecting airfares

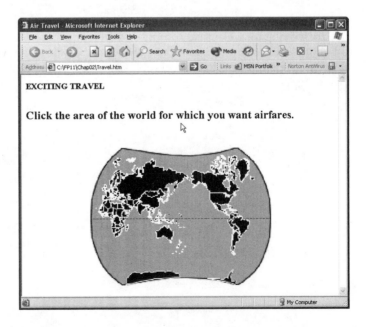

Because of that, these schemes are often very useful. Four less-obvious orders are topical, task, priority, and metaphor.

**Topical** Many, if not most, sites provide a topical index to their contents, because people tend to know the topic they are looking for rather than a specific item, and because the list of specific items is often too large to search. For example, the Amazon.com music page lists music by type, like this:

If you are looking for a classical composer, you would click Classical, and then use an alphabetical search to find the composer. If you are just looking for a classical album without a clear preference as to composer, you can click Classical, and then select from this second list of topics:

But are the topics clear? Is there a definite understanding of what constitutes "General" or "Forms & Genres"? Isn't Symphonies a form of classical music and therefore included in "Forms & Genres" (it is)? And who is included in "Essentials by Artist"? There isn't always a clear definition, but it is still useful to categorize them this way even though you may run into some gray areas. It is important to organize topics in a sensible way that makes things easy to find. It is frequently better to organize topics in order of interest rather than alphabetical order, because it allows people to quickly find what they are looking for. Try to keep the gray areas to a minimum. Keep it simple!

**Task**    Task schemes are organized around things that you do. The menus in a web browser are set up that way with selections for *File, Edit,* and *View.* Task-oriented schemes are useful if the web application is dealing with processes, tasks, or actions that you want the user to do. Task lists always start with or include a verb, like "Track," "View," "See," or "Return" in the following task list on Amazon.com:

**Priority**    Sometimes things need to be arranged around their importance or priority. If you are organizing the departments of a corporation alphabetically, you would put *Accounting* in front of the *Office of the President.* But if you are organizing by importance, or priority, the *Office of the President* will be first.

Unfortunately, this type of organizational scheme can be fraught with political implications, for what constitutes an obvious order of importance to those inside an organization may be completely different to those outside it. But if your web site aids customers looking for their own account information, Accounting would be more important than Office of the President (unless they want to complain!).

**Metaphor**    *Metaphor* is the use of one object's meaning transferred to another to make an idea easier to understand. One of the great metaphors on the computer desktop is Apple's use of the trashcan as a metaphor for deleting files. Figure 1-5 shows a site organized around metaphors.

Metaphorical organization must be used carefully because not all metaphors have the clear connection of the Macintosh trashcan. The associations people make may be unexpected, or there may be no association at all. For example, what is the Lounge in Figure 1-5? It also may not be clear what the Mailroom and the Reception areas are.

### Mixing Organizational Schemes

One of the greatest causes of confusion to the user is the mixing of organizing schemes. The organizing scheme is what helps the user create a mental map of the web application. When you mix schemes, it becomes very difficult to develop a mental map of the web application, and this causes confusion. It is the old apples-and-oranges comparison. While apples and oranges share the status of fruit, they are also dissimilar enough to be seen as completely

FIGURE 1-5
Web page options
organized
metaphorically

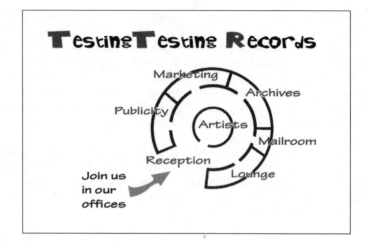

different. So it is with organizing schemes. The mind tries to make patterns out of what it sees, and when things the mind expects to be the same are actually quite different, there is a mental grinding of gears in trying to reconcile them.

Put yourself in the mind of the users. How will they perceive and use the information? Figuring this out often requires a pair of fresh eyes—something you may not be equipped with if you're too close to your material. Therefore, it's often worthwhile to get users to look at what you have done. If they don't understand your organizing scheme, don't assume it's their fault. At least you know there's a problem, and you can correct it.

With the material now organized, you can begin laying out the structure of the web application.

## Structuring the Web Application

How you have organized your material will determine how you structure your web application. Three major ways to structure a web application are hierarchical, hypertext, and database. These methods can be used alone or in different combinations, as the material requires.

### Hierarchical Structure

*Hierarchical* structure is the traditional top-down approach. It is creating high-level categories and then arranging material underneath in logical subcategories. You can divide music into:

- Types (Rock, Classical, and so on)
- Musical periods (Baroque, Classical, and so on)
- Composers of the period (Schubert, Rachmaninoff, and so on)
- Forms of music the composer wrote (symphonies, sonatas, and so on)
- Specific pieces the composer wrote (*Symphony No. 41, Eine Kleine Nachtmusik,* and so on)

Each of these is a level in a hierarchical structure, like this:

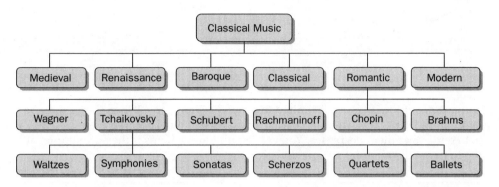

This is a very common classification scheme that most people are familiar with. It helps users create a mental map of the structure of the site that in turn helps them move around it without getting confused or lost.

In designing a hierarchical structure, keep a balance between the width and depth of the hierarchy. The extremes are the *narrow and deep hierarchy* and the *broad and shallow hierarchy*.

**Narrow and Deep Hierarchy**    A narrow and deep hierarchy is organized so that there are just a few classifications at the top. As a result, the user is forced to move down through many levels to get the information desired. This constitutes extra work for the user, making it difficult to keep track of where he or she is in the web application. In this example, it takes seven clicks to get from *Page A* to *Page B:*

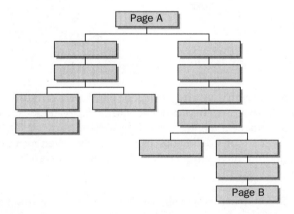

A good rule of thumb for depth is to structure the web application so that users access the information they want in three levels. Once they hit four or five levels without getting what they want, confusion and frustration set in.

**Broad and Shallow Hierarchy**    The opposite problem occurs when classifications at the top level greatly outnumber the levels underneath. This can present the user with too many choices to keep track of, as illustrated next.

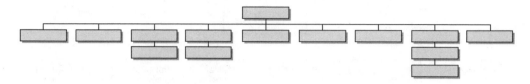

Human short-term memory is limited to around seven items. When they get to the eighth or ninth, users start forgetting earlier ones. As the items become more complex, the ability to remember them decreases. You can list up to nine items if they are simple, or keep it down to five if the material is more complex.

**NOTE**   *It is useful to draw a diagram of your site hierarchy showing the pages and their relationships to one another. You can refer to this diagram, or storyboard, when you create your web pages.*

### Hypertext Structure

Hypertext is text or images linked to other text, images, or audio or video pieces without a specific structure. These links can be located throughout the page and provide a way to move quickly to related data. This is a very nonlinear approach to structure, and looks like this:

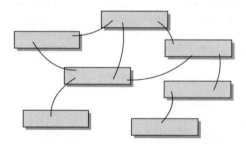

Using hypertext can be confusing and should be employed carefully. It works best as a secondary, or supporting, structure. Because of its nonlinearity, the user can get lost quickly and will find it difficult to make a mental map of the web application. Using hypertext works best if the link is to data that is at a dead end. The user would then move back to the main hierarchical structure and not have other choices that would move him or her further away.

### Database Structure

A database can be used for structuring a site by building pages of information out of a database as the information is requested. This works well for large sites with related information. Using a database can also give a lot of flexibility in presenting only the information requested. Chapter 17 describes using databases with FrontPage.

Once you have a structure for your web application, you will next develop the tools the user needs to navigate through this structure.

## Developing a Navigation Scheme

The navigation scheme of your web application is highly dependent on the structure you have developed and directly affects how the user will move around your site and access the material you present.

There are a lot of ways to provide navigation. If you have been on the Web for a while, you have seen many of them and probably have gotten lost using some. Web developers naturally tend to come up with new ways to dazzle their audience. But it is often best to keep navigation simple, or your audience may end up more confused than dazzled.

The next several sections discuss the major issues that need to be considered in setting up navigation schemes, including browser navigation, maintaining the hierarchy and structure of your design, providing flexibility in navigation, and the use of navigation bars, frames, and menus. This will be followed by an example of a navigation scheme.

### Browser Navigation

Because your web application will run inside a web browser, it has navigation tools before you even start building it. Most modern web browsers provide the following variety of tools independent of your web application:

- Forward and backward arrows, which let the user move forward and backward through web pages
- *Bookmark* or *favorites* lists, which allow the user to save the URL of a page and return directly there without going through the front door of the web application
- Page URLs, which allow the user to go directly to any page desired
- Status bar display of a link's URL, which gives users a sense of where they are going if you have carefully labeled your folders and files

However, one of the most useful navigation features that the browser provides is one that web developers underrate—the use of blue underlined type to indicate an unvisited text link, and purple underlined type to indicate a visited link. It is a navigation scheme common to all browsers and one that every beginning web user learns very early. It makes it easy to scan a page and see where the links are and to know whether you have used a particular link. No other navigation scheme provides that much information or is as universally understood. To use any other scheme is to force your user to stop and learn your scheme before being able to proceed.

### Maintaining the Design Hierarchy and Structure

Your navigation scheme will be the primary way for the user to get a sense of the structure of your web application. The user is not just using the navigation scheme to find places to go, but also to see where they are and how they are related to the rest of the web application.

When using a hierarchical structure, it is useful for the navigation scheme to reflect that. But many such schemes do not differentiate between pages that are at different levels of the hierarchy. They treat them as if they are equal, as the following hypothetical navigation bar would imply:

| <u>Music Home Page</u> | <u>Alternative</u> | <u>Blues</u> | <u>Classical</u> | <u>Folk</u> | <u>Jazz</u> | <u>Rock</u> |

One of the most recognized ways of showing hierarchy and structure is the outline form. The top levels of the hierarchy are flush left, and each level down is indented to the right an equal amount, as shown next.

1. **Classical Music**
   A. Modern
   B. Romantic
      1. Brahms
      2. Chopin
      3. Rachmaninoff
      4. Shubert
      5. Tchaikovsky
         a. *Ballets*
         b. *Quartets*
         c. *Scherzos*
         d. *Sonatas*
         e. *Symphonies*
         f. *Waltzes*
   C. Classical
   D. Baroque
   E. Renaissance
   F. Medieval

This outline structure shows where each section is and how it relates to the hierarchy. Your navigation scheme should provide this kind of information. One way is to show users where they are as they progress down a structure, which Amazon does like this:

## Providing Flexibility in Navigation

Providing flexibility in navigation is a balancing act. The web developer is acting as director of traffic when designing the navigation scheme. How do you get the users to their destination quickly without getting them lost? Let's look at the extremes in order to see the middle.

The least flexibility is provided by links that only go down or up the hierarchy tree one level at a time with no lateral links, as you can see here:

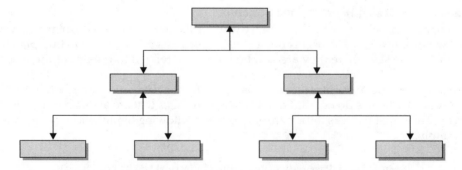

This forces the user to travel back up, one page at a time, and then back down the tree, one page at a time, to go from one part of the web application to another. This may keep users from getting lost, but they are not going to be able to get around the web application quickly.

The most flexibility, the other extreme, is when everything is linked to everything else, like this:

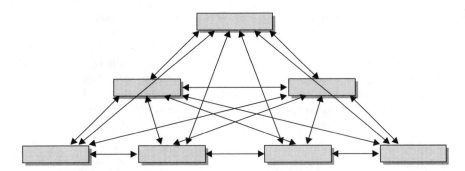

The user has maximum flexibility to move around the web application and, as you can see, a maximum opportunity for confusion. This presents the user with too much information. The trick is to balance the amount of information to maximize flexibility without confusing the user.

As you move down the hierarchy tree, it is recommended that you provide links back up the tree to the home page so that the user can quickly return there. It is also useful to provide lateral links to pages on the same level since these pages should all be related information if the hierarchy tree is set up correctly. Lateral links to pages one level above may be useful, but be careful not to offer so many choices that the user becomes confused. Here is a reasonable set of links:

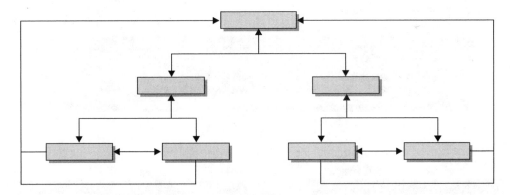

### Consistent Labeling

The labels used for navigation links need to reflect the material they represent. This isn't the place to get fancy. Users need to be able to scan your navigation links and have a clear understanding of where they are going.

If you have organized your material well, your labels should fall into place. If the material is arranged by task, the labels should identify those tasks. If it is arranged by topic, the labels should identify the topics.

The wording for the labels should be consistent. The words should use the same verb tense, punctuation, capitalization, and so on. Put yourself in the place of users new to your material: will your labels be clear to them? To make sure, keep your labels concise, but avoid abbreviations and acronyms, because the confusion they cause is always greater than the space they save.

Once you have labels that are consistent and clear, be sure to use the same ones throughout the web site. A useful technique is to repeat the navigation link in the heading of each page. This should show the links used to arrive at that page using the same labels users selected to get there. If the labels are different, users will think they have clicked the wrong link and gone to the wrong page. As important, if users are not where they want to be, they are reminded of the choices they made and can go back and change those choices.

### Navigation Bars

When you have come up with a navigation scheme and identified all the labels for the links, you need to determine where to put the links. The simplest answer is to gather all the navigation links on a *navigation bar,* which is a set of buttons or text links that allow you to jump to another place in your web application. Navigation bars can be on the top, the bottom, the left side, or the right side of a web page. The major concern is that the location is consistent. Every page must use the same scheme for navigation. The home page defines where it is and what it looks like. All the other pages of the web application should follow that lead.

There are certain limitations with navigation bars on top of the page. The horizontal layout makes it difficult to show hierarchy, and the width of the page limits the entries in the navigation bar unless you go to a smaller font. The top navigation bar can be in the way of the object of the page, which is its content. Here are horizontal navigation bars used by MSN.com, Amazon.com, and eBay.com:

Navigation bars on the bottom of the page should only be there if there is also one on the top. Bottom navigation bars have the same limitations as far as content, and become yet another element to maintain. There may be a bit of confusion here, too. When you look at the navigation bar, are you at the top or the bottom of the page? When the navigation bar is in one place, it acts like an anchor to the page. It becomes a consistent visual point of reference as to where you are on that page. When it is in two places, it doesn't provide that reference.

The left side of the page has become a standard place to put navigation bars. It is not so limiting on the length of the labels and gives more room to show hierarchy without getting in the way of the content. The vertical navigation bar should be placed high so that when the users are at the top of the page, they will also see the top of the navigation bar. Here are vertical navigation bars from MSN.com (CNBC content), Amazon.com, and eBay.com (many sites use both horizontal and vertical navigation bars):

Putting the navigation bar on the right side is not a common approach, but is useful in certain limited conditions. Often in a large web application, the home page becomes more of an index of links to the rest of the application. In such cases, it makes sense to use a right navigation bar to link to important pages within the web application, as long as it's set up so a user with a small display will not have to scroll horizontally.

**Text vs. Icons**    They say a picture is worth a thousand words, but it took words to say that. Try saying it in a picture. Try saying it in a small picture. Icons have limited use unless it is for a very common function, such as returning to the home page. Whenever you see an icon, there is usually a text link along with it. So what is the purpose of the icon? Typically, it is no more than eye candy, as shown here:

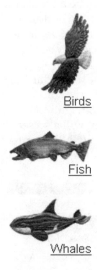

At most, an icon can supplement a text link. It can provide some additional visual information that supports the text link, but the text link is still the primary link that users will focus on. Icons also take additional time to create, maintain, and download, so use them carefully. Seldom can they stand on their own.

**Text Links vs. Navigation Buttons**    In a navigation bar, you can use either *text links* (text with a link associated with it) or *navigation buttons* (small graphics with a text label and an associated link). Navigation buttons allow the web developer to use a variety of fonts and backgrounds for the link. This is usually done for aesthetic reasons, to better integrate the text of the links into the design of the other graphics used on the page. The following example shows navigation buttons and text links:

However, whenever you use something other than the default text links, you slow users down because they have to decipher what are links and what are not. The default text link has the advantage of already being familiar to many users. Using alternatives also forfeits the ability to tell if you have used that link or not. With the default text link, the color changes when it has been used. It is also easier to modify a text link in a navigation bar than it is to change or create a new graphic every time you want to edit or insert a new link.

### Drop-Down List Boxes

Drop-down list boxes can put a number of selections or links in a small space. The drop-down list (or pull-down menu) only takes up one line until it is selected, and then it opens and displays its contents for selection. The user, though, cannot see what is in the drop-down list until it is selected. If there are several drop-down list boxes, users will not be able to remember what is in each one and will end up clicking back and forth to find what they want. The following example shows how a drop-down list box will show its information when selected:

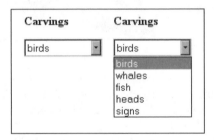

It is better to have everything the user needs clearly visible. Navigation is not a treasure hunt. Make it easy.

### Image Maps

*Image maps* (graphics with "hotspots" that are essentially links the user can click) can be especially useful if your information is organized around geographical locations. It is often not clear that an image can be used to select links. Any navigation system should be usable without instructions on how to use it. To force users to wave their cursor over an image to see if there are any links is to put them on another treasure hunt, which they don't often have the patience for. Even when it is clear that there are hotspots on the image for selection, care must be taken to make it obvious where those hotspots are. Figure 1-6 shows the image map first seen in Figure 1-4 with boxes defining the hotspots. Image maps and hotspots are discussed further in Chapters 2 and 6.

### Additional Navigation Aids

Sometimes a site map, an index, and/or a table of contents are used to supplement the primary navigation scheme. Generally speaking, these are admissions of defeat. They are mostly used as an alternative to good organization and a well-designed navigation scheme. They have possibilities as a supplement to the primary navigation scheme, but usually the time spent on these aids would be better spent on improving the organization and primary navigation.

### Subsites

Despite all the emphasis on consistency of navigation devices throughout your web application, in some situations, it makes sense to change the navigation: in large sites, particularly large

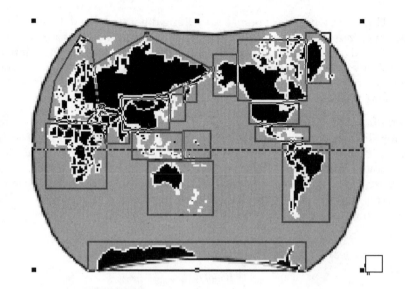

**FIGURE 1-6**
Navigational links
provided by
hotspots on an
image map

corporate intranets. As you move down the tree to lower levels, you come to sections where the content is very different and therefore needs to be organized differently. Sites representing various organizations in a large corporation are a good example of this. These become *subsites*, and there is often a lot of latitude in how they are presented, as long as they are consistent within themselves and still provide navigation links back up to the primary site.

## An Example Navigation Scheme

What does a navigation scheme that meets the preceding requirements look like? The following is an example of one acceptable scheme. Users have found it easy to use this scheme, but that doesn't mean there aren't other ways to get them to where they need to go. If you find a better way that's even easier to use, then use that scheme. Just remember to keep your focus on the needs of the user when designing it.

The following navigation scheme is for classical music. It will start at the top level and break down into individual types of music by composer. Figure 1-7, example A, shows the top level.

The home page is at the top. Since this is the page you are on, there is no link. It is frustrating to users to have the page they are on have a link to itself. The unlinked text is bold to distinguish it from the linked text. The links are all text links in the default colors, and they are all indented evenly like an outline. This shows they are all on the same level and one level below the home page in the web application hierarchy. Users will thus know where they are and what the structure is for one level.

This example is built with a table within a table to align and indent the links. The link labels are for the different standard genres of classical music. The genres are date-related and are chronologically ordered, with the most recent on top. The dates could have been included in labels. This is also a good illustration of how not to do labels. The label "Classical" appears in both levels. Since this is common usage, it is used here, but it always causes confusion.

Next, go down one level by selecting the link "Romantic." Figure 1-8, example B, shows what this would look like.

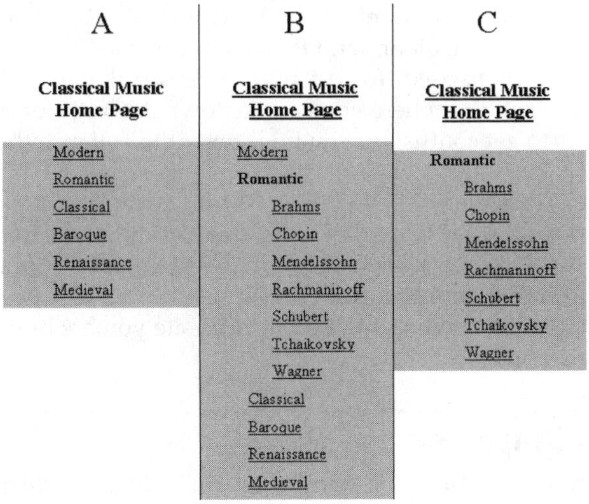

**FIGURE 1-7**
Sample navigation scheme, first and second levels

Another level opens up that has composers from the Romantic period. It is indented to the right, indicating another level down in the web application hierarchy. Since the page you are on is Romantic, it is bold and not linked. You can see where you are. You can also see the pages one level below, as well as those at the same level and the page one level up. This allows you to move down, laterally, and up.

Figure 1-7, example C, shows another way this might be displayed.

Here the lateral moves have been eliminated, but you can still move up and down from this point. Whether you want to collapse the structure like this depends on the material and the number of links shown.

Go down one more level by selecting Tchaikovsky. Figure 1-8, example A, shows what the navigation bar might now look like.

**FIGURE 1-8**
Sample navigation scheme, third level

Now Tchaikovsky is unlinked and bold since that is where the user is. The pages one level below are shown, along with those on the same level. But the pages on the level above have been collapsed. To add all the pages at that level would start overloading the navigation bar. From here you can go down, laterally, or up to either level above.

If it starts to get confusing, you might want to collapse the lateral links as in Figure 1-8, example B.

Using this scheme will tell you where you are and what is around you in the web application. You can collapse the levels, depending on the material and number of links, so that the resulting navigation bar provides the most flexibility in moving up, down, and laterally without becoming too confusing.

With the navigation bar designed for the site you are building, look at how to handle the graphics.

# Working with Graphics

The work you have done on organizing, structuring, and developing the navigation of your web application results in a site that is easy to use. All the graphics in the world are not going to make a poorly organized site any easier to use. Graphics can, however, make your site attractive and fun to use. This section will provide some highlights on graphics for the Web and encourage you to learn more.

## What Are Graphics For?

What are graphics, anyway? Most people think the term indicates pictures, icons, and illustrations. And, for the purpose of this section, that is what it will mean (in FrontPage they are all "pictures"). But the term really includes much more. Graphics include not only picture elements but also *typography*. And typography isn't just about the shapes of letters and typefaces, but also about white spaces: the spaces between letters, lines, and paragraphs. The term "graphics" refers to how all the visual elements on a page are put together.

What are graphics for? In a broad sense, they support the content. They make the information visually interesting and understandable. As such, they play a supporting role. The content—the message—is the primary consideration. If the graphics help that message jump off the page and be easily understood, they are good graphics. If they become dominant, if they are done for their own sake, if they get in the way of the message, they are bad graphics.

Do you really need graphics? Graphics—and here we shift back to their definition as picture elements—are useful but not always necessary. Using pictures and illustrations is often a case of less is more. A lone red rose lying on a white sheet becomes a much more powerful image than the same rose lying on a multicolored background. There are many beautiful pages with only text and white spaces. It is how the graphics are arranged and how they serve the content that are important.

## What Kinds of Graphics Are There?

There are several different formats for digital images. Many are unique to the graphics program they are created in, and many formats are created to be universal formats that can be read by many programs. Another consideration in digital formats is file size, because of the time they take to download on the Web. Some digital formats have been created that can compress their file size yet still retain their universal file types.

The Web uses two of these compression formats: GIF and JPEG. There are new file types being developed, but these two are the most widely supported and used today.

### GIF

The *Graphics Interchange Format (GIF)* was originally developed by CompuServe and is a *lossless* compression scheme. Lossless compression compresses and decompresses a file, restoring it without losing any pieces.

GIF files contain only 256 colors or less. This is compatible with many computers, which have 8-bit, or 256-color, displays. The user can define the 256 colors.

The way a GIF file is compressed gives us some clues as to how it is best used. The GIF compression is based on horizontal pixel transitions. It creates a number that defines the color and the horizontal span of the color. If you have a solid color or solid horizontal lines, there is a much higher compression than if you had a lot of changes in color horizontally, or have nonhorizontal lines. For example, if you took the graphic shown next with horizontal lines and compressed it as a GIF, the GIF file size would be very small. If you rotate the graphic so that it is not perfectly horizontal and compress it as a GIF this way, the file size increases to six times the size of the previous compression.

One of the best ways to keep file size down when using GIF compression is to create illustrations that use large areas of solid colors. When you have continuous-tone images, like a photograph where the colors change every pixel, the file size will be much larger.

---

***TIP***   *Create your web graphics at 72 pixels per inch since the GIF compression scheme converts your graphic to 72 pixels per inch.*

---

There are two types of GIF compressions: GIF87a and GIF89a. GIF89a builds on the older GIF87a by adding interlacing, transparency, and animation.

**Interlacing**   When an image is *interlaced,* it is loaded and displayed at full size, but not all the information is immediately used. The image appears "out of focus" and gets sharper in a series of passes. It takes four passes to display an interlaced GIF in its final form. Interlaced GIFs are only used for larger graphics that will take a while to download. They can be annoying. *Noninterlaced* GIFs are displayed one stripe at a time, and each stripe is displayed at the final resolution. FrontPage has an option that allows you to make a GIF file interlaced.

**Transparency**    *Transparent backgrounds* are created when one color in the GIF is replaced by the color of the background it is displayed on. This is a very useful feature for placing text closely around an irregular-shaped image rather than around a rectangular box that includes the original background. The fish on the left, shown next, is the full graphic where you can see the rectangular shape with its original background, while the fish on the right has a background that has been made transparent:

**Animation**    *Animated GIFs* are a series of static GIF images that are displayed in succession to create the illusion of movement. These static GIFs, along with the timing information, are saved as a single animated GIF image file. Animated GIFs are supported by Netscape Navigator 2.0 and later, and by Internet Explorer 3.0 and later. To create animated GIFs, you need a program such as the GIF Construction Set for Windows (available at **http://www.mindworkshop.com/alchemy/gifcon.html**).

---

***Tip***    *Take care to keep an animated GIF's file size down because there is no compression between GIF frames. If you create an animated GIF file with ten 4KB files, you will have a 40KB file.*

---

Animated GIFs should be used with caution. Any motion, particularly repetitive motion, is very distracting. It draws the eye every time it moves.

### JPEG

The *Joint Photographic Experts Group (JPEG)* format is a *lossy* format. Image data is lost whenever the file is compressed. Compression can be as much as 100:1. The amount of compression is variable depending on the graphic program.

Low compression will change the picture little, while high compression will cause noticeable change. Run some tests to see how much you can compress and still get an image you like.

Create your graphics at 72 pixels per inch. Unlike GIF compression, JPEG compression will retain the resolution of the original graphic. The screen resolution on a Macintosh computer is 72 pixels per inch. Windows monitors have a slightly higher resolution but use 72 pixels per inch. If you exceed 72 pixels per inch, you will create detail that will not be seen, and you will have a large file because of the extra detail.

JPEG is a 24-bit format, which gives it over 16.7 million colors. However, if the viewer's computer only has an 8-bit display, it will only display 256 colors. JPEG compression works best on continuous-tone images like photographs.

## Where Do Graphics Come From?

Graphics for your web application can be purchased as clip art, created in graphics programs, scanned from existing images, or taken with a digital camera.

## Clip Art

Clip-art images are already created and usable as they are. "Clip art" used to mean little line drawings, but that has changed. Now the term includes all manner of images including large collections of photographs on CDs.

A good place to get clip art is on the Web. Go to Yahoo and search for "clip art." You will find sites with collections of clip art that are both free or for sale over the Web. Always be aware of copyright infringement when using clip art. When people give away free clip art, it may not be theirs to give away.

---

***Tip***   *Make sure you have the right to display an image before using it in your web application.*

---

There are many collections of clip-art CDs available at computer stores. Many stock photo houses also put their photo collections on CDs or the Web. The reputable photo CDs are not inexpensive, but you do get the legal right to use high-quality images.

The big disadvantage of clip art is that you aren't the only one using these images. They show up all over the place. You've probably seen print ads from different companies that used the same image. Clip art also often has a sameness about it that screams, "clip art!" Originality does count, after all.

## Graphics Programs

When you decide you want to be original and create your own graphics, you can use one of a number of different graphics programs. The problem is that using them isn't simple. You can choose among paint programs, draw programs, and combinations of the two. (Also, image viewing programs for many different formats come with most versions of Windows with limited or no drawing capabilities.)

**Paint Programs**   Paint programs are the mainstay of web graphics. A paint program is a pixel based, or bitmap, program. Whether you bring in a photograph, put in some type, or create some shapes, the program only recognizes the pixels it has created. It doesn't know what the pixels represent. It only knows that they are pixels and what the hue and values are. This is also called *raster graphics*. But a paint program has a lot of flexibility in color control for creating web graphics. It is the best program for dealing with photographic images.

Adobe Photoshop is the most popular paint program used for web graphics. Fractal Paint offers a lot of artistic flexibility in making interesting graphics and is a good supplement to Photoshop. Corel PHOTO-PAINT is also widely used. In addition, there are some good shareware programs if Photoshop is too expensive for you. Paint Shop Pro is very popular. Microsoft PhotoDraw is another option for a paint program.

**Draw Programs**   Draw programs use vector graphics. They are not pixel based. The shapes are defined mathematically and are always editable. For example, text always remains editable (it doesn't become mere pixels when you leave the text function), and you can change the font, colors, or any other characteristic at any time. When you zoom in on a graphic created by a paint program, you see the individual pixels. There are no pixels in a draw program. You can zoom in all you want and still have sharp edges and clean colors.

However, paint programs like Adobe Photoshop are better for final preparation of web graphics since GIFs and JPEGs are pixel based. It often works well to use the draw program for elements, such as text, that it does well and then to export the file to the paint program. You can see the difference between paint and draw programs (or between raster and vector graphics) here, where the draw program with vector graphics is on the left and the paint program with bitmap or raster graphics is on the right.

CorelDRAW and Adobe Illustrator are two very popular draw programs and provide much better control of text and precise line drawings than do paint programs.

### Scanners

A scanner can be a powerful tool to use with a paint program. You can convert any image on a flat surface into a digital image. These images are scanned into bitmapped graphic files or directly into a paint program where they can be manipulated and integrated into your web graphics. Scanners often come with a low-end paint program not really suitable for serious web graphics.

While high-end flatbed scanners go for up to $600, you can get a very good scanner in the $100 to $200 range.

---

**NOTE**  *Scanners can be used for more than copying images. They also come with optical character recognition (OCR) programs. These programs scan text documents, turn them into bitmap images, compare the shapes of the text to the shapes of letters in its memory, and create a text file that can be edited in a word processing program.*

---

### Digital Cameras

One of the new ways to get images is with a digital camera, or cell phones/wireless PDAs with built-in digital cameras. Although they are more expensive than a film-based camera, they allow you to eliminate all the film and developing costs.

The images can be downloaded into your computer and manipulated with a paint program. Actually, digital cameras come with their own paint programs, but unfortunately, they are fairly simple and are no substitute for a higher-end paint program when it comes to doing web graphics.

## Monitor Color Settings

On a PC, the number of colors a monitor displays can be 16, 256, 64,000 (16-bit Medium), or 16 million (24-bit High) or more. Keep in mind, though, you have no control over how many colors will be displayed when your work goes onto the Web; some monitors still display only 256 colors.

---

**NOTE**  *You can expect the number of colors available to continue increasing; you may even have 32-bit Highest on your own system. Regardless, you can count on your work being displayed at minimum on a 256-color system.*

---

The decision you have as a web page designer is whether to limit yourself to the lowest common denominator (256-color, 800×600 resolution) or to work at a higher standard. If you are designing a simple page with minimal graphics, limiting your design to 256 colors may make sense. It ensures compatibility with virtually all the systems your work will be displayed on. (If someone is using a monochrome monitor to view your work, the point is moot, of course.)

However, if you limit yourself to 256 colors, you will not be able to effectively use scanned photographs or graphics with subtle shadings. In that case, it would be better to use at least 16-bit colors. You cannot limit yourself to the lowest common denominator in every case. You simply have to accept that your work will not look its best on lower-end systems. (The people with these systems hopefully will upgrade them as they discover that other people's systems look a lot better!)

Another point to remember about color is that every monitor will display colors a little differently. There are many factors at play here, ranging from the age of the monitor to the amount and type of light in the room. If you've worked with programs like Adobe Photoshop and have output to color printers, you know how difficult it can be to get the printed output to exactly match the colors you see on the monitor. If it's important that a particular color appear exactly the correct shade on a web page—when it's part of a logo, for example—you're simply out of luck. You can calibrate your own monitor and ensure the color is correct on a calibrated system, but once you turn it loose on the Web, you have no control over how it will appear.

If you design your web pages to be displayed on a 16-bit-color, 800×600-resolution monitor and bear in mind it will look different at other video resolutions, you can count on most people seeing your work the way you intended. See "Monitor Display" later in this chapter for more information on how a monitor's resolution affects the way a web page appears to the user.

---

*TIP*    *In calibrating your monitor, a reasonably safe middle ground is to use 24-bit color, High 1024×768 resolution.*

## Some Tips for Professional Looking Graphics

Information on creating web graphics can fill up a whole book—actually, many books, judging from bookstore shelves. But the following three tips cover a lot of mistakes that beginners make.

### Browser-Safe Palette

GIFs use up to 256 colors. But which 256 colors? It can be any 256 colors. And this is not good. You painstakingly create a graphic with a nice solid color, and when you look at it on your monitor, it isn't solid anymore. What happened? If your monitor is set to display 256 colors, it is displaying a defined set of 256 colors. And they may not be the same colors you used in your graphic.

When the computer runs across a color outside of its 256-color palette, it approximates that color by combining two of its colors. This is called *dithering*. When you look closely,

you can see that the dithered color has clumps of different-colored pixels, while the non-dithered example does not—as in the dithered example on the left.

Fortunately, browsers use a common palette of colors, although it has been reduced to 216. If you use these 216 colors when creating your graphics, they will display as solid, non-dithered colors.

FrontPage's standard palette (labeled "More Colors") displays 134 of these colors, and if you stick to these, you are safe. You can find out more about these colors at an excellent web site on web graphics: Lynda Weinman's site at **http://www.lynda.com/hex.html**.

Lynda's site has two graphics that give the red, green, blue (RGB) values for all 216 browser-safe colors. You can use these RGB values in FrontPage for defining the background colors, or in your graphics program to make sure your colors will not dither. Her site has a graphic with these colors that you can load into Adobe Photoshop and turn into a palette that will allow you to select the colors directly.

### Anti-aliasing

Why do some web graphics have little jagged edges while others do not? It is because the smooth-edged web graphics use *anti-aliasing*. GIFS are created at 72 pixels per inch.

 When you put a solid-color, irregular-shaped image on top of a solid-color background, the edge is visibly jagged. Anti-aliasing creates a buffer zone of transition colors between the shape and the background. This tricks the eye into seeing the edge as smooth. Make sure your paint program has anti-aliasing turned on when you create text and shapes. Here's a comparison of aliased (on the right) and anti-aliased characters (on the left).

### Halos

A possible problem with anti-aliasing is that halos appear around an image when the image has been anti-aliased, compressed as a GIF, and had the background made transparent. That process causes the white line or halo to appear around this fish head.

The buffer pixels between the image and background that anti-aliasing introduces are color-keyed to the background color of the graphic and not to the web page background. The solution is to not use the transparent function of GIF89a, but to create the graphic with the graphic background using the same browser-safe color as the web page background. Then the rectangular edges of the graphic blend in with the web page background. Of course, if you change the page background, you must change the graphic background.

This won't work with textured or tiled backgrounds since there is no way to control the registration of the background image with the graphic.

---

**NOTE**   *It is not recommended to use images as a background since the background then starts to fight with the foreground for attention, and it is the foreground that has your content.*

Next, put together all you have previously learned and make a set of web pages or a web application.

# Laying Out Web Pages

Successfully laying out a web page, like many things in life, is making the most of a less than perfect situation. You must live within a number of limitations inherent in the web environment, and you have a fixed set of tools and techniques that are available to you. How you use those tools and techniques to work around the limitations will determine your success.

## Layout Limitations

Layout limitations include those in the language used to create a web page (HTML), the limitations of both a browser and the user's monitor in displaying a web page, and the fact that everything on your page must be downloaded to users at the speed of their modem or LAN connection. All of these factors require serious consideration when laying out a page.

### HTML Limitations

Your web application is created using the Hypertext Markup Language (HTML). As you read earlier in this chapter, HTML is a formatting language that consists of ASCII text and, since ASCII text contains extremely limited formatting information, a system of formatting tags is used to contain the formatting information.

There are tags that begin and end a web page, define the sections of the web page, call for images, execute programs, and affect how the text is displayed. There are lots of tags, and more on the way. In fact, there are far more tags than you probably want to deal with, and with a program like FrontPage, thankfully, you really don't have to deal with tags at all. Just in case you do have to work with tags, however, Chapter 12 goes into some depth on HTML.

FrontPage is a WYSIWYG (what you see is what you get) HTML editor. It allows you to create the page layout much as you would if using a word processor—a pretty stupid word processor, unfortunately. This is not a shortcoming of FrontPage, but a result of HTML's limitations. Like everything on the Web, though, this is changing.

Although you don't need to know HTML to produce excellent web applications with FrontPage, there will come a time when you have to look at the HTML to troubleshoot something, and it is a great help to know what you are looking at. Chapter 12 will give you a good start on this.

---

**NOTE**   *As a historical aside, in the early 1980s, personal computer word processing programs were ASCII text editors with formatting tags that were interpreted when the document was printed, much like a web browser does today when it displays a web page.*

### Browser Display

When you want to view a web page on your browser, you are requesting an HTML document with its ASCII text and HTML tags. The browser analyzes the HTML tags to determine what formatting to use. When it comes to a tag that indicates an image, it sends another request to the server for that image. Each time it comes to an image, it sends another request. It goes through the entire document getting images and other secondary files, and then displays the page.

The HTML document leaves all the actual decisions of how the text is to be displayed up to the browser software. This wouldn't be a problem if there were just one browser. But there are different browser manufacturers, and each manufacturer has different versions of their browser. Each manufacturer displays the standards slightly differently, each version of a browser adheres to different standards, and each manufacturer has created their own nonstandard standards. This is why browsers display web pages differently.

If you keep to the industry-standard tags, everything works pretty well even though the display will look slightly different from one manufacturer's browser to the other. When you move into the more advanced browser capabilities, like cascading style sheets or Java scripts, you may run into headaches, because what works on one browser may not work on a competitor's. And they won't work at all on older browsers.

---

**NOTE** *Scripting languages like JavaScript and VBScript give the web developer a lot of capabilities, but there are so many problems if you use them on the client (browser) side that it is recommended you keep them on the server side.*

---

There is no one good source that documents all the differences among browsers. The only way to deal with these is to keep your design and layout simple and look at your page in recent versions of Netscape Navigator and Microsoft Internet Explorer. If you are working in an intranet environment where everyone has the same browser, you are blessed.

### Monitor Display

Monitor resolution affects the width of the page displayed. It is measured by the width of the screen in pixels by the height of the screen in pixels. The two most common displays are 800×600 pixels and 1024×768 pixels, with 1024×768 being the most common. Many monitors are now designed with higher resolutions. However, most web sites today are still created using 800×600 pixels so that they can service lower-resolution monitors. With 800×600, even a lower-resolution monitor will be able to see all the content, and the result for higher-resolution screens is that some of the space on the monitor screen is empty so that a user can see both the web site and the desktop beneath it. In other words, viewing a web site does not take the whole screen and force a user to close one window to see something else.

When you lay out your page, you need to consider that it will be viewed in various formats and that it should look good, or at least acceptable in all of them. It certainly isn't going to look the same, however. Figures 1-9 and 1-10 show how a web page designed for 800×600 will look in the two formats.

The best way to tell how your design will appear is to test it on your monitor at each of the two different sizes.

---

**TIP** *You can set the dimensions of your web browsers using the FrontPage Preview In Browser command (located on the File menu). If you are using Windows, you can often change your resolution without rebooting by right-clicking the desktop, choosing Properties, selecting Settings, and changing the Screen Resolution.*

**FIGURE 1-9**   Web page at 1024×768 resolution

**FIGURE 1-10**   Web page at 800×600 resolution

**NOTE**    *If you design your pages to display full screen on an 800×600 display, as many pages are, users viewing a 640×480 display will have to scroll both horizontally and vertically to see the full page. It can be disorienting to scroll in both directions, but there are increasingly fewer users still using 640×480. In fact, the newest Windows operating system doesn't even provide for 640×480 in its display settings.*

### Data Transfer

Making people wait too long for your web page to download is a sure way to get your viewers to go elsewhere. And elsewhere is only a few clicks of the mouse away. The two major factors in long downloads are the user's connection speed, usually a modem being the slowest, and the total file size of your HTML and any other files, such as images, that your web page uses. Some users are still on 28.8- or 33.6-Kbps modems, but these are becoming rarer. Try to keep your download times less than 30 seconds for a 56-Kbps modem user.

**TIP**    *FrontPage tells you in the lower-right corner of the Page view window the average download time of a page with a 56-Kbps or other speed modem.*

You can't control the user's modem speed, but you can control the size of the files that make up your web page. Keep unnecessary graphics off your page. When you do have graphics, make their file size small. You can keep the user's attention longer if there is text to read while images lower down in the page are loading. You also can make the page shorter so that there is not as much on it. Users are not nearly as impressed with pages that have lots of fancy graphics and a long download time as they are with quick-loading pages.

## Page Elements

There are some page elements to consider adding to every web application, such as banner identification, a simple page background, short line length, and contact information. On the other hand, some page elements such as horizontal lines and bullets may be overused and so are better left off the site.

### Banner Identification

Using a banner at the top of every page is the best way to identify the web application from page to page. Using the same banner on all the pages provides an effective visual anchor. If the banner always stays the same, and the page underneath it changes, it is clear to the users that they are in the same web application.

It also helps to visually differentiate the banner on the home page from the following pages. Making the banners on the following pages smaller than the home page helps establish the position of the home page in the hierarchy of the web application.

### Page Background

The default background for web pages is either white or, in older browsers, gray. This color can be changed to other solid colors, or an image can be tiled in the background. Always be careful about placing anything other than a solid color under text. If there is a textured background, the text can be hard to read, which will only get in the way of your message. If you use a dark color, you will have to use a lighter-colored text to make it readable. This is called *inverted text* and is more difficult to read. Using colored text on a colored background may be useful, as is inverted text, for setting off a piece of text, but for larger areas of text it is better to maximize contrast for readability. Black letters on a white background are the easiest to read. Ever read a book that was anything other than black letters on a white page? If you have (remarkable in itself since non–black-and-white books are hard to find), you have probably discovered why black on white is the standard.

### Line Length

In the early days of web design, most web developers let their text run the width of the page. Some still do. This makes reading very difficult; when the eye gets to the end of the line it is reading, it must traverse back to the beginning of the line below. If it's a long line, the eye gets confused about which is the next line, and the text becomes tiring to read. This concept is even more important for screen text than print text. It is ideal to have no more than 10 to 12 words on a line or no more than 60 to 80 characters. Putting your text in a table whose cells are 400 to 420 pixels wide will accomplish this.

### Contact Information

One of the beauties of the Web is its interactivity. The user can speak back. Provide a way for this to happen with at least an e-mail address. Let the user of the site communicate directly with the owner of the site. This is normally done at the bottom of the home page with a copyright notice and the name, address, e-mail address, and sometimes the phone number of the owner of the web application.

### Horizontal Rules

Horizontal rules are seen everywhere on the Web and are sometimes misused to separate elements of a page. Horizontal rules can separate too much. They don't cause the eye to pause; they cause it to come to a halt. It is often better to use well-organized white space for vertical separation. On the other hand, when you want the eye to make a clear break, such as between a banner and a navigation bar, or between a navigation bar and the body text, then a horizontal rule may make sense. When there is a need to provide a stronger break between two sections, you can use what's called a *printer's mark*. This is a small graphic such as a 10×10-pixel square or diamond, as shown here:

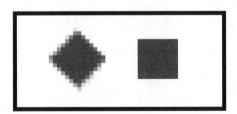

If you want to use a horizontal line, try something other than the 2-pixel-high, full-width horizontal rule. It is easy in FrontPage to make the horizontal rule thinner and shorter. Try a 1-pixel-thick rule at 50 percent of your page width.

## Page Layout

Page layout is about placing all these elements along with the text, images, and navigation bars on the page, then controlling where everything goes. This can sometimes be a sporting proposition using HTML, but there are some tools—most importantly, tables—that let you put things down and have them stay there whether the display is 640 or 1024 pixels wide.

### Tables vs. Frames

There are two basic approaches for controlling space on the web page: tables and frames. Frames, which are like pages within a page and allow separate scrolling of different areas of a web page, can lead to navigation and printing difficulties because each frame is a separate page. Frames also present problems for page layout. They take up valuable real estate on the page and do not begin to offer the much finer control that tables offer. Tables do not offer the same degree of control that you get from a page layout program such as PageMaker or Microsoft Publisher, but tables are the best tool currently available for complex layout of a web page.

FrontPage makes using tables much easier than doing it directly in HTML since the table structure is easy to see and manipulate in FrontPage's Page view. Trying to use tables extensively in a text editor is almost impossible, but in FrontPage they can be constructed quickly and modified easily. This doesn't mean that they don't do weird things sometimes, so keep checking the page in a browser to see just how it is going to look. Tables and frames are discussed in depth in Chapter 7.

### Invisible Tables

When you use tables, you normally want to turn off all borders since they often get in the way of the information they surround. Borders are a visual element meant to provide separation for the text they enclose, but unfortunately they often fight for the eye's attention. It is better to use vertical and horizontal white space to separate and accentuate a table's contents.

### Nested Tables

A table within a table is called a *nested table*. After establishing the table and cell structure for the overall page, it may be necessary to control page elements within individual cells. The indented links in the navigation bar are accomplished with nested tables. The following example, which is used to indent options in a navigation bar, has the table borders turned on so you can see where the tables are and how a nested table is used within a cell of an outer table. Nested tables are a very powerful tool for controlling the layout of a web page.

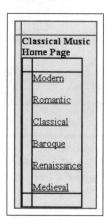

### Absolute and Relative Cell Size

Tables can be very elastic and change size based on the screen resolution and the screen area given to the browser. To control where elements are placed on the page, you need to control cell width, which can be unconstrained, relative, or absolute.

**FIGURE 1-11**
A table with unconstrained cell width in both 640×480 and 1024×768 resolutions

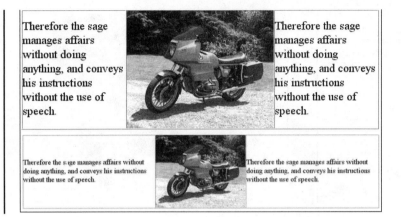

**Unconstrained Width**    If the width of the cell is not otherwise defined, the text and images that are in it will define its width. When you create a table with undefined sizes for both the table and the cells, put in text and images, and move the width of the browser in and out, you will see how the cells change their size to match the browser width. It is impossible to control how a page looks with this scheme. The top of Figure 1-11 shows how this looks in a 640×480-pixel display, while the bottom shows how it changes in a 1024×768-pixel display.

**Relative Size**    Tables and cells can be defined as a percentage of the browser width. This becomes an improvement over the undefined size, but it is still not enough to accurately control the page layout. When using relative size, the look of the page changes significantly between a 640×480 display, shown at the top of Figure 1-12, and a 1024×768 display, shown in the bottom of that figure.

**Absolute Size**    Defining table and cell size by pixels is the only way to control the placement of the elements in your page. If you apply pixel values to a table's width and move the browser width in and out, the page stays the same, independent of whether your

**FIGURE 1-12**
A table with relative cell width in both 640×480 and 1024×768 resolutions

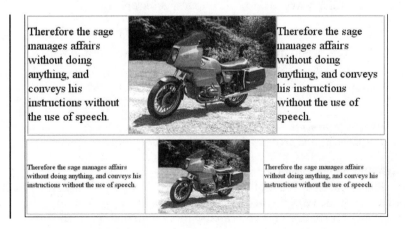

**FIGURE 1-13**
A table with
absolute cell width
in both 640×480
and 1024×768
resolutions

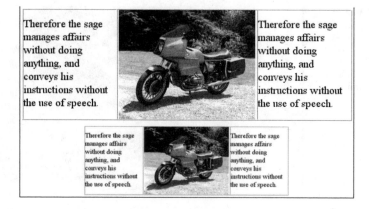

display is 640×480, as shown in the top of Figure 1-13, or 1024×768, as shown in the bottom.
The page and its elements are stable.

### Table Weirdness

Even when using absolute-size tables, weird things can happen. When you stuff a big image
in a smaller cell, the table will try to adjust the best it can. If you are using empty cells to
control vertical space, they may not display, which means you will need to specify the
height and width of the image cell. Always look at the page in a browser at several
resolutions to see how the table is going to display.

FrontPage makes it easier to work with tables, but when you start nesting tables, you
need to be careful that they don't start interacting with each other. Pay attention to the
widths of the tables being nested, and keep checking them in the browser.

## Using Color in Page Layout

Separate colors are often used to separate areas of a page. For example, a separate color can
be placed behind a navigation bar to separate it from the rest of the page, or a separate color
can be placed behind a particular article to call attention to it.

There are three ways to add colors to a specific area of a page:

- Create a background image for the page with the desired area separately colored.
- Use frames and make the desired area a separate frame with its own color.
- Create a table with the desired area occupying one or more cells containing a
  unique color.

---

***TIP***    *FrontPage presents some predefined Themes that give you color combinations (as well as
design elements and organizational attributes) for your web pages.*

### Background Image Layout

The background image layout was developed before table cells could be colored, but
it still has its uses. With it you can color any area of a page including circles and other
non-rectangular shapes, and you can use more than one color. The greatest drawback to
a background image is that an image that is balanced at 640×480 becomes unbalanced at

800×600 and very unbalanced at 1024×768 because of all the extra white space that is added at the higher resolutions. For example, if a background image is created with a colored stripe on the left that highlights a navigation bar and has a balancing white stripe on the right that fills a browser in a 640×480 display, it will become unbalanced when white space is automatically added on the right at 800×600 and 1024×768.

*TIP   The scroll bar in a browser takes up screen width, so make a background image or table no more than 600 pixels wide to fit within a 640-pixel-wide window.*

### Frame-Colored Layout

You can create separate frames only in designated areas of a page including the top, the left and right sides, and the bottom. If you want any of those areas colored, you can use a frame to do it. Each frame is considered a separate page to which you can assign a separate background color. Also, within each frame you can use a background image or a table with separate cell colors. The frame itself is the biggest drawback to this approach at coloring a part of the layout, suffering from the navigation, printing, and page space problems mentioned earlier in the chapter.

### Cell-Colored Layout

The cell-colored layout uses the coloring of individual cells within a table to highlight specific areas of a web page. Because of table offset within a page, the color cannot go to the edge or to the top of the screen. You are also limited to one color within a cell, but since there is not an image to download and possibly tile, a cell-colored layout will be a little quicker to load. Since you don't have to place your content over a background, you can center the layout, allowing white space to be added on all sides at higher screen resolutions. Figure 1-14 is an example of the cell-colored layout with the table borders turned on so you can see the added white space on either side at 1024×768.

**FIGURE 1-14**
A cell-colored layout with the table borders turned on

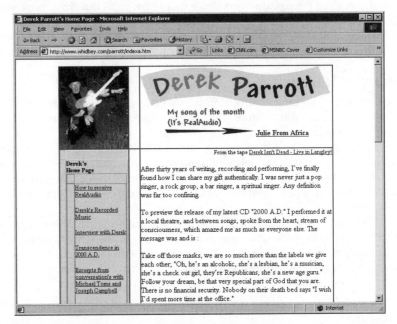

The cell-colored layout in Figure 1-14 has a fixed width and is centered in the browser. It is set up to fill the browser in a 640×480 display. In an 800×600 or 1024×768 display, there will be equal amounts of white space on the sides.

The basic table structure is a three-cell table. The left cell holds the navigation bar, and the right cell holds the content of the page. The middle cell acts as a spacer between the right and left cells. The width of this cell is adjusted so that the content has enough white space between itself and the navigation bar background. The left cell uses nested tables to lay out the content.

There is a built-in offset in a browser between the left edge of the browser and the left edge of the table, so the left side of the image is not the same as the left side of the table. To make it worse, the offset is different between Microsoft and Netscape browsers. All you can do is look at it in both browsers and adjust as best you can.

To control what you want colored, you can set the background color of a single cell, a group of cells, such as a column, or you can set the color of individual nested cells. This is the most precise of all the methods, as shown here.

## Testing, Testing, Testing

When you finish laying out the pages of your web application, you have to test them to see if they actually work the way you want them to. This process is in two parts: functional testing and usability testing.

### Functional Testing

Functional testing determines whether the web application works at the functional level. Do all the links work? Do all the forms work? Do all the images load? FrontPage offers a lot of checks to make sure everything will work well, but there is no substitute for clicking all the links and using all the functionality you have designed into the web application in a real-world situation. Surprises always appear. Use the web application under the same conditions the user will experience to see what really is going to happen.

### Usability Testing

The most enlightening testing is usability testing. This is where you test the human element—how a human other than you interacts with your web page. And those pesky humans always seem to do things you didn't expect.

Large corporations hire focus groups to do this testing. All you need to do is invite some friends over and, without telling them anything, watch them use your web application. No coaching! Look at what they click. Notice how they move through your web application. Watch when they pause. Are they confused? Are they getting the message? Again, no coaching!

They are giving you a lot of valuable information just by how they use your web application. And if they do something wrong, it is probably because your design is unclear and needs more work. Listen to them carefully. Afterwards, ask them for their comments. They may have some solutions for you.

# Keep Them Coming Back

No matter what the subject of your web site or application, you should expect competition. So how do you keep people coming back to your web application? If it is a hobby, such as an application for a favorite pastime, encouraging return visits may not matter to you. However, if you want it to be profitable, you have basically three paths: advertising, subscriptions, or selling merchandise. In each case, you need to build and maintain a high volume of users.

Good design for your web pages is only half the battle. You must also make them interesting—people must have a reason to visit them. Keep the following guidelines in mind when creating your web pages: they have to be rich in content, they must stay fresh, and they must make the user feel part of a community.

## Rich Content

First and foremost, your web application has to be rich in content, not hype. For example, if it was created for marketing your line of kayaks, include the history of the sport, stories (with photos) of trips your users have taken, information for people new to the sport, hyperlinks to related sites (not necessarily your competitors'), and anything else you can think of that might be interesting to kayakers. Don't just put up an online catalog and expect people to come back.

## Stay Fresh

Keep your web application fresh. Update as often as you can. People are not going to come back to see the same old stuff. In the kayaking example, consider updating the trips featured every month. In winter (in the Northern Hemisphere), feature trips in New Zealand. Compare your web application to a magazine—no one would subscribe to a magazine that was the same every month; it would be boring. Your web application is no different.

## Community

Design and content only go so far in getting people to come back. The final element for a successful web application is a sense of community. The Web is not a one-way environment. It allows the user to respond back to the owners of the web application and also to other users.

There are four tools that can help you achieve this: Instant Messaging, guest books, message boards, and chat.

- **Instant Messaging**  A popular way to communicate with persons working at their computers at the same time. When this feature is enabled, you will see a small message that tells you when another person has signed onto his or her computer. You can send and receive messages to two or more persons in real time.

- **Guest books**  The simplest way for the user to interact with the owner of the web application and other users. Users enter their comments in a form, and these comments are added on top of a page with the other users' comments.

- **Message boards**  The familiar electronic bulletin boards that have been a mainstay of electronic communication. By creating a place for your users to post their ideas and engage in conversation with other users, you give them an additional reason to come back to your site often. With FrontPage's Discussion Web (see Chapter 3), you can easily create your own message boards.

- **Chat**   A more immediate form of message board. The conversation takes place in real time, with each user's comments appearing on the other users' screens shortly after they are typed in. Due to the inevitable delays, this can be similar to having a conversation at a party, with several conversational threads going at once. You must be careful with chat rooms to stay focused on supporting your application, or it can get out of control. You need to monitor what is going on. FrontPage's Discussion Web can also be used for this purpose.

The proper balance of design, content, and community is the foundation of a successful web application.

## Do It!

Putting together a useful web application can be a lot of work. There's a lot to know, but the best way to learn it is to just do it. Build your web application, and see what works and what doesn't work. Change it and remember what to do for the next time. Not all web applications need to be high-powered business applications. You could just be putting up pictures of your daughter's wedding, or your child's first birthday, or pictures of your vacation.

You can communicate throughout the world using the Web. This book will show you how to do it using FrontPage.

# CHAPTER 2

# Exploring FrontPage

Microsoft FrontPage is an authoring and publishing system for creating and delivering formatted content over the Internet or over a local area network (LAN). FrontPage provides the means to design, organize, and deliver an online application, called a *web*, which may be one or more pages on the Internet's World Wide Web (the *Web*) or on a LAN's intranet. To both create and deliver web content requires two or, for the best results, four major modules:

---

**NOTE** *In this book, we use the terms "web application," "web," and "web site" to mean the same. They can be used interchangeably.*

- **FrontPage** Allows you to create, format, and lay out text; add pictures created in or outside of FrontPage; establish hyperlinks; and organize your webs and their links by using several views of the pages in a web in a drag-and-drop environment.

- **A web server such as Microsoft's Internet Information Services (IIS)** Included in 2000 Server (IIS 5.0), Server 2003 (IIS 6), and in a limited edition in Windows XP Professional (IIS 5.1). A web server allows you to directly deliver your webs to someone seeking them and provides file-management support for your webs.

- **FrontPage Server Extensions** Used in previous releases of FrontPage, it is available for most popular web servers, and adds the functionality needed to implement the interactive parts of a FrontPage web. It ran with SharePoint 1 used in FrontPage 2002. FrontPage Server Extensions are replaced in FrontPage 2003 with Windows SharePoint Services (SharePoint2). FrontPage Server Extensions are no longer being upgraded. Instead, Windows SharePoint Services are the preferred vehicle to add interactive web features. However, if you have older web sites created with FrontPage Server Extensions, you may prefer to continue using that.

- **SharePoint** A web-based program for collaboration set up and customized with FrontPage. In addition, FrontPage makes use of some of the SharePoint facilities in its templates and wizards.

## Creating a Web

The FrontPage process of creating a web is unique. The following steps provide an overview:

1. Plan the web: what the goals are; what text, pictures, forms, and hyperlinks it will contain; how it will flow; how the user will get around; and roughly what the pages will look like, including which areas on all pages will be fixed and which will be variable (for example, company name and address on all web pages would be fixed, while the name of the web page would vary).

2. If desired, in FrontPage create a Dynamic Web Template, which will define a master page containing the fixed and variable areas, style theme, and any other text, hyperlinks, or design elements that are consistently displayed throughout the web site.

3. In FrontPage, create the structure of the new web by using a wizard and/or template, or simply by starting with a blank page. If desired, you can also import existing webs into yours. Attach the Dynamic Web Template if you created one to help define the basis of the web site.

4. Open FrontPage's Tasks view and create the items you want to include on the list of tasks to be completed before your web is ready to publish. If you used a wizard to create your structure, you will automatically have items in the Tasks list you can edit.

5. Open FrontPage's Folders view and double-click the first page you want to work on to open it in Page view.

6. In FrontPage's Page view, enter, format, and position the text you want to use. Insert the pictures, sound, video, hyperlinks, frames, tables, and forms.

---

**NOTE**   *In FrontPage, you can directly edit HTML, DHTML, or XML code as well as the scripting languages and the Active Server Pages (ASP.NET). You can see how to do this in depth in Chapters 12 to 16. Later in this chapter, you will see how to view/edit the HTML, DHTML, and XML code.*

---

7. As each page is completed, save it and mark the task as complete. From Folders view, select the next page you want to work on and open it in Page view.

8. Periodically open a web browser such as Microsoft Internet Explorer or Netscape Navigator from Page view using the Preview In Browser (where "Browser" is replaced with the name of the default browser you are using) toolbar button, and look at the web you are creating. (Better yet, use both browsers to see what your web will look like.) This allows you to test the full functionality of your web with your local web server. You will be able to see and interact with the web as the user will. You can then revise the web by changing or updating the content, adjusting the page layouts, and reordering the pages and sections using one or more of the FrontPage views.

9. In FrontPage's Reports view, look for errors and potential problems with the web in the reports that are available on files, links, tasks, and themes.

10. In FrontPage's Hyperlinks view, verify the hyperlinks that you have placed in your web.

11. When you are satisfied with your web, publish it using Remote Web Site view on the server from which you want to make it available.

12. Using your browser, download, view, and manipulate the web as the user would. Note the load times and the impression you are getting of the web. Ask others to view and use your web and to give you their impressions and suggestions.

13. Revise and maintain the web as necessary, either by directly editing the copy on the server, or by editing your local copy and then replacing the server copy.

---

***TIP***   *If someone other than you has permission to edit a web you are about to work on, you should import the current version from the server and then edit it, rather than trusting the copy on your local machine. This avoids the "Twilight Zone Effect," where more than one person edits a web simultaneously.*

Creating a web with FrontPage gives you important advantages over using other authoring systems. You can

- Graphically visualize and organize a complex web with a number of pages, images, and other elements by using Folders view

- Create and edit a complex web page in a WYSIWYG (what you see is what you get) environment by using Page view without having to use or know HTML, the language of the Web

- Easily edit HTML code and see the results using a split pane that shows the design of the page in one pane and the code creating it in another

- Easily manage the tasks that are required to build a web, who has responsibility for them, and their completion by using Tasks view

- Quickly create an entire web, a page, or an element on a page by using wizards or templates

- Easily add interactive functions such as forms, text searches, and discussion forums without the use of programming by using Web Components

- Integrate your web with a database

- Work with and maintain a SharePoint Services web site (you'll read about SharePoint later in this chapter)

- Directly view and use a web on your hard disk by using a local web server

FrontPage is a true client/server application that provides all of the pieces necessary to create and deliver formatted text and graphical information over both a LAN and the Internet. FrontPage is the client side, while a combination of a web server (IIS) and the FrontPage Server Extensions (or SharePoint Services) constitutes the server side.

## FrontPage Views

FrontPage offers eleven different views you can use when creating or managing a web:

- **Page view**   Contains four views that you can access by way of a view bar at the bottom of the pane:

  - **Design view**   Allows you to create and edit a web page by adding and laying out formatted text, pictures, sounds, video, frames, tables, forms, hyperlinks, and other interactive elements. Page view provides a WYSIWYG editing environment where you can edit new webs and existing webs, including those created elsewhere on the Web. In Page view you can use page wizards, templates, and themes, attach Dynamic Web Templates, apply Web Components for interactive functions, create forms and tables, add image maps with clickable hotspots, and convert popular image formats into GIF and JPEG formats used on the Web.

  - **Split view and Code view**   Allow access to the HTML code. With the Split view, you can see both the Design and the Code views, each in their own pane. You can work with the design of the web and its code at the same time. The Code view displays the HTML code in a full pane view where you can edit it at will.

  - **Preview view**   Displays the web using the default browser. With a simple click you can see how your web will look using a browser.

---

**TIP**   *You can display a pseudo-XML view by choosing View | Toolbars | XML View. It contains a toolbar that allows you to Reformat XML or to Verify Well-formed XML code.*

---

- **Folders view**   Allows you to look at and manage an entire web from its files and folders level.

- **Reports view**   Allows you to look at a Site Summary, Shared Content reports such as Dynamic Web Templates or Themes, Files reports on Recently Added or Changed Files or Older Files, Problems reports such as Slow Pages or Unlinked Files, Workflow reports such as Review Status or Publish Status, and Usage reports showing a variety of web site usage and hit counts, including statistics on referring domains and uniform resource locators (URLs) and browsers used. Thirty-one reports are available from the Reports view.

- **Navigation view**   Allows you to check and change the hierarchy of pages that determine the way a user would get from one page to another and then back to the home page using a drag-and-drop technique.

- **Hyperlinks view**   Allows you to check and organize the hyperlinks in a web in a drag-and-drop environment.

- **Tasks view**   Displays the Tasks list, allows you to track the tasks required to produce a web, identifying who is responsible for them, their priority, and status.

- **Remote Web Site view**   Provides a way for you to open and view files and folders in a remote site, and to coordinate files and folders between a local and remote site. You can use this when you publish a web site, for instance, or synchronize files between two locations.

In the next several sections of this chapter, you will further explore the FrontPage views. While it is not mandatory, it will be beneficial if you are looking at these on your own computer. To do that, start FrontPage by opening the Windows Start menu, choosing All Programs, choosing Microsoft Office, and selecting Microsoft Office FrontPage 2003.

## Page View

When you first start FrontPage, Page view (Design) is normally the view that you will see. If you have chosen to use a template or a wizard to create a web, or you have imported a web, FrontPage may open in Folders view. In that case, double-click the page you want to work on to open it in Page view. You can also choose Page in the View menu. In any case, when you are in Page (Design) view, you'll see a window that looks very much like most word processors—in particular, Microsoft Word—as you can see in Figure 2-1. This is where you can enter and edit text. It is also where you can add pictures, frames, tables, forms, sound, video, hyperlinks (including hotspots on pictures), and active Web Components to your page, as you'll read about in a moment.

As you read in Chapter 1, a web page is a lot of HTML (Hypertext Markup Language) and a little bit of text. If you use a normal word processor or text editor (without any optional HTML features added) to create a web page, you must learn and use HTML. With the

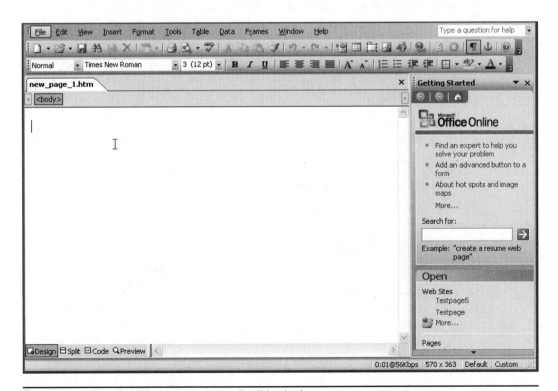

**FIGURE 2-1**    FrontPage Page view, where all editing is done

FrontPage Page view, you don't need to know HTML. You simply enter the text you want, format it using normal word processing formatting tools, and add pictures, tables, forms, and other elements. As you are doing this, FrontPage is generating the HTML for you. However, if you want to edit the code, you easily can. The code is displayed by clicking either Split to see both the Design pane and a Code view, or just Code to see only the HTML code created by the features on the web page. Creating a web page complete with HTML code is no harder than creating and formatting any other document, and what you see on the screen is very close to what you would see in a web browser. Not only does Page view convert the text and formatting that you enter to HTML, but you can also import RTF, ASCII, and Microsoft Office files into Page view, and they will have the HTML added to them.

---

***TIP*** *If you are comfortable with directly editing HTML, you can do so in the Split or Code views of Page view. If you're not familiar with editing HTML, directly changing the HTML could create a problem by changing the page in unintended ways.*

## Formatting Text

The formatting that is available from Page view is quite extensive, but it is limited to the type of formatting that is available with HTML. For example, HTML predefines a number of formatting styles whose names and definitions are unique to the Web. Some formatting tags are dependent on the web browser being used to display your web page. For example, both Internet Explorer and Netscape Navigator accept a Font tag that allows you to change the font (for example, <FONT FACE="Arial">*text to be formatted*</FONT>), but other browsers may not. Some of the paragraph styles supported in FrontPage are described in Table 2-1 and shown in Figure 2-2. They are applied from the Style drop-down list on the left of the Formatting toolbar.

---

***TIP*** *To have text displayed in a specified font, the browser must support the Font tag, and the specified font must be installed on the user's computer. More information about using fonts on the Web, as well as a selection of fonts that can be downloaded, can be found on Microsoft's web site, **http://www.microsoft.com/truetype/**.*

**TABLE 2-1**
Paragraph Styles

| Paragraph Style | How It Looks |
|---|---|
| Normal | Displayed with the proportional font, normally Times New Roman. |
| Formatted | Displayed with the fixed-width font, normally Courier. |
| Address | Displayed with the proportional font in an italic style. Often used to display information on how to contact the owner of the web. |
| Heading 1–6 | Displayed with the proportional font in a bold style in six sizes. |

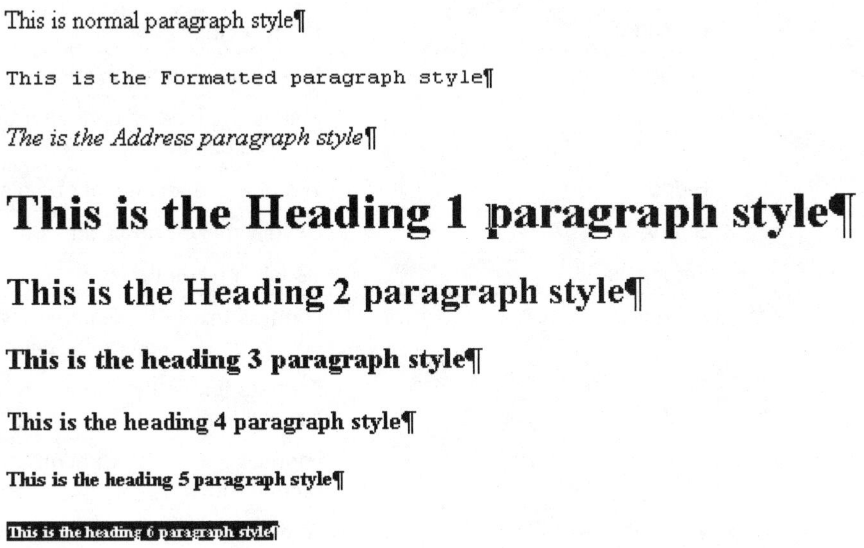

This is normal paragraph style¶

```
This is the Formatted paragraph style¶
```

*The is the Address paragraph style*¶

# This is the Heading 1 paragraph style¶

## This is the Heading 2 paragraph style¶

### This is the heading 3 paragraph style¶

This is the heading 4 paragraph style¶

This is the heading 5 paragraph style¶

This is the heading 6 paragraph style¶

---

**FIGURE 2-2**    Examples of the paragraph styles

---

**NOTE**   *The Formatted paragraph style is the only tag that allows you to use multiple spaces in text. HTML throws out all but one space when it encounters multiple spaces, except when the Formatted style is used. This can be used for forms, to get labels to right-align and text boxes to left-align. You can also use tables to align labels and form fields (see Chapters 7 and 8).*

Any of the paragraph styles can use left, center, right, or justify (both left and right) paragraph alignment applied either from the Paragraph dialog box (accessed by opening the Format menu and choosing Paragraph) or with the alignment buttons on the toolbar.

Standard font (or character) styles that are available are regular, bold, italic, and bold italic. These are applied using the Formatting toolbar buttons for that purpose. In addition, there are 18 font effects described in Table 2-2 (some samples are shown in Figure 2-3). The font effects are applied in the Font dialog box, which is opened with the Font option on the Format menu.

**TABLE 2-2**
Font Effects

| Font Effect | What It Does |
|---|---|
| Underline | Makes text underlined. |
| Strikethrough | Puts a line through text. |
| Overline | Puts a line above the text. |
| Blink | Makes text blink (defined only in Netscape Navigator). |
| Superscript | Raises text above the baseline. |
| Subscript | Lowers text below the baseline. |
| Small Caps | Makes normally lowercase letters small capitals. |

| Font Effect | What It Does |
|---|---|
| All Caps | Makes all letters capitals. |
| Capitalize | Makes the leading character of all words a capital. |
| Hidden | The affected text will not be displayed. |
| Strong | Usually makes text bold. |
| Emphasis | Usually makes text italic. |
| Sample | Formats text in the Sample style, normally in a fixed-width font. |
| Definition | Formats text in the Definition style, normally italic. |
| Citation | Formats text in the Citation style, normally italic. |
| Variable | Formats text in the Variable style, normally italic. |
| Keyboard | Formats text in the Keyboard style, normally the fixed-width font with a bold style. |
| Code | Formats text in the Code style, normally the fixed-width font. |

Strong, Emphasis, Sample, Definition, Citation, Variable, Keyboard, and Code styles are *logical* styles. The appearance of the text with these tags is determined by the browser. Older

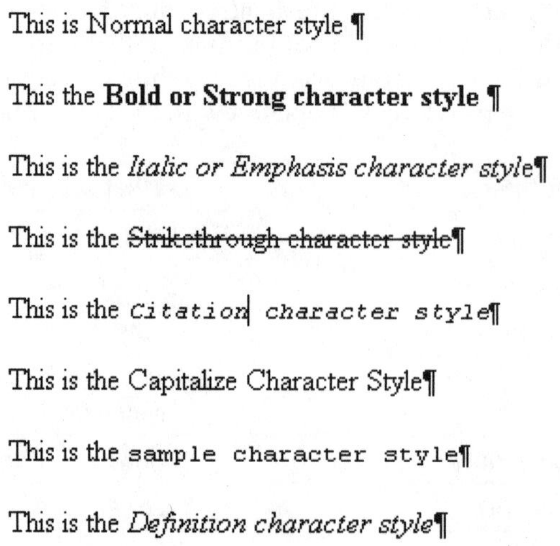

This is Normal character style ¶

This the **Bold or Strong character style** ¶

This is the *Italic or Emphasis character style*¶

This is the ~~Strikethrough character style~~¶

This is the `Citation character style`¶

This is the Capitalize Character Style¶

This is the `sample character style`¶

This is the *Definition character style*¶

**FIGURE 2-3**   Examples of some of the available font effects

browsers allowed you to change the defaults for these tags, but this feature seems to have disappeared. Bold, Italic, Underline, Strikethrough, Overline, Blink, Superscript, Subscript, Small Caps, All Caps, Capitalize, and Hidden are *physical* styles that are not changeable by the browser.

---

***Tip*** *Beginning with FrontPage 2000, FrontPage generates the <B> tag for bold and the <I> tag for italic. If you want the <STRONG> and <EM> tags, you must select Strong and Emphasis from the Font dialog box.*

---

Characters in any style can be one of seven preset sizes from 8 points to 36 points (as shown in Figure 2-4), one of 16 preset colors or a custom color, and designated as either superscript or subscript. Character size and color can be changed with the respective toolbar drop-down list or the Increase Font Size and Decrease Font Size buttons, shown here, or through the Format | Font dialog box.

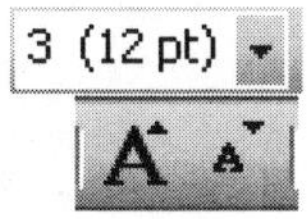

In addition to the paragraph styles that you have already seen, HTML and FrontPage allow you to define several types of lists. Table 2-3 describes the available list styles, which are shown in Figure 2-5. Note that at this time there is no difference between bulleted, directory, and menu lists, so only the Numbered List is shown. This may change. These list styles are available from the Style drop-down list on the left of the toolbar.

---

***Tip*** *You can end any list by pressing* CTRL-ENTER.

---

Not all web browsers treat the formatting in a web the same; they may even ignore some formatting. Blink, in particular, is a style that is ignored by all but Netscape Navigator. Also, several styles may produce exactly the same effect in many browsers. For example, in most instances, the Emphasis, Citation, Definition, and Italic styles often produce the same effect. If you are creating a web for a broad public audience, it is worthwhile to test it in recent versions of the two primary web browsers: Netscape Navigator and Microsoft Internet Explorer.

**FIGURE 2-4**
The seven preset font sizes

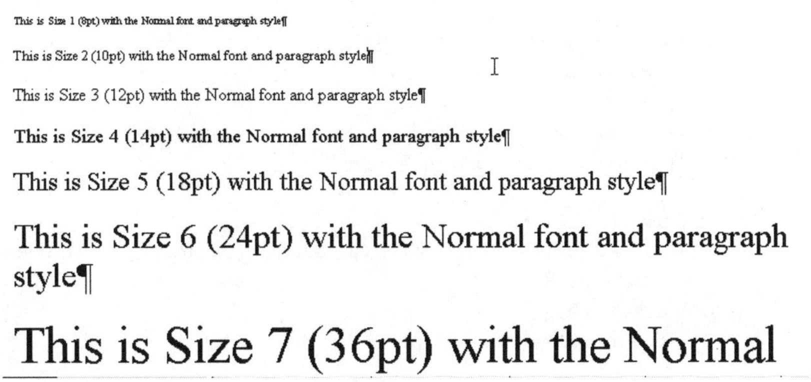

This is Size 1 (8pt) with the Normal font and paragraph style¶

This is Size 2 (10pt) with the Normal font and paragraph style¶

This is Size 3 (12pt) with the Normal font and paragraph style¶

This is Size 4 (14pt) with the Normal font and paragraph style¶

This is Size 5 (18pt) with the Normal font and paragraph style¶

This is Size 6 (24pt) with the Normal font and paragraph style¶

This is Size 7 (36pt) with the Normal

**TABLE 2-3**
List Styles

| List Style | How It Looks |
|---|---|
| Numbered List | Series of paragraphs with a hanging indent and a number on the left |
| Bulleted List | Series of paragraphs with a hanging indent and a bullet on the left |
| Directory List | Series of short (normally less than 20 characters) paragraphs |
| Menu List | Series of paragraphs, one line or less in length, in a vertically compact format |
| Definition and Defined Term | Pairs of paragraphs as terms, which are left-aligned, and definitions, which are indented similarly to dictionary definitions |

**TIP**    *Use only the physical styles other than Blink to be assured of the greatest consistency.*

The Font dialog box and the Font Color button on the toolbar allow you to set the color of selected text. You can also set the color of text for an entire page through the Formatting tab on the Page Properties dialog box, which is opened from the File menu Properties option (you may have to extend it) and shown in Figure 2-6. (Yours may not have a Workgroup tab depending on the configuration and operating system of your computer.) Colored text is useful on colored backgrounds to create an unusual look on a page.

This is a Normal style paragraph.¶

- This is line one of a bulleted list. In lists such as this, a hanging indent is created that lets the bullet stick out on the left.¶
- This is line two of the bulleted list.¶

1. This is line one of a numbered list. In lists such as this, a hanging indent is created that lets the number stick out of the left.¶
2. This is line two of the numbered list.¶

- This is line one of a directory list.¶
- This is line two of a directory list.¶

- This is line one of a menu list.¶
- This is line two of a menu list. ¶

This is a term.¶
This is a definition. In lists such as this, a hanging indent is created that lets the term stick out on the left.¶
This is the second term.¶
This is the second definition. ¶

**FIGURE 2-5**    Examples of list styles

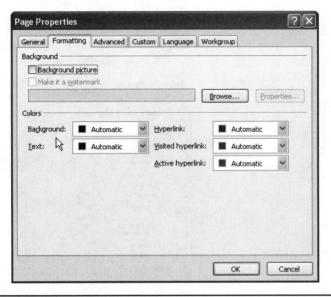

**FIGURE 2-6**    Setting background colors in the Page Properties dialog box

---

***TIP***    *You can open the Page Properties dialog box by right-clicking the page and selecting Page Properties from the context menu.*

### Formatting with Themes

Themes are predefined combinations of formatting and layouts that are available for creating web pages. They offer a professional look using design elements, color, and page layout. When you choose Format | Theme, you will see a pane offering thumbnail descriptions of many different themes, as shown in Figure 2-7. When you click one of the thumbnails, its effects are immediately reflected in the Design view pane.

### Inserting Pictures

FrontPage allows you to add pictures to a web page in these ways:

- You can copy a picture onto the Clipboard and then paste it onto a page.

- You can drag and drop a picture onto a page. In this case, you need to arrange the desktop so that the source and destination for the picture are both visible.

- You can add a background picture that fills a page, which you can specify in the Page Properties dialog box (Figure 2-6). By placing a picture in the background, you can enter text on top of it.

---

***NOTE***    *A background picture will be tiled if it doesn't fill the screen. Even if it fills the screen at 640×480, it may be tiled at higher resolutions.*

- You can add a group of pictures in a photo gallery by opening the Insert menu and choosing Picture | New Photo Gallery. This opens the Photo Gallery Properties

**FIGURE 2-7**
Theme thumbnails display predefined web design and layout options.

dialog box, where you can select the pictures to be in the gallery, as well as choose the gallery's layout. Figure 2-8 shows a group of pictures in the horizontal layout.

- You can add a stand-alone picture from the Picture dialog box opened from the Insert menu (Insert | Picture) and then specify if the picture is from a clip-art library, a file, a scanner or camera, the photo gallery, or an animation product such as MicroGraphics Flash. You can also use the Insert Picture From File button on the toolbar. You can size the picture either before you insert it (using a graphics program) or after using FrontPage. You can place a picture and other objects on a page with varying degrees of precision, up to specifying a pixel coordinate. Once it is inserted, you can open the Pictures toolbar by choosing View | Toolbars | Pictures and then place it either as a floating toolbar in the FrontPage window or as an additional toolbar (on the top of the window, as shown in Figure 2-9). You also can right-click the picture and select Picture Properties to open the Picture Properties dialog box, where you can enter the alignment; the amount of space to place above and to the left of a picture; the thickness of a border, if any; and, on the General tab, the alternative text to display if the picture is not displayed. You can also identify a hyperlink to follow if the user clicks the picture.

---

***TIP***    *You can left-, center-, or right-align a picture by selecting it and clicking the Align Left, Center, or Align Right buttons on the toolbar normally used to align text.*

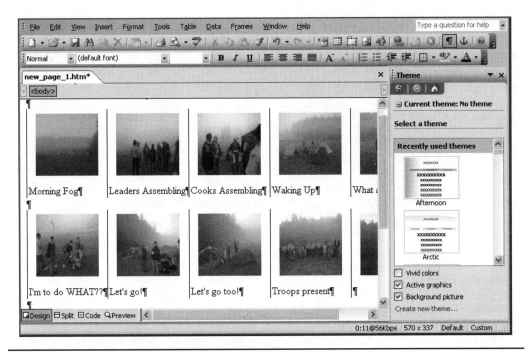

**FIGURE 2-8**    A group of pictures in Photo Gallery

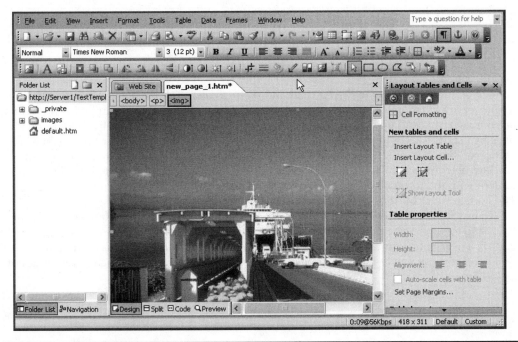

**FIGURE 2-9**    The Picture toolbar, shown here on the top of the screen, appears when a picture is selected and allows you to edit it.

Pictures that are included in web pages must be GIF, JPEG, or PNG format. This has presented a problem in the past, because many clip-art and graphics programs use other formats. FrontPage has solved this problem by allowing you to import other file formats that FrontPage will convert to GIF, JPEG, or PNG-8 or PNG-24. The file formats that FrontPage can accept are the following:

| | |
|---|---|
| Graphics Interchange Format GIF (.gif) | JPEG (.jpg, .jpeg, .jff, .jtf) |
| Portable Networks Graphics (.png) | Kodak PhotoCD (.pcd) |
| PCX (.pcx) | Encapsulated PostScript (.eps) |
| SUN Raster (.ras) | Targa (.tga) |
| Tag Image File Format TIFF (.tif) | Windows Metafile (.wmf) |
| Windows or OS/2 Bitmap (.bmp) | PC PaintBrush (.pcx) |

**NOTE**   *FrontPage converts pictures with up to 256 colors to GIF files and pictures with more than 256 colors to JPEG files.*

Remember, pictures take a long time to download and therefore become frustrating for the user who has to wait for them. Even though a picture may look really neat, if users have to wait several minutes for it to download, they probably are not going to appreciate it or stick around to look at it.

**TIP**   *You can tell how long a page will take to download using a 28.8-Kbps modem* `0:09@56Kbps` *(or whatever speed you choose through right-clicking it) by the time@speed notation on the right of the status bar, like what you see here.*

## Adding Forms

So far, you have seen how to display text and pictures on a web page—in other words, how to deliver information to the user. In Page view, you can also add a form in which the user of your web can send you information. You can create a form either field-by-field, or all at once by using the Form Page Wizard. You'll see how the Form Page Wizard works in a later section of this chapter ("Working with Templates and Wizards"). For now, let's look at the field-by-field approach. You can use the Form option on the Insert menu to create a Form toolbar with the forms options on it by "dragging off" the menu, as shown in Figure 2-10. The Form toolbar buttons are described in Table 2-4.

To use the Form toolbar, simply place the cursor or insertion point where you want the field, and then click the type of field you want. The form field will appear on the page. After adding a new field, you can right-click it and choose Form Field Properties. A dialog box will open and ask you to name the field and specify other aspects of it, such as the width of

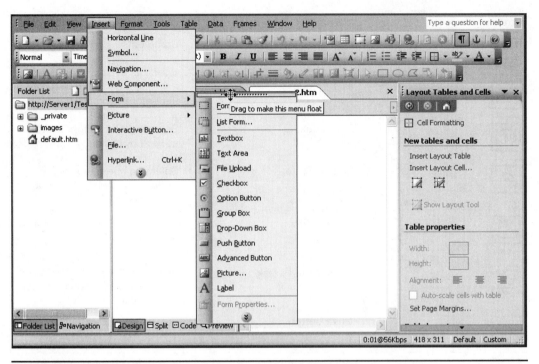

**FIGURE 2-10**    You can create a Form toolbar by dragging it off the Insert menu.

| Button | Name | Use This For: |
|--------|------|---------------|
| | Form | Dashed outline of form |
| | List Form | Adding a list form. Used with SharePoint lists |
| | List Field | Adding a list field. Used with SharePOint lists |
| | Form Web Part | Adding a unit of information containing web content. See Chapter 8 |
| | Textbox | Address |

**TABLE 2-4**    Form Field Creation Buttons

| Button | Name | Use This For: |
|---|---|---|
|   | Text Area | Comments |
|   | File Upload | Allowing a user to browse for a file before submitting it |
|   | Checkbox | Selecting one option from several by clicking a button |
|   | Option Button | Selecting one mutually exclusive option, such as a list of ages |
|   | Group Box | Adding a border and label with which to group a set of controls within a form |
|   | Drop-Down Box | Select from a menu of options, such as which product do you want to explore? |
|   | Push button | Submit and Reset buttons |
|   | Advanced Button | A sizable, editable push button |
|   | Picture | Adding a picture |
|   | Label | Providing descriptive text for a field, such as to enter an e-mail address |
|   | Form Properties | Opening the Form Properties dialog box |

**TABLE 2-4**   Form Field Creation Buttons *(continued)*

the box on the form and the number of characters that can be entered. Figure 2-11 shows an example of a form being built using a template and the toolbar. In Chapter 8, you'll go through the detailed steps of designing and building a form.

*TIP*   *If you put form fields in the same form block (area created by the Form button and enclosed by a dashed line) and use* SHIFT-ENTER *to create a new line, you can stack the fields closer together, and they will all have the same form properties.*

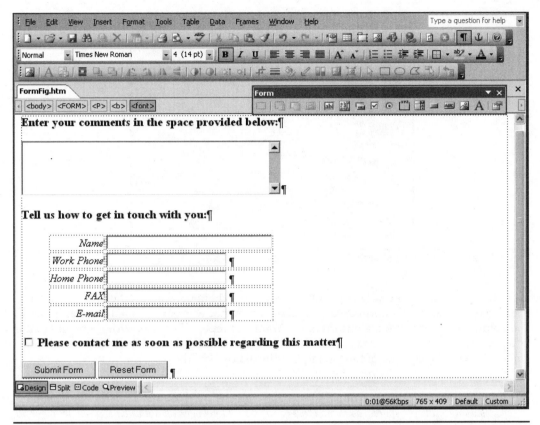

**FIGURE 2-11**    A form created with all fields in the same block using the Formatted paragraph style

When you create a form field-by-field, you need to provide a means of gathering the data that is entered on it. With FrontPage, you can handle the form data in a number of ways:

- You can save the information to a file as HTML, as formatted text, as a text database that can be imported into most database programs, or directly into an Access (.mdb) database.

- You can have the results sent as an e-mail or posted to a discussion group, or register the sender to access a password-protected area of a web, too.

- You can also have the form results sent to a custom script for processing.

To choose how your form results will be handled, right-click the form, and then choose Form Properties. This opens the Form Properties dialog box, shown in Figure 2-12, where you can select or create a file to save the form information, specify an e-mail address to send it to, send it to a database, or select a custom script to process the information. Clicking the

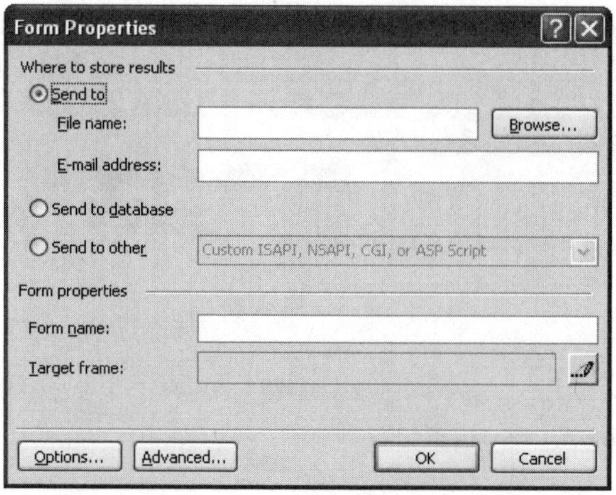

**FIGURE 2-12**    Determining what to do with the contents of a form

Options button opens the Saving Results dialog box, where you can set the options for each method of processing the form data. You may or may not want to include the field names in the output or in the additional information. You must repeat these steps for each field that is in a separate *form block* (the area enclosed within the outermost dashed line) with the options under the Saved Fields tab of the Saving Results dialog box.

*TIP    If you format form fields with the Formatted paragraph style, you can align the labels and text boxes using multiple spaces, as shown in Figure 2-11. However, it's not always possible to get all the form elements to line up exactly by using Formatted text. This is because a space in a form text box is not the same width as a character space. As you will see in the section "Working with Templates and Wizards" later in this chapter, you can also use tables to align form elements, often with better results.*

When you create a form, you may have certain fields that must be filled in (such as first and last name) or fields that have to contain a certain type of information (such as numeric for a phone number). To force the user to enter the proper type of information where required, you can create validation rules for each form field. You do this by right-clicking the form field you want validated, then selecting Form Field Properties from the context menu and clicking Validate to open a validation dialog box. The Text Box Validation dialog box is shown in Figure 2-13. (Different types of form fields will display different validation dialog boxes, while some do not display validation dialog boxes at all.)

### Using Tables

In webs, tables provide a means of dividing some or all of a page into rows and columns. Tables can be used to display tabular data as well as to simply position information on a page, perhaps with a border around it. FrontPage has the extensive ability to create and work with tables such as the one shown in Figure 2-14.

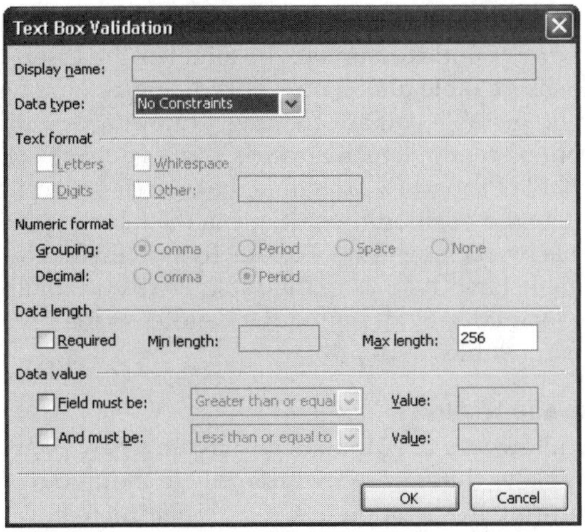

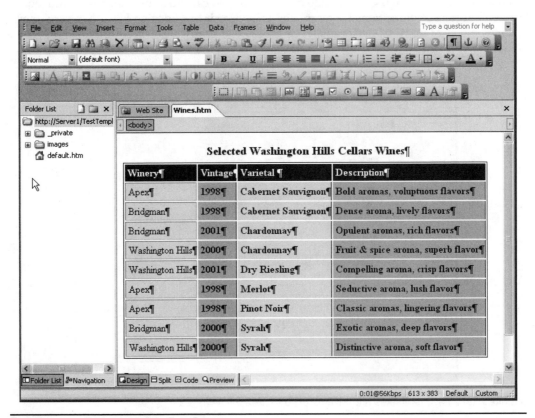

**FIGURE 2-13**   Validate a field to force the information you need.

**FIGURE 2-14**   Table created in FrontPage

Tables are created by use of either the Insert Table button in the toolbar (which allows you to set the number of rows and columns in the table) or the Insert option on the Table menu, which opens the Insert Table dialog box. This dialog box allows you to specify the size, layout, and width of the table you are creating. Once a table is created, you can modify it through the table's context menu, which appears when you right-click the table. From the menu, you can choose Table Properties to change the overall properties of the table or a single cell. You can change the positioning of items in the table at pixel precision. A Table Layout tool (made visible by clicking Show Layout Tool on the Layout Tables and Cells pane or by choosing Enable Layout Tools in the Table Properties dialog box) enables you to manipulate the table manually, by dragging the handles to the precise measurement you want. Chapter 7 will go into tables in depth.

### Working with Templates and Wizards

Templates and wizards allow you to automatically create a new page or a new web with many features on it. Templates differ from wizards only in the amount of interaction between you and the computer during the creation process. *Templates* create a ready-made page or web without interacting with you. *Wizards* use one or more dialog boxes to ask you a series of questions during creation. Based on your answers to these questions, a customized page is created. Whether you use a template or a wizard, you can customize the resultant web pages. You can see the options for templates and wizards by choosing File | New and then clicking either More Web Site Templates or More Page Templates. Selecting More Page Templates from the New task pane opens the Page Templates dialog box shown in Figure 2-15.

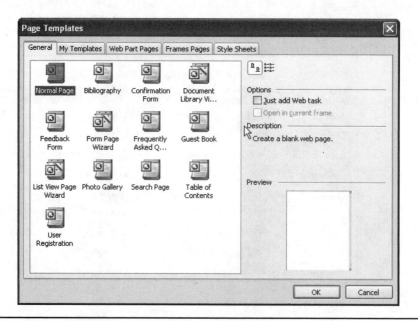

**FIGURE 2-15**   Page templates and wizards used to create new pages

**NOTE**   *Two wizards, Document Library View Page Wizard and List View Page Wizard, not shown in Figure 2-15, are available only when you install SharePoint Services. SharePoint and the Team Web Site that uses SharePoint are discussed briefly at the end of this chapter, again in Chapter 4, and at some length in Chapter 22.*

**NOTE**   *Both CTRL-N and the New Page button on the toolbar give you a new page using the Normal Page template—they do not open the New task pane, which provides access to templates and wizards. The down arrow on the right of the New Page button gives you a choice of Page or Web Site (among other choices), which in turn directly opens the Page Templates or Web Site Templates dialog box, bypassing the New task pane.*

For example, to use a wizard to create a custom form similar to the one created earlier, you would select the Form Page Wizard. This opens a series of dialog boxes that ask you questions about what you want on the form you want to build. One such dialog box is shown in Figure 2-16. When you are done, a form is automatically created, which you can see in Figure 2-17.

**NOTE**   *The form in Figure 2-17 was created by use of a table. The Form Page Wizard mentioned above can also generate Formatted text for aligning labels and form fields.*

Web templates and wizards, like their page counterparts, create multipage webs that you can customize as you see fit. Web templates and wizards are discussed later in this chapter under "Folders View." Page templates and wizards provide an excellent way to get a quick start on a large variety of web pages, as described in Table 2-5.

**FIGURE 2-16**   A series of questions guides you through the Form Wizard, such as the Contact Information shown here.

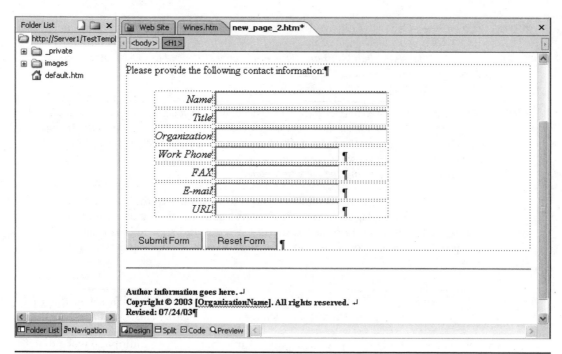

**FIGURE 2-17** A form created with the Form Page Wizard

**TABLE 2-5**
Page Templates
and Wizards

| Template or Wizard | What Is Created on a New Page |
|---|---|
| Normal Page | Blank page |
| Bibliography | List of references to other pages or works |
| Confirmation Form | Acknowledgment of the receipt of input from the user |
| Feedback Form | Form for a user to give you comments |
| Form Page Wizard | Custom form you have designed using this wizard |
| Frequently Asked Questions | List of questions and their answers |
| Guest Book | Form for users of your web to leave their identification and comments |
| Photo Gallery | Thumbnail pictures and captions |
| Search Page | Search engine for finding keywords within the pages of a web |
| Table of Contents | List, in outline format, of hyperlinks to the other pages in your web |
| User Registration | Form for registering to use a secure web |

*TIP   Templates and wizards quickly get you over the "where do I start" hurdle and give you a "first cut" that you can customize.*

### Frames

Frames are a way to organize a web page by combining several pages onto one, each in a tile or *frame.* You use the Frames Pages tab of the Page Templates dialog box to create the several pages necessary for a given layout, called a *frameset.* In the Frames Pages tab, you can click a frames option, and you will see it displayed in the Preview thumbnail on the right of the dialog box. When you choose a frames template, each of which is a frameset (described in Table 2-6), it will be created using the layout in the thumbnail. You are shown the layout and asked how you want to determine the page contents, as shown in Figure 2-18. Frames are discussed in depth in Chapter 7.

*NOTE   Frames are another area of HTML programming that is not supported by all browsers, though Netscape Navigator has supported them since version 2.0, and Internet Explorer has supported them since version 3.0. As you will learn in Chapter 7, you can create alternate pages meant to be loaded by browsers that do not support frames when a frames page is encountered. (As explained above, a "frames page" or Frameset defines and identifies the set of pages, each containing the contents of one frame, which go together to create the single frames page in a browser.)*

**TABLE 2-6**
Frames Templates

| Template | What Is Created on a New Frames Page |
|---|---|
| Banner and Contents | Creates three frames: a banner across the top, a contents frame on the left, and a main frame |
| Contents | Creates two frames: a contents frame on the left and a main frame |
| Footer | Creates a main frame with a narrow footer frame across the bottom |
| Footnotes | Creates a main frame with a footnote frame across the bottom |
| Header | Creates a main frame with a narrow header frame across the top |
| Header, Footer and Contents | Creates four frames: a header frame across the top, a contents frame on the left side, a main frame, and a footer frame across the bottom |
| Horizontal Split | Creates two frames, split horizontally |
| Nested Hierarchy | Creates a full-height contents frame on the left, a header frame, and a main frame |
| Top-Down Hierarchy | Creates three frames, split horizontally |
| Vertical Split | Creates two frames, split vertically |

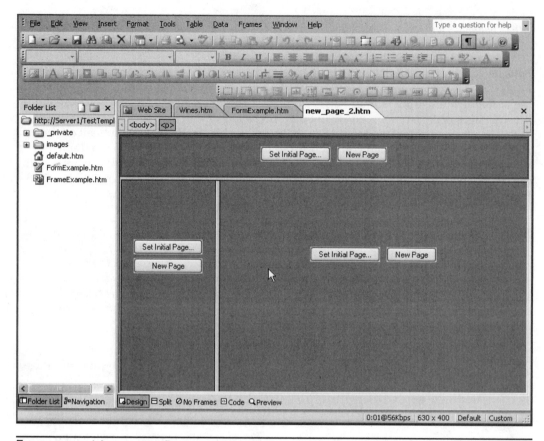

**FIGURE 2-18**    A frames page (Banner and Contents) layout allows you to create the content in each frame.

All of the frames pages discussed so far require that you create a frameset that divides the "page" a user sees into a set of frames that cover the entire page. Also, an *inline frame* allows you to have a single floating frame anywhere on a regular page. This does not require a frameset, but is a single frame that has all the properties of a normal individual frame. Examples of an inline frame are a form or a complex list of items that the user would scroll to fully see.

### Using Web Components

Web Components provide automation in a web, giving you the ability to do more than just provide text and pictures on a page. For example, components return information to you that has been entered on a form, or enable users to participate in a discussion group. Most of FrontPage's components, though, just make creating and maintaining a web easier. In other web-authoring packages, this same capability requires various levels of programming. In FrontPage, you simply have to set up and enable a component.

The Discussion Component is automatically enabled when you create a new web using the Discussion Web Wizard. The Save Results Component is automatically enabled when you use the Form Page Wizard. All other components are enabled through the Insert Web

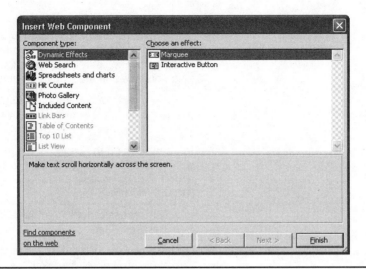

**FIGURE 2-19**    Adding components to a web page

Component dialog box (shown in Figure 2-19), opened by choosing Web Component from the Insert menu. The components that you can place on a page are described in Table 2-7.

| Component | Capability Added to a Web Page |
|---|---|
| Dynamic Effects Interactive Button | Creates a button that can change color, display a picture, or play a sound when the mouse pointer hovers over it. |
| Dynamic Effects Marquee | Inserts a marquee on a web page in which text is scrolled or slid across the marquee. |
| Web Search – Current Web | Adds a search form to allow the user to search the current web. |
| Spreadsheets and Charts | Adds an interactive Office Spreadsheet, Chart, or PivotTable to a web page in which the web viewer can change the data and see the results. |
| Hit Counter | Allows you to choose from several counters, which record the number of times a page has been downloaded. |
| Photo Gallery | Provides for the automatic display of a series of photos on a page with a horizontal, vertical, montage, or slide show layout. |
| Included Content | Allows you to include one web page's content, picture, banner, or creation information (such as author and date last changed) on another page. For example, a page header can be put on one page and included on every other page. |

**TABLE 2-7**    Components Inserted from the Insert Web Component Dialog Box

| Component | Capability Added to a Web Page |
|---|---|
| Link Bars | Adds a link bar with hyperlinks to other pages specified by the user, or to the next or previous page, or based on the structure of the current web. |
| Table of Contents | Creates a table of contents that lists all of the pages in a web either hierarchically or based on chosen categories. |
| Top 10 List | Reports back on the usage of a site: the top ten visited pages, referring domains, referring URLs, search strings, visiting users, operating systems (OSes), and browsers. |
| List View | Provides access to lists in a SharePoint Team Services Web Site. |
| Document Library View | Provides access to document libraries in a SharePoint Team Services Web Site. |
| Expedia Components | Accesses Expedia components. |
| MSN Components and MSNBC Components | Adds content from Microsoft web sites, such as stock quotes, weather forecasts, and news headlines, and lets you exchange banner ad time. |
| Additional Components | Adds an Additional Component, for example, a Visual InterDev type of navigation bar. |
| Advanced Controls | Adds controls such as HTML content, a Java applet, a plug-in, an ActiveX control, a Flash movie, or design-time control to a web page. |
| Advanced Controls: Confirmation Field | Echoes the information entered on a form by users, so you can show them what they entered. |

TABLE 2-7    Components Inserted from the Insert Web Component Dialog Box *(continued)*

### Adding Hyperlinks and Mapping Hotspots

In Page view, you can add hyperlinks (or *links*), which allow the user of a web to quickly jump from one page to another, or to a particular element on the same page or another page (called a *bookmark*), or to a different web or web site. You can make either text or a picture the element the user clicks to make the link, and you can map certain areas of a picture to be designated as different links (called *hotspots*). You create a link by first selecting the object that you want the user to click and then clicking the Insert Hyperlink button in the toolbar, or by choosing Hyperlink from either the context menu (opened by right-clicking the item) or the Insert menu. In either case, the Insert Hyperlink dialog box will open, as shown in Figure 2-20.

Within the Insert Hyperlink dialog box, you can select a bookmark that has been previously placed on any open page or just an open page without a bookmark, any page in the current web with or without a bookmark, any URL or address on the World Wide Web, a new page yet to be defined in the current web, or an e-mail address. When you have

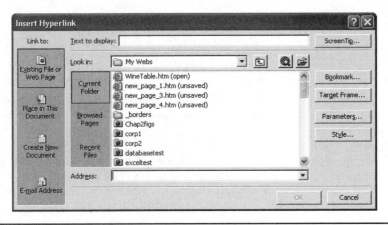

**FIGURE 2-20**   Insert Hyperlink dialog box

created a hyperlink, the object on which the user is to click changes to a different color and may become underlined.

A picture can have its entire area defined as a link, or you can identify specific areas in a picture as separate links, while any unidentified areas are assigned a default link. For example, you could provide a map that allows the user to quickly get to information about a particular area of the world by simply clicking that area, as you can see in Figure 2-21.

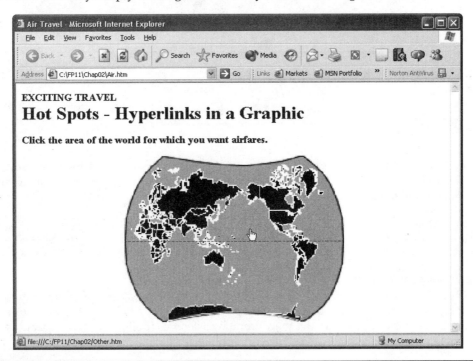

**FIGURE 2-21**   Selecting a hyperlink that is a hotspot in a picture

---

***TIP***   *The left end of the status bar informs you of the link under the mouse pointer.*

You place hotspots on a picture by using the hotspot drawing tools (shown to the right) located on the Pictures toolbar. You can display the  Pictures toolbar by choosing View | Toolbars, Pictures, if it isn't already displayed. (If you don't see the Pictures toolbar, it may be partially hidden by another toolbar. At the end of the toolbar is a small arrow, which, when clicked, displays additional tools, such as the hotspot tools.)

First select the picture, and then select the rectangle, circle, or polygon tool. Use it to draw a border around the area of the picture you want to be the hotspot. When you complete a closed area, the Insert Hyperlink dialog box will be displayed, and you'll be asked to enter the URL (bookmark, web site, or page reference) where the browser should transfer when that area is clicked. When you are done identifying all the hotspots, your picture will look something like this (although users won't see the lines in a browser):

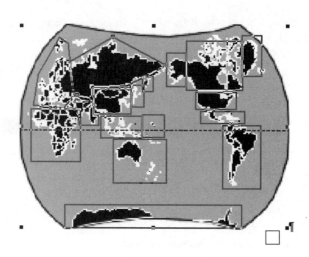

 Another useful tool on the Pictures toolbar is the Set Transparent Color tool, shown here. This tool lets you click any color in the picture and make it transparent, allowing the page background to show through.

---

***NOTE***   *Transparent backgrounds only work with GIF89a files. If you try using a transparent background with a JPEG, you'll get a dialog box that says the JPEG will be converted to a GIF.*

### Using Drawing, AutoShapes, and WordArt

Besides adding clip art and pictures, FrontPage gives you the capability of adding your own drawings, AutoShapes, and WordArt. The Drawing toolbar provides the tools for the drawing tasks. It is opened from the View menu by selecting Toolbars | Drawing and is shown next.

PART I

*TIP*    *Another drawing tool that's available is the Drawing Canvas that defines a drawing area accompanied by a small toolbar to expand the canvas, fit it to the pane, or insert scale handles to fine-tune the sizing of the canvas; you can also get it from the New Drawing option on the Insert | Picture menu.*

The Drawing toolbar provides a number of tools, described in Table 2-8, that allow you to create and enhance simple line drawings. Two of the tools on the Drawing toolbar, AutoShapes and WordArt, are themselves clusters of tools and can be separately opened from the Insert | Picture menu.

**AutoShapes**    AutoShapes are a set of ready-made shapes that includes basic shapes, various arrow shapes, and flowchart elements, as well as lines, stars, banners, and callouts. To get the toolbar, choose Insert | Picture | AutoShapes. To then choose a shape, click the

| Tool | Name | Purpose |
|---|---|---|
| Draw ▾ | Draw menu | Manipulate a drawing, including group, ungroup, order, and align objects; snap, nudge, and rotate an object; and edit points on a line or curve. |
| ▨ | Select object | Select elements in a drawing such as lines, curves, and text. |
| AutoShapes ▾ | AutoShapes | Insert predefined shapes. See following section. |
| ╲ | Line | Draw lines, initially straight, but through editing make curved. |
| ↘ | Arrow | Draw lines with an arrowhead at the end. Lines are initially straight, but through editing can be made to curve. |
| ▭ | Rectangle | Draw rectangles that can be edited. |
| ○ | Oval | Draw ovals that can be edited. |
| ▨ | Text Box | Insert a text box. |

**TABLE 2-8**    Drawing Toolbar

| Tool | Name | Purpose |
|------|------|---------|
|   | WordArt | Give text an artistic flair. See upcoming section. |
|   | ClipArt | Insert clip art. |
|   | Picture | Insert a picture from a file. |
|   | Fill | Fill a closed object with a color, texture, pattern, or picture. |
|   | Line Color | Change the color or pattern of a line. |
|   | Font Color | Change the color of text. |
|   | Line Style | Change the type and width of lines. |
| 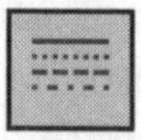  | Dash Style | Make a line dashed in various ways. |
| 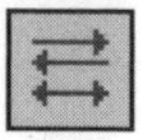  | Arrow Style | Change the arrow type. |
|   | Shadow | Add a shadow to an object. |
|   | 3-D | Add 3-D effects to an object. |

**TABLE 2-8**    Drawing Toolbar *(continued)*

category, such as Lines, Basic Shapes, Block Arrows, Flowchart, Stars and Banners, Callouts, and More AutoShapes. An extension of the toolbar will display, allowing you to choose the specific shape you want, as seen next in the Flowchart shapes:

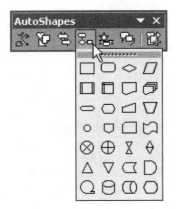

Once you have selected the shape, you can place it anywhere on the page by moving the mouse pointer to that area and clicking. In this manner, you can lay down a "normal-sized" object, or size it by dragging the mouse. To resize the object once it's on the page, simply select it and drag one of the selection handles in or out. You can also fill an enclosed shape with color and/or change its outline color by using the Fill and Line Color tools.

**WordArt**   WordArt takes selected text that you have entered and applies one of 30 effects that you select from the WordArt Gallery, shown in Figure 2-22. You can get to WordArt by choosing Insert | Picture | WordArt or by clicking the WordArt button on the Picture toolbar. After you have selected the effect, the Edit WordArt Text dialog box opens, allowing you to make any changes to the text you want. When you click OK, the text with the applied effect will appear on your current work page. When the text is selected, a WordArt toolbar appears,

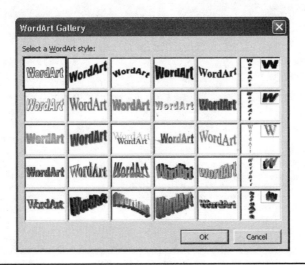

**FIGURE 2-22**   WordArt effects that can be applied to your text

allowing you to edit the text; select a different effect from the gallery; change the color, size, layout, and rotation of the text; make all the characters the same size; make them vertical; change their alignment; and alter their spacing.

## Other FrontPage Views

While Page view is the place where you construct the individual pages that make up a web, edit and view the HTML code, and preview the page with a browser, FrontPage offers you six more views that let you look at the web in other ways. You can look at the complete web and see all of its pages, files, and links, or you can look at a segment of the web and see the components of that segment. As you saw earlier in this chapter, the other views are Folders view, Reports view, Navigation view, Hyperlinks view, Tasks view, and Remote Web Site view.

### Folders View

Folders view is similar in a number of ways to the Windows Explorer. You show it by choosing View | Folders view. The Folders view should not be confused with the Folder List that often is displayed in the left pane, showing a more hierarchical structure of folders. Folders view is displayed in the content pane (center or right pane, depending on whether there are two or three panes being displayed). It displays a list of the files supporting the web, as shown in Figure 2-23.

By clicking the plus and minus icons in the left pane, you can expand or collapse the view of the folder hierarchy. If you right-click an object in either pane, its context menu will open, which, among other options, allows you to open the object's Properties dialog box. A final way that Folders view is like the Windows Explorer is that in Folders view, you can sort the list of files by clicking the column name immediately above the list.

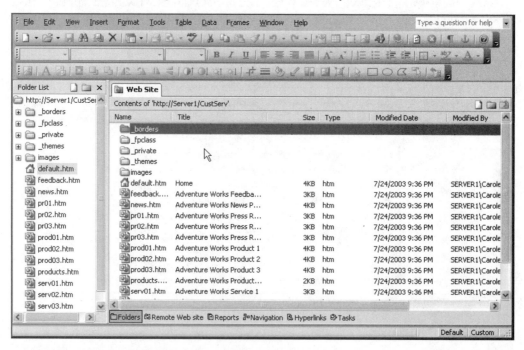

**FIGURE 2-23** A web displayed in Folders view

In either Page or Folders view, you can use wizards and templates to automatically create entire webs, including a full set of pages, links, and other elements. As in page wizards and templates, web site wizards and templates differ only in the amount of interaction between you and the computer during the creation process. Web templates create a ready-made web without interacting with you. Web wizards, on the other hand, use one or more dialog boxes to ask you a series of questions during creation. Based on your answers to these questions, a customized web is created. You can customize the resultant web pages and elements with Page view. You can also create an empty web by choosing More Web Site Templates in the New task pane and clicking the Empty Web Site icon in the Web Site Templates dialog box, or import an existing web by double-clicking the Import Web Site Wizard icon.

The web templates and wizards that are currently available in FrontPage are shown in Table 2-9. You can use these templates and wizards to create either new webs or additions to existing webs. Also, wizards and templates automatically create the tasks in Tasks view that support the created pages. As you'll see in Chapter 4 and Appendix C, you can build your own templates to create a standard look—for example, across all departments in a corporate intranet.

| Template or Wizard | Characteristics of Web Created |
|---|---|
| **Templates** | |
| One Page Web Site | Has a single blank page. |
| Customer Support Web Site | Tells customers how to contact you and provides a form where they can leave information so you can contact them. Includes an FTP download area, a frequently asked questions (FAQ) area, and a form for leaving suggestions and contact information. |
| Empty Web Site | Has no pages, so you can import pages from another web. |
| Personal Web Site | Has a single page with personal and professional information and ways to be contacted. |
| Project Web Site | Provides a way to communicate the status of a project including its schedule, who is working on it, and its accomplishments. |
| SharePoint Team Site | Has pages for collaboration among team members. This template and other SharePoint Services templates, discussed in Chapter 22, are to be used with SharePoint (see brief discussion later in this chapter in the "SharePoint" section). |
| **Wizards** | |
| Corporate Presence | Provides information about a company, including what it does, what its products and services are, how to contact it, and a means to leave feedback for it. |
| Database Interface | Sets up a connection with a database whose records can then be viewed and modified. |
| Discussion Web Site | Is an electronic bulletin board where users can leave messages and others can reply to those messages. |
| Import Web Site | Provides assistance in collecting all of the components of a web and bringing them into FrontPage. |

**TABLE 2-9**   Web Templates and Wizards

### Reports View

If you choose View | Reports and then select Site Summary, you will see a summary of some of the reports available in FrontPage, as shown in Figure 2-24. To see the detail of any report, click its name. You can then return to the Site Summary by clicking the drop-down report list at the top of the report pane and choosing Site Summary (see Tip that follows). A great amount of valuable information is in the reports that FrontPage provides. The best way to get familiar with them is to open each of the reports and study the contents.

**NOTE**   *Some of the reports do not open and only provide information at the summary level.*

**TIP**   *The drop-down reporting options automatically appear whenever you open the Reports view. They enable you to select what is displayed in the Reports view.*

### Navigation View

Navigation view, displayed by clicking View | Navigation, is shown in Figure 2-25 in the content pane. It gives you a graphical overview of how the web is organized. The Navigation view shows a graphical representation of the hyperlinks used to go from page to page. By clicking the plus and minus signs in the right pane, you can expand or collapse the hierarchy of links. You can also drag a page from one position to another and change its link by doing so.

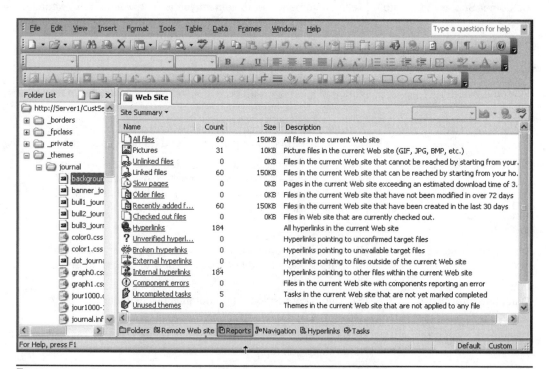

**FIGURE 2-24**   Reports view showing some of the reports that are available

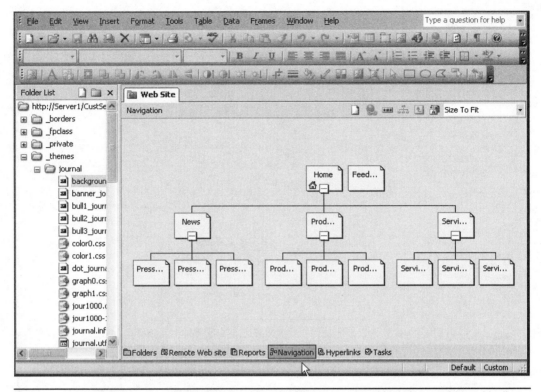

**FIGURE 2-25**    Navigation view shows the structure of the web pages and how they are hierarchically connected.

The Folder List in the left pane shows the files that are connected to the Home Page. By dragging a file from the Folder List to the Navigation pane, you can place the file exactly where you want it to be in the hierarchy.

*TIP    Instead of the Folder List, you may sometimes see a Navigation pane, a list of the files supporting the web, in the left pane.*

### Hyperlinks View

Hyperlinks view, displayed by choosing View | Hyperlinks, allows you to look at the links among the pages in a web, as well as the links to external sites (see Figure 2-26). Web pages and their links create a hierarchical structure that can be created either by adding pages one at a time and then linking them, or by using one of the web wizards or templates to automatically create the desired pages and their links. Click the plus signs to extend the hyperlinks. In the left pane, the Folder List shows the files that are used to create the hyperlinks.

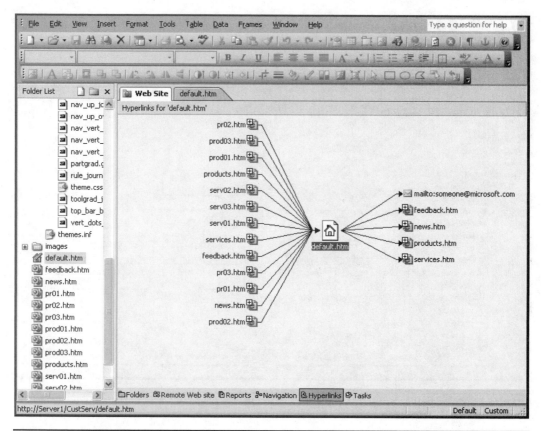

**FIGURE 2-26** Hyperlinks view shows how the hyperlinks to and from the Default.htm page.

## Tasks View

Tasks view (Figure 2-27) lists the tasks that must be accomplished to complete the web application you are building. The items on the Tasks list are placed there either by a web wizard or by you. You can add tasks in any view by choosing Edit | Tasks. A list of options will be displayed, allowing you to choose between add, edit, start, mark complete, or show the history of a task. You can add a new task by clicking the arrow to the right of the New button and choosing Task.

When you add a new task, the New Task dialog box will appear in which you can give the task a name, assign it to an individual, give it a priority, and type in a description. Use the Tasks list to list the work that remains on the various sections of a web. You can right-click a task and select Start Task. This will open Page view and display the page that needs work. When you have completed the task, you can return to Tasks view, right-click the task, and select Mark Complete from the context menu, which will mark the task as completed and leave it in the list; or select Delete Task from the context menu to delete the task from the list. By right-clicking an uncompleted task and selecting Edit Task from the context menu, you can modify who is assigned to do the task, its priority, its description, and the task name. For a completed task, you can only edit the description.

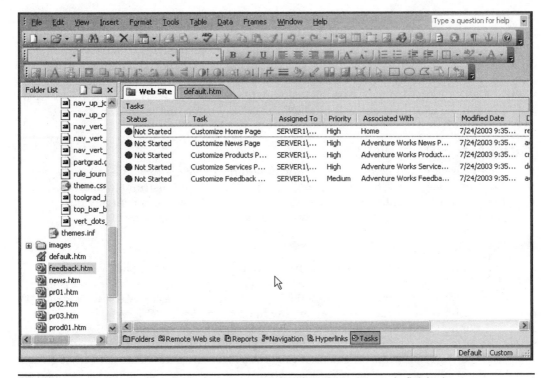

**FIGURE 2-27**    Tasks view lists tasks to be completed before the web page is finished.

---

*TIP*    *You can sort the tasks in Tasks view on any column by clicking the column name at the top of the list.*

---

### Remote Web Site View

The Remote Web Site view is displayed during functions that require you to synchronize files between two sites, or to copy files from one site to another. For example, when you publish a web site, the Remote Web Site view is created to tell you whether the files exist on both sites, whether they are different, and allow you to choose which files to copy in which direction—from your local computer to your remote web server, for instance. This view is discussed later in the chapter and will be shown in Figure 2-28.

### Accessing Other Functions in FrontPage

As you are working on your web, you can open Page view in several ways. The following are just a few methods:

- Use the Page option in the View menu.
- Double-click the page filename (or icon) you want to edit in one of several views of FrontPage.
- Select Start Task, as just discussed.

When you are done creating a web, you can display the Hyperlinks view and see if any of the links are broken. If they are, the line will be broken in the view. Also, if you have edited a web and removed or changed some of the pages, use the Recalculate Hyperlinks option in the Tools menu to update all of the internal links so there is no reference to a nonexistent page. Finally, when everything is the way you want it, you can publish your web on a server (provided you weren't already working on the server) by using the Publish Site option in the File menu or by using the Publish Site button on the toolbar.

## Distributing FrontPage Webs

So far, this chapter has dealt with the creation of FrontPage webs—that, after all, is the purpose of FrontPage. A web page, though, is worthless if it isn't distributed to those who wish to see it. The distribution side of FrontPage has at least one and potentially three components: web servers, FrontPage Server Extensions, and SharePoint.

### Web Servers

You must have a web server in order to distribute web pages. You can use any web server to publish FrontPage webs. As mentioned at the beginning of this chapter, this book assumes you are using Microsoft's Internet Information Services (IIS) web server. Windows Server 2003 comes with IIS 6, Windows 2000 Server comes with IIS 5, Windows NT Server 4.0 comes with IIS 4, and Windows XP and 2000 Professional come with limited editions of IIS 5. The web server can be on your computer, another computer on your LAN, or a computer on the Internet. If your web server is on your computer or a local computer on your LAN, it gives you added flexibility to test your webs. IIS on your computer simply sits in the background as a task and takes very little management. IIS is often on a dedicated server and is all the web server you need to run a full World Wide Web site.

Appendix A details the installation and setup of IIS. From here on, this book will assume that IIS is running and available to you.

### Publishing a Web

When you are ready to launch your web site, you will publish it to your server. This is how others will be able to log onto your web site using their browser. You can then use the published web site to more thoroughly verify that all links work the way you anticipated, that the forms are easy to use, that the web is attractive and easy to use, and all the other elements of a web that you want to verify.

To publish a web, you select File | Publish Site. Then, in the Remote Web Site Properties dialog box Remote Web site tab, select the correct Remote Web Site Server Type option and type the remote server location. In the Publishing tab, select options on how to move the files from their current location to the web server. The Remote Web Site pane will gather information on where and how you want it published, as shown in Figure 2-28. Here you tell FrontPage which files you want to move from the local to the remote site. You then click Publish Web Site to move the web site folders and files to the server site. When you are finished, you will see a status note in the left side of the publish pane that tells you whether the published task has been successful. We will discuss publishing webs in several other chapters, primarily in Chapter 23, Publishing and Promoting Webs on the Internet.

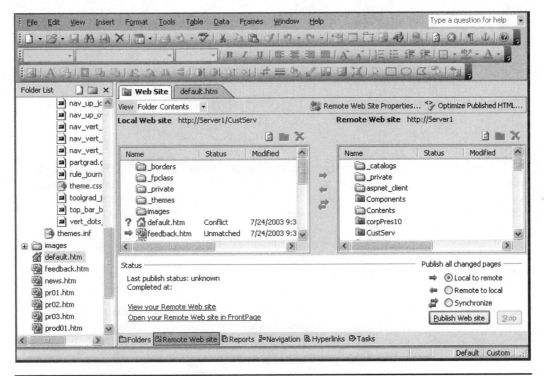

**FIGURE 2-28**    The Remote Web Site view lets you see which files and folders will be moved between the local web site and the remote server.

## FrontPage Server Extensions

Since the earliest versions of FrontPage, some of its components, such as searching and building a table of contents, required that the FrontPage Server Extensions (FPSE) be installed on both the server you used to build your webs and the server your Internet service provider (ISP) or web presence provider (WPP) was using. The FPSEs are a set of programs that run on the server and provide the capabilities required by the web components. The most recent version of FPSE is Front Page Server Extensions 2002 that came out in the fall of 2001 with FrontPage 2002.

***

**NOTE**    *Though the terms "Internet service provider" (ISP) and "web presence provider" (WPP) are sometimes used interchangeably, they differ. An ISP provides access to the Internet, usually through a dial-up (modem) connection. A WPP hosts web sites. That is, a WPP stores the web files on a server that is accessible over the Internet. Often, your ISP and your WPP will be the same company. In this book, the terms "presence provider" and "web host" refer to a WPP.*

Among the components and advance features in FrontPage that require FPSE are

- Forms
- Hotspot image maps

- Web Components that are active while a web is being used in a browser, such as
  - Confirmation Field Component
  - Discussion Component
  - Registration Component
  - Save Results Component
  - Search Component
  - Table of Contents Component

There will not be a FrontPage Server Extensions 2003. Your FrontPage 2003 webs can use FPSE 2002, and some web components are supported by the newest version of SharePoint (see the next section). If you are working on an Internet web site which will be hosted by a WPP, you will need to determine whether the WPP has FPSE 2002 available to you before you use the web components mentioned above. For an intranet web site, you may want to not only determine if the FPSE 2002 is available but also which, if any, version of SharePoint is available.

## SharePoint

SharePoint is the capability to build and host a web site that facilitates collaboration and management in an organization. SharePoint provides several unique tools including lists, calendars, surveys, document libraries, and discussion groups. With these tools, the following functions can be set up and made available to an organization:

- Tasks can be documented and tracked.
- Events can be scheduled and followed up.
- Announcements can be made and archived.
- Contacts can be identified and maintained.
- Favorite references, styles, procedures, web sites, and other preferences can be cataloged.
- Opinions can be sought and documented.
- Libraries of documents, drawings, pictures, sounds, video images, scripts, and code can be indexed and maintained.

Microsoft has come out with two versions of SharePoint. FrontPage 2002 shipped with both FPSE 2002 and SharePoint 1, called SharePoint Team Services on the FrontPage distribution CD. SharePoint 2, called Windows SharePoint Services, will eventually be distributed with Windows Server 2003, but it is not ready for the initial distribution of the Server, so it will initially be distributed as a download from Windows Update ("THEY" think, per the newsgroup). Unless otherwise mentioned, when you see "SharePoint" in this book, we are talking about Windows SharePoint Services or SharePoint 2.

## SharePoint Web Sites

To use SharePoint, you must separately install it from the Windows Server 2003 CD or download it from Windows Update (see Chapter 4 for a discussion of this). You can then create a SharePoint Team web site using FrontPage 2003 and the SharePoint Team Site template, which is shown in Figure 2-29. You can tailor your SharePoint web to have just the features you want to use, and the organization members can have the set of permissions to use the features that are appropriate both for the team and for the individual.

SharePoint depends on an SQL database to store the lists, libraries, and surveys that make up each web. (A run-time version of SQL comes with SharePoint.) You can set up the database in a manner appropriate to the web site. Chapter 4 describes SharePoint further and Chapter 22 describes how to use SharePoint in detail.

## SharePoint Web Components

In addition to using the features on the SharePoint Team Site template, SharePoint 1, but NOT SharePoint 2, provides two web components, List View and Document Library View. List View allows you to determine the format of a list that can be used to share information among a team. Examples of lists are contacts, team members, events, dates, milestones, and products. Document Library view allows you to determine the format of a library that is

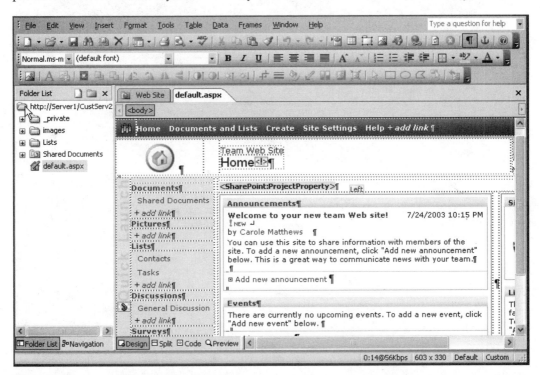

**FIGURE 2-29**   SharePoint web site created with the SharePoint Team Site template

used to share documents among a team. Examples of items in a library include correspondence, reports, procedures, plans, and policies. You can create and manage lists and document libraries in FrontPage using the List View and Document Library View FrontPage component described earlier in the section "Using Web Components."

### SharePoint Administration

SharePoint is administered through the SharePoint Central Administration pages that are opened on Server 2003 through Start | Administrative Tools | SharePoint Central Administration. This provides the page shown in Figure 2-30, which contains the primary controls that allow you to change the configuration settings as well as manage SharePoint users.

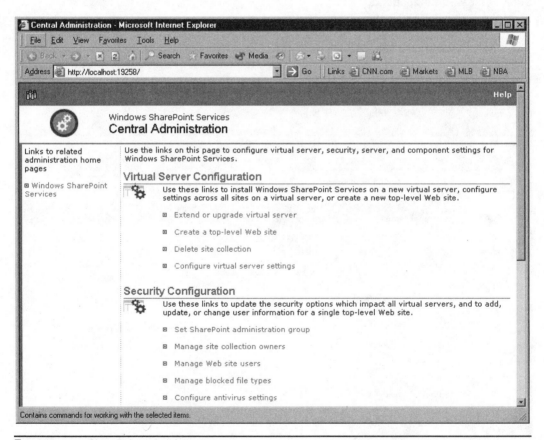

**FIGURE 2-30**    SharePoint administrator page

# CHAPTER 3

# Using Wizards

As you saw in Chapter 2, the easiest way to create a web with FrontPage is by using a wizard or a template. You'll remember that *wizards* ask you questions about the web you want to create and then build a web template based on your answers. *Templates* create a particular kind of web without input from you. In this chapter, you'll see how to use wizards to create web sites and to use other building blocks, such as link bars and web themes. This will acquaint you with the wizards and demonstrate many of FrontPage's features, which have been included in the wizard-produced web templates.

---

**NOTE** *Most of the wizards are web wizards, which create the folder structure and pages that make a complete web template. A few are page wizards, which create only a single page template.*

---

## Web Wizards

Begin looking at the FrontPage wizards by loading FrontPage as you did in Chapter 2. For the remainder of this book, it is assumed you have Internet Information Services (IIS) and either the SharePoint 1 and FrontPage Server Extensions or SharePoint 2 running on your computer or on another computer on your network, as explained in Appendix A. Because we use both in this book, some of the screens and responses will be different depending on the SharePoint being used.

After FrontPage has loaded, you can start a new web in three ways:

- You can simply begin creating the first web page and then add additional pages to it as necessary.
- You can click the down arrow of the Create a New Normal Page toolbar button (called New or New Page in this book) and choose Web Site, as shown here.

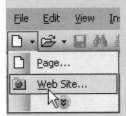

You can open the File menu and choose New to open the New task pane. Click More Web Site Templates.

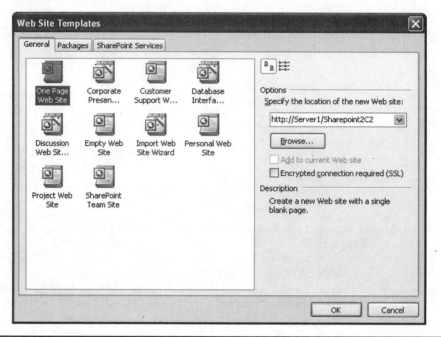

**FIGURE 3-1**     Web Site Templates dialog box

In the last two alternatives, the Web Site Templates dialog box will be displayed, as shown in Figure 3-1. This dialog box displays icons for the following web wizards:

- **Corporate Presence Wizard**   Creates a complete web site to promote your company or business. With it you can
  - Create web pages that tell customers what's new with your company (for example, by using press releases)
  - Inform customers about your products and services
  - Create a table of contents to help visitors navigate your web site
  - Provide a feedback form so your customers can give you their opinions
  - Provide a search form that visitors to your web site can use to quickly find specific information on your site
- **Database Interface Wizard**   Builds a web site with which you can connect to and manage a database, including viewing, adding, changing, and deleting database records.
- **Discussion Web Wizard**   Creates web pages that allow the web user to submit comments to a discussion. It also provides a table of contents, a search form, a page to follow threaded replies, and a confirmation page so users know their comments have been received. *Threaded replies* link multiple comments on the same subject. This allows the reader to go directly from one comment to the next on a given subject.

- **Import Web Wizard**   Lets you quickly convert existing web pages and content into a FrontPage web by collecting web pages from your local drive, or from an intranet or the Internet, and organize them into a FrontPage web. This is an important feature if you need to convert a number of existing webs into FrontPage, to update them, or to incorporate any of FrontPage's active elements, Web Components, or other dynamic FrontPage elements in them.

## Using the Corporate Presence Wizard

The Corporate Presence web is one of the more sophisticated webs that FrontPage creates. By using a wizard, you get to do a lot of customizing as you build. In this section, you will create a Corporate Presence web ("Corporate web," for short). Do that now with these instructions:

1. Open the File menu, choose New, and the New task pane will be displayed. Then click More Web Site Templates.

2. The Web Site Templates dialog box will be displayed, as shown in Figure 3-1. In addition to selecting the web you want, you also want to select the location and name of the web under Options. We used "CorporateWeb" on our IIS 6 server. Double-click the Corporate Presence Wizard in the Web Site Templates dialog box. The Corporate Presence Web Wizard will be displayed.

3. This first dialog box explains that you will be asked a series of questions. Click Next, opening the second wizard dialog box (shown next), which displays the list of pages that can be included in the web.

---

**NOTE**   *This is an example of where your screen might differ depending on whether you have SharePoint 1 (STS) or SharePoint 2 (WSS). With SharePoint 2, you will not have a Search or Table of Contents page.*

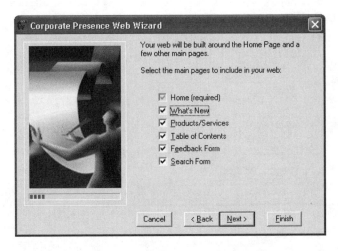

4. Select all of the options (to include all the possible pages) and click Next. This brings up a list of topics that can be included on the Home Page.

5. Choose all the check boxes and default options in this and the following wizard dialog boxes, and supply requested information about your company or organization. (One of the choices is whether you want to use the Under Construction icon on your pages. See the following Tip on this choice, although in the illustrations here it was included.) Any object, such as links, a company logo, or product image, can be selected now; you can insert the actual objects later. After you select web options and supply information about your site, you will reach the dialog box that gives you the option of displaying the Tasks view after the web is uploaded. Choose to do this and click Finish to complete the Web Site Wizard creation.

***T*IP** *If your site will be placed on the server for public consumption prior to all tasks being completed, then using the Under Construction icon is generally not a good idea, since the promise of something to come someday is confusing and irritating to users. (The icon, shown in the wizard, is shown again on the screen shots later in this chapter so you can see what it looks like.)*

The web site will be displayed with the Folder List view in the left pane and the Tasks view in the right, as shown next:

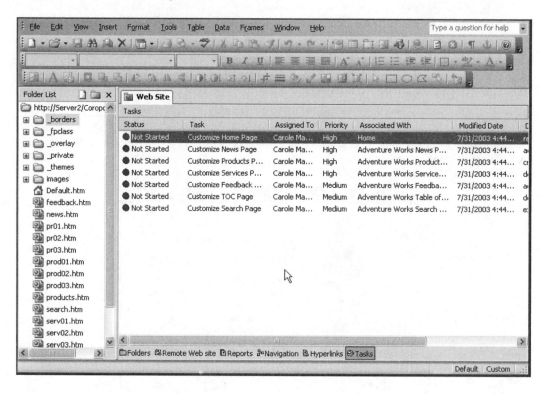

You can easily show the various views of the web site, as discussed in Chapter 2, by clicking the buttons on the bottom of the right pane: Folders for the Folders view, Remote Web Site to set up the remote web properties, Reports to see a list of reports about the web site, Navigation to see the structure of the web site, Hyperlinks to see the network of links between the pages of the web site, and Tasks to keep track of your progress in building the web site. Follow these steps to see these views:

6. Click the Navigation view button in the view bar on the bottom of the FrontPage window to show the Corporate web in Navigation view, as shown next. This shows all of the main web pages and their relationship to each other.

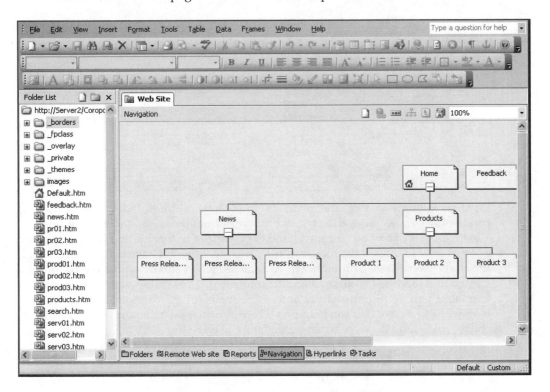

7. Select Hyperlinks view by clicking the Hyperlinks view button in the view bar. As you can see next, the Corporate Presence Web Wizard has not only created all the pages you selected in the wizard, but it has also created the basic hyperlinks

between the pages, represented by the arrows in the right pane of the FrontPage window.

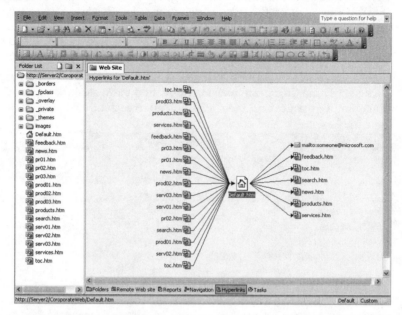

8. Right-click the Home Page file, which is either Default.htm or Index.htm, in either pane of Hyperlinks view, and choose Properties from the context menu that opens. The Properties dialog box for the Home Page, similar to the one shown next, will open. Here you can see the filename, title, and location that have been generated for the Home Page. In the Summary tab you can see when and by whom the page was created and modified. You can also add comments. The Workgroup tab allows you to establish group responsibilities and assignments for the web site. Each category is attached to a page that can help you locate information on a page. You can also choose to exclude the page when publishing the web site.

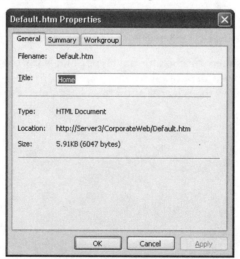

**NOTE** *If you are using IIS as your web server, FrontPage will name the Home Page Default.htm. With other servers or with none, FrontPage would name the Home Page Index.htm. The name of the home page for a web is important since this will determine whether your web server will display the home page when accessed without the home page filename (http://webname/) or whether the full URL will be required (http://webname/pagename.htm). Different web servers have different default settings for the home page name. Check with your web server administrator for the default home page name on your web server.*

9. Click OK. The Properties dialog box closes. Click the Tasks view button in the view bar to return to the Tasks list (shown previously).

10. Right-click the first task (Customize Home Page), and choose Start Task from the context menu. Design view will open with the Home Page displayed, as shown in Figure 3-2. (Note the yellow Under Construction icon above the News, Products, Services link bar.)

11. As you will recall from Chapter 2, you can use themes to lend a consistent look to all pages of the web site. When you use a wizard, a theme is automatically assigned, which you can easily change. From the Format menu, click Theme. The Theme task pane will be displayed on the right. You can see that the web site default theme is "Journal." You can click a few other themes to see how the Home Page can be instantly revised with a new look. When you are finished, or find the theme you want to use, click the Close button on the Theme task pane. The theme you have chosen will become part of the page when it is saved.

12. On the Home Page, seen in Figure 3-2, you can see some of the features incorporated in this web (scroll through the page to make sure you see everything). Here are some of the features to note:

**TIP** *If the Folder List is still open, click the Close button in the pane title bar. To turn it back on, use the Toggle Pane button in the toolbar (sixth button from the left, as shown here, which toggles between no pane on the left, a Folder List pane, or a Navigation pane) to close it and gain more screen area to display the page.*

- Hyperlink buttons ("Home," "Feedback," "Contents," and "Search") at the top of the page, called a *link bar*, allow visitors to jump to other pages in your web site.

- The page title, "Home," called a *page banner,* and the page background are graphics. You can create graphics in Microsoft PhotoDraw, CorelDRAW, Adobe Photoshop, Fractal Design Painter, or other graphics packages and then place them here in FrontPage.

- The link bar down the left side, similar to the one at the top, is a series of graphics, one for each of the hyperlinks, and is included in a common border, called Shared Borders, that is used at the top, left, and bottom of each regular web page.. In Figure 3-2, there are three link bars: one at the top ("Home," "Feedback," "Contents," and "Search"); one under the Home banner (you must edit it for the buttons to be visible); and one on the left ("News," "Products," and "Services"). There is also a link bar in the bottom-shared border that you cannot see in Figure 3-2.

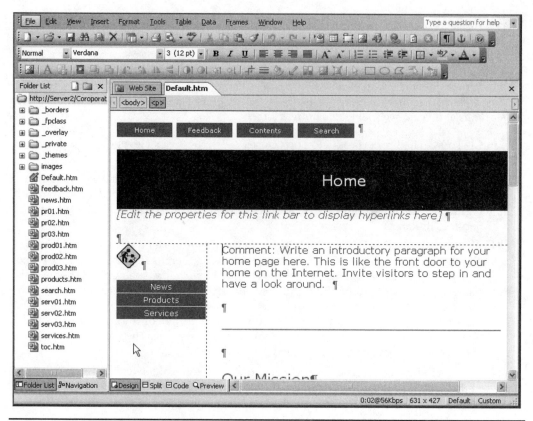

**FIGURE 3-2**   Corporate web Home Page in Design view

***NOTE*** *"Shared borders" (a name which wonderfully expressed the concept) were used in previous releases and have been upgraded by the use of Dynamic Web Templates in FrontPage 2003 with Windows SharePoint Services. If you want to enable using Shared Borders, you can do so by selecting Tools | Page Options, and then clicking Authoring. Click Shared Borders under FrontPage and SharePoint Services specific technologies.*

- The line beneath the first Comment is a graphic.

- The phone numbers, postal address, and e-mail addresses near the bottom of the page are entered and maintained through Insert | Web Component | Included Content, where Substitution is selected as the type of content. (Web Components are discussed in Chapter 9.)

13. Select Open from the File menu or click Open on the toolbar to display the Open File dialog box.

14. Double-click News.htm. (You can also just double-click news.htm in the Folder List, if it is open.) When the News.htm file is loaded in Page view, you can see the common elements that are included on each page created with the Corporate Presence Web Wizard. Notice that the "Home" page banner below the top link bar has been

replaced by one that says "News." Each page in the Corporate web will have its own page banner to identify it.

---

***TIP***    *If you do not see file extensions (the ".htm" in "News.htm"), you can turn them on by opening the Windows Explorer and its Tools menu, choosing Folder Options, selecting the View tab, and clearing the Hide Extensions For Known File Types check box.*

On any of the pages, you can enter and format text, insert graphics, and add forms, tables, and other elements, as you saw in Chapter 2. In later chapters, you will see how to do all of these tasks. The purpose here is simply to show that the Corporate Presence Web Wizard does, in fact, create a complete web. It also creates all of the structure (shown earlier) behind a web in FrontPage.

The web pages generated by the Corporate Presence Web Wizard include text and graphics, as well as content stored in common borders. The common borders—on the top, bottom, and left of the page—will be explored later in this chapter, after you have examined the rest of the page contents.

### Looking at the News Page

The News page of your Corporate web serves as a central location to list press releases, information on media coverage, changes to your web site, and to provide hyperlinks to the individual pages that describe the items in more detail.

Each element on the page has its own properties, which you can view and change by right-clicking the object and selecting Properties from the context menu. In the following steps, you will look at the Properties dialog boxes for the different types of objects on the News page.

1. Scroll down the News page, and right-click the small "NEW" image on the left of your company name ("Adventure Works Inc." if you didn't change the wizard default). In the context menu, select Picture Properties to open the Picture Properties dialog box, as shown here. (Your image may differ slightly if you have Windows SharePoint Services.)

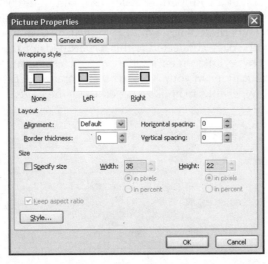

- In the Appearance tab of the Picture Properties dialog box, you can choose the wrapping style, set the alignment of the graphic within text on the page, specify horizontal and vertical spacing around the graphic, create a border for it, and specify the size.

- In the General tab, you can select the image to be shown, provide text that will appear in browsers that do not display graphics (this text will also be displayed for a few seconds if you point on the graphic in a browser), and create a hyperlink for the graphic.

- The Video tab is where you select a video file and modify how the video appears, how long it plays, and when it starts.

2. Close the Picture Properties dialog box, and right-click any of the horizontal lines on the page. Select Horizontal Line Properties from the context menu. Many of the properties for the horizontal line on this page are defined by the web's theme, but you can edit these settings in the dialog box, as shown next. (Your image will differ somewhat with Windows SharePoint Services.)

3. Close the Horizontal Line Properties dialog box, and right-click the hyperlink Press Release in the line following the "NEW" image. Select Hyperlink Properties to display the Edit Hyperlink dialog box shown next. You can see next to the Address that the name of the page connected to this hyperlink is pr01.htm. You use this dialog box to set hyperlinks on either text or graphics in your web pages that connect to other locations in your web, to other intranet webs, or to the Internet. You can also set hyperlinks to bookmarks on the same page.

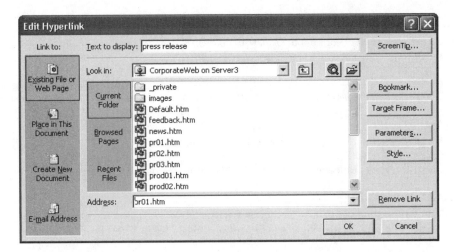

4. Click Cancel to close the Edit Hyperlink dialog box. Right-click the same Press Release hyperlink again, and select Follow Hyperlink in the context menu (or press and hold CTRL while clicking the hyperlink) to open the Press Release 1 page (pr01.htm) in Page view, as shown next. The Press Release 1 template includes space for the title of your announcement, the date of the release, and contact information for the press.

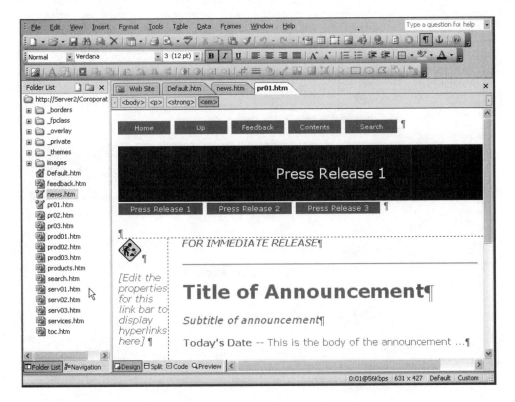

***Tip***    *In Page view, you have to press and hold* CTRL *while clicking the hyperlink, or you can open the context menu and select Follow Hyperlink to open the target of a link. In a web browser or when using the Preview, you simply click the hyperlink.*

***Note***    *The Press Release pages, as well as the Product and Service pages, are all numbered 1 through 3. As you recall, the Corporate Presence Web Wizard set the default number of pages to be created as three. The next time you create a web with this wizard, you can choose the number of Product and Service pages that best fits your needs.*

    5. Close the Press Release 1 page by selecting Close from the File menu.

## The Table of Contents Page

The Table of Contents page provides the user with a single location to open any page in a web. It is not available with Windows SharePoint Services or SharePoint 2.

    1. Open the Table of Contents page in Page view by double-clicking toc.htm in the Folder List or from the Open File dialog box. (Recall you can display the Folder List by clicking the Toggle Pane button in the toolbar, and that the Open File dialog box is accessed either by use of the Open toolbar button or by selecting File | Open.) Figure 3-3 shows the page in Page view.

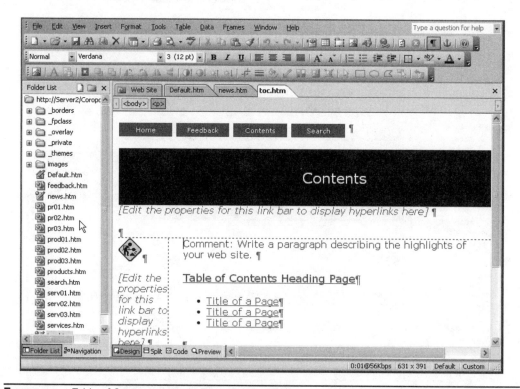

**Figure 3-3**    Table of Contents page in Page (Design) view

2. The pages listed in the Table of Contents are automatically generated, starting from the Home Page. In Page view this does not look like much, but in a browser this is automatically expanded to include references to each page and to each bookmark on those pages.

3. Open the File menu and select Preview In Browser. (You may have to fully extend the menu.) In the Preview In Browser submenu that appears, you can select a web browser to view your page, including selecting the size at which the browser will be opened. (If you click the Preview In Browser toolbar button—the name of the toolbar button will be Preview In *Name Of Your Default Browser*—you do not get a choice of browsers; your default browser automatically opens instead. Of course, if you have only one browser installed, that is what you get in either case.) Depending on your server and network configuration, you may be prompted to log onto the Internet first.

*TIP*    *To add, remove, or modify the browsers contained on the submenu, select Edit Browser List from the submenu.*

4. Click the Preview In Browser tool to open the Table of Contents page in your selected browser. Figure 3-4 shows the Table of Contents page after the Web Component has created the hyperlinks.

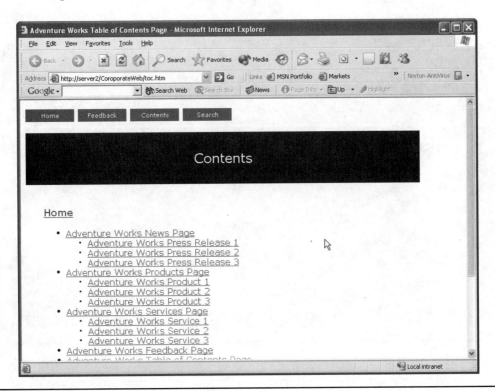

**FIGURE 3-4**    Table of Contents page in a web browser

5. Close your browser, return to Page view, and close the Table of Contents page.

---

*Tip*    *A quick way to close a page or save it is to right-click the tabbed filename (toc.htm for Table of Contents) and select Close or Save from the context menu.*

### The Feedback Page

There are many reasons to get feedback from the people who visit your web site. If your site is designed to promote a product or service, you will want to know what visitors think of your products, and as a result you'll give users a simple way of contacting you with questions. The Feedback page in the Corporate web does exactly that, as you will see by following these instructions:

1. Open the Feedback page in Page view by selecting feedback.htm in the Open File dialog box and clicking Open, or by double-clicking feedback.htm in the Folder List.

2. When the Feedback page is opened, scroll through it to see all the elements. The lower part of the page should look like this:

3. The body of the Feedback page is a form. As you saw in Chapter 2, a form is used to gather information on a web page and then transfer the information to a Web

Component or another application. This Feedback form includes a scrolling text box to enter the users' comments, a drop-down menu for users to select the subject of their comments, seven one-line text boxes for users to enter information about themselves, and buttons to submit or clear the form.

**TIP** *To see the contents of a drop-down menu on a form field in Page view, double-click the drop-down menu. Click Cancel when you are done looking at this dialog box.*

4. Right-click anywhere on the form except on one of the form fields, and select Form Properties from the context menu. The file in the File Name box of the Form Properties dialog box shows the file to which the input data will be saved.

5. Click the Options button to open the Saving Results dialog box, shown in Figure 3-5. (If you are using Windows SharePoint Server, your dialog box may be slightly different.) Here, you can set the name and location of the file to which the data is being saved, as well as the format of the file. Additional information (for example, date, time, and username) can be selected in the Saved Fields tab of the dialog box and included in the file. The Confirmation Page tab displays where you might find an e-mail response to the person filling in the feedback form. The E-mail Results allows you to set up the specifications for saving e-mail communications, such as e-mail address, format of text, and E-mail Message Header text for the Subject Line and Reply-to Line.

6. Close the Saving Results dialog box and then the Form Properties dialog box. Then close the Feedback page in Page view.

### The Search Page

In a large web site, a table of contents does not always provide the quickest method for a user to find specific information. The Search page, on the other hand, allows users to search

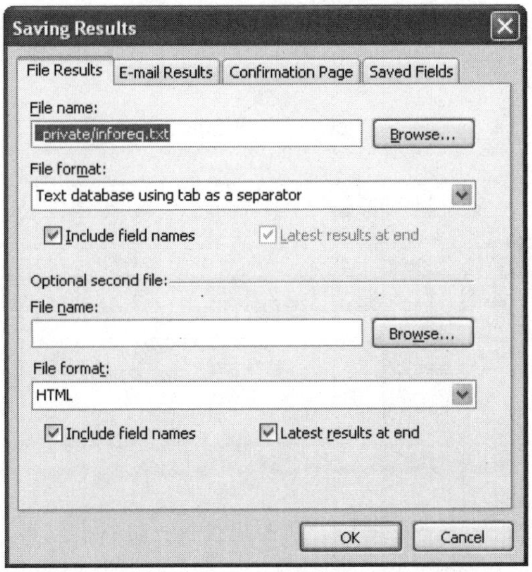

**FIGURE 3-5**
Setting where, what, and how to save feedback information

your web using any of the keywords that describe the information they are looking for. The Search page uses the Web Search Component to search the web and generate a results page that contains hyperlinks to web pages matching the search criterion. The Search Page is not available with Windows SharePoint Services. Figure 3-6 shows the results of a search of the Corporate web for the word "products."

---

**TIP** *You can hide pages, such as style pages or pages you only want to include in other pages, from the Web Search Component by placing the pages in the special web folder Webname\_private. The Search Form does not search this folder.*

1. Open the Corporate web Search page in Page view (search.htm in the Open File dialog box), and click Preview in the bottom left views bar to see the Search page shown in Figure 3-7.

2. The body of the Search page is a simple form with a single text box and two buttons. The user enters the word(s) to search for in the text box and then clicks the Start Search button. Click Design in the views bar to return to the working Page view.

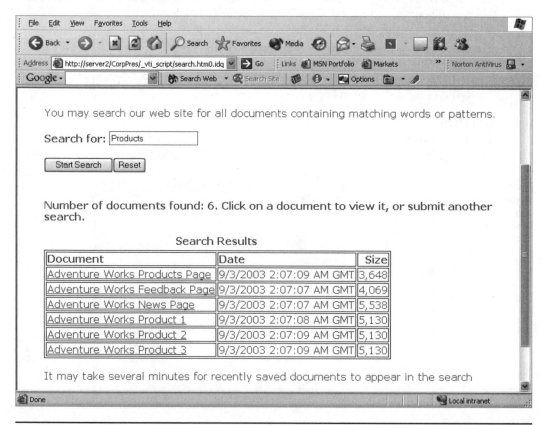

**FIGURE 3-6** Search results for the word "products"

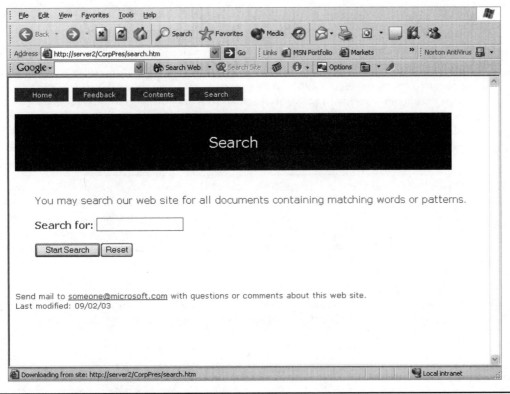

FIGURE 3-7    The Search form in Preview

3. Right-click the form (the Search For text box) and select Search Form Properties from the context menu. In the Search Form Properties dialog box (shown next), you can set the labels for the text box and the buttons, as well as set the width of the text box. In the Search Results tab of the dialog box, you can set the options for the search results. If you have Windows SharePoint Services, your dialog box may be different.

4. Click Cancel to close the Search Form Properties dialog box.

5. At this point, it would be useful to look at the entire web. Close all open pages, except for Default.htm or Index.htm, the Home Page.

6. Click the Preview In Browser toolbar button to examine your web.

7. From the Corporate home page, use the navigation buttons (hyperlinks) to look at other pages in the web. Go to the Search page and search for the word "press." After you generate a list of pages that match that criterion, go to the Feedback page and enter some constructive criticisms of the site. Notice that when you click the Submit Feedback button in the Feedback form, you will see a confirmation page that tells you that your feedback was received.

*TIP*   *On a Windows XP or Windows Server 2003 computer, if your search is unsuccessful or you get the message "Service is not running" when you do a search, it is because the Indexing Service is not started. To do that, right-click My Computer and choose Manage. Open Services And Applications and select Indexing Service. Open the Action menu and choose Start. Click Yes to begin the Indexing Service when the computer is started. Be aware that it may take a few minutes for the Indexing Service to create an index.*

8. When you are finished viewing the Corporate web in your browser, close your browser, and then delete the Corporate web by choosing Delete Web from the File menu, selecting Delete This Web Entirely in the Confirm Delete dialog box that appears, and clicking OK.

*TIP*   *If you do not have Delete Web in your File menu, you can add it by opening the Tools menu and choosing Customize. Under the Commands tab of the Customize dialog box, select File in the Categories list. Scroll the Commands list until you see Delete Web; then drag Delete Web to the File menu and drop it just below Close Site. This is a very useful command to have in your File menu.*

The Corporate web shows how easy it is to create a complete web site with the FrontPage wizards. To actually put the web on the World Wide Web, you need only add your content to the pages. In Chapter 11, you'll learn how to import word processor documents and other files into a FrontPage web.

## Connecting with the Database Interface Wizard

Connecting a web site to a database allows you to dynamically change the web site's content based on the selections made by the user. This can be a complex subject and is fully described in Chapter 17. To make the process easier, FrontPage includes a Database Interface Wizard that leads you through the process. This feature may be unavailable with SharePoint 2. See how the Database Interface Wizard works with these steps:

1. Click the down arrow on the right of the New toolbar button, choose Web Site, and then, when the Web Site Templates dialog box opens, select Database Interface Wizard. On this dialog box, you can also enter a location and name for the web site and click OK. The first Database Interface Wizard dialog box will open, as you can see here:

2. Click Use A Sample Database Connection, and then click Next. When you are told the database connection is made, click Next again. You are asked to select a table or view to use for the database connection.

3. Select Customers from the drop-down menu and then Next. You will be shown a list of fields that will be used to display data within the database. For an existing database, you can modify only the field type on the right, but for new databases, you can add and delete records and modify all fields. For now, accept most of the defaults. However, click Customer ID, click Modify, click Primary Key, and then click OK to establish the Customer ID as a Primary Key.

4. Click Next. You are asked to select the database interface pages you would like created. Select all three page types, and click Next. If you want the database protected with a username and password, enter them, or click Don't Protect My Database Editor (the example shown in this chapter is not protected). Click Next.

5. You are told the Database Interface Wizard will create the pages you selected and place the results in a specified folder. Click Finish. The Database Interface page will be displayed. On it are the three pages that were specified in the wizard.

6. Open the Database Editor by pressing CTRL and clicking the hyperlink. Figure 3-8 shows the screen.

7. To see the page with data, as it will be, you must first publish the web site to a remote location and then view it with a browser. From the File menu, select Publish Site.

8. The Remote Web Site Properties dialog box will be displayed, as shown in Figure 3-9. You have these choices:

   - **FrontPage or SharePoint Services**   Selected when you are using a server with FrontPage Server Extensions or the SharePoint Services. In this case, you enter the **http://*servername*/*webname*** address. Using this option guarantees that FrontPage functions will work.

   - **WebDAV**   Used when you want to use Web Distributed Authoring and Versioning servers.

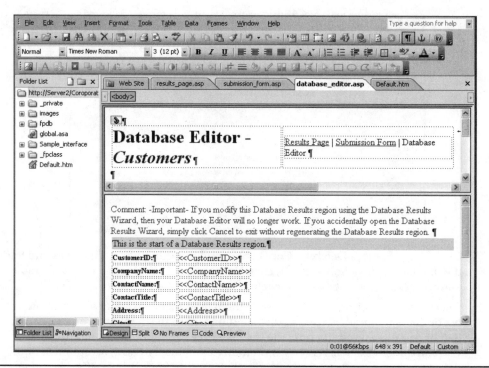

**FIGURE 3-8**    The Database Editor allows you to view and change a database.

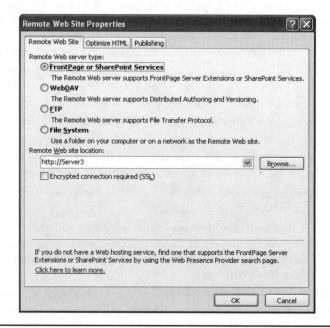

**FIGURE 3-9**    The Remote Web Site Properties dialog box specifies the server's location.

- **FTP**   Used when you want to publish the web site to an older server using File Transfer Protocol. In this case, you enter **ftp://servername/webname**.

- **File System**   Used when the web site is to be published to a folder on your computer or network. In this case, you enter the path and filename, such as **c:\folder\webname**.

9. Enter or browse to your remote web site location and click OK. The Publish Web Site panes will open, as shown next, which allow you to publish files from one location to another. Under Publish All Changed Pages in the lower right, select Local To Remote and click Publish Web Site.

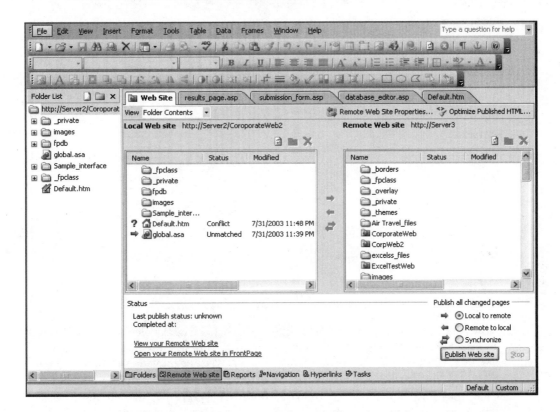

**TIP**   *If you see question marks next to some files, you are being warned of a conflict between the files on the local web site and the remote web site (that is, files on the remote site are different from those on the local site). You can resolve it by replacing one file (or files) with another that you select. The Files In Conflict view will show you when the files were created. Select the file to be retained, and click the arrow in the direction of the copy to be discarded. The selected file will overwrite the file in conflict. Then click the Publish Web Site button again.*

10. Under Status, click View Your Remote Web Site, and then click Database Editor while pressing CTRL. The web site will be displayed, as shown next. As you can see, the empty fields have been filled in with the sample data. The data will appear when you look at the pages with a browser.

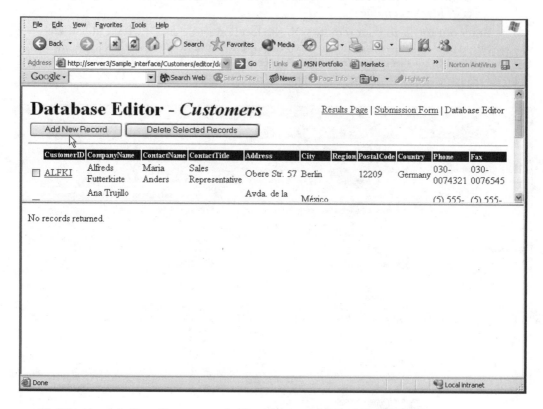

11. Now back in FrontPage, open the Results page (click the tab labeled results_page.asp) and the Submission page (submission_form.asp). At first, these pages don't look like much, but when you look at them with a browser, as they are meant to be seen, they look fine. Look at them with the Preview In Browser button on the toolbar.

12. Close the browser, reopen the Database Editor page, and click Preview In Browser. If you are told you haven't saved your changes (creating the web site), click Yes to do so. The Database Editor will then open in a browser, as shown next. The window is divided into two panes. The list of customers is in the top pane, and the lower will be used to edit or modify the database records.

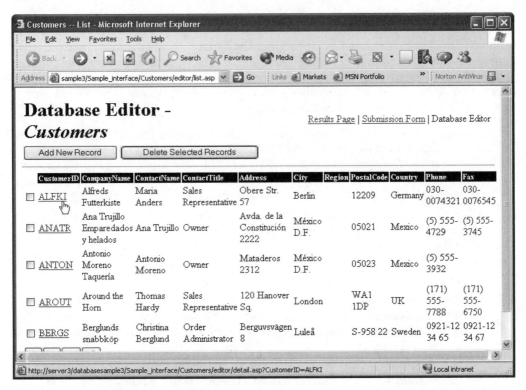

13. Click the CustomerID hyperlink for a name, and it will be displayed in the lower pane. You can edit and delete a record here. Click Results Page at the top of the Database Editor page. Here, a set of five or fewer database records is displayed along with a group of navigational buttons that enable you to move from one set to the next, or to jump to the first or last set of records.

14. Click Submission Form at the top of the Results page. Here you can enter a record into the database by entering the desired contents into each field and clicking OK at the bottom of the form.

15. Return to the Database Editor page, and note how you can either add or delete records here. Click Add New Record. The Submission form you just saw opens in the lower pane. As you saw earlier, to delete a record, you would select a record and click Delete Selected Records, and the edit/delete pane would open.

16. Close the browser and then delete the web entirely.

This gives you a brief introduction to the Database Interface Wizard. Besides using the sample database, you can create a new database in FrontPage with which you can interface, or create an interface to an existing Access database, an external SQL, or an Oracle database. In Chapter 17, you'll see how to directly work with a database.

## Working with the Discussion Web Wizard

Discussion groups provide a means for people to have online conversations. They provide a simple way for you to link comments about a single subject, or to find comments about a specific subject in the discussion group. You can create a separate discussion web or incorporate a discussion group in another web by using the Discussion Web Wizard (this is unavailable in Windows SharePoint Services):

1. Choose New from the File menu and click More Web Site Templates on the New pane, or click the down arrow next to the New toolbar button and select Web Site. The Web Site Templates dialog box will open. Enter the location and name for the web site, and double-click Discussion Web Site Wizard. The first Discussion Web Wizard dialog box will explain how the wizard works.

2. Click Next. The second dialog box will ask you the features of a discussion group that you want to include, as you can see in Figure 3-10. Your choices include the following:

   - **Submission Form**    The form is used to submit comments to the discussion and is required for a discussion group.

   - **Table of Contents**    Provides a means of organizing and finding previously submitted comments by subject. If you want readers to read and comment about what previous contributors have submitted, then you need to include a table of contents.

   - **Search Form**    An alternative way for readers to find previously contributed information. It allows a reader to find a contribution containing words other than those in the subject.

   - **Threaded Replies**    Links multiple comments on the same subject. This allows the reader to go directly from one comment to the next on a given subject.

   - **Confirmation Page**    Shows the person making a submission what the system has received.

**FIGURE 3-10**
Discussion Web
Site Wizard's
second dialog box

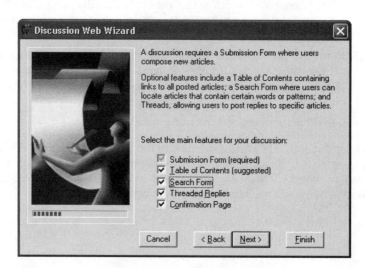

3. Select all of the options if they are not already checked, so you can look at them, and click Next. The third dialog box will open and ask for the title you want to use as well as the folder name for the discussion group messages. Accept **Discussion** for the title, and accept the default folder name (note that discussion folder names must begin with an underscore). Click Next.

4. You will be able now to choose input fields for the discussion, such as the default fields named "Subject" and "Comments." Accept the defaults. You will be able to add more later in Page view. Again, click Next.

5. For the next five dialog boxes, accept the defaults and click Next. You will see these subjects:

   - Restrict contributors to the discussion group or allow anyone to contribute.

   - Sort the list of posted articles by time entered.

   - Home page to be the Table of Contents.

   - Select the information to be searched using a selection of one or a combination of Subject, Size, Date, and Score.

   - Using frames with browsers or not, and how to arrange them between contents and the displayed article.

6. Finally, click Finish and you will see the Web Site Folders view.

7. Click Navigation view in the views bar and double-click the single box in the right pane of Navigation view to open the Discussion Group Home Page in Page view. From here, you can open any of the pages and make any changes you desire.

8. To try a page, though, you need to look at it in a browser. And to do that, you need to publish the web site to a server that has the FrontPage Server Extensions before it will function properly.

---

**TIP**  *If your server does not have FrontPage Extensions, you may need to publish the web to a remote web site that does. In this case, select File | Publish Web, set up the specifications and location of the server, click OK, and then click Publish Web Site.*

---

9. Preview your web in your Internet browser, and your Discussion Group web Home Page will appear, as shown in Figure 3-11.

10. Click Post A New Article. In the form that appears, enter a subject, your name, and some comments; then click Post Article. (If you get a message saying you are about to send information over the Internet and other people might see it, click Yes.) The confirmation should appear showing the subject you entered.

11. In the Confirmation page, you are told that the article has been submitted to the discussion group. Click the Refresh The Main Page hyperlink. Back at the Home Page you saw in Figure 3-11, you should again see the subject you entered under Contents. You may need to click the Refresh button in your browser to see articles that were just entered. Click your subject and that message will appear in the bottom frame, as shown in Figure 3-12. You will see the name, the date and time you made the submission, and the comments you entered. Depending on the

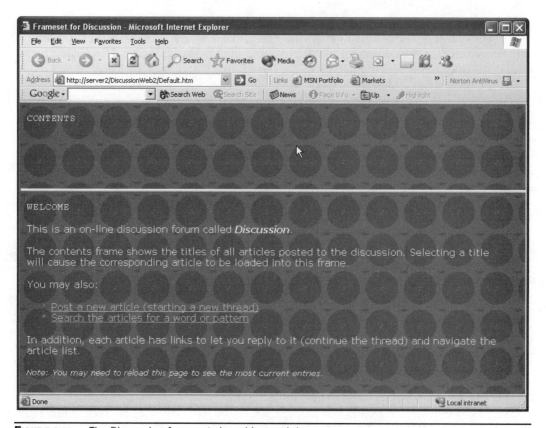

**FIGURE 3-11**    The Discussion frameset viewed in a web browser

options you selected for your discussion group, you may see other information about the person who submitted the comment as well.

12. The link bar in the top of the bottom frame now has several new entries: Contents, Search, Post (to start a new thread), Reply (to add a comment to an existing thread), Next and Previous (to go forward and backward, respectively, in the current thread), and Up (to go to the next thread).

13. Try these new link bar entries by making several submissions, both independent and in reply to another submission, so you can see how the navigation works. When you are done, close the browser and delete the web.

A discussion group can be a powerful means of communication, and FrontPage offers an easy way to create one.

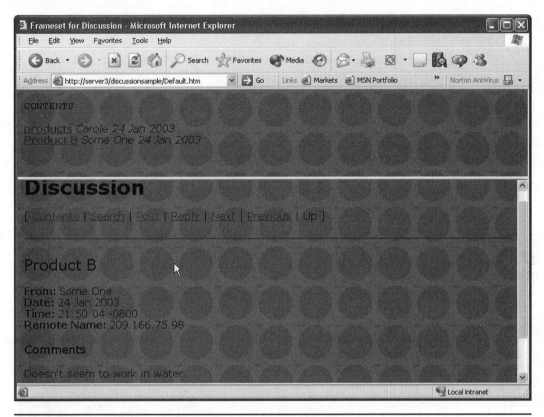

**FIGURE 3-12**    Message selected in the Contents frame and displayed in the Discussion frame

## Using the Import Web Wizard

If FrontPage 2003 is the first version of FrontPage you've used, you may have a number of existing webs that you will want to convert to FrontPage webs. The process is extremely simple when you use the Import Web Wizard.

1. If it isn't open already, open the New task pane on the right, and as you have done previously, select More Web Site Templates, provide a name, and double-click Import Web Site Wizard.

2. In the Import Web Site Wizard dialog box, select a source for your web—either from your local computer or network, or from the World Wide Web. If you choose a source on your local computer or network, enter the complete pathname of the folder where the web is located, or click the Browse button to locate the folder. Select the Include Subsites check box. If you choose the World Wide Web, enter the complete URL and whether it requires a secure connection. Then click Next.

3. Now specify where you want to create a local copy. Click Add To Current Web Site for this exercise.

4. Click Next and the next wizard dialog box will be displayed. Click Finish to complete the import function.

5. You will now see the Folder Contents view showing the Local Web Site on the left and the Remote Web Site on the right, as shown in Figure 3-13. Here you can specify the files you want to import.

6. If you are updating the local web site with the remote web site, you can just verify on the lower right corner that it says "Publish All Changed Pages," verify "Remote to Local" is selected, and click Publish Web Site. If you want to move only selected files, then select the files and folders on the right to be imported, since you are moving files from a remote site to a local one, and click the left arrow. The files will be copied.

That's all there is to it. Your imported web will be displayed in FrontPage, ready for you to work on it. Be sure to delete your imported web site.

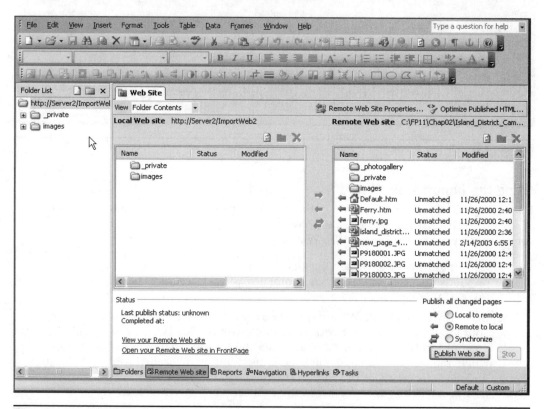

**FIGURE 3-13**    The Folder Contents view allows you to select the files to be imported.

## Page Wizards

In addition to the wizards that create a full web site, FrontPage comes with several wizards that create a single page template. Depending on your installation, you may see either one or three page wizards in the Page Templates dialog box. If you see only one wizard, it is the Form Page Wizard, which leads you through the creation of a single page form by allowing you to select the information you want the form to collect. This was briefly demonstrated in Chapter 2 and will be covered further in Chapter 8. The other two page wizards will only appear if you are connected to a server with SharePoint installed (see "Teaming Up with the SharePoint Team Web Site" in Chapter 4) and have an open web in FrontPage. These are the Document Library View Page Wizard, which creates a page to view the Team Web Site's document library, and the List View Page Wizard, which creates a page to view a Team Web Site list. SharePoint and the Team Web Site are described briefly in Chapter 4 and in more detail in Chapter 22.

## Themes

Overall, the purpose of a theme is to provide a unifying, cohesive look-and-feel to your entire web site. You can create many of the same attributes by using Dynamic Web Templates, your own templates, or other templates that FrontPage supplies. But FrontPage can do much of the work if you choose. Themes apply and control various elements of a web page and consistently apply these elements to pages you select. Having coordinated graphic elements, background images, and link bars gives a familiar feel to your web site. Visitors will see the same color schemes, navigation tools, and graphic images at each page in your site.

Some of the elements that are applied to pages incorporating a theme include the following:

- Text colors
- Bullet styles and colors
- Font sizes and types
- Link bars and buttons
- Heading styles
- Horizontal lines
- Page background images
- Page banners

As you will see, FrontPage 2003 comes with a generous selection of themes that can be applied to an entire FrontPage web or to individual pages.

### Assigning Themes to Web Sites

When you generate a web site using a wizard, a theme is automatically applied to most of the web sites or pages. However, you can choose to accept the theme or choose another, regardless of whether the web already has a theme applied to it.

1. Open or create a FrontPage web. A good example would be the Corporate Web Site Wizard. Open the Home Page in Page view. If you want to open an existing web,

you can simply choose File | Recent Sites and then choose the site you want to open.

2. From the Format menu, choose Theme. The Theme pane will open on the right, as shown in Figure 3-14. It shows a series of thumbnails that contain a small image of the themes. They are organized into three sections: Web Site Default Theme, the Recently Used Themes, and All Available Themes. (If this is the first time you have used Themes, all categories may not appear.)

3. You can see that the top theme is the one used on your web. In Figure 3-14, the theme used on the Corporate web site was Journal. Yours may differ depending on which web site you opened, or you may not have one at all if your web didn't originally have one. Scroll through the web site, and note some of the objects that are included in a theme, such as these in the Corporate web site:

   - A banner at the top of the page
   - Navigation buttons at the top of the page
   - A horizontal line above the Mission comment
   - A matching set of different-sized bullets for bullet lists

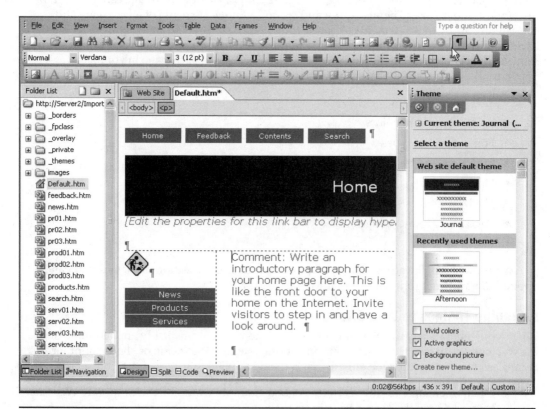

**FIGURE 3-14**   Themes, found in the Theme pane, are used to apply theme formats to your web site.

- A color scheme that color coordinates page text, banners, bullets, and horizontal lines

- A unified color scheme for links, followed links, and active links

4. Now experiment by selecting several themes and seeing their schemes on the Theme pane.

5. Below the list of themes are three check boxes that add special effects to a selected theme. As soon as you click one of two check boxes (the first or third check box), the effect of that selection is applied immediately in the sample thumbnail in the theme area.

   - Choosing the Vivid Colors option brightens the color scheme or applies a background color, and generally transforms your site from subtle to brash.

   - Choosing the Background Picture check box replaces the solid color background with a tiled graphic image.

   While you can test the effects of the Vivid Colors and Background Picture check boxes in the thumbnails in the Theme pane, you will not see the full effect of active graphics when you select the Active Graphics check box. This option transforms navigation buttons in your web pages into dynamic hover buttons. To test these hover buttons, you will have to apply your theme and open your web page using a browser that interprets Java applets.

6. After you decide which theme and theme options to apply to your web pages, click the down arrow on the right edge of the thumbnail theme you want (you will have to place the cursor over the thumbnail before you see the arrow). From the context menu, shown here, you can select one of several options:

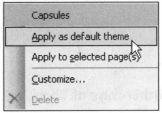

   - You can select to apply the theme as a default. In this case, all pages of a web site use this theme, and all future pages will be automatically created with it. Any modifications to a theme will be applied to all pages as well.

   - You can apply the theme to selected pages. In this case, only the selected pages will have the theme.

   - You can customize an existing theme by varying its fonts, colors, and so on.

7. To apply a theme as a default, display the context menu of the theme you have chosen. If you are applying the theme as the default to an existing web, you are warned that applying the theme will permanently change some existing formatting, and that individually themed pages will not be changed. If you want to do that, click Yes. Then look at the effect in your web pages by opening them in Page view or in your browser.

---

**NOTE**  *If you select Apply As Default Theme to a web site with an existing theme, all pages of the web site will be reformatted with the new theme, except for pages having individual themes.*

## Assigning Themes to Selected Web Pages

As you have seen, themes can be assigned to one or more selected web pages as well as to an entire FrontPage web. Because the purpose of a theme is to provide a unifying look and feel to your entire web site, themes are usually applied to entire webs. However, you might want to assign themes to an individual page for a number of reasons. You could decide that one or more pages in your web should not look like they are part of the overall web site. These pages might include legal disclaimers, pages that provide information that isn't integral to the overall message of the web, or pages you want to stand out from the rest of the web.

To apply a theme to one or more selected web pages, you will open it in Page view and use the following steps:

1. With your web Home Page open in Page view, open the Format menu and choose Theme.

2. The Theme pane will open. Find the theme you would like to have applied to your selected page. This can be one of the many themes defined for you, or it can be No Theme, one of the choices.

3. Select the files to which you want the theme applied. You do this in the Folder List, which you can toggle on and off with the Toggle Pane button on the toolbar if it is not already showing. To select the pages, simply hold CTRL and click the pages you want.

4. From the context menu, select Apply To Selected Pages.

5. Once you have previewed your theme in Page view, you can close the Theme pane.

That does it. However, there are some other ways of seeing the theme applied to a web page.

## Other Ways of Checking a Web Page Theme

There are a couple of other ways to see what theme is applied to a page, as well as to remove a theme from a page. You can remove themes using the Page Properties dialog box. With your web page open in Page view, right-click anywhere on the page, and choose Page Properties from the context menu. If a theme has been applied to the web page, the Page Properties dialog box has a Custom tab (see Figure 3-15) that lists the applied theme in the User Variables section. You can delete a theme by selecting the theme from the User Variables list and clicking the Remove button.

You can also view or remove themes in the HTML view by clicking the Code button in the bottom of the Page view window. The HTML code will be displayed, such as:

```
<meta name="Microsoft Theme" content="topo 111">
```

This code indicates that the Topo theme has been applied to the page. You can remove a theme by selecting this line of HTML code in the Code view and pressing DEL.

## Customizing Themes

Even though you have applied a new theme to an open web page, you can still edit many of the page format elements using page formatting. For example, you can change font color,

**FIGURE 3-15**
The Page Properties dialog box is another place you can change the theme.

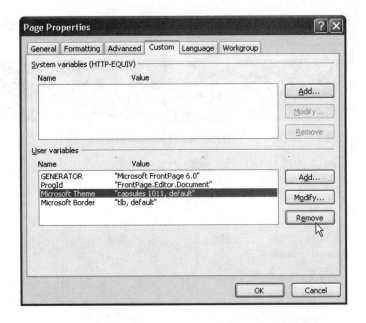

font size, and paragraph alignment. However, other formatting options cannot be changed after applying a theme, such as the background and the default text and hyperlink colors. To change these elements, you must customize a theme. Here is how you can do this:

1. With a web site open in Page view, select Format | Theme. The Theme pane will be displayed on the right.

2. Find the thumbnail image of the theme you wish to customize, and click the down arrow on it to display a context menu. Select Customize.

**NOTE**  *The Web Site Default Theme cannot be customized since it would change web site pages that may not be displayed.*

3. The Customize Theme dialog box will be displayed, as shown in Figure 3-16. On it are three buttons allowing you to modify Colors, Graphics, and Text. Click Colors. You can see the color schemes on the left and the preview of the color scheme on the right. Click a few color schemes on the left to see the differences. You can switch back and forth between Normal Colors and Vivid Colors while you click color schemes to see how colors can be emphasized. Sometimes the theme schemes are very subtle and sometimes dramatic. Click OK when you are finished.

4. Click Graphics. Here you can change the graphic or fonts. The Picture tab is showing the file that identifies the current graphic, which is previewed on the right. Click the Item drop-down menu, and select an item, such as Horizontal Navigation. You will see the graphics for that item. With the Browse button, you can replace a graphic with one you prefer.

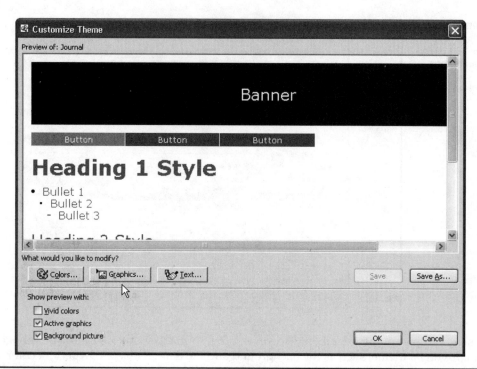

**FIGURE 3-16**    You can customize a theme by changing color, graphics, and text attributes.

5. Click the Font tab. This is how you change text on graphic elements. Select an item from the drop-down menu. As you click a font on the left, you can see it previewed on the right. You can also change the style, size, horizontal alignment, and vertical alignment by changing those attributes. When you are finished, click OK.

6. Click Text. Here you will see how the fonts can be changed for text in a web page. From the Item drop-down menu select a text item. Then click a Font to see how it appears in the Preview side. When you are done, click OK.

7. You can Save a theme to overwrite the existing one, or Save As a theme to create an entirely new theme. When you are done, click Cancel and then No, if prompted, to close the Customize Theme dialog box.

Themes have many advantages, including the fact that they create attractive, professional, coordinated, and useful web pages very quickly. The downside is that your ability to fine-tune the look-and-feel of your web site is constrained by themes.

While learning about FrontPage, you may choose to use predefined themes to provide layout and design ideas. As you become proficient with FrontPage, you may want to customize the theme or use other tools to create coordinated pages that are completely unique to your site.

# Dynamic Web Templates and Shared Borders

In previous releases of FrontPage, *shared borders* have been an important part of creating a web site. In FrontPage 2003, shared borders are usurped by Dynamic Web Templates. Both of these define common sections of a web page that are set aside for content that will appear on each page of a web. The common areas are usually located at the top, bottom, left, or (rarely) right side of a page.

These common areas often include link bars. All the FrontPage webs generated by wizards or templates include link bars in the common areas. Here are some other examples of useful common attributes of Dynamic Web Templates:

- A top banner with page titles
- A bottom area with copyright information, site contact information, and other text or images you want to appear on the bottom of every page in your site
- A left border with general information you want to place in every page in your site, such as links to other pages in a web site

---

**NOTE**   *Dynamic Web Templates rarely define common areas placed on the right side of web pages because your users may not see them. Depending on the size and resolution of the users' screen, and the size of their browser window, the right side of your web pages may not be visible to them unless they use the horizontal scroll bar to see it. Since common areas often include link bars, you will normally want them to be visible as soon as your web page downloads.*

---

All FrontPage themes assign some combination of common areas to web pages. As you have seen, these can be changed. So, for example, even though a theme may apply three common areas to every page in a FrontPage web, you can change it so only two appear on a given page.

If you did not create your FrontPage web from a template or wizard, you can still assign a Dynamic Web Template to your web. Chapter 4 discusses this feature in more depth.

## Link Bars

Link bars are generated automatically in FrontPage. They include hyperlinks to other pages within your web site. How does FrontPage know the relationship between pages in your web site? FrontPage uses the page relationships shown in Navigation view to place navigation buttons. The hierarchy you assign when you create a web (as shown in Navigation view) determines the options available for link bars.

If you created your FrontPage web using a wizard or template, link bars were created automatically, defined by the way the pages are related. The actual page-to-page relationships utilized by the link bars are best viewed and changed in Navigation view. Try defining new relationships by following these steps:

1. Open a new FrontPage Empty Web Site template, choose Navigation view, and open the Folder List by clicking the Toggle Pane button on the toolbar.

---

*TIP*   *To create an empty web, you can open the Empty Web Site template, and then add blank pages to it by clicking File | New. You must save each new page individually as part of the new web site. When you save them, you can name them. You'll see how this is done in greater depth in Chapter 5.*

---

2. Drag web pages from the Folder List (left pane) into the Navigation view (right pane), as shown in Figure 3-17.

---

*NOTE*   *The view shown in Figure 3-17 is the default portrait view (that is, horizontally displayed) of a web hierarchy and the one referred to in the following points. You can switch to a landscape (vertical) display by using the Navigation toolbar, which is normally open when you are in Navigation view. Click a page to see the Navigation toolbar.*

You can define the relationship between pages by how you place them in relation to each other. For example:

- A page that is connected to and below another page in Navigation view is referred to as a *child-level* page.

- A page that is connected to and above another page is a *parent-level* page.

- Pages that are connected by a horizontal line are referred to as *same-level* pages. These relationships determine the buttons that can be included in link bars.

Once you have defined page relationships in Navigation view, you can assign link bars in Page view:

1. Open a web page in Page view.

2. Click an area in which you will place or edit an existing link bar.

3. If a link bar already exists, double-click it. If there is no link bar, select Navigation from the Insert menu, choose Link Bars | Bar Based On Navigation Structure, click Next, and then select a style, click Next, select an orientation, and finally, click Finish. The Link Bar Properties dialog box appears, as shown in Figure 3-18.

4. In the Hyperlinks To Add To Page area, choose one of the six options: Parent Level, Same Level, Back And Next (navigates between pages on the Same Level that are next to each other in Navigation view), Child Level, Global Level (Home Page and other pages at that top level), or Child Pages Under Home.

---

*TIP*   *To fully understand where the link bar hyperlinks go, turn off the Home Page and Parent Page check boxes, try each of the six options (several times) in the Hyperlinks To Add To Page area, and look at the diagram on the left (keep turning off the Home Page and Parent Page check boxes to see just the effect of the six options).*

---

5. Regardless of which option you choose, you can include a link to the home page and/or the parent page for the open page by selecting one or both of the Additional Pages check boxes.

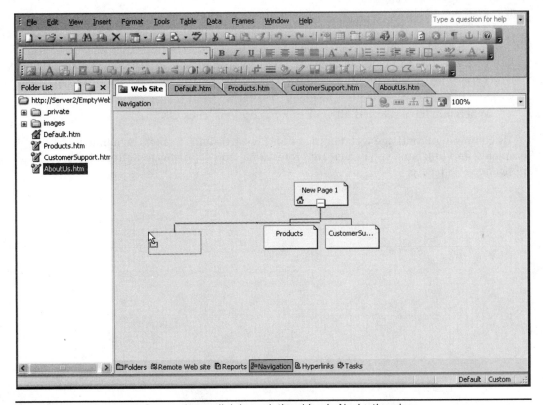

**FIGURE 3-18**    You can define or change link bar relationships in Navigation view.

**FIGURE 3-17**
The Link Bar
Properties dialog
box determines
the function of
navigation buttons.

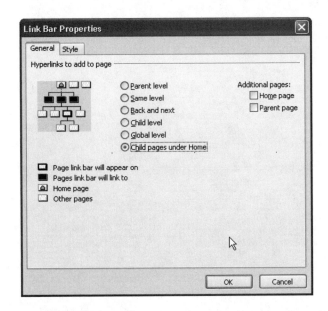

6. In the Style tab, you can choose a style or theme for the link bar by scrolling down the list and clicking the one you want. In the Orientation And Appearance area of the dialog box, you can define the layout of navigation buttons that will appear on your link bar and whether they use vivid colors and active graphics. Horizontal and vertical layouts are previewed in the small preview area on the left side of the Orientation And Appearance area of the dialog box.

7. When you have selected all your link bar options, click OK.

By combining FrontPage web templates and wizards with themes, Dynamic Web Templates, and link bars, you can create professional and sophisticated integrated web applications with ease.

# Using Templates

A s you now know, wizards and templates provide easy ways to create webs with FrontPage. In Chapter 3, you saw how to use wizards to create complete webs and pages by answering questions about the web you want to build. You briefly looked at one of the building blocks of a web, a Dynamic Web Template, which defines common areas of pages of a web. In the first part of this chapter, you'll learn how to create a Dynamic Web Template. Then you will see how to use *predefined* templates that come with FrontPage to build both webs and pages. Among these templates is the SharePoint Team Web Site template, which you can use to coordinate a group's work. In the second part of this chapter, you'll learn how to create your own page templates. The templates can then be used in creating new webs or to add pages to existing webs without having to re-create a design or layout each time.

## Dynamic Web Templates

Dynamic Web Templates, as you saw in Chapter 3, allow you to define areas of a page that contain the same or different content on all pages of a web. For instance, on all web pages you may have a common title or company name, common links to pages on the web or to other web sites, or a common footer with additional hyperlinks to other pages or copyright information. You also may have different page titles on various web pages, such as "Customer Comments Page," "Search Page," or "Product Information Page." In addition to common links on each page, you may have different ones for individual pages, such as links to different products available from the Product Information Page. You define these areas in a Dynamic Web Template and then attach to it new pages you create. Or you can attach the Dynamic Web Template to existing web pages.

A Dynamic Web Template may be attached to several web sites, for example, in an organization where departments create their own web sites using a standard preserved by the Dynamic Web Template. In this case, the departments would change the editable parts of a page to reflect the information they wish to display, while being restricted from changing the information frozen by the Dynamic Web Template.

**NOTE** *Dynamic Web Templates are replacing the Shared Borders used in earlier releases of FrontPage.*

## Creating the Common Areas

To create a Dynamic Web Template, you can create an empty web or even use a page in an existing web and then define the common and non-common areas you will use. To see how to create a Dynamic Web Template from scratch, follow these steps:

1. Select File | New and click More Web Site Templates from the New pane.

2. Under Options, fill in the location and name of the Dynamic Web Template you will create. For this purpose, call it **TestDWP** for "test Dynamic Web Page." Double-click the Empty Web Site icon. After a short pause, the test web will be displayed.

3. You will need to add a blank page to the empty web. Click Create A New Normal Page on the toolbar. A new page entitled "new_page_1.htm" will be created. In addition to the new page, a pane called "Layout Tables And Cells" is displayed. These tables and cells offer ways to organize and arrange common information, hyperlinks, and other data on your web page. You will insert a table into the blank page and then define the information contained within the common areas. (Chapter 7 explains tables and cells in depth.)

4. Choose the layout table shown in Figure 4-1 by scrolling down the Table Layout list and clicking the indicated layout.

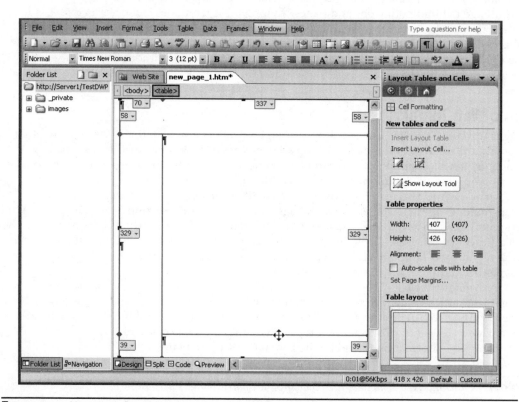

**FIGURE 4-1**    You can define the layout of a new page by selecting a predefined layout.

5. First, you might fill in the parts of the web page that you want to remain constant; for instance, you might type in the company name and address, plus any other information that you wanted to keep the same on all pages of the web site. In our test example, we typed in a company name in the top banner of the page and the address in the bottom banner.

6. Now you can define the variable areas of the Dynamic Web Template. Click the top bar or banner area beneath the company title on the table to select it, and select Format | Dynamic Web Template. Then click Manage Editable Regions. The Editable Regions dialog box will be displayed, as shown in Figure 4-2.

7. Type the name of the region, click Add, and then Close the dialog box. Beginning with selecting the region to be named, repeat the steps for each common area you want on a page. For this test, we will define three areas: the page title named **Page Name**, a side area named **Page Links**, and the **Page Body**, where the content of the page resides. The dialog box will look like Figure 4-3 when you finish.

**FIGURE 4-2**
The Editable Regions dialog box establishes common areas of a page.

**FIGURE 4-3**
Areas of a region entered into the Editable Regions dialog box

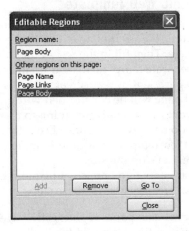

## Defining the Common Areas

After you have defined or mapped the editable areas of a Dynamic Web Template, you can enter the information they are to contain. Follow these steps to continue the process:

1. You'll notice that beneath the area name "Page Name" (the blue text within an orange outlined box) is a larger orange outlined box containing normal text within parentheses. Highlight the normal text to select it, and type the name of the page, for instance, Home Page. You can change the font size and boldness to make it stand out.

---

*Tip*    *You can click the Show All icon on the standard toolbar to expose the paragraph marks.*

2. Click within the orange box below the Page Links, and type in placeholder text that will be replaced when you create each page of the web site. For example, if you envision each page having three pages that you might link to, you might name them Link 1, Link 2, and Link 3. Later, you would replace or add to these names with buttons or actual link names.

3. You might add a couple of lines of text to the orange box for the Page Body to expand the text box.

4. Now choose a theme by selecting Format | Theme and clicking a theme from the Theme pane, for example, Afternoon.

5. Right-click on the new_page_1.dwt tab and choose Save. In the Save dialog box, give the Dynamic Web Template a name. If you do not, the name will default to the first words on the page, in this case, the company name, which might be fine with you.

6. Save the Dynamic Web Template by selecting File | Save As. Under Save As Type, choose Dynamic Web Template if not already selected and click Save.

7. Close the Dynamic Web Template by right-clicking the Name.dwt tab and choosing Close. Do not close the web site TestDWT; we'll use it next.

## Attaching a Dynamic Web Template

When you create a new web site, or change an existing web site, attach the new web page or pages to the Dynamic Web Template as one of the first actions, to define the constant and variable areas of a page. Then fill in the rest of the information. You can create the Dynamic Web Template as a separate template to be used in creating a collaborative web site, where, for example, each department or team creates its own web page as part of a greater web site. Each individual page will be constrained within the structure of a standard Dynamic Web Template. However, if you only are going to use the Dynamic Web Template for a single web site, you do not have to create a DWT that is separate from the web site. You can create the Dynamic Web Template within the single web site and then attach it to newly inserted pages as you develop the site.

For example, assume that you are creating a three-page web page using the Dynamic Web Template we just created. Follow these steps:

1. Add three new blank pages to the TestDWT web site by clicking the Create A New Normal Page icon three times in the toolbar.

2. Save the individual three pages by right-clicking the tab and selecting Save. The Save dialog box will be displayed. On it, you can rename the latter two pages if you wish, with names that describe what the pages will be used for, for example, CustServ.htm and Products.htm. Then click Save. The names will appear in the tabs above the task pane. Do not rename the home page, which will be named default.htm or index.htm.

---

**NOTE** *If you change the name of index.htm or default.htm, the page will not be automatically displayed when the web site is opened. The IIS handler opens default.htm or index.htm first, assuming it is the site's home page. However, when you don't want the page to open first, do rename it.*

3. Display the home page in Design view by clicking the Default.htm tab (or index.htm). Select Format | Dynamic Web Template and selecting Attach Dynamic Web Template. In the Attach Dynamic Web Template dialog box, click the name of the Dynamic Web Template you created (should be the DWT file in the TestDWP web site) and click Open. The new Home page with the accompanying Dynamic Web Template elements will be displayed, as shown in Figure 4-4. Repeat this for each of the other two pages.

---

**TIP** *You can attach the Dynamic Web Template to all three pages at one time by selecting the filenames in the Folder List in the left pane (click each name while holding down CTRL). Then select Format | Dynamic Web Template and select Attach Dynamic Web Template. Click Open. All three pages will be attached to the Dynamic Web Template.*

4. At this point, you can verify how the page is divided into areas that are accessible and those that are not. Place your cursor over the company name and the address. Both of these areas should be unchangeable.

5. However, the Page Name, Page Body, and Page Links can be edited freely. Change the text for the Page Name from "Home Page" to **Customer Service** for CustServ.htm and to **Products** for Products.htm. You can see how the Dynamic Web Template is used to map your pages.

6. Save each of the new pages with the attached Dynamic Web Template to retain them for use in the next section, dealing with templates. Keep the web site open for now.

When you are finished looking at the web site, continue to the next section to find out more about Dynamic Web Templates.

## Detaching, Opening, and Updating Dynamic Web Templates

When you have a web site with an attached Dynamic Web Template, you can continue to work with the common areas defined by it. You can use additional commands at this time. Select Format | Dynamic Web Template and view these commands:

- **Detach From Dynamic Web Template** Allows you to separate the Dynamic Web Template from the web page. Perhaps you have several Dynamic Web Templates, and you want to view each of them to find the correct one.

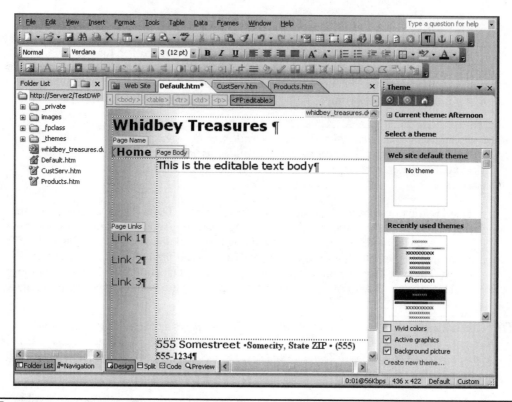

**FIGURE 4-4** The Dynamic Web Template design elements attached to a new page

- **Open Attached Dynamic Web Template** Accesses the original Dynamic Web Template. Perhaps you have determined that you need to do additional work with it. You can open it to add or remove features or refinements.

- **Update Selected Page** Updates the active web page with any changes that have been made to the Dynamic Web Template.

- **Update Attached Pages** Updates all pages that have been attached to the Dynamic Web Template.

- **Update All Pages** Updates all pages in the web site.

This has been a quick look at how you can create and attach a Dynamic Web Template for the common areas of your web sites. You can close the web site now. Future chapters will explain elements of creating these common areas in more detail, for example, Chapter 6, which discusses adding and managing hyperlinks and hotspots.

## Web Templates

FrontPage provides templates at both the web level and the page level. To take a look at the web templates, load FrontPage and then select File | New and choose More Web Site Templates from the New task pane. The Web Site Templates dialog box will open and display the templates and wizards, as shown in Figure 4-5. There are six web templates:

- One Page Web Site
- Customer Support Web Site
- Empty Web Site
- Personal Web Site
- Project Web Site
- SharePoint Team Site

## Using the One Page Web Site Template

The usual starting place for creating a general-purpose web is with the One Page Web Site template. This template creates a web folder structure for your server with a single page. Begin now with these instructions (the Web Site Templates dialog box should be open on your screen):

1. Select the One Page Web Site in the General tab of the Web Site Templates dialog box.

2. On the right of the dialog box, enter the server and folder names where you want the new web stored in the Specify The Location Of The New Web Site combo list box. For the name, type **OnePage**, and then click OK.

3. If the Folder List pane is not displayed, click Folder List in the View menu. As you can see in Figure 4-6, this creates a web with a single page, the home page named either Index.htm or Default.htm.

**FIGURE 4-5**
The Web Site Templates dialog box contains six web templates, as well as wizards.

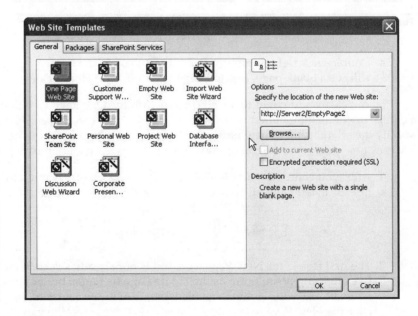

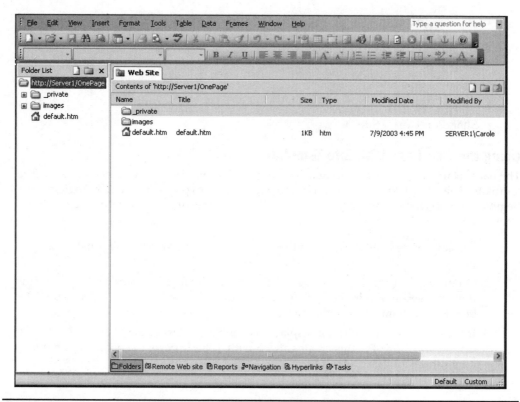

**FIGURE 4-6**    The folders and page created with the One Page Web Site template

4. Double-click Default.htm (or Index.htm) to open the home page in Page view. You will see a blank page. Just to keep track of it, type **Home Page**.

You can easily add pages to a web created with the One Page Web Site template in Page, Folders, or Navigation view, but in Navigation view you can also easily and graphically specify the relationship of new pages to existing pages. Try the following instructions and see how new pages are integrated into the web that was created in Navigation view:

1. After you generate a new One Page web, select View | Navigation. You will see a toolbar in the view title bar, as shown here:

2. The first icon is the New Page icon. If it is not already selected, click the Default.htm (we are using default.htm as the Home Page filename, but you might have index.htm as your Home Page filename) icon in the center of the page to select it, click the New Page icon on the Navigation toolbar (on the view title bar), and a new page will be inserted in the Navigational chart under the Default.htm. Click five

more times for a total of six new pages in all. The first page you generate is called "New Page 1" and is a child page to the Home Page. The rest are named in a like manner sequentially.

**NOTE** *To create a new page, you can also click the Home Page icon in the right pane, click File | New, and then click Blank Page from the New task pane on the right. You can create as many pages as you need by following these steps.*

3. Edit the navigational relationships between pages by dragging the pages in the right (Navigation) pane of the Navigation view such that pages 4 and 5 are under page 2, and page 6 is under page 4, as shown in Figure 4-7.

**TIP** *Right-click an empty area of the right pane of Navigation view, and choose Zoom | Size To Fit to see all the pages in case some are outside the window. If it is open, you can also do this using the Navigation toolbar (rightmost drop-down menu).*

**NOTE** *To refresh the file list in the Folder List, select View | Refresh.*

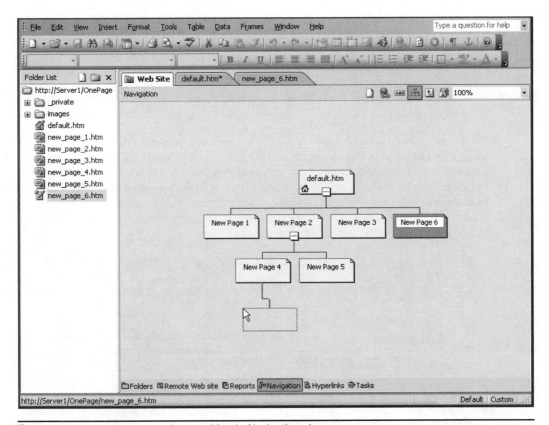

**FIGURE 4-7** Dragging a page into position in Navigation view

4. At this point, you might want to rename the pages with names you can relate to. So right-click on each page icon and choose Rename; then type the name you want, such as Customer Service, About Us, or Products. The name will not change the name of the file. It changes the Title of the name in the Page Properties. To change the filename, right-click on the filename in the Folder List and select Rename.

5. Return to the home page by clicking the Default.htm tab. In the Folder List, select all seven pages by clicking each as you press CTRL. Then select Format | Dynamic Web Template. Click Attach Dynamic Web Template, as shown in Figure 4-8. Supply the location and name of the Dynamic Web Template and click Open (see Note). A Choose Editable Regions for Content dialog box will be displayed to help you map a new page to the Dynamic Web Template regions. Click OK. The pages of the web will be updated, and you will see the effects of the Dynamic Web Template on all pages of the web.

---

***TIP***   *The attached DWT name is shown in the upper-right corner of the page.*

---

***NOTE***   *The Dynamic Web Template used here is the one created in the previous example. It can be found in My Network Places/TestDWT/yourname.dwt or Servername/TestDWT/yourname.dwt.*

---

6. Double-click the first new page (not default.htm), and replace the heading in the Page Name with the name on the page tab. You are customizing each of the pages. Before you go to the next page, save the current page by right-clicking the tab and choosing Save.

---

***NOTE***   *If you cannot save the page with a name change using Save, select File | Save As and enter the new name of the page.*

---

7. Now you will insert some hyperlinks. Click the home page tab (default.htm or index.htm) to see it in Page view. Select the text "Link 1" and replace it with the name of one of the main pages, such as Customer Service. Select the new name and right-click in the selected text area. Select Hyperlink. In the Insert Hyperlink dialog box, shown in Figure 4-9, select the file corresponding to the newly named page, "*custserv*.htm" (or whatever your new name is) and click OK. If you want, repeat this to insert hyperlinks for other named pages.

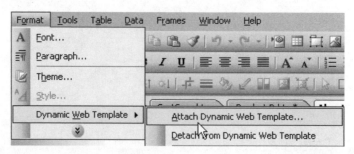

---

**FIGURE 4-8**   You can apply a Dynamic Web Template to all pages of a web by selecting the pages and attaching the Dynamic Web Template.

PART I

FIGURE 4-9
Inserting
hyperlinks can be
done on the web
pages.

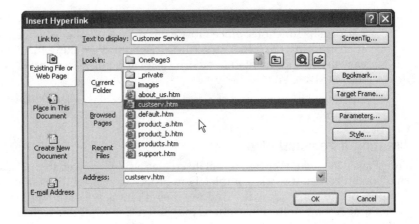

8. Finally, to verify that the hyperlink connects to the correct page, right-click the hyperlink and select Hyperlink Properties. You can see in the Address that the hyperlink refers to the page you intended.

9. When you are ready, open the File menu, choose Delete Web, click Delete This Web Site Entirely, and click OK. (If you don't see a Delete Web option on the File menu, you need to drag it there from Tools | Customize | Commands as described in Chapter 3.)

This has given you an idea of how you create a multipage web site from the One Page template, manipulate the structure of the web with the Navigation view, attach a Dynamic Web Template, and insert hyperlinks.

As you create your own webs, you'll probably often use the One Page Web Site template to build the small or custom webs that you'll need.

## Applying the Empty Web Template

If you are going to import web content (see Chapter 11 for more on this subject) and want a FrontPage structure in which to place it, then the Empty Web template is the way to start. This template creates a web folder structure for your server, but does not generate any web pages. Do that now with these instructions:

1. Click the down arrow next to New on the toolbar, click Web Site, click Empty Web Site in the Web Site Templates dialog box, enter a server and folder name, and click OK.

2. If the Folder List is not showing, select View | Folder List, and you will see that the folder structure has been created for the web, but with no pages, like this:

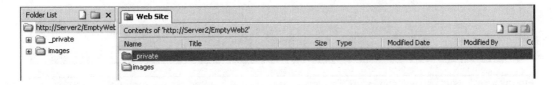

Why go to all this trouble for an empty web? FrontPage needs the folder structure to perform its functions. Since most webs have a number of pages and other elements, such as forms, the folder structure is used for organizing the web and making it easy to use and maintain. You can easily add pages to this web just as you did with the One Page Web Site.

3. Open the File menu and choose Delete Web, click Delete This Web Site Entirely, and click OK.

## Creating a Personal Web

FrontPage's Personal Web Site template creates a six-page web to publicize a person or small organization. It works completely in FrontPage Server Extensions 2002, but some components do not work with Windows SharePoint Services (SharePoint 2). If you are using SharePoint 2, some of the illustrations may differ. See what this web is like by building it with the following steps:

1. Select File | New and choose More Web Site Templates. Enter a server and folder name, and double-click Personal Web Site. The new web appears and if you look at Folders view, you will see the six pages (the six HTM files) that you can customize, as shown in Figure 4-10.

**FIGURE 4-10**     Folders view shows six filenames for six pages created by the Personal Web Site template.

2. Double-click the Welcome Page (the Index.htm or Default.htm file) to open it in Page view. The page that opens has a lot of features incorporated into it, some of which are shown in Figure 4-11. These features are only suggestions and can be removed or customized. They provide a starting set of elements that you can use or delete depending on your needs, and you can add any other features you want. Among the important features are the following:

- **Page title**    At the top of the page is a Page Banner that contains a graphic with the page title text overlaid. To change the text, you must change the page title ("Welcome to my Web site" in this case) by right-clicking the banner and selecting Page Banner Properties. Or in Navigation view, right-click the page and choose Rename. Changing the name in the Page Banner Properties dialog box or editing the text on the page does not permanently change the title.

- **Table framework**    Separates the various parts of the page. Each of the cells is identified by a dotted line in Design view, but in Preview view, you only see the lines that have been drawn. Tables are discussed in Chapter 7.

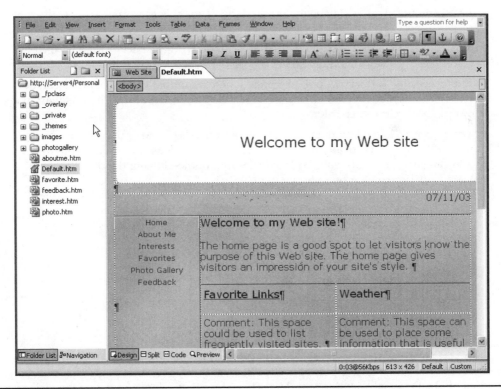

**FIGURE 4-11**    Home page created with the Personal Web Site template

- **Link bars**   On the left side and at the bottom of the page, these lines of text are hyperlinks to other pages in the web. You can edit a link bar by right-clicking the text that is or represents the link bar and then choosing Link Bar Properties. The Link Bar Properties dialog box will open, where you can change the hyperlinks used for navigation and the orientation and appearance of the buttons. You'll work with this dialog box later in the chapter. Link bars are discussed more in Chapter 3.

---

**TIP**   *The Link Bar Properties dialog box, in the Hyperlinks To Add To Page area, allows you to determine how the selected link bar buttons are hierarchically organized, and you can alter the hierarchy from among pages above (Parent Level), below (Child Level), or on the same level. By clicking a radio button, you choose which links will be displayed on the selected link bar.*

---

- **Plain text**   Text that you can replace with your own words by simply editing it as you would in a word processor. For example, you would normally replace "The home page is a good spot…" with your own words.

- **Hyperlinks**   Marked with underlines, hyperlinks are links to other pages in your web site or other sites on an intranet or the Internet.

- **Background image**   May be included in the page. This is a small graphic file that is *tiled* or repeated across the background of the web page.

- **Text font and colors**   Assigned attributes, along with the background image or color, these are part of a theme that has been attached to this web.

- **Photo Album/Gallery**   A link to a page where a number of photographs can be automatically displayed with captions. See the discussion of the Photo Gallery page template later in this chapter.

- **Time stamp**   Placed on the page using the Date And Time option of the Insert menu. It will automatically display the date the page was last updated or edited. You can change the time-stamp properties by double-clicking the date to open the Date And Time dialog box, shown here:

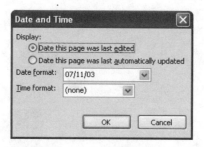

When you are done looking at the home page, double-click the HTM files listed on the Folder List (or you can choose Open from the File menu) to view other pages that were generated by the Personal Web Site template. Then close Page view and delete the web you created. The "simple" personal web you can create with the Personal Web Site template is a good starting point for many webs and offers a number of useful features. Consider using it as you create your own webs.

## Using the Project Web Template

The Project Web template creates a multipage web, which is used to keep people up-to-date on a project. As with the Personal Web Template, the Project Web Template works completely in FrontPage Server Extensions 2002, but some components do not work with Windows SharePoint Services (SharePoint 2). The structure is shown in Figure 4-12. It lists a project's staff members, schedule, an archive, a search engine, and a discussion bulletin board. On each page, you will see independent page headers and footers. (You've seen how some of these features are used in the webs you created with wizards in Chapter 3.) Follow these steps to look at some of the features that are unique to this template:

1. Open the Web Site Templates dialog box, select Project Web Site, enter a server and folder name for the web, such as "Project," and click OK. A new web will be created and will appear. In Navigation view, it will look like Figure 4-12.

2. Double-click the Home icon in Navigation view to open Page view. The page shown in Figure 4-13 will be displayed.

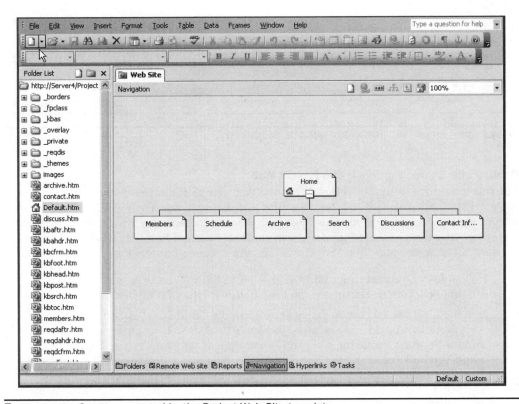

**FIGURE 4-12**    Structure created by the Project Web Site template

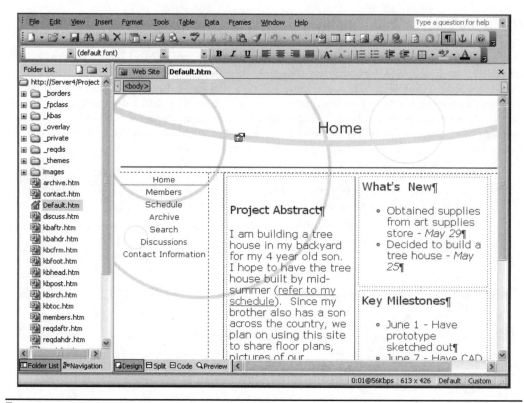

**FIGURE 4-13**    Project web home page with title and link bars

## Dealing with Shared Borders in the Project Web

The previous chapter explained how Dynamic Web Templates have replaced shared borders in FrontPage 2003. You saw how both features add common areas to a web, and you created a Dynamic Web Template in the One Page web discussion earlier in this chapter. You may have webs that contain shared borders from earlier releases of FrontPage. See how shared borders can be edited here. The Project web has three shared borders that can be edited.

1. Double-click discuss.htm. Edit the link bar in the left shared border by double-clicking it. This opens the Link Bar Properties dialog box.

2. In the Link Bar Properties dialog box, select the Child Level option from the Hyperlinks To Add To Page area, and leave the Home Page check box selected. In the Style tab, leave the style and orientation as they are set (use Page's Theme and Vertical) and click OK. The names that appear in a link bar are the names of the other pages in the web as determined by the Link Bar Properties dialog box.

---

***TIP***    *To change the actual words used in the link bar, you can change the page names in Navigation view by right-clicking a page, selecting Rename, and entering a new name over the original one, followed by pressing* ENTER.

3. On the home page, scroll to the bottom of the page. Note the bottom shared border, as shown next. It has the automatic Date and Time component (although it is showing only the date here).

Home | Members | Schedule | Archive | Search | Discussions | Contact Information ↵
↵
Copyright or other proprietary statement goes here. ↵
For problems or questions regarding this Web site contact [ProjectEmail]. ↵
Last updated: 07/11/03. ¶

4. Open and review the Members, Schedule, and Archive pages. On each you'll see the shared borders, as well as other features you saw on the Project Web Home Page. Keep this web site open; you will continue to work with it in the next section.

---

*NOTE*  *Since you chose Child Level in the Link Bar Properties dialog box for the left shared border, you only have Home in the link bar of the pages below the Home page. If you change it on the child pages so you have links there, you won't have any links on the Home page (try it and see), but the original default of Child Pages Under Home works for both page types.*

### Searches and Discussion Groups

The Project web that you produced incorporates two other FrontPage-created features—text searches and discussion groups—that add interactivity to the web. You saw how these features worked in the Corporate Presence web you created in Chapter 3. To review how these work in the Project web:

1. Open the Project Web Search page in Page view by choosing Open from the File menu and double-clicking Search.htm. Your screen should look like Figure 4-14. This page includes a one-field form that allows you to search the documents in the current web for a particular text string that you have entered in the form.

---

*NOTE*  *Depending on how you left your link bar properties, your link bar may differ from what is shown in Figure 4-14.*

2. This search form is another FrontPage Web Component. You can edit its characteristics by right-clicking the search area and choosing Search Form Properties. (You can also just double-click the search area.) On the Search Form Properties tab, you set specifications for the search function, for example, how it is labeled, width for the text string, the Start button label, and the Reset button label. On the Search Results tab, you can set search results characteristics, such as the scope of the search, the number of maximum records recorded, and some display options.

3. Close the dialog box and the Search page (File | Close or right-click the tab) and open the Project web Discussions page (Discuss.htm), which contains links to two discussion groups (Requirements Discussion and Knowledge Base). The discussion

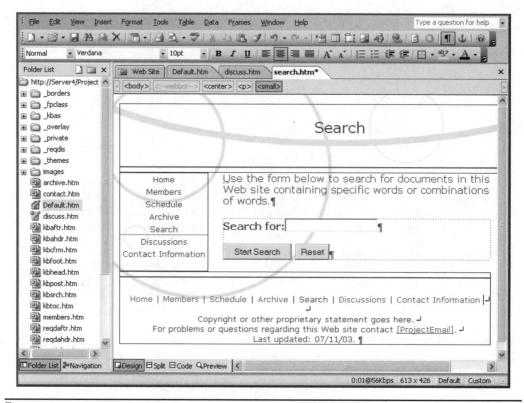

**FIGURE 4-14**    Search page for doing a text search of the web that contains it

groups are separate. They allow people to enter comments, and others to comment on the original comments, thereby creating threads on a given subject. Most online forums follow this format.

4. To get a better perspective of the Project web, click Preview In Browser on the toolbar. (You may be asked whether to save the changes. Respond Yes.) Follow the navigation buttons to look at the various pages. When you are finished viewing the Project web, close your browser. Then delete the Project web.

A web that has been created with the Project Web Site template provides an excellent communications tool, not only for projects, but also for any team, operation, or department.

## Applying the Customer Support Web Site Template

The Customer Support Web Site template, shown in Navigation view in Figure 4-15, makes a lot of information available to users in several ways and allows users to provide information to you in two ways. In doing this, the web uses FrontPage features you have already seen, but with different twists. As with the Personal Web Site template, the Customer Support Web Site template works completely in FrontPage Server Extensions 2002, but some components do not work with Windows SharePoint Services (SharePoint 2). We'll look at those differences next.

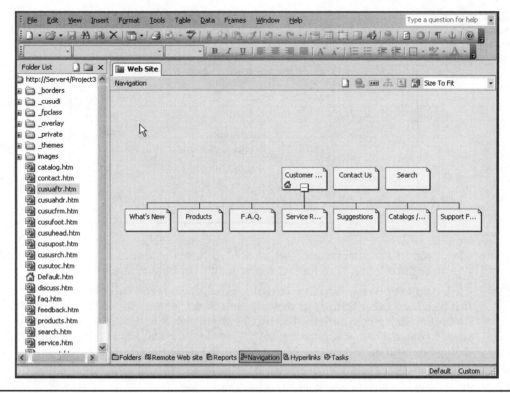

**FIGURE 4-15**   Customer Support Web Site template structure

1. Create a Customer Support web using the Customer Support Web Site template in the Web Site Templates dialog box. Then, in Navigation view, your result should look like Figure 4-15. (Use the Size To Fit tool in the Navigation toolbar if it does not fit in the pane.)

2. Double-click the Customer Support Web Site page, the home page for this web. This page has top, bottom, and left common areas, with link bars in all three.

3. Close the home page and then open, look at, and close the What's New and F.A.Q. (frequently asked questions) pages. These pages, well-designed for their purposes, are simply combinations of text and hyperlinks with the included header and footer.

4. Double-click the Service Request page (Service.htm). If you scroll down the page, you'll see a special form for collecting information about a problem with a product. As with all other features in a wizard- or template-created web, you can customize this, changing the text, size, and content of the fields.

5. To experience changing one of the fields on the form, right-click the drop-down list box that displays Select Product/Service and choose Form Field Properties. The field's (Drop-Down Box) Properties dialog box will open, as shown in Figure 4-16. Here you can change the name of the field in the top text box and change the choices the field presents to the user by using the Add, Modify, and Remove buttons.

**FIGURE 4-16**
Changing the
contents of a
drop-down menu

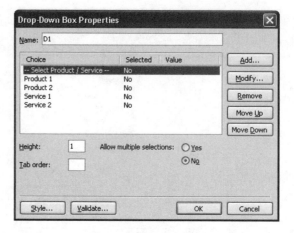

6. Click Product 1 to select it, and then click Modify. In the Modify Choice dialog box, type over the selected "Product 1," replacing it with **Blue Widget**. Click OK.

7. Click Add to open the Add Choice dialog box. Type **Green Widget** in the Choice text box, leave other settings as they are, and click OK. Back in the Drop-Down Box Properties dialog box, click the Product 2 entry to select it; then click Move Down twice to move it below Service 2. Click OK to close the Drop-Down Box Properties dialog box, and then save and close the Service Request page.

8. Next open, look at, and close the Suggestions page (Suggest.htm), which allows customers to use a form to submit suggestions.

---

**NOTE**   *Remember that to close a page, you can simply click the tab and select Close from the context menu.*

---

**TIP**   *When you select View | Hyperlinks while you are in Page view, you will see the hyperlinks to and from that page. When you click the plus sign next to a link name, you will expand the view to see hyperlinks coming from or going to that page.*

9. Open the Suggestions From Customers page (feedback.htm), which is used to contain the suggestions that customers have entered using the Suggestions page. Notice that it has no links at this point. Close the Suggestions From Customers page.

10. Then open, look at, and close the Support and Search pages. These contain a discussion group and a search form similar to those you saw in the Project web. At this point, all pages should be closed.

11. Open your Customer Support (Default.htm) web in a browser and try its features, submitting a service request and a suggestion. This will show you how these pages work. You should then see a confirmation page, as shown in Figure 4-17.

12. After you enter and submit input in the Suggestions and Service Request pages, close the browser and return to the home page in Page view.

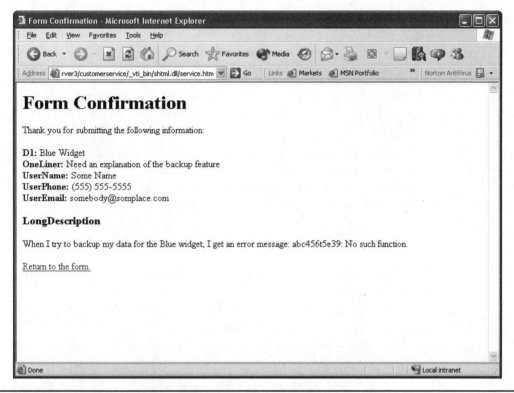

**FIGURE 4-17**    Confirmation page from the Customer Support Service Request form

13. When you are done, completely delete the Customer Support web.

**NOTE**    *As noted in Chapter 3, these webs are deleted when you are done looking at them because they take a fair amount of disk space.*

## Teaming Up with the SharePoint Team Web Site

The SharePoint Team Web Site is used to share information among a team of people, such as a project group, a marketing team, a department, or a small company. It is a special-purpose program that facilitates collaboration among team members. The Team Web Site provides a way for a team to collect and group information that is useful to all members. There are two versions of SharePoint, each with different components. SharePoint Team Services (STS or SharePoint 1) offers components that often use the FrontPage Server Extensions (FPSE). Windows SharePoint Services (WSP or SharePoint 2) is the newer version that does not require FPSE.

This chapter introduces both versions of SharePoint; however, Chapter 22 talks about them in depth, and you can learn how to install SharePoint in Appendix A.

### Using Team Web Site with SharePoint 1

As you can see in Figure 4-18, SharePoint 1 (using FPSE) Team Web Site allows team members to add announcements, calendar events, and links on the home page, as well as to create and share documents, participate in a discussion group, use a common contacts list, use a common Tasks list, and add another link as needed.

From the home page of the Team Web Site, you can see how you would use it to collaborate with other team members on one or more documents. Follow these steps to get a feel for how this works:

1. Select File | New, click More Web Site Templates, and after specifying the name and address of the web site, double-click SharePoint Team Site.

2. Double-click the home page, default.htm or index.htm, and click the Preview In Browser button in the toolbar to see the web site with your default browser.

3. Click Documents from the link bar on the top of the page. Here you can see the contents in Shared Documents and set up specifications for a New Document Library.

4. If you click Lists from the link bar, you will see shared Announcements, Contacts, Events, Links, and Tasks.

5. Click Discussion Boards to set up a New Discussion Board, Discuss A Document, or hold a General Discussion on a topic the team wishes.

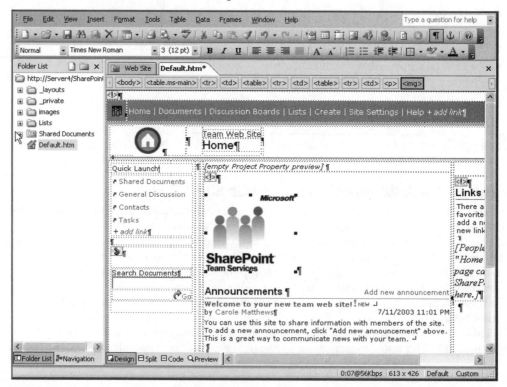

**FIGURE 4-18**    The SharePoint 1 Team Web Site for collaborating within a web site

6. Click a few of the links to see how your team might use this information. Perhaps you need other items that are not contained here, or perhaps you don't need some of the ones shown. If you are planning on using SharePoint, get acquainted with the items listed.

7. Click Create from the link bar. This is where you would add a new Document Library or Custom List, Discussion Board, Survey, Links, Announcements, Contacts, Events, or Tasks. The Custom List feature lets you define the columns of a list you want or a spreadsheet environment for entering data. You can import a spreadsheet to contain the data, or synchronize with your custom spreadsheet.

8. Continue to explore the site. When you are finished, you can close the browser and delete the web site completely.

As mentioned earlier, SharePoint and the Team Web Site are discussed further in Chapter 22; Appendix A discusses how to install it.

### Using Team Web Site with SharePoint 2

Now, as shown in Figure 4-19, you can see what Windows SharePoint Services (SharePoint 2) offers, by following these steps:

1. Select File | New, click More Web Site Templates, and after specifying the name and address of the web site containing Windows SharePoint, double-click SharePoint Team Site.

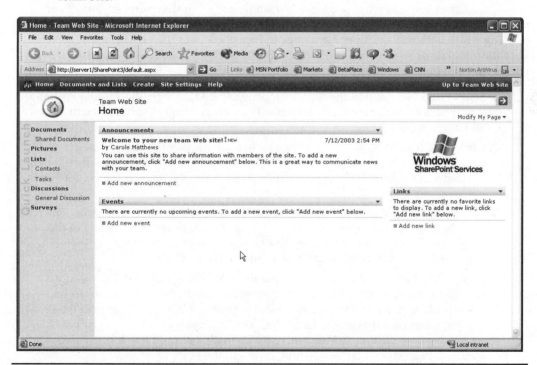

**FIGURE 4-19**    The Windows SharePoint 2 Team Web Site using the Preview In Browser option

2. Double-click the home page, default.htm or index.htm. Click the Preview In Browser button in the toolbar to see the web site with your default browser. You will see a screen like the one shown in Figure 4-19. On the home page, you can add announcements and events and additional links that you want your web team to be able to share.

3. Explore the web site by clicking the links at the top of the page. First, click Documents And Lists to go quickly to pre-established site links, such as Shared Documents, Announcements, Contacts, Events, Links, Tasks, and Discussion boards. Then click Create to add new libraries, lists, discussion boards, and so forth. Finally, click Site Settings to set up and maintain the web site itself.

4. Return to the home page, and down the left side of the web page you will see additional links that allow you to go quickly to the page you want by clicking Documents, Pictures, Lists, Discussions, or Surveys.

5. When you are finished, close the browser and delete the web site completely.

Again, you can learn more about both SharePoints 1 and 2 in Chapter 22, and about installing them in Appendix A.

## Page Templates

The Web Site templates create webs with many different page types and features on each page. Sometimes, though, what you want is a single page. For that purpose, FrontPage provides page templates. For example, you can add a page like the Search Page to a web by opening a web in FrontPage, opening a page in Page view, and then creating a new page with the template or wizard you want to use. In this section, you'll see some of the more useful page templates. Begin with these steps:

1. Select File | New and in the New task pane, click More Web Site Templates. In the dialog box, fill in the location and name the web **TestPage**. Double-click the Empty Web Site template.

2. Click the Create A New Normal Page tool, and new_page_1.htm will be created. Save the page by right-clicking the tab and choosing Save. Accept the default name of what will be the home page and click Save to save the page. If the Folder List is not showing, choose View | Folder List.

3. Choose File | New and select More Page Templates in the New task pane. The Page Templates dialog box appears with the General tab selected. Click a few of the templates to see the resulting thumbnails displayed under Preview, as shown in Figure 4-20. Open Feedback Form by double-clicking it.

4. Right-click the tab and choose Save. The Save As dialog box will allow you to change the name of the file. Name the file according to the function, for example, feedback.htm. Click Save. That name will appear as both the filename in the Folder List pane and the tab name in Page view. (An example is shown in Figure 4-21, which displays the Empty Web Site template with a normal blank home page and a feedback page shown on the tab and as files in the Folder List pane.)

5. Use this web structure to try out some of the page templates. It will be deleted later.

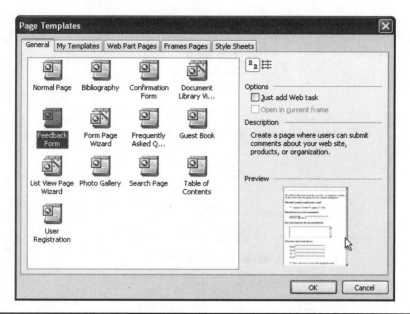

PART I

**FIGURE 4-20**    The Page Templates dialog box allows you to preview predefined templates before selecting one.

***TIP***    *The Create A New Normal Page toolbar button itself (not the arrow) gives you a new page using the Normal Page template (a blank page); it does not open the New task pane or the Page Templates dialog box, where you can choose other templates. For that, you must click the arrow on the right of the Create A New Normal Page toolbar button.*

The templates and wizards listed in the Page Templates dialog box General tab represent a tremendous resource that you can use to build your own webs. Chapter 2 provided a brief description of all the page templates and wizards. Let's look at several of them. As each template is discussed, use it to create a page and look at the results, at least in Page view (and possibly in your browser).

## Feedback Form Template

The Feedback Form template creates a general-purpose form page (as you can see in Figure 4-21) that allows a user to send you comments. The template creates several types of fields, gives them names, and generates files needed to capture the information submitted. Afterward, it's saved in the Feedback.txt file in the _Private subfolder under the web's folder. (If you use the default folder scheme and your web is named TestPages, then the full path for Feedback.txt with Microsoft IIS is C:\Inetpub\Wwwroot\ TestPages\_Private\Feedback.txt.)

***NOTE***    *If you are using Windows SharePoint Server 2003 with SharePoint2, the web files are stored in \Documents and in Settings\Adminstrator.Servername\NetHood\TestPage\_private\ Feedback.txt.*

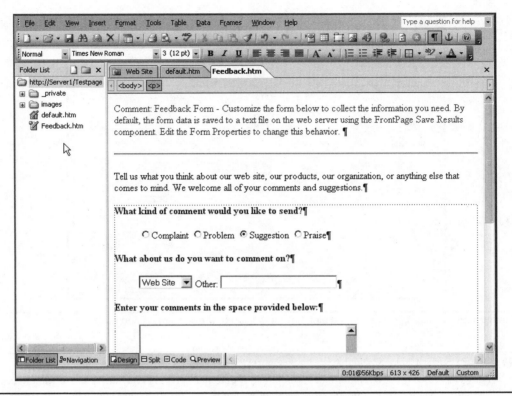

**FIGURE 4-21** Form page created with the Feedback Form page template

**NOTE** *Both "folder" and "directory" describe a container of disk files. In this book, we'll use "folder" when talking about the file structure in FrontPage and other Windows applications, and "directory" when referring to the real or "virtual" file structure on many web servers such as Windows Server 2003.*

## Confirmation Form Template

A *confirmation page* is used to show someone submitting information to you that his or her submission was received. When you create a submission form—for example, a feedback form or a registration form—FrontPage automatically generates a default confirmation page. You can create a custom confirmation page by using the Confirmation Form template, but you must specify that you want to use your own confirmation page in the Form Properties dialog box of the submission form (from a form's context menu, click Form Properties, click Options, select the Confirmation Page tab, and fill in the URL of the confirmation page). In Hyperlinks view, after saving both the submission form and the confirmation page, you can see the link between them, like this:

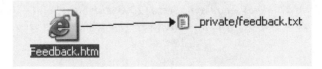

***NOTE*** *To get the page names shown here, the pages are saved with their template names (Feedback and Confirmation), and then their page title is changed in Navigation view by right-clicking the page and choosing Rename or by using Change Title in the Save As dialog box.*

The Confirmation Form template creates a confirmation page, as shown in Figure 4-22. This page contains fields from the form the user submitted. You can add fields to a confirmation page by opening Insert | Web Component and choosing Advanced Controls | Confirmation Field, as well as change the text and move the existing confirmation fields. The only requirement is that the name of a field on a form must be the same as the name used in the confirmation page. Several submission forms can share the same confirmation page if the forms use identical field names.

***NOTE*** *You must know the field names from the submission form when you are building the confirmation page, because the Insert | Web Component | Advanced Controls | Confirmation Field option and the Confirmation Field Properties dialog box, opened by right-clicking a confirmation field, both require the field name and do not allow you to browse for them.*

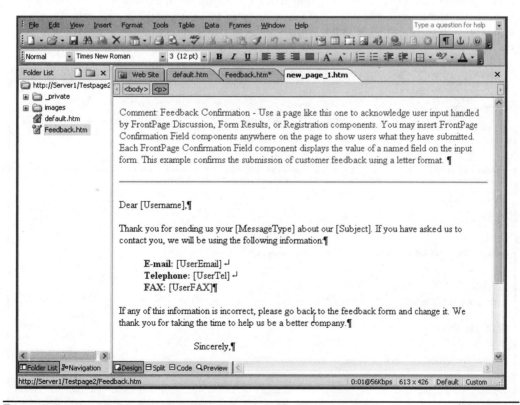

**FIGURE 4-22**   Confirmation Form template

## Search Page Template

The Search Page template, which requires the FrontPage Extensions, provides all the text search features that you saw in the webs earlier in this chapter. It is completely self-contained, including the query language instructions. When you include this page in a web, it will search all of the text in the web without any further effort on your part.

When visitors to your web site use your search page, they will receive a list of pages with content that matches their search criteria, as shown in Figure 4-23. Visitors can click the entries in the list of pages to view the one they want.

---

**NOTE**    *In Windows 2000 and XP and in Windows Server 2003, you must have the Indexing Service turned on (right-click My Computer, choose Manage, open Services and Applications, right-click Indexing Service, and choose Start) for a search to work. Also, after saving the web pages, you may have to wait several minutes for the indexing to take place.*

---

## Table of Contents Template

The page, or more likely a portion of it, created by the Table of Contents template is one of the more useful page templates. All the components do not work with SharePoint 2. When you have finished adding all of the pages to a web, giving them each names and creating links from a home page, add a table of contents page, or incorporate its contents on another page. This will not look like much in Page view, but when you open the page in a browser, you'll have a complete table of contents of all the pages in the web.

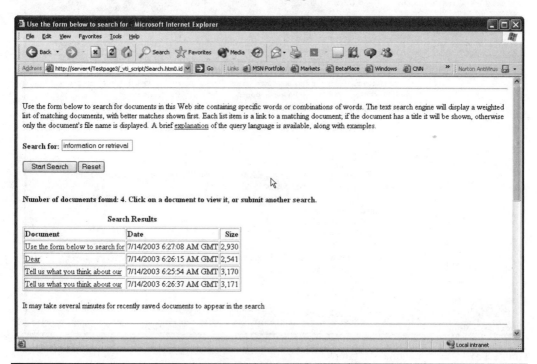

**FIGURE 4-23**    Search results using the Search Page template

Figure 4-24 was taken from a web that contained the pages created with templates discussed in the preceding sections, including the home page of the web. To display the names properly, you must supply the page title by right-clicking each page, selecting Page Properties, and typing the name you want to appear in the Table of Contents in the Title text box. To specify the filename of the home page, where the Table of Contents is to begin its search, open the Table Of Contents Properties dialog box (on the Table of Contents page, right-click the line that says "Table of Contents Heading Page" and click Table Of Contents Properties), and specify the filename of the home page, as shown here:

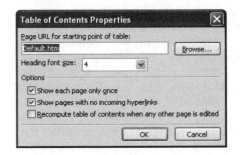

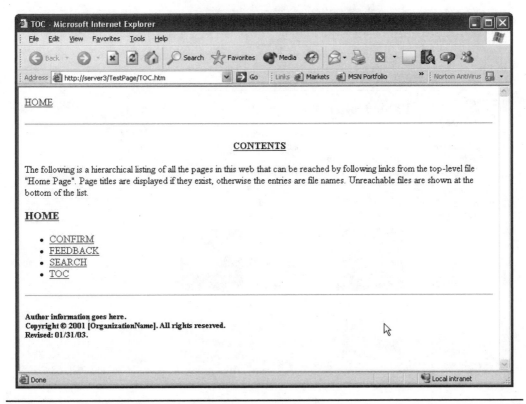

**FIGURE 4-24**    The Contents page in a browser

## Photo Gallery Template

The Photo Gallery template provides a page on which you can display one or more photographs along with their captions, as shown in Figure 4-25. You add photos, captions, and descriptions to this page by right-clicking the photo-thumbnail area and choosing Photo Gallery Properties. Next, you click Add | Pictures From Files or Pictures From Scanner Or Cameras. You then select the files you want to display and enter their captions and descriptions.

## The Web Part Pages

The templates you have examined so far used components like search boxes, tables of contents, input forms, and a photo gallery. These templates generated valuable features by using the components. Other page templates do not use components or any usable text. They provide features you can use to create your web pages. You find them by choosing File | New, clicking More Page Templates, and then clicking the Web Part Pages tab. These are used on web servers running SharePoint 2 and allow you to easily connect sets of data (XML files, Web services, and SharePoint lists) from different data sources, in a modular manner, without advanced programming. The intent of Web Parts is to provide preprogrammed Web Components that can be picked from a library of Web Parts to be

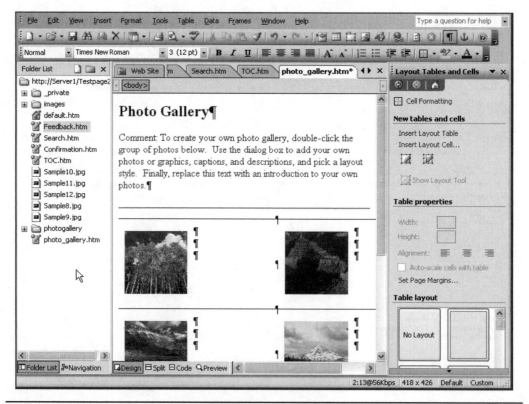

**FIGURE 4-25**    Adding a Photo Gallery page template

inserted into your web site. They perform the common chores that web sites must perform. In this way, you do not "program" a new web site, as much as "assemble" it. You are free to concentrate on your real task of creating the content for a meaningful and useful web site for your users rather than on programming the common web chores. This is the way of the future, using .NET Framework components like Web services and ASP.NET.

Preview some of the various layout Web Part pages by clicking on them to select them and seeing a thumbnail view under Preview. In addition to these, other Web Parts will be available on Web Part Galleries. They may be developed by Microsoft or by third-party vendors, and many will be available with Windows SharePoint Services, others online from various sources. Some examples of the layout design Web Part pages available are as follows:

- Full Page Vertical
- Header and Footer with 2 columns and 4 rows
- Header and Footer with 3 columns
- Header and Footer with 4 columns and a top middle row
- Header with a left column and larger body on the right
- Header with body on the left and a right column
- Left column with Header, Footer, a top row, and 3 columns
- Right column with Header and Footer, a top row, and 3 columns

Before going on to create your own templates, delete the TestPages web you have been using.

## Creating Your Own FrontPage Templates

As you have been working with templates, you have probably had some ideas for templates that you wished were available. If you are setting up an intranet, this is especially true, because it makes excellent sense to have a template for the entire organization to use to get a consistent web across the company. In any situation where several similar webs are needed, you can use a template to create them. If you are creating a large web with a number of pages that look alike, you can create a page template that will speed up the process.

In the next couple of sections, you'll look at the types of templates you can create and their common characteristics, and then see how to build the different types. Building templates does not require programming, as does creating your own wizards, but templates do require getting the right files in the right place. We'll spend some time clarifying the file management and then lead you through a few complete examples so you can see how templates are built.

### Types of Templates

*Templates* are model or prototype webs or web pages, identical in every detail to an actual web or web page. The only thing that distinguishes them is that they are in a special folder. You can view a template in a browser and use it like any other web or web page. In fact, a template is just a web or web page that has been set aside to serve as a model for other webs or web pages.

Because they are stored in different folders, think of web templates and page templates as two distinct types of templates, although there are many similarities. *Page* templates generally create a single page that becomes part of a separately created web, although a page template can include additional linked pages. A *web* template creates a full FrontPage web with one or more interconnected pages. This means that it includes all of the folder structure that is a part of FrontPage. In both cases, though, you create the web or the page in the same way that you would create any other web or page. When the web or page is the way you want it, you then place it in a special folder set up for templates with the extension .tem. For example, Test.tem is a folder containing the files for a template named "Test." The files within the template folder are just the normal .htm extension HTML web files plus an INF template information file and a DIB file, which is a thumbnail of the page template that appears in the Page Templates dialog box Preview section.

## FrontPage Folder Structure

The TEM template folders that come with FrontPage are stored in different folders depending on whether they are pages, webs, frames, or styles. If you used the default installation, these folders have the path

C:\Program Files\Microsoft Office\Templates\1033\Webs

or

C:\Program Files\Microsoft Office\Templates\1033\Pages

Figure 4-26 shows the contents of the Webs folder within that path.

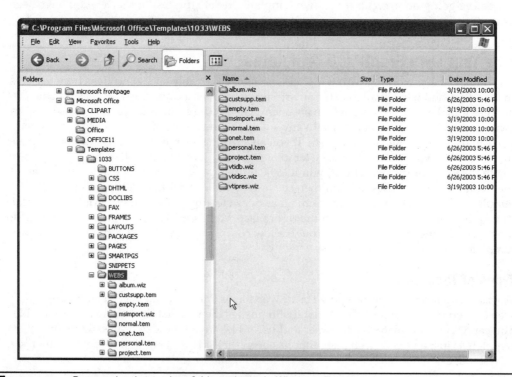

**FIGURE 4-26**    Page and web template folders shown in Windows Explorer

If you are using Windows XP with IIS, Windows 2000, or Windows Server 2003 along with the default installation, you have a folder with this path (see earlier note if you are using SharePoint2):

C:\Inetpub\Wwwroot

This folder is the root directory for the webs that you want to let people access with IIS on your computer. The folder can store all of the FrontPage webs that you create. It is *not* used to store templates, but comes into play when you create them.

Use the Windows Explorer to open your C:\Program Files\Microsoft Office\ Templates\ 1033\Pages folder now, and then open the feedback.tem template folder. Within the folder, you will see three files, like this:

| | | | |
|---|---|---|---|
| FEEDBACK.DIB | 15 KB | Bitmap Image | 1/5/1999 12:07 AM |
| FEEDBACK.HTM | 3 KB | HTML Document | 9/4/2002 5:43 PM |
| FEEDBACK.INF | 1 KB | Setup Information | 10/23/2002 12:30 PM |

One of these files is an HTM web file that, if you double-click it, will open your default browser and display the web page produced by the template. In any other folder, this file would be considered just another web page; there is nothing to distinguish it except for the folder it is in. The other files within the template folder are an INF setup information file and a DIB image file, which is a thumbnail of your page template automatically generated by FrontPage and used in the Preview area of the Page Templates dialog box. Look at the INF file next.

## The INF (Setup Information) File

The INF (Setup Information) file is used to hold descriptive information about the template. It is similar to a Windows INI file and is read by FrontPage's Page view when it is working with templates. The INF file must have the same name as the TEM folder it is in; so, for example, the Test.tem folder will contain the Test.inf file.

If it isn't open already, open the Pages and feedback.tem folders; then double-click the feedback.inf file. If the INF file type is not associated with an application that can read it on your computer, select Notepad as that application. Notepad will open and display the file's short contents, like this:

```
File  Edit  Format  View  Help
[info]
_LCID=1033
_version=11.0.4628.0
title=Feedback Form
description=Create a page where users can submit comments about your web site, products, or or
```

### The Setup Information File [info] Section

The INF information file will always have an [info] section with at least two items in it—the title of the template and its description—as you just saw. These items are used in the Page Templates or Web Site Templates dialog box to provide the name of the template and its description.

If the INF file is not included, FrontPage uses the base name of the template folder ("Test" if the template folder is Test.tem) as the title and leaves the description blank.

Under most circumstances, the INF file will automatically be created for you, as you will see in later sections of this chapter. When it isn't created automatically, you must create it using the INF file format that you saw earlier. There must be a section named "[info]," and it must contain the title and description lines spelled correctly and with the equal signs. Whatever is on the right of the equal sign is data that will appear in the Description area or below the icon representing its title of the Page Templates or Web Site Templates dialog box. Each of the fields in the [info] section can be up to 255 characters long, including the attribute name ("title" and "description") and the equal sign. As a practical matter, though, to be completely visible within the Page Templates or Web Site Templates dialog box, the title should be fewer than 30 characters, and the description should be fewer than 100 characters.

---

***TIP***    *If you do have to create an INF file, the easiest way is to copy an existing file and change the name, title, and description.*

For page templates, which are displayed in Page view, only the [info] section of the INF file is used. For web templates, with one or more pages within them, the INF file can have additional sections, including [FileList], [MetaInfo], and [TaskList], that are used when the template is loaded into a server.

### The Information File [FileList] Section

The [FileList] section, which is shown in Figure 4-27, tells FrontPage how you want the files in the template stored in a web. If a [FileList] section is not included, FrontPage loads all of the files in the TEM folder, but does nothing with any subfolders. The filenames in the TEM folder are converted to all lowercase and become URLs in the web. Also, any JPG or GIF files in the TEM folder are placed in the Images subfolder of the web. The [FileList] section should be included if you have any of the following situations:

- You have subfolders to the TEM folder containing files you want in the web.

- You want to specify the URL and/or the case it uses.

- You want to indicate the specific files in the TEM folder to be placed in the web (files in the TEM folder and not in [FileList] are ignored).

- You want the files to go to folders in the web other than the root folder for the HTM files and the Images subfolder for the JPG and GIF files. Another available subfolder is _private, used for files that you do not want to be found in a web search.

When you use the [FileList], you must list all of the files you want transferred. If you do not want to change the filename or the path, list just the filename with an equal sign after it. If you want to specify the path, you need to switch from the MS-DOS/Windows use of the *backslash* between subfolders on the *left* of the file list to the URL use of a *slash* between subfolders on the *right* side, as shown about three-quarters of the way down the list in Figure 4-27.

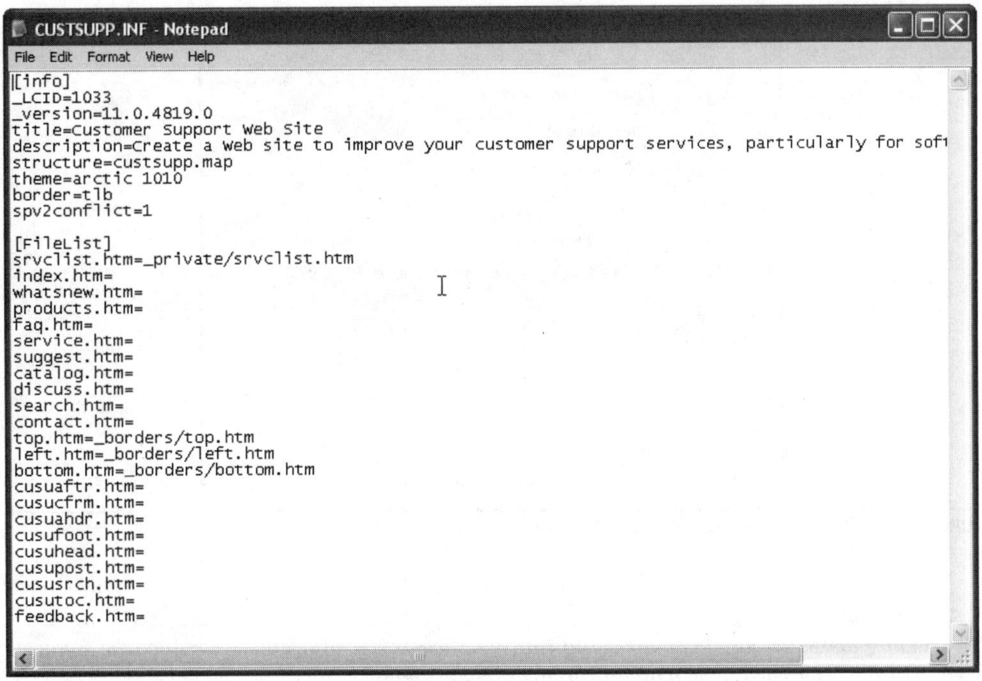

**FIGURE 4-27** A web template INF file with a [FileList] section

## The Information File [MetaInfo] Section

The [MetaInfo] section can be used to store configuration variables used in the Substitution component (discussed in Chapter 9). In this way, the [MetaInfo] section supplies the custom configuration variables that would otherwise have to be manually loaded into the Parameters tab of the FrontPage Site Settings dialog box for each web (opened by selecting Site Settings from the FrontPage Tools menu). For example, you might provide the following company information for all users of a template:

```
[MetaInfo]
CompanyName=Wines 'N Things
CompanyAddress=1234 W 23rd St., Ourtown, ST 01000
```

## The Information File [TaskList] Section

The [TaskList] section is used to provide a list of tasks to be placed in the FrontPage Tasks view for a web template. The tasks in the list have the following format:

TaskNumber=TaskName | Priority | CreatedBy | URL | Cookie | Comment

The elements in the task list are separated by a vertical bar and are described in Table 4-1. Figure 4-28 shows a Tasks view Task Details dialog box in which you can see how the elements are used.

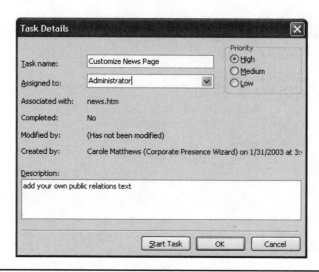

**FIGURE 4-28**    The elements of a task in the Task Details dialog box

**TIP**   *Adding tasks to a web template significantly increases its value and can reduce the amount of support that is needed to help organizations use your template.*

| Element | Description | Comments |
|---|---|---|
| TaskNumber | A unique number or a key | For example, "t01," "t02," "t03," and so on |
| TaskName | A short task description | A three- or four-word phrase used as the task name |
| Priority | An integer describing relative importance | 1 = High, 2 = Medium, 3 = Low |
| CreatedBy | Name of user and template | Used in the Created By field of the dialog box |
| URL | The URL for the task | The page or image that the task refers to |
| Cookie | The location on the page where work is required | Only bookmarks are supported, in the form #bookmark |
| Comment | Description of task | A longer description of what needs to be done (cannot contain newline characters) |

**TABLE 4-1**    Description of [TaskList] Elements

### Home Page Renaming

As a default, FrontPage names the home page in its webs Index.htm if you don't specify a server type. If you are using IIS, the name is automatically changed to Default.htm. On an NCSA server (a common UNIX-based server), Index.htm is used for the home page and can be left off the URL for a web. For example, the fictitious URL **http://www.fairmountain.com/wine** opens the Index.htm page in the Wine web on the Fairmountain NCSA server. Depending on the server to which the web is eventually uploaded, the name for a home page can differ. On a CERN server (another UNIX server), it normally is Welcome.htm. When FrontPage creates a web from a web template, it will automatically rename any file named "Index.htm" to the name appropriate for the specified server. FrontPage, though, *does not change any links to the home page.* To use the automatic renaming feature, you can make all links to the home page be a special *./* (period-slash) link that will force the server to locate the correct home page. If you do not want to use the automatic renaming feature, put the following line in the [info] section of the INF information file:

NoIndexRenaming=1

## Creating Page Templates

FrontPage makes it easy to create customized page templates. These templates can then be reused, just like the page templates that come with FrontPage. FrontPage even generates a thumbnail graphic illustrating your page that you can see in the Preview in the Page Templates dialog box.

Building a single-page template is simplicity itself. Just create a normal web page with the material you want on it, and then save it as a template. That's all there is to it! Try it:

1. Select File | New and in the New task pane, click More Web Site Templates. Type in the name, such as TestTemplate, and the location of the web. Double-click Empty Web Site. The web opens in Folder view.

2. Click the Create A New Normal Page tool to insert a blank new page.

3. To create the content of the template, you can put anything you may want on a page you commonly use: title, text, theme, hyperlinks, additional pages, and so on.

4. When your page is as you want it for the new template, select File | Save As. In the Save As Type drop-down list, select FrontPage Template. Click Save. The Save As Template dialog box opens, and you will change it as shown next.

5. Change the Title to **Home Page Template**, accept the Name, type **Create a custom home page.** (including the period) in the Description box, and click OK. Click OK to save any embedded files.

**NOTE**   *You'll remember from Chapter 3 that if you are using IIS as your web server, FrontPage names the home page Default.htm. However, using other servers or no servers at all will result in the filename Index.htm for the home page. This name determines which page is automatically displayed as the home page without specifying the filename. Unless your web server has a different default name for the home page, it is important to keep "default.htm" or "index.htm" as the name of the home page.*

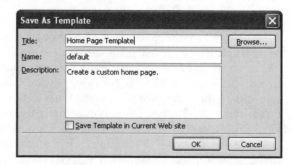

**NOTE**   *Do not check the Save Template In Current Web Site check box. If you check the box, the template won't be globally available—that is, it won't be in the Pages folder, it will be in a _sharedtemplates folder in the current web.*

## Opening Your Custom Template

At this point, you can open and begin to use your custom template. First, however, open Windows Explorer and locate the new template. In Windows 2000, XP Professional, or Windows Server 2003, it will be in the folder located at C:\Documents and Settings\\*username*\Application Data\Microsoft\FrontPage\Pages\ homepage_t.

---

**TIP**   *If you do not see the template name in the \Pages subfolder, press F5 to refresh Windows Explorer.*

1. Open the Homepage_t folder. You should see the three files that were automatically created when you saved the page as a template. These are the HTM web file, the INF information file, and the DIB image file (which is used for a thumbnail picture of the template in the Page Templates dialog box). Double-click the INF (Setup Information) file. It should open and reflect your entries earlier, as shown here:

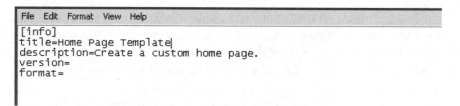

2. Close Notepad, close Windows Explorer, and in FrontPage, choose File | New. In the New task pane, click More Page Templates, and in the My Templates tab, select Home Page Template. Figure 4-29 shows what your template should look like in the Page Templates dialog box with the description and a thumbnail image.

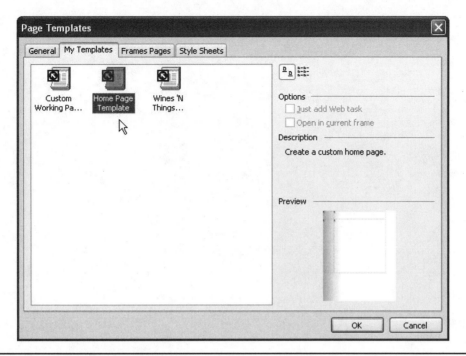

**FIGURE 4-29** The templates you create are available from the My Templates tab in the Page Templates dialog box.

   3. Double-click Home Page Template, and a new page based on your template will open ready for you to customize. When you are finished, save the page with a unique name, and close the web, or delete it entirely.

Although this example was very simple, you can see that with your template you should be able to substantially reduce the time it takes to create additional pages, and that all the pages you create using templates will be consistent. In Chapter 5, you will learn about the various elements you can use to customize your web pages and templates. In Appendix C, you can read about creating a web template, which is a not as easy as creating a page template.

# Creating Web Sites

Part I gave you an overview of webs and how they are built in FrontPage. In Part II, you will see how to actually build a web using many of the tools that FrontPage provides. In Chapter 5, you will build a foundation web using only the most basic of web tools. In Chapter 6, you will see how to add hyperlinks and hotspots to your foundation web. In Chapter 7, you will add tables and frames, while in Chapter 8 forms will come into play. Chapter 9 uses Web Components, and Chapter 10 looks at advanced formatting techniques. Finally, Chapter 11 discusses how Office and other files can be brought in and used in FrontPage.

# Creating and Formatting a Web Page from Scratch

In Chapters 3 and 4, you saw how to build a web and its pages by using a wizard or a template. You learned that using a wizard or template is the easiest way to create a web that incorporates many FrontPage features. Often, though, you will want to build a web from scratch. In this chapter, you'll see how to do that (and consequently increase your knowledge of the parts of a web).

## Planning a Web

Chapter 1 talked about the process of designing a web application or web site, and Chapter 2 listed the steps necessary to build a web. In both chapters, planning was the first and probably most important step in making a good web—and the one most often shortchanged. Planning seeks to answer four questions:

- What are the goals of the web?
- What will its content be?
- How will it be organized?
- What do you want it to look like?

Pick a smaller organization for which you would like to build a web site with the objective of promoting the organization and its products or services. Go through each of the four questions with that in mind. (This can be either an Internet or an intranet web site.)

Whatever your need for a web site, you should begin by defining your goals.

### What Are Your Goals?

Setting the goals of a web is very important—if the goals are well thought out, you will probably end up with an effective web. Keep it simple. Having one or two obtainable goals for your web is better than having a number of goals that cannot all be met. Too many goals will scatter the focus of the web, making it much more difficult to accomplish any one of them.

## What Is the Content?

To accomplish your goals, you'll need to include supporting information. The information needs to be complete enough to capture your readers' interest but concise enough for them to read quickly. Therefore, include not only a brief description of your products or services, but also general information such as exchange rates and anything that is needed to use your product or service.

## How Is It Organized?

How well a web is organized determines how easily users can get the information they seek. The desired information should be within two or three clicks of your Home Page, and the path should be clear—users shouldn't have to guess how to get what they want. The Home Page mainly provides links to other pages. The pages below the Home Page contain the desired information and are a single click or link away from the Home Page. In a web site with a limited amount of content, this is a relatively simple process, but a web site with a great deal of content requires more planning. The user will have to "drill down" into the web's structure, going from the general to the specific to reach the desired information. How you organize your content will determine the path the user follows. This path should be clear and logical, and should allow the user to jump back to the starting points without having to retrace every step. The Home Page's links to detailed information give relatively quick answers to those viewers who are willing to take a couple of minutes, but following the links may not appeal to those who are in a hurry. For quick answers, you need to have some special products or services that you want to promote prominently listed on the Home Page.

Your web needs to be based on a simple and obvious tree structure, similar to the one shown in Figure 5-1, so that users always know where they are and how they got there. The lines connecting the pages show how the pages should be hyperlinked. In this example, no page is more than three clicks from the Home Page, and most of the content is within two clicks. The third-level pages within each second-level area are linked, but the user has to move back up the tree to reach the third-level pages in the other second-level area. While a cross-link between two third-level branches may seem like a quick way to get users from one place to another under certain circumstances, it can easily confuse users about where they are. It is often better to force users back up the tree and down another branch. If you never have more than two levels from your Home Page, it is not a big chore to backtrack. Besides, the previously visited pages are already on the users' disk in their browser's cache, so they can quickly backtrack.

---

**NOTE**   *Web browsers store the web pages and pictures they download in temporary files, called a "cache," on the user's local machine. This speeds up subsequent loading of the pages by reading from the user's hard disk rather than again downloading the file over the Internet. The browsers check to see if the file on the web server is newer than the files in the cache. If the pages are the same, the cached page is used. If the version on the web server is newer, it is downloaded. In Netscape 4.0 through 6.0, the users control the cache (called "History" by Netscape) in the Preferences dialog box, opened by choosing Edit | Preferences. You can clear the cache or History anytime, and you can set a time limit for saving cached files. Internet Explorer calls its cache "Temporary Internet Files." ("History" in IE is a set of links to pages you have viewed, not the pages themselves.) The cache is controlled from the General tab of the Internet Options dialog box, opened by choosing View | Internet Options (IE 4.0) or Tools | Internet Options (IE 5.0 and on).*

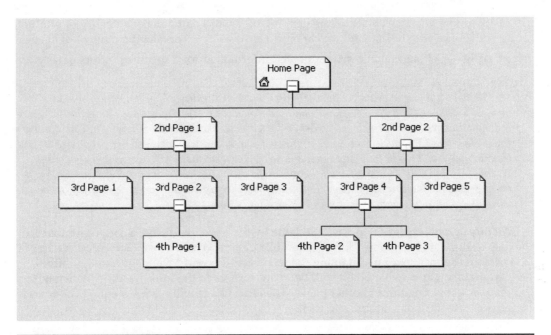

**FIGURE 5-1**    A simple but efficient web tree structure

This tree structure can be expanded to hold hundreds or even thousands of pages, all within two or at most three clicks of the Home Page. The important thing is to remember that no matter how small your web is at the beginning, a well-organized tree structure will allow you to expand your web to any size in the future.

*TIP*    *Each page in your web, regardless of the level, should have a direct link back to the Home Page. This allows users to quickly return to the starting point in one click. (Figure 5-1 shows the hierarchical structure of a web, not the links that are needed.)*

## What Will It Look Like?

With all the concepts just discussed, what will your web look like? Consider the graphic design as well as the structure of each page, although it's best to begin with the structure and then to add the graphic elements. This gives you the functionality first; no web site, no matter how good looking, will be successful if it isn't well structured and easy to use.

The best approach is to begin by sketching the primary types of pages that you will be using. Figure 5-2 shows one way that the information in a web could be laid out to satisfy the desired points brought out in the plan. To keep to the desired three levels, you will have three types of pages:

- A Home Page with a list of special offerings and links to all the major categories of products or services, each of which is contained on a second-level page

- Second-level pages that contain general information for a major category of product or service with links to individual products or services contained on third-level pages
- Third-level pages that contain detailed information for a specific product or service

---

**NOTE**    *To make it easier to visualize this structure, think of a real-world organization you are familiar with. For example, consider a small wine merchant. His Home Page shows the individual wines he has on sale plus a list of the varietals like Cabernet Sauvignon, Chardonnay, Pinot Noir, and Zinfandel. Each entry in this list is a second-level page, so there is a page for Chardonnay and another for Pinot Noir, and so on. Each second-level page presents general information and a list by region of all the wines the merchant has for a particular varietal. Each entry in this list is a third-level page. Each third-level page gives a detailed description of one particular wine along with ordering and other information.*

All three types of pages will have the same footer, which will have a copyright notice, the date last updated, a postal address, and information on how to contact the *webmaster* (the person responsible for maintaining the web). Each second-level page and the third-level pages below it, of which there will be many, will share the same heading, which will be a *link bar*, providing links to other pages. The Home Page will have a unique header and larger, separate sections with links in each.

**FIGURE 5-2**
One approach to laying out a web site

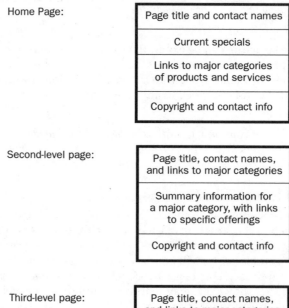

The trick is to maintain a balance that neither overwhelms users with dozens of links on a page, nor makes them click until their finger cramps to reach the information they want.

As you create the pages, you will fine-tune how they look by adding pictures and by positioning and formatting text. The final web that you build in this book is the product of several chapters, so you'll have to be patient to see the final image on your screen.

## Starting a Web

In this chapter, you will work with text and pictures, and in the next four chapters you will work with hyperlinks and hotspots, tables and frames, forms, and Web Components, respectively. The reason for this approach is to focus on one topic at a time. As a result, you'll see areas, especially in this chapter, that may be better handled with, for example, a table or a Web Component. That discussion will be put off until the appropriate chapter, so each topic can be fully developed without interfering with others.

Developing all but the simplest webs is a long and tedious chore. Here you will work on a Home Page, a single second-level page, and a single third-level page. In a real web, though, there could be 10 to 20 second-level pages and as many as 10 or more third-level pages for each second-level one—so a 200-page web would not be unusual. One way around this large size is to use databases to build web pages in real time as they are requested, which you will read about in Chapter 17. It is important to consider, though, how the page count explodes as you develop a web and how adding levels makes the web grow geometrically.

*TIP    Allow enough time to complete the development of a web. Material created electronically, such as text files and pictures, is the easiest to work with, but you may need to use text for which you only have printed copies. One way to speed the process is to scan printed documents that you want incorporated (like travel brochures for the details of a travel offering) and then to use optical character recognition (OCR) to convert them to text. Be sure to carefully edit any OCR-generated text (the process is less than perfect), and make sure you have written permission to reproduce other people's copyrighted material.*

1. Start FrontPage. In the Getting Started (or Home) task pane on the right, choose Create A New Page Or Site. (If your Home task pane is not open, select View | Task Pane or press CTRL-F1.) In the New task pane, under New Web Site, click One Page Web Site. The Web Site Templates dialog box will open with One Page Web Site selected.

2. Enter the folder name for your site (we're using "winesnthings" for a wine shop), which becomes the web name, with the path you want to use (the path and folder name should follow the format **http://servername/foldername**), and click OK.

3. Right-click the Home Page (Index.htm or Default.htm) icon in either the Folder List (if displayed) or in the Folders view pane to open its context menu. Choose Properties to open the page's Properties dialog box. Type **Home Page** for the page title. Observe that the URL for this page includes the page's filename of Index.htm or Default.htm. The filename of the Home Page should match the default for the server your web will be hosted on (check with the webmaster of your server if you're not sure). Default.htm is the default filename for IIS. Click OK to close the Properties dialog box.

> **NOTE**   *FrontPage will detect the correct default filename for the selected server and name the Home Page accordingly. If you are developing your web on IIS but intend to move it to another server later, you should set the default filename to match the final web server.*

4. Click the Navigation button in the view bar at the bottom of the Web Site pane, or select View | Navigation to look at the web site in Navigation view. Click New Page on the Navigation pane's toolbar on the right of the pane. A new page will appear in the Navigation pane under the Home Page. Slowly click twice (don't double-click) in the title area of the new page in the middle of the navigation pane, type **Second Page**, and press ENTER.

5. Again, click New Page on the Navigation pane's toolbar, slowly click twice in the title area of the new page, type **Third Page**, and press ENTER. You should see three pages, one under the other, as shown in Figure 5-3.

> **NOTE**   *The web server that webs are developed on is often called the "staging server." In this book, IIS is assumed to be the staging server. When the web is ready to go "live," it will be copied, or "published," to a production server. All work on a web should be done and tested on the staging server before you publish it to the production server.*

There is a very good structural reason for organizing your web pages in folders. Web servers, like IIS, allow you to create *virtual* directories. These are simply folders that are *aliased* or *mapped* to names that are easier to work with. For example, if you have set up

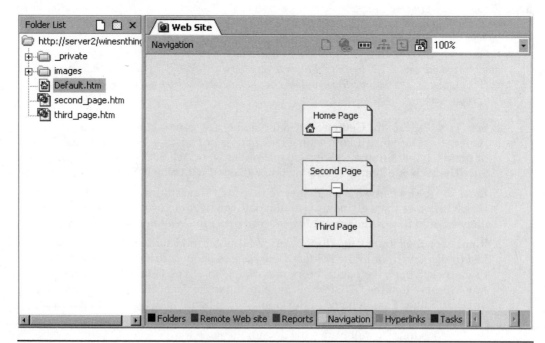

**FIGURE 5-3**   The initial three pages in Navigation view

FrontPage and IIS as recommended in Appendix A, the physical path to this new web folder (assuming that Windows SharePoint Services [WSS or SharePoint 2] is not installed) is C:\Inetpub\wwwroot\*webname*\, as displayed with the Windows Explorer in Figure 5-4. This can be mapped to the virtual directory /*webname*. In your web, you can reference any pages in the web folder using the /*webname* virtual directory rather than the full path.

When you installed IIS, certain virtual directories were created by default. The most important is the root directory of the web server. The physical path is, by default (without WSS), C:\Inetpub\wwwroot\. This was mapped to the Home virtual directory. This means the URL http://*servername*/ will load the web page whose path is C:\Inetpub\wwwroot\ Default.htm. Only one Home virtual directory can be with IIS on a client computer running Windows XP Professional or Windows 2000 Professional. Web servers like Windows Server 2003 or Windows 2000 Server running IIS can have multiple home directories, but each one must have a unique IP address.

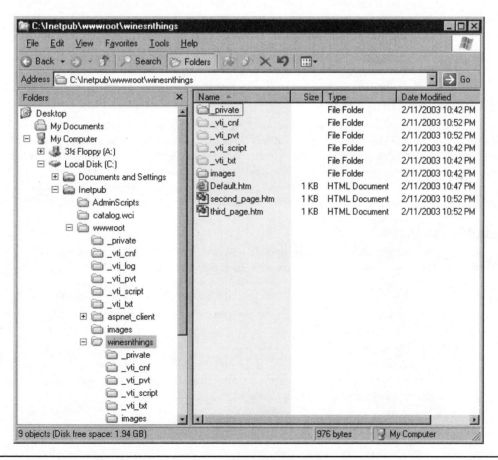

**FIGURE 5-4**    In Windows Explorer, you can see where the new web is placed.

**NOTE** *The terms "folder" and "directory" are interchangeable. FrontPage and Windows Server 2003, Windows XP, 2000, and 98/Me use "folder," while Windows NT and IIS use "directory." In this book, we'll use "folder" when talking about the file structure in FrontPage and other Windows applications, and "directory" when referring to the real or "virtual" file structure on most web servers.*

Using virtual directories also allows you to set different levels of permissions for web pages. If you have some web pages that you want to be available to the public, but others to which you want to limit access, you can place the restricted pages in a separate folder and control access to the folder. In a FrontPage web, the _private folder serves this purpose. Chapter 20 covers security on the web in more detail.

The next step in creating your web is to add text and pictures to your pages. In Chapter 6, you will add the hyperlinks that will give the web a structure.

**NOTE** *By creating the three pages in FrontPage Navigation view, you automatically established a relationship among the pages, as shown by their relative position and the lines between them. This relationship will be used in creating the automatic links in a link bar. Since you will be working with hyperlinks and hotspots in Chapter 6, you won't do anything more with links in this chapter.*

## Adding and Formatting Text

The text will be entered in sections corresponding to the Home Page sections shown in Figure 5-2—for example, the title, the footer (copyright and contact information), and the current specials. Where applicable, this information will be entered and formatted on the Home Page and then copied to other pages. Begin by entering the footer. Here, we'll do it the old-fashioned way by entering it on one page and manually copying it to the other pages. In Chapter 10, we'll come back and do this with a Dynamic Web Template.

### Entering the Footer

The footer goes at the bottom of all the pages and contains the copyright notice and information on how to contact the webmaster. To create the footer:

1. Double-click the Home Page icon in the Navigation pane to open the Home Page.

2. Press ENTER ten times to move to the bottom of the pane, type **Copyright**, and press SPACEBAR.

3. With the cursor where you left it after step 2, open the Insert menu, expand the menu, and choose Symbol. In the Symbol dialog box, scroll down the set of characters, and select the copyright symbol, as shown next, click Insert (you can also just double-click the symbol), and then click Close.

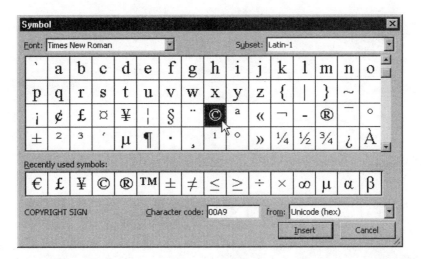

4. Press SPACEBAR once again to insert a space after the copyright symbol, and then type text that is similar to what follows for your web site. Press SHIFT-ENTER (newline) at the end of each of the first two lines. Insert the bullet from the Symbol dialog box.

   **2003 Wines 'n Things, Inc. All rights reserved.**
   **1234 W 23rd St, Ourtown, ST 12345 • (999) 555-1234**
   **Please send comments and suggestions to webmaster@winesnthings.com**

---

**NOTE**   *Using* SHIFT-ENTER *instead of* ENTER *reduces the amount of space between lines and helps to group related material.*

5. To see the newline and paragraph marks, click Show All on the right of the toolbar.

6. If you look at the paragraph style in the Style drop-down list box on the left of the Formatting toolbar, it should be Normal. This is a little large for the footer, so click the down arrow in the Style drop-down list shown next and select Heading 5. This reduces the size and makes it bold, but it is still easy to read, as you can see in Figure 5-5.

7. Click Save on the toolbar or press CTRL-S to save your Home Page with its new footer.

8. Press CTRL-A or select Edit | Select All to select the footer and the paragraph marks that placed the footer at the bottom of the page. Click Copy in the toolbar, select Edit | Copy, or press CTRL-C.

9. In the Folder List, double-click second_page to open that page. Click Paste in the toolbar, select Edit | Paste, or press CTRL-V. Double-click third_page and click Paste to place the same footer on all three pages.

You now have the footer entered and correctly formatted on each page. Next, work on the Home Page title.

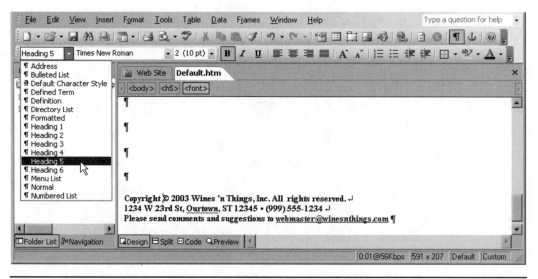

**FIGURE 5-5**    Formatting the footer text as Heading 5

## Creating the Home Page Title

The Home Page title is the introduction to a web. It needs to be inviting and to reflect the company. In our web, we also want to communicate how the owners can be reached and where the store is. To start out, create a text-only title with the following instructions. You can replace the text with a graphic later.

1. Click the Default.htm tab and press HOME to place the insertion point at the left of the paragraph mark at the top of the Home Page in preparation for creating the title.

2. Type the following text, pressing SHIFT-ENTER at the end of the first and fourth lines below, and pressing ENTER at the end of the second and sixth lines. (The fourth and sixth lines are just continuations of the third and fifth lines.) Look at Figure 5-6 to see what the final title will look like (you'll do the formatting in a moment).

   **WINES 'N THINGS**
   **Grand Wines and Accoutrements**

   **Visit us at 1234 23$^{rd}$ Street, Ourtown,**
   **Call us at 555-1234 or 555-1235 or fax 555-1236**
   **Jim Maynard and John Staley, Wine Merchants**
   **jim@winesnthings.com or john@winesnthings.com**

3. Click anywhere in each of the two paragraphs you just typed, and then, for each paragraph, click Center on the Formatting toolbar.

4. Drag across the first two lines to select them, open the Style drop-down list, select Heading 1, and then click Italic on the Formatting toolbar.

5. Drag across just the first line, open the Font Size drop-down list on the Formatting toolbar, and select 7 (36 pt) to increase the font size to the 36-point maximum.

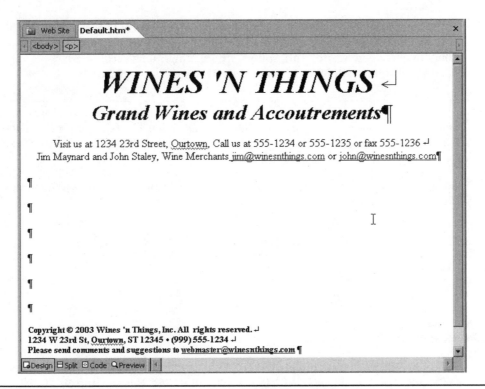

**FIGURE 5-6**    The Home Page with the title and footer in their initial form

6. Click Save on the toolbar to protect your work. Your final product should look like Figure 5-6. (The figures and illustrations in this book may look different than your screen because of differences in resolution.)

## Listing the Current Specials

The current specials are promotional sale items for a particular week. Listing them gives buyers immediate access to these items instead of having to go to the third-level page to find them.

---

***TIP***    *It is very important to keep the list of specials updated. First, it provides a reason for people to come back and look at the page. Second, it prevents information in the list from getting out of date.*

To create the list of current specials:

1. With the insertion point on the blank line immediately following the two e-mail addresses, make sure that the paragraph style is Normal and the text is left-aligned.

2. Type or copy the text that you want for the specials on your web site. Ours are shown next. Press ENTER at the end of each line (see Figure 5-7).

**CURRENT SPECIALS**
**1998 Apex Cabernet Sauvignon, deep color, rich, complex flavor, $31.99**

2001 Santa Barbara Chardonnay, exceptional, with a touch of oak, $14.95
2001 Bridgman Chardonnay, opulent bouquet, creamy fruit flavor, $10.99
2000 Ravenswood Merlot, full, round, ripe flavor, intense aroma, $9.95
2000 Washington Hills Syrah, dark, lush flavor, rich aroma, $10.99

---

**NOTE**   *A single paragraph cannot have more than one paragraph style, nor can a single paragraph contain more than one bulleted or numbered line. For that reason, all of the lines in both the Current Specials and Major Varietals and Regions sections have* ENTER *placed at the end of each line, even though it takes more space.*

3. Click line 1 of the Current Specials text, and from the Style drop-down menu box, choose Heading 2.

4. Drag across lines 2 through 6, and click Bullets on the Formatting toolbar.

5. Click Save. Your Current Specials section should look like Figure 5-7.

## Adding the Major Categories

The major categories section provides a list (really an index) of the products and or services that are available from this web site. In Chapter 6, you'll come back and make these links to the second-level pages.

To create the major categories section:

1. With the insertion point on the line immediately below the last line typed above, type your web's major categories of products and/or services. Ours are shown next. Press ENTER at the end of every line.

**MAJOR VARIETALS AND REGIONS**
**CABERNET SAUVIGNON: Washington, Northern Calif., Australia**

# *WINES 'N THINGS* ⏎

## *Grand Wines and Accoutrements*¶

Visit us at 1234 23rd Street, Ourtown, Call us at 555-1234 or 555-1235 or fax 555-1236 ⏎
Jim Maynard and John Staley, Wine Merchants jim@winesnthings.com or john@winesnthings.com¶

## CURRENT SPECIALS¶

- 1998 Apex Cabernet Sauvignon, deep color, rich, complex flavor, $31.99¶
- 2001 Santa Barbara Chardonnay, exceptional, with a touch of oak, $14.95¶
- 2001 Bridgman Chardonnay, opulent bouquet, creamy fruit flavor, $10.99¶
- 2000 Ravenswood Merlot, full, round, ripe flavor, intense aroma, $9.95¶
- 2000 Washington Hills Syrah, dark, lush flavor, rich aroma, $10.99¶

---

**FIGURE 5-7**   The completed Current Specials section

**CHARDONNAY: Washington, Oregon, Northern Calif., Central Coast**
**MERLOT: Washington, Oregon, Northern Calif., Central Coast**
**PINOT NOIR: Oregon, Central Coast, France**
**SAUVIGNON BLANC: Oregon, Northern Calif., Central Coast, France**
**ZINFANDEL: Washington, Northern Calif., Central Coast**

2. Click line 1 and choose the Heading 2 style.

3. Select lines 2 through 7 and click Numbering on the Formatting toolbar.

4. Delete any blank lines between the last line of the wine options and the beginning of the footer.

5. Save the Home Page, the bottom of which should look like Figure 5-8.

This completes the text that you will need on the Home Page.

## Building the Title for Pages 2 and 3

On all but the Home Page, you want to have a brief title or heading. In ours, we also want ways to contact the owners and links to other pages. This keeps the contacts in front of buyers and gives them the primary way to navigate or get around the web. Use the next set of instructions to enter the text related to these items on page 2, and copy them to page 3. Later in this chapter, you'll do some graphics work on this, and in Chapter 6, you'll establish the actual links to implement the navigation.

1. Scroll to the top of the Home Page, drag over the first four lines of text that represent the title of the web, and click Copy on the toolbar.

2. Click the second_page.htm tab. After the page opens, click the top-left corner to place the insertion point there and click Paste on the toolbar. The title appears on page 2.

3. If you have an extra blank line above the just-pasted title, press CTRL-HOME to move the insertion point to the very top of the page, and then press DEL to delete the leading paragraph mark.

4. Select the first two lines of what you just pasted and choose Heading 2 as the paragraph style. The size doesn't change, because you applied the special character size to these words. The size of the second line ("Grand Wines and Accoutrements," in our case) changes because it is part of the same paragraph, and you did not apply a special character size to it.

5. Select Format | Font, scroll up in the font size, and select Normal. This will change the first line to the actual Heading 2 size. Click OK to close the Font dialog box and resize your text.

---

**NOTE**   *"Normal" font size is not a particular size, but rather allows the default size of a given paragraph style to take precedence.*

6. Select the second line of what you pasted in step 2 and press DEL twice to delete the line as well as the paragraph mark. This also changes the phone numbers and e-mail addresses to Heading 2. In our case, you want to delete all but the contacts and their e-mail addresses.

## CURRENT SPECIALS¶

- 1998 Apex Cabernet Sauvignon, deep color, rich, complex flavor, $31.99¶
- 2001 Santa Barbara Chardonnay, exceptional, with a touch of oak, $14.95¶
- 2001 Bridgman Chardonnay, opulent bouquet, creamy fruit flavor, $10.99¶
- 2000 Ravenswood Merlot, full, round, ripe flavor, intense aroma, $9.95¶
- 2000 Washington Hills Syrah, dark, lush flavor, rich aroma, $10.99¶

## MAJOR VARIETALS AND REGIONS¶

1. CABERNET SAUVIGNON: Washington, Northern Calif., Australia¶
2. CHARDONNAY: Washington, Oregon, Northern Calif., Central Coast¶
3. MERLOT: Washington, Oregon, Northern Calif., Central Coast¶
4. PINOT NOIR: Oregon, Central Coast, France¶
5. SAUVIGNON BLANC: Oregon, Northern Calif., Central Coast, France¶
6. ZINFANDEL: Washington, Northern Calif., Central Coast¶

Copyright © 2003 Wines 'n Things, Inc. All rights reserved. ↵
1234 W 23rd St, Ourtown, ST 12345 • (999) 555-1234 ↵
Please send comments and suggestions to webmaster@winesnthings.com ¶

**FIGURE 5-8**    The completed major categories section

7. Select all *except* the first line, open the Font Size drop-down list, and choose 3 (12 pt) for all of the contact information. In our case, we have put the e-mail addresses on a third line, so our finished heading looks like this:

### *WINES 'N THINGS* ↵
Jim Maynard and John Staley, Wine Merchants ↵
jim@winesnthings.com or john@winesnthings.com¶

**NOTE**    *If you see a wavy red line under any words, the spelling checker is telling you that these words are not in the spelling dictionary and may be misspelled. You can right-click these words and get a list of alternative correctly spelled words, as well as commands to ignore the suspected misspelling or to add the word to the dictionary.*

8. Click Align Left to left-align all three lines and then move the insertion point to the line following the tree you pasted.

9. Type what in Chapter 6 will become a link bar with links to the rest of the web. (Note that there is a space, a vertical bar, and a space between each option.) Here is ours:

**| Home | Cabernet | Chardonnay | Merlot | Pinot Noir | Blanc | Zinfandel |**

10. With the insertion point still in the future link bar, choose Heading 4 for the paragraph style. The top of your second page should now look like this:

11. Click Save to save the changes to page 2. Select the three lines pasted above, and the link bar, and click Copy on the toolbar.

12. Click the third_page.htm tab, click the top-left corner of the page to place the insertion point there, and click Paste on the toolbar. The heading appears on page 3. If a small Paste Options icon appears, click it to open and select Keep Source Formatting.

13. If you have an extra blank line above the just-pasted title, press CTRL-HOME to move the insertion point to the top of the page. Then, if necessary, press DEL to delete the leading paragraph mark.

14. Click Save to save page 3.

## Entering the Offerings for a Major Category

The body of information on the second page is a listing of specific offerings for a major category of products or services. In our case, we have a single variety of wine, such as Chardonnay, under which we will list all the offerings by region where the wine is produced. That is, of course, a long list. For this example, to keep the typing to a minimum, we have a single page for Chardonnay, with only a couple of regions and a couple of offerings in each. You, of course, can make this as complex as you wish. Here are the steps we took to build one major category page:

1. Click the second_page.htm tab. When the page opens, place the insertion point at the first blank line under the link bar.

2. Type **CHARDONNAY**, choose Heading 1, click Center, and press ENTER.

3. Type **WASHINGTON**, choose Heading 2, click Align Left, and press ENTER.

4. Choose Heading 3 and click Increase Indent on the Formatting toolbar to format and indent the list of Washington Chardonnays.

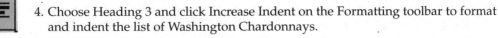

5. Type the following list, like this:

| Home | Cabernet | Chardonnay | Merlot | Pinot Noir | Blanc | Zinfandel |¶

# CHARDONNAY¶

## WASHINGTON¶

**2001 Apex Chardonnay, rich golden hue, complex flavors, $19.99¶**

**2001 Bridgman Chardonnay, opulent bouquet, rich flavors, $10.99¶**

**2000 Washington Hills Chardonnay, balanced, creamy finish, $9.99¶**

Press ENTER after each line:

**2001 Apex Chardonnay, rich golden hue, complex flavors, $19.99**
**2001 Bridgman Chardonnay, opulent bouquet, rich flavors, $10.99**
**2000 Washington Hills Chardonnay, balanced, creamy finish, $9.99**

6. Click Decrease Indent, choose Heading 2, type **OREGON**, and press ENTER.

7. Choose Heading 3, click Increase Indent, and type the following list, pressing ENTER after each line:

   **2000 Chateau Benoit Chardonnay, silky texture, tropical aroma, $16.95**
   **1998 Argyle Chardonnay, seductive aroma, toasted nut flavor, $22.95**
   **2001 Duck Pond Chardonnay, rich aroma, creamy, fruit flavor, $9.95**

8. Click Decrease Indent, choose Heading 4, and type the following notice:

   **Note: Excellent case prices are available on these wines call for quotes.**

9. If you have more than one blank line between the last line entered and the beginning of the footer, delete the extra lines. When you are done, click Save; your second-level page should look like Figure 5-9.

## Importing the Details of an Offering

The third-level page contains the detailed description of one particular product or service. Since this is often better described by the manufacturer or service provider, it may be helpful to use their material if you have permission to do so (check with your legal department or advisor on the need for this). You can do this by typing in the material, copying it from a web site, or in some cases, it might be faster to scan it in.

---

**NOTE**    *Scanning text from brochures and other promotional pieces and then using optical character recognition (OCR) has a much lower success rate than OCR with text on plain white paper. For small amounts of text, it is often easier to type it than to use OCR.*

---

In the following exercise, we use information from a web site, which we have gotten permission to use on the third page. You, of course, can use any source information or a

**FIGURE 5-9**    The completed second-page detail

combination of sources of information for your third page. If you have a scanner with OCR capability, you are encouraged to use it with something like a brochure or catalog—anything that is on slick paper with a mixture of text and pictures, and possibly with the text printed on a background image. You'll then get an understanding of how that works.

---

**NOTE**    *FrontPage can import files from many word processors. Chapter 11 will cover in detail how to import word processor and other files into FrontPage.*

To build the body of the third page of the web site by use of imported, scanned, and typed text, use the following steps:

1. Using your scanner and its software in the normal manner, scan an article of approximately 100 words. Use your OCR program (included with most scanners) to convert the text so that it can be read by Microsoft Word or your word processing program.

2. Similarly, scan and convert to text one or two other short articles. Finally, scan and convert to text a table of approximately four columns and four rows.

3. In Microsoft Word or your word processing program, edit the articles and table for scanning errors, and make any changes you'd like. Then save the articles.

4. Click the Third_page.htm tab. Place the insertion point at the first paragraph mark after the link bar and type the following text. Use SHIFT-ENTER at the end of the first line and ENTER on the second. Format these lines with Heading 2. Click Center in the Formatting toolbar, drag across the second line, and change its size to 4 (14 pt).

**Washington Hills 2000 Chardonnay**
**Released April 2002**

5. Move the insertion point below the heading you just typed, and then select Insert | File. In the Select File dialog box, shown next, open the Files Of Type drop-down list, and choose the type of word processor file you used.

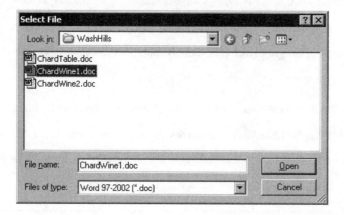

6. Locate the folder, select the name of your first article, and click Open. You may be told that FrontPage needs to install a converter to display this file. If so, click Yes. If needed, follow the instructions to convert the text. The article will appear on your page.

7. In a similar way, import the one or two short articles, and finally import your table.

8. On the line after the table, type the following text:

**Material on this page originated from and is used with the permission of**
**Washington Hills Cellars.**

9. Select the line you just typed, select Heading 4, click Italic on the Formatting toolbar, and then save the page, which should look like Figure 5-10.

---

*TIP    Getting permission to use other people's work generally depends on whether it is to the advantage of the originator. For example, permission for the material used here from Washington Hills Cellars was obtained because it publicizes them and one of their wines, and it doesn't detract from them (not to mention that they are nice people!).*

The text and pictures used on page three of the Wines 'n Things web site originated from, are owned by, and are used with the permission of Washington Hills Cellars. The Washington Hills web site is http://www.washingtonhills.com. You may contact the winery at 1-800-814-7004 or contact the executive offices at 1-425-889-4581.

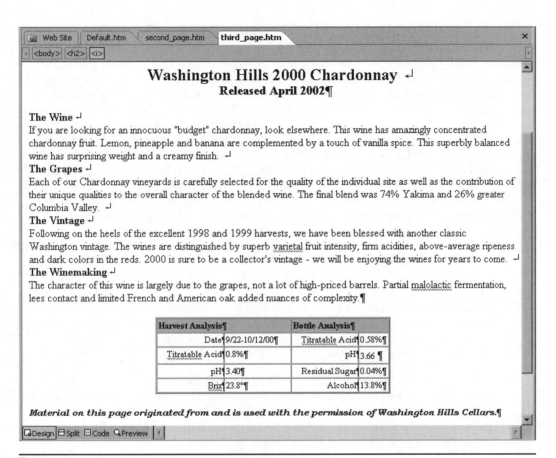

**FIGURE 5-10**   Text imported and typed onto the third page

The table in this example was imported from the Washington Hills Cellars web site. In Chapter 7, you'll see how to create FrontPage tables.

This completes the entry of all the text you need in this web. Now let's look at sprucing up the text with different fonts and then add pictures.

## Working with Fonts

The web site at this moment is nothing but text using the default typeface. One way to give it more appeal is to change the fonts to something that is more eye-catching. A *font* is a set of characters with the same design, size, weight, and style. A font is a member of a *typeface* family, all members of which have the same design. The font 12-point Arial bold italic is a member of the Arial typeface with a 12-point size, bold weight, and italic style. Using FrontPage, you have numerous fonts that you can choose from, including a number of fonts (over 100) that come with FrontPage and many, many more that you can add from other sources. With so many choices, it is easy to misuse fonts.

Fonts used correctly can be a major asset in getting a message across, but they also can detract from a message if improperly used. Two primary rules are to not use too many fonts, and to use complementary fonts together. In a one-page document, two typefaces should be enough (you can use bold and italic to have as many as eight fonts). In a longer document, using three—and at most four—typefaces is appropriate. Determining what fonts are complementary is more subjective. Arial and Times Roman are generally considered complementary, as are Futura and Garamond, and Palatino and Optima. In each of these pairs, one typeface (for example, Arial) is *sans serif* (without the little tails on the ends of a character) and is used for titles and headings, while the other typeface (for example, Times Roman) is *serif* (it has the tails) and is used for the body text. You have, of course, many other options and considerations in the sophisticated use of fonts.

One nice feature of recent versions of FrontPage and other Office products is that they show what a font looks like in the list of fonts when you go to select one. The only way to find out the right font for your web is to try several that look appealing. Do that now.

1. Click the Default.htm tab to open the Home Page. Drag across the first two lines on the page.

2. Open the Font drop-down list, and look at the fonts that are displayed. Choose a font that looks interesting by clicking it, and see how the title looks with that font. Try this several times to find the font that is just right for you. The final font you select should be the font that you use for all the headings in your web site. We chose Tempus Sans ITC.

   | Tempus Sans ITC | ▾ |

3. Select each of the headings in the three pages, and change their font to the one you just chose. For headings that are otherwise the same, you can use the Format Painter to copy the font in one heading to another. For example, select the first heading on page 1, and change its font to the one you chose in step 2. Then click the Format Painter and drag it across the second heading.

4. Return to the Home Page and select the two lines of address and contacts under the title. Open the Font drop-down list and select a complementary font to the one you are using for the title. This will be the font you use for all body (vs. heading) text. We are using Bookman Old Style.

---

**NOTE**   *Some fonts are much larger than others at the same point size, so you need to consider what the size means to you. We had to reduce the size of the two lines of address and contacts under the title to get them to fit within a reasonable width.*

5. Apply the body font to all of the nonheading text in your web. When you are done, save all three pages. Click Preview at the bottom of the pane to turn off the paragraph marks, and your Home Page should look like Figure 5-11.

---

## Obtaining and Working with Pictures

There are four sources of pictures for a web:

- Programs like Microsoft PhotoDraw, CorelDRAW, Windows Paint, or Adobe Photoshop allow you to create your own pictures.

# WINES 'N THINGS ↵
## Grand Wines and Accoutrements¶

Visit us at 1234 23rd Street, Ourtown, Call us at 555-1234 or 555-1235 or fax 555-1236 ↵
Jim Maynard and John Staley, Wine Merchants jim@winesnthings.com or john@winesnthings.com¶

## CURRENT SPECIALS¶

- 1998 Apex Cabernet Sauvignon, deep color, rich, complex flavor, $31.99¶
- 2001 Santa Barbara Chardonnay, exceptional, with a touch of oak, $14.95¶
- 2001 Bridgman Chardonnay, opulent bouquet, creamy fruit flavor, $10.99¶
- 2000 Ravenswood Merlot, full, round, ripe flavor, intense aroma, $9.95¶
- 2000 Washington Hills Syrah, dark, lush flavor, rich aroma, $10.99¶

## MAJOR VARIETALS AND REGIONS¶

1. CABERNET SAUVIGNON: Washington, Northern Calif., Australia¶
2. CHARDONNAY: Washington, Oregon, Northern Calif., Central Coast¶
3. MERLOT: Washington, Oregon, Northern Calif., Central Coast¶
4. PINOT NOIR: Oregon, Central Coast, France¶
5. SAUVIGNON BLANC: Oregon, Northern Calif., Central Coast, France¶
6. ZINFANDEL: Washington, Northern Calif., Central Coast¶

**FIGURE 5-11**    Home Page with new fonts applied

- Clip art from any number of sources—including the Internet, FrontPage, PhotoDraw, and CorelDRAW—give you ready-made images that you can immediately place into your work.

- Scanners allow you to scan existing photographs and other printed art and to put the results into your work.

- Digital cameras, both still and video, enable you to take photos and video and immediately place them in a web.

All of these sources have advantages and disadvantages. Using clip art is fast and easy, but it is often difficult to find exactly what you want. Scanned art gives you a lot of versatility, but you must have access to a scanner, and you must get permission from the art's creator to copy it. Digital cameras are very quick and easy, but you must be in the location where you want the picture taken, and some skill helps to create a good image. Also, you may need to get permission to take and publish a picture. Creating your own art in a drawing program has the ultimate versatility, but it takes time and skill. This section will look at several types of pictures.

Pictures can communicate a lot very quickly, and to some people they are far better at communicating than text. Therefore, make pictures an important part of your web, whether it is on the Internet or an intranet. Adding pictures to an intranet page is slightly different from adding them to an Internet page. Intranet pages, for internal consumption, usually emphasize information. Internet pages, for external consumption, usually emphasize selling. Also, LAN connections used by most intranets are much faster at downloading pictures than the modem connections generally used on the Internet. Just keep in mind the objectives of your web and the time pictures take to load.

## Creating and Inserting Pictures

In creating pictures for your web pages, you are limited only by your skill, imagination, and time. There are, of course, an infinite number of ways to create your own graphic and a number of different programs to do so.

---

**TIP**    *Before exporting a graphic from a graphics program to a web, it's best to size the graphic as desired. Though you can resize it in FrontPage, you cannot add more pixels. Enlarging a graphic will make it appear jagged. Also, choose a moderate number of colors or even switch to grayscale to reduce the file size and therefore the download time.*

What we have done here is to take four clip-art images, put them on the Home Page behind the title, and changed the title color to white so it could be seen. Here is how we did it:

Visit us at 1234 23rd Street, Ourtown, Call us at 555-1234 or 555-1235 or fax 555-1236
Jim Maynard and John Staley, Wine Merchants jim@winesnthings.com or john@winesnthings.com

CURRENT SPECIALS

1. If you are not already there, click the Default.htm tab. At the left of the title, press ENTER to create a blank line above the title with the insertion point in that line.

2. Locate the clip art and save it on your hard disk. In FrontPage, select Insert | Picture From File. Locate the file on your hard disk and double-click it. In our case, the picture came in very large, and the Pictures toolbar opened. We had to locate the lower-right corner, click the picture, and then drag the lower-right corner up and left until the picture was just a little larger than the two lines of the title.

---

**NOTE**    *If your Pictures toolbar doesn't open, right-click the picture and then click Show Pictures Toolbar in the context menu that opens.*

3. Leaving the insertion point on the right of the inserted picture, repeat step 2 three more times to insert the remaining three pictures, sizing them so they are the same height.

4. Drag across the row of four pictures to select them all at once. They will be displayed as a negative image.

5. Click Position Absolutely (the fourth icon from the left in the Pictures toolbar). The title will disappear behind the pictures.

6. Click Send Backward (the sixth icon from the left in the Pictures toolbar) to send the pictures behind the title.

7. Click somewhere else on the page to deselect the pictures, and you will see the title, although if your pictures are dark, like ours, it will be difficult.

8. Drag across just the title text to select it. Open the Font Color drop-down list on the right of the Formatting toolbar and choose the white color. Click somewhere else on the page to deselect the title, and you will see that it is white and stands out from the pictures, as you saw before the start of these steps.

9. Save the changes to the Home Page. The Save Embedded Files dialog box will open, allowing you to save the images you are using in this web (the pictures behind the title, in this case) with the web files. Click OK.

**CAUTION**  *Always save your images with your web files so that when you copy the web to another server, they will all be together, and FrontPage can do the copying for you.*

## Adding Horizontal Lines

Horizontal lines help separate sections of a web page. FrontPage provides an easy way to add such lines through the Insert menu. You can also add your own lines by placing them as pictures. Try both techniques now with these steps:

1. With the Wines 'n Things Home Page displayed, place the insertion point at the left end of "CURRENT SPECIALS."

2. Select Insert | Horizontal Line. A horizontal line will appear on your page above "CURRENT SPECIALS," separating the top two sections on your Home Page, like this:

Visit us at 1234 23rd Street, Ourtown, Call us at 555-1234 or 555-1235 or fax 555-1236
Jim Maynard and John Staley, Wine Merchants jim@winesnthings.com or john@winesnthings.com

## CURRENT SPECIALS

3. Move the insertion point down to the left end of the line that reads "MAJOR VARIETALS AND REGIONS." Press ENTER to create a blank line just above it, move the insertion point to that line, and make it Normal style. Here you'll add a horizontal line graphic that comes with FrontPage.

4. Select Insert | Picture | Clip Art. The Clip Art task pane will open. Type **lines** in the Search For text box and click Go. A number of different lines appear, like this:

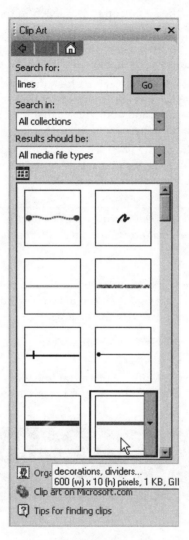

5. Click the line that you want to use (the right one in the fourth row was used here), and the line will appear on the page. You can also choose to open a fly-out menu by clicking the arrow on the right of each image and then clicking Insert.

6. If the line isn't long enough, as ours wasn't, click the line to turn on the sizing handles, move the mouse pointer to the right end of the line until the pointer becomes a horizontal two-headed arrow, and then drag the line to the right as necessary, like this:

- 2000 Washington Hills Syrah, dark, lush flavor, rich aroma, $10.99

## MAJOR VARIETALS AND REGIONS

*Picture Actions*

*TIP    When the line is selected, a rectangular box with an icon in it and a drop-down arrow appears below the line near the right end. If you move the mouse pointer into the box, you'll see that the box is called Picture Actions. When you click the drop-down arrow, the box opens. You can choose to only modify the size, which uses the original pixels, or to resample the pictures getting the needed additional pixels for a change in size. (You don't get the Picture Actions box on the first line because you can't change it and it automatically sizes itself.)*

   7. Close the Clip Art pane, save your Home Page, and click OK to save the embedded file that is the last line you placed.

### Placing Clip Art

Clip art gives you that quick little something to create interest in a page. We would like something next to the Current Specials heading to call attention to it. Searching the Office Insert Clip Art collection with the keyword "wine," we find a glass of wine and a wine bottle. Here is what we do with it (you can use similar steps to place your own piece of clip art):

   1. With the Wines 'n Things Home Page open in FrontPage, move the insertion point to the left edge of the Current Specials heading.

   2. To locate the piece of clip art in the Office clip art collection, select Insert | Picture | Clip Art, type the keyword on which you want to search (**wine**, in our case), and press ENTER or click Go. Scroll through the images that appear and choose one. When you find it, double-click it and it will appear on your page.

*NOTE    The Clip Art pane gives you several methods of locating a picture file. To get an image from the Internet, open the Search In drop-down list and choose Web Collections while if necessary deselecting the other choices. To get an image from your own file, open the Search In drop-down list and select My Collections while deselecting the other choices. The Results Should Be drop-down list can help you narrow the search by deselecting Movies and Sounds and possibly only selecting Clip Art or Photographs, depending on what type of "picture" you want.*

   3. If necessary, select the graphic, which opens the Pictures toolbar. (If your Pictures toolbar doesn't open when you select a picture, you can open it by selecting View | Toolbars | Pictures.) You've already seen several things you can do with the Pictures toolbar; another is to crop a picture (remove some of the outer edges).

   4. Select the Crop tool just a little right of center in the Pictures toolbar. When you do that, a dotted line appears in the picture you have selected. Either use the sizing handles to move the dotted line to where you want to crop, or drag the cropping tool across the rectangle of your final image. When you have the final image you want inside the dotted line, press ENTER.

5. As discussed under "Creating and Inserting Pictures," size the picture as you need. To move the picture between lines so that it is not constrained by text lines, click Position Absolutely and drag the picture to where you want it. You may need to adjust the text and line size to fit the picture. We had to move "CURRENT SPECIALS" to the right by putting spaces on the left. We also had to add a Normal (12 pt) line above "CURRENT SPECIALS."

6. Periodically click Preview at the bottom of the pane to see how it looks without the various marks. When you are ready, save the Home Page. The Save Embedded Files dialog box again appears, allowing you to save the graphic to the current FrontPage web. Click OK to do so, which closes the dialog box.

7. The final test is to look at your page in a browser. Do that by clicking Preview In Microsoft Internet Explorer in the Standard toolbar. The result is shown in Figure 5-12. You can try various resolutions in Internet Explorer by clicking the drop-down arrow next to Preview In Microsoft Internet Explorer.

8. When you are done, close your browser, leaving FrontPage open.

It's easy to get carried away with adding small clip-art images. They are neat and don't use much memory, so people think that they add little to the load time. But if you put several of them on a page, such as one for every paragraph, all of a sudden you have a loading problem, and the page begins to look cluttered.

**FIGURE 5-12**
Finished Home page with graphics in place

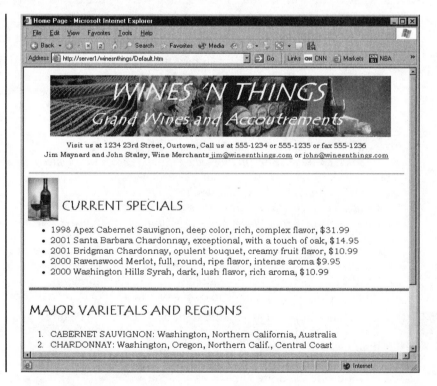

## Adding Colored Text

FrontPage makes it very easy to color text, as you saw with making the title text in front of the pictures white. As with clip art, it is easy to get carried away. Also, it is very important that whatever you use does not impair readability. You want the color to have a high contrast with its background. Use the following steps to learn more about coloring text:

1. In the Wines 'n Things Home Page, which should be open on your screen, drag across the words "CURRENT SPECIALS" or your first heading.

2. On the Formatting toolbar, click the down arrow on the right of the Font Color button to open the color palette, as shown next:

 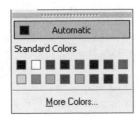

> **TIP**    *The color palette can be "torn off" the toolbar to become a floating menu by dragging the bar at the top of the palette. When you move the mouse pointer to this bar, the mouse pointer becomes a four-headed arrow.*

3. Click the color from the palette that you like best for your first heading. We chose Maroon, the fourth selection from the left in the first row, to give these words a burgundy color.

4. Select the words "Major Varietals and Regions" and, using the preceding process, make them the same or a complementary color. We chose the same color.

5. Close the Font Color palette, and once again save your Home Page.

## Adding a Background

The default background used by FrontPage is white, which you have seen in all the figures and illustrations so far in this chapter. You can change this to any color you wish or to a background image by using the Page Properties dialog box. Again, you have to be aware of the load-time impact as your background gets more sophisticated. There are several possibilities for a background.

### Creating a Solid-Color Background

Begin by looking at solid-color backgrounds:

---

***TIP*** *If you choose black for your text—and there is no reason you need to—then your backgrounds should be very light colors. In any case, you should maintain a very high contrast between the background and text colors so they are easy to read.*

1. In the Wines 'n Things Home Page, right-click in a blank area of the page, choose Page Properties, and click the Formatting tab. The Page Properties dialog box Formatting tab will appear as shown in Figure 5-13.

2. Click the down arrow for the Colors Background drop-down list. A palette of 16 colors, the default color, possibly a set of custom colors, the colors currently in use in the document, and a More Colors option are displayed, as you saw with font colors.

3. By selecting More Colors, you display the More Colors dialog box, shown in Figure 5-14. You can use any of the predefined 128 colors, or you can use one of the 6 shades of gray. You can also create your own colors with the Custom button, which opens the Color dialog box, where you can use either of two numerical schemes, or more simply by clicking a color in the color selector and then adjusting the brightness on the right. One possible color is a very light beige being selected in the More Colors dialog box in Figure 5-14.

4. Select a color of your own, and then click OK. The color appears in the Page Properties dialog box; click OK again. Now the color appears on the web page.

---

***TIP*** *Be sure to check how both Netscape Navigator and Microsoft Internet Explorer display any custom color you create. Some colors may end up being "dithered" (motley colored instead of a single smooth color because it displays the component colors instead of blending them) and won't look right.*

---

**FIGURE 5-13**
Setting a page's
background

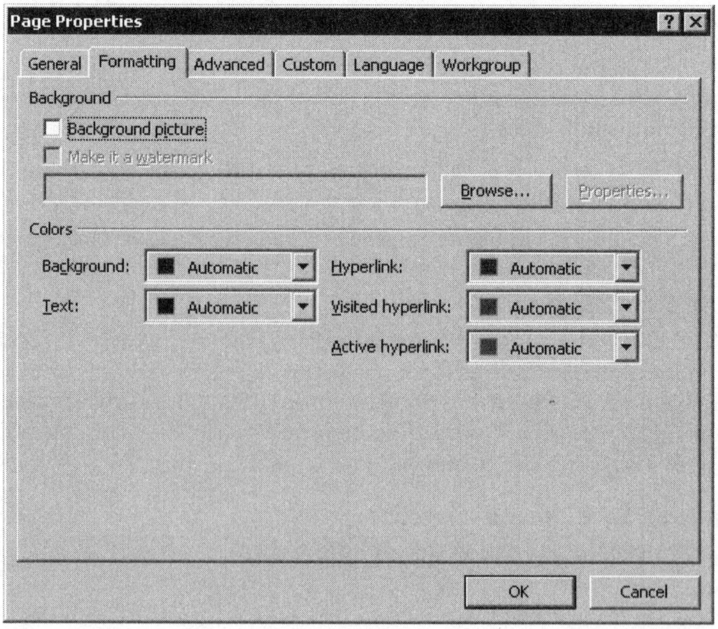

**FIGURE 5-14**
Selecting a
background
color for the
Home Page

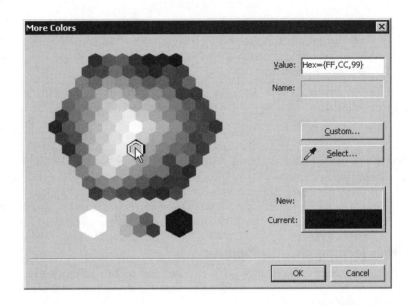

5. If either your page title or the clip art you added now shows a different background, click the graphic to select it and open the Pictures toolbar. Select the Set Transparent Color tool, and click the color you want to be transparent.

---

**NOTE**    *Doing this with a .jpg opens a message box saying the graphic will be converted to a .gif and warning it may reduce the number of colors and/or increase file size.*

6. Save your Home Page.

### Using a Textured Background
You can also choose one of the many textured backgrounds offered with Office or FrontPage, as well as any of those available on the Internet and elsewhere.

---

**NOTE**    *Most textured backgrounds are made by tiling a small graphic. You can make your own with any small image, optimally 96×96 pixels. If the image has a repeatable pattern, it is possible to get it to be reasonably seamless, as FrontPage has done in its samples.*

To add a textured background:

1. Click the second_page.htm tab. Press CTRL-HOME to place the insertion point in the upper-left corner of the page. Select Insert | Picture | Clip Art. The Clip Art task pane will appear.
2. Type **texture** in the Search Text box and click Go. Select the one you want and click it. A block of the pattern will appear on the page.
3. Save the second_page. When the Save Embedded Files dialog box appears, note the name of the texture, and then click OK. Once the page and the texture image are saved, delete the texture image on the page and close the Clip Art pane.

4. Right-click a blank area of the page, choose Page Properties, open the Formatting tab, and click Background Picture. Click Browse and double-click the texture image you just saved. Finally, click OK to close the Page Properties dialog box. The background appears.

5. Save your second-level page. Click Preview In Microsoft Internet Explorer, and you should see an image similar to that shown in Figure 5-15. When you are ready, close your browser.

> **NOTE**   *We do not like this textured background because it makes the text hard to read and readability is of primary importance. We chose this texture as the least offensive of the ones in the Microsoft Clip Art collection. We also searched on "pattern," "background," and "stationery" and found nothing that is better, and most of the images were the same in all those categories. If we really wanted a textured background, we would search for a very light-colored image.*

## Other Techniques with Pictures

You can do many other things with pictures and text to enhance a page. Use two small images on the third page to see what you can do to position text relative to a picture. Here is what we did:

1. Select third_page.htm from the Window menu. Place the insertion point to the left of the detail item heading ("Washington Hills…," in our case).

**FIGURE 5-15**    The second page with a textured background

2. Select Insert | Picture | From File, browse to locate a small image. (The image we've used is the Washington Hills logo with a bottle of wine from the Washington Hills web site and used by permission of Washington Hills.) Click Insert to close the dialog boxes and insert the image.

3. Select the image you just brought in, and click Position Absolutely in the Pictures toolbar. Move the image to the left edge of the text in the paragraph below the heading.

4. Click in the heading at a point where it makes sense to split it into two lines. We did it between "Hills" and "2000." That gave us enough room to fit our image on the left, like this (you may need to do some more playing with your text to get it to fit):

| **Home** | **Cabernet** | **Chardonnay** | **Merlot** | **Pinot Noir** | **Blanc** | **Zinfandel** |

*Washington Hills*
*2000 Chardonnay*
**Released April 2002**

**The Wine**
If you are looking for an innocuous "budget" chardonnay, look elsewhere. This wine has amazingly concentrated chardonnay fruit. Lemon, pineapple and banana are

5. Move the insertion point to the middle of the text on page 3, select Insert | Picture | From File, browse to locate a second small picture, and click Insert. The picture will come into the page.

6. Right-click the picture and choose Picture Properties. In the Appearance tab, click the Right wrapping style, like this:

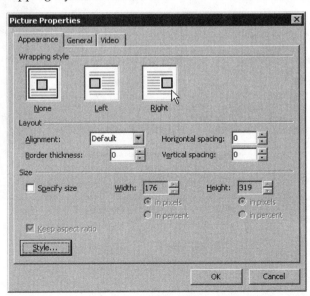

and Sem
: of Eleme
finish. ⅃

7. Click OK and the picture will reappear with the text wrapped on its left. If you want to move the picture, you will find that you can't drag it. Instead, you must drag a small arrow icon you will find in the text and shown on the left. When we had the picture positioned the way we wanted, the body of our third page looked like Figure 5-16 in Preview.

8. Save your third-level page, clicking OK to save the images with the web.

Text and pictures are the foundation of any web, whether you create the web or it is created with a template or wizard. You've just seen the tip of what you can do with them and have just begun the process of creating a web site. In Chapter 6, you'll learn about adding hyperlinks to both text and pictures. In future chapters, you'll see how to change the look of this web to achieve a more professional feel.

**FIGURE 5-16**    Finished third page with the text wrapping around a picture

# Adding and Managing
# Hyperlinks and Hotspots

When you open a web page in a browser, you have access to only the single page in the address given to the browser. You can't get to another page without giving the browser its address, unless there is a hyperlink on the first page that provides the address of (and therefore takes you to) another page.

A *hyperlink* or *link* is an object, either text or graphic, that, when you click it, tells the browser to move to a bookmark on the same page or to open another page. The hyperlink, when clicked, gives the browser an address called a *uniform resource locator (URL)*. The browser then opens the page at that address. The page can be part of the current web, part of another web at the same site, or part of any web at any site anywhere on the Internet, anywhere in the world (unless your intranet limits you to its domain).

A hyperlink is an essential part of a web page. It is the element that allows the page to be interconnected with other pages, producing the "web." Hyperlinks are also why the original language behind web pages, HTML, is called *Hyper*text Markup Language. Hyperlinks provide the first and most important interactivity in a web page: they give users a choice of where to go when they are done with the current page.

When a hyperlink is viewed in a browser, it is normally a different color than the surrounding text and it is usually underlined. (The person controlling the browser may be able to determine what color a hyperlink is and whether it is underlined.) Also, when you move the mouse pointer over a hyperlink, the pointer normally turns into a pointing hand, and either the full or partial URL related to that link is displayed in the status bar at the bottom of the window, as you can see next. (This shows a full path, http://server1/winesnthings/Default.htm. A partial URL would be just the page name, Default.htm.)

In this chapter, you will see how to add hyperlinks to text and graphics, how to assign areas of a graphic, or hotspots, to a hyperlink, and how to manage the hyperlinks in a web page.

# Adding Hyperlinks to Text and Graphics

Hyperlinks can be assigned to anything you enter on a web page. Any piece of text—be it a word, a phrase, or a paragraph—or any graphic (from a bullet to a large image) can be assigned a link. While there are many similarities, some differences also exist, so let's look separately at assigning hyperlinks to text and to graphics.

## Assigning Hyperlinks to Text

Within a web, hyperlinks provide the principal means of getting from one page to another and back again. Begin by assigning hyperlinks for that purpose:

1. If it isn't already loaded, start FrontPage. In FrontPage, open the web site that you created in Chapter 5 (Wines 'n Things, in our case), and then open the three pages, one after the other.

---

***TIP*** *A fast way to open a web you have recently worked on (Wines 'n Things, in our case) is to open the File menu and select Recent Sites | http://yourserver/yourwebsite.*

---

2. Display the Home Page, and then scroll the page so you can see the list of major offering categories below the second heading. In our case, this was the list below Major Varietals And Regions.

3. Drag across the word in the list that references your second page to select that word. In our case, the word is "CHARDONNAY" in the second line. You'll make this word a link to the second page, displaying, in our case, a list of Chardonnay wines.

4. Click Insert Hyperlink on the toolbar. Alternatively, you can choose Hyperlink from the Insert menu, right-click the word and choose Hyperlink, or press CTRL-K. The Insert Hyperlink dialog box will open.

5. The second page is the one you want to link to, so double-click the filename (second_page.htm), as shown in Figure 6-1. The Insert Hyperlink dialog box will close. When you return to the Home Page, you'll see that the word you had selected ("CHARDONNAY," in our case) has changed. If you move the highlight off it, you'll see that it has changed color and is underlined. Also, a tooltip appears and the link destination is displayed in the status bar when the mouse moves over it, like this:

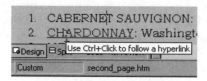

6. Right-click your word like "CHARDONNAY," and choose Hyperlink Properties to again open the hyperlink dialog box, now called Edit Hyperlink. You'll see that it is similar to what was shown in Figure 6-1 as the Insert Hyperlink dialog box, except that it has a Remove Link button. Click Cancel to close the dialog box.

7. Click Save on the toolbar to save the Home Page.

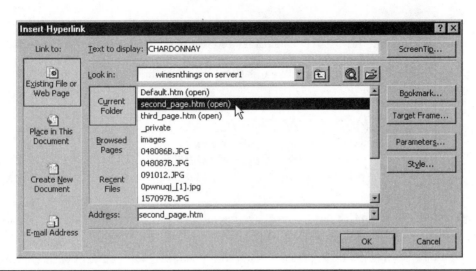

**FIGURE 6-1**    Selecting the destination of a hyperlink

8. Press and hold CTRL while clicking (called "CTRL+click") your link similar to CHARDONNAY to follow the hyperlink and see where it will take you. You should end up on the second page. (If you didn't, you somehow did not select the correct page in step 5.)

**NOTE**    *When you simply choose a page as a link, you are taken to the top of that page. This may or may not be what you want. You can control where you go on a page through bookmarks, which are discussed in "Establishing Bookmarks" later in this chapter.*

## Creating or Activating a Link Bar

Once you are on the second page (when viewing in a browser), you need a way to return to the Home Page (ignore for the moment that there is a Back button). To do that, you need a link back to the Home Page as well as to other pages. This is what a link bar is used for. In Chapter 5, you mocked up a link bar and put it in both the second and third pages. One way to provide the links back to the Home Page and to other pages is simply to activate the words in the existing link bar mockup. An alternative is to let FrontPage build a link bar for you. Let's look at both of these approaches next.

**Activating the Mockup Link Bar**    Activating the mockup link bar is the same as turning any word into a hyperlink, as you can see with these steps:

1. At the top of the second page, drag across the word "Home" in the link bar, and click Insert Hyperlink on the toolbar. (From now on, this will just be called the "Link" button.)

2. Double-click the Home Page (Default.htm) to establish that as the destination of the link.

3. Since you'll copy the link bar to other pages, drag across your equivalent to Chardonnay in the link bar, click Link, and double-click the second page. Home and Chardonnay are the only two link bar elements you can activate at this time, so your link bar should look like this (We turned off the background to make the text easier to read):

### WINES 'N THINGS ↵

Jim Maynard and John Staley, Wine Merchants ↵
jim@winesnthings.com or john@winesnthings.com¶

| **Home** | Cabernet | **Chardonnay** | Merlot | Pinot Noir

**Having FrontPage Create a Link Bar**    FrontPage uses the relationships established and shown in Navigation view to create a link bar for you. See how with these steps:

1. Open the View menu and click Navigation. The Navigation view of your web site should look like Figure 6-2. If your second and third pages are not as shown in Figure 6-2, drag them from the Folder List to the Navigation pane, and they will automatically be connected to the page above where they are being dragged.

2. In the Navigation toolbar on the right of the Navigation pane, the Included In Link Bars button, shown on the left, allows you to turn a particular link in the automatic link bars on or off. If you select the second page and click the Included In Link Bars button, both the second and third pages are removed from the automatic link bars and become gray. Try this for yourself with different pages selected. When you are done, make sure that all pages are included in link bars and that your Navigation view looks like Figure 6-2.

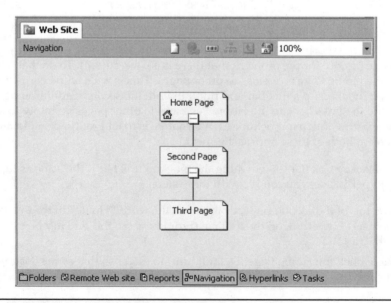

**FIGURE 6-2**    Navigation view relationships establish the links in a link bar

3. Click the tab for the second page to open that page. When the page opens, place the insertion point at the right end of the manual link bar and press ENTER.

4. Open the Insert menu and choose Navigation. In the Insert Web Component dialog box, Link Bars should be selected as the Component Type. If not, select it, choose Bar Based On Navigation Structure, and click Next.

5. Choose any style that you like. For the Wines 'n Things web, we chose one called Canyon (select the options to see the name). Click Next, accept the horizontal orientation, and click Finish. The Link Bar Properties dialog box opens. Select the Child Level option and Home Page check box, as shown in Figure 6-3. Click OK.

---

**NOTE**  *In the Insert Web Component dialog boxes or in the Style tab of the Link Bar Properties dialog box, you can choose to have the hyperlinks displayed as either graphical buttons or text. For buttons, you apply a theme to the web or choose from a number of styles. Alternatively, you can choose to have the links displayed as text.*

As you can see next, in SharePoint Team Services (STS or SharePoint 1) a link bar is inserted on the page, displaying the links you established in Navigation view and selected in the Link Bar Properties dialog box. In Windows SharePoint Services (WSS or SharePoint2), a statement "*[Edit the properties for this link bar to display hyperlinks here]*" is displayed where the link bar should be. You don't see the actual links until you save the page and open it in a browser.

In step 5 of the preceding exercise, you created links to the Home Page and child pages in the link bar. If you were to repeat these steps on the third-page link bar, since it doesn't have a child page, the link bar with the same settings as the second page would have only one link, back to the Home Page. The third page does have a parent page—the second page—and you'll want to provide a link to that page. You'd do that by changing the link bar properties on the third page to include the parent page. Do that with these steps:

1. Click the tab for the third page. On that page, place the insertion point at the right end of the manual link bar and press ENTER.

2. Open the Insert menu and choose Navigation. In the Insert Web Component dialog box, make sure Link Bars is selected as the Component Type, select Bar Based On Navigation Structure, and click Next.

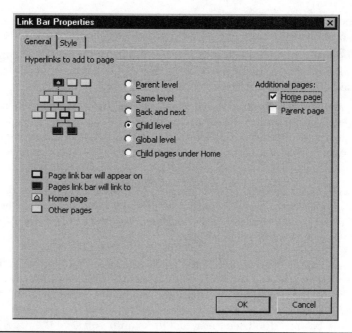

**FIGURE 6-3**   Establishing the links in an automatic link bar

3. Choose the same bar style as you chose earlier, click Next, accept the horizontal orientation, and click Finish.

4. In the Link Bar Properties dialog box, click Same Level to pick up any future pages that are created at the third level, and click Home Page and Parent Page to create links to those pages. Click OK. A link bar with Home and Up will appear if you are using STS. In WSS, it will appear in Preview or in a browser.

5. Save both your second and third pages.

### Establishing Bookmarks

Since some web pages can be quite long and you may want to direct exactly where on a page a link will take the user, you need to identify a spot on a page where a link will end up. This is done by use of bookmarks. *Bookmarks* are objects (text or graphics) that have been selected as destinations for a link. Follow these steps to create a bookmark:

---

***TIP***   *You must identify the bookmark before you establish the link, unless you want to go back and edit the link after it is established.*

---

1. Return to the second page and drag across the heading that refers to a group of detail offerings. In our case, that is "WASHINGTON."

2. Press CTRL-G or open the Insert menu and choose Bookmark (you may have to extend the menu). The Bookmark dialog box will open, as shown next.

3. Click OK to make your word similar to "WASHINGTON" a bookmark. You'll see a dashed line appear under "WASHINGTON."

4. Drag across the heading "OREGON," press CTRL-G or open the Insert menu, choose Bookmark, and click OK in the Bookmark dialog box. A dashed line will appear under the selected word.

Selecting the bookmarks is only half the procedure; you must also establish the links to the bookmarks. Before going back to the Home Page to do that, establish the link to the third page.

### Linking to the Third Page

The third page is a detailed description of, in our case, one Washington wine listed on the second page. Therefore, set the line that lists the wine as the link to the page that describes it, using these steps:

1. With the second page displayed, scroll the page so you can see the list of Chardonnay wines under the Washington heading.

2. Drag across the first part of the line that begins "2000 Washington Hills Chardonnay."

3. Click Link on the toolbar to open the Insert Hyperlink dialog box, and then double-click Third_Page.htm. Your second page with the activated link bars, the two bookmarks, and the link to the third page should look like Figure 6-4 when created with STS.

4. Click Save on the toolbar to save the second page.

5. CTRL-click your equivalent to the 2000 Washington Hills Chardonnay link you established in step 3 to follow the hyperlink. Your third page should open.

6. Clean up the page and recapture some room by selecting and deleting the manual link bar mockup, leaving the link bar created by FrontPage on the third page, as you can see in Figure 6-5.

7. Click Save on the toolbar to save the third page.

8. In STS, CTRL-click the word "Home" in the link bar to return to the Home Page.

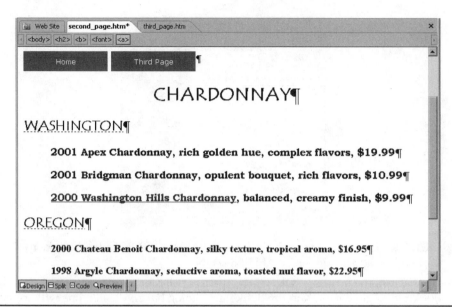

**FIGURE 6-4**    Links and bookmarks on the second page

You have now followed the links you established from the first to the second page, from the second to the third page, and from the third page back to the first. You can see that they

**FIGURE 6-5**
Cleaned up
third page with
activated link bar

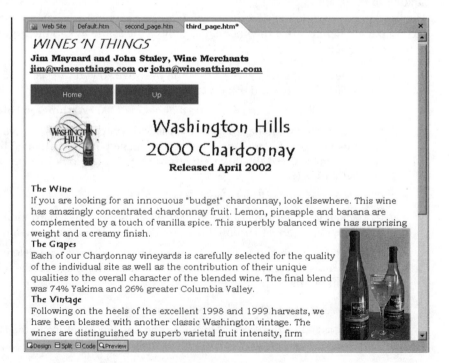

provide a good means of navigating a web. Later in the chapter, you'll try them in a browser, where all you'll need to do is click them.

## Using Bookmarks in Links

On the Home Page, use the two bookmarks you set to create two detail links within what on our site are the Chardonnay regional options:

1. On the Home Page, scroll the page so you can see the numbered list of your major offering categories.

2. Drag across your equivalent to our word "Washington" in the list of Chardonnays, as you can see here:

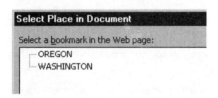

3. Click Link on the toolbar to open the Insert Hyperlink dialog box.

4. Click Second_Page.htm in the list of pages, and then click Bookmark. Your two bookmarks will appear, like this:

**Select Place in Document**

Select a bookmark in the Web page:

- OREGON
- WASHINGTON

5. Double-click your equivalent to WASHINGTON to select that bookmark, and then click OK to close the dialog box and establish the link. The Address in the bottom of the Insert Hyperlink dialog box now includes the bookmark, as shown next:

6. Drag across what in our case is the word "Oregon" (in the same lines as the "Washington" you selected in step 2 earlier), click Link, select Second_Page.htm, click Bookmark, and double-click OREGON.

7. Click OK to close the dialog box and to set the link.

## Setting Links to Other Than Web Sites

All of the links that you have created so far have been to other pages within this single web application. Later in this chapter, you'll make a link to another web site. FrontPage allows you to make a link to:

- An existing page in the current web
- A new page in the current web

- Another web
- A bookmark in either the current web or another web
- A frame in either the current web or another web
- A file on a local hard disk
- An e-mail address to send e-mail

A link to an e-mail address using the mailto link is commonly found in the footer on a web page. This allows the user to easily contact the webmaster or the page's creator by using e-mail. FrontPage will create a mailto link when you enter text that looks like an e-mail address (two text strings, without spaces, separated by the @ character). In Chapter 5, you saw that the footer for the Wines 'n Things web had the e-mail address webmaster@ winesnthings.com. FrontPage has automatically created the mailto link, as you can with these steps:

---

**NOTE**    *If your webmaster e-mail address is not underlined, telling you it is recognized as an e-mail address, place the insertion point on the right of ".com" and press the* SPACEBAR. *This should turn it into an address—or, in other words, a link to the person's e-mail mailbox. You can delete the extra space by moving the insertion point to the left of the space and pressing* DEL. *If you press* BACKSPACE, *you will get rid of the link.*

---

1. Scroll to the bottom of the Home Page so you can see the copyright and other information in the footer.
2. Right-click your equivalent to "webmaster@winesnthings.com," and then select Hyperlink Properties.
3. In the E-mail Address text box on the Edit Hyperlink dialog box, you can see that the URL for the hyperlink is mailto:webmaster@winesnthings.com, as shown next:

4. Click OK to close the Edit Hyperlink dialog box, and then click Save on the toolbar to save the Home Page.

You now have a number of links, so it is time to see if they work.

### Testing Your Links in a Browser

The only way to know if your links are really working is to try them in a browser:

1. If you didn't save each of the three pages in the preceding steps, do that now by opening the File menu and selecting Save All.

---

**TIP**    *You can tell if a page has been saved since it was last changed by looking at the tabs at the top of the window. If the page name has an asterisk beside it, it needs to be saved.*

2. Your Home Page should still be displayed. Click Preview In Microsoft Internet Explorer on the toolbar. Your browser will open.

**TIP**   *You should always look at your work in both 640×480 and 800×600 resolution. Remember that you have no control over the user's browser resolution, so your work must look good in both resolutions. If your site looks good at 800×600, it will also look fine at 1024×768. Very few people today use 640×480, so if your web is readable at that resolution, that is all you need.*

3. If your web browser is already open, you can enter the address or URL for your web in the Address drop-down list. The address should be in the form **http://servername/webname/**. In FrontPage, you can see this in the title bar, or you can find this in the Page Properties dialog box for any page in a web (right-click the page and choose Page Properties). For example, here is the URL for the Home Page in its Page Properties dialog box opened from Page view:

| Location: | http://server1/winesnthings/Default.htm |
|-----------|-------------------------------------------|
| Title: | Home Page |

**NOTE**   *If you include a page filename in the URL when you open a browser, you will open that page, which may not be the Home Page. You do not need to include the page filename if you want to open a home page.*

**TIP**   *You can drag across the URL in the FrontPage Page Properties dialog box, press* CTRL-C *to copy it to the Clipboard, open a browser, click the Address box, and press* CTRL-V *to paste the URL there.*

4. If you have previously opened your web in your browser, click Refresh on the browser's toolbar to make sure you are using the latest files.

5. Scroll down the page until you can see your equivalent to MAJOR VARIETALS AND REGIONS. Move the mouse pointer until it is over your word similar to "CHARDONNAY." The mouse pointer will turn into a pointing hand, and the URL for the second page will be shown in the status bar at the bottom of the window, as you can see in Figure 6-6.

**TIP**   *If you don't see the URL at the bottom of the Internet Explorer window, you need to turn on the status bar by opening the View menu and choosing Status Bar.*

6. Click your equivalent of CHARDONNAY, and your second page will be displayed. Your first hyperlink has now opened the second page.

7. Click Home in either link bar. Your Home Page should again be displayed.

8. If you are not already there, scroll down so you can see the line with the links to the bookmarks on the second page (Washington and Oregon, in our case), and then click

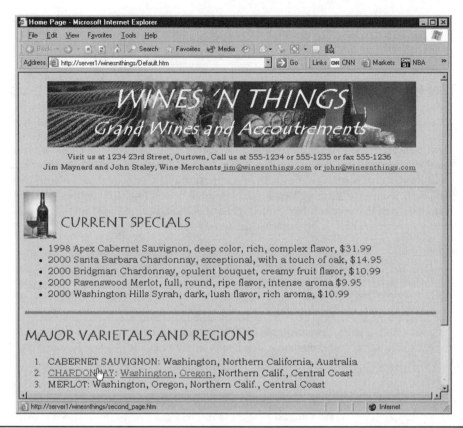

**FIGURE 6-6**    When the mouse pointer is over a hyperlink, its URL is displayed in the status bar

one of those links (we're clicking Oregon). The bookmarked heading will be positioned as far up in the window as information below it allows (if there is enough information below the bookmark, the bookmark will be at the top of the window), as shown in Figure 6-7.

9. Click the line with your third-page link (2000 Washington Hills Chardonnay, in our case). The third page will open.

10. Click Up in the link bar, and you'll be returned to the second page. Notice how the page is positioned at its top.

11. Click Home on the link bar. When the Home Page opens, it will be positioned at its top.

12. Scroll to the bottom of the Home Page and click the webmaster address. Your e-mail system should start and display a new message window with the webmaster address in the To text box, as you can see in Figure 6-8.

13. Close down your e-mail system without sending a message, and then close your browser and return to FrontPage.

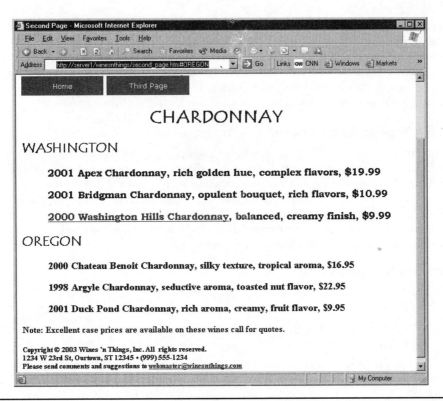

**FIGURE 6-7**    A bookmark in a link will position the bookmark toward the top of the window

**FIGURE 6-8**
Clicking a mailto link opens your e-mail New Message window.

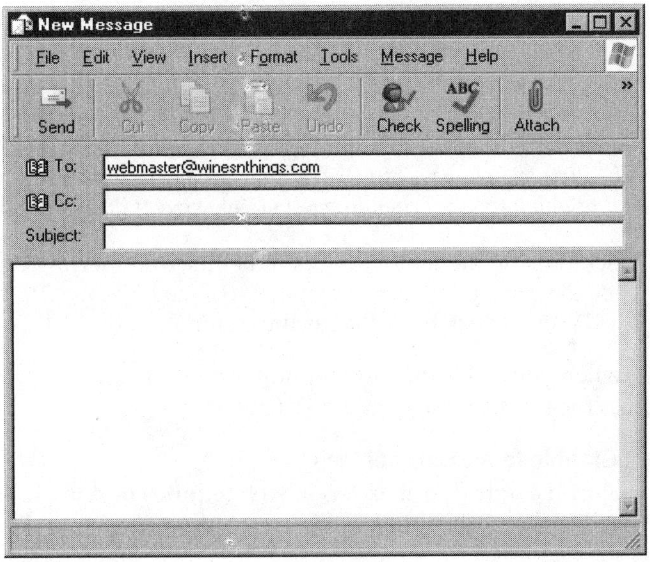

All of your links should have worked, providing an excellent navigation system around your web. If you find that a link did not work, right-click it in FrontPage, click Hyperlink Properties to open the Edit Hyperlink dialog box, and correct where the link is pointing. Checking your work in a browser not only confirms that your links work as expected, but it also gives you a visual check of the page design. You cannot count on the appearance of a page carrying over to your browser. Check your work on your browser often.

## Assigning Hyperlinks to a Graphic

Although text makes for good links, graphics have even greater possibilities. You can assign a single link to a graphic, or you can divide a graphic into sections, called *hotspots,* and make each section a separate link. All of the concepts that you learned about with text links also apply to graphics. You can have links to the existing web, both with and without bookmarks. You can have external links to web sites as well as to other types of Internet sites. In addition, you can make either a single graphic that has been divided or multiple graphics into a link bar, and you can test graphic links in your browser.

### Making a Graphic a Single Link

Making a graphic a single link is very much like what you did with a piece of text. To do this for a graphic:

1. Open the Home Page. Scroll the page down, if necessary, so you can see the picture next to the first heading.

2. Click the picture so it is selected, showing the sizing boxes in the four corners as well as in the middle of each side, like this:

<No ID>

CURRENT SPECIALS ↵

- 1998 Apex Cabernet Sauvignon, deep color, ric
- 2001 Santa Barbara Chardonnay, exceptional,

---

**NOTE**    *The Picture Actions menu (the drop-down menu under the picture) provides the ability to do pixel resampling when changing the picture size. It disappears after you choose to resample.*

---

3. Click Link on the toolbar to open the Insert Hyperlink dialog box, and then double-click the third page (you may need to click Existing File Or Web Page first to see the third page) to establish that as the destination of the link.

Now when you move the mouse pointer over the graphic, you'll see "third_page.htm," the address for the third page, in the status bar.

### Linking a Graphic to an External Web

Linking a graphic or text to an external web requires nothing more than specifying the external web's URL in the link:

1. Open the third page (or do a CTRL-click on the picture link you just created), and position the page so you can see the picture you placed next to the page title. In our case that is a logo for and a wine bottle from Washington Hills Cellars. We're going to create a link between that picture and the Washington Hills Cellars web site.

2. Click the picture to select it, and then click Link to open the Insert Hyperlink dialog box. Click the Address text box at the bottom of the dialog box.

3. Type a URL—for example, **http://www.washingtonhills.com/**—and click OK. You should see the URL in the status bar when you move the mouse pointer over the graphic.

---

*TIP*   *If you click the Browse The Web button in the Insert Hyperlink dialog box, locate the web site you want to link to, and then, without closing your browser, return to the Insert Hyperlink dialog box, the URL will be automatically copied to the Address text box in the Insert Hyperlink dialog box.*

---

**FIGURE 6-9**   External web site opened from a link in the web being created here

4. Save the third page and then click Preview In Microsoft Internet Explorer. When the browser opens, move the mouse over the picture to which you just added a hyperlink, and you'll see the URL in the status bar.

5. Click the picture and, since you are connected to the Internet, the web site you put in the URL will open, as you can see mine did in Figure 6-9. When you are ready, close your browser.

### Adding Hotspots to Graphics

FrontPage has a feature that allows you to divide a graphic into sections that can be rectangles, circles, or polygons, and to assign each of those sections a different link. Each linked, or clickable, section is called a *hotspot*. When FrontPage generates the actual web that is downloaded by the user, it creates an *image map* of the graphic and all of its hotspots. In the Wines 'n Things web site, we're going to add a new page with a map containing hotspots for several of the wine producing regions of the United States. When a particular region is clicked, it will open a page listing the wines of that region. Here is how we do that (use similar steps to create your own graphic with hotspots):

1. Open the Home Page of the Wines 'n Things web and, if necessary, scroll down the page until MAJOR VARIETALS AND REGIONS can be seen.

2. Drag across the word "REGIONS" and click Link on the toolbar.

3. Click Create New Document on the left of the dialog box, type the name **Regions.htm**, accept the other defaults, and click OK. This will create a new page in the current web and link it to the selected object. A new page is generated and opened.

4. Separately, we will copy the title and link bar for the page. For now, enter several blank lines to leave room for the header, and then type **Click the region from which you want a list of wines:** (including the colon), format it as Heading 3, and then press ENTER.

5. Open the Insert menu, choose Picture, and select either Clip Art or From File, search Clip Art for "US Map" or locate one you have, and double-click the map to insert it on the page. Select the map and size it, as shown in Figure 6-10.

6. With the U.S. map selected, use the tools on the right in the Pictures toolbar, which automatically opens when you click a picture (if yours doesn't open automatically, open the View menu and choose Toolbars | Pictures), to draw the hotspots on the map.

7. Select the Rectangle tool and draw a rectangle around a rectangular region, such as the state of Washington in the U.S. map. When you complete the rectangle and release the mouse button, the Insert Hyperlink dialog box will open. You have all the normal choices for a new link including an existing page, with or without a bookmark, any other site on the Internet, or a new page. If you create a new page, be sure to save it and give it a name that can be used for the link, but also choose to Edit The New Document Later, not the default.

8. Using a similar procedure, select the Circular tool to draw circular areas, and the Polygonal tool to draw polygonal areas. Using these three tools, create the hotspots on the map that you want.

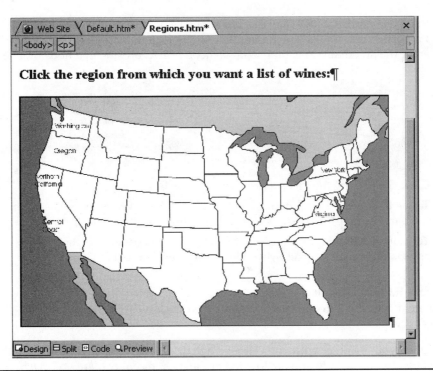

**FIGURE 6-10**     A new page created with a U.S. map

9. When you have completed drawing the shapes you want over the various areas of your map, you'll see all of the shapes on your map. The shapes will not be visible in a browser. When you move the mouse pointer over one of the areas, you'll see the URL, absolute or relative, in the status bar:

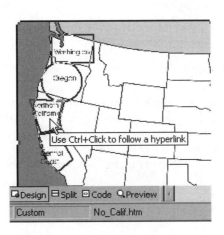

10. Right-click an area of the map that has not had a hotspot drawn over it, choose Picture Properties, and in the General tab Default Hyperlink section's Location text box, enter the link that you want used if someone clicks outside of a hotspot, like this:

11. Click OK to close the Picture Properties dialog box.

12. To see the hotspots uncluttered by the map, click Highlight Hotspots on the Pictures toolbar. The map will disappear, leaving only the shapes you drew.

13. Turn off Highlight Hotspots, save the new Regions page, save the associated image, return to your Home Page, and save that page.

### Testing Your Graphic Links in a Browser

Once again, it is prudent to open your browser and see how your links are working:

1. Open your browser with your Home Page displayed, and click Refresh on the toolbar to make sure you are looking at the most recent copy of your web.

2. Scroll down the Home Page until you can see the second heading, what in our case is Major Varietals And Regions, and then click Regions. The new Regions page will open and display the map that was placed there.

3. Move the mouse pointer around the map to see the various hotspots you created and their URLs in the status bar. Click several to see that they work, using Back to return to the Regions map page. When you are done looking at the map, click Back to return to the Home Page.

4. Close your browser. If you have any problems, edit the links to see what the trouble is. When all your links are working, open the View menu and choose Hyperlinks.

## Managing Hyperlinks

The Wines 'n Things web displayed in Hyperlinks view now looks very different than it did when you started this chapter, as you can see in Figure 6-11. With this ability to display your links, FrontPage is an excellent tool for managing them. Besides the obvious visual checking that you can do in Hyperlinks view, it has the ability to verify that the link exists through the Verifies Hyperlinks button on the Reporting toolbar. FrontPage also has a command in the

Tools menu that helps you in link management: Recalculate Hyperlinks updates the display of all links as well as the server databases used by the Include and Search components. To check out your links:

1. Click Reports in the view bar at the bottom of the Web Site tab. Click Verifies Hyperlinks on the right of the Reporting toolbar. You are given a choice of verifying all hyperlinks or just unknown ones, which are listed behind the dialog box, and given a tip that all open modified pages should be saved.

2. Click Verify All Hyperlinks and click Start. Each of your links is checked (if you are not currently connected to the Internet, your system will attempt to connect if you have an external link). If broken, the link is entered on the Broken Hyperlinks report shown next (we intentionally renamed one of the map links to show a broken link):

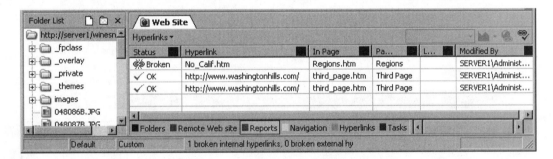

3. Select a broken link and click Edit Hyperlink on the Reporting toolbar. The Edit Hyperlink dialog box will open, as shown next, allowing you to replace the current link with a new one. You can change all pages with this link, or only selected ones.

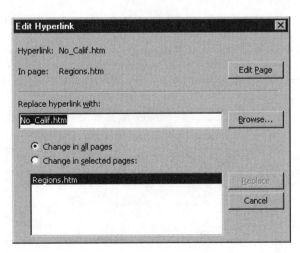

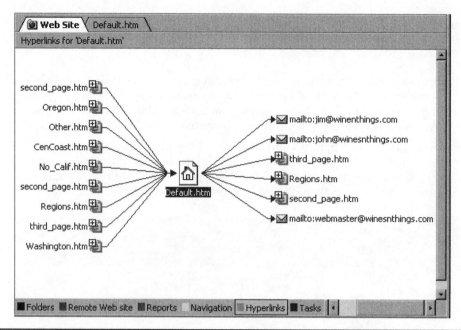

**FIGURE 6-11**    Hyperlinks view showing the links to and from the Home Page

4. If you click Browse in the Edit Hyperlink dialog box, the Insert Hyperlink dialog box will open, although it is still called Edit Hyperlink. Here you can select a page in the current web, enter any URL, browse for a site on the Web, search for a file on your disk, or create a new page.

5. When you have fixed all of your broken links, return to Hyperlinks view for your Home Page, and select Recalculate Hyperlinks from the fully extended Tools menu. You are told what the process will do, and that the procedure will take several minutes, as shown next. Click Yes to proceed. When the process is complete, your web will be redisplayed in FrontPage with any repairs it was able to do.

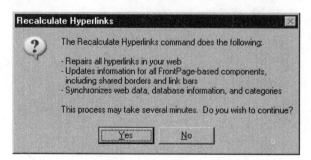

***NOTE***   *When you have broken a link, the icon for the linked page is broken in the Hyperlinks view of FrontPage, like this:*

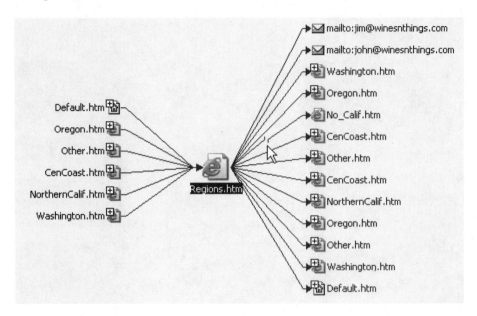

You have seen in this chapter how easy it is to establish links in FrontPage both with text and with graphics, within a web and externally, and how you can manage those links with some powerful tools. Next, we'll look at the great tools FrontPage provides to add and work with tables and frames in your webs.

# Using Tables and Frames

S o far in this book, you have used the full width of a web page for placing all text and graphics. Good layout designs can be accomplished this way, but it does not allow for text or graphics to be placed in independent columns, and the only way to align text within a line (other than at the ends) is to add spaces with the Formatted paragraph style. FrontPage has two features that allow you to break up some or all of a page into sections that can contain text or graphics. These two features are tables and frames. You can also position page elements using cascading style sheets, which are covered in Chapter 10, but support for style sheets is available only in the latest browsers. Tables and frames are supported in older browsers, which means your design is more likely to appear as you intended.

*TIP*    *Browsers usually ignore multiple spaces in text; only the first space is displayed. The two exceptions to this are when the spaces are formatted with the Formatted paragraph style and when the nonbreaking space HTML character ( ) is inserted from the Symbol dialog box (the first character in the first row). Using HTML code is covered in Chapter 12.*

## Designing with Tables

*Tables* allow you to divide a portion of a page into rows and columns that create *cells* by their intersection. Tables can be used to systematically arrange information in rows and columns, or they can be used to lay out text and graphics on a page. In web design, tables are probably the most important tool for creative page layout. Just a few of the ways that you can use tables are as follows:

- Tabular data display, with and without cell borders
- Side-by-side columns of text
- Aligning labels and boxes for forms
- Text on one side, graphics on the other
- Placing borders around text or graphics
- Placing graphics on both sides of text or vice versa
- Wrapping text around a graphic
- Adding color to backgrounds, to text, and to graphics

When you create a table, you can determine the number of rows and columns in the table, the horizontal percentage of a page that will be used by the table, the percentage of the table's width in each column, and whether the table has a caption. Within the percentage limits set for the table and column, a cell will automatically expand both horizontally and vertically to contain the information placed in it.

---

**TIP**   *Although you can create a table based on a percentage of the screen, with columns as a percentage of the table, there are often problems getting the table to display the way you want. If you use fixed pixel widths based on the minimum 640×480 screen, you'll be able to create a more consistent look. Each method has advantages and you will probably use both, depending on the function of the table.*

After a table has been created, you can

- Add or remove rows and/or columns
- Combine adjacent cells
- Split one or more cells
- Add to or remove from a cell or group of cells any formatting available to the table's contents
- Split the table into two or more tables
- Edit the border of the table
- Enter repetitive information into the table using Fill Right and Fill Down
- Automatically format a table
- Add rounded corners, shadows, and other visual effects to tables
- Mix fixed-size columns with variable-size columns using Autostretch
- Apply formatting to a cell background, border, and contents

## Displaying Tabular Data in a Table

The classic table, such as you might create in a spreadsheet application, segments text into rows and columns. To build such a table, take the following steps:

1. If it's not already loaded, start FrontPage.

2. If the New task pane is not open, click the File menu and choose New.

3. In the New task pane, select the One Page Web Site option. In the Specify The Location Of The New Web Site combo box, select your web server and type **Tables** for the title of the new FrontPage web, and then click OK.

4. In the Folder List on the left, double-click the Home Page (Default.htm). Press ENTER to move down the page one line and leave room at the top. If you see a paragraph mark, click Show All to turn off the display of the various formatting marks so they won't clutter the tables we will be working with.

5. Open the Table menu and choose Insert | Table. The Insert Table dialog box will open. Figure 7-1 shows what this book will use as the default values in this dialog box. If your dialog box has different values in it, change them to match the values

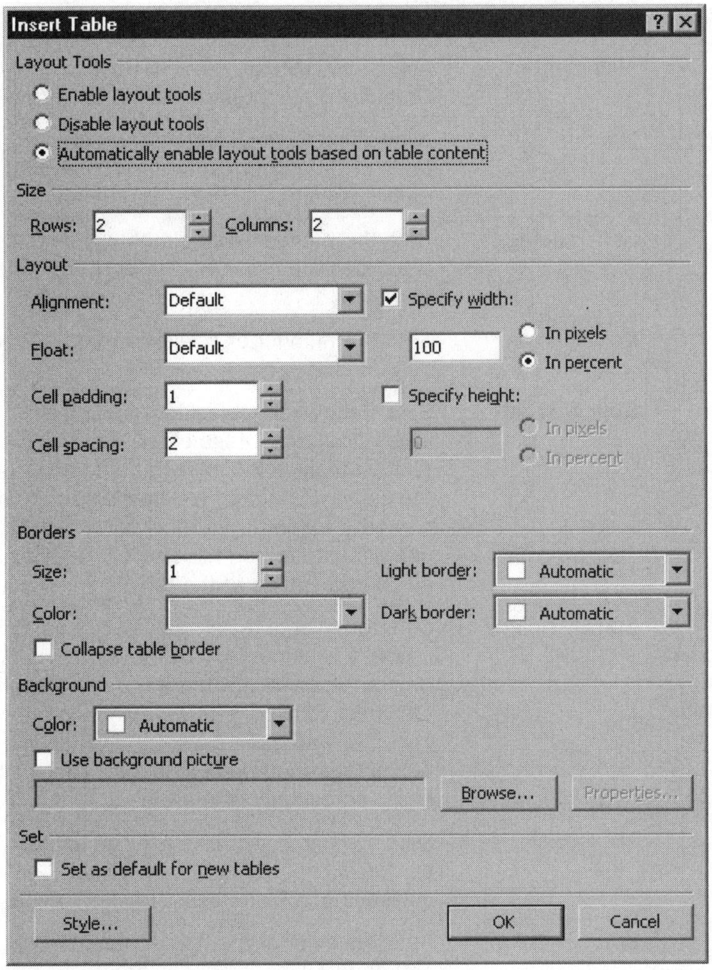

**FIGURE 7-1**    The defaults for new tables

here and then click Set As Default For New Tables. In the dialog box, take a look at the options available when you create a table; they are described in Table 7-1.

**TABLE 7-1**
Table Options

| Option | Description |
|---|---|
| Layout Tools | Enables/disables the precision layout tools either full time for the table being constructed or enabled only if the content requires it. |
| Rows | Specifies the number of horizontal rows in the table. |
| Columns | Specifies the number of vertical columns in the table. |

**TABLE 7-1**
Table Options
*(continued)*

| Option | Description |
|---|---|
| Alignment | Aligns the table on the left, center, or right of the page. Default alignment is the same as Left alignment. |
| Float | Allows text to wrap around the table by placing the table at the left or right edge of the page. Default is the same as Left. |
| Cell Padding | Sets the number of pixels between the inside edges of a cell and the cell contents on all four sides. The default is 1. |
| Cell Spacing | Sets the number of pixels between adjacent cells. The default is 2. |
| Specify Width | Sets the overall table width to be a fixed number of pixels or a percentage of the window size, if Specify Width is selected. Otherwise, the table is the sum of the cells, which are individually sized to contain their contents within the size of the window. If the percentage method is selected, each cell is given an equal percentage of the table. |
| Specify Height | Sets the overall table height to be a fixed number of pixels or a percentage of the window size, if Specify Height is selected. Otherwise, the table is the sum of the cells, which are individually sized to contain their contents within the size of the window. If the percentage method is selected, each cell is given an equal percentage of the table. |
| Border Size | Sets the number of pixels in the border. A 0-pixel border will not appear in a browser, but you'll see a dotted line in FrontPage. The default is 1. |
| Borders Color | Sets the color of the border itself as well as the light and dark 3-dimensional elements of the border. |
| Collapse Table Border | Removes the 3-dimensional elements of the border that gives it thickness and height so it becomes just a simple line. |
| Background | Sets the color or allows the choosing of a picture behind the table. |

**NOTE**  *The Collapse Table Border option in the Insert Table and Table Properties dialog boxes was called in prior editions of FrontPage "Show Both Cells And Table Borders," which in our mind was a clearer statement of what the option accomplishes.*

6. Click OK. A two-row, two-column (four-cell) table is displayed with the cursor in the first column of the first row. Select the table by pressing and holding SHIFT-CTRL

while pressing END (to select everything to the end of the page, see the following Tip), and then remove it by pressing DEL. If the new line you entered in step 5 is also removed, press ENTER to place a blank line at the top of the page.

7. Click the Insert Table button on the toolbar. In the drop-down table that opens, click the second cell from the left in the second row, as shown next. Another four-cell table appears on your page.

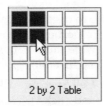

2 by 2 Table

The Insert Table button on the toolbar offers a quick method for creating a table using the defaults, while the Insert Table option in the Table menu allows you to set the properties for the table as it is created.

---

**TIP**    *If you want more than the 4×5 rows and columns shown in the Insert Table drop-down table, simply drag the lower right cell of the drop-down table to the size you want. The box will expand to display the number of rows and/or columns you select.*

### Working with Table Properties

Table properties affect all of the cells in a table and establish how the overall table will look. To see that for yourself:

1. In the new table that was just created, type **1** in the upper-left cell, press TAB to move to the cell on the right, and type

   This is a longer statement

   Your table should look like the one shown next. The table takes up almost 100 percent of the window's width, and the two cells in each row proportionately share that width based on their contents.

   | 1 | This is a longer statement |
   |---|----------------------------|
   |   |                            |

2. Press the DOWN ARROW twice to move out of the table, and then press ENTER to leave a blank line.

---

**TIP**    *Pressing TAB in the last cell of a table will insert a new row at the bottom of the table.*

3. Open the Table menu and choose Insert | Table. In the Insert Table dialog box, click Specify Width to clear it, and then click OK. A second, much smaller table appears.

4. Type **1**, press TAB, and type

   This is a longer statement

5. Press TAB again to move to the left cell in the second row, type **2468**, press TAB once more, and type

   A statement

   Each column in the table is as wide as the cell in that column with the longest content, as shown in Figure 7-2.

6. Right-click the second table to open the context menu. You can see that it has both Table Properties and Cell Properties options. Choose Table Properties, opening the dialog box, which is exactly the same as the Insert Table dialog box you saw in Figure 7-1 and was explained in Table 7-1.

7. Change Cell Padding to **6**, Cell Spacing to **8**, Border Size to **5**, check Collapse Table Border if it is not checked, and click OK. Your table should look like the following one on the left. Reopen Table Properties, uncheck Collapse Table Border, and click OK. The table should now look like the one on the right.

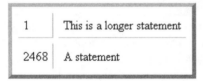 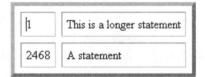

8. Right-click the upper-left cell in the upper table (see Figure 7-2) and select Cell Properties. The Cell Properties dialog box will open, as you can see in Figure 7-3. Take a moment and look at the options it contains. They are described in Table 7-2.

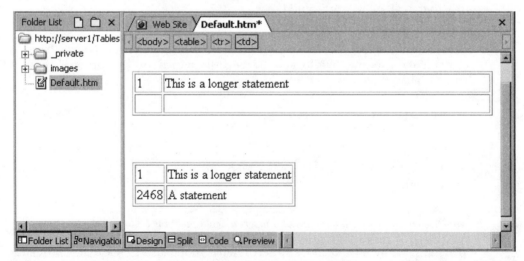

**FIGURE 7-2** Tables with (above) and without (below) a specified width

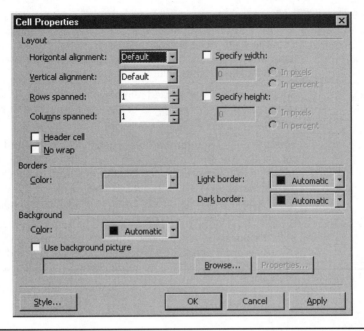

**FIGURE 7-3**   Changing cell properties

| Option | Description |
|---|---|
| Horizontal Alignment | Horizontally aligns the contents of the cell. It can be Left, Center, Right, Justify, or Default, which is the same as Left. |
| Vertical Alignment | Vertically aligns the contents of a cell. It can be Top, Middle, Baseline, Bottom, or Default, which is the same as Middle. Baseline aligns the baseline of text in a cell with the baseline of the largest text in the row. |
| Rows Spanned | Joins adjacent vertical cells to make a single larger cell that spans two or more rows. |
| Columns Spanned | Joins adjacent horizontal cells to make a single larger cell that spans two or more columns. |
| Header Cell | Identifies the cell as the label for a row or column and makes the text in the cell bold. (You can also do this with the paragraph or character formatting options.) |
| No Wrap | Indicates that the web browser should not wrap the text in the cell; otherwise, the text will be wrapped if the browser window is too narrow to display the text. |

**TABLE 7-2**   Cell Properties

| Option | Description |
|---|---|
| Specify Width | Sets the width to be a fixed number of pixels or a percentage of the table size, if Specify Width is selected. Otherwise, the cell width is automatically sized to hold its contents. |
| Specify Height | Sets the height to be a fixed number of pixels or a percentage of the table size, if Specify Height is selected. Otherwise, the cell height is automatically sized to hold its contents. |
| Borders | Sets the color used for the border, which can consist of one or two colors. Use the Border Color drop-down to specify a single-color border, and use the Light and Dark drop-downs to specify a two-color border, which will have a three-dimensional effect if you select a lighter color in the Light Border drop-down, which will appear on the top and left of the cell. |
| Background | Sets the background for a cell. This can be either a picture, for which you can browse and set its properties, or a background color. |

**TABLE 7-2**    Cell Properties *(continued)*

### Applying Cell Properties

Cell properties apply to just the one or more selected cells in a table, as shown in the following steps:

**NOTE**    *If you change the cell width, you should do so for an entire column, and you should make sure that the sum of the cell widths in a row does not exceed 100 percent, or you will get unpredictable results.*

1. With the insertion point still in the upper-left cell of the upper table and the Cell Properties dialog box open, change Horizontal Alignment to Center, Vertical Alignment to Top, and click OK. You should see the contents of the cell you selected (a "1") change accordingly.

**NOTE**    *Cell padding and spacing may prevent much movement, especially vertically, in a cell when you change the alignment.*

2. Select the bottom row in the upper table by pointing to the left border of the table and clicking when the pointer changes to a heavy arrow. Then right-click the selected row, choose Cell Properties, change Columns Spanned to **2**, and click OK. Your table should look as shown next. The leftmost cell does span the two upper cells, but you now have an extra cell on the right (although it might look like an extra column was created, it is actually only an extra cell).

*TIP*   *To select either a row or a column, move the mouse pointer to the outer edge of the table—the left edge for a row, the top edge for a column—until the mouse pointer changes to a heavy arrow, and click. If you drag the heavy arrow, you can select multiple rows or columns.*

*NOTE*   *The width of your columns may be different than the illustration due to differences in screen resolution.*

3. Press CTRL-Z or choose Undo Edit Properties from the Edit menu to undo step 2. In a moment, you'll see another way to do this that is probably closer to what you want.

4. Select the top row of the upper table, open the Cell Properties dialog box, increase Rows Spanned to **2**, and click OK. The top two cells come down and push the bottom two to the right, like this:

5. Click the Undo button on the toolbar.

6. Select the two cells in the left column, open Cell Properties, check Specify Width, select In Percent, type **20** for the width, and click OK. The two left cells will occupy about 20 percent of the table width, as you can see here:

*TIP*   *To select multiple cells not in a row or column, press and hold CTRL while clicking the additional cells.*

7. Click Undo, click the bottom right cell, open the Table menu, and extend it to its full length. Look at the options in this menu, which are described in Table 7-3.

| Option | Description |
| --- | --- |
| Layout Table and Cells | Opens the Layout Table And Cells task pane, which provides a number of predefined table configurations used for laying out a web page, specialized cell formatting, as well as other features. |
| Cell Formatting | Allows the formatting of an individual cell within a layout table to add, for example, color, graphical borders, and drop-shadows. |
| Draw Table | Creates a table by enabling you to draw the outside border and then insert columns and rows. |
| Insert \| Table | Opens the Insert Table dialog box, where you can select the properties of a table to place at the current insertion point. If the insertion point is in the cell of another table, a second table is placed in that cell. |
| Insert \| Rows Or Columns | Opens the Insert Rows Or Columns dialog box, where you can select the number of rows or columns above, below, to the left, or to the right of the current selection. |
| Insert \| Cell | Inserts a new cell to the left of a selected cell, pushing any cells on the right farther to the right. |
| Insert \| Caption | Inserts a blank line, with an insertion point for typing text, immediately above the active table. This line is aligned with and attached to the table. If you select or delete the table, the caption is also selected or deleted. The initial alignment is for the caption to be centered on the table, but it can also be left- or right-aligned on the table. |
| Delete Cells | Deletes the selected cells, which must be in whole columns or rows. |
| Select Layout Table, Table, Cell, Column, or Row | Selects a particular area so that it can be merged, split, sized, deleted, or formatted. You can also select a cell by pressing ALT while clicking the cell. |
| Merge Cells | Joins two or more selected cells in a row or column—including an entire row or column—into a single cell that spans the area originally occupied by the cells that were merged. |
| Split Cells | Opens the Split Cells dialog box, where you can split the selected cell into multiple rows or multiple columns. |
| Split Table | Splits the table into two separate tables immediately above the current row. |
| Table AutoFormat | Opens the Table AutoFormat dialog box where you can choose from 38 different table formats and select whether to apply the format to the borders, shading, font, and color of a table. |
| Distribute Rows or Columns Evenly | Equalizes the width or height of the selected rows or columns. |

**TABLE 7-3**     Table Menu Options

| Option | Description |
|---|---|
| AutoFit To Contents | Reduces the width of each column in a table to the minimum width needed to display the longest content in the column. This has the same effect as clearing the Specify Width check box in the Cell and Table Properties dialog boxes. |
| Convert Text to Table | Opens the Convert Text To Table dialog box, where you convert selected text into a table. See the "Building a Tabular Table" section later in this chapter for a detailed explanation of how to do this. |
| Convert Table to Text | Converts a table into text with the contents of each cell becoming a separate paragraph. |
| Fill Down or Right | Repeats the contents of the top- or left-most cell in the selected cells of a row or column. |
| Table, Cell, or Caption Properties | Opens the Table, Cell, or Caption Properties dialog box. |

**TABLE 7-3**    Table Menu Options *(continued)*

### Employing the Table Menu Options

The Table menu provides some important options for working with tables. To see for yourself:

1. In the Table menu, choose Insert | Table, accept the existing settings in the Insert Table dialog box, and click OK. You should now have a 2×2 table in the cell of your original table, as shown here:

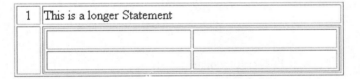

2. Click Undo and click the upper-left cell in the same table. Open the Table menu and choose Insert | Rows Or Columns. The Insert Rows Or Columns dialog box will open:

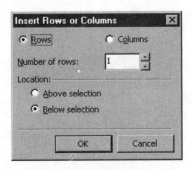

3. Accept the default options, Rows, 1, and Below Selection, and click OK. A new row appears in the middle of the table.

4. Reopen the Table menu and choose Insert | Rows Or Columns again. Click Columns, Left Of Selection, and then OK. A new column appears on the left so that your table now looks like this:

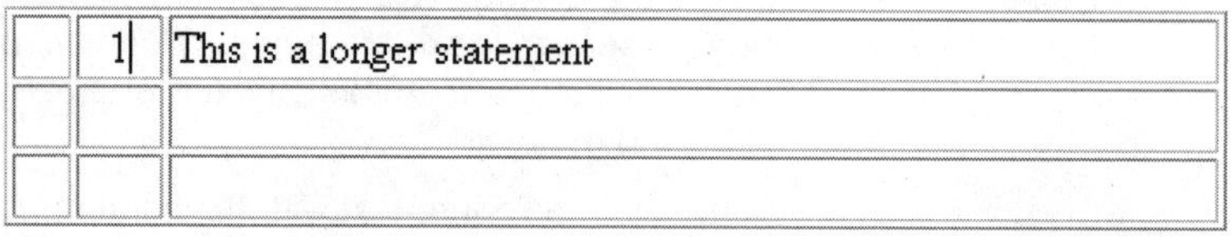

| | 1| This is a longer statement |
|---|---|---|
| | | |
| | | |

5. Open the Table menu and choose Insert | Cell. A new cell appears in the table, pushing the right cell in the row out to the right. The insertion point also moves to the new cell, like this:

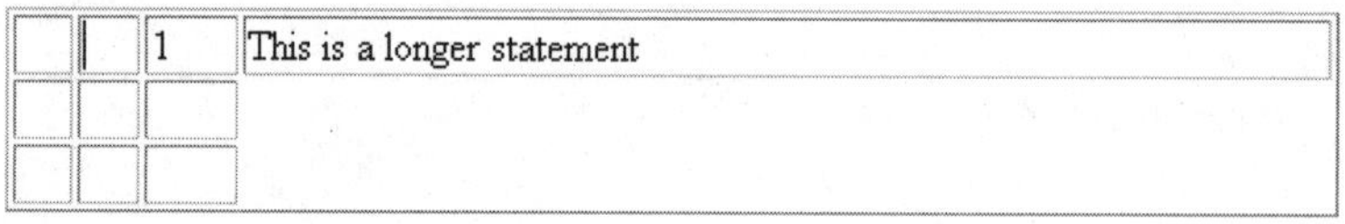

| | | 1 | This is a longer statement |
|---|---|---|---|
| | | | |
| | | | |

6. From the Table menu choose Select | Cell, or ALT-click the cell, and then choose Delete Cells from the Table menu. The new cell disappears.

7. From the Table menu, choose Insert | Caption. An insertion point appears above and centered on the table. Type

This is a Caption

8. Select the bottom row of the first table. Then, from the Table menu, choose Merge Cells. The bottom row now only contains a single cell, as shown next:

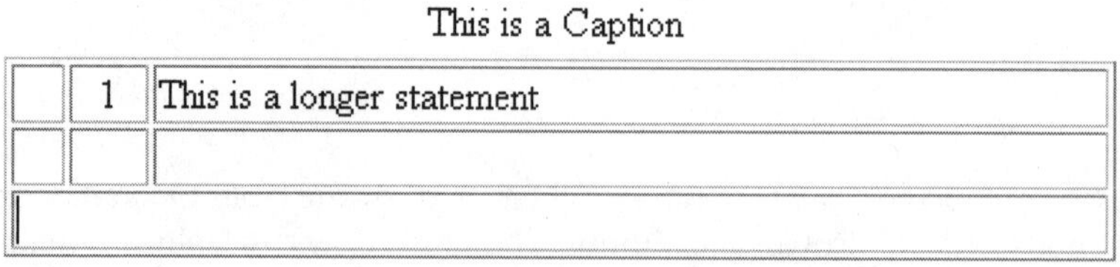

This is a Caption

| | 1 | This is a longer statement |
|---|---|---|
| | | |
| | | |

9. Click in the upper-right cell of the first table, and then choose Split Cells in the Table menu. The Split Cells dialog box will open:

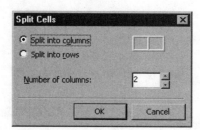

10. Accept the defaults and click OK. Your original cell is now split into two, as shown here:

This is a Caption

| | 1 | This is a longer statement | |
|---|---|---|---|
| | | | |

11. Click at the top of the second column to select the column, the top cell of which contains "1." From the Table menu, choose Fill | Down. A "1" appears in the other cell that is selected.

12. Click in the bottom cell, open the Table menu, and choose Split Table. The upper table is now two tables, like this:

This is a Caption

| | 1 | This is a longer statement | |
|---|---|---|---|
| | 1 | | |

---

***TIP***    *Tables can be selected from the Table menu and by double-clicking in the left margin of the page opposite the table.*

13. With the insertion point in the new single-cell second table, open the Table menu and choose Select | Table. Now press DEL. In FrontPage 2003 this again deletes the table. In FrontPage 2002 it didn't, unlike earlier versions of FrontPage that did.

14. Click in the upper table, open the Table menu and choose Table AutoFormat. The Table AutoFormat dialog box will open, as you can see in Figure 7-4.

15. Select each of the 38 formats to look at them in the Preview area. After looking at them all, select the one you want to use here. Then turn on and off each of the options under Formats To Apply and Apply Special Formats. Select the options you want to use and click OK. The format will be applied and appear on the page. Press CTRL-Z to undo the formatting.

16. Open the Table Properties dialog box and set the Border Size to **0**; then click OK. The table border will become a dotted line. Click Preview. There is now no indication that your text is being formatted by a table, as shown next. Click Design and then click Undo.

This is a Caption

1   This is a longer statement

1

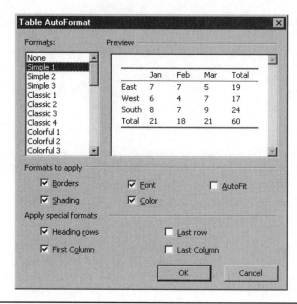

**FIGURE 7-4**   Applying a ready-made format to a table

## Drawing a Table

The Table menu and Table Properties dialog box allow you to create complex tables easily, but you can also simply draw a complex table, as described next.

1. Place the insertion point in the blank line between the two tables, press ENTER twice, and then press the UP ARROW once.

**NOTE**   *If you need a blank line between the tables, place the insertion point in the upper-left cell of the lower table to the left of the cell contents and press* CTRL-ENTER.

2. Open the Table menu and choose Draw Table. The Tables toolbar will be displayed, and the cursor turns into a pencil. Table 7-4 describes the Tables toolbar options.

| Button | Option | Description |
|---|---|---|
| Show Layout Tool | Show Layout Tool | Places a grid around a table and each of its cells that you can drag to precisely size it all. |
| | Draw Layout Table | Allows you to draw a table, which, when you are done, has a layout grid placed around it. |

**TABLE 7-4**   Tables Toolbar Options

| Button | Option | Description |
|---|---|---|
|   | Draw Table | Allows you to draw the overall dimensions of a table, and row and column borders. |
|   | Draw Layout Cell | Allows you to draw a cell, which, when you are done, has a layout grid placed around it. |
|   | Eraser | Removes rows and columns from a table. |
|   | Insert Rows | Inserts rows without opening the Insert Rows or Columns dialog box. |
|   | Insert Columns | Inserts columns without opening the Insert Rows or Columns dialog box. |
|   | Delete Cells | Deletes the selected cells. |
|   | Merge Cells | Merges the selected cells. |
|   | Split Cells | Opens the Split Cells dialog box. |
|   | Align Top | Aligns the cell's contents with the top of the cell. |
|   | Center Vertically | Centers the cell's contents vertically. |
|   | Align Bottom | Aligns the cell's contents with the bottom of the cell. |
|   | Distribute Rows Evenly | Equalizes the height of the rows in the table. |
|   | Distribute Columns Evenly | Equalizes the width of the columns in the table. |
|   | AutoFit To Contents | Reduces the width of each column in a table to the minimum width needed to display the longest content in the column. |
|   | Fill Color | Changes the background color of the selected cell, row, column, or table. |
| 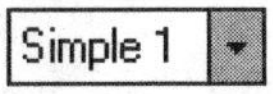 Simple 1 ▾ | Select Format | Choose one of 38 different table formats. |

**TABLE 7-4**    Tables Toolbar Options *(continued)*

| Button | Option | Description |
|--------|--------|-------------|
| | AutoFormat dialog box | Opens the Table AutoFormat dialog box where you can choose from 38 different table formats and select whether to apply the format to the borders, shading, font, and color of a table. |
| | Fill Down | Repeats the contents of the first cell in the selected cells of a column. |
| | Fill Right | Repeats the contents of the first cell in the selected cells of a row. |

**TABLE 7-4**    Tables Toolbar Options *(continued)*

3. Place the pencil-cursor between the two existing tables and drag it horizontally across the page, and then vertically so that the new table is approximately the height of the second table. The exact dimensions are not important.

4. Place the cursor on the top border of the new table approximately in the center. Drag down to the bottom border.

5. Create three rows in the right column by pointing to the column divider you just created and dragging to the right table border twice. Don't worry about the height of the rows.

6. Click Distribute Rows Evenly on the toolbar, and the three rows will be adjusted to equal heights, as shown here:

7. Draw a vertical line dividing the second row in the right column into two columns.

8. Draw two vertical lines dividing the third row in the right column into three columns. The second new column will align with the column divider in the row above it, as shown next:

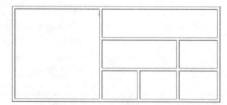

9. Point on the right column border of the first (left) column. The cursor will turn into a double-headed arrow.

10. Drag the column border to the right to make the column wider.

11. Select the Eraser tool in the Tables toolbar and drag it across the left column divider in the bottom row so that the bottom row of the right column is divided into two columns, like this:

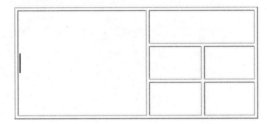

12. Click the Eraser tool to deselect it, and then point on the top border of the table, over the second column. When the pointer turns into a heavy arrow, click to select the column.

13. Press SHIFT and move the pointer to the right, over the column that wasn't selected, and click again. The first column of the table should *not* be selected, and the remaining two columns should be selected.

14. Click Distribute Columns Evenly on the toolbar. Your drawn table should now look similar to this (probably not much change):

15. Select the table and then press DEL to remove it.

Through the preceding exercises you saw the incredible flexibility in FrontPage's table capability. And it is all WYSIWYG; you instantly see the table you are building very much as it will appear in a browser. Next, build a real table and then look at all three of your tables in a browser.

## Building a Tabular Table

A tabular table is what is generally thought of when one thinks of a table. It is a columnar listing of something. You are encouraged to locate a tabular subject of your own to use for this exercise, but since we have been talking about wine shops, we will build a table of wines as might be prepared by one. Here is how it's done, starting with a text-based table:

1. With Default.htm of the Tables web open in FrontPage, click New Page, right-click the new_page_1.htm tab and click Save. In the Save As dialog box, change the Page Title to **Wines** and the file name to **Wines.htm**. Click Save. Double-click the new page to open it. Press ENTER to leave a blank line at the top of the page.

2. Prepare, scan, or copy a text-based table with a .txt extension. Here is the one we used:

| Winery | Vintage | Varietal | Description |
|---|---|---|---|
| Apex | 1998 | Cabernet Sauvignon | Bold aromas, voluptuous flavors |
| Bridgman | 1998 | Cabernet Sauvignon | Dense aroma, lively flavors |
| Bridgman | 2001 | Chardonnay | Opulent aromas, rich flavors |
| Washington Hills | 2000 | Chardonnay | Fruit & spice aroma, superb flavor |
| Washington Hills | 2001 | Dry Riesling | Compelling aroma, crisp flavors |
| Apex | 1998 | Merlot | Seductive aroma, lush flavor |
| Apex | 1998 | Pinot Noir | Classic aromas, lingering flavors |
| Bridgman | 2000 | Syrah | Exotic aromas, deep flavors |
| Washington Hills | 2000 | Syrah | Distinctive aroma, soft flavor |

3. Open the Insert menu, choose File, select your path and the file you want to bring in, and click Open. Select Formatted Paragraphs in the Convert Text dialog box and click OK.

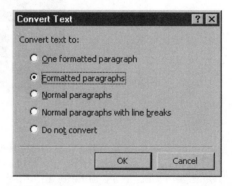

**NOTE** *Which option you select in the Convert Text dialog box is determined by the format of the file you are inserting. The Wine.txt file was created with tabs and paragraphs, so Formatted Paragraphs was the correct choice for that text. Try the various options with your file to see which works best.*

4. Select all the text that was inserted, open the Table menu, and choose Convert | Text To Table.

5. In the Convert Text To Table dialog box, select the option that is correct for you (we're using Tabs) and click OK. Figure 7-5 shows the table created from the text file.

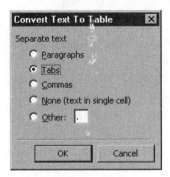

NOTE  *In the beta software we used to write this book, when you do the conversion mentioned in step 5, the result is that each cell looks like it is double-spaced. It is our understanding that this will be fixed in the final released version of FrontPage 2003, but if you encounter this problem, select the entire table, click Code, click Edit Find, click the Replace tab, in the Find What enter* **\<pre\>**, *leave Replace With blank, and click Replace All. Repeat this procedure with* **\</pre\>**. *This will eliminate the double-spaced look.*

6. Right-click the table and choose Table Properties. Choose Center alignment, enter a cell padding of **4**, turn off Specify Width if it is selected, Collapse Table Border should be not be checked, and click OK.

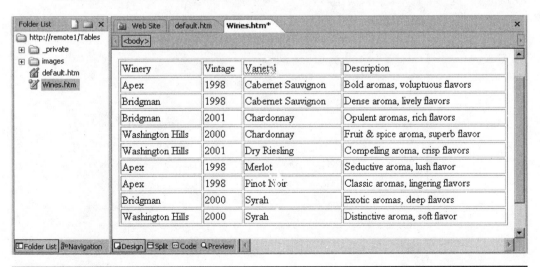

| Winery | Vintage | Varietal | Description |
|---|---|---|---|
| Apex | 1998 | Cabernet Sauvignon | Bold aromas, voluptuous flavors |
| Bridgman | 1998 | Cabernet Sauvignon | Dense aroma, lively flavors |
| Bridgman | 2001 | Chardonnay | Opulent aromas, rich flavors |
| Washington Hills | 2000 | Chardonnay | Fruit & spice aroma, superb flavor |
| Washington Hills | 2001 | Dry Riesling | Compelling aroma, crisp flavors |
| Apex | 1998 | Merlot | Seductive aroma, lush flavor |
| Apex | 1998 | Pinot Noir | Classic aromas, lingering flavors |
| Bridgman | 2000 | Syrah | Exotic aromas, deep flavors |
| Washington Hills | 2000 | Syrah | Distinctive aroma, soft flavor |

**FIGURE 7-5**  Table converted from a text file

**NOTE**   *The cell padding puts pixels on all four sides between the cell's contents and the cell walls. Cell spacing puts pixels between the walls of adjacent cells on as many sides as there are adjacent walls. If you check Collapse Table Border, you eliminate the interior cell borders and therefore the cell spacing. Try these for yourself and see the effects. When you are done, return your table properties to a cell padding of 4, a cell spacing of 2, and Collapse Table Border should not be checked.*

7. Select the top row, right-click a cell in the first row, open the Cell Properties dialog box, click Header Cell and Left Horizontal Alignment, and click OK.

8. From the Table menu, choose Insert | Caption. Click the Bold button and select 4 (14 pt) from the Font Size drop-down list (both on the Formatting toolbar), then type a caption for your table. Ours is

   **Selected Washington Hills Cellars Wines**

9. Select the first row of the table, then click the down arrow of the Fill Color button in the Tables toolbar. Select Aqua from the Color drop-down list (the third color square from the left in the second row).

10. Select the remaining rows of the table, and then open the Cell Properties dialog box. Select Yellow from the Background Color drop-down list and click OK. When you are done, your table should look like the one in Figure 7-6. You may have further ideas about how to improve the table. Try them. You can always click on Undo if you don't like a change.

11. Click Save to save the table you have built.

12. Open the File menu and choose Preview In Browser and select the browser and resolution you want to use. You should see the Washington Hills Cellars Wines table, or your equivalent, appear.

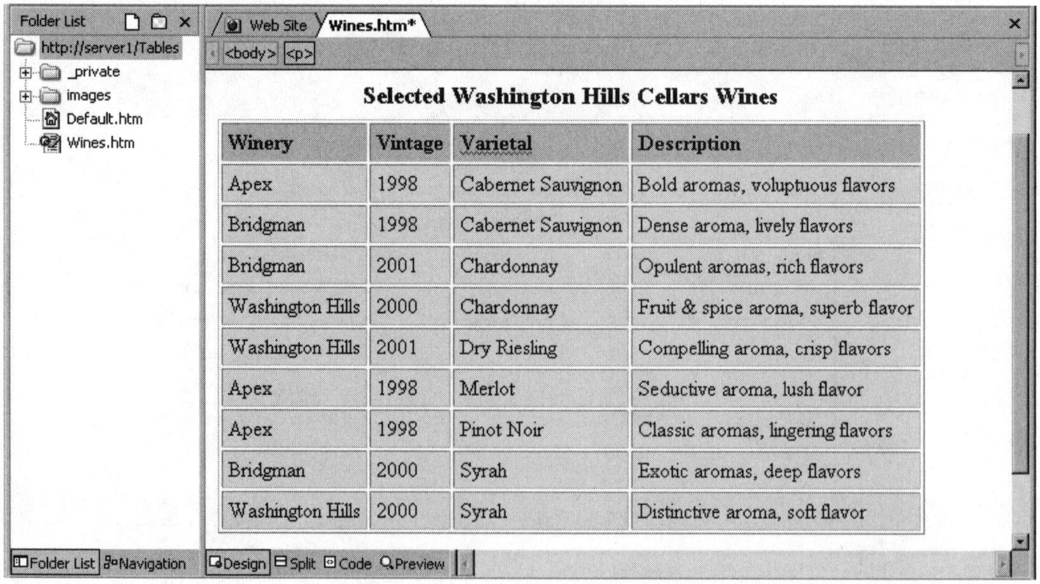

| Winery | Vintage | Varietal | Description |
|---|---|---|---|
| Apex | 1998 | Cabernet Sauvignon | Bold aromas, voluptuous flavors |
| Bridgman | 1998 | Cabernet Sauvignon | Dense aroma, lively flavors |
| Bridgman | 2001 | Chardonnay | Opulent aromas, rich flavors |
| Washington Hills | 2000 | Chardonnay | Fruit & spice aroma, superb flavor |
| Washington Hills | 2001 | Dry Riesling | Compelling aroma, crisp flavors |
| Apex | 1998 | Merlot | Seductive aroma, lush flavor |
| Apex | 1998 | Pinot Noir | Classic aromas, lingering flavors |
| Bridgman | 2000 | Syrah | Exotic aromas, deep flavors |
| Washington Hills | 2000 | Syrah | Distinctive aroma, soft flavor |

**FIGURE 7-6**   Improved table formatting

13. If you have another browser, open it and view your table page. Figure 7-7 shows the table in both Internet Explorer 6 and Netscape Navigator 7. The only differences are the added spacing under the caption and the "3-D" cell borders, both in Internet Explorer. Close your Tables web in your browser(s) when you are done looking at it.

14. Back in FrontPage, with the insertion point in the table, open the Table menu and choose Table AutoFormat. Select several of the formats and look at your table with that format. There are many choices with a lot of different types of table formatting. At the least these should give you some ideas that you can use in the future.

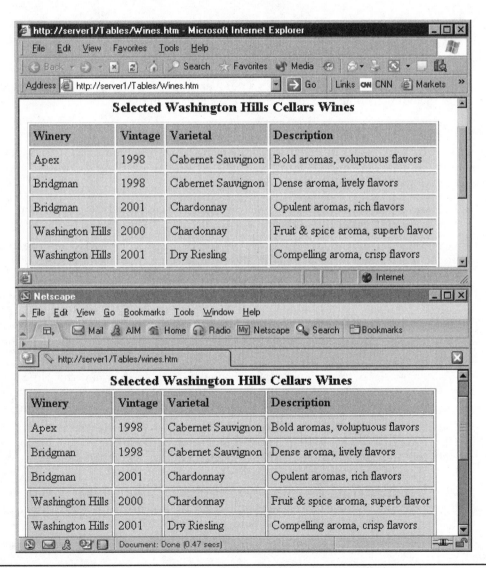

**FIGURE 7-7**    Comparing a table in Internet Explorer 6 and Netscape Navigator 7

15. When you have either tired of looking at various formatting alternatives or found one you want to keep, save your Wines page or its equivalent as well as the Default.htm page and then close the Tables web.

Support for tables has improved greatly in current browsers. There used to be considerable differences in how various browsers display tables. You need to view your work in various browsers to decide how these differences affect you. In the Internet arena, Netscape and Microsoft have the lion's share of the market, and both support tables quite well.

## Using Tables for Page Layout

While tabular tables are the classical way tables are imagined, in web page design, tables are extensively used for some or all of a page's layout. Rarely are you aware that there is a table behind the layout. FrontPage 2003 has a number of new facilities for laying out pages with tables including a number of ready-made layouts you can use.

### Using Tables with Pictures and Text

You can see how tables work in a page layout by using tables to separate pictures and text in the web you created in Chapters 5 and 6. Put the picture, the heading, and the bulleted items on the Home Page in a layout table with these steps:

1. In FrontPage, open the web you created in the last two chapters, then open the Home Page (Default.htm) in Design view.

2. Open the File menu and choose Save As. Change the page title to **Home Page in a Table**, rename the page **Home_table.htm,** and save it in your existing web. This prevents any of your changes from affecting your original page.

3. If the Tables toolbar isn't already open, open the View menu and select Toolbars | Tables. Choose the Draw Table tool, then draw a table between the title and first heading, around the picture, the heading, and the bulleted items. When you are done drawing the table, the picture, heading, and items may be pushed below it.

4. About a quarter of the way from the left edge of the table, draw a vertical line from the top to bottom edges of the table. Draw a horizontal line from about a quarter of the way down the new line you just drew to the right edge, as shown in Figure 7-8.

5. Click the Draw Table tool to deselect it, then drag the picture into the left cell of the table. Drag across the heading, click Cut in the Standard toolbar, click in the top right cell, and click Paste. Similarly, select and cut the bulleted items and paste them in the bottom right cell.

6. Work with the sizing of your picture and the size and positioning of your text to get them to fit in your table (we actually edited our text to make it fit better). Open the Table Properties dialog box. Set the Border Size of 0. Click OK.

7. Click Preview. Our results are shown in Figure 7-9. Return to Design view and save your work.

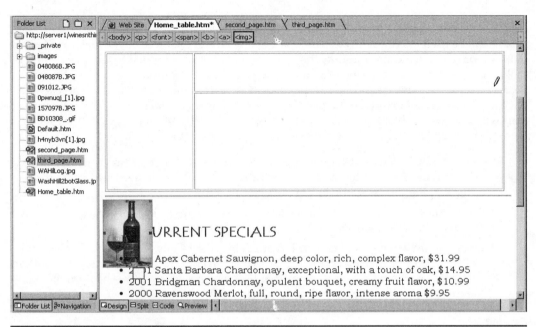

**FIGURE 7-8** Drawing a table

Using a table is an easy way to relatively position a picture and text, as you can see. That is the reason that the majority of web pages use tables.

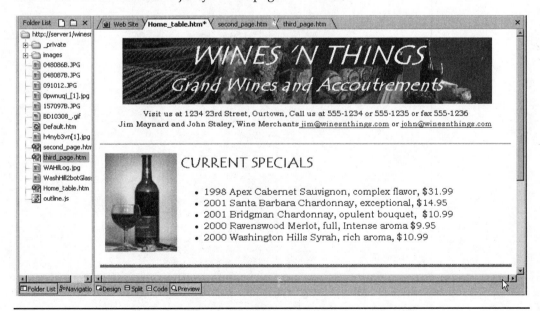

**FIGURE 7-9** Results of using a table to position a picture, a heading, and a list

## Using a Table to Lay Out a Page

A table can be used to lay out all or a large part of a page and therefore be the major influence in how a page will look. Look at how the Third page of the web created in Chapters 5 and 6 looks if a table is used to control the layout of the page. In this example, we will use FrontPage 2003's new Layout Table And Cells task pane to add a ready-made table layout to an existing page and copy items already on the page into the table. In a normal situation, you would start with a table on a blank or mainly blank page and initially place the items in the table. Here are the steps we used to transform our third page to a table layout:

1. In the web you built in Chapters 5 and 6, open the file for the Third page in Design view and use Save As to make a copy of the page with the name Third_table.htm and changing the page title to **Third Page in a Table**.

2. Press CTRL-HOME to place the insertion point in the upper-left corner (on the left of the web title if the instructions in Chapter 5 were followed).

3. Open the Table menu and choose Layout Tables And Cells. The Layout Tables And Cells task pane will open on the right of your screen. Scroll the layouts at the bottom of the task pane and choose the one that best matches your page. The right one in the third row is used here, as shown in Figure 7-10.

**FIGURE 7-10**
Selecting a table layout to apply to the Third page

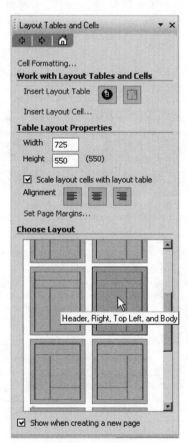

*TIP  You can drag the left edge of the Layout Tables And Cells task pane to adjust its width and see as many as one to four layouts in a single row.*

4. Cut and paste or drag the web title and the next two rows of text to the top cell. Cut and paste or drag the link bar to the second cell from the top. You will get a message after pasting the link bar that reads "[Add this page to the Navigation view to display hyperlinks here]." After doing that (click Navigation and drag the table page under Second_Page), the link bar will appear. Right-click in the second cell, choose Cell Properties, open the Vertical Alignment drop-down list, choose Middle, and click OK.

5. Select the Draw Table tool from the Tables toolbar. Down about an inch and a half into the third cell ( the "Body" cell) draw a horizontal line across the cell, creating a new cell. About an inch and a half from the left side of the new cell, draw a vertical line from the top to the bottom of the new cell. Click the Draw Table tool to deselect it.

6. Drag the picture that was next to the page heading to the leftmost or smaller of the two new cells and drag the page heading to the rightmost of the new cell. Right-click the page heading cell, choose Cell Properties, choose Center for the Horizontal Alignment and Middle for the Vertical Alignment, and click OK.

7. Select the main body of text and drag it to the bottom-left cell. Note how the cell expands to accept it. Finally, drag the second picture to the right-hand cell. Right-click that cell, choose Cell Properties, change the vertical alignment to Middle, and click OK.

8. Finally, copy the footer information below the table and delete any remaining empty lines above the table.

9. Save Third_table.htm and click Preview In Browser. Figure 7-11 shows what our page looks like.

*NOTE  If in the cut and paste process you lose some of the original formatting, redo it to get the page to look as it did before.*

10. Close your browser, but leave your web open in FrontPage.

You may have some other ideas of how to apply tables to this page. Try them. Play with your ideas until you have the look you want—that is how good designs are created. FrontPage's table capability gives you an extremely powerful tool to create what you want.

## Precision Sizing of Tables and Cells

You may have noticed as you are working with tables that you would like to just "tweak" the size of a cell or side of the table. FrontPage 2003 now allows you to do that with great precision using the Table Layout tool. Prior to FrontPage 2003, if height and width were not a percentage of the page or table size you could drag the border between two cells, increasing the size of one cell and decreasing the size of the other. There was no way, though, of knowing the precise dimensions as you were dragging (you have to go into the Cell Properties dialog box), and there was no way of adjusting one cell border without adjusting its neighbor at the same time. You now can now do all that with the Table Layout tool. See how next:

1. With Third_table.htm open in FrontPage, right-click within the table and choose Table Properties. In the Table Properties dialog box, if it isn't already, select Enable

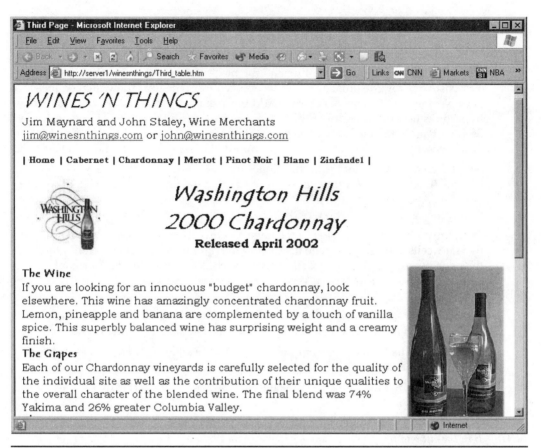

**FIGURE 7-11**    The Third page laid out with a table

Layout Tools. Also, if it isn't already, select Specify Width, click In Pixels, with a width value in the 700 to 800 range (we're using 725). Click OK to close the Table Properties dialog box.

2. With the Third_table positioned so you can see the top border of the table and hopefully a little area above the table, move the mouse pointer above the table so it is an insertion point (an I-beam cross section). Then, without clicking, very slowly move the mouse down over the top border of the table.

As you first come to the table border, it should turn green. This is the outside border of the entire table. If you keep moving the mouse down, the border will turn blue. This is the border of the top cell in the table. If you keep moving the mouse down until you get to the bottom border of the top cell, the border around the top cell will again be blue, and, with further movement down the border around the second from the top cell will be blue.

3. Move the mouse pointer back up to the top border until it turns green and then click. The table and all cells will be highlighted and pixel dimensions will be displayed, as you can see in Figure 7-12.

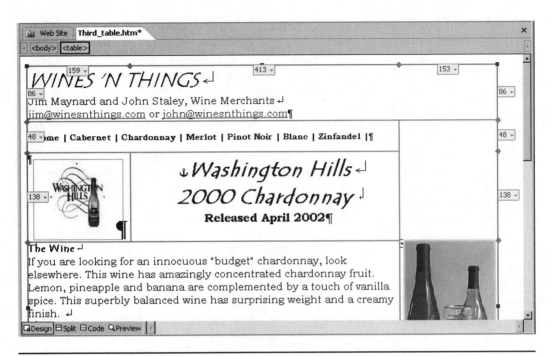

**FIGURE 7-12**    Layout tools shown on a table

In the table used here, we would like the second row (the second cell from the top on the left) to span the entire table and the second cell on the right to be a little shorter to allow this to happen. That is done as follows. Do similar steps with your table.

4. Move the mouse pointer until the border surrounding the second cell on the right is selected, and then click so the sizing handles appear around that border.

5. Point at the center sizing handle on the top border and drag it down until it is even with the bottom border of the second cell on the left. Note that the border will jump to and stick to this spot.

6. Select the border of the second cell on the left and drag the middle sizing handle on the right to the right to fill the space just vacated by shortening the right cell, like this:

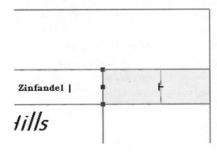

7. Try changing some other cells. Note that you must first make a neighboring cell smaller before enlarging a cell. Also, you can't make a cell smaller than its contents.

8. Select the table border again. Click the downward pointing arrowhead in one of the little dimension boxes. A menu opens that allows you to directly enter a row height or a column width, make the row or column Autostretch, which is the same as making the table have a specified height or width equal to 100 percent of the window displaying it, and insert an empty image to use as a row or column spacer.

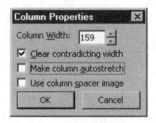

9. Click Change Column Width. The Column Properties dialog box will open. Here you can directly enter a width you want and automatically change the width of an adjacent column to accommodate the change. This option, Clear Contradicting Width, also works the opposite way. If you reduce the width of a cell and this option is selected, the adjacent cell will expand to fill the space created. Try this.

10. With the table border still selected, double-click it and the Layout Tables And Cells task pane will open, as you saw earlier in Figure 7-10. If you select a cell border and double-click it, the Cell Formatting task pane opens. This allows you to set a number of options that are available in the Cell Properties dialog box

11. When you are done working with the Table Layout tool, if you want to save the results, do so by clicking Save, otherwise right-click the page tab and click Close, clicking No to Save Changes. If the Home_table.htm is still open, close it, saving it if desired.

## Laying Out with Frames

Both frames and tables allow you to divide a page into sections, but they do so in different ways and with different results. *Tables* divide a page into fixed or static segments whose relationship to each other cannot be changed by the viewer. *Frames* are actually several independent pages that have each been allocated a section of a single viewing window. The viewer can scroll each of the pages or frames independently of the other frames, and the viewer can change the size of each of the frames if the web designer allows that.

The structure of pages used with frames along with the HTML to control them is called a *frames page* or a *frameset*. In FrontPage, frames are built by use of the Frames page templates. The Frames page templates establish a structure of blank pages and the HTML to view them as frames within a single window. This makes the new pages appear as independent segments of a single page.

**NOTE**    *Frame pages created quite a bit of excitement when they were first introduced. This has died down to some extent, and some sources now recommend that they not be used at all. Because frame pages actually load several pages, the total loading time is longer than for a single normal web page. There has also been a tendency to overuse frame pages. Regardless, they are a useful tool for the web designer. They should simply be used with care. Ask yourself if the pages you are creating really benefit from frame pages, and avoid using them simply for a whiz-bang effect.*

There is a different type of frame called an *inline frame* that allows you to place a single frame on an existing web page. The inline frame can float or be anchored on the page and displays the contents of another page, which you can scroll. Inline frames are discussed later in this chapter.

## Creating a Traditional Frames Page

Explore FrontPage's traditional frames capability and compare it to using tables by building a frames page alternative for your Home Page in your web site from Chapters 5 and 6. Create the frames page with these steps:

1. With your previous web site still open, open the File menu and choose New. In the New task pane, click More Page Templates. In the Page Templates dialog box, click the Frames Pages tab, shown in Figure 7-13.

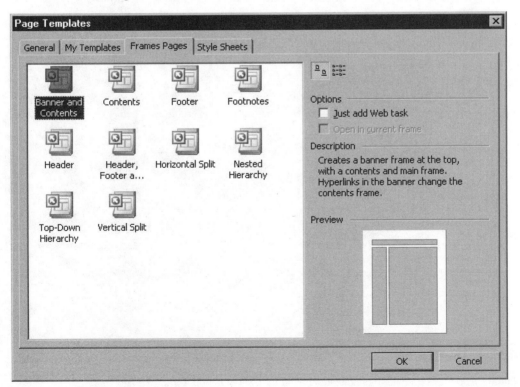

**FIGURE 7-13**    Selecting a frames layout

In the Frames Pages tab, there is a list of the frames page templates, a description of the template, and a preview of the frames page.

2. Click the Header, Footer, and Contents frames page template icon (second one in the second row). The preview shows that this frames page displays four separate web pages: a header, a footer, a contents page on the left, and the main page. Click OK. Figure 7-14 shows the frames page in FrontPage.

Each frame contains two buttons of which you can choose one or the other: Set Initial Page, which you use to choose an existing web page that will be displayed in the frame by default, and New Page, which you use to create a new page to be displayed in the frame.

3. Right-click a frame, and then click Frame Properties. The Frame Properties dialog box shown in Figure 7-15 is displayed. The options are described in Table 7-5.

4. Click the Frames Page button in the Frame Properties dialog box. This displays the Page Properties dialog box that you have used before.

With a frames page there is an additional tab, Frames, which has two options. The Frame Spacing option is similar to the border width of a table in that it sets the width of the borders between frames in a frame page. The Show Borders check box determines if borders will be displayed between frames. Clearing this check box has the same effect with frames as setting the border width to 0 in a table.

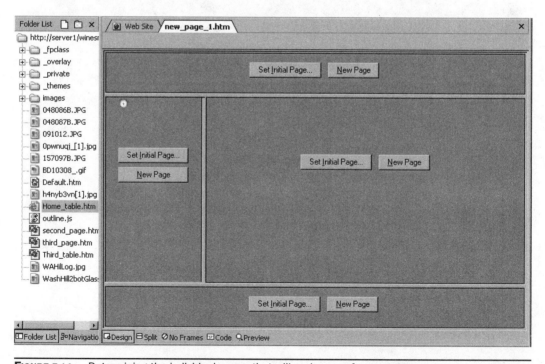

**FIGURE 7-14**    Determining the individual pages that will make up a frames page

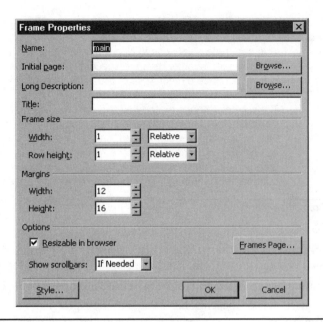

**FIGURE 7-15**   Setting the properties of an individual frame

5. Click Cancel to close the Page Properties dialog box; then click Cancel to close the Frame Properties dialog box.

6. In the Top (header) frame, click New Page. A new blank page is opened in the Top frame.

| Option | Description |
|---|---|
| Name | The name of the frame itself, not the page displayed in the frame. This is the name used as a target by hyperlinks in the frames page and the one that determines in which frame a page will be displayed. |
| Initial Page | The URL of the page that will be displayed in the frame when it is first loaded by the user's browser. |
| Frame Size | This has two options, Width and Row Height, that can be set to pixel, percent, or relative values. These function the same way as table dimensions. If your frame contains a graphic, you may want the frame to be no larger than the graphic itself. In that case, you can set the dimensions of the frame to match the graphic using pixel values. The other frames can then use relative or percent values. |
| Margins | Sets the margins, in pixels, of the selected frame. |
| Resizable In Browser | Determines if the frame can be resized in the user's browser. If this option is cleared, the user cannot resize the frame. |

**TABLE 7-5**   Frame Properties

| Option | Description |
|---|---|
| Show Scrollbars | This has three selections: If Needed, which displays scroll bars if the page content is larger than the space available; Never, which will never display scroll bars regardless of the page content; and Always, which will always display scroll bars.<br><br>The correct settings for the last two options depend on the page content being displayed in the frame. If it is a menu, you would want the scroll bars to be displayed as needed, and you would probably want the user to be able to resize the frame. If the frame is displaying a header with a graphic, and you've sized the frame to the graphic using the Frame Size options, then you might want to disable both these options. |

**TABLE 7-5**  Frame Properties *(continued)*

7. Open the original Home Page (Default.htm). Select the picture(s) behind the title and the title itself and copy them. Paste them into the new header page.

8. Drag the bottom border of the Top frame up or down until the entire graphic is visible.

9. In the Bottom (footer) frame, click New Page. In the Home Page, scroll to the bottom, select the three lines in the footer, click Copy, reopen the frameset page, and with the insertion point in the Bottom frame, click Paste. The footer will be pasted into the bottom frame.

10. In the Main frame (the right pane in the center of the frames page), click New Page, copy and paste first the two address lines and then the body of text from the original Home Page, including the headings.

11. In the Contents frame (the left frame in the center of the frames page), click New Page and type a heading and the detail you want for the links to the other pages in your web. Format both the heading and the links as you want and attach the links to the pages and bookmarks you want them to go to. At this point, our Frameset page looks like Figure 7-16.

12. Open the File menu and choose Save As. The Save As dialog box for frames pages opens, as shown in Figure 7-17, and includes an outline of the frames page on the right. This indicates which frame will be saved. To save the frames page itself, there must be a border around the entire page, as shown in Figure 7-17.

13. Click Change Title, type **Frames Page**, and click OK. Then enter the File Name Frameset.htm and click Save.

14. After the overall frames page is saved, the Save As dialog box will be redisplayed with one of the individual pages in the frame selected. The title and filename you enter will apply to the page in the selected frame. We use the following titles and filenames:

| | |
|---|---|
| Header | HdrFrame.htm |
| Main | MainFrame.htm |
| Footer | FooterFrame.htm |
| Contents | ContsFrame.htm |

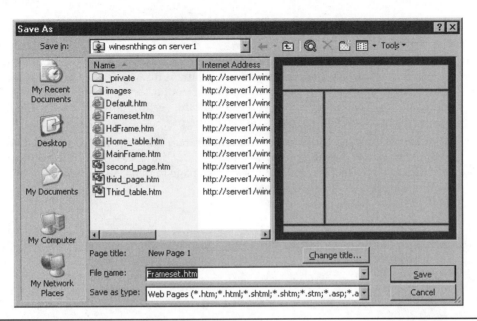

**FIGURE 7-16**　Saving a frames page

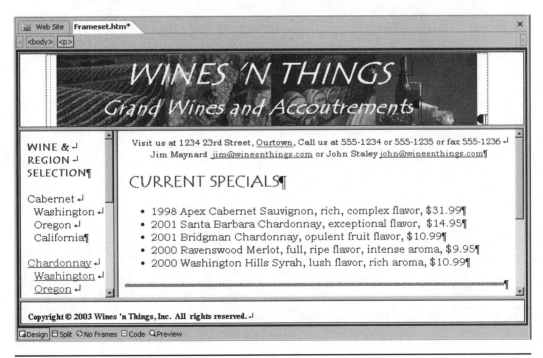

**FIGURE 7-17**　Final set of pages making up a frames page

15. Enter the titles and filenames for each frame and click Save. When you are done, you are returned to the Frameset page.

16. Click Preview In Browser. Figure 7-18 shows the frames page in Internet Explorer 6. Notice there is no scroll bar in the footer, so there is no way to see the rest of the footer. Also, note that you cannot drag the horizontal border between the Main frame and the Footer frame, but you can drag the vertical border between the Contents and Main frames in the middle of the page.

17. Click one of your hyperlink in the Contents frame. The page linked to is displayed in the Main frame, which you can scroll. Click Back and the Main frame is returned its primary page. Test the rest of your frames page to make sure everything is working properly. Close your browser.

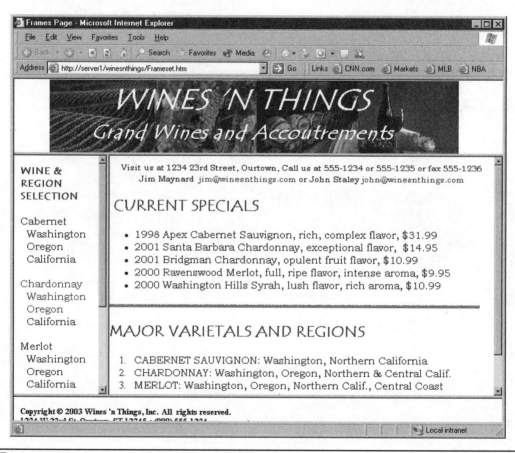

**FIGURE 7-18**   Frames page displayed in Internet Explorer

18. Back in FrontPage, fix the footer so it will scroll by right-clicking in the Footer frame and choosing Frame Properties. In the bottom of the dialog box, open the Show Scrollbars drop-down list, select If Needed, as shown next, and click OK. Note that you could have also made this area resizable if you had wanted.

19. Fix the Contents frame so it is not resizable (there is no need for it). Right-click the Contents frame and choose Frame Properties. Under Options, clear the check box opposite Resizable In Browser and click OK.

20. Save the frameset and reopen it in a browser. Check to make sure everything is working the way you want it to. When you are ready, close your browser.

One problem with frames pages is that not all browsers support them. Frames were introduced in Netscape Navigator 2.0, and Microsoft followed suit in Internet Explorer 3.0. Support for frames was made official with the adoption of HTML 3.2 early in 1997. Older versions of these browsers, as well as other browsers, do not support frames. Some people still use these older browsers, so you must assume a small, but possibly significant, percentage of your audience will not be able to view your frames pages correctly.

This problem is dealt with by creating a No Frames page. If the user's browser does not support frames, the No Frames page is displayed instead. FrontPage will automatically create a No Frames page when a frames page is created, as you can see by clicking No Frames at the bottom of the page when a frames page is open. Here is what the default No Frames page looks like:

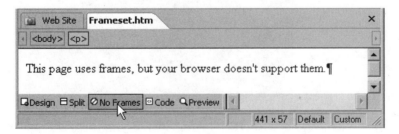

You can add anything you like to this page either to direct the user to download a browser that supports frames by creating hyperlinks to Microsoft's or Netscape's browser-download pages on their web sites, or to re-create your frames pages without frames. This is a case where you could use tables to place the categories list in one column and other pages in a second column. Your table could have one row with two columns.

Frames provide some powerful layout capabilities, in particular, the target frame concept and the ability of a frame to scroll. Based on the default target frames, anything that you open by clicking a link in a Contents frame will appear in the Main frame.

## Creating an Inline Frame

An inline frame is a single frame on a normal web page. This allows you to have a window on one page that displays the contents of a second page. For example, if the table of wines that was prepared as an example of a tabular table at the beginning of this chapter was used as a scrollable inline frame in place of the list of Current Specials, it might take less space on the page, allow a longer list, and potentially keep the reader on the original page. See how this is done using the following steps:

1. Open the original Home Page (Default.htm) in Design view. Resave the page as Home_inline.htm.

2. Open the File menu, choose Import, click Add File, navigate to your Tables web site (by default it is C:\Inetpub\Wwwroot\Tables with STS), double-click the page containing the table you created, (in my case, Wines.htm), and click OK twice. This puts a copy of that page and table in the current web site.

3. Scroll down the page to the list of Current Specials heading, select that list and press DELETE. If needed, enter a blank line between the heading and the separator line.

4. With the insertion point on the blank line, open the Insert menu, extend the menu if necessary, and choose Inline Frame. A frame appears on the page, like this:

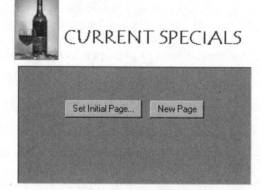

5. Click Set Initial Page. The Insert Hyperlink dialog box will open. Scroll down until you find the page you imported in step 2, and then double-click that page. It will be displayed in the inline frame.

6. Move the insertion point to one of the borders of the frame where it becomes a pointer and click to select the entire frame. Selection handles appear around the frame.

7. Drag the lower-right selection handle to size the frame so it fits the width of the table and is the height you want. With the full frame still selected, right-click the frame border and choose Inline Frame Properties to open its dialog box, shown in Figure 7-19.

8. Change the frame Name to **Wines**, change the Width and Height margins to 10, and click OK.

9. Save the page and click Preview In Browser. Figure 7-20 shows this scrollable frame within an otherwise normal page. Close your browser and the current web.

Tables and frames add real depth to your ability to create sophisticated, state-of-the-art web pages in FrontPage. You can do it very easily, aided by FrontPage's true WYSIWYG ability that allows you to see the final results.

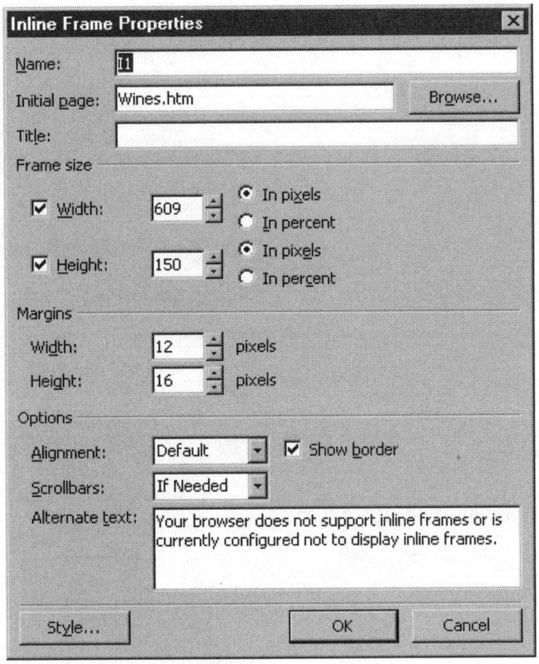

**FIGURE 7-19** Setting the inline frame properties

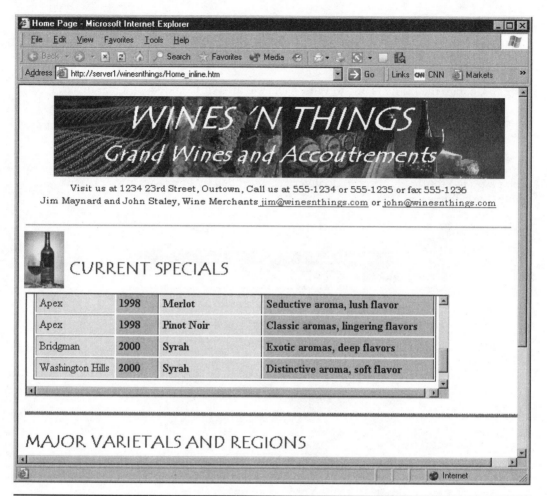

**FIGURE 7-20**    An inline frame in Internet Explorer

# Working with Forms

F orms in a web are very similar to those on paper, as you saw in Chapter 2. You are given boxes to fill in, options to select, and choices to make. The advantages of computer forms over paper forms are that computer forms can be easily modified, you don't have to decipher someone's handwriting, and the data starts out in computer form, so it does not have to be retyped into a computer. As with paper forms, though, the design of a form is very important if you want the user to fill it out willingly and properly. The three cardinal rules of forms are

- Keep it simple.
- Keep it short.
- Make it very clear what the user is supposed to do.

## Using Forms

FrontPage provides a comprehensive Form Page Wizard to lead you through the development of a form. In addition, FrontPage has a complete set of tools both in the Forms toolbar and in the Insert menu to allow you to create any form you can dream up. You'll work with both of these in this chapter, beginning with the Form Page Wizard.

### Creating Forms with the Form Page Wizard

To create a form, you need to figure out what questions to ask and what fields are necessary for the user to answer them. Go through that process with the idea of creating a questionnaire for prospective project team members. First, use the Form Page Wizard to generate the form; then examine and modify the results.

### Generating the Form

Like the other wizards you have seen, the Form Page Wizard asks you a series of questions, which it then uses to build a form. To work with the Form Page Wizard, follow these steps:

1. If necessary, start FrontPage.
2. Create a new one-page web and name it **Forms**.

3. Click the arrow to the right of Create A New Normal Page on the toolbar and choose Page. Select Form Page Wizard in the Page Templates dialog box and click OK. The Form Page Wizard's introductory dialog box will appear, telling you about web forms, what the wizard will do, and what you can do with the result. Click Next after reading this.

4. The Form Page Wizard dialog box that opens will eventually show the questions that you are asking on your form. Currently, it is blank. Click Add to select the first question.

5. The top of the next dialog box lists types of input that can be collected. Click Contact Information. As you can see in Figure 8-1, a description of the fields that will be placed on the form appears in the middle of the dialog box, and the actual question is displayed at the bottom, where you can change it as you want. Accept the default and click Next.

6. You are then asked to select the specific fields that you want on the form for your first question. All of these are related to an individual contact. For the Name entry, you can use one, two, or three fields. Leave the check boxes that are selected as is, and click First, Last, which is the two-field choice. Also click Postal Address and Home Phone, and then click Next, leaving the suggested name for the group of variables (Contact) as is (see Figure 8-2). Notice that if you have done this before, the base name will have to be unique.

7. You are returned to the list of questions, which now shows the contact information question you just selected. Use steps 5 through 7 to include additional questions dealing with Account Information and Personal Information. In the dialog box that appears once you choose Account Information, select the As First And Last Names Fields option for the Username, and then accept the other defaults. For the Personal Information dialog box, you don't want to repeat the Name field, so clear the Name check box; but you do want to accept the other defaults.

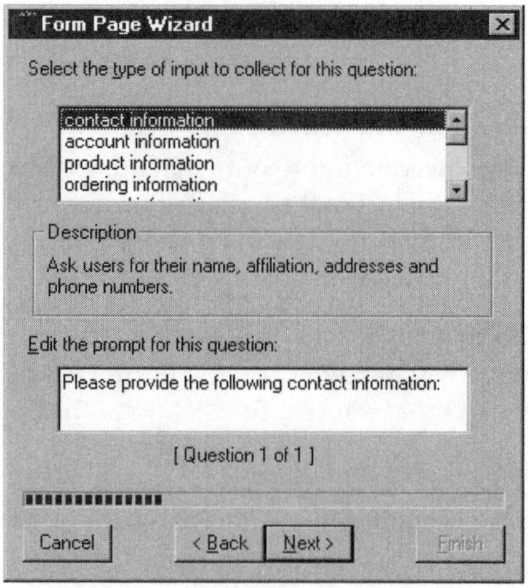

**FIGURE 8-1**
Choosing the type of questions to be on the form

FIGURE 8-2
Selecting the
specific fields to
use for gathering
contact
information

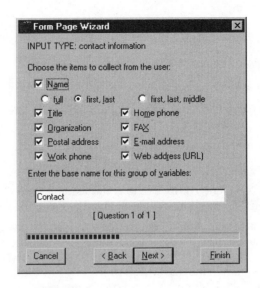

**NOTE** *After you are done using the Form Page Wizard, you can add to, change, and delete what the wizard has produced.*

8. Click Add in the dialog box that shows the list of questions, select the One Of Several Options question, and change the prompt in the lower section of the dialog box to

   **Choose the city where you want to be located:**

9. Click Next and enter **New York, Austin,** and **San Francisco** as three separate labels on three lines in the upper list box (press ENTER after the first and second label). Then click Radio Buttons, enter the word **Location** as the variable name, and click Next.

**NOTE** *If* ENTER *does not work, you can fill the line with spaces to force it to the next line. It is important that the options be on separate lines.*

10. Click Add, select the Any Of Several Options question, and change the prompt to

    **Select two areas you want to be associated with:**

11. Click Next and enter

    **Initial Design**

    **Detail Plan**

    **Project Management**

    **Plan Implementation**

    **Evaluation**

on five separate lines. Enter **PreferredAreas** (without a space) as the name for the group of variables and click Next.

12. Click Add, select Date, change the prompt to

    **Enter the date you are available:**

13. Click Next, leave the default top date format, enter **Availability** for the variable name, and click Next.

14. Click Add, select Paragraph, change the prompt to

    **Why do you want to be on this project?**

15. Click Next, enter **Why** as the variable name, and click Next. When you are done, your list of questions will look like the one in Figure 8-3.

16. Look at your list of questions. Do you want to change any of them or reposition them in the list? While you can change the finished product, it is easier to change it now, before the form is generated. Click No. 6, the availability date. Click Move Up twice to move the date ahead of the city question. Click any question you want to edit and click Modify. When you are done editing and have returned to the list of questions, click Next to continue with the form creation.

17. You are asked how the list of questions should be presented. Leave the defaults: As Normal Paragraphs, No Table Of Contents, and Use Tables To Align Form Fields. Then click Next.

18. You are asked how you want to save the results of the questionnaire. Choose Save Results To A Text File, enter the filename of **Proj_ans** for the results file, click Next, and then click Finish to generate the form page, which appears as shown in Figure 8-4 (with the Folder List closed). Scroll down the form in Page view to see all the types of form fields created.

**FIGURE 8-3**
Final list of
selected questions

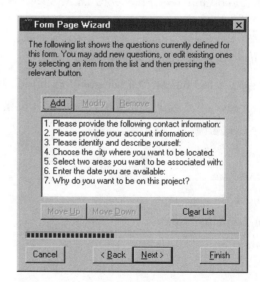

**FIGURE 8-4**
The form as generated by the wizard

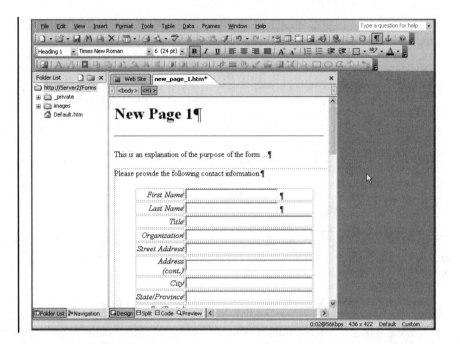

19. Save your form by clicking Save on the toolbar, entering the filename of **ProjForm.htm**, changing the page title to **Project Team Questionnaire**, and clicking Save.

---

***TIP*** *If you want to transfer the results of a web form to a database or spreadsheet, you can use a text file to collect the information. You can choose a comma-, tab-, or space-delimited file (tab probably being the best for exporting from FrontPage), which is fairly easy to import into most products. In Chapter 17, you will learn how to record the form results directly to a database. In Chapter 11, you will see how spreadsheet information can be displayed in web pages.*

---

Forms can be formatted by use of either a table or the Formatted paragraph style. The Formatted style was often used in the past for two reasons: it is the only paragraph style that can display more than one consecutive space, which can then be used to align the form fields; and many browsers did not support tables. Most browsers now support tables, and this has become the preferred method for aligning forms. Using tables greatly simplifies aligning the labels and fields in a form, and it allows you to use any available font. As you have seen, Chapter 7 describes how to use tables.

### Reviewing and Editing a Form

As with most documents that you create, you'll want to go through your form in detail and make any necessary changes. In the real world, you would need to replace the introductory paragraph with an explanation of the form. This should tell users how the form will be used and why they should fill it out. In this case, you might use something like "This form will be used to qualify prospective members of the Project Team. If you are interested in being a member, please fill out this form."

You can customize many areas of the form. The things that you can do are discussed in the following sections.

**Changing the Field's Label or Text**   Change the label or text on the left of each field by simply typing over or adding to the existing text. This may change the width of the table column. For example, add **& Middle** to the first label, and you'll get the column width change, as shown next. Click Undo to restore your form.

*First Name & Middle*
*Last Name*
*Title*

---

***TIP***   *If you use the Formatted paragraph style to format your form, changing the label for one field may necessitate adjusting other fields to restore the form's alignment. If you use a table to format the form, the realignment will occur automatically.*

**Changing the Field's Alignment**   Change the alignment by opening the Cell Properties dialog box for the cell (right-click the text box and select Cell Properties) and changing the horizontal or vertical alignment. You can select the entire column to change the alignment for all the labels or fields at one time. For example, move the mouse pointer to the top of the label or left column until the arrow pointer appears, drag it down to select the column, and click Align Left in the toolbar. All the labels will move to the left, as shown next. Click Undo. If you are using the Formatted paragraph style, you change the alignment by adding or deleting spaces.

*First Name*
*Last Name*
*Title*
*Organization*
*Street Address*

---

***TIP***   *If you use the Formatted style and change the paragraph style on the form fields from Formatted to any other style, you'll lose all the leading spaces that produce the original field alignment. This can easily happen if you backspace up to the first paragraph. If this happens to you, click Undo to quickly recover.*

**Deleting a Field**   If you want to delete a field and its label, select the table row and choose Cut from the Edit menu (pressing DEL clears the label but does not delete it). If you select either the label or field individually and press DEL, you leave the table row available for placing another label or field. Delete an entire section by selecting the question, labels, and fields, and choosing Cut from the Edit menu.

**Changing a Field's Properties**   Right-clicking a
field (not its label) and selecting Form Field
Properties opens the field's Properties dialog
box, shown here (the dialog box displayed
depends on the type of field selected).
   Here you can

**Text Box Properties**

Name: Contact_FirstName

Initial value:

Width in characters: 25   Tab order:

Password field:   ○ Yes   ● No

Style...   Validate...   OK   Cancel

- Change the field's name (not the label
  displayed on the web page).

- Establish an initial value, such as a state
  abbreviation if most people filling out a form are from one state.

- Set the order in which the fields will become active when the user presses TAB.
  (This feature doesn't work with all browsers.)

- Determine if the field contains a password so its contents can be encrypted.

- Set the width of the text box, which can also be changed by dragging the end of
  a field, as shown here.

Changing the width of a text box does not affect the maximum number of characters
the field can contain. To do that, you use the Form Field Validation dialog box opened
by clicking Validate in the Form Field Properties dialog box. For a text field, the Text Box
Validation dialog box shown in Figure 8-5 is displayed. The Max Length text box displays
the maximum number of characters the field will accept, regardless of the width of the field.
If the maximum length is greater than the width, the text will scroll in the text box until the
maximum length is reached. The other options in the Validation dialog box will be covered
later in the chapter in the section "Validating a Form." For now, close all open dialog boxes.

**NOTE**   *Even if you set the field width and maximum length to the same number, all the text might
not fit in the text box without scrolling. This is because the width of a character as determined by
the HTML is not always the same as a character displayed on the screen. Test your form fields in
a browser by entering the maximum number of characters and setting the width accordingly.*

**Changing the Field's Placement**   The table created with the Form Page Wizard has two
columns, each with one label and data entry area on a single line. You may want to have
more than one field on a line, such as the State and Zip fields. To do that, you need to split
a single cell into multiple cells, like this:

1. Reduce the width of the State/Province field (not the label or the table) to about
   a third of its original size by selecting it and dragging the right-middle selection
   handle to the left.

FIGURE 8-5
Validating a
text box

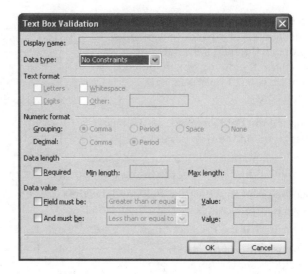

2. With the cursor in the same cell, select the cell by choosing Select | Cell from the Table menu.

3. Right-click the selected cell and select Split Cells. Accept the default Split Into Columns, and then enter **3** in the Number Of Columns spinner and click OK.

4. Cut and paste first the Zip/Postal Code label, and then separately cut and paste the Zip/Postal Code form field into the new cells.

5. Right-click the cell containing the Zip/Postal Code label and open the Cell Properties dialog box.

6. Set the Horizontal Alignment to Right and click OK. Your form fields should look like this:

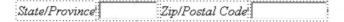

7. Select the vacated row and select Delete Rows from the Table menu to remove the row.

**Validating a Form**    Fields in a form often need to be limited to specific types of information, such as allowing only numbers (no letters), or requiring that a field not be left blank. Form validation traditionally has been done on the web server by the form handler (*server-side* validation). This has the disadvantage of requiring the form to be sent to the server, validated, and then sent back to the user if the validation fails. Besides the time involved, server-side validation places a greater demand on the web server's resources. If your web site is receiving a large number of hits each day, this can slow down the server. Validating a form before it's sent (*client-side* validation) has the advantages of speeding up the process and placing less demand on the web server.

*NOTE Client-side validation is performed by the web browser. FrontPage generates a JavaScript or VBScript script (see Chapter 15) that is run by the browser to validate the form. JavaScript (the default) is supported by both Netscape and Microsoft, while VBScript is supported mainly by Microsoft. Some browsers do not support either scripting language. If the browser being used does not support the scripting language used, the client-side validation is ignored. This is another reason to encourage visitors to your web sites to upgrade to the latest versions of either Netscape Navigator or Microsoft Internet Explorer.*

Validation criteria for one-line and scrolling text boxes are set by use of the Text Box Validation dialog box that you saw in Figure 8-5. The options are explained in Table 8-1.

Radio buttons or option buttons are validated by use of the Option Button Validation dialog box, shown next, which allows you to make the field required and to set a display name for error messages:

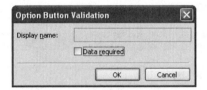

| Option | Description |
|--------|-------------|
| Display Name | Displays the name when an error message is generated. If no name is entered, the contents of the Name field in the form field's Properties dialog box are displayed. |
| Data Type | Sets the type of data that will be accepted: No Constraints (any characters), Text (alphanumeric characters), Integer (numbers, including "," and "–", without decimals), or Number (numbers with decimal places). |
| Text Format | Sets the acceptable formats for a text form field: Letters, Digits (numbers), Whitespace (spaces, tabs, returns, and newline characters), and Other. If Other is selected, you must type the characters (such as hyphens or commas) that will be accepted in the text box. |
| Numeric Format | Sets both the Grouping and Decimal punctuation characters for numeric fields. Grouping characters can be Comma (1,234), Period (1.234), Space (1 234), or None (1234). Decimal sets the character used as a decimal point: either a Comma or a Period. You cannot use the same character for both Grouping and Decimal. |
| Data Length | Sets the acceptable length of the data. Required means that the field cannot be left blank. Min Length and Max Length set the minimum and maximum number of characters that can be entered, respectively. |
| Data Value | Sets a test for the data entered. The value entered in the Value text box is used for the comparison. You can set two tests for each field: Less Than, Greater Than, Less Than Or Equal To, Greater Than Or Equal To, Equal To, or Not Equal To. |

**TABLE 8-1**    Text Box Validation Options

Drop-down lists, or menus, have an additional validation option: Disallow First Choice, as shown here. When this is selected, the first item in the drop-down box cannot be chosen. This enables you to place an instruction or comment, rather than an option, as the first item in the drop-down list.

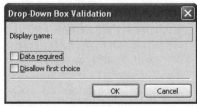

You can validate all the fields in a form except check boxes and push buttons by right-clicking them, selecting Form Field Properties, and clicking Validate. A dialog box, such as the one shown next, is displayed for each form field that fails the validation criteria. This dialog box was generated by making the First Name field required and then submitting the form with the field left blank. In this case, the Display Name field in the Text Box Validation dialog box was set to First name. If the Display Name field had been left blank, the error message would have displayed the form field name "Contact_FirstName."

Make the First and Last Name fields required with these steps:

1. Right-click the First Name form field, select Form Field Properties from the context menu, and click Validate.

2. In the Text Box Validation dialog box, select Required for a Data Length, type **First name** as the Display Name, and click OK twice.

3. Repeat steps 1 and 2 for the Last Name form field, using **Last name** as the Display Name.

4. Save the page and then open it in your web browser. Without entering any information, click Submit Form. The validation error dialog box just shown is displayed.

5. Click OK to close the validation error dialog box, and then type any characters in the First Name field of the form. Click Submit Form again. The validation error dialog box will now state that a value is needed for the Last Name field.

6. Click OK to close the validation error dialog box; then close your browser.

**Changing the Form's Properties**    A *form* is a group of fields enclosed within a dashed border on a page. From the context menu of any field in the form or from any open space within the form boundaries, click Form Properties to open the Form Properties dialog box shown in Figure 8-6. This allows you to set the following properties:

- The form handler, labeled Where To Store Results, will return the contents of a form to you. You have a choice of a file (the default), an e-mail, a database, a custom

FIGURE 8-6
Setting the
properties
for a form

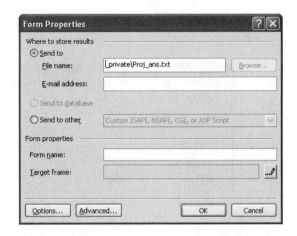

script that you create, and the Discussion or Registration Form Handlers for those types of web forms.

- The Form Name.
- The Target Frame in which you want the form to appear.
- The Options for the form handler. By clicking Options, you open the Saving Results dialog box, shown in Figure 8-7. Here you can change the name and format of the results file, include (or exclude) the field names, and set up a second file to save the results with its format and the selection of fields to be included. The E-mail Results tab allows you to change the address and format of the results e-mail, and to set the Subject and Reply-to Line values. The Confirmation Page tab establishes the URL for a confirmation page to be sent on the receipt of a form and establishes the Validation Failure Page to be displayed if the form fails the client-side validation. In the Saved Fields tab, you can select the form fields to be saved and add information to the results file.

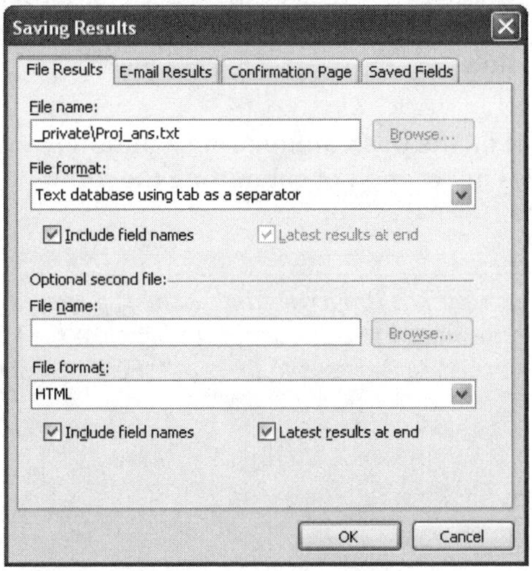

FIGURE 8-7
Setting options
for saving the
results of a form

If the Send To Other option is selected in the Form Properties dialog box, clicking Options displays the Options For Custom Form Handler dialog box shown next. The Action is the URL of the script that will process the form input. This can either be the default or a custom script. The Method is either Post or Get; Post is the default. The Encoding Type sets how the form data will be encoded; this should be left blank to use the default. You should use the defaults for both the Method and Encoding Type fields unless you have a specific reason for changing them. The finer points of these options relate to the HTTP protocol itself.

Clicking Advanced in the Form Properties dialog box displays the Advanced Form Properties dialog box, where you can add hidden fields. The hidden fields are information you want to appear in the data collected from the form but not on the form itself.

With the Add, Modify, and Remove buttons, you can add a field name and a value that appear in the data. For example, if you use the same form on several web pages, you could add a field named Source that identifies where this set of data originated, like what you see here.

The lower part of the form that was created by the wizard contains different types of fields, as shown in Figure 8-8. Each of these fields has slight variations in its Properties dialog box. Open each of these in turn and look at their differences. Note the following features:

- The group of option buttons is a single field, and the value is the button selected.

- Each of the check boxes is its own field, and the value is "on" if a box is selected.

- In the scrolling text box, you can select the number of lines as well as the width. The total content, though, can be far greater than you might think by looking at the width and number of lines (five lines of 35 characters, or 175 characters total), since each line can contain up to 256 characters, not just the 35 characters per line used here.

- You can change the label on the push buttons. Push buttons can submit or reset a form (erasing any entries made and not submitting the form) or link the form to a custom script (using the Normal option).

---

**TIP**   *The Normal option in the Push Button Properties dialog box is a new feature, supported by HTML 4.0. This option allows the button to call a script, rather than the normal form handler. When the button is clicked, the form data is passed to the script. Scripting is covered in Chapter 15.*

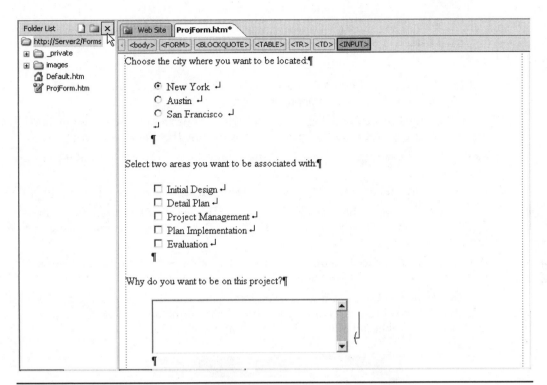

**FIGURE 8-8** The variety of fields created by the Forms Wizard

Given the considerable customization that can be done to a wizard-created form, if your form looks anything like a form the wizard can build, it will probably save you time to use the wizard. The wizard also makes the necessary settings for handling the form results that you otherwise would have to remember to do. Next you'll see what it is like to build a form from scratch. Before going to that, close any open dialog boxes and save your project form one more time.

## Building Forms from Scratch

As good as the Form Page Wizard is, there will always be the need for forms that are different enough from the standards that it is worthwhile building them from scratch. Now that you're familiar with wizard-created forms, take on the building of a form from scratch, and see the differences in the following exercise using the Form toolbar, shown here. (Display the Form toolbar by choosing Form from the Insert menu and dragging the title bar of the submenu away from the main menu to create a "floating" toolbar.)

Here you will build a request for literature, which could be built with a wizard, but this design calls for it to be laid out with Formatted text quite differently from what the wizard would do.

1. With the Project Team Questionnaire still open in FrontPage, click Create A New Normal Page on the toolbar to open a blank page.

2. Open the Page Properties dialog box by selecting Properties on the File menu and type **Literature Request** for the title. Click OK to close the dialog box.

3. At the top of the new page, type **Literature Request**, center it, and format it as Heading 1.

4. Insert a horizontal line under the title by selecting Insert | Horizontal Line.

5. On the first line below the horizontal line, select the Text Box tool from the Form toolbar. A text box will appear beneath the line followed by the Submit and Reset form buttons.

6. If it isn't there already, place the cursor to the left of the Submit button and press ENTER several times to move the buttons several lines down.

7. Right-click the text box, and from the context menu, select Form Field Properties to open the Text Box Properties dialog box, type **First** for the name, change the width to **25**, leave the other defaults as shown next, and click OK.

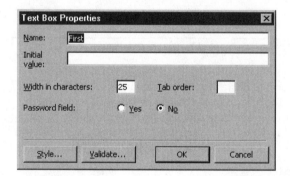

8. Move the insertion point to the left of the new text box, select the Formatted paragraph style, type **First Name:**, and leave a space before the text box.

9. Move the insertion point to the right of the text box, leave two spaces, type **Last Name:**, leave a space, and insert a second text box named **Last** with a width of **25**. Press RIGHT ARROW, and then SHIFT-ENTER to start a new line within the form.

10. Type **Company:**, leave four spaces, insert a text box named **Company**, change the width to **66** characters, and press RIGHT ARROW and then SHIFT-ENTER. (The 66 characters make the second line equal to the first line on *my* screen; yours may be different. You can change this number if you want.)

11. Type **Address:**, leave four spaces, insert a text box named **Address1** with a width of **25**. Press RIGHT ARROW, leave two spaces, type **Address 2:**, leave one space, insert a text box named **Address2** with a width of **25**, and press RIGHT ARROW and then SHIFT-ENTER.

12. Type **City:**, leave seven spaces, insert a text box named **City** with a width of **25**, press RIGHT ARROW, leave two spaces, type **State:**, leave a space, insert a text box named **State** with an initial value of **WA**, change the width to **9** characters, press RIGHT ARROW, leave two spaces, type **Zip:**, leave a space, insert a text box named **Zip** with a width of **11** characters, and press RIGHT ARROW and then SHIFT-ENTER.

13. Type **Phone:**, leave six spaces, insert a text box named **Phone** with a width of **25**, press RIGHT ARROW, leave two spaces, type **E-mail:**, leave four spaces, insert a text box named **Email** with a width of **25**, and press RIGHT ARROW and then SHIFT-ENTER.

14. Click Checkbox on the Form toolbar, give it the name **Literature**, and accept the defaults shown next. Press RIGHT ARROW, but do not enter a space, and then type

   **Click here if you wish literature.**

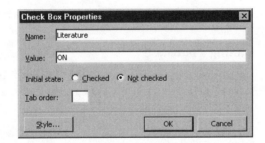

(include the period). Leave four spaces. (The number of spaces you need to vertically align the lines of text may be different.)

15. Type **Which Products?**, leave a space, and click Drop-Down Box on the Form toolbar. In the Drop-Down Box Properties dialog box, type **Lit_Products** for the Name, and click Add to open the Add Choice dialog box. Type **Portable Model** and click Selected as the Initial State, as shown here:

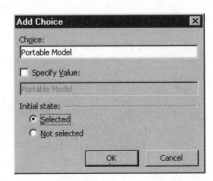

16. Click OK and then click Add twice more to add the choices of **Desktop Model** and **Floor Model**. In both cases, leave the Initial State as Not Selected. In the Drop-Down Box Properties dialog box, click Yes to Allow Multiple Selections so that your dialog box looks like Figure 8-9.

17. Click OK. Select both the "Which Products?" label and the drop-down box by dragging across them and press CTRL-C to copy them to the Clipboard. You'll use this twice again. Move the insertion point to the end of the line and press SHIFT-ENTER.

18. Insert a check box named **Use** and accept its defaults. Press RIGHT ARROW and immediately type

    **Click here if you use our products.**

    Leave three spaces (the number of spaces you need to align the labels may be different on your system), and press CTRL-V to paste in your "Which Products?" label and drop-down box. In the Drop-Down Box Properties dialog box, change the Name to **Use_Products**. Move the insertion point to the end of the line and press SHIFT-ENTER.

19. Insert a check box named **Plan** and accept its defaults. Press RIGHT ARROW, and immediately type

    **Click here if planning a purchase.**

    Leave four spaces and press CTRL-V to paste in the "Which Products?" label and drop-down box. Name the field **Plan_Products**, move the insertion point to the end of the line, and press SHIFT-ENTER.

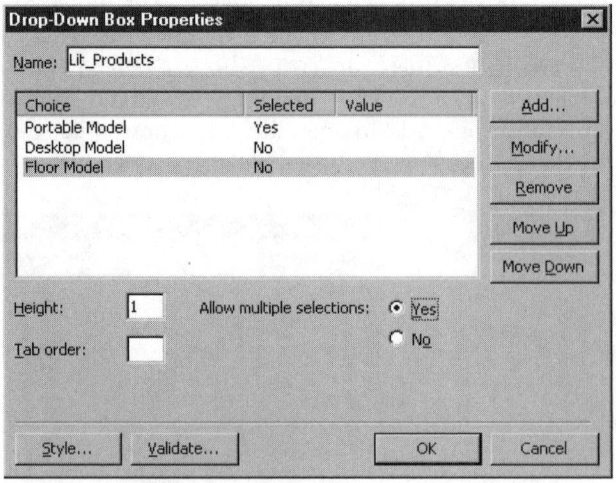

**FIGURE 8-9**
Setting the
options for a
drop-down box

**NOTE** *When you right-click a drop-down box, if FrontPage finds any words in the drop-down box text that are not in the dictionary, the Spelling context menu is displayed. Select an option on the context menu for each word found. When the spell-check is complete, right-clicking the drop-down box will display the standard context menu.*

20. On the new line, type

    **What is your company size?**

    Leave three spaces and click Option Button on the Form toolbar. In the Option Button Properties dialog box, enter a Group Name of **Size**, a Value of **Less than 50**, and choose an Initial State of Not Selected, as shown next:

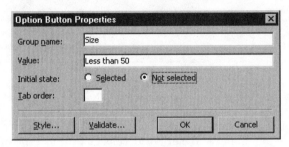

21. Press RIGHT ARROW, and immediately type

    **Less than 50**

22. Leave three spaces, insert a Not Selected option button with a Group Name of **Size** and a Value of **50 to 500**, press RIGHT ARROW, and immediately type

    **50 to 500**

23. Leave three spaces, insert a third Not Selected option button with a Group Name of **Size** and Value of **Over 500**, press RIGHT ARROW, type

    **Over 500**

    and press SHIFT-ENTER.

24. Type

    **Please give us any comments you wish:**

25. Click Text Area on the Form toolbar, type a Name of **Comments** in the TextArea Box Properties dialog box, and enter a width of **32**, as shown here. Click OK.

26. Right-click the Submit button and choose Form Field Properties to open the Push Button Properties dialog box. Type a Name of **Submit** and a Value/Label of **Submit Form**. Make sure the Button Type is Submit, as shown next, and click OK:

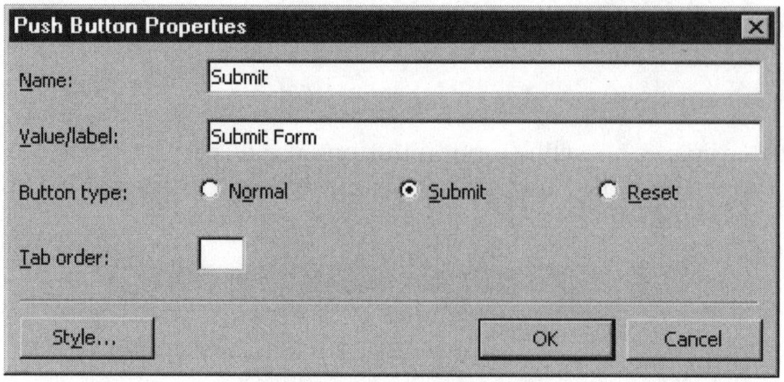

---

***TIP***    *Push buttons are placed in forms by use of the Push Button button on the Form toolbar.*

27. Right-click Reset and open the Push Button Properties dialog box. Name the button **Reset** with a Value/Label of **Reset Form**, select a Button Type of Reset, click OK, save your form with a File Name of **Literature.htm**, and you're done! The result should look like Figure 8-10.

28. Well, almost done. You still need a handler to process the input from the form. Right-click the form inside the dotted line and choose Form Properties. In the Form Properties dialog box, the Send To option button should be selected.

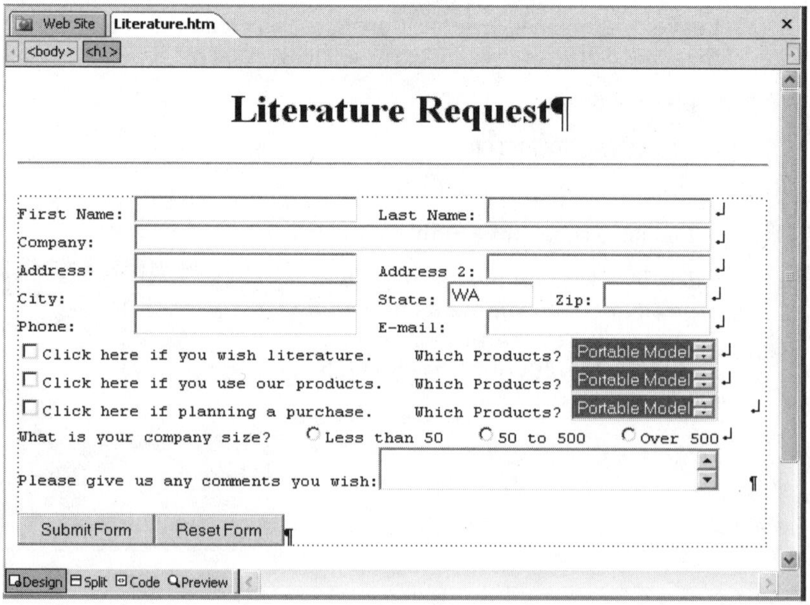

**FIGURE 8-10**
Completed form
built from scratch

29. In the File Name text box, type **_Private/Literature.txt** for the filename, and then click Options. In the File Results tab of the Saving Results dialog box, select Text Database Using Tab As A Separator for the File Format, and turn off Include Field Names. In the Saved Fields tab, under Additional Information To Save at the bottom, click Username, and in the Date Format drop-down list, select the first option after None, and then click OK twice to get back to your form. Now you are done, so save your form once more.

---

**NOTE** *Much of the spacing and wording in this form was done interactively—in other words, by use of the "try it and see what it looks like" approach. The beauty of a WYSIWYG form editor is that you can immediately see what the form you're building looks like and change it if needed.*

Part of the purpose of this "from scratch" example was to see what the Form Page Wizard does for you. You must admit it's a lot. The wizard saves you the hassle of naming, spacing, and layout, not to mention the setup of the form handling. For longer forms like this, the Form Page Wizard offers a lot of advantages.

## Handling Form Input

The next step is to look at your forms in a browser. The web called Forms should still be active on your screen and should have three pages: a blank page, a Project Team Questionnaire page built with the Form Page Wizard, and a Literature Request form built from scratch. To use the web, you'll need to put some links on the Home page to the two forms. To do that and then try out the forms in a browser, follow these steps:

1. In FrontPage, open the Home page (Default.htm) in Page view. At the top of the page, type **Forms Examples**, format it as Heading 1, and press ENTER.

2. On the next line, type **Form Page Wizard**, format it as Heading 3, select the three words you just typed, and click Link on the toolbar. In the Insert Hyperlink dialog box, select ProjForm.htm and click OK. Move the insertion point to the end of the line and press ENTER.

3. Type **Custom Form**, format it as Heading 3, select the words, and click Link on the toolbar. In the Insert Hyperlink dialog box, select Literature.htm and click OK. Your Home page should now look like Figure 8-11. Save this page, put a Home link back to the Home page at the bottom of each form, and save each of them.

4. Open your favorite browser and display the Forms web. Select the Form Page Wizard to open the Project Team Questionnaire and submit it without filling in the First Name field. Immediately an error message is displayed, as you saw earlier in the chapter.

5. Fill out the form and submit it again. Almost immediately, you'll see another benefit of FrontPage—an automatic confirmation form is created for you and is used here to verify your input, as you can see in Figure 8-12. Click the Return To The Form link at the bottom of the confirmation page.

**FIGURE 8-11**
Home page with
hyperlinks to the
forms

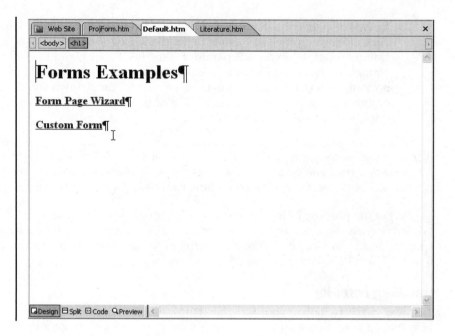

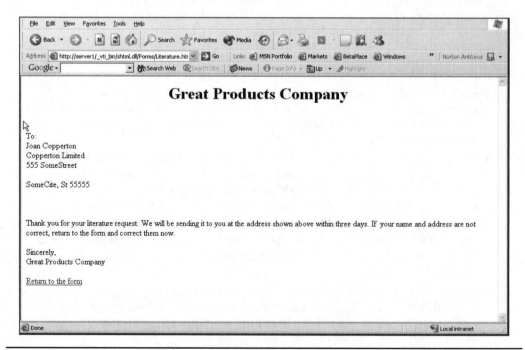

**FIGURE 8-12**     Automatic confirmation page created by FrontPage

6. Use the Home Page link to get back to the Home page, and then select Custom Form to open the Literature Request form. Fill it out and click Submit Form. Again you'll see the automatic confirmation report. Click Return To The Form, and then close your browser.

---

**NOTE** *The "beautiful" symmetry of the form in FrontPage Page view (previously shown in Figure 8-10) has not totally carried over to the browser, as shown in Figure 8-13. If you look at the form in different browsers, you'll notice different spacing. The user can also change the spacing by selecting different fonts in the browser. In a table, the form's appearance would be much improved.*

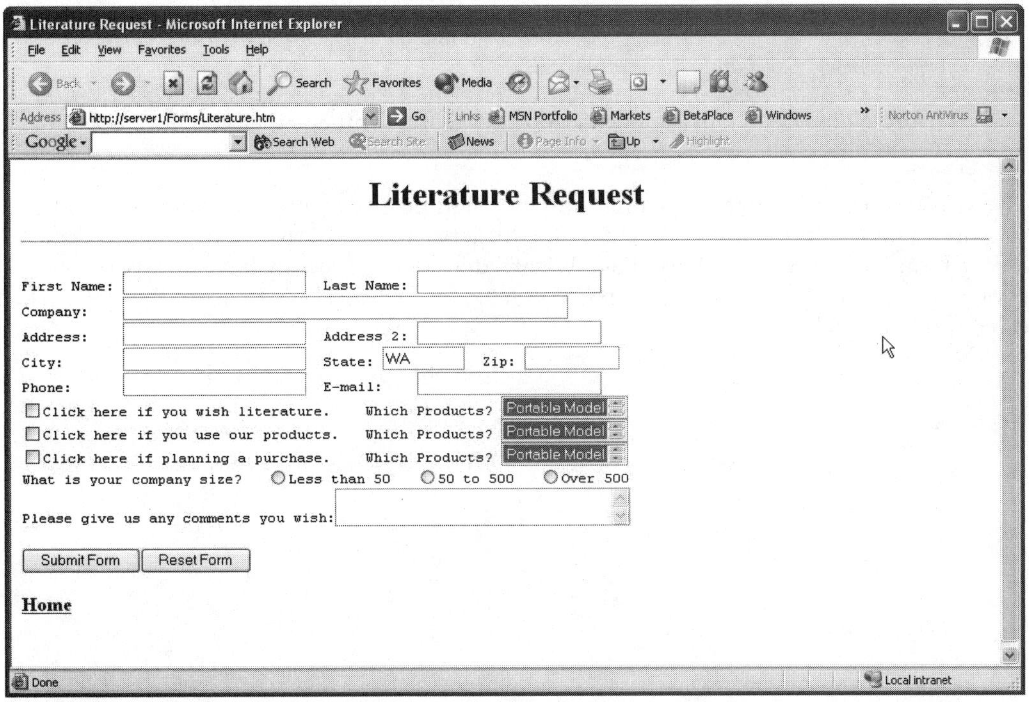

**FIGURE 8-13** The Literature Request form loses some of its symmetry in a browser.

7. Open the file that was created by the Save Results Component from the Literature Request Questionnaire. If you used the default directories when you installed FrontPage, this should be located at C:\Inetpub\Wwwroot\Forms\_Private\ Literature.txt. Use Windows Explorer or My Computer to locate it, and then double-click it to open it in Notepad. What you see should look something like this:

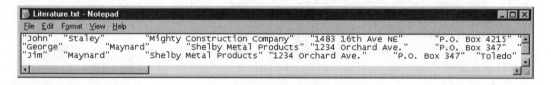

**TIP**    *You can also open the files saved from either form in a database program or in a spreadsheet, such as Microsoft Excel and Microsoft Access.*

8. Close Notepad and any applications other than FrontPage that you have open. In FrontPage, close your Forms web.

As you can see, FrontPage not only provides significant power for creating a form, but it also does a lot to get the data collected on the form back to you. Also, in the data collection area, a form created with the Form Page Wizard does not necessarily have an advantage over a properly set up custom form. In Chapter 17, you'll learn how to insert the form data directly into a database.

# CHAPTER

# Using Web Components

As you have read in earlier chapters, a web component is a way you can add automation to your web, often to provide interactivity with the user. Some components are buried in other features, such as the form-handling components that you saw in Chapter 8, while others are stand-alone tools that you can use directly. The majority of the stand-alone components are accessed through the Insert Web Component dialog box shown in Figure 9-1 and are briefly described in Chapter 2's Table 2-7.

Web components are discussed in a number of places throughout this book. Here is where to look for particular component information:

- Dynamic Effects Interactive Button and Marquee components are covered in Chapter 18.

- Web Search Current Web, Spreadsheets and Charts, Hit Counter, Photo Gallery, Included Content, Table of Contents, and Top 10 List are discussed in this chapter.

- Link Bars are described primarily in Chapter 6.

- List View, Document Library View, and Full Text searches, all of which are used with the SharePoint Team Web Site, are discussed in Chapter 22.

- Expedia, MSN, MSNBC, and Additional Components are discussed in this chapter, as is Advanced Controls Confirmation Field.

- Advanced Controls HTML component, which allows you to include HTML commands not modified by FrontPage is covered in Chapter 12. Advanced Controls Java Applet, Plug-In, ActiveX Control, Design-Time Control and Flash are discussed in Chapter 18.

There are three components that are opened from the Insert menu rather than, or in addition to, opening them from Insert Web Component dialog box. These are the Date and Time component, opened with the Date And Time option; the Comment component, opened with the Comment option; and the Link Bar component, opened with the Navigation option, which just opens the Insert Web Component dialog box at the Link Bar option. The Date and Time and Comment components are described in this chapter.

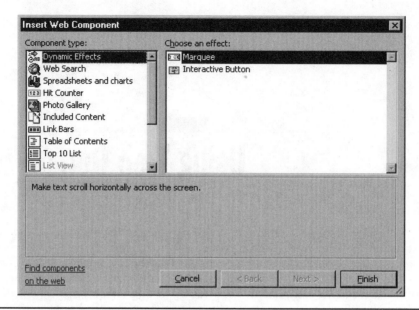

**FIGURE 9-1**    Accessing stand-alone web components

**NOTE**    *In earlier versions of FrontPage, Web Components were referred to as FrontPage Components and before that as WebBots or bots. In some cases, Microsoft still uses the term WebBots, and it appears in the code generated by FrontPage. For all practical purposes, the terms WebBots, bots, FrontPage Components, and Web Components can be used interchangeably.*

## Incorporating Components in Your Webs

See how you can incorporate Web Components in your own webs by trying out several of the stand-alone components in the following sections. Begin by opening a new One Page Web Site named Components.

### Date and Time Component

The Date and Time component inserts either the date (and optionally, the time) the page was last edited and saved, or the date and time (optional) the page was last automatically updated and saved. A page is edited when someone makes a change and resaves it, while a page is automatically updated when a page's content is changed without direct editing. For example, a page is automatically updated when a component of a Dynamic Web Template is changed, even if there were no changes to the active page. To see this, follow these next steps:

**NOTE**    *As this book goes to press, the beta version of FrontPage 2003 is not showing a difference between updated and edited time in Windows SharePoint Services (WSS or SharePoint 2), although that is the intent. This may or may not be fixed in the final released version of the software. SharePoint Team Services (STS or SharePoint 1) does show this difference.*

1. Click New Page. If the Layout Tables And Cells task pane is not already open, open the Table menu and select it. Select a layout with a header and footer and then close the task pane.

2. In the Footer, type **This page was last edited on** and leave a space. Fully open the Insert menu, and choose Date And Time to display the Date And Time dialog box.

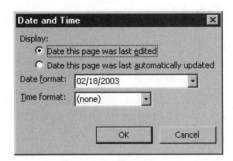

3. Open the Time Format drop-down list, and select the time format with seconds that ends with "AM TZ." (May be "PM TZ.") This means *time zone* and will automatically insert the difference between Greenwich Mean Time (GMT) and the time zone your computer is set to. For example, Pacific Standard Time (PST) is eight hours behind GMT, so the date and time are displayed like this:

> This page was last edited on 02/19/2003 07:53:02 AM -0800

4. Click OK. The date and time your page was last edited should appear, as you just saw.

5. Press SHIFT-ENTER, type **This page was last updated on** leave a space, again open the Insert menu and the Date And Time dialog box, select Date This Page Was Last Automatically Updated, choose the AM/PM TZ Time Format, and click OK.

6. Make any cells that you want, editable (see Chapter 4), and then save the page as a Dynamic Web Template with a filename of "Template.dwt."

7. Open Default.htm, open the Format menu, choose Dynamic Web Template | Attach Dynamic Web Template, and double-click Template.dwt. The template with the footer will come in to the Home Page. Click Close.

8. Save the Home page. Return to Template.dwt. In the Footer, click to the left of the top line, press ENTER, move up to the new line that is created, and type **Copyright ©** **2003, Acme Industries** (insert the copyright symbol by opening the Insert menu, choosing Symbol, double-clicking the copyright symbol, and clicking Close).

9. Save Template.dwt page, click Yes to update the page attached to the template, and click Close.

10. Reopen the Home page and click Preview in Browser and click Yes to save changes. You should see a difference between the time you edited the footer on that page and

the time you made the changes on Template.dwt, which, because of the Dynamic Web Template, updated the footer on the Home page, as you can see next:

Copyright © 2003, Acme Industries

This page was last edited on 02/19/2003 07:53:02 AM -0800
This page was last updated on 02/19/2003 07:55:41 AM -0800

11. Close your browser.

---

**NOTE** *As you have probably observed, the changes in times are not observable in FrontPage, even in Preview mode, unless you close and reopen the web. You have to look at them in a browser. This is often true of Web Components.*

## Comment Component

The Comment component allows you to insert notes that you want to be visible while the web is edited in FrontPage, but invisible or hidden while the web is being viewed in a browser. To see how that works, follow these steps:

1. On the Home page, click a cell you previously made editable, type **This is normal text.** (include the period), and press ENTER.

2. From the Insert menu, choose Comment. The Comment dialog box opens. Here you can type any text you want to see in FrontPage, but not in a browser. Type

   **This is a comment that should not be visible in a browser.**

   (include the period) and then click OK. Press ENTER twice. The comment text will appear as shown next.

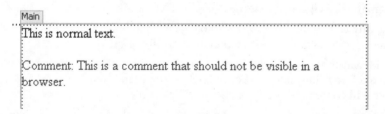

3. Save your web page, open it in a browser, and all you'll see is the normal first line.

## Web Search Component

The Web Search Current Web Component creates a form in which users can enter any text that they want to search for in the current web. After users enter such text and click the Search button, the Search Form component carries out the search and returns the locations where the text was found. This is similar to the search forms that are built into FrontPage wizards and templates and described in Chapters 3, 4, and 22. To look at how the Web Search component is used, take these steps:

1. If it isn't already open, open your Components web in FrontPage; then open the Home page in Design view.

2. Leaving at least one blank line beneath the Comment inserted previously, fully open the Insert menu and choose Web Component. In the Insert Web Component dialog box, select Web Search under Component Type. Current Web should automatically be selected under Choose A Type Of Search.

---

**NOTE**    *The Current Web search option is not available with WSS.*

---

3. Click Finish. The Search Form Properties dialog box will open, as shown next. The Search Form Properties tab displays the selections for searching, and the Search Results tab sets how the results are displayed.

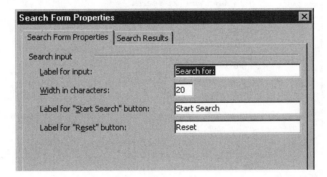

4. Accept the defaults in this dialog box and click OK. The search form will appear on the Home page.

5. Save the web page, open the page in your browser, and the search form will appear on the page.

6. In the Search For text box, type **Acme** and click Start Search. In a moment, you will get the results, which should look like Figure 9-2.

---

**NOTE**    *On a computer running Windows 2000, XP, or Server 2003, if you get the message "Service is not running" when you do a search, it is because the Indexing Service is not started. To get it started, right-click My Computer and choose Manage. Open Services And Applications and select Indexing Service. Open the Action menu and choose Start. Click Yes to begin the Indexing Service when the computer is started. Be aware that it may take a few minutes for the Indexing Service to create an index.*

---

7. Close your browser.

---

**TIP**    *If you want certain pages not to be found by the Search Form Component (like style pages, templates, and included pages), place the pages in the _private folder of the current web; that folder is not searched. If you're using FrontPage's default folder structure and the Components web, the full path to the private folder for that web is C:\Inetpub\Wwwroot\Components\_private.*

**FIGURE 9-2**
Results of doing
a search

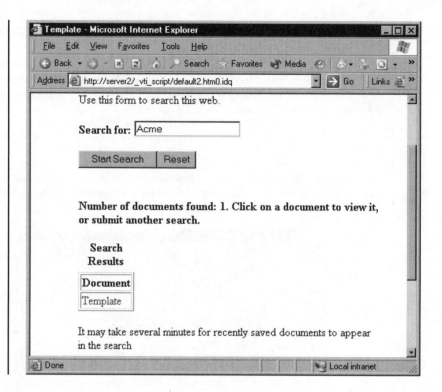

**FIGURE 9-2**
Results of doing
a search

Web Components provide a level of sophistication that you can use to build the web you want. Much of the "gee whiz" that you saw in the wizards and templates in Chapters 3 and 4 came from these tools.

## Spreadsheets and Charts Component

The Spreadsheets and Charts component allows you to add an Excel spreadsheet, chart, or pivot table to a FrontPage web and have someone viewing the web page interactively work with the spreadsheet, chart, or pivot table. In other words, while on the Internet or an intranet, the user of the web page can make a change to the spreadsheet, have it recalculate, and see the result in real time, as if they were in Excel. This is in contrast to inserting an Excel spreadsheet file or cutting and pasting from Excel to a web page in FrontPage, both of which come in as static tables without interactivity. In the following example, notice the various ways in FrontPage of using the Excel spreadsheet in Figure 9-3:

1. After creating the Excel spreadsheet in Figure 9-3 using formulas in the sixth and eighth rows (for example C6 is =(C3*$B$3)+(C4*$B$4)+(C5*$B$5) and C8 is =$B$8*C6) and the total column, save it as Commissions.xls and copy it to the Clipboard.

2. In the Components web that should be open in FrontPage, click New Page to add another page to the web. Press ENTER twice to leave several lines at the top of the page.

**FIGURE 9-3**
Excel spreadsheet brought into FrontPage

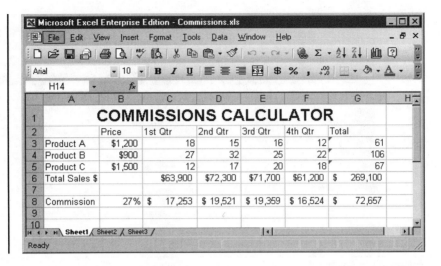

3. Move the insertion point to the second line (there should be a blank line both above and below this line). Click Paste in the Standard toolbar. The spreadsheet comes into FrontPage as an ordinary static table, like this:

| COMMISSIONS CALCULATOR | | | | | | |
|---|---|---|---|---|---|---|
| | Price | 1st Qtr | 2nd Qtr | 3rd Qtr | 4th Qtr | Total |
| Product A | $1,200 | 18 | 15 | 16 | 12 | 61 |
| Product B | $900 | 27 | 32 | 25 | 22 | 106 |
| Product C | $1,500 | 12 | 17 | 20 | 18 | 67 |
| Total Sales $ | | $63,900 | $72,300 | $71,700 | $61,200 $ | 269,100 |
| | | | | | | |
| Commission | 27% $ | 17,253 | $ 19,521 | $ 19,359 | $ 16,524 $ | 72,657 |

---

**NOTE** *Depending on how you installed Office, you may be requested to insert the Office installation CD to install the Excel converter.*

4. Move the insertion point to the blank line beneath the table that was just created, press ENTER to add another blank line, open the Insert menu, and choose Web Component.

5. In the Insert Web Component dialog box, choose Spreadsheets And Charts | Office Spreadsheet, and click Finish. A small, blank spreadsheet area looking very similar to Excel opens in FrontPage.

6. Click cell A1 to select it and then click Paste in the spreadsheet area's toolbar. The Commissions Calculator spreadsheet opens in the spreadsheet area. Right-click the spreadsheet, choose Commands And Options, click Advanced, change the Column Width to 9.57, press ENTER, and close Commands And Options. Your page should look like the one in Figure 9-4.

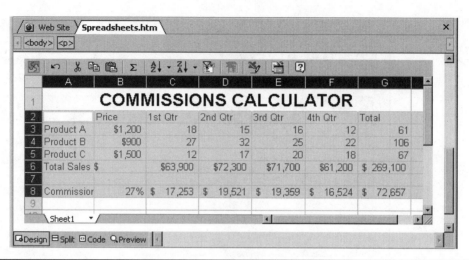

**FIGURE 9-4**   An interactive spreadsheet in FrontPage

7. Save your page, naming it **Spreadsheets**, and then open it in a browser. You should see the static spreadsheet at the top and the interactive one at the bottom. Try out its interactiveness by changing the commission rate, for example, pressing ENTER, and witnessing the changes in the calculated numbers.

8. Close your browser.

***TIP***   *You can also get an interactive spreadsheet in a web by saving an Excel spreadsheet as a web page and choosing Add Interactivity.*

## Hit Counter Component

Hit counters have lost much of their popularity because they are not very useful for compiling any real information about traffic on a web site. What they record is *page views,* the number of times a particular web page has been loaded by a browser. Advertisers are generally more interested in *visits,* the actual number of people who access a site. One visit may have a number of page views. If the visitor reloads a page, the hit counter will record it as a separate hit, which is what limits the hit counter's usefulness. Hit counters can be fun to have on a page, though, especially if you don't take them too seriously.

Adding a hit counter to a page requires only a few steps:

1. Open Template.dwt in the Components web and place the insertion point on the left end of the top line in the Footer. Press ENTER, move the insertion point up into the new line, and type **The number of times this page has been viewed is:** including a space.

2. Open the Insert menu, choose Web Component, select Hit Counter as the Component Type, choose a counter style, and click Finish. The Hit Counter Properties dialog box is displayed.

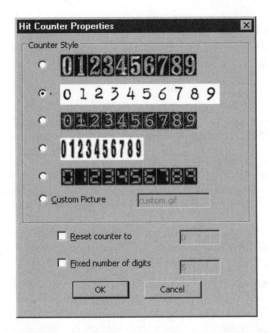

3. In the Hit Counter Properties dialog box, you can select the counter style to be displayed, the starting number for the counter ("Reset The Counter To), and a fixed number of digits to be displayed. Each digit is actually a graphic; you can use the ones included with FrontPage, download others from the Web, or create your own. The Reset Counter To option lets you set the starting number for the counter. The Fixed Number Of Digits option will always cause the number of digits selected to be displayed. If you accept the default of 5, the first visit will be 00001; when the count reaches 99999, the next visit will roll the counter over to 00000 again.

---

**TIP**    *To create your own counter graphic, create a single GIF file with the numbers 0 to 9. Each number is 10 percent of the total width of the graphic. If your graphic is 120 pixels wide, zero would be the first 10 percent of the graphic (12 pixels), one would be the next 10 percent, and so on.*

4. Select any of the Counter Style options and click the Fixed Number Of Digits check box. Accept the default of 5. Click OK. In Design view, a text placeholder is inserted.

5. Save the template page and Default.htm and view the home page in your browser. The hit counter will appear similar to this:

The number of times this page has been viewed is:  0 0 0 0 1

Copyright © 2003, Acme Industries

6. Close your browser.

## Photo Gallery Component

As you saw with Photo Gallery page template in Chapter 4, the Photo Gallery Component provides an area on which you can display one or more photographs along with their captions. An example of how to do this is described next:

1. In the Components web, open a new page in Design view. With the insertion point in the upper left, press ENTER twice to add two blank lines and then place the insertion point on the middle line so that a blank line exists both above and below it.

---

*TIP*   *As you are working on a web page, it is a good idea to always leave a blank line above and below an object that is being inserted so that you can more easily get on either side of it. You can very easily remove the blank lines if desired when you are done with the insert.*

---

2. Open the Insert menu, choose Web Component, select Photo Gallery as the component type, pick one of the gallery layouts (the vertical arrangement is used here), and click Finish. The Photo Gallery Properties dialog box will open.

3. Click Add | Pictures From Files. Select the pictures that you want from the File Open dialog box. Hold CTRL to select several pictures that are not next to each other, or hold SHIFT to select the first and last of several contiguous pictures. When you are done selecting pictures, click Open. You are returned to the Photo Gallery Properties dialog box.

4. Select each of the pictures you chose and add a caption and/or description while looking at the picture in the preview area of the dialog box, as shown in Figure 9-5.

5. When you have added the captions and descriptions that you want, click OK. Thumbnails of the pictures with their captions and descriptions will appear on your web page, like those in Figure 9-6.

6. Save the page with a name similar to "Photos.htm," including the embedded graphics files you used, and display it in a browser where you can click a thumbnail and have it displayed full-size. When you are done looking at your pictures, close your browser.

The Photo Gallery component or template provides the ability to quickly and easily display a number of pictures without using a lot of page space or download time.

## Included Content Components

The Included Content components allow you to incorporate repeated web content that you enter once in one place in the web and have it display in several locations. There are five Included Content Components that are described in the following sections:

- **Substitution component**   Defines variables such as author and URL that may be repeatedly used on the pages of a web.

- **Include Page component**   Allows you to include one page's contents on another page.

**FIGURE 9-5**
Adding captions
and descriptions
to a photo gallery

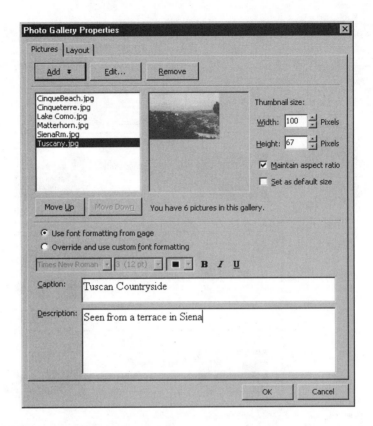

- **Scheduled Page component**   Allows you to schedule when one page's contents will be included on another page.

- **Scheduled Picture component**   Allows you to schedule when a picture will be included on a page.

- **Page Banner component**   Allows you to include either a graphic or simple text as the page's heading based on a set of circumstances.

### Substitution Component

The Substitution component replaces a value on a web page with a configuration variable when the page is viewed by the user. A *configuration variable* contains specific information about either the current page or the current web. There are four predefined configuration variables, as shown in Table 9-1, and you can define additional variables in the FrontPage Web Settings dialog box Parameters tab, which you can open from the Tools menu. You can see how this works with the following instructions:

1. With the Components web still open in FrontPage, in the Folder List right-click the Home page (Default.htm) and choose Properties. The page's Properties

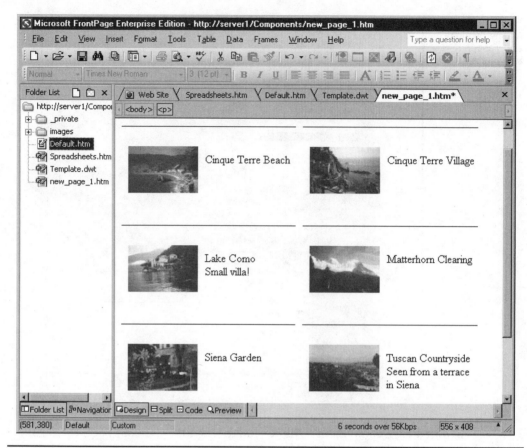

**FIGURE 9-6** A photo gallery's thumbnails and captions in FrontPage

| Variable | Description |
|----------|-------------|
| Author | Name that is in the Created By field of the FrontPage current page's Properties dialog box Summary tab (opened by right-clicking a page in the Folder List or Folders view and choosing Properties). |
| Description | Contents of the Comments scrolling text box of the FrontPage current page's Properties dialog box Summary tab. |
| Modified By | Name of the person who most recently changed the page, contained in the Modified By field of the FrontPage current page's Properties dialog box Summary tab. |
| Page URL | Filename in the Location field of the FrontPage current page's Properties dialog box General tab. |

**TABLE 9-1** Configuration Variables

dialog box will open with the General tab showing, the top of which is shown here:

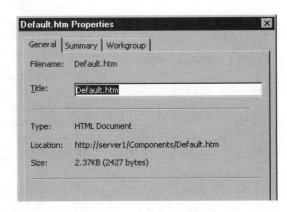

2. If it isn't already open, click the General tab of the page's Properties dialog box so you can see the Location field, this is also the URL. Click the Summary tab to see the Created By and Modified By fields and to both see and change the Comments scrolling text box.

3. In the Comments scrolling text box, type **This is a great web!**, click Apply, and then click OK to close the Properties dialog box.

4. Open Template.dwt, on a new line inserted immediately above the line preceding the Hit Counter, type **This page was last modified by**, insert a space, open the Insert menu, choose Web Component, select Included Content, and double-click Substitution. The Substitution Properties dialog box will open.

5. Click the down arrow to see the list of variables shown next. Click Modified By and then OK. You'll see the name of the person who last modified the page appear on the page.

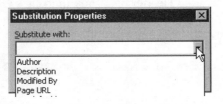

6. Insert a space and then type **who left these comments:**, insert a space, reopen the Substitution Properties dialog box, choose Description, and click OK.

7. Save the template, click Yes to update the attached pages, click Close, save the Home page, and then click Preview In Browser. The comments you left should appear, as you can see next.

This page was last modified by SERVER1\Administrator who left these comments: This is a great web!

8. Close your browser.

### Include and Scheduled Include Page Components

The Include Page component allows you to include one web page on another. For example, if you wanted a section with identical contents on every page, you could put the contents on a web page and then include that page on all others in the web. Future changes to the contents of that page will then automatically appear on all the pages that include the page. The Scheduled Include Page component allows you to include one page on another for a given period. When the time expires, that page is no longer included.

---

**NOTE** *Include Page has been largely replaced with Dynamic Web Templates, which provides all the Include Page features plus improved flexibility and control.*

To try Include Page, follow these steps:

1. With the Home page of the Components web open in FrontPage, click New Page on the toolbar to create a new page. At the top of the page, type

   **This is a page heading; it should be on all pages.**

   (include the period) and format it as Heading 2.

2. Save this page with a filename of Inchead.htm.

3. Open another page that does not have the Dynamic Web Template attached, like the Spreadsheets page, place the insertion point at the top of the page, open the Insert menu, choose Web Component, select Included Content, and double-click Page to open the Include Page Properties dialog box.

4. Click Browse to get a list of pages in the current web.

5. Double-click the Included Header page, and then click OK to return to the web page. You should see the heading appear on this page and the WebBot icon appear when you move the mouse pointer over it, as shown next:

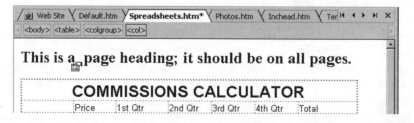

The real beauty of using the Include Page component is that not only are you saved from retyping or copying the heading onto each page, but also changes you make need only be typed once. This is of course also true with Dynamic Web Templates.

The Scheduled Include Page component works like the Include Page component, except that it has a start and stop date and time, as will be demonstrated next, with the Scheduled Picture component.

### Scheduled Picture Component

The Scheduled Picture component, which is not available with WSS, allows you to display a picture on a page for a fixed period. When the time expires, the picture disappears. To see how this works, take these steps:

1. On the Home page of the Components web, move the insertion point to the line following the Search form and press ENTER to create a blank line after the Search form.

2. Open the Insert menu and choose Picture | Clip Art. In the Clip Art task pane, type **lion** and click Go. Double-click the lion you want to use. Close the task pane and, if necessary, drag the lower-right-corner sizing handle up to the left to reduce the size to about one-inch square.

3. Save the page and, in the process, save the embedded file (the lion) with the name Lion.gif. When the files are saved, select the lion on the Home page and delete it. Once more save the page. Leave the insertion point on the second line below the Search form.

4. Open the Insert menu, choose Web Component, select Included Content, and double-click Picture Based On Schedule. In the Scheduled Picture Properties dialog box, shown in Figure 9-7, click the first Browse to open the Picture dialog box. In the Picture dialog box, select Lion.gif, and click OK.

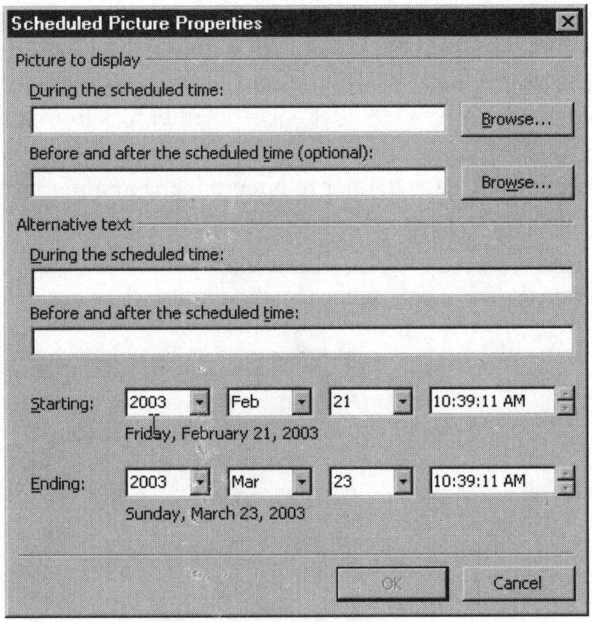

**FIGURE 9-7**
Scheduling when a picture will be displayed

5. In the Alternative Text During The Scheduled Time, type **Lion**. Set the ending time for a couple of minutes past the current time in the Ending date and time spinner. (The default is to display the picture for one month.) Click OK. You should see the picture appear.

6. Save your web page and open your browser and the Components web. If necessary, click the Refresh button in the Internet Explorer Standard toolbar or the Reload button in the Netscape Navigator Link bar.

7. After the time has expired, close your browser, go back to FrontPage Design view displaying the Components web Home page and click Refresh on the toolbar or select Refresh from the View menu.

8. The lion graphic will be replaced with the message "[Expired Scheduled Picture]." If you resave the page and return to your browser and refresh it, the graphic will also disappear from there.

9. Close your browser.

### Page Banner Component

The Page Banner component is similar to the Include Page component; it allows you to select a picture or text to use as a banner at the top of a web page. Banners are usually larger graphics that identify the site or the page contents.

If the web page does not use a theme or a shared border, then the page title is inserted, and choosing Picture in the Page Banner Properties dialog box has no effect. If a theme has been applied, the theme's banner picture is inserted when Picture is selected.

1. Open a new page. Save the page with the name Banner.htm. Click the Web Site tab and then Navigation in the View bar at the bottom of the pane. Drag your Banner.htm from the Folder List to under your Default.htm in Navigation view.

2. Slowly click twice (don't double-click) on the title of Banner.htm and type **Page Banner** and press ENTER. Reopen Banner.htm in Design view.

3. Open the Insert menu, choose Web Component, select Included Content, and double-click Page Banner to open the Page Banner Properties dialog box, shown next.

---

**TIP**    *You can also add a page banner by clicking Insert | Page Banner to get the same dialog box.*

4. The Page Banner text box should contain the title you gave the page above. Click OK. The page banner text will appear on the page.

5. Save your work, preview it in a browser, and, when done, close both the browser and the Components web.

## Table of Contents Components

FrontPage provides two ways of generating a table of contents: one based on the links that are contained in the web and one based on categories that you establish. See how both of these work in the next two sections.

### Contents Based on Links

The Table of Contents component creates and maintains a table of contents for a web with links to all the pages in the web. Whenever the web's contents are changed and resaved, the table of contents is updated. The Table of Contents co/mponent builds the structure of the table of contents based on the links that are on each page. For example, if the home page has three pages directly linked to it and the second page has two other pages linked to it, the structure shown in Figure 9-8 would be built.

---

**NOTE**   *This component is not available with WSS.*

---

If there are pages in the web that are not linked to other pages, they are listed at the end of the table of contents.

Chapters 3 and 4 discuss (and have several examples of) the Table of Contents component as used in web and page wizards and templates. See the "Using the Corporate Presence Wizard" section in Chapter 3 and the "Table of Contents Template" section in Chapter 4.

**FIGURE 9-8**
The web structure for the sample table of contents

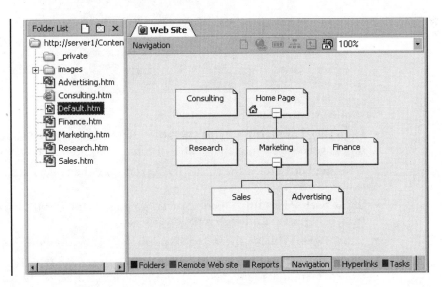

---

**NOTE** *When you add the Table of Contents component to a page, you do not see the full table of contents. It is only when you open the page in a browser that the full table is displayed.*

Look at how a table of contents based on links is constructed from scratch. With nothing open in FrontPage, you can do that with these steps:

1. Click the down arrow next to New on the toolbar and choose Web Site. Select One Page Web Site, name it Contents, and click OK.

2. Open Navigation view and click New Page in the Navigation pane three times to place three new pages under the Home page. Then select New Page 2 and click New Page twice more to place two pages under that page. Finally, click New Page again and drag that page up next to the Home page; this will give you the structure that you saw in Figure 9-8.

3. Rename the files, by selecting and changing the filename in the Folder List, and the title, by selecting and changing the name in the Navigation pane, to the names shown in Figure 9-8 (if necessary, click Refresh on the right end of the Standard toolbar to get the files' names to appear).

4. Double-click the Home Page to open it. Open the Insert menu, choose Web Component, select Table Of Contents, and double-click For This Web Site. The Table Of Contents Properties dialog box will open, as shown here:

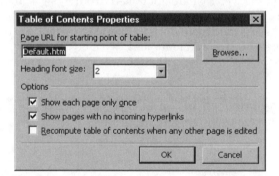

5. The options in this dialog box are as follows:

   - **Page URL For Starting Point Of Table**  Should be the home page of the web, unless you want a subsidiary table of contents for a section of a web.

   - **Heading Font Size**  The size of the top entry in the table. Each subsidiary entry is one size smaller.

   - **Show Each Page Only Once**  Prevents a page that has links from several pages from being listed under each page.

   - **Show Pages With No Incoming Hyperlinks**  Allows unlinked pages to be listed.

   - **Recompute Table Of Contents When Any Other Page Is Edited**  Forces the table to be rebuilt if any page in the web is changed. Since this can take a significant amount of time, you may not want to do this. A table of contents is also rebuilt every time the page it is on is saved, which should normally be adequate.

*TIP*   *Using the Table of Contents component can be a good way to initially establish a link from the home page to all the other pages in the web.*

6. Accept the default entries in the Table Of Contents Properties dialog box and click OK. The initial table of contents entries will appear on the page like this:

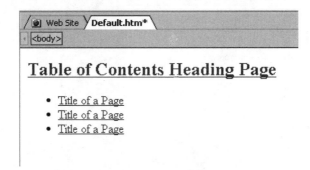

7. Save the page and then view it in a browser. As you can see next, a full table of contents is generated providing links to all the other pages in the hierarchical structure that you created:

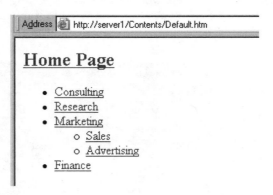

8. Close your browser.

### Contents Based on Page Categories

The Page Category component provides an automated method for creating hyperlinks to web pages based on the category that has been assigned to each of the pages. The Page Category component then creates the links to the page based on the assigned category. When a page is added or removed from a category, the hyperlink is also updated. The first step is to create Master Categories for your web, discussed next.

1. In the Contents web, right-click the Home page (Default.htm) in the Folder List and choose Properties. In the Properties dialog box that opens, select the Workgroup tab, shown in Figure 9-9.

2. Click the Categories button to open the Master Category List dialog box, shown next:

3. In the New Category text box, type **Internal Functions** and click Add.

4. Delete any text in the single-line text box, type **External Functions**, and click Add. Delete the other functions except Miscellaneous by selecting them and clicking Remove, then clicking OK and Yes that you want to remove the categories.

**FIGURE 9-9**
Assigning categories to a page

The Master Categories you created will be displayed in the Available Categories list box on the Workgroup tab of the current page's Properties dialog box.

5. Click the Internal Functions check box to select it and then click OK.

6. In the Folder List, right-click first Research.htm and then Finance.htm; for each, choose Properties | Workgroup tab, click the Internal Functions check box to select it, and then click OK.

7. Similarly, right-click first Marketing.htm and then Consulting.htm; for each, choose Properties | Workgroup tab, click the External Functions check box to select it, and then click OK.

8. Open the Home Page. Add two blank lines below the table of contents (if you are using STS), type **Internal Functions:** (include the colon), format it as Heading 3, and press ENTER.

9. Open the Insert menu, choose Web Component, select Table Of Contents, and double-click Based On Page Category. The Categories Properties dialog box, shown here, is opened:

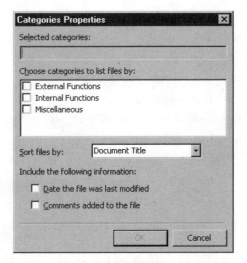

10. The Categories Properties dialog box displays the Master Categories you created previously and several options for how the hyperlinks will be displayed. Using the Sort Files By drop-down list, you can choose to display the hyperlinks sorted by either the date the page was last modified or by the document (page) title. You can also include the date the page was last modified and/or any comments for the page (comments are added using the Summary tab of the current page's Properties dialog box).

11. Click the Internal Functions category and the Date The File Was Last Modified check boxes to select them. Accept the other defaults and click OK.

12. Press ENTER, type **External Functions:** (include the colon), format it as Heading 3, and press ENTER. Open the Insert menu, choose Web Component, select Table Of

Contents, and double-click Based On Page Category. The Categories Properties dialog box opens.

13. Click the External Functions category and the Date The File Was Last Modified check boxes to select them. Accept the other defaults and click OK.

14. Save the page and then open the Contents web Home page in your browser. Hyperlinks, showing the page title of the web's main pages and the date they were last modified, are displayed in their respective categories, as shown in Figure 9-10.

15. Close your browser and the Contents web.

---

**NOTE**   *There is no reason that a page cannot have more than one category checked and appear in more than one list.*

## Top 10 List Components

The Top 10 List components provide seven pieces of information that you can gather about visits to the current web site. These are the top 10:

- Visited pages in the current web site
- Referring domains for the current web site
- Referring URLs for the current web site
- Search strings used to find the current web site
- Visiting users for the current web site
- Operating system used to view the current web site
- Browser used to view the current web site

**FIGURE 9-10**
Pages grouped by their category assignment

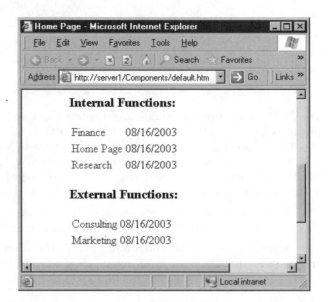

To use any or all of these components, place them on a page of the web as described in the next set of steps.

---

**NOTE**  *To keep the usage statistics to yourself, the page that contains them should probably not be referred to on any other page, and you will have to know the full URL to open the page.*

1. Open the Components web that you were using earlier in the chapter, create a new page named **Stats**, and open it in Design view. Place the insertion point at the upper-left corner of the page, press ENTER twice, and then move the insertion point up one line.

2. Open the Insert menu, choose Web Component, select Top 10 List, and double-click Visited Pages. The Top 10 List Properties dialog box will open, as you can see here:

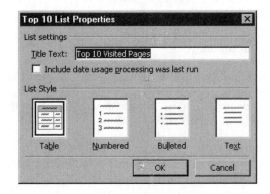

3. Click Include Date Usage Processing Was Last Run and click OK to accept the other defaults. A table will appear with a mockup of the pages to be reported when viewed in a browser.

4. Save the page and view it in a browser. If your server logs have been recently updated, you will see statistics about page visits. If you don't initially see anything, come back in a couple of days and look for it.

5. Close your browser and the Stats page but leave the Components web open.

---

**NOTE**  *The Top 10 components require that the FrontPage 2002 Server Extensions or Windows SharePoint Services be installed on an IIS 5 or 6 server since the components are simply displaying information in the IIS server logs. By default, server logs are only updated weekly. If you have administrative authority over your server, you can change the Usage Analysis settings by clicking Start | Administrative Tools | Microsoft SharePoint Administrator, selecting Administration for the default web site, clicking Go To Site Administration For* http://servername, *and scrolling down and clicking Change Usage Analysis Settings.*

---

**NOTE**  *The Top 10 List works in both SharePoint 1 and 2, but in SharePoint 2 you need to open Microsoft SharePoint Administrator in the first page click Extend; things then appear correctly.*

## Microsoft Site Components

The Microsoft site components are items from various Microsoft web sites that you can include on your site.

- **Expedia Link To A Map** Provides a link to Expedia and the ability to use a dynamic map pointed at a specific location.
- **Expedia Static Map** Displays a static map of a specific location.
- **MSN Stock Quote** Provides the ability to look up a stock quote through MSN's MoneyCentral.
- **MSN Web Search** Provides the ability to search the Internet using MSN's search engine.
- **MSNBC Weather Forecast** Provides a weather forecast from MSNBC on your web page.
- **MSNBC Headlines** Displays headlines in five areas: business, living and travel, news, sports, and technology.

There may be additional MSN, MSNBC, and other components in the future. These components are very powerful and can really make the difference between an ordinary web site and one that shouts for attention. Look at how a couple of these components are implemented with the following instructions:

1. Open the Components web's Home page. Place the insertion point on the left end of "This is normal text," press ENTER three times, and move the insertion point up one line so there is a blank line above and below it.

2. Open the Insert menu, choose Web Component, select MSN Components, and double-click Search The Web With MSN. A small search form will appear on the page. You will be prompted to connect to the Internet if you are not connected already. Save the page and view it in a browser. The search form in a browser should look like this:

3. Enter some word in the search form (we entered "Autos") and click Search. The MSN Search page will open with the results of your search, as you can see in Figure 9-11.

4. Close your browser and return to the Components Home page in FrontPage. Below the MSN search form, add the blank lines and move the insertion point so there is a blank line separating it from the search form and another below it.

5. Open the Insert menu, choose Web Component, select MSNBC Components, and double-click a Weather Forecast From MSNBC. The Weather Forecast From MSNBC Properties dialog box will open, asking you for the name of a city or a U.S. ZIP code.

6. Enter a city name or ZIP code and click Next. The city or ZIP code will be confirmed. Click Finish. A sample weather forecast will appear in FrontPage. Save the page and view it in a browser. The current weather forecast will look like this:

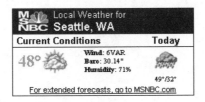

7. Close your browser and the Components web.

## Confirmation Field Component

The Confirmation Field component allows you to build a confirmation page that echoes the contents of a web form that has been submitted. Such a page would replace the automatic confirmation form you saw in Chapter 8 (Figure 8-12). To build a confirmation page for your Literature Request form:

1. In FrontPage, open the Forms web you created in Chapter 8, and then open the Literature Request form (Literature.htm).

2. Create and open a new page. On the new page, create a brief confirmation letter. Begin by putting a heading on the page, such as

   **Great Products Company**

   formatting it as Heading 1, centering it, and then pressing ENTER.

3. Click Align Left on the toolbar; then at the left margin, type **To:** and press SHIFT-ENTER.

4. Open the Insert menu, choose Web Component, select Advanced Controls, and double-click Confirmation Field. In the Confirmation Field Properties dialog box, type **First**, as shown next, and then click OK:

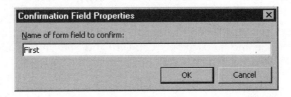

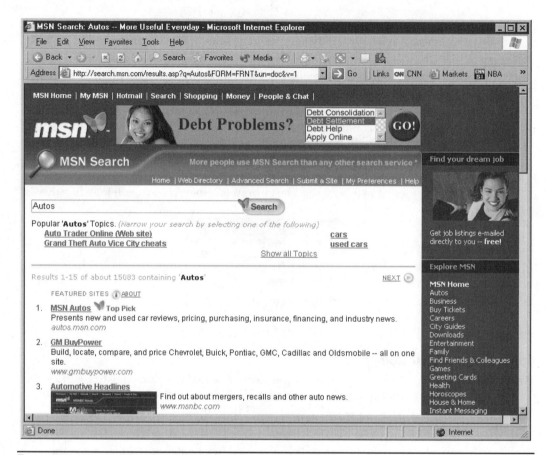

**FIGURE 9-11**   Results of a web search from your page

5. Leave a space, again open the Confirmation Field Properties dialog box, type **Last**, click OK, and press SHIFT-ENTER for a new line.

**NOTE**   *There is no easy way to get a list of field names—you need to either remember them, write them down as you are creating a form, or open the Properties dialog box for each field. Suggestions have been made to Microsoft that a Browse feature be added to the Confirmation Field Properties dialog box.*

6. Repeat step 4 to enter confirmation fields for **Company**, **Address1**, and **Address2** all on separate lines ending with SHIFT-ENTER.

7. Again repeat step 4 to enter confirmation fields for **City**, **State**, and **Zip** all on one line, with a comma and a space between *City* and *State*, and a space between *State* and *Zip*.

8. Enter two blank lines and type the body and ending of the letter, something similar to that shown in Figure 9-12. Follow this with a link that says **Return to the form** and points to the Literature Request form (Literature.htm). When you are done, save the confirmation letter with a page title of **Literature Request Confirmation** and a filename of **Litreqcf.htm**.

9. Open the Literature Request form, right-click the form inside the dotted line, choose Form Properties, click Options, and then click the Confirmation Page tab. Click the first Browse and double-click Literature Request Confirmation. Litreqcf.htm should appear in the text box. Click OK twice. Save the Literature Request form.

10. In your browser, open the Forms web (Default.htm), click Custom Form, fill out the form, click Submit Form, and you'll see a confirmation letter similar to the one shown in Figure 9-13.

11. Close your browser and your Forms web.

For more on confirmation forms, see Chapter 4.

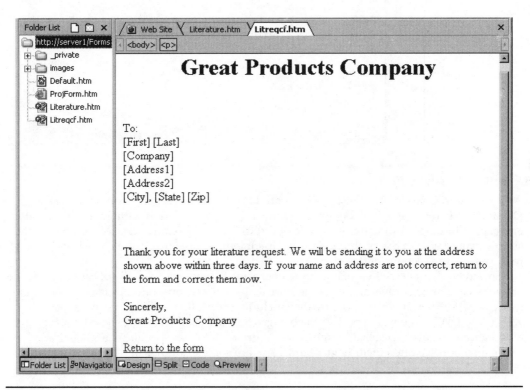

**FIGURE 9-12**    Custom confirmation letter in FrontPage

FIGURE 9-13
Filled out
confirmation page
in a browser

## Using Shared Borders

As you read in Chapter 3 and elsewhere, shared borders have largely been replaced by Dynamic Web Templates (DWTs), which perform a similar function with greater flexibility and capability, and do so without the use of FrontPage server extensions. Nevertheless, the simplicity and ease of use of shared borders is sometimes useful and so its use is described in the remaining sections of this chapter.

Shared borders are sections of a web page set aside for content that will appear on each page of your web. Shared borders are *borders* because they are at the top, bottom, left, or (rarely) right side of a page. They are *shared* because they include content that is shared by every page in a web. (With DWTs, you must specify which pages they are used on, while shared borders are automatically on every page, although you can turn them off on specific pages.)

Shared borders often include link bars. Here are some examples of other useful shared borders:

- A top shared border with page titles
- A bottom shared border with copyright information, site contact information, and other text or images you want to appear on the bottom of every page in your site
- A left shared border with general information you want to place in every page in your site, such as links

***TIP***   *Shared borders are rarely placed on the right side of web pages because your users may not see them. Depending on the size and resolution of the users' screen, and the size of their browser window, the right side of your web pages may not be visible to them unless they use the horizontal scroll bar to see it. Since shared borders often include link bars, you will normally want the shared border to be visible as soon as your web page downloads.*

***NOTE***   *You cannot insert link bars in shared borders unless you use the Navigation view to assign how the pages in your web relate to each other.*

## Assigning Shared Borders to a FrontPage Web

Global changes can affect the layout of shared borders in every page. Use the following steps to see how this works (shared borders are deactivated by default, so the first step must be to activate them):

1. Start FrontPage if it is not already running, open Tools | Page Options, and then click the Authoring tab. Click Shared Borders under FrontPage And SharePoint Technologies. Click OK.

2. Using the Web Site Templates dialog box, create a One Page Web Site with a name similar to **Shared**, and then select Shared Borders from the Format menu. (You may have to fully extend the menu.) The Shared Borders dialog box will open.

3. Use the Top, Left, Right, and Bottom check boxes in the Shared Borders dialog box to select or turn off any of the four borders; use the three Include Navigation Buttons check boxes to add navigation buttons to the borders. If All Pages is selected, the borders you select will be applied to or removed from every page in your web by default, although you can turn them off or change them for specific pages. Our choices are shown in Figure 9-14.

**FIGURE 9-14**
Specifying where you want shared borders

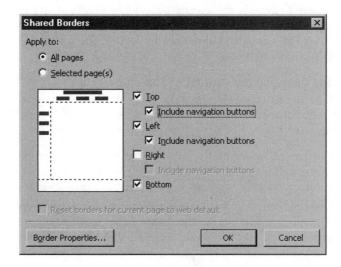

4. When you have chosen which shared borders to add or remove, click OK. The shared borders are applied immediately to the pages in your web that do not have specific shared borders.

---

**NOTE**   *In both WSS and STS, a borders folder is added to the web, though it takes a Refresh to get it to show in STS.*

## Assigning Shared Borders to a Web Page

Shared borders can be edited and customized for individual web pages. For example, you can apply a bottom shared border to some but not all pages in your web:

1. Open a new page in Page view on which you will customize the shared borders.

2. Open the Format menu and select Shared Borders (you may have to extend the menu).

3. Choose the Current Page option in the Shared Borders dialog box, and define additional shared borders or remove current shared borders by selecting or clearing the applicable check boxes.

After you create a new shared border for a page, the content of that shared border is available to other pages.

## Changing Shared Borders

You can define a maximum of four shared borders for a FrontPage web. You can elect to apply or not apply different borders to different pages, but you can make only limited changes to shared borders on individual pages. If you want to place different content on each web page (and you will), do so independently of shared borders. The purpose of shared borders is to place the same content on multiple pages.

Think of shared borders as being similar to headers and footers in printed documents. They are there to include content that you want to repeat on each page. Therefore, when you change a shared border in one page, for the most part you change that shared border on every page to which the shared border is applied. Both the content and the properties of shared borders can be changed.

### Adding and Changing the Content of Shared Borders

When you add shared borders to a site, place-holding text appears on the pages showing you where the shared borders content goes, as shown in Figure 9-15. There are three types of place holders, each of which is handled in a different manner:

- The page title is automatically placed in the top shared border and is changed by changing the title (not the filename) in Navigation view. You can delete the placeholder for the page title to remove it, BUT removing on one page, removes it on all pages.

- The navigation or link bars in the top or side borders are changed in two ways. The relationship among the pages that is established in the Navigation view is automatically reflected in the link bar, where applicable. Also, in all cases you can

FIGURE 9-15
Standard
placer-holder text
in shared borders

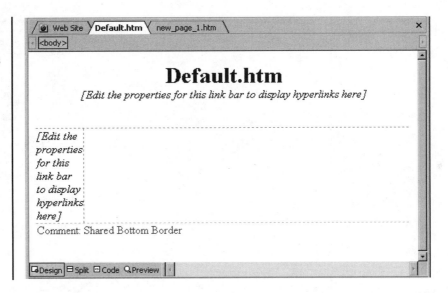

right-click the link bar placeholder, choose Link Bar Properties, and identify the hyperlinks you want to add.

- Comments, as shown in the bottom border are simply replaced with any desired text you want on all pages.

See how you can work with shared borders with the following steps:

1. Open the Navigation view by clicking the Web Site tab and clicking Navigation in the View bar at the bottom. Create or drag web pages onto the Navigation pane to create the structure you want reflected in the link bar. Change the title of a page by slowly clicking twice (don't double-click) on the page title in the Navigation pane and then typing the title you want to use.

2. Change the links on a navigation bar in Design view by right-clicking the placeholder, choosing Link Bar Properties, and selecting the links that are appropriate.

3. Select the comment in the Bottom shared border to edit it. Type **Copyright © 2004, A Company, Inc.** (You can add a copyright symbol after the word "Copyright" by opening the Insert menu, choosing Symbol, locating and double-clicking the copyright symbol, and clicking Close.)

4. Click outside the shared border when you are done entering or editing its contents.

After you edit a shared border for a particular page, the shared border content will appear on all other pages. In Figure 9-16, the page title, the link bar on the left, and the bottom-shared border has been set for a page in a web. The link bar in the top shared border still shows a placeholder, but that will disappear when viewed in a browser (not in Preview view, though).

FIGURE 9-16
Content in shared
borders

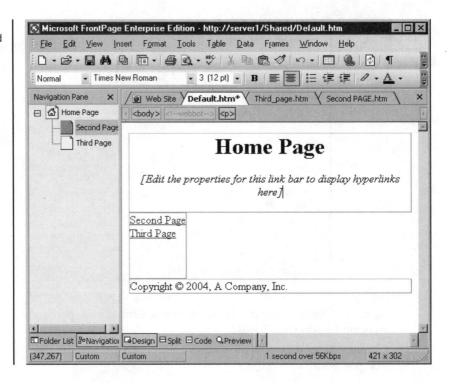

FIGURE 9-16
Content in shared
borders

### Changing the Properties of Shared Borders

Besides the content of a shared border, you can also change the border properties that include either or both the background color and/or a background picture. You can do this by right-clicking any shared border and choosing Shared Border Properties, or by choosing Border Properties in the Shared Borders dialog box you saw in Figure 9-14. This opens the Border Properties dialog box, like this:

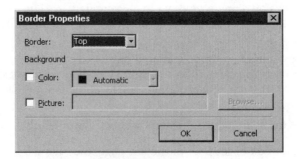

In the Border Properties dialog box, you can choose the border you want to change and the color and/or picture you want contained in that border.

Shared borders are easy to use and still have a place in web design when you want simple, repeated content on every page.

# Advanced Formatting Techniques

In the preceding chapters, you have seen many ways to lay out, format, and enhance a web page. These are, for the most part, classic techniques that have been available to web authors for some time. FrontPage additionally brings you several advanced techniques for doing this. The purpose of this chapter is to cover these advanced techniques, including:

- Customizing existing themes
- Creating and using style sheets
- Positioning and wrapping text around objects
- Easily choosing web-safe colors
- Creating graphics within FrontPage
- Customizing the look of Tables

## Customizing Existing Themes

If you have used the themes that are available in FrontPage and looked at the many alternatives, you may have come to the conclusion that while there are many neat elements in a number of the themes, no one theme is exactly the way you would like it to be. You can solve this by customizing one of the existing themes to add your own logo; change the styles, colors, and graphics used; and save the theme with your name. In this way, you create your own theme.

### Modifying a Theme

You begin the process of creating a customized theme by picking an existing theme, preferably one that is close to what you want, and opening it for modification.

1. With FrontPage open in Page and then Design view (you don't need to have a web open), open a new page if one isn't already, and then select Format | Theme. The Theme pane will appear as shown in Figure 10-1.

**FIGURE 10-1**
Selecting an
existing theme
to modify

2. Click each of the themes in the list and look at them with and without their Vivid
   Colors, Active Graphics, and Background Picture options.

3. Select the accompanying options (Vivid Colors, Active Graphics, and/or Background
   Graphics) and then right-click a theme that comes closest to the theme you want to
   create, open the drop-down menu on the theme's right, and choose Customize.

The Customize Theme dialog box opens, as you can see in Figure 10-2. This allows you
to modify the colors, graphics, and text styles in the selected theme and then save the
resulting theme with a new name. You'll see how to change each of these elements in the
next several sections.

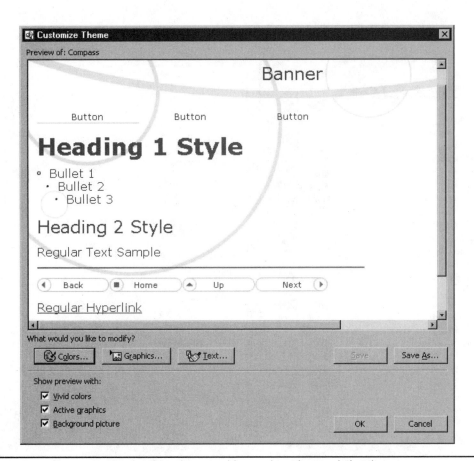

**FIGURE 10-2**    You can customize the colors, graphics, and text in an existing theme.

## Changing the Colors in a Theme

The colors in a theme control the coloration of all parts of a web page including the background, headings, hyperlinks, banner text, and table borders. You can set these in the Customize Theme dialog box with the following steps:

1. Click Colors. A different Customize Theme dialog box opens, as shown in Figure 10-3. It provides three ways to set the colors used in a theme: ready-made color schemes, a color wheel, and custom color selection.

2. With the Color Schemes tab selected, click a number of the ready-made schemes and scroll the Preview Of Theme preview box to see how the colors are applied.

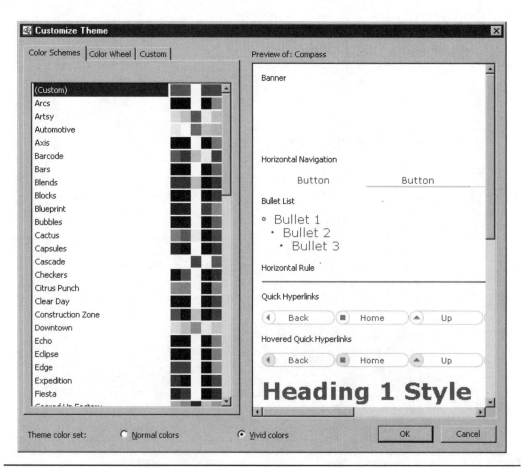

**FIGURE 10-3**   Choosing or creating a custom color scheme

3. Click the Color Wheel tab. Drag the small circle in the color wheel to see how the color schemes change. Also, change the Brightness slider and observe its effects.

4. Click the Custom tab. Click the down arrow under Item and observe the list of items on a web page for which you can set a particular color, as shown here:

---

***TIP*** *You can combine all three color selection methods by first choosing color scheme, then adjusting the colors with the color wheel, and finally changing a few selected items in the Custom tab.*

5. Select several of the page items one at a time—say, Background, Heading 1 and 2, and Banner Text—and choose a color to use for each.

6. Click the Color Schemes tab and you will see a new (Custom) scheme with the colors you chose.

---

***NOTE*** *As in the original Customize Theme dialog box, you can select normal or vivid colors at the bottom of the dialog box.*

7. Click OK to close the color Customize Theme dialog box.

## Replacing the Graphics in a Theme

The graphics that can be used on a page and set in a theme include the background, the banner, bullets, and buttons. You can change any or all of these with the following steps:

1. Click Graphics. A third version of the Customize Theme dialog box opens. This time it allows you to change the picture and font used for a particular item on the page, as you can see in Figure 10-4.

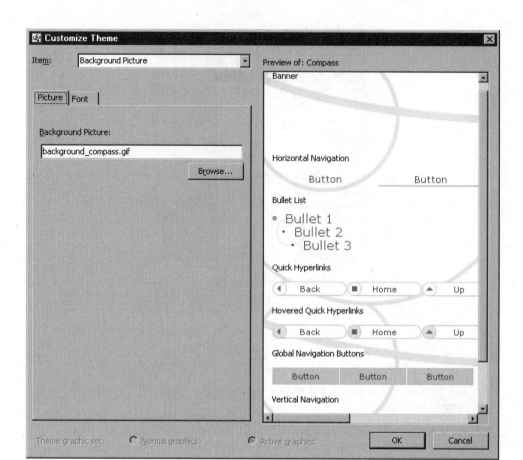

**FIGURE 10-4**    Choosing the pictures and fonts to be used in a theme

2. Open the Item drop-down list to see the list that can be changed, like this:

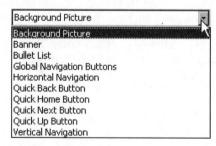

3. Select several items from the drop-down list at the top and look at what you can select a picture for. In some cases—for example, Horizontal Navigation—there are three elements that need pictures (the regular button, the selected button, and the button that is hovered over).

4. Click Browse and find an alternative graphic to use for the selected item.

5. When you have selected a graphic to use for an item, click the Font tab. Here you can choose from a variety of fonts and select the style, size, and alignment you want to use. Graphics that don't have text associated with them, such as Background Picture, have a grayed out Font tab.

6. After the graphics and fonts are the way you want them for all the items you are using on the page, click OK to return to the original Customize Theme dialog box.

## Applying Different Text Styles to a Theme

As you just saw, the Graphics button allows you to set the fonts, sizes, and font styles (bold, italic) to be used for text on the graphic items in a theme such as banners and buttons. The Text button allows you to do the same tasks for normal text (called "Body") and headings on a web page. You can also create or modify a style sheet related to the theme. Explore theme text modification with these steps:

1. Click Text. The fourth version of the Customize Theme dialog box will open. In this case, you can choose Body or one of the heading types and then select the font you want to use for that particular type of text.

2. Open the Item drop-down list. You can see that you have six levels of headings and Body to choose from:

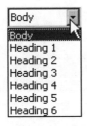

**NOTE**   *Body text refers to regular text as well as hyperlinks (regular, followed, and active).*

3. With Body selected, look at the Regular Text Sample in the Preview pane, and then click several fonts you might like to see how the text looks in the sample area. Once you find a family, look at the weights that are available and decide how you are going to assign those weights to the body and heading items. For example, here are the assignments we made, as shown in Figure 10-5:

   • Heading 1: Arial Black

   • Heading 2: Arial Unicode MS

   • Heading 3: Arial

   • Heading 4: Arial Narrow

   • Heading 5: Arial Narrow

   • Heading 6: Arial Narrow

   • Body (Regular Text): Bookman Old Style

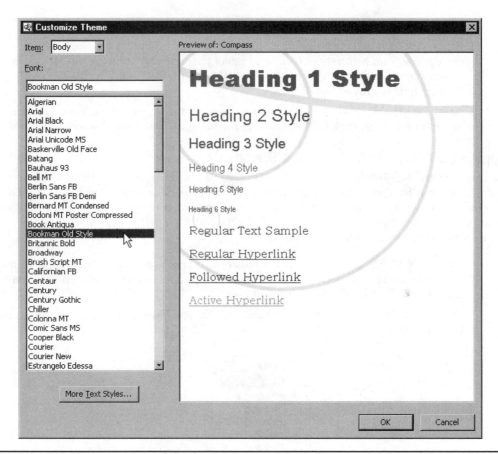

**FIGURE 10-5**     Assigning fonts to types of text

**NOTE**   *Your fonts may be different than those shown here.*

4. Select a text item (Body or one of the headings) and click a font. Repeat this for all the text items.

5. When you have completed selecting the font you want to use for all of the text items, click More Text Styles. The Style dialog box will open, like the one in Figure 10-6.

6. With User-Defined Styles selected in the List drop-down box, click Body in the Styles list. A description of that style will appear along with examples of it.

7. Click Modify to open the Modify Style dialog box and then click Format | Font. Here, choose the font style, size, color, and effects that are to be used for the selected style. When you set the characteristics of the style, click OK twice.

**NOTE**   *The next section, "Creating and Using Style Sheets," will describe style sheets and how to create them and use them in more detail.*

**FIGURE 10-6**
Identifying the
formatting for a
particular style

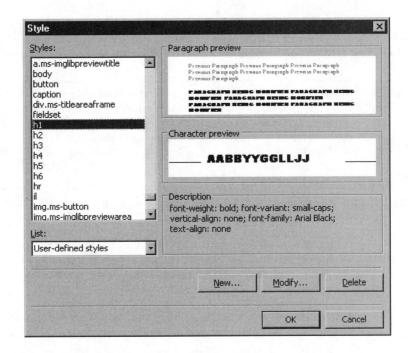

8. Repeat steps 6 and 7 for all the styles you want to modify. After defining all the styles, click OK to close the Style dialog box and click OK again to close the Text Customize Theme dialog box.

9. In the initial Customize Theme dialog box, click Save As to save your changes under a new name. Enter a name and click OK. The new theme name will appear in the list of themes. Click Cancel to close the Customize Theme dialog box.

10. Apply the new theme by opening a new or existing web, select Format | Theme, right-click the theme, and click Apply As Default Theme, or Apply To Selected Pages. The theme's styles become part of the web page and are available for use from the style drop-down list. As you build the web pages, select the style you want to use for a particular item (heading, body text, and so on) from the style drop-down list on the left of the Formatting toolbar.

Themes are a very powerful device to maintain a consistent look and feel when a number of people are creating parts of a web site or an intranet.

## Creating and Using Style Sheets

Style sheets, which are also called cascading style sheets (CSS), allow you to predefine a number of styles and then consistently apply them throughout a web site. This not only gives a consistent look to your site, it saves you time and allows you to change the entire site by simply changing the style sheet. As you saw previously, you can use style sheets with themes, but you can also define your own style sheets and use them to control the webs you create.

There are two types of style sheets: *embedded style sheets* that apply only to the page on which they reside and *external style sheets* that are linked to and used in a number of pages. How these two types of style sheets are created is different, although their usage is the same.

---

**NOTE** *Early web browsers (before Internet Explorer 3.0 and Netscape Navigator 4.0) cannot use style sheets, and pages that are formatted with them probably will not look as they are intended to. There are two style sheet standards: CSS 1.0, which covers formatting, and CSS 2.0, which covers the positioning and layering of page elements. Internet Explorer 3.0 supports CSS 1.0, and Internet Explorer 4.0 and later and Netscape Navigator 4.0 and later support both CSS 1.0 and 2.0.*

## Creating Embedded Style Sheets

An embedded style sheet is created in the page in which it will be used. Follow these instructions to create an embedded style sheet.

---

**NOTE** *If the Style option is dim (not available) in the Format menu, it has been disabled. It can be enabled by selecting Tools | Page Options | Authoring, and making sure both CSS 1.0 and CSS 2.0 are checked under the Browsers section.*

1. Create a new page in which you want the style sheet. Then select Format | Style. A Style dialog box will open similar to the one you saw in Figure 10-6.

2. In Figure 10-6, the Styles list shows user-defined styles, while here it shows HTML tags. If you select User Defined Styles in the List box, you will see it is empty. To build a style sheet, you can either choose an HTML tag to attach the style to or you can create a style from scratch. If you choose an HTML tag, the style is automatically applied when the tag is used (for example, the Body tag is automatically used in every web page, while the H1 tag is used whenever you use a Heading 1). With user-defined styles, you must manually apply them to the page element you select.

3. Click Body in the Styles list and then click Modify to create a style for the body text on the page (you can also just double-click Body). The Modify Style dialog box opens showing a preview of the style and giving a description of it, which is initially blank.

4. Click Format and choose Font. The Font dialog box opens, as you can see in Figure 10-7. Choose the font, font style, size, color, and effects you want (remember this is the body text, the majority of text on a page).

5. Click the Character Spacing tab. Open the Spacing drop-down list. Here you have expanded and condensed options, and in the spinner to the right you can set the amount of either by 1 point increments. In the Position drop-down list, you can raise or lower the text from a normal baseline to subscript and superscript positions or to five other positions above and below the baseline.

6. Click OK to close the Font dialog box and, back in the Modify Style dialog box, again click Format and choose Paragraph. The Paragraph dialog box will open and you can select the paragraph alignment from the drop-down list and set indentation and line and word spacing from spinners.

7. Click OK to close the Paragraph dialog box. In a similar manner, look at the Borders And Shading, Bullets And Numbering, and Position dialog boxes.

**FIGURE 10-7**
Choosing the font characteristics for a given style

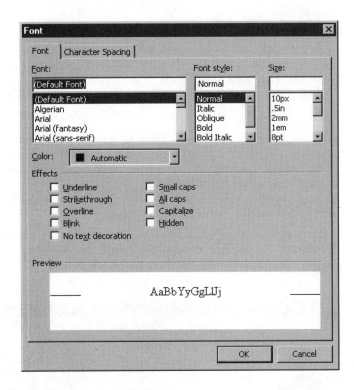

8. When you are back in the Modify Style dialog box, click OK to return to the Style dialog box. Notice that you now have Body in your User Defined Styles, and its description is as you defined it.

9. To define styles for other tags, such as H1 (Heading 1), select HTML Tags from the List drop-down box, click the tag in the Styles list, click Modify, and repeat steps 3 through 7.

10. To define your own style—for example, Red H1 for a red Heading 1—click New, enter the name, such as **Heading1(red)**, click Format, and follow steps 3 through 7.

11. When you have defined all the styles you need, click OK to close the Style dialog box, save your page, and close it.

You'll see in a minute how to apply your new styles, but if you want to sneak a peek, open the Style drop-down list on the left of the Formatting toolbar and you'll see the standard styles at the top (Body is Normal) and your custom styles at the bottom of the list. For example, the custom styles Special and Heading1(red) defined here are shown at the bottom of this Style list:

## Creating External Style Sheets

An external style sheet gives you the benefit of being able to apply a set of styles to a number of pages, a whole web site, or even several web sites. Then, with a single change in the style sheet you can change all of the pages to which it is linked. External style sheets provide a very powerful means to maintain a consistent look to all of the pages in a site. Here are the steps to create an external style sheet:

1. Click New | Page to open the Page Templates dialog box. Click the Style Sheets tab, which will open as you can see in Figure 10-8. This tab allows you to either create a style sheet from scratch (the Normal Style Sheet) or to start with one of 12 ready-made style sheets, which are also used in the themes. The description will give you an idea of the style sheets, but there are no previews available. In any case, you can add to and modify the style sheet you start with.

2. Click Blueprint to see what you have when you start with a ready-made style sheet. Note from the description that you should have Century Gothic text and headers, purple hyperlinks, and a bright yellow background.

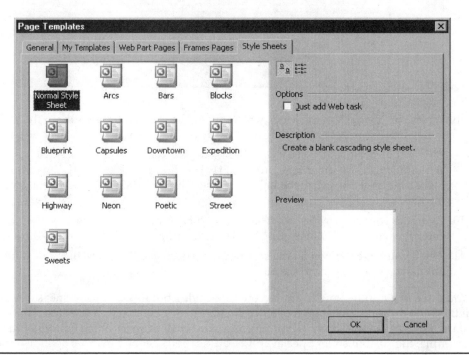

**FIGURE 10-8**    Selecting a starting point for a style sheet

**NOTE**    *If you open the Page Templates dialog box from within an open web, there's an option that is a true procrastinator's dream, Just Add Web Task, instead of adding a new page, frame page, or style sheet.*

3. Click OK. A new page opens in Page view with a .CSS extension and displaying the HTML code used in the page, as shown in Figure 10-9. Notice that there is no View bar at the bottom of the page. For this type of page, Code view is the only way you can look at it.

4. You can edit the style sheet in two ways: you can directly edit and add to the HTML on the page, being sure to follow the rules for writing HTML (see Chapter 12); or you can use the Style option in either the Format menu or the floating Style toolbar.

5. Scroll down the page until you see first the group of heading styles and then the individual heading styles. The group defines the font to be used for all the headings, while the individual styles define their color.

6. Click Style in the floating Style toolbar. The Style dialog box will open with a number of user-defined styles, as you can see next, which you can add to or modify as you did in the previous section:

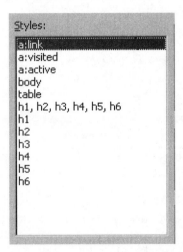

7. After you have made the additions and changes that you want to make, click OK to close the Style dialog box. In FrontPage, open the File menu and save the page with a .CSS extension in your root web. Close the web.

Had you used the Normal Style Sheet instead of a ready-made one, you would have opened a blank page and a blank style sheet to which you could add your own styles— either for HTML tags or user-defined styles.

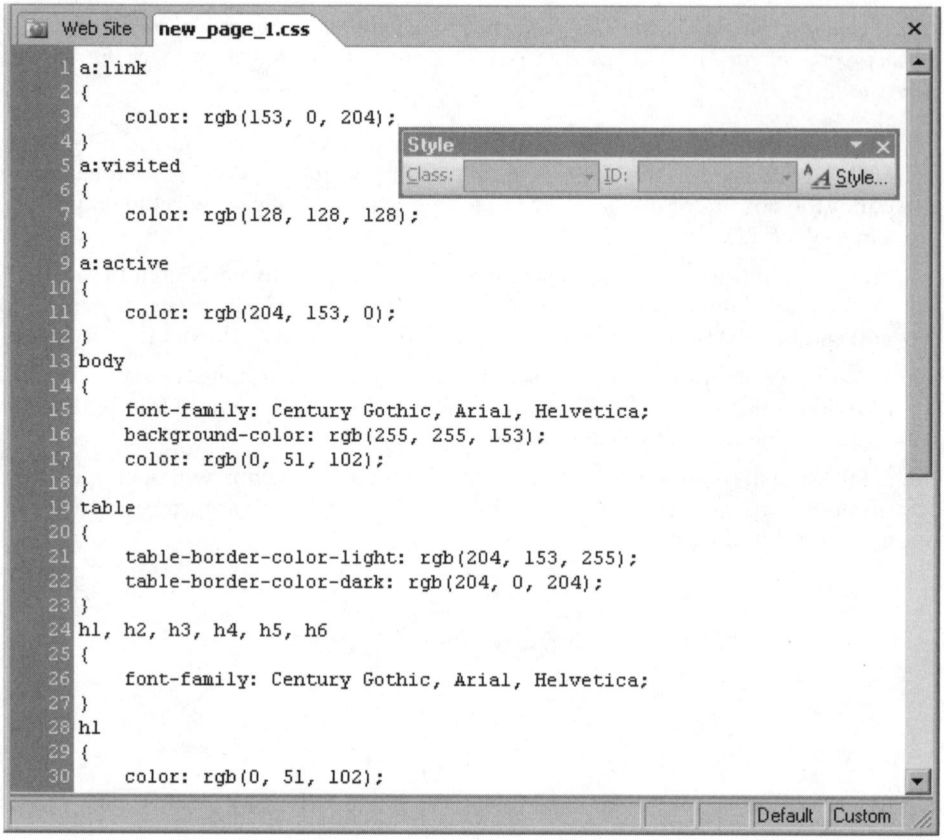

**FIGURE 10-9**    An external style sheet can only be viewed in Code view.

## Linking to External Style Sheets

For a page to use an external style sheet, it must be linked to the style sheet. Once that is done, the linked style sheet behaves as though it is an embedded style sheet. All the styles in the external style sheet are available in the Style drop-down list in the Formatting toolbar. Here's how to link to an external style sheet:

1. With the page that you want linked to the external style sheet open in FrontPage, open and fully extend the Format menu and click Style Sheet Links. The Link Style Sheet dialog box will open.

**NOTE**    *In the Link Style Sheet dialog box, you can choose to link the style sheet to all the pages in a web or to only the pages you have selected.*

2. If the URL list does not show any style sheets, click Add. The Select Style Sheet dialog box will open, followed almost immediately by the Select File dialog box.

Select the drive and path to the folder in which you stored your style sheet, normally your root web, and then double-click your style sheet. The Select File and Select Style Sheet dialog boxes will close, and you will see the path to your style sheet in the Link Style Sheet dialog box, like this:

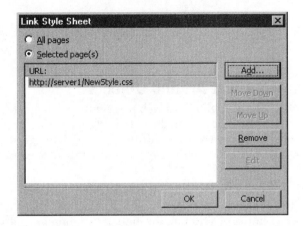

**TIP**  *If your Select File dialog box did not open immediately and you are left looking at the Select Style Sheet dialog box, click the Select A File On Your Computer button to the far right of the URL text box.*

3. Click the link to select it, and then click OK to close the dialog box. The styles on the external style sheet are now available on the page.

The external style sheet does not have to be on your hard disk; it can be anywhere on your network or your intranet—theoretically, it could be on the Internet. The potential problem of that is that you would have to be connected to the Internet to access the styles.

## Using Style Sheets

Using a style sheet, as has been implied, is very easy—you just select the style you want to use from the style drop-down list, like this:

1. Open either the page with an embedded style sheet or use the page that is linked to a style sheet currently open. (The page linked to the external style sheet just described is used in the following steps and figures.)

2. Open the Style drop-down list on the Formatting toolbar and select Heading 1. Type the heading and press ENTER. The next line should be Normal or Body text. Type a line and again press ENTER.

3. From the style list, select Heading 2. Type the heading and press ENTER. Again, the next line is Normal style.

4. Type some text to be a hyperlink, select the text, click the Hyperlink button on the toolbar, and select a destination to which to link. The line will be formatted as a hyperlink.

5. Try out any other styles you have defined. Using these steps and the linked style sheet, my page looks like Figure 10-10. If you had different styles, yours, of course, will look different.

6. Close your page without saving it.

---

***TIP*** *While it may be a bit of a hassle to set up a style sheet initially, you'll find it more than pays you back for the time you spend.*

---

## Positioning and Wrapping Text Around Objects

When you place an object like a picture on a web page with text, the default is for the picture to be flush left and for the text to flow from the bottom right corner of the picture from left to right and top to bottom, as you can see in Figure 10-11. FrontPage gives you several tools to position objects in different ways on the page and to wrap text around the objects.

### Positioning Objects on a Page

The default positioning of objects on a page can be changed through the positioning properties of the object. Simple positioning through the alignment controls on the Formatting toolbar is supported by all browsers. Use of tables for positioning is also supported by most browsers, but the advanced positioning described here requires web browsers that support CSS 2.0, specifically Internet Explorer 4.0 and above. This advanced positioning can be *relative* to the other objects on the page or *absolute* to a specific set of coordinates and can be assigned a layer or *z-order* in the stack of objects on the page. Advanced positioning is done through the object's Properties dialog box, the Position dialog box, and the Positioning toolbar.

**FIGURE 10-10**
Style sheet styles applied to text on a page

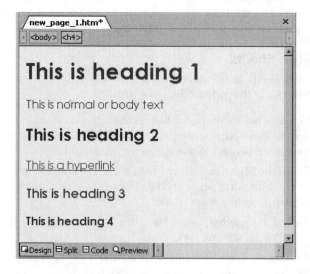

**FIGURE 10-11**
The default positioning of a picture and text on a web page

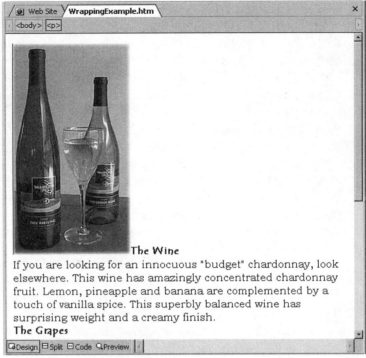

The pictures and text in this section are from Washington Hills Cellars and are used with their permission.

**NOTE**  *Advanced positioning may conflict with Dynamic HTML and cause unpredictable results, so the two should not be used together.*

## Using Absolute Positioning

Absolute positioning allows you to specify the exact pixel position for the upper left-hand corner of an object. You can do that by dragging an object to that position or by specifying that position in either the Position dialog box or Positioning toolbar. When you place an object at an absolute position, it is taken out of the text stream and text will no longer flow around it or be impacted by its position—the text will be either above it or below it on a separate layer. Absolute positioning means that the object is located at a specific set of pixel coordinates independent of the screen resolution and therefore will not change even though the layout of text and other relative objects have changed with a different resolution. So it is important to test a page with absolute positioning on all the common resolutions (at least 800×600, and 1024×768, and possibly higher), as well as in both Netscape Navigator and Internet Explorer. The following steps demonstrate how absolute positioning works:

1. Open a new page in FrontPage. Open the Insert menu, choose a picture you have, either from a file or from clipart. Cut and paste a couple paragraphs of text immediately following the picture, so you have a page similar to Figure 10-11. Save this page as WrappingExample.htm in your default folder, as well as the embedded picture file.

2. Click the picture to select it, select Format | Position (you must open the menu all the way to do this). The Position dialog box will open, as shown in Figure 10-12.

3. Click Absolute. Notice how the Left and Top location spinners become active. This is the number of pixels from the left edge and from the top edge of the page—its absolute position on the page. You can change that position by changing the numbers.

4. Change the left spinner to 130, and click OK to close the dialog box. The picture will now be on top of the text and in its approximate center.

5. Select View | Toolbars | Positioning. The Positioning toolbar will appear showing the position of the selected picture.

6. Move the mouse pointer to the picture border, where it becomes a four-headed arrow. Drag the picture around. Notice that it is independent of the text and that the Positioning toolbar shows you your position in pixels, as you can see in Figure 10-13.

7. Save your page as Absolute.htm in your default folder, My Documents\My Web Sites, then select File | Preview In Browser | Internet Explorer. Internet Explorer will open and display the exact same positioning that you had in FrontPage if the two are sized the same, as shown at the bottom of Figure 10-14 (compare to Figure 10-11).

8. Return to FrontPage, select File menu | Preview In Browser | Netscape Navigator. Again, you have almost exactly the same positioning as that in both FrontPage and Internet Explorer 6, as shown in the top of Figure 10-14.

9. Close Internet Explorer, Netscape Navigator, and your current page in FrontPage. Also close the Positioning toolbar.

You should also try different screen resolutions. The preceding figures were shot at 1024×768; when switched to 800×600, there did not seem to be a significant difference.

**FIGURE 10-12**
Controlling the positioning of an object relative to the text on a page

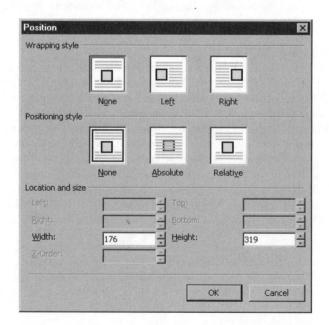

**FIGURE 10-13**
The Positioning toolbar reflects a picture's absolute position.

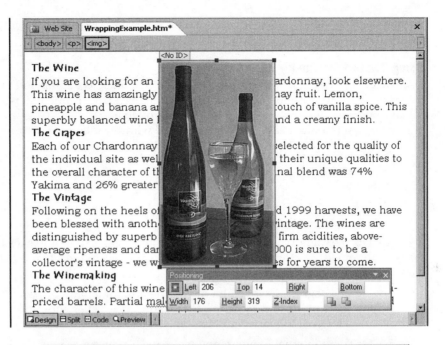

**FIGURE 10-14**
Absolute positioning in Netscape Navigator 7 and Internet Explorer 6

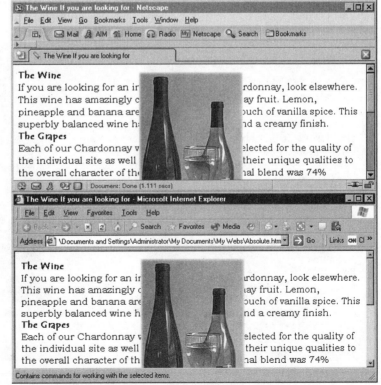

But that will not always be the case. You need to test your pages at those resolutions, especially if you are using absolute resolution.

### Using Relative Positioning and Wrapping Text

Relative positioning allows you to set the position of an object in relation to other objects on the page, so no matter how the size of the page changes, the objects will remain in the same relative position. This allows you to wrap text around a picture and keep it that way with various screen resolutions. This is demonstrated with the following instructions:

1. In FrontPage with nothing open, open the WrappingExample.htm file that you saved earlier. You can use File | Recent Files (extend the File menu) to quickly open the file.

2. Click the picture to select it, select Format | Position (you may have to extend the menu) to open the Position dialog box you saw in Figure 10-12.

3. Click the Right Wrapping Style, Relative Positioning Style, and click OK. The picture will move over to the right and the text will move to the left and below of the picture, as you can see in Figure 10-15.

4. Save this page as Relative.htm in your default folder and preview the page in both Internet Explorer and Netscape Navigator and in several resolutions. Figure 10-16 shows Internet Explorer and Netscape Navigator at 1024×768.

5. Close both Internet Explorer and Netscape Navigator as well as your page in FrontPage.

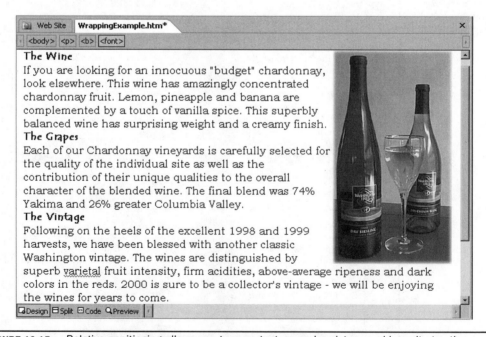

**FIGURE 10-15**    Relative positioning allows you to wrap text around a picture and have it stay there.

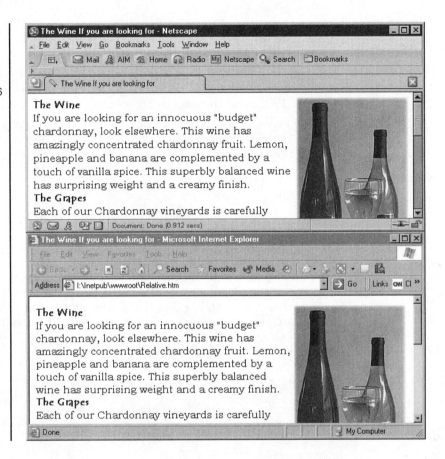

**FIGURE 10-16**
Relative positioning in Netscape Navigator 7 and Internet Explorer 6

In our case, both Internet Explorer and Netscape Navigator displayed the page almost exactly the way it was intended to be displayed. You may have a different experience. This demonstrates the need to preview your pages in both browsers.

---

**NOTE**   *The placement of photos and text can also be done with a table, which would ensure that everyone would see it as you intended, and is the way most web designers do it.*

---

## Easily Choosing Web-Safe Colors

FrontPage brings substantial capability to applying web-safe colors to graphics, backgrounds, tables, hyperlinks, and text and to picking up existing colors. In HTML, color is specified as a six-character hexadecimal (hex) value that is difficult to use. Early versions of FrontPage allowed you to select a color without having to use the hex value but gave you only 48 colors that were web-safe and then a more difficult way to pick any custom color. Later versions of FrontPage give you 134 web-safe colors, a way to pick up an existing color from anything on your screen, even outside of FrontPage—for example, in a browser—and a way to create any custom color. If you create custom colors, they are available throughout FrontPage and are even maintained between editing sessions. Look at where and how color is created in FrontPage with the following steps:

1. Open a new page in FrontPage. Type some Heading 1 text, create a 3×3 table, type a hyperlink, and place a horizontal line, which you can use to work with color, as shown in Figure 10-17. Save the page as Color.htm.

2. Right-click the heading text and choose Font. In the Font dialog box, there is a Color drop-down list. If you click the down arrow, a small color palette opens showing the 16 primary colors and allowing you to choose more colors, like this:

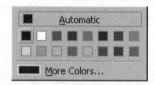

3. Close the Font dialog box, right-click the table, and choose either Table Properties or Cell Properties (the dialog boxes are close to the same; one applies to the entire table, the other to a single cell). The Table or Cell Properties dialog box opens and shows four of the Color drop-down controls—three for the border and one for the background, as you can see next. If you open any of these drop-down lists, you'll see the 16-color palette from the previous step.

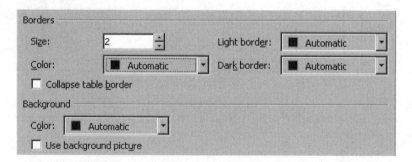

**FIGURE 10-17**
Page items, which will be colored

4. Close the Table or Cell Properties dialog box, right-click the horizontal line, and choose Horizontal Line Properties. Again you see the same Color drop-down control, and if you open it, you see the 16-color palette.

5. Close the Horizontal Line Properties dialog box, right-click any blank area of the page, and choose Page Properties. In the Formatting tab, you see five Color drop-down controls—three for hyperlinks, one for the background, and one for text, like this:

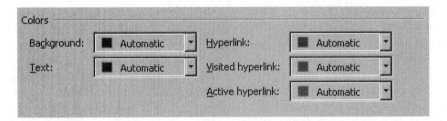

6. Click the Background color drop-down control to display the 16-color palette and then click More Colors. The More Colors dialog box will open, as you can see in Figure 10-18. Here are the 134 web-safe colors (127 in the hexagon and 8 below, but since white is both in the hexagon and in the colors below, the total is only 134). When you click a color either in or below the hexagon, the color's hex value is displayed in the upper-right of the dialog box. If the color has an official color name, it is displayed beneath the hex value.

7. Click the eyedropper Select button. The mouse pointer turns into an eyedropper, and with it you can go anywhere on your screen, including outside of FrontPage. Hovering over a color will cause that color to be identified in the More Colors dialog box; clicking that color will select it.

**FIGURE 10-18**
Selecting one of 134 web-safe colors

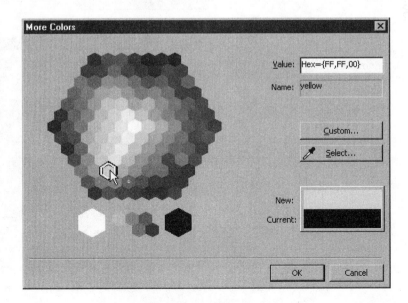

***TIP*** *You can press* ESC *to return the eyedropper mouse pointer to a normal pointer.*

8. Click Custom to open the Color dialog box, which is the same as the Color Selection dialog box in FrontPage 97 and 98, shown in Figure 10-19. Here, there are 48 web-safe colors and the ability to pick any color there is by clicking the color matrix and dragging the brightness level, or by choosing one of the numeric color schemes. When you have chosen a custom color, click Add To Custom Colors; it will be displayed in the Custom Colors blocks in the lower left. Close the Color dialog box to return to the More Colors dialog box.

9. Choose a color and click OK to close the More Colors dialog box. You are returned to the Page Properties | Background tab. Open the Text color drop-down palette and specify a color using any of the schemes that have been discussed. Click OK to close the Page Properties dialog box; you'll see the background color you have chosen on the page. Reopen the font color palette you saw in step 2, and notice how new sections have been added entitled Custom Colors and Document's Colors, like this:

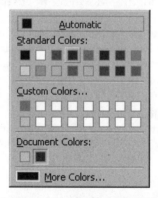

**FIGURE 10-19**
Selecting any color, not all of which are web-safe

10. Close the open dialog boxes. Open any of the other Color drop-down controls' palettes and see that the new sections are repeated there.

11. Close all dialog boxes and close the Color page.

The color features of FrontPage allow you to easily define a set of web-safe colors and then use those colors anywhere in a web site. Like the other features in this chapter, the color features significantly enhance your ability to easily produce outstanding web sites.

## Creating Graphics within FrontPage

While most of the graphics you use to build a web site in FrontPage will be created elsewhere, FrontPage does have a fair capability to directly create some graphics. Much of this capability is centered on the Drawing toolbar, shown next, which was described in Chapter 2. Two major components on the drawing toolbar that are discussed here are AutoShapes and WordArt. In addition, several other layout tools are discussed in this section.

### Using AutoShapes

AutoShapes are a set of ready-made shapes that include basic shapes, block arrows, and flowchart elements, as well as lines, stars, banners, and callouts, as you can see next. Once you have selected the shape, you can place it anywhere on the page by moving the mouse pointer to that area and clicking. In this manner, you can lay down a "normal-sized" object or size it by dragging the mouse. To resize the object once it's on the page, simply select it and drag one of the selection handles in or out. You can also fill an enclosed shape with color and/or change its outline color by using the Fill and Line Color tools. The AutoShapes menu as well as its six submenus can be "torn off" and become independent toolbars, as shown in Figure 10-20. The seventh option on the AutoShapes menu, More AutoShapes, opens the Clip Art pane with clip art shapes.

Build a simplified schematic diagram for selecting a wine using AutoShapes and following these steps:

1. Open a new page in FrontPage. Type **Steps In Selecting Wine**. Format the line as Heading 2, and press ENTER twice.

2. Select View menu | Toolbars | Drawing. In the Drawing toolbar, open AutoShapes, point to Flowchart, and click the upper-left rectangle called Process. The pointer becomes crosshairs.

3. Place the crosshairs under and to the left side of the heading and drag a rectangle that is roughly two inches wide by one inch tall, like this:

**Steps In Selecting Wine**

4. From AutoShapes | Flowchart, select the diamond, the third shape in the top row, and drag a diamond roughly the same width as the rectangle beneath the rectangle. Click the rectangle to select and press CTRL-C to copy it.

5. Press CTRL-V twice to paste two copies of the rectangle. Drag one rectangle below the diamond and the other to the right of the diamond.

6. From AutoShapes | Lines, choose the single-headed arrow. Drag the arrow from the bottom of the top rectangle to the top of the diamond. Similarly, drag one arrow from the bottom of the diamond to the bottom rectangle and another one from the right of the diamond to the rectangle on the right.

7. In the Drawing toolbar, click the Text Box button and drag a text box just inside the existing top rectangle. Type the following:

**Take a sip of wine and before swallowing swirl it around your tongue.**

This should be formatted as Normal, which is Times Roman size 3 (12 point).

8. Right-click the border of the text box, choose Format Text Box, change the Line Color to No Line, and click OK. In a similar manor, create a text box, turn off the border, and insert the text in the other flowchart objects, including the Yes and No text outside the objects, as shown in Figure 10-21.

9. Save your page (the name WineSelection.htm is used here) and leave it and FrontPage open. Close any AutoShapes toolbars you have open.

**FIGURE 10-20**
AutoShapes and its submenus can be "torn off" to become toolbars.

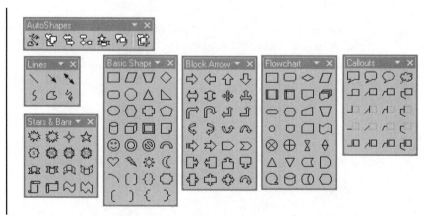

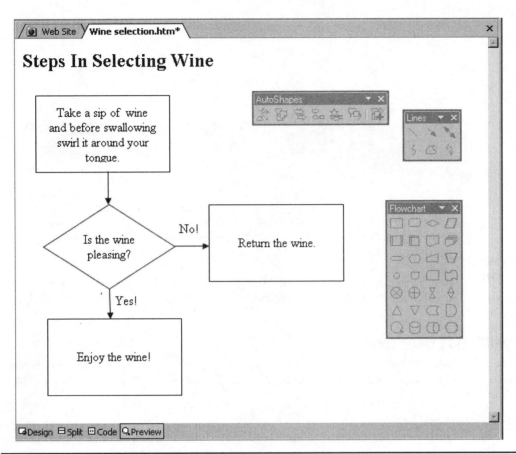

**FIGURE 10-21**   Creating schematic diagram using AutoShapes

## Using WordArt

WordArt takes text that you have entered and selected and applies one of 30 effects that you select from the WordArt Gallery. After you have selected the effect, the Edit WordArt Text dialog box opens, allowing you to make any changes to the text you want. When you click OK, the text with the applied effect will appear on your current page. When the text is selected, a WordArt toolbar appears allowing you to edit the text; select a different effect from the gallery; change the color, size, layout, and rotation of the text; make all the characters the same size; make them vertical; change their alignment; and alter their spacing. See how in this set of steps:

1. On the current page, insert enough blank lines to move the insertion point below the bottom rectangle and type **CHARDONNAY**.

2. Select the word CHARDONNAY and click Insert WordArt in the Drawing toolbar. Select a style that you want to use (the second column, third row was chosen

here) and click OK twice. The word art will appear on the page with its menu, like this:

3. Save the page and then view it in a browser. The WordArt and the schematic diagram should appear as you saw them in FrontPage.

4. Close the page.

The Drawing toolbar, AutoShapes, and WordArt have a number of features that are not described here, but they are easy for you to explore on your own. We recommend that you do that.

## Additional Layout Tools

There are three additional layout tools that have not been discussed elsewhere and deserve to be reviewed. These are the use of rulers and grid, the use of layers, and the ability to trace an image.

### Using Rulers and Grid

In order to more precisely position elements on a page, you can turn on both horizontal and vertical rulers in Design view, as well as turn on a set of gridlines demarcating the major points on the rulers, as you can see in Figure 10- 22. You can set the units that are used on the rulers to be pixels, inches, centimeters, or points, and you can also determine the spacing and the look of the grid line. Finally, you can determine how close an object has to be to a gridline before it "snaps" to it. The next set of steps describe how to turn on, configure, and use rulers and grid:

1. Open a new page. Select View | Ruler And Grid | Show Ruler. Right-click a ruler and select Show Grid. Your page should look like Figure 10-22, unless the defaults have been changed.

2. Right-click a ruler and choose Configure. The Page Options dialog box will open, like this:

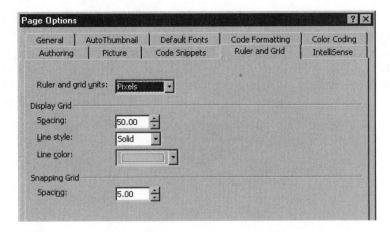

3. Open the drop-down list opposite Ruler And Grid Units. Look at the options and choose a different unit of measure. While the dialog box is open, look at and change each of the other settings and click OK.

4. On the page, place a picture and a table. Select first one and then the other and for each use Format | Position to make them both absolute position. Then drag them to specific grid intersections. Try this with Snap To Grid on and off to see the difference. Change the granularity of the Snapping Grid to see how that works.

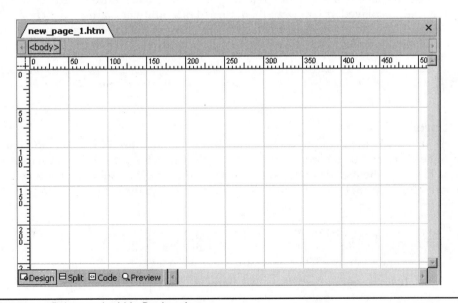

**FIGURE 10-22**    Rulers and grid in Design view

Notice how, when you drag the mouse over the page, you can see where the mouse is in the rulers.

5. Drag the intersecting lines in the topmost and leftmost corner of the rulers into the grid. Notice how the origin (the 0/0 point) changes, allowing you to set the origin at any place on the page. You can reset the origin at the upper-left corner of the page by double-clicking at that point or by right-clicking a ruler and choosing Reset Origin.

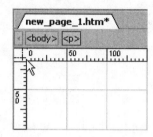

6. Select an object on the page, like the picture you place there, right-click a ruler, and choose Set Origin From Selection. The origin moves to the upper-left corner of the object.

7. Right-click a ruler and choose Configure. Click Reset Defaults to return the rulers and grid to the original settings. But, the origin remained where it was.

8. Close the page without saving it and open a new page. Notice the rulers and grid are still displayed. If you want them turned off, right-click a ruler and choose first Show Grid and Show Ruler to do so (if you turn off the rulers first, you will not have anything to click to turn off the grid except to do so from the View menu).

---

**NOTE**   *Even though you turn off the rulers and grid, you can leave the Snap To Grid on and objects will adhere to the grid.*

### Using Layers

Layering allows you to put multiple objects (pictures, tables, or text blocks) on different layers in the same space and then use DHTML code to select which layer is visible. Chapter 13 will describe how to write the DHTML code to do this, and here we'll show you how to create and control the layers. The latter is principally done through the Layers task pane. See how with the following steps:

1. In the new page created in the previous section, with or without rulers and grid, select Format | Layers. The Layers task pane opens with only two options: to insert a layer and to draw a layer (you can also insert a layer from the Insert menu).

2. Click Insert Layer in the Layers task pane. A blue square appears in the Design view pane and an entry appears on the task pane.

3. Right-click the entry in the task pane and a context menu opens. This shows you that you can cut, copy, and paste a layer, change its visibility (which is shown by the eyeball in the first column), modify its ID or name, modify its position on the Z-axis

(the vertical axis coming out of the screen at you), and determine how its borders and positioning are handled.

4. When you selected the layer entry in the task pane, the blue square in the Design pane was also selected and given sizing handles. Drag the lower-right handle to the lower-right so the square becomes a rectangle approximately 400×300 pixels (wide and tall).

5. Click Positioning at the bottom of the task pane. In the Position dialog box, click Absolute so you can move the pane anywhere on the page, fix the width and height so they are exactly 400×300 pixels, and click OK.

6. Insert a picture into the layer and size the picture so it fills the entire layer. Draw a new layer over the first, insert and size another picture in the second layer, give it absolute positioning, and move it so it is on top of the first layer. Your FrontPage window should look like Figure 10-23.

7. Using the Layers task pane, click first one layer and then the next. With DHTML, you will be able to do that automatically in a browser, as described in Chapter 13. Save the page with the name **Layers,** save the embedded files, and close your web page.

### Tracing Images

Tracing Images allows you to place an image behind the Design pane that the user of the page will never see, only the author, and use that image as a guide while building the web

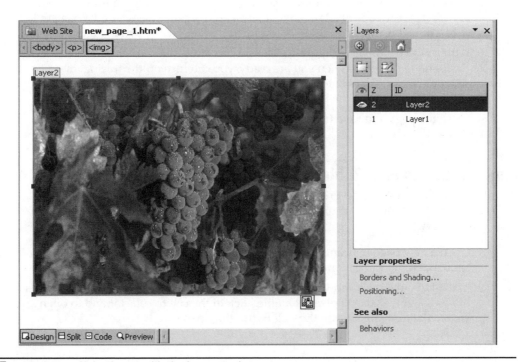

**FIGURE 10-23**    Using layers with the Layers task pane

page. This can be drawing an outline around some object, building a table at a given location, or the relative positioning of objects on a page. Try out Tracing Images next:

1. Open a new page in FrontPage Design view. Select View | Tracing Image | Configure. The Tracing Image dialog box opens like this:

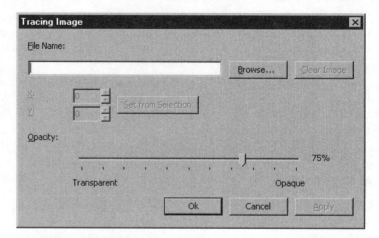

2. Click Browse to locate the image you want to trace, set the opacity at about 60 percent and click OK. The image should appear on your page, a little dim because of the 60 percent opacity. We did a quick sketch of what we wanted a page to look like, scanned it, and brought it in as a tracing image, as shown in Figure 10-24.

3. With a sketch similar to Figure 10-24, you can draw a table over it and then insert the identified objects. When you are ready, you can turn off the tracing image by selecting View | Tracing Image | Show Image (of course, at any time you can look at your page without the image by clicking Preview).

4. Close the page and save the results with a name like "Tracing," or not, as you choose.

## Customizing the Look of Tables

FrontPage allows you to do several things with tables that gives them a possibly more appealing look. This includes rounding the corners and giving the table a 3-D look. See how that is done next:

1. Open a new page in FrontPage. If the Layout Tables And Cells pane is not already open, open the Table menu and choose that option.

2. In the Layout Tables and Cells pane, click Draw Layout Cell and draw a single cell that is roughly 200×100 pixels. Double-click in the cell to select it and to open and enable the elements within the Cell Formatting pane.

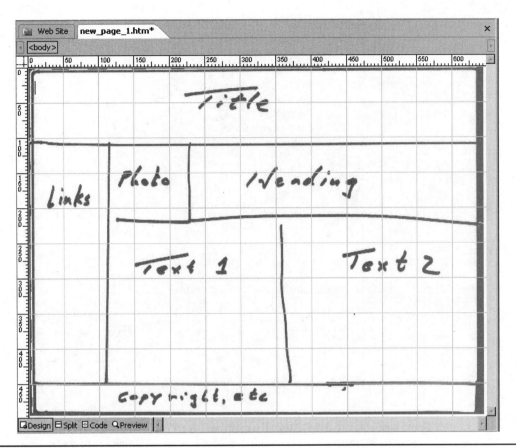

**FIGURE 10-24**     Tracing a sketch of a proposed layout

3. Click the leftmost square in Apply Borders to apply the default black border 1 pixel thick around the four sides, like this:

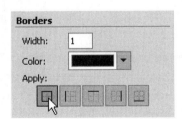

4. Click Cell Corners And Shadows to open it, as shown next:

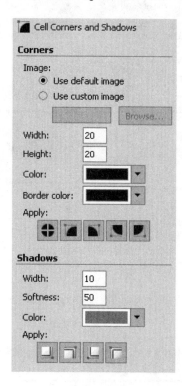

5. Under Shadows, if there aren't already numbers for Width and Softness, enter **10** and **50**, respectively, and click the rightmost shadow to add a shadow on the lower right of the cell. Click Preview. Your cell should look like this:

6. Return to Design view and use Draw Layout Cell to draw another approximately 200×100 pixel rectangle beneath the first one, select the cell, add the default 1 pixel border, and open Cell Corners And Shadows.

7. Click the leftmost square below Apply under Corners. You will see rounded corners appear in the cell.

8. Save your page with the filename Cells.htm along with the embedded corner files and click Preview In Browser. Netscape Navigator 7, shown in Figure 10-25, does not do as good a job of rounding the corners as does Internet Explorer 6.

9. Close your browser and close FrontPage.

You can see that there are a number of ways to vary both the shadow and the rounded corners. Try some of these on your own.

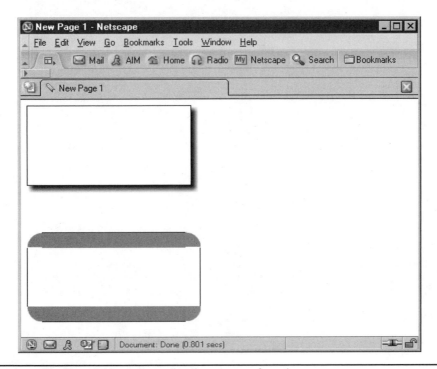

**FIGURE 10-25**   Shading a table and rounding the corners of another

# Importing and Integrating Office and Other Files

Y ou will probably want to augment your FrontPage web with files imported from other applications—if for no other reason than because the files you want already exist in another format. This is especially true with multimedia files, since FrontPage does not have the capability to create multimedia files. FrontPage has several ways of working with information created outside of it, including importing information onto an existing page, importing information onto a new page, and attaching or linking to a non-FrontPage file from a web. Look at this from the standpoint of Microsoft Office 2003 and other productivity applications. (Working with multimedia files will be covered in Chapter 19.)

## Importing Microsoft Office 2003 and Other Productivity Files

FrontPage 11 is part of the Microsoft Office 2003 family and thus is tightly integrated; in several editions, it is bundled with the other Office products. If you use the Office products Word, Excel, PowerPoint, and Access, you can see a definite similarity in the menus, toolbars, and behavior of FrontPage. Of equal or even greater importance, though, is how easy it is to bring files created in the other Office products into FrontPage. Here, you'll look at several Office products and see how you can import information they create into FrontPage. If you use other productivity applications, such as those from Corel, WordPerfect, or Lotus, you will find that they are not as tightly integrated as the Office applications, but you can still easily import these files into FrontPage.

**NOTE**  *Microsoft Access is covered in depth in Chapter 17.*

### Using Text from Microsoft Word and Other Word Processors

FrontPage can bring externally created text, especially Microsoft Word text, into a web in a number of ways. Among these are

- Pasting text from the Windows Clipboard onto an existing page in Page view.

- Inserting a file onto an existing page in Page view. The file can be in any of the file formats listed in Table 11-1.

- Opening a file onto a new page from within Page view. The file can be in any of the file formats listed in Table 11-1.

- Importing a file onto a new page in either HTML format or its native format, if that format has been associated with its native editor in FrontPage. (Microsoft Word's DOC format is an example of this.)

- Dragging and dropping a file into FrontPage.

| File Format | Extensions |
| --- | --- |
| Hypertext Markup Language | .HTM, .HTML |
| Hypertext Templates | .HTT |
| Preprocessed HTML | .HTX, .ASP |
| HTML Document | .HTM, .HTML, .HTX, .OTM, shtml, .shtm, .stm |
| Lotus 1-2-3 | .WK1, .WK3, .WK4 |
| Microsoft Excel Worksheet | .XLS, .XLW |
| Recover Text from Any File | *.* |
| Rich Text Format | .RTF |
| Text Files | .TXT, .CSV, .LOG, .ASC, .ASX, .BAK |
| Windows Write | .WRI |
| Word (Asian Versions) 6.0/95 | .DOC |
| Word 2.x for Windows | .DOC |
| Word 4.0–5.1 for Macintosh | .MCW |
| Word 6.0/95 for Windows and Macintosh | .DOC |
| Word 97/2000/2002 | .DOC |
| WordPerfect 5.x/6.x | .DOC, .WPD |
| Works 6.0/7.0 | .WPS |
| Active Server Pages | .ASP, .ASPX |
| Single File Web Page | .MHT, MHTML |
| HyperText Template | . HTT |
| HyperText Style Sheet | .CSS |
| XML | .XML, .XSL, .XSD, .WSDL, .VXML, .SMI, .SMIL |
| Javascript/Java | .JS, .JAVA, .J JAV, .JSP, .JHTML |

**TABLE 11-1**     File Formats that can Be Brought into FrontPage in Page View

To see how these methods differ, you'll need documents from Microsoft Word or another word processing application to use as examples.

### Pasting Text from the Clipboard

Probably the easiest way to bring in a small amount of text from almost any Windows application is through the use of the Windows Clipboard. Follow these steps to see how it works with FrontPage:

1. Select all the text (CTRL-A) of a Microsoft Word document and copy it to the Windows Clipboard by pressing CTRL-C.

---

**NOTE**   *As you would expect, if you want to copy and paste only part of a Microsoft Word document, highlight the part you want to copy and press* CTRL-C

2. Close Microsoft Word and start FrontPage.

3. Create or open a web, name it if new, and double-click its home page to open it in Page view. An example of the Customer Support Web Site is shown in Figure 11-1. We will replace the What's New statement with our own.

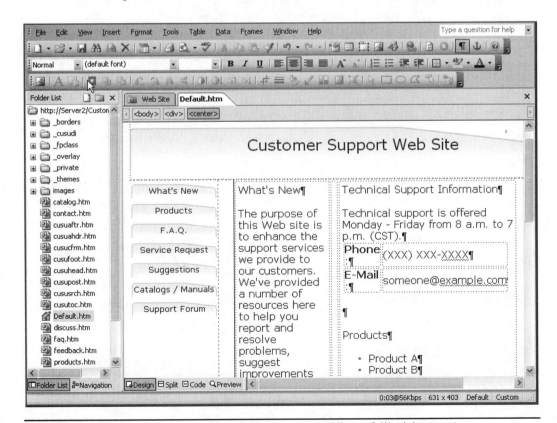

**FIGURE 11-1**    An example of a web site before we paste our Microsoft Word document

---

**NOTE** *If you are using Windows SharePoint Services, SharePoint 2, you will see a warning box saying that some components will not display correctly using Windows SharePoint Services.*

4. In Page view, highlight the area to be replaced, or click your cursor where you want to the text to be inserted, and press CTRL-V to paste the contents of the Clipboard there. Your result should look like Figure 11-2.

As you can see, most of the formatting is retained when you bring text into FrontPage from the Windows Clipboard. The only significant changes are that the vertical spacing between paragraphs is different, and you could experience a difference in the font.

---

**NOTE** *FrontPage and some browsers support the use of fonts other than the default Times New Roman. However, the font used must be installed on the user's computer to be displayed correctly, even if the browser supports the use of other fonts. More information about using fonts on the Web can be found at **http://www.microsoft.com/truetype/**.*

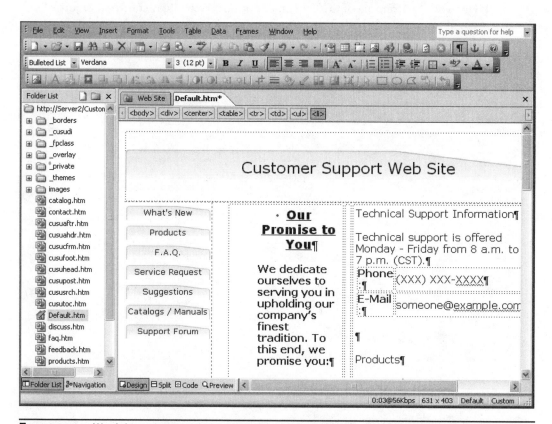

**FIGURE 11-2**    Word document pasted into FrontPage with most of its formatting

### Inserting a File onto an Existing Page

You can insert a file onto an existing page by using any of the supported file formats. You'll look at the Word DOC, HTML, RTF, and TXT files next. The steps are similar for all the supported formats.

**Inserting TXT Files**    The Text (.TXT) option of inserting a file has several alternatives. Follow these steps to see how it is done:

1. Select Insert | File. The Select File dialog box will open.

2. Click the DOWN ARROW in the Files Of Type drop-down list box. Here you can see some of the types of files you can bring into FrontPage:

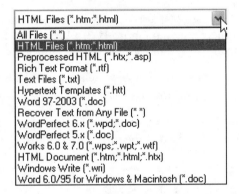

```
HTML Files (*.htm;*.html)                               ▼
All Files (*.*)
HTML Files (*.htm;*.html)
Preprocessed HTML (*.htx;*.asp)
Rich Text Format (*.rtf)
Text Files (*.txt)
Hypertext Templates (*.htt)
Word 97-2003 (*.doc)
Recover Text from Any File (*.*)
WordPerfect 6.x (*.wpd;*.doc)
WordPerfect 5.x (*.doc)
Works 6.0 & 7.0 (*.wps;*.wpt;*.wtf)
HTML Document (*.htm;*.html;*.htx)
Windows Write (*.wri)
Word 6.0/95 for Windows & Macintosh (*.doc)
```

3. Click Text Files.

4. Find the TXT file you want to insert into the web page. Use Look In to specify the path and the filename and click Open.

5. In the Convert Text dialog box, select the option you want from among the following:

   - **One Formatted Paragraph**    Contains no paragraph breaks, only new-line breaks where either new-line or paragraph breaks exist in the original document.

   - **Formatted Paragraphs**    Contains paragraph breaks wherever you had paragraph breaks in the original text. Much of formatting from Microsoft Word will be gone.

   - **Normal Paragraphs**    Retains paragraph or line breaks where you had paragraphs in the original, multi-line paragraphs would still be wrapped, and the numbered paragraphs, as expected, would be numbered.

   - **Normal Paragraphs With Line Breaks**    Uses FrontPage's Normal style, with paragraph breaks in the places you had them, multi-line paragraphs wrapped to fit the page, and numbered paragraphs with their designated numbers. All remaining formatting is lost.

   - **Do Not Convert**    Copies the file without attempting to convert the formatting.

6. Click OK.

---

***NOTE*** *When you are copying documents created in earlier versions (before Word 2002), you'll see that the numbered paragraphs will be numbered and that paragraph breaks are replaced with new-line (SHIFT-ENTER) breaks. If you turn on Show All on the right of the toolbar, you can see the paragraph marks.*

---

***TIP*** *Notice that when you insert the TXT file with Formatted Paragraphs, the first paragraph is one line, or rather it is formatted without word wrap. With the Normal Paragraphs option, the text is wrapped to the width of Page view.*

The text format does not give you much, unless you want to bring in some plain text in FrontPage's Formatted paragraph style.

**Inserting a DOC File**    As you saw in Table 11-1, many word processors use the .DOC extension for their files. In this example, shown in Figure 11-3, a Word 2003 file is used. The steps will be similar for any of the word processors supported by FrontPage.

1. From the blank home page in Page view, select Insert | File.
2. In the Select File dialog box, find and double-click the file you want to use.

The sample file shown in Figure 11-3 is again shown in Figure 11-4 after being inserted into FrontPage. You can see how some of the formatting is lost.

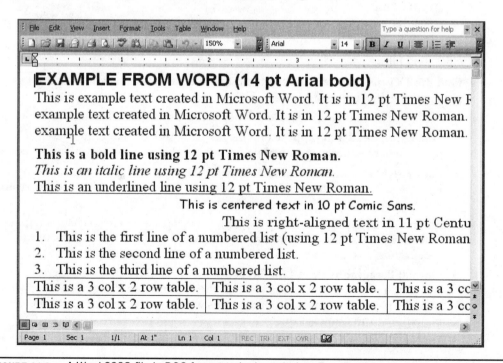

**FIGURE 11-3**    A Word 2003 file in DOC format to be brought into FrontPage

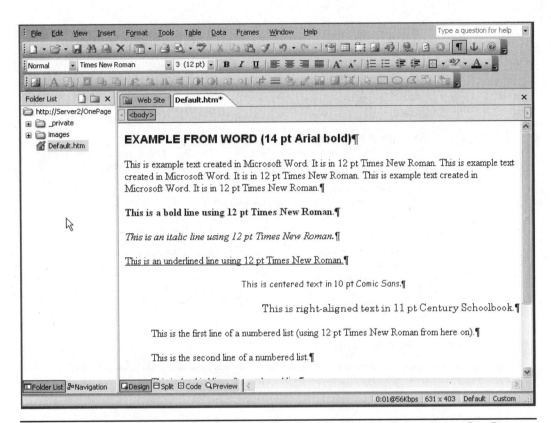

**FIGURE 11-4**   Some formatting is lost when a Word 11 file in DOC format is brought into FrontPage

---

**NOTE**   *If this is the first time you are bringing a DOC file into FrontPage, you may be told that you need to install the import filter. In that case, insert your installation CD and follow the directions on the screen.*

An inserted DOC file retains some, but not all, of the formatting in the original document. There are two major differences between the original DOC and the inserted HTML version—the numbers are missing from the numbered list and the original 11-point right-aligned line is 12 points (because there is no standard HTML size of 11 points; the closest standard sizes are 10 or 12 points). Additionally, it is Times New Roman, not Century Schoolbook.

**Inserting an HTML File**   An HMTL file (with a file extension of .HTM or .HTML) is the normal format of all text files on the Web, including FrontPage text files. For that reason, it is the default when you insert a new file. The HTML files come into FrontPage nicely, as you can see in Figure 11-5. In this example, a duplicate of the DOC file displayed in Figure 11-3

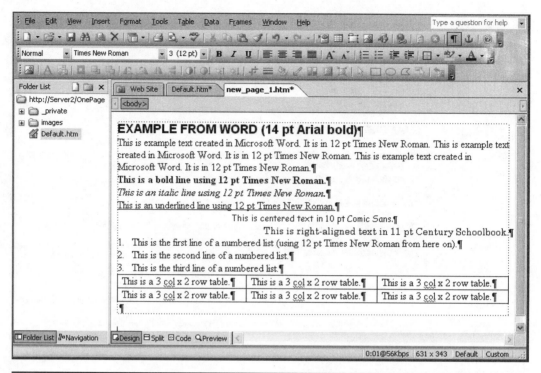

**FIGURE 11-5**    A Word file in HTML format brought into FrontPage

is converted into an HTML file and then inserted into FrontPage. Follow these steps to insert an HTML file:

---

**NOTE**   *Microsoft Word 97 through 2003 allows you to save files directly in HTML format (.HTM extension). Microsoft has a free add-in called Internet Assistant you can download for Word 6 or 7/95 that will do the same thing, at* **http://www.microsoft.com/downloads/ release.asp?ReleaseID=13796**.

---

1. Open a New Normal Page in Page view and choose Insert | File.

2. Change the file type to HTML Files and double-click the filename.

3. The file will appear on the open page, a sample of which is shown in Figure 11-5.

The HTML file has maintained more of the original formatting than any other method. There are no significant features missing in this example.

**Inserting an RTF File**    RTF (Rich Text Format) was created to communicate the majority of text formatting. Many applications, not just word processing programs, have the ability to export files in RTF. To see how FrontPage inserts these files, follow these steps:

1. Open a new normal page in Page view, and then, as in the preceding description, select Insert | File.
2. In the Select File dialog box, change the Files of Type to Rich Text Format. Then find the RTF file you want to insert and double-click it. The file will appear on the new page, as you can see in the example in Figure 11-6.

The results of the RTF import are very good—with the only exception being that the 11-point text is converted to 12 point and some of the line spacing is different.

### Opening a File onto a New Page

The third way (in addition to pasting and inserting) that you can bring text files into a FrontPage web is through the Page view File | Open command. This displays the Open File dialog box, shown in Figure 11-7, from which you can again select any of the supported file

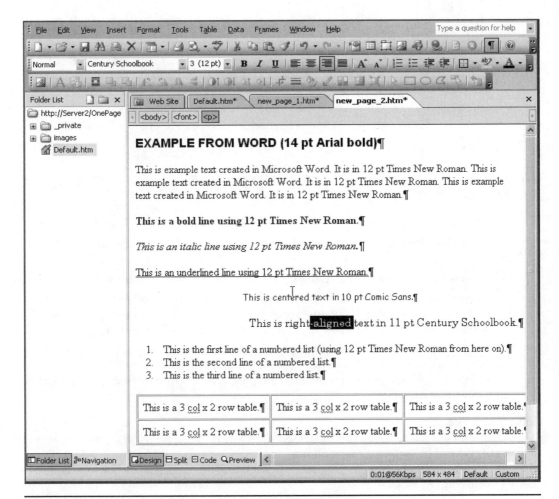

**FIGURE 11-6**    A Word file in RTF format inserted into FrontPage

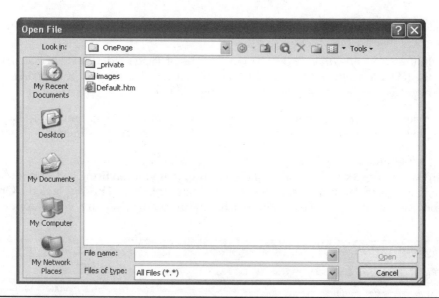

**FIGURE 11-7**   Selecting a file to directly open in FrontPage

types. In this case, the parent application is opened. The steps to opening a file are as follows:

> **NOTE**   *Even though the .RTF file type is not listed in the Open File dialog box, it still is accessible. When you open a .RTF file, Microsoft Word is opened.*

1. From the Page view of a web page, choose File | Open.
2. In the Open File dialog box that is displayed, select the file type and double-click the filename of your text file.

   The results vary depending on the type of text file you are opening:
3. If you open a Word, HTML, or RTF file in FrontPage, the parent application, for example Microsoft Word, will open and display the file. You can edit the file in Word and then copy and paste the text you want into a web page in FrontPage.
4. If you open a TXT file in FrontPage, the TXT file will be opened in FrontPage without specifying the conversion type. It will be copied into FrontPage perfectly into its own page. Then you can copy and paste the text into the web page in which you want it to appear.

## Importing a File

The fourth method for bringing text files into FrontPage is to use FrontPage's File | Import command. When you import a file, it allows you to import a file in its native mode. When the file is opened in FrontPage, its parent application will be opened in most cases. Follow these steps to import a file:

1. In FrontPage Folders view, choose File | Import. The Import dialog box opens. (If you get the Web Site Templates dialog box, you need to create a One Page Web Site and then try to Import.)

2. Click Add File and the Add File To Import List dialog box opens. Click the down arrow in its Files Of Type drop-down list. Notice that you do not have all the choices here that you had in Page view Insert and Open methods, as you can see here:

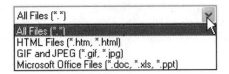

3. At this point, you can add a number of files that you want to import into FrontPage. Use the Look In drop-down list box to find each file, set the Files of Type, and click Open.

4. The file is added to the Import dialog box. You can then repeat the Add File and select additional files to import, as shown in this example of five different file types.

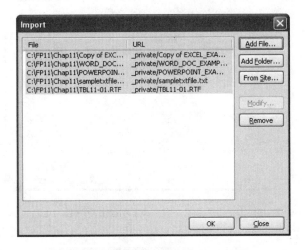

5. When you have imported all the files you want, click OK. In Folders view, you will see the imported files listed. The files will be in their native format.

The ability to import a file in its *native format* is very important because it means you don't have to convert it before you use the file. But this process has limitations in that the contents must be edited in the parent application, in most cases. You'll see how this works next (only the TXT files can be imported directly into FrontPage):

1. To open a text file in FrontPage, double-click the file in Folders view of FrontPage.

2. The Parent application, such as Microsoft Word with .DOC, .HTML, or .RTF files, will load, and the file will be displayed and ready to edit as you saw when opening a text file.

---

**NOTE**    *If you right-click on the file and select Open With, you will see a selection of applications that may be used to open the file, such as Microsoft Word, FrontPage (Open as HTML), FrontPage (Open as Text), Notepad, Internet Explorer, Microsoft PowerPoint, and Microsoft Excel. The application listed first will be the default application but by clicking another one, you can open the file where you want it.*

**Setting Extension Associations**    The .HTM and .DOC extensions may be associated with Microsoft Word, for example, and that application is opened to edit the file. These extension associations are determined by your Windows Registry. Follow these steps to associate a file extension with the application that FrontPage will open to edit the file:

1. In FrontPage, select Tools | Options.

2. In the Options dialog box, click the Configure Editors tab, shown next. You can use this dialog box to associate a file extension with the application that FrontPage will open to edit the file:

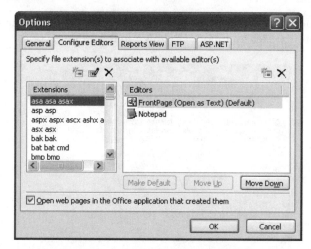

3. Click the New Extension icon (the first of the three) to add a new extension. The Open With dialog box will open, as shown here:

4. Enter a new file Extension that makes sense for you. Then choose the program to associate with the extension. For example, to add an association between the application CorelDRAW and the extension .CDR, type **cdr** as the Extension and select the program to use from the list displayed below. If needed, you can click Browse to locate the application.

5. Click OK to close the dialog box.

---

**NOTE**    *There is one catch to using a file in its native format in a web—you are assuming that users have the application on their computer so they can view the file. This assumption is best made on an intranet where you can control the desktop environment of your users.*

Later in the chapter, in "Bringing Files from Other Productivity Applications," you'll also see how to work with applications other than Microsoft Word.

## Drag and Drop Files Into FrontPage

Another way to bring files into FrontPage is to drag and drop a file into Folders or Page views. You will get slightly different results.

### Drag and Drop in Folders View

The first task is to arrange the windows so that you can see both the source and destination of the files you want to copy. Here is how you do it with Windows Explorer and FrontPage:

1. Minimize any running applications besides Windows Explorer and FrontPage.

2. Open Windows Explorer and find the file you want to drag and drop into FrontPage.

3. In FrontPage, select Folders view.

4. Right-click an empty portion of the taskbar and click Tile Windows Horizontally. The Windows Explorer window and FrontPage window are arranged so that both are visible on your screen, as shown in Figure 11-8.

5. Select the file in Windows Explorer, and then drag it onto the left pane of FrontPage, on top of a folder or file where you want it to be placed. If the file is placed on top of a folder, the file will be copied within it. If the file is on top of another file, it will be contained in the folder that contains that file. The pointer changes to an arrow with a plus sign, indicating the selected file will be copied to the new location, as shown here. Release the mouse button to copy the file to the selected folder.

---

**NOTE**    *Regardless of which view is being displayed In FrontPage (Folders, Remote Web Site, Reports, Navigation, Hyperlinks, Tasks, or Page views), if the Folder List is turned on, you can drop the file into the selected folder.*

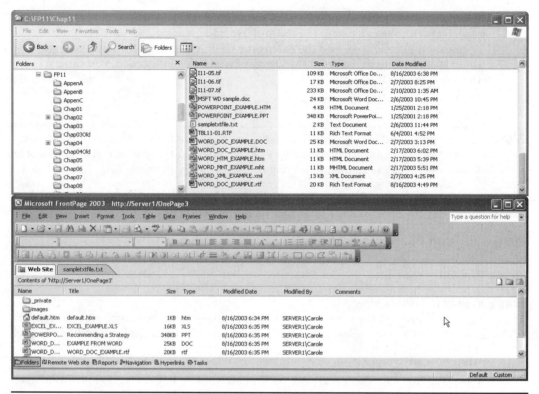

**FIGURE 11-8**  Windows Explorer and FrontPage arranged to drag and drop files

6. You can double-click the dropped file to verify that it opens correctly.

Dragging and dropping a file onto FrontPage has the same result as importing a file by use of the Import option on the File menu.

---

**NOTE**  *Dropping an HTML file onto FrontPage imports only the HTML page; any images on the page are not imported and must be imported separately.*

### Drag and Drop in Page View

You can also use drag and drop to insert files into Page view. The dragged file becomes the content of the page rather than a separate file.

1. Arrange your screen (as shown in Figure 11-8) so that both the source and destination in the Windows Explorer and FrontPage Page view windows are visible.

2. In Windows Explorer, select the file to be copied and drag it onto the new page in Page view. (If you are copying TXT data, you will see the Convert Text dialog box where you must choose how you want the content on the file formatted. Choose OK.)

3. The contents of the document will be copied onto the page open in FrontPage.

## Bringing Files from Other Productivity Applications

By using HTML, RTF, or a file in its native format (if you think the user can open it), you can bring files from many applications into FrontPage. Now you'll see how this works with Microsoft Excel and PowerPoint files.

### Using Microsoft Excel Files

In Microsoft Excel, as in most spreadsheet applications, you can create both tabular information and charts or graphs, as shown in Figure 11-9. When you bring this material into FrontPage, you must use either the native format—which means that Excel will be opened in FrontPage to handle both tabular and graphic data—and hope the user has the product or the viewer, or you must handle the tabular data and graph or chart separately by saving them as .htm files or web pages. Here are the steps to do both:

To Save the file in native format:

1. In Microsoft Excel, open the.xls file you want to bring into FrontPage, an example of which is shown in Figure 11-9.

2. In Excel, choose File | Save As. In the Save As dialog box, click My Network Places, select your destination web (or go to the location where you have saved your webs), click Open, and then click Save. You may be asked whether you want to save the workbook even if all the features cannot be saved in FrontPage. Click Yes.

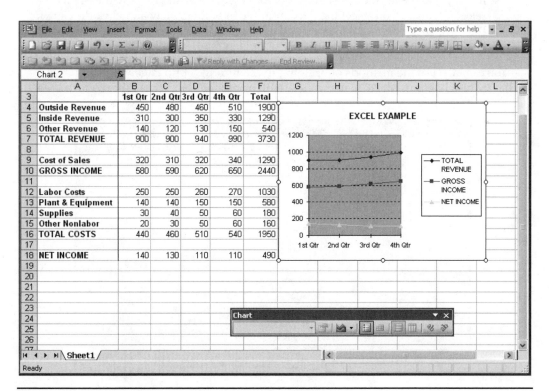

**FIGURE 11-9**    Excel example with both tabular and chart data

3. In FrontPage, click Refresh on the toolbar and the Excel file will appear in Folders view.

4. If you open the native Excel file (.xls) in your browser (for example, as a link on your web page or by selecting the file in Folder view and then clicking the Preview in Browser View tool) and your browser is Internet Explorer 5 or later, but not Netscape, it will open; open Excel within it and display your workbook. (If you try to open the native Excel file in a browser and are told that you are trying to download the file, choose to open it and not save it to disk.)

To save the data types separately or together as a web page:

1. In Excel, choose File | Save As Web Page. The Save As dialog box will open, as shown in Figure 11-10. Here, you can save either the current selection (tabular or chart) or the entire workbook. In the example in Figure 11-10, the tabular data and the chart will be saved as one file.

2. Make sure that the Save As Type is Web Page. To change the title on the browser title bar, click Change Title and type the name you want and click OK. At this point, you can close Excel.

3. In FrontPage, click Refresh on the toolbar and the Excel files will appear in Folders view.

4. If you double-click the Excel .htm file, Excel will open and display the file with the selected data. If you select the Excel.htm file in Folders view and click Preview In Browser, your browser will open and display the web page complete with a chart if it is available, as you can see in our example in Figure 11-11.

You can also use the methods of bringing Excel .htm files into Page view discussed earlier in this chapter with DOC files to insert all or part of your spreadsheet onto a web

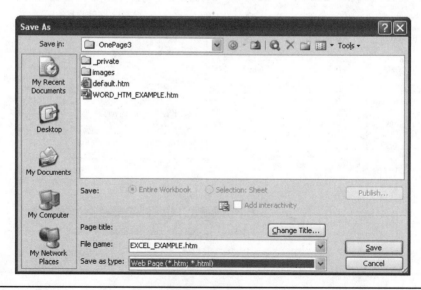

**FIGURE 11-10**    Excel Save As dialog box saving an entire workbook as a web page

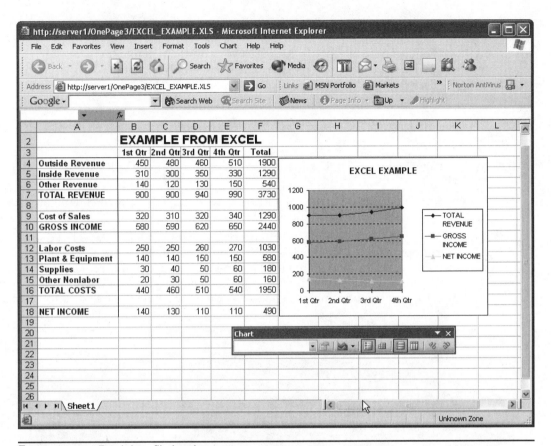

**FIGURE 11-11**    Excel .htm file in a browser

page in FrontPage. Also, both spreadsheet tabular and chart data can be copied to the Clipboard and pasted onto a web page, and the .xls files can be dragged and dropped into Folders view.

---

**TIP**    *When you save an Excel spreadsheet as a web page and choose Add Interactivity, and then open that spreadsheet in a browser, you will get an interactive spreadsheet where you can change the numbers and see both the totals and the chart change without having Excel on the browser machine. This is independent of FrontPage and allows you to save the changed spreadsheet back to Excel. This Add Interactivity is the same thing we did in Chapter 9, using the Web Component: Spreadsheets and Charts | Office Spreadsheet.*

### Bringing in PowerPoint Files

In PowerPoint, like Word and Excel, you have two choices for getting its files on the Internet: in native format and in HTML format. To handle each of these, follow the next steps.

To Save as a PPT file, in native format:

1. In PowerPoint, choose File | Save As. Select your destination folder where your web is stored. Select Presentation (*.ppt) as the Save As Type, name your file, and click Save. Close PowerPoint.

---

**NOTE**   *You may need to click Open first and then Save, depending on how you choose to locate the destination.*

---

2. In FrontPage Folders view, click Refresh on the toolbar and you will see the PowerPoint .PPT file.

3. If you double-click the file in the Folder List, PowerPoint will be loaded with the presentation, as seen in the example in Figure 11-12.

4. To see how it looks with the browser, from the FrontPage Folders view, select the PowerPoint.ppt file and click Preview In Browser on the toolbar. You will see just the PowerPoint presentation without the buttons or frames that incorporate the outline. (If you are told that you are trying to download the file or a warning that some files can harm your computer, choose to open it and not save it to disk.)

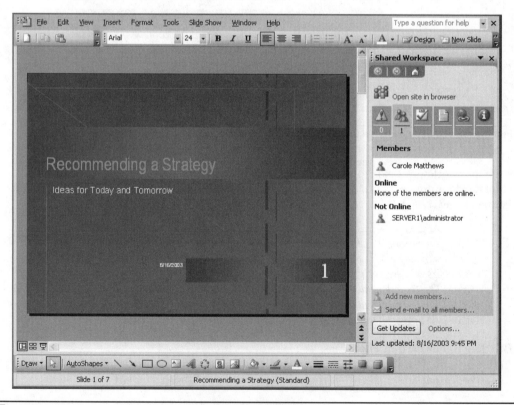

**FIGURE 11-12**   An example of a PPT file loaded in FrontPage

To Save as an HTML file or web page:

1. In PowerPoint, in the Home pane, choose File | Open. In the Open dialog box, locate the PowerPoint file you wish to save to a web and open the file.

2. Choose File | Save As Web Page. The Save As dialog box will open. Make the Save As Type to be Web Page and specify the destination folder as your Save In location, as shown in the following example. Click Save.

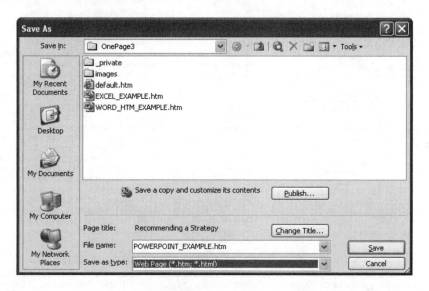

**NOTE**   *In PowerPoint, when Saving As Web Page, the file extension will default to "Single File Web Page" (.mhtm) not a Web Page (.htm) as we've been using in the chapter. As the name implies, all the supporting files that are contained in a separate folder when doing a save to Web Page are contained in one larger file. For example, the size of an example .htm file was 3KB in size plus a folder of files; the same presentation saved as an .mhtm file was 68KB with no extra folder.*

3. In FrontPage Folders view, click Refresh on the toolbar and you will see the PowerPoint .HTM file.

**NOTE**   *Using Windows Explorer, open the folder in which you saved the PowerPoint HTM file, then open the PowerPoint HTML folder and observe the complete web that has been created (as seen in the example in Figure 11-13).*

4. In FrontPage Folders view, double-click the PowerPoint.htm file in the destination folder to open it in PowerPoint. What you get is your original presentation, as you do with the .PPT file.

5. To see the presentation in the browser, select the PowerPoint.htm file in the Folder List and click Preview In Browser on the toolbar to see the presentation as it will appear in the browser.

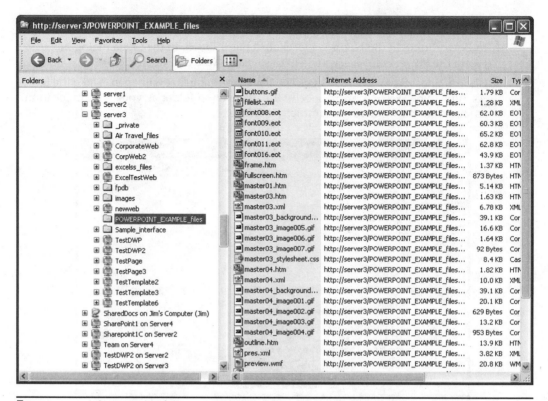

**FIGURE 11-13**   An example of the complete set of files created for a PowerPoint web

All of the Microsoft Office applications, including Access and Outlook, have the impressive ability to create HTML and other files that are usable in a web and importable with FrontPage. This is a great way to quickly generate web content.

## Using Legacy Files on an Intranet

An intranet provides an excellent opportunity to make good use of, or even improve, *legacy* (previously created) files. Manuals and sets of procedures are particularly good examples of this. Instead of maintaining 20 (or 50 or 500!) sets of company manuals that rarely get used except to settle an argument, maintain one set on your intranet. Here people can use a search capability to quickly find what they are looking for, whenever they want and wherever they are.

Manuals and sets of procedures almost surely exist as word processing files that can be easily transferred to FrontPage. Once you do that, you can add the Table of Contents Web component to quickly index the files, the Web Search component to search all of the text, and Dynamic Web Templates to place headers and footers on each page with link bars, time stamps, and contacts.

---

**NOTE**   *The Web Search component and the Table of Contents | For This Web Site are not supported in Windows SharePoint Services, SharePoint 2.*

Company reports and periodicals are also good candidates for your intranet—current editions and previous issues can be searched and read in one easily accessible place.

The availability of FrontPage's search capability to easily find information on an intranet could be the primary reason for putting information on it. In the same vein, the Table of Contents and Dynamic Web Templates can significantly improve usability of existing documents. In other words, putting your legacy documents on your intranet with FrontPage not only gives them a new way to be distributed and read, but features such as the Search, Table of Contents, and Dynamic Web Templates also make them substantially more usable, and therefore more likely to be used. Finally, and far from least important, putting information on an intranet ensures that everyone in the organization is getting the same information and the latest version of it.

## Looking at Imported Files in a Browser

You have seen how Excel and PowerPoint files look in a browser, but take a peek at how the Table of Contents Web component can be used to provide both an overview and navigation within a web site. Again, note that the Web Component Table of Contents | For This Web Site is not available with Windows SharePoint Services.

### Using the Table of Contents Web Component

The Table of Contents Web component can automatically create links to all the HTM pages and the DOC, XLS, and PPT files. It will include any internal links that those pages may contain, as you'll see below. Follow these steps:

1. Open a web page in Page view. The page opened should be your Home page with a filename of Default.htm. You can use this page for your Table of Contents, or from Page view, you can create a blank page, which is what we do in this example.

2. Enter a title for the page—for example, **Table of Contents**—format it with Heading 1, center it, and press ENTER.

3. Choose Insert | Web Component, then select Table Of Contents | For This Web Site and click Finish.

4. Accept the defaults for the Table of Contents Properties; this gives you a link to all of the HTM files (although they won't appear until you open the web in a browser), and click OK. (To close the dialog box, you may need to Browse the current web to select Default.htm.)

5. Save any pages changed, including any page titles (see the following Note). Display the Table of Contents page and then click View | Hyperlinks. You should see all of the links for the Table of Contents page, as shown in Figure 11-14.

---

**NOTE**    *You can change the title of an indexed page by changing the Title in the Page Properties dialog. Right-click the page and select Page Properties from the context menu. Be sure to save the page.*

6. Click Preview In Browser on the toolbar. The Table of Contents page will appear, an example of which is shown in Figure 11-15.

---

**NOTE**    *Links to seemingly duplicate pages are a result of the many secondary files in the PowerPoint example.*

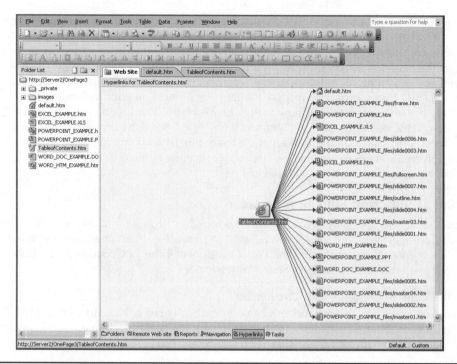

**FIGURE 11-14**   Hyperlinks created by the Table of Contents Web component

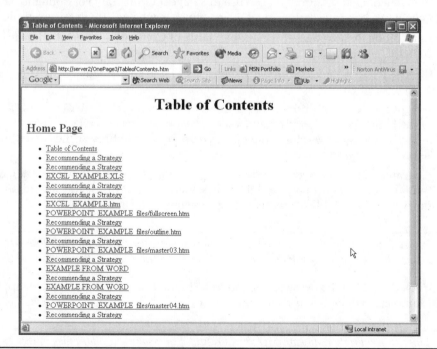

**FIGURE 11-15**   Table of Contents give you links to each page in a web.

You can click a number of the links to view the imported (or opened or inserted) files, using the browser's Back button to return to the Table of Contents page. You will not find many surprises.

## Importing Hyperlinks

One of the better examples of Office integration is the ability of FrontPage to recognize and preserve hyperlinks present in imported files. Not only does FrontPage display the hyperlinks in FrontPage views, but also when affected files are moved or renamed within the FrontPage web, FrontPage will update the hyperlink references in the Office files. As an example, one file with links to four others has been imported into a blank, one page web. Figure 11-16 shows an excerpt from this book cut and pasted into a web page, including

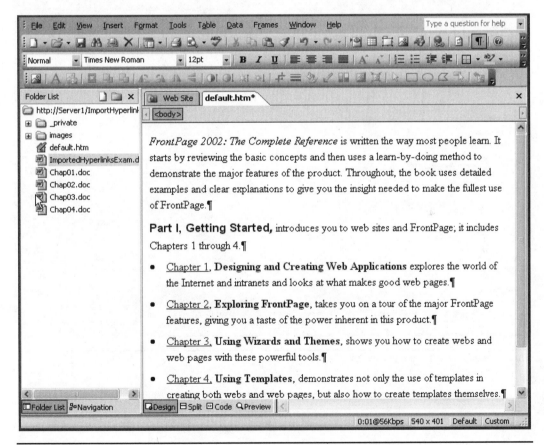

**FIGURE 11-16**   Imported document with hyperlinks

hyperlinks to references of other chapters in the book. After importing the file, along with the four chapter files (Chap01.doc, Chap02.doc, Chap03.doc, and Chap04.doc), into a FrontPage web, the hyperlink relationships are displayed in FrontPage's Hyperlinks view, as shown in Figure 11-17.

Importing files into a FrontPage web—whether they are text, tables, presentations, or databases (covered in Chapter 17)—provides a great deal of ready-made content. When these files are artfully used, they can quickly give a web a lot of depth. As you are building a web site, remember the many existing files available. Their use in a web will further leverage their original investment.

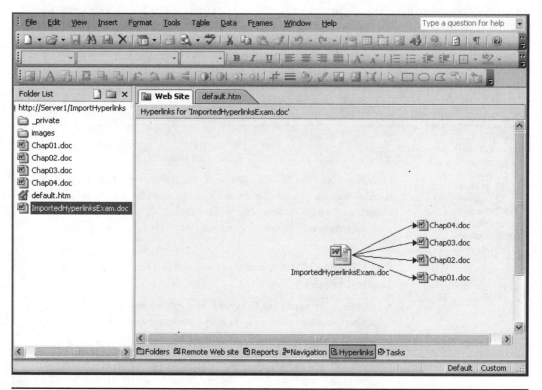

**FIGURE 11-17**   Hyperlinks carried over into FrontPage

# Working Behind the Scenes

In the previous chapters, you've learned how to use FrontPage to build webs without extensive knowledge of HTML or other Web technologies. With FrontPage, you can build great webs without this knowledge, but the Web is an evolving creature with a growing array of new technologies (most of which are still evolving themselves). This section contains the information you need to better understand how your webs work and how to add features that can raise your webs to the next level where web pages have dynamic content and your audience can truly interact with your webs.

Chapter 12 explains Hypertext Markup Language (HTML), the foundation language of the Web. Chapter 13 covers Dynamic HTML (DHTML), the first major evolutionary step in Web languages. Chapter 14 discusses Extensible Markup Language (XML), which enables content and presentation to be treated separately—a major step forward for the Web. Chapter 15 describes scripting for the Web using JavaScript and Visual Basic Script (VBScript), the most common scripting languages used on the Web. Chapter 16 discusses Active Server Pages (ASP).NET, a technology that empowers you to create truly interactive webs. Chapter 17 explains how to integrate databases with your webs, a necessity for advanced Web applications, and Chapter 18 discusses how to add active elements (such as animations) to your webs using FrontPage.

# Working with HTML

With FrontPage, you don't have to learn HTML (Hypertext Markup Language), the foundation programming language of the Web, you can build great web pages without ever knowing anything about it or even reading this chapter. But for those who either want to go further—to put the last bit of flourish on their web page—or who just want to understand the HTML behind their FrontPage-created web, this chapter will be useful. With access to FrontPage, you probably will not have to create many webs from scratch in HTML, so this chapter will not provide exhaustive coverage of that topic, nor will it cover every nuance of every HTML tag. Both areas are fully covered by sites on the Web, as listed at the end of this chapter. What this chapter will cover is how to understand the HTML that is generated by a FrontPage web and how to add specific capabilities to a FrontPage web with HTML.

---

***NOTE*** *Stephen Le Hunte's HTML Reference Library, HTMLib, is a valuable resource that provides, in Windows Help format, a detailed reference to every HTML tag and its attributes. It is strongly recommended that you download and install HTMLib and refer to it as you read this chapter. You can download this reference library from a number of sites, but the primary site is **http:// www.htmlib.demon.co.uk.** (Download and save this to a folder named "HTMLib" and then from the Windows Explorer, open this folder and double-click Hlbsetup.exe. This installs HTMLib, which you can then use as you do Windows Help. Once installed, use the library by opening Start | All Programs | HTML Reference Library.)*

---

***NOTE*** *Even though there is a standards body for the Web (the World Wide Web Consortium— http://www.w3.org), compliance with its standards is somewhat voluntary. As a result, you cannot count on all web browsers interpreting your HTML code identically. Some differences are relatively minor, while others are not. It's always best to test your work in the major browsers before publishing it. At the time of this writing, Microsoft's Internet Explorer is the dominant browser, with a market share of over 90 percent. Netscape's Navigator is a distant second. (There was a time when these positions were reversed.) You also need to be aware of the versions of the various browsers as not everyone updates to the latest versions when they are released. It's reasonable to design for versions 4.0 and later of Internet Explorer and Navigator, but this will not absolutely cover everyone surfing the Web.*

## Introducing HTML

*HTML* is a series of tags that identify the elements in a web page. *Tags* or *markup tags* consist of a tag name enclosed in angle brackets and normally come in pairs. Tags are placed at the beginning and end of an element, generally text, which you want to identify, with the ending tag name preceded by a slash. For example,

```
<TITLE>This is a title</TITLE>
```

uses the Title tag to identify text that will be placed in the title bar of the browser window. Tags are not case-sensitive, so they can be all uppercase, all lowercase, or a mixture. Tags are placed around text to control its formatting and placement on a page, to identify a hypertext link, to identify a graphic, sound, or video to be loaded, or to identify a particular area of a web page.

---

***TIP***    *While HTML is not case-sensitive, this is an exception in the realm of programming languages. For example, both XML (covered in Chapter 14) and JavaScript (Chapter 15) are case-sensitive. Webs today rarely contain only HTML, as you will learn in the following chapters. Treating your HTML as if it is case-sensitive is a good programming habit that will reduce headaches when working with multiple languages.*

---

In addition to a tag name, a tag may contain one or more *attributes* that modify what the tag does. For example, if you want to center a paragraph on the page, you could use this tag:

```
<P ALIGN="CENTER">This will be a centered paragraph</P>
```

ALIGN="CENTER" is an *attribute* for the Paragraph tag.

---

***TIP***    *HTML does not require that attribute values be enclosed in quotes, as just shown, but other languages, such as XML, do. Again, it's best to be consistent. In this case, this means enclosing all attribute values in quotes.*

---

***NOTE***    *In the listings and HTML examples in this chapter, tags are shown in all capital letters and bold, while attributes are just all capital letters. Also, continuation lines are indented from their parents. These conventions are used solely for readability. By default, HTML created by FrontPage is lowercase, indented using spaces, and attribute values are enclosed in quotes. In the Code Formatting tab of the Tools | Page Options dialog box, you can change these settings. HTML is also by default color-coded for readability when a page is viewed in Code view (by clicking the Code option in the View bar at the bottom of the Page view pane). The colors used for tags, attribute names, attribute values, and comments are set in Tools | Page Options Color Coding tab.*

---

***NOTE***    *Code view options (Word Wrap, Auto Indent, Line Numbers, and Selection Margin) are available at Tools | Page Options General tab under Code View Options. Their functions are covered in Table 12-10.*

## Using Basic Tags

All web pages must contain a basic set of tags. These tags identify the document as being an HTML document and identify the major parts of the document. With the exception of DOCTYPE, these are the only tags that must be included in a web page to conform to the HTML standard. The Body tag is also used to identify the page defaults, such as the background color or image and the text color. The basic tags, some of which are shown in Listing 12-1, are described with their attributes in Table 12-1.

**Listing 12-1:**
Basic set
of HTML

```
<!DOCTYPE HTML PUBLIC "-//W3C//DTD HTML 4.0//EN">
<HTML>
  <HEAD>
    <META HTTP-EQUIV="Content-Language" CONTENT="en-us">
    <META HTTP-EQUIV="Content-Type" CONTENT="text/html;
      charset=windows-1252">
    <TITLE>Listing 1</TITLE>
    <META NAME="Microsoft Border" CONTENT="none">
  </HEAD>
  <BODY TEXT="#FFFFFF" BGCOLOR="#0000FF">
    <P>This is the text that is the body of this web document.</P>
  </BODY>
</HTML>
```

**TABLE 12-1**
Basic Set of HTML
Tags with Their
Attributes

| Tag or Attribute | Description |
|---|---|
| `<!DOCTYPE ...>` | Identifies the document as adhering to the given HTML version. This tag is optional and often left off. |
| `<HTML> </HTML>` | Identifies the intervening text as being HTML. |
| `<HEAD> </HEAD>` | Contains the title and document identifying information. The `<TITLE>` tag is required in the `<HEAD>` tag. |
| `<TITLE> </TITLE>` | Identifies the title that is placed in the browser's title bar. |
| `<META ...>` | Assigns content to an element that can be used by a server or browser and cannot otherwise be assigned in HTML; "Microsoft FrontPage 5.0" is assigned to "GENERATOR" in Listing 12-1. Placed within the `<HEAD>` tag. |
| `<STYLE> </STYLE>` | Defines a style sheet that prescribes specific styles that are to use certain elements such as normal paragraph (`<P>`) and first-level headings (`<H1>`). See "Style Sheets" later in this chapter. |
| `<BODY> </BODY>` | Specifies the part of the page that is shown to the user and defines overall page properties. |

PART III

**TABLE 12-1**
Basic Set of HTML
Tags with Their
Attributes
*(continued)*

| Tag or Attribute | Description |
|---|---|
| ALINK | Identifies the color of the active link as either a color name or hexadecimal number representing a color value. |
| BACKGROUND | Identifies the background image that will be tiled if necessary to fill the window. |
| BGCOLOR | Identifies the background color that will be used, as either a color name or a hexadecimal number representing a color value. The hexadecimal value for blue is shown in Listing 12-1. |
| BGPROPERTIES | Specifies that the background image will not scroll with the window if BGPROPERTIES =FIXED. |
| LEFTMARGIN | Sets the left margin for the entire page and overrides any default margin (a margin of 0 will be exactly on the left edge). |
| LINK | Identifies the color of links that have not been used, as either a color name or a hexadecimal number representing a color value. |
| TEXT | Identifies the color of text on the page as either a color name or a hexadecimal number representing a color value. The hexadecimal value for white is shown in Listing 12-1. |
| TOPMARGIN | Sets the top margin for the page and overrides any default margin (a margin of 0 will be exactly on the top edge). |
| VLINK | Identifies the color of links that have been used as either a color name or a hexadecimal number representing a color value. |

**NOTE**  *In HTML (and other programming languages), you will often see numbers written using hexadecimal notation, as in the numerical values for the BODY tag attributes TEXT and BGCOLOR in Listing 12-1. Hexadecimal is a base-16 numbering system where the basic "numbers" are 0 through F and are used in pairs; 0 in decimal notation (base-10) is written 00 in hexadecimal. In HTML, hexadecimal numbers are preceded by a pound sign (#). The section "Using Color" explains how colors are defined using hexadecimal notation.*

**NOTE**  *In the tables of tags and attributes in this chapter, tags are shown with their angle brackets, and attributes are indented from the left.*

**TIP**  *Just because an HTML tag exists doesn't mean you have to use it. As in most other endeavors, the KISS principle applies to the use of HTML.*

## Using Color

Color names that can be used with ALINK, BGCOLOR, LINK, TEXT, and VLINK, as well as other tags with Microsoft Internet Explorer 2.0 and 3.0, are Black, White, Green, Maroon, Olive, Navy, Purple, Gray, Red, Yellow, Blue, Teal, Lime, Aqua, Fuchsia, and Silver. Microsoft Internet Explorer 4.0 and later, and Netscape Navigator or Communicator 3.0 and later, support 140 named colors (for a complete listing, open Stephen Le Hunte's HTML Reference Library, HTMLib; in the left pane, open The HTML Language Reference | Document Structure Elements | Body | Possible Colour Names, and then point on a color to see both its hexadecimal number and its English name). In addition to the named colors, a color value may be used that is a combination of three hexadecimal numbers, one each for Red, Green, and Blue. (This is often called a hexadecimal triplet.) Each primary color can have 256 tones (ranging in value from 0 to 255 decimal or 00 to FF hexadecimal), and these combinations allow a total of over 16 million colors, compared with the 16 or 140 named colors. The video card and monitor must be configured to support Medium Color Quality (16-bit, which produces over 65 thousand colors), High Color Quality (24-bit) or Highest Color Quality (32-bit color, which displays over 16 million colors) to get the full benefit of these colors.

---

*TIP*   *An easy way to convert between decimal and hexadecimal notation is to use the Windows Calculator in Scientific mode. Open the calculator from Start | All Programs | Accessories | Calculator, then select View | Scientific. Click either the Hex or Dec option, enter a hexadecimal or decimal number, and click the appropriate mode to convert the number. Hexadecimal may seem a bit complicated but it makes a great deal of sense to a computer, which is really using binary (base-2) arithmetic and internally converting all numbers.*

In the past, any discussion of color on the Web focused on the Web Safe palette—216 colors that would display correctly on virtually any monitor. One reason the earliest browsers had only 16 named colors was that many systems wouldn't support more than 16 colors. Today, this situation, like everything else connected with the Web, is vastly different. As this is written (in the Summer of 2003), very few computers surfing the Web are limited to 256 colors. At this point, it makes little sense to adhere to a standard that has been made obsolete by advancing technology. This doesn't mean that named colors should not be used when they fit the application, only that the importance of adhering to this standard has greatly diminished.

One of the best sources for information on color and web browsers is *The DMS Guide to Web Color* at **http://csu.colstate.edu/webdevelop/design/color/dms_guide_to_color_for_the _web.htm**. This site includes palettes that can be used with Adobe Photoshop and other graphics programs. Stephen Le Hunte's HTML Reference Library (HTMLib) has a Color Wizard, which gives you three ways to visually create the hexadecimal values for any possible color.

## Setting Paragraph Styles

Paragraph styles include basic paragraph definition and alignment, headings, the line break, bulleted, numbered, and definition lists, preformatted (called "Formatted" in FrontPage) paragraphs, comments, and horizontal lines or rules. Unless the preformatted style is used, normal line endings, extra spaces of more than one, and tabs are ignored in

HTML. Lines simply wrap to fit the space allotted for them unless you use the Paragraph tag. Listing 12-2 shows examples of paragraph styles. This listing is combined with the tags in Listing 12-1 to produce the web page shown in Figure 12-1. Paragraph styles are described in Table 12-2.

**Listing 12-2:**
Example
of using
paragraph
style tags

```
<H2 ALIGN="CENTER">This is a 2nd-level heading and is centered</H2>
<P>This is the first line of a paragraph which ends with a line break.<BR>
This is the second line of a paragraph.</P>
<HR WIDTH="70%" SIZE="3">
<UL>
  <LI>This is item 1 in a bulleted (unordered) list</LI>
  <LI>This is item 2 in a bulleted list</LI>
</UL>
<OL>
  <LI>This is item 1 in a numbered (ordered) list</LI>
  <LI>This is item 2 in a numbered list</LI>
</OL>
<!-- This is a comment, it is ignored by a browser and not displayed -->
<PRE>This line will be reproduced with
 all its spaces, tabs, and line endings.</PRE>
<ADDRESS>This text will be italicized</ADDRESS>
```

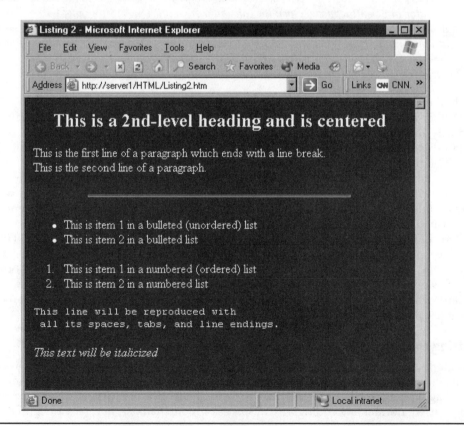

**FIGURE 12-1** The web page listing resulting from placing Listing 12-2 between the Body tags of Listing 12-1

**TABLE 12-2**
Paragraph Style
HTML Tags

| Tag | Description |
|-----|-------------|
| `<P> </P>` | Identifies the start and end of a paragraph and its alignment with `ALIGN=` and `LEFT`, `CENTER`, or `RIGHT`. |
| `<Hn> </Hn>` | Identifies a heading in one of six heading styles ($n = 1$ to 6) and its alignment with `ALIGN=` and `LEFT`, `CENTER`, or `RIGHT`. |
| `<BR>` | Forces a line break similar to pressing SHIFT-ENTER in FrontPage. |
| `<HR>` | Creates a horizontal rule or line where you can specify the alignment, color, shade, size (height), and width across the page. |
| `<OL> </OL>` | Contains an ordered (numbered) list. |
| `<UL> </UL>` | Contains an unordered (bulleted) list. |
| `<LI> </LI>` | Identifies an item in a numbered or bulleted list. |
| `<DL> </DL>` | Contains a definition list. |
| `<DT> </DT>` | Identifies a term to be defined, displayed on the left of a window. |
| `<DD> </DD>` | Identifies the definition of the term that immediately precedes it, indented from the left. |
| `<ADDRESS> </ADDRESS>` | Identifies a paragraph of italicized text. |
| `<BLOCKQUOTE> </BLOCKQUOTE>` | Identifies a paragraph that is indented on both the left and right, as you might do with a quotation. |
| `<CENTER> </CENTER>` | Centers all text and images contained within it. |
| `<!-- -->` or `<COMMENT> </COMMENT>` | Identifies a comment that the browser will ignore and not display. `<COMMENT> </COMMENT>` is not used in Netscape Navigator. |
| `<DIV> </DIV>` | Identifies a division of a page for which the alignment is set with `ALIGN=` and `LEFT`, `CENTER`, or `RIGHT`. |
| `<PRE> </PRE>` | Identifies preformatted text in which all spaces, tabs, and line endings are preserved (called "Formatted" in FrontPage). The maximum number of characters in each line can be set with `WIDTH=` (generally 40, 80, or 132). |

**TIP** *In HTML, it is not always necessary to have a closing tag, for example, the List Item tag `<LI>` can be used without the closing `</LI>` tag. It is also not necessary to have a `</P>` if it would be immediately followed by a `<P>`. All browsers will assume the last item or paragraph has ended when a new one starts. However, XML does require that every tag be closed. To ensure future compatibility between the languages, FrontPage inserts the closing tags.*

**NOTE** *You can nest lists within lists and get automatic indenting.*

## Applying Character Styles

Character styles, which determine how one or more characters will look or behave, come in two forms. *Logical* character styles are defined by the browser and may be displayed in any way that the browser has established. *Physical* character styles have a strict definition that will be the same in all browsers. Examples of character style tags are shown in Listing 12-3, while Figure 12-2 shows how Microsoft Internet Explorer 6 and Netscape Navigator 7 display them. Note the lack of differences. Table 12-3 describes most character styles.

**NOTE** *Figure 12-2 demonstrates that browsers ignore line endings unless they are marked with* `<P>`, `<BR>`, *or other paragraph styles.*

**Listing 12-3:**
Examples
of using
character
style tags

```
<B>This text is bold</B>
This text is normal size, <BIG>this is larger</BIG>
This text is normal size, <SMALL>this is smaller</SMALL>
<CODE>This is normally fixed-width font</CODE>
<EM>This text is normally italic</EM>
<FONT COLOR="#0000FF" SIZE="5">This text is size 5 and
  in blue</FONT>
<I>This text is italic</I>
<STRIKE>This text is struck through</STRIKE>
<STRONG>This text is normally bold</STRONG>
<U>This text is underlined</U>
```

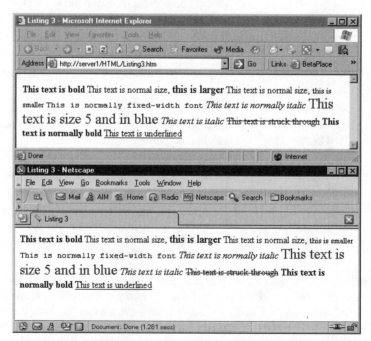

**FIGURE 12-2**   Character style tags displayed in Microsoft Internet Explorer 6 and Netscape Navigator 7

| Tag | Description |
|---|---|
| `<B> </B>` | Applies the Bold physical character style to the enclosed characters. |
| `<BASEFONT>` | Establishes the font size and/or color and/or typeface for a web (`<STYLE>` is now often used in place of `<BASEFONT>`; see "Style Sheets" later in this chapter). |
| `<BIG> </BIG>` | Makes the enclosed characters one size larger. |
| `<BLINK> </BLINK>` | Applies the Blink physical character style to the enclosed characters; introduced by Netscape, this tag is not part of the HTML standard and is not recommended. |
| `<CITE> </CITE>` | Applies the Citation logical character style to the enclosed characters; normally italic. |
| `<CODE> </CODE>` | Applies the Code logical character style to the enclosed characters; normally a fixed-width font. |
| `<DFN> </DFN>` | Applies the Definition logical character style to the enclosed characters; normally italic. |
| `<EM> </EM>` | Applies the Emphasis logical character style to the enclosed characters; normally italic. |
| `<FONT> </FONT>` | Applies the font size and/or color and/or typeface specified to the enclosed characters; if `<BASEFONT>` is used, `<FONT>` size can be relative to the base font size. |
| `<I> </I>` | Applies the Italic physical character style to the enclosed characters. |
| `<KBD> </KBD>` | Applies the Keyboard logical character style to the enclosed characters; normally a fixed-width font. |
| `<S> </S>` or `<STRIKE> </STRIKE>` | Applies the Strikethrough physical character style to the enclosed characters. |
| `<SAMP> </SAMP>` | Applies the Sample logical character style to the enclosed characters; normally a fixed-width font. |
| `<SMALL> </SMALL>` | Makes the enclosed characters one size smaller. |
| `<STRONG> </STRONG>` | Applies the Strong logical character style to the enclosed characters; normally bold. |
| `<SUB> </SUB>` | Applies the Subscript physical character style to the enclosed characters. |
| `<SUP> </SUP>` | Applies the Superscript physical character style to the enclosed characters. |
| `<TT> </TT>` | Applies the Typewriter Text physical character style to the enclosed characters; a fixed-width font. |
| `<U> </U>` | Applies the Underline physical character style to the enclosed characters. |

**TABLE 12-3**    Character Style HTML tags

## Displaying Special Characters

HTML defines that the less-than, greater-than, and ampersand characters have special meanings and therefore cannot be used as normal text. To use these characters normally, replace them as follows:

| To display a: | Type these characters: |
| --- | --- |
| Less-than (<) | &lt; or &#60; |
| Greater-than (>) | &gt; or &#62; |
| Ampersand (&) | &amp; or &#38; |

All other characters that you can type on your keyboard will be displayed as they are typed. In addition, HTML has defined a number of other characters that can be displayed based on entering an *escape sequence* where you want the character displayed (in FrontPage, these characters are also available from the Insert | Symbol window). The escape sequence can take either a numeric or a textual format, as was shown with the three special characters just mentioned. In either case, the escape sequence begins with an ampersand (&) and ends with a semicolon (;). In the numeric format, the ampersand is followed by a number symbol (#) and a number that represents the character. All characters, whether they are on the keyboard or not, can be represented with a numeric escape sequence. The textual format has been defined only for some characters and excludes most characters on the keyboard. Additional examples of the two formats are shown in Table 12-4.

---

**NOTE**   *Unlike the rest of HTML, escape sequences are case-sensitive—for example, you cannot use &LT; for the less-than symbol.*

For complete lists of the character escape sequences, open Stephen Le Hunte's HTML Reference Library, HTMLib; in the left pane, open The HTML Language Reference | Character Data | Character Entity References, and scroll the right pane to see both the complete ISO Latin-1 character set and the additional HTML 4.0–specified characters.

| Character | Name | Numeric Sequence | Text Sequence |
| --- | --- | --- | --- |
| … | Horizontal Ellipsis | &#133; | &hellip; |
| · | Bullet | &#149; | &bull; |
| ™ | Trademark | &#153; | &trade; |
| © | Copyright | &#169; | &copy; |
| Æ | AE ligature | &#198; | &aelig; |
| Ä | a umlaut | &#228; | &auml; |
| É | e acute accent | &#233; | &eacute; |
| Õ | o tilde | &#245; | &otilde; |

**TABLE 12-4**   Samples of Character Escape Sequences

## Style Sheets

*Style sheets*, or *cascading style sheets* (*CSS*), allow you to define and apply paragraph and character styles to an entire document or web. Style sheets can be part of (embedded in) an HTML document within the Head tag using the Style tag, or can be a separate document referenced by the HTML page using the Link tag. Listing 12-4 shows the definition of a simple embedded style sheet that defines two heading and two paragraph styles.

**Listing 12-4:**
Definition
and use of a
style sheet

```
<HTML>
  <HEAD>
    <TITLE>This is the title</TITLE>
    <STYLE>
      <!--
        H1.red { font-family: Arial; font-size: 18pt;
                 font-weight: bold; color: red}
        H1.blue { font-family: Arial; font-size: 18pt;
                  font-weight: bold; color: blue}
        P.main { font-family: Times; font-size: 12pt}
        P.special { font-family: Times; font-style: italic;
                    font-size: 12pt}
      -->
    </STYLE>
  </HEAD>
  <BODY>
    <H1 CLASS="red">This is a heading in red</H1>
    <P CLASS="main">This is a main paragraph</P>
    <H1 CLASS="blue">This is a heading in blue</H1>
    <P CLASS="special">This is a special paragraph</P>
  </BODY>
</HTML>
```

A style is a set of properties that can be attached to any HTML tag, such as <H1> (level-1 heading). In effect, you can redefine HTML tags. For example, to have all your level-1 heads display as 18 pt Arial bold in blue, you would redefine the level-1 head like this:

```
H1 {font-family : Arial; font-size : 18 pt
    font-weight: bold; color: blue}
```

You can also have classes of styles. For example, if you want some of your level-1 heads to be blue and some red, you could define two styles: H1.blue and H1.red, as shown in Listing 12-4. The HTML to use the red style would then look like this:

```
<H1 CLASS="red">This heading would be in the H1.red style</H1>
```

Style sheets use a single tag, Style, and within that tag define the various styles you want to use. To keep older browsers that do not know how to handle styles from generating an error, comment tags are placed at the beginning and end of the definitions. These are ignored by the more recent browsers and keep the older browsers from choking on the style definitions.

For more information on the HTML related to style sheets, see the Style Sheets Reference section of the HTML Reference Library (HTMLib) and the Style Sheet resource page at W3C (**http://www.w3.org/Style/**).

## Working with Images and Image Maps

Images are added to a web by use of the Image (<IMG>) tag, which specifies the path and filename of the image as well as a number of attributes such as size, positioning, margins, and border. One of the attributes, ISMAP, identifies the image as having an image map attached to it. The image map is a separate MAP file used by the server to relate areas of the image to URLs. To use ISMAP, you must include the Image tag in an Anchor tag (see the next section, "Adding Hyperlinks and Bookmarks"). A couple of examples are given in Listing 12-5 and shown in Figure 12-3. Many of the Image attributes are described in Table 12-5.

---

**NOTE** *The   (which can also be  ) in Listing 12-5 is a nonbreaking space and is used with the Paragraph tags to create a blank line (paragraph) that HTML will not get rid of.*

---

**Listing 12-5:**
Examples of using the Image tag

```
<P><IMG SRC="hibiscus.jpg" ALT="A picture of a hibiscus"
  ALIGN="bottom" BORDER="2" HSPACE="3" WIDTH="166"
  HEIGHT="190"> This is a picture of a hibiscus ...</P>
<P> </P>
<P ALIGN="center"><IMG SRC="undercon.gif" ALT="Under
  Construction" ALIGN="top" WIDTH="40" HEIGHT="38">
  This image is centered...</P>
```

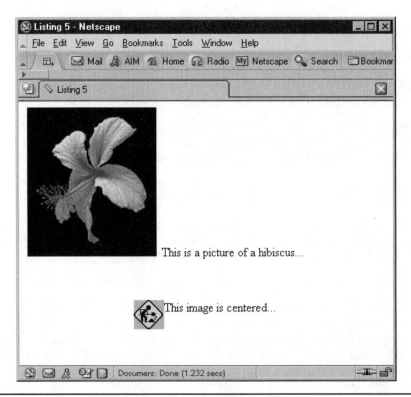

**FIGURE 12-3** Example using the Image tag in Listing 12-5

| Attribute | Description |
|---|---|
| ALIGN | Positions text at the TOP, MIDDLE, or BOTTOM of the image, or positions the image on the LEFT or RIGHT of the text. |
| ALT | Identifies alternative text that is displayed when the mouse pointer is placed on the image or if the image cannot be displayed. |
| BORDER | Specifies that a border of so many pixels be drawn around the image. |
| HEIGHT | Specifies the height, in pixels, of the image. |
| HSPACE | Specifies the blank space, in pixels, on the left and right sides of the image. |
| ISMAP | Indicates that the image has an image map. |
| SRC | Identifies the path and filename or URL of the image. |
| USEMAP | Indicates the name of the image map that is to be used. |
| VSPACE | Specifies the blank space, in pixels, on the top and bottom of the image. |
| WIDTH | Specifies the width, in pixels, of the image. |

**TABLE 12-5**   Image Tag Attributes

*TIP   Specifying the HEIGHT and the WIDTH speeds up loading, because a quick placeholder will be drawn for the image, allowing the text to continue to be loaded while the image is drawn. Without these dimensions, the loading of the text must wait for the image to be drawn and thereby determine where the remaining text will go. Netscape Navigator 3.0 and above and Internet Explorer 4.0 and above will automatically scale the other dimension based on the current aspect ratio of the image if just one of the dimensions (HEIGHT or WIDTH) is given.*

## Adding Hyperlinks and Bookmarks

Hyperlinks provide the ability to click an object and transfer what is displayed by the browser (the *focus*) to an address associated with the object. HTML implements hyperlinks with the Anchor tag (<A> </A>), which specifies that the text or graphic that it contains is a hyperlink or a bookmark or both. If the tag is a *hyperlink* and the contents are selected, then the focus is moved either to another location in the current page or web, or to another web. If the tag is a *bookmark*, then another Anchor tag may reference it and potentially transfer the focus to it.

An image used as just described assumes that the entire image is the hyperlink. An image may also be broken into sections, where each section is a link or a *hotspot*. To break an image into multiple links requires an *image map* that is implemented with the Map tag. The Map tag contains Area tags that define the shape of a specific area of the image and the link that it is pointing to.

Listing 12-6 provides some examples of the Anchor, Map, and Area tags, which are shown in Figure 12-4. Table 12-6 describes these tags and their attributes.

PART III

> **NOTE**    *The pointer in Figure 12-4 is pointing to the hotspot labeled "Screen," as shown at the bottom of the window (.../Listing6.htm#Screen).*

**Listing 12-6:**
Examples of
hyperlinks
and
bookmarks

```html
<P>This is a link to the <A HREF="default.htm">Home
   Page.</A></P>
<P><A NAME="This ">This </A>is a bookmark.</P>
<P>This <A HREF="#This ">link </A>takes you to the bookmark.</P>
<P><MAP NAME="ComputerMap">
  <AREA SHAPE="POLYGON" COORDS="163, 121, 197, 145, 91, 183, 55,
     157" HREF="#Keyboard">
  <AREA SHAPE="POLYGON" COORDS="6, 90, 147, 87, 148, 115, 46, 145,
     2, 124" HREF="#Processor">
  <AREA SHAPE="RECT" COORDS="30, 6, 124, 70" HREF="#Screen"></MAP>
  <A HREF="computer.map">
    <IMG ALIGN="bottom" SRC="computer.gif" WIDTH="200" ISMAP
       USEMAP="#ComputerMap" HEIGHT="186"></A></P>
```

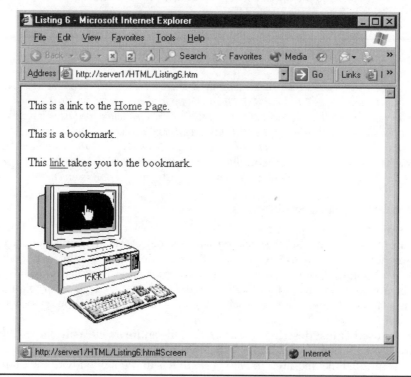

**FIGURE 12-4**    Hyperlinks and bookmarks defined in Listing 12-6

| Tag or Attribute | Description |
|---|---|
| `<A> </A>` | Specifies the definition of a hyperlink. |
| HREF | Identifies the destination URL, which can be a bookmark, page, or web. |
| NAME | Identifies the bookmark at this location. |
| TARGET | Identifies a specific frame in the link destination. |
| TITLE | Identifies a name for a link that is displayed when the mouse passes over the link; otherwise, the link address is displayed. |
| `<MAP> </MAP>` | Specifies the definition of an image map. |
| NAME | Identifies the name of the image map. |
| `<AREA> </AREA>` | Specifies the definition of one image area. |
| SHAPE | Identifies the type of shape being defined to be CIRC, CIRCLE, POLY, POLYGON, RECT, or RECTANGLE. |
| COORDS | Identifies the coordinates of the shape being defined using x and y positions in terms of image pixels for each point. |
| HREF | Identifies the bookmark or URL to which the focus is transferred. |
| NOHREF | Indicates that a given area causes no action to take place. |

**TABLE 12-6**   Anchor, Map, and Area tags and Their Attributes

**NOTE**   *The SHAPE attribute of the Area tag may be left out, and a rectangular shape will be assumed.*

## Defining Forms

A form in HTML is defined by the input fields that it contains. Each input field is defined by its type, name, and potentially a default value. There are a number of field types around which you can wrap text and formatting to get virtually any form you want to define. One example is shown in Listing 12-7 and displayed in Figure 12-5. Table 12-7 describes the tags and attributes related to forms.

**Listing 12-7:**
Example
of a form

```
<H1>This is a form</H1>
<FORM ACTION="saveresults" METHOD="post">
  <PRE>
    Name: <INPUT TYPE="TEXT" SIZE="50" MAXLENGTH="256"
      NAME="Name"><BR>
    Address: <INPUT TYPE="TEXT" SIZE="50" MAXLENGTH="256"
      NAME="Address"><BR><BR>
    Send Data? Yes <INPUT TYPE="RADIO" NAME="Send" Value="Yes">
    No <INPUT TYPE="RADIO" NAME="Send" Value="No">
    For what type of product? <SELECT NAME="Product" MULTIPLE
      SIZE="1">
      <OPTION SELECTED VALUE="Laptop"> Laptop
      <OPTION VALUE="Desktop">Desk Top
        </SELECT><BR>
    Check if a member <INPUT TYPE="CHECKBOX" NAME="Member"
      Value="TRUE">
    <BR><BR>
    <INPUT TYPE="SUBMIT" VALUE="Send It"> <INPUT TYPE="RESET"
      VALUE="Forget It">
  </PRE>
</FORM>
```

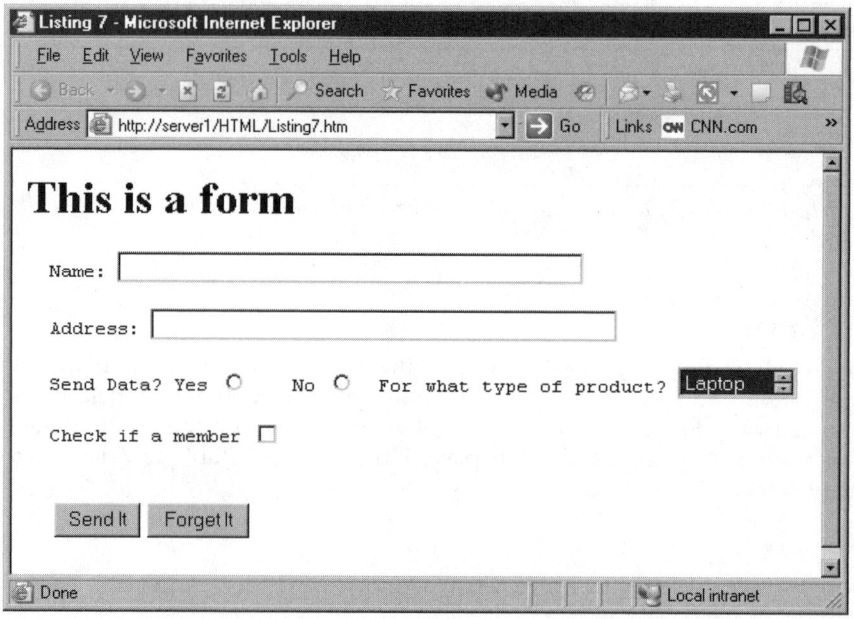

FIGURE 12-5   Form created with Listing 12-7

| Tag or Attribute | Description |
|---|---|
| <FORM> </FORM> | Specifies the definition of a form. |
| <INPUT> | Identifies one input field. |
| TYPE | Specifies the field type to be CHECKBOX, HIDDEN, IMAGE, PASSWORD, RADIO, RESET, SUBMIT, TEXT, or TEXTAREA. |
| NAME | Specifies the name of the field. |
| VALUE | Specifies the default value of the field. |
| ALIGN | If TYPE=IMAGE, positions text at TOP, BOTTOM, or CENTER of image. |
| CHECKED | If TYPE=CHECKBOX or RADIO, determines if by default they are selected (TRUE) or not (FALSE). |
| MAXLENGTH | Specifies the maximum number of characters that can be entered in a text field. |
| SIZE | Specifies the width of a text field in characters, or the width and height in characters and lines of a text area. |
| SRC | Specifies the URL of an image if TYPE=IMAGE. |
| <SELECT> </SELECT> | Specifies the definition of a drop-down menu. |
| NAME | Specifies the name of a menu. |
| MULTIPLE | Specifies that multiple items can be selected in a menu. |
| SIZE | Specifies the height of the menu. |
| <OPTION> | Identifies one option in a menu. |
| SELECTED | Specifies that this option is the default. |
| VALUE | Specifies the value if the option is selected. |

**TABLE 12-7**    Form Tags and Attributes

## Creating Tables

HTML provides a very rich set of tags to define a table, its cells, borders, and other properties. As rich as the original HTML table specification was, there have been many extensions to it by both Microsoft and Netscape. Since these extensions are not consistent between the two companies, they need to be used with caution. Listing 12-8 provides an example of the HTML for creating the simple table shown in Figure 12-6. Table 12-8 shows the principal table tags and their attributes.

**Listing 12-8:**
Table
example

```
<H2>A New Table</H2>
<TABLE BORDER="2" CELLPADDING="3" CELLSPACING="4" WIDTH="100%"
    BGCOLOR="#FFFFFF" BORDERCOLORDARK>
  <CAPTION ALIGN="CENTER">THIS IS THE TABLE CAPTION</CAPTION>
  <TR VALIGN="BOTTOM">
    <TH ALIGN="LEFT" WIDTH="25%">Cell 1, a header</TH>
    <TD COLSPAN="2" WIDTH="25%">Cell 2, This cell spans two
      columns</TD>
    <TD WIDTH="10%">Cell 3</TD>
    <TD WIDTH="10%">Cell 4</TD></TR>
  <TR><TD WIDTH="25%">Cell 5, 25%</TD>
    <TD WIDTH="25%">Cell 6, 25%</TD>
    <TD WIDTH="25%">Cell 7, 25%</TD>
    <TD WIDTH="10%">10%</TD></TR>
  <TR><TD ROWSPAN="2" WIDTH="25%">Cells 9/13, These cells were
    merged</TD>
    <TD WIDTH="25%">Cell 10</TD>
    <TD WIDTH="25%">Cell 11</TD>
    <TD WIDTH="10%">Cell 12</TD></TR>
  <TR><TD WIDTH="25%">Cell 14</TD>
    <TD WIDTH="25%">Cell 15</TD>
    <TD WIDTH="10%">Cell 16</TD></TR>
</TABLE>
```

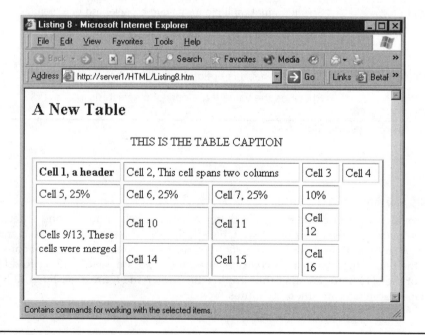

**FIGURE 12-6**     Table created with Listing 12-8

| Tag or Attribute | Description |
|---|---|
| `<TABLE> </TABLE>` | Specifies the definition of a table. |
| `ALIGN` | Specifies that the table will be aligned on the `LEFT` or `RIGHT` of the page, allowing text to flow around it. |
| `BACKGROUND` | Specifies that a URL containing an image be used as a background; works in Internet Explorer 3.0 and above and Netscape Navigator 4.0 and above. |
| `BGCOLOR` | Specifies a background color for an entire table. |
| `BORDER` | Specifies the size, in pixels, of a border to be drawn around all cells in a table. |
| `BORDERCOLOR` | Specifies a border color if a border is present; works in Internet Explorer 3.0 and above and Netscape Navigator 4.0 and above. |
| `BORDERCOLORLIGHT` | Specifies the lighter of 3-D border colors if a border is present; not used in Netscape Navigator. |
| `BORDERCOLORDARK` | Specifies the darker of 3-D border colors if a border is present; not used in Netscape Navigator. |
| `CELLSPACING` | Specifies the amount of space, in pixels, between cells; a default of 0 is used when not specified (although you may have set this to 2 in an earlier chapter). |
| `CELLPADDING` | Specifies the amount of space, in pixels, between the cell wall and its contents on all sides; a default of 0 is used when not specified (although you may have set this to 1 in an earlier chapter). |
| `COLS` | Specifies the number of columns in the table. |
| `FRAME` | Specifies which of the outside borders of a table are displayed— `VOID` (none), `ABOVE` (only the top), `BELOW` (only the bottom), `HSIDES` (horizontal sides), `VSIDES` (vertical sides), `LHS` (left-hand side), `RHS` (right-hand side), `BOX` (all); not used in Netscape Navigator. |
| `HEIGHT` | Specifies the height of a table as either a certain number of pixels or a percentage of the window. |
| `RULES` | Specifies which of the inside borders of a table are displayed— `NONE`, `BASIC` (horizontal rules between the heading, body, and footer sections), `ROWS`, `COLS`, `ALL`; not used in Netscape Navigator. |
| `STYLE` | Specifies a style sheet for the table. |
| `WIDTH` | Specifies the width of a table as either a certain number of pixels or a percentage of the window. |

**TABLE 12-8**    Table Tags and Attributes

| Tag or Attribute | Description |
|---|---|
| `<TR> </TR>` | Identifies the cells in a single row of a table. `BACKGROUND`, `BGCOLOR`, `BORDERCOLOR`, `BORDERCOLORLIGHT`, `BORDERCOLORDARK`, `HEIGHT`, and `STYLE` are the same as described for `<TABLE>`. |
| ALIGN | Specifies that the text in the cells of this row is aligned on the `LEFT`, `CENTER`, or `RIGHT` of each cell. |
| VALIGN | Specifies that the text in the row can be aligned with the `TOP`, `CENTER`, `BASELINE`, or `BOTTOM` of the cells; if not specified, text is center-aligned. Not used in Netscape Navigator. |
| `<TD> </TD>` | Identifies a single data cell in a table. `BACKGROUND`, `BGCOLOR`, `BORDERCOLOR`, `BORDERCOLORLIGHT`, `BORDERCOLORDARK`, `HEIGHT`, `WIDTH`, `STYLE`, and `VALIGN` are the same as described for `<TABLE>` or `<TR>`. |
| ALIGN | Specifies that the text in this cell is aligned on the `LEFT`, `CENTER`, or `RIGHT` of the cell. |
| COLSPAN | Specifies the number of columns a cell should span. |
| ROWSPAN | Specifies the number of rows a cell should span. |
| NOWRAP | Specifies that the text in the table cannot be wrapped to fit a smaller cell, forcing the cell to enlarge. |
| `<CAPTION> </CAPTION>` | Identifies the caption for a table. |
| ALIGN | Specifies that the caption is aligned to the `LEFT`, `CENTER`, or `RIGHT` of the table; not used in Netscape Navigator. |
| VALIGN | Specifies that the caption should appear at the `TOP` or `BOTTOM` of the table; not used in Netscape Navigator. |

**TABLE 12-8**    Table Tags and Attributes *(continued)*

---

**TIP**    *A table without the BORDER attribute will not have a border, but will take up the same space as if it had a border of 1. Therefore, specifying a border of zero (0) will take up less space.*

## Incorporating Frames

HTML frames allow the definition of individual panes or *frames* within a browser window. Each frame contains a separate page that can be scrolled independently of the other frames. HTML defines frames in terms of a *frames page,* which contain Frameset tags, which in turn contain Frame tags. In a frames page, the Frameset tag replaces the Body tag and provides the overall structure of the frames to be created in a browser window. Similarly, the Frame tag is used to define the structure of a single frame. Figure 12-7 shows a simple frames page that was created with the tags displayed in Listing 12-9. (The banner, contents, and main pages are separately defined to contain the information you see.) The tags and attributes related to frames are described in Table 12-9. Because the browser in Figure 12-7 correctly displays frames, the body message "This web page uses frames, but your browser doesn't" is not displayed.

**Listing 12-9:**
A frames page with Frameset and Frame tags

```
<HTML>
  <HEAD>
    <TITLE>Listing 9</TITLE>
  </HEAD>
  <FRAMESET ROWS="12%,*,11%">
    <FRAME SRC="frtop.htm" NAME="top" NORESIZE>
      <FRAMESET COLS="35%,65%">
        <FRAME SRC="frconten.htm" NAME="contents">
        <FRAME SRC="frmain.htm" NAME="main">
      </FRAMESET>
    <FRAME SRC="frbottom.htm" NAME="bottom" NORESIZE>
    <NOFRAMES>
      <BODY>
        <P>This web page uses frames, but your browser doesn't</P>
      </BODY>
    </NOFRAMES>
  </FRAMESET>
</HTML>
```

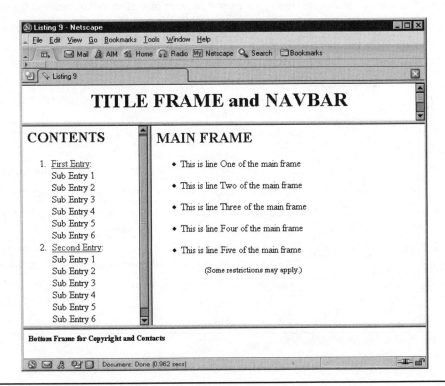

**FIGURE 12-7**   A frames page produced with Listing 12-9

| Tag or Attribute | Description |
|---|---|
| `<FRAMESET> </FRAMESET>` | Specifies the definition of a set of frames. |
| COLS | Identifies the number of vertical frames (columns) in the frameset and their absolute or relative size (see comments on this attribute). |
| ROWS | Identifies the number of horizontal frames (rows) in the frameset and their absolute or relative size (see comments on this attribute). |
| FRAMEBORDER | Turns the border around a frame on (FRAMEBORDER="Yes" or "1") or off (="No" or "0"). |
| FRAMESPACING | Identifies extra space, in pixels, inserted between frames; not used in Netscape Navigator. |
| BORDERCOLOR | Specifies the color of the frame border; not used in Internet Explorer 3.0, but is in 4.0. |
| `<FRAME> </FRAME>` | Specifies the definition of a single frame. |
| FRAMEBORDER | Turns the border around a frame on (FRAMEBORDER="Yes" or "1") or off (="No" or "0"). |
| FRAMESPACING | Identifies extra space, in pixels, inserted between frames. |
| MARGINWIDTH | Identifies the size, in pixels, of the left and right margin in a frame. |
| MARGINHEIGHT | Identifies the size, in pixels, of the top and bottom margins in a frame. |
| NAME | Identifies the name of the frame so it can be referred to by TARGET attributes. |
| NORESIZE | Prevents the frame from being resized by the user. |
| SCROLLING | Turns the appearance of scroll bars on or off with SCROLLING="Yes"/"No"/"Auto"; Auto is the default. |
| SRC | Identifies the URL of the web page that will occupy the frame. |
| BORDERCOLOR | Specifies the color of the frame border; not used in Internet Explorer 3.0, but is in 4.0 and later. |
| `<NOFRAMES> </NOFRAMES>` | Specifies HTML that will be displayed by browsers that cannot display frames, but ignored by browsers with frame capability. |
| `<IFRAME> </IFRAME>` | Specifies the definition of an inline frame; WIDTH, HEIGHT, HSPACE, VSPACE, and ALIGN are the same as described for `<IMG>`. |

**TABLE 12-9**    Frame Tags and Attributes

**NOTE** *If FRAMEBORDER and FRAMESPACING are specified in the Frameset tag, they will automatically apply to all the Frame tags contained within it and only need to be specified for the Frame where a change is desired.*

**NOTE** *The* TARGET *attribute, which you have seen with other tags, is used to load pages into specific frames.*

Internet Explorer 3.0 introduced *inline frames* (also called floating frames). These are individual frames that can be placed anywhere in a standard HTML document. If the browser does not support floating frames, the HTML within the <IFRAME></IFRAME> tags is displayed on the page in the usual manner.

**NOTE** *No tags that would be within a Body tag can precede the first Frameset tag, although Frameset tags can be contained within another Frameset tag.*

Within the ROWS and COLS attributes is a list of values separated by commas, one for each horizontal frame ("row") or vertical frame ("column") in the frameset. These values can be

- The absolute width of a column or height of a row, in pixels. For example, COLS="200, 100, 300" sets up three columns that, from left to right, are 200, 100, and 300 pixels wide, respectively.

- A percentage of the window's width for a column or the window's height for a row. For example, ROWS="15%, 85%" sets up two rows, one taking 15 percent of the window and the other, 85 percent.

- A relative value to the other rows or columns. For example, COLS="*, 2*" sets up two columns, the right one getting twice as much space as the left one (this is the same as using "33%, 67%").

- Any combination of absolute, percentage, and relative. For example, ROWS="100, 65%, *" sets up three rows: the top is 100 pixels high, the middle is 65 percent of the window, and the bottom gets the remaining space.

**CAUTION** *Using absolute pixel values with the ROWS and COLS attributes can result in some weird-looking frames, due to the many differences in screen sizes and resolutions.*

## Using Multimedia

*Multimedia* is the inclusion of audio, video, and animation pieces in a web. You can simply offer a user a multimedia file to be downloaded by clicking its link, and then, depending on the availability of players, the file can be automatically or manually played. If you want to make multimedia an automatic part of a web (called *inline* audio or video)—for example, to automatically play an audio piece when a web opens—you must use some extensions to HTML. These include the <BGSOUND> tag for playing inline audio and the DYNSRC attribute for the Image tag to play inline audio-video. Also <MARQUEE>, which is a scrolling bar of text across the window, is included here as a form of animation. Netscape Navigator 3.0 and above support the <EMBED> tag, which allows you to include audio and video files with one of the Netscape plug-ins. Netscape plug-ins for standard audio and video files are included with Navigator 3.0 and above, and more can be found on the Netscape web site (**http://home.netscape.com/developer/**). Internet Explorer 4.0 (and later) also supports the <EMBED> tag. Listing 12-10 provides some examples of using multimedia with Internet Explorer, and Table 12-10 describes the related tags and their attributes.

**Listing 12-10:**
Examples of
the HTML to
use multimedia

```
<BGSOUND SRC="all.wav" LOOP=2>
<IMG SRC="hibiscus.jpg" DYNSRC="goodtime.avi" CONTROLS
   START=MOUSEOVER>
<MARQUEE BEHAVIOR=SLIDE, DIRECTION=RIGHT>The marquee will
   scroll this text</MARQUEE>
```

**NOTE**  *The Image tag attributes in Table 12-10 are in addition to the regular Image tag attributes listed in Table 12-5, which can all be used with video and animation clips.*

| Tag or Attribute | Description |
|---|---|
| <BGSOUND> | Specifies a sound to be played automatically as a page is loaded. Not used in Netscape Navigator. |
| SRC | Identifies the URL of the WAV, AU, or MID file that will be played as soon as it is downloaded. |
| LOOP | Identifies the number of times the sound will play; if LOOP=-1 or INFINITE, the sound will play until the page is closed. |
| <IMG> | Specifies a video or animation clip is to be played. |
| DYNSRC | Identifies the URL of the inline video AVI file to be played. Not used in Netscape Navigator. |
| START | Identifies when the file should start playing (START=FILEOPEN or MOUSEOVER); FILEOPEN is the default, and MOUSEOVER means the file will start playing when the mouse is moved over the alternative image. |
| CONTROLS | Specifies that the video player control panel should be displayed. |
| LOOP | Identifies the number of times the video will play; if LOOP=-1 or INFINITE, the sound will play until the page is closed. |
| LOOPDELAY | Identifies how long to wait, in milliseconds, between repetitions in a loop. |
| SRC | Identifies the image to display if the browser cannot play the video. |
| <MARQUEE> </MARQUEE> | Specifies the definition of a scrolling bar of text across the browser window. Not used in Netscape Navigator. |
| ALIGN | Identifies the alignment of the text in the marquee to be at its TOP, MIDDLE, or BOTTOM. |

**TABLE 12-10**  Multimedia Tags and Attributes

| Tag or Attribute | Description |
|---|---|
| BEHAVIOR | Identifies how the text should behave. BEHAVIOR=SCROLL means the text will continuously scroll from one side to the other; =SLIDE means it will move from one side to the other and stop; =ALTERNATE means the text will continuously bounce from one side to the other. SCROLL is the default. |
| BGCOLOR | Identifies the background color. |
| DIRECTION | Identifies the direction that the text will scroll (=LEFT or =RIGHT); LEFT is the default. |
| HEIGHT | Identifies the height of the marquee in either pixels or percentage of the window. |
| HSPACE | Identifies the right and left margins of the marquee in pixels. |
| LOOP | Identifies the number of times that the text will loop; if LOOP=-1 or INFINITE, the text will display until the page is closed. |
| SCROLLAMOUNT | Identifies the number of pixels between successive loops of text. |
| SCROLLDELAY | Identifies the number of milliseconds between successive loops. |
| VSPACE | Identifies the top and bottom margins of the marquee. |
| WIDTH | Identifies the width of the marquee, either in pixels or as a percentage of the window. |
| <EMBED> | Specifies a sound or video file to be played by the appropriate plug-in; SRC, WIDTH, HEIGHT, BORDER, HSPACE, and VSPACE are the same as for <IMG>. |

**TABLE 12-10**    Multimedia Tags and Attributes *(continued)*

# Understanding FrontPage-Generated Code

Many of the example listings in the "Introducing HTML" section have been created with FrontPage and only slightly modified to fit the needs of the section. Let's look at two more examples of web pages and get a feeling for the code generated by FrontPage. First, though, we'll explore the ways of looking at FrontPage's HTML.

## How to Look at FrontPage Code

You have at least three ways to look at the HTML code generated by FrontPage. In FrontPage, you can look at it in either Code view, where you see nothing but the code, or in Split view, where you can look at both the code and the page it produces at the same time. In addition, you can also look at the code in your browser. If you have more than one browser, you can look at the HTML code in each. Use the following steps to see the differences among the views.

1. Load FrontPage if it's not already loaded. If the New task pane is not open, select File | New. In the New pane, click One Page Web Site.

2. In the Web Site Templates dialog box, the One Page Web Site should be selected. Enter your default web directory and name the web (I use "HTML"), then click OK.

3. Open the home page in Design view and enter a heading, a couple of short paragraphs with some formatting, and place an image with text after it, as shown in Figure 12-8. Save the page.

4. Select View | Reveal Tags. The HTML web home page with the HTML tags revealed is displayed. You can click a tag to select it and its contents, as shown in Figure 12-9, right-click a tag to display a context menu, and double-click a tag to open the tag's property sheet. This method is not as complete as using Code view. For example, the line break or the IMG tag for the graphic is not displayed.

5. Click Code in the View bar at the bottom of home page. The HTML source will appear as shown in Figure 12-10, except that on your screen, you will see at least five colors:

   • Line numbers are white on a bluish-gray background

   • Tags are maroon

   • Attribute names are red

   • Attribute values are blue

   • Text you enter is black

   • Comments (if present) are gray

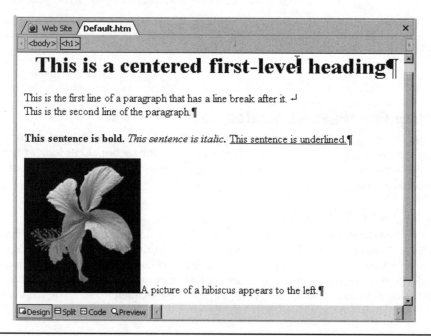

**FIGURE 12-8**    A simple web page

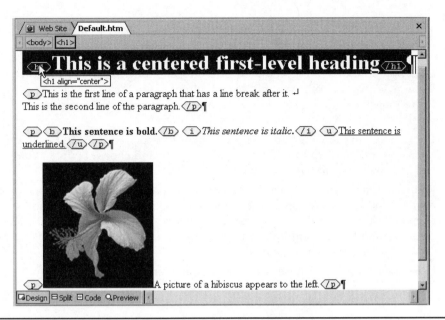

**FIGURE 12-9**    The HTML home page with the HTML tags revealed

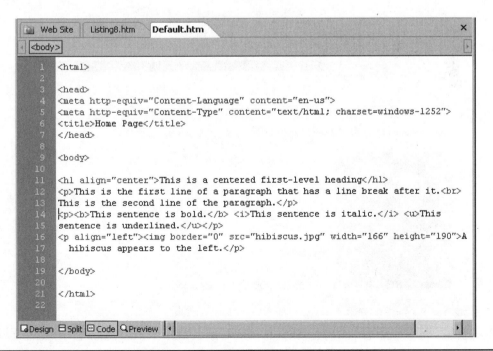

**FIGURE 12-10**    Code view of the HTML home page shown in Figure 12-8

6. Click Split in the View bar and then click on something like the picture on the Design view of the split. You will see it highlighted in the Code view of the split. Make some small change to your web page like centering the image, and you will see the change in Code view, as shown in Figure 12-11.

7. Click Design in the View bar, save your page, and open the HTML Home Page in Microsoft Internet Explorer. Open the View menu and choose Source. Windows Notepad will open and display the code behind the web page.

8. Return to FrontPage and open the HTML home Page in Netscape Navigator if you have it. Open the View menu and choose Page Source. A Netscape window will open and show the code. As you can see on your screen and in Figure 12-12, the Netscape and Internet Explorer source looks similar, but Navigator uses a color coding that makes it easier to read.

9. Close the listing and browser windows and reopen FrontPage in Design view.

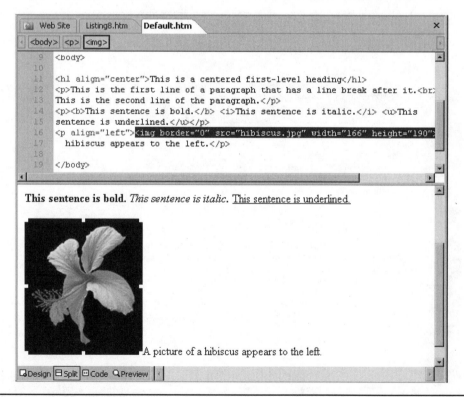

**FIGURE 12-11**    Split view allows you to see both the Design view and the Code view at the same time.

**FIGURE 12-12**   Source code listings in Internet Explorer and Netscape Navigator

In the code views, you have just seen that there are no major differences, although you may see some with other pages. In this example, it just depends on your preference and what you want to do with what you are looking at. If you just want to look, Netscape and Internet Explorer offer a quick way to do that. If you want to directly change the code, you can do that in FrontPage or Microsoft Internet Explorer with Notepad editor. In all three views, you can select and copy the code to the Windows Clipboard, copy it to another editor, and then easily move the code from both FrontPage and Navigator to, for example, Notepad.

In the next several sections of this chapter, you will try all three methods (if you have both browsers). By the end of the chapter, you'll be able to decide which you like best.

## Looking at the HTML Example

Take a closer look at the tags and attributes that were created by FrontPage in the above HTML example. Listing 12-11 shows the code for this example. It was copied to the Clipboard and then pasted in the manuscript for this book. The tags and attributes were put in uppercase letters, the tags were made bold, and tags contained in other tags or lines that were a continuation of the previous line were indented. Otherwise, this listing has not changed from that generated by FrontPage.

**Listing 12-11**:
A simple HTML
example

```
<HTML>
  <HEAD>
  <META HTTP-EQUIV="Content-Language" CONTENT="en-us">
    <META HTTP-EQUIV="Content-Type" CONTENT="text/html;
      CHARSET=windows-1252">
    <TITLE>Home Page</TITLE>
  </HEAD>
  <BODY>
    <H1 ALIGN="center">This is a centered first-level heading</H1>
    <P>This is the first line of a paragraph that has a line break
      after it.<BR>
      This is the second line of the paragraph.</P>
    <P><B>This sentence is bold.</B>
      <I>This sentence is italic.</I>
      <U>This sentence is underlined.</U></P>
    <P><IMG BORDER="0" SRC="hibiscus.jpg" width="166" height="190">
      A picture of a hibiscus appears to the left.</P>
  </BODY>
</HTML>
```

There are no surprises in Listing 12-11. All of the tags and attributes were discussed in the "Introducing HTML" section earlier in the chapter. There are, however, a few interesting items to note:

- FrontPage uses the ALIGN=CENTER attributes of Heading and Paragraph tags instead of embedding the tags in a Center tag.

- The Bold (B) and Italic (I) tags are used; in versions of FrontPage prior to FrontPage 2000, you would see the Strong and Emphasis tags.

- The HEIGHT and WIDTH attributes are automatically added to the Image tag to establish the area to be occupied by the image and to allow the following text to be displayed while the image is loaded.

## Looking at Your Chapter 5 Web

For a second example, close your HTML web example and open the home page you created in Chapter 5. The top of the page that we created for Wines 'n Things is shown in Figure 12-13,

**FIGURE 12-13**    Top of Chapter 5's home page

and the code that creates it is provided in Listing 12-12 (to reduce the bulk and repetition, only the first two items in the bulleted list and the first two items in the numbered list were included).

**Listing 12-12:**

```
<HTML>
  <HEAD>
    <META HTTP-EQUIV="Content-Language" CONTENT="en-us">
    <META HTTP-EQUIV="Content-Type" CONTENT="text/html;
      CHARSET=windows-1252">
    <TITLE>Home Page</TITLE>
  </HEAD>
<BODY>
    <DIV STYLE="position: absolute; top: 15; left: 10; width:
      727; height: 125; z-index: -10">
      <H1 ALIGN="center"><IMG BORDER="0" SRC="048086B.jpg" WIDTH="167"
        HEIGHT="116"><IMG BORDER="0" SRC="091012.jpg" WIDTH="162"
        HEIGHT="116"><IMG BORDER="0" SRC="048087B.jpg" WIDTH="160"
        HEIGHT="116"><IMG BORDER="0" SRC="157097B.jpg" WIDTH="158"
        HEIGHT="116"></H1>
    </DIV>
</DIV>
```

```
<H1 ALIGN="center"><I><FONT FACE="Tempus Sans ITC" SIZE="7"
      COLOR="#FFFFFF">WINES 'N THINGS<BR></font>
         <FONT COLOR="#FFFFFF" FACE="Tempus Sans ITC">Grand Wines and
      Accoutrements</FONT></I></H1>
         <P ALIGN="center"><FONT FACE="Bookman Old Style" SIZE="2">Visit
      us at 1234 23rd Street, Ourtown, Call us at 555-1234 or
      555-1235 or fax 555-1236<BR>
      Jim Maynard and John Staley, Wine Merchants<A HREF="mailto:
      jim@winenthings.com"> jim@winesnthings.com</A> or<A HREF="mailto:
      john@winesnthings.com"> john@winesnthings.com</A></FONT></P>
<HR>
<P ALIGN="left" STYLE="margin-top: 0; margin-bottom: 0">
         <FONT FACE="Tempus Sans ITC"><SPAN STYLE="position: absolute;
      left: 9; top: 210"><B><A HREF="third_page.htm">
         <IMG BORDER="0" SRC="h4nyb3vn[1].jpg" width="57" HEIGHT="82">
         </A></B></SPAN></FONT></P>
         <H2 ALIGN="left"><FONT FACE="Tempus Sans ITC"><B>
              
         <FONT COLOR="#800000">CURRENT SPECIALS</FONT></B></FONT></H2>
<UL>
         <LI>
            <P STYLE="margin-left: 0in" ALIGN="left"><FONT FACE="Bookman
            Old Style">1998 Apex Cabernet Sauvignon, deep color, rich,
            complex flavor, $31.99</FONT></LI>
         <LI>
<P STYLE="margin-left: 0in" ALIGN="left"><FONT FACE="Bookman
            Old Style">2001 Santa Barbara Chardonnay, exceptional, with
            a touch of oak, $14.95</FONT></LI>
</ul>
      <P ALIGN="left"><IMG BORDER="0" SRC="BD10308_.gif" width="722"
         height="11"></P>
      <H2 ALIGN="left"><B><FONT FACE="Tempus Sans ITC" color="#800000">
         MAJOR VARIETALS AND REGIONS</FONT></B></H2>
         <OL>
<LI>
<P STYLE="margin-left: 0in"><FONT FACE="Bookman Old Style">
         CABERNET SAUVIGNON: Washington, Northern California,
         Australia</FONT></LI>
<LI>
<P STYLE="margin-left: 0in"><FONT FACE="Bookman Old Style">
         CHARDONNAY: Washington, Oregon, Northern Calif., Central
         Coast</FONT></LI>
</OL>
<H5>copyright <FONT FACE="Times New Roman">© 2003 Wines 'n
      Things, Inc. All rights reserved<BR>
      1234 W 23rd St, Ourtown, ST 12345 Ã (999) 555-1234<BR>
      Please send comments and suggestions to
      <A HREF="mailto:webmaster@winesnthings.com">
      webmaster@winesnthings.com</A> </FONT></H5>
   </BODY>
</HTML>
```

If there is one feeling that you should come away with after looking at the HTML generated by FrontPage, it is a much greater appreciation for FrontPage and what it saves you in creating web pages. Just the amount of reduced typing is mind-boggling, but more important are all the automatic features, where you simply don't have to worry about some minutiae that is important to the browser but not to anyone else. For example, the following items are totally handled by FrontPage:

- The hexadecimal triplet for the custom color in the theme
- The height and width of images
- The particular font size for a piece of text
- Making sure you have all the ending tags for your beginning tags
- Translating some characters into their escape sequence

## Adding Capability to a FrontPage Web with HTML Code

Besides understanding the HTML code that FrontPage generates, the other reason to learn about HTML is to be able to augment FrontPage when it doesn't provide an HTML-supported function. There is actually very little strict HTML that FrontPage does not support, but the techniques that will be described are still very useful. HTML is no longer the only web language, as you will see in the following chapters. DHTML and other languages can greatly enhance a web, and all the features of these languages are not always directly supported by FrontPage.

First, look at how you'd add HTML code to FrontPage, and then look at an example of a feature not directly supported in FrontPage: modifying a table.

### How to Add HTML Code to FrontPage

There are three ways to add HTML code to FrontPage:

- Directly edit the HTML produced by FrontPage outside of FrontPage and resave it. This technique is strongly discouraged, because it potentially removes the ability to maintain the web with FrontPage, and there is an excellent way to add HTML within FrontPage.

- Use the Code or Split view in Page view, which allows you to see and edit the HTML code that describes a given page.

- Use the HTML Web Component, which is available anywhere on a normal page in Page view, by positioning the insertion point where you want to add the HTML, selecting Insert | Web Component | Advanced Controls | HTML and clicking Finish. The HTML Markup dialog box, shown here, will open and allow you to directly enter HTML:

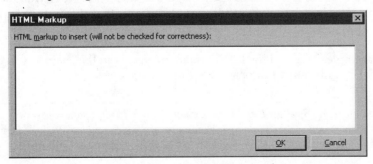

Code or Split view provides the most flexibility and a complete picture of the HTML code behind a page. The HTML Web Component allows you to encapsulate the HTML you are adding and keep it separate from the FrontPage-generated-and-checked HTML. You will use Split view in the next section to modify the HTML for a table.

## Inserting HTML to Modify a Table

The table that you saw in Figure 12-6 had an outside border or frame around the entire table and individual borders around each cell. In Design view, you control how a table looks with the Table Properties dialog box, where the border controls allow you to change the size and color of the border, but not turn off the outer frame while leaving the cell borders. You can do that by changing the HTML code. Here, you will use the Split view to remove the borders of any simple table. For illustration purposes, the table created earlier in this chapter and shown in Figure 12-6 is used, but you can use any table with the following steps.

---

**NOTE**    *In the Design view, you can achieve the same effect of cell borders without a table border by first turning off all borders in the Table Properties dialog box by making the Borders Size 0. Then, select the cells you want to have borders, open the Cell Properties dialog box, click Style, click Format, choose Border, click Box, make the Width something larger than 0, and click OK three times. The HTML technique is easier!*

1. From FrontPage, either create a new web or open an existing web with a table in it. In either case, select Split view of that table. (If necessary, create a simple 4×4 table with a little text in each cell (like "Cell 1," "Cell 2," and so on).

2. Right-click the table and choose Table Properties. In the Table Properties dialog box, make the Borders Size **0**, close the Properties dialog box, and look at the results in Preview and in the Code pane of the Split view.

3. Reset the border to **2** and then, one at a time, make each of the three border colors white (or the same color as the background), and look at the results, both in Preview and in the Code pane. You can see that either all the borders are showing or all the borders are not visible. When you are done, return the Table Properties dialog box to its default settings.

4. In the Code pane, click between <table and border to place the insertion point there.

5. Type **frame="void"** (including both quotation marks). Make sure there is a space on either side of the newly typed material.

6. Click Save on the toolbar to save the page, and then click Preview in the View bar or look at it in a browser. Your result should resemble the table in Figure 12-14.

7. Close your browser.

With the examples here and the HTML reference earlier in the chapter, you can see how easy it is to make significant additions to your FrontPage webs.

---

**TIP**    *When you are using Split view and make a change in the Design pane, the code is automatically updated as soon as you make the change. When you make a change in the Code pane nothing happens in the Design pane until you either click in the Design pane or press F5.*

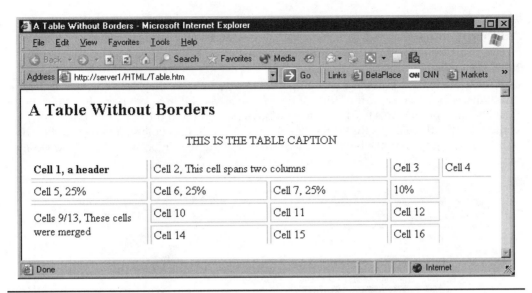

**FIGURE 12-14**    Changing code produced a table without an outside border.

## Code Authoring Tools

FrontPage 2003 added some significant new tools to work directly with code. You have just used one of them, the Split view. (Figure 12-15 shows the table you were just working on in

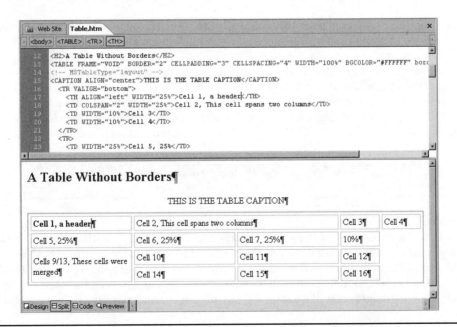

**FIGURE 12-15**    Split view lets you work on a web page in both Design and Code view at the same time.

Split view, which shows the borders in Design view.) Others include the Quick Tag toolbar, Code IntelliSense and code typing aids, and storing and using code snippets.

### Quick Tag Toolbar

The Quick Tag toolbar is at the top of either the Design or Split view, immediately under the tabs. It displays a hierarchy or outline of the tags at any point in a web page. For example, if the insertion point is in a bold sentence within a paragraph in the body of a page, you would have the three tags **<BODY> <P> <B>** in the Quick Tag toolbar. If you click the **<B>** in the Quick Tag toolbar, the bold sentence will be highlighted in both the Code and Design panes, like this:

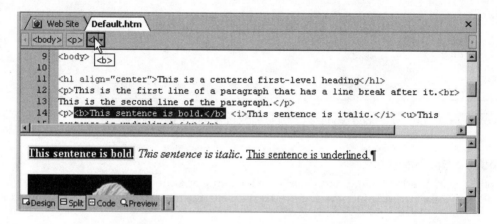

The Quick Tag toolbar allows you to quickly see what tags are impacting a particular spot on a web page and constantly changes as you click in various spots on a page. This is particularly important if you have a table within a table. The tags on the toolbar also allow you to edit just the code related to the immediate tag without opening either Split or Code view using the Quick Tag Editor. If you right-click a tag or click the down arrow on its right, a context menu opens that allows you to select and edit the tag, among other choices. If you choose Edit Tag, the Quick Tag Editor opens, as shown next, and allows you to change just that particular tag:

For example, in the tag just shown, you could very easily change the border thickness to something other than 0. In addition to editing the tag, the Quick Tag Editor allows you to also wrap a tag with another tag and to inset HTML code. These are very similar, but have an important difference. If you select a paragraph, right-click the tag, choose Insert HTML, and enter the tag **<LI>** to make the paragraph a bulleted paragraph, a new bulleted paragraph will be inserted before the current paragraph. If you choose

Wrap Tag with the same steps, the current paragraph will becomes a bulleted paragraph, like this:

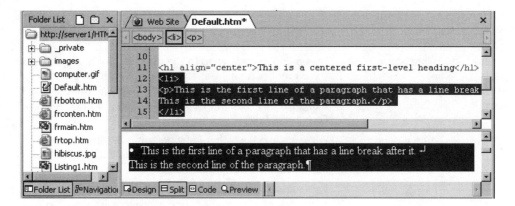

### Code IntelliSense and Typing Aids

FrontPage 2003 has done a lot to make the laborious job of typing code easier. One of the features you just saw was upon entering an opening tag (**<LI>**), the closing tag (**</LI>**) is automatically entered. This was done with Code IntelliSense, which works in the same way that IntelliSense works in other Microsoft products; it attempts to complete the code statement you are currently entering. Code IntelliSense allows you to not only write code faster, but do so more accurately. You can control Code IntelliSense through the Page Options dialog box, IntelliSense tab, shown next, where you can also get an idea of what it will do:

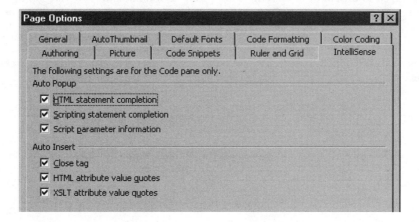

The code typing aids that are available in FrontPage are extensive. They consist of features that you can enable or not and menu options and shortcut keys that speed your progress through code.

**Optional Coding Features**    The features that you can enable are in the Page Options dialog box (opened from the Tools menu) on several different tabs. Table 12-11 shows a list of them by tab.

| Tab | Name | Description |
|---|---|---|
| General | Word Wrap | Lets a line of code wrap to the next line if it is longer than the current pane allows. The default is to have the code extend out of the pane to the right, although there is a right margin set by default at 80 characters. See the Code Formatting tab. |
| General | Auto Indent | When enabled, which it is by default, new lines are automatically lined up with the previous line. When disabled, new lines start at the left margin. |
| General | Line Numbers | When enabled, which it is by default, line numbers are placed to the left of each line of code allowing you to use Go To Line to jump to a particular line number. |
| General | Selection Margin | When enabled, which it is by default, adds a space between the line numbers and the first character of code allowing you to place the pointer there to select the line, which you can also do from the line numbers. |
| Default Fonts | Font And Size | Allows you to select the font and font size that will be used in the Code pane. The default is Courier New and 9 point type. |
| Code Formatting | Base On Current Page | Allows you to pick up and use the formatting on the current Code page for all the formatting options on the Code Formatting tab. |
| Code Formatting | Tags Names Are Lowercase | Makes all tag names lowercase, which is the default. |
| Code Formatting | Attribute Names Are Lowercase | Makes all attribute names lowercase, which is the default. |
| Code Formatting | Allow Line Breaks Within Tags | Provides for breaking a code line within a tag. |
| Code Formatting | Tab Size | Determines the number blank characters or spaces that are added when you press TAB. |
| Code Formatting | Indent | Defines what an indent is when code is indented either automatically or by you. |

**TABLE 12-11**    Coding Features Enabled in Various Page Options Tabs

| Tab | Name | Description |
|---|---|---|
| Code Formatting | Right Margin | Sets the number of characters in a line if word wrap is not used. By default, this is 80 characters. |
| Code Formatting | Tag Line Breaks | Sets the number of line breaks before and after the start and the end of each type of tag, as well as whether to omit either the starting or ending tag and indent the contents of the tag. |
| Color Coding | Set Colors | Allows you to set the color used for line numbers, tags, attribute names, attribute values, comments, and script. |
| IntelliSense | HTML Statement Completion | When enabled, which it is by default, IntelliSense pops up the completion of an HTML statement. |
| IntelliSense | ScriptingStatement Completion | When enabled, which it is by default, IntelliSense pops up the completion of a script statement. |
| IntelliSense | Script Parameter Information | When enabled, which it is by default, IntelliSense pops up script parameter information. |
| IntelliSense | Close Tag | When enabled, which it is by default, IntelliSense automatically supplies the closing tag for every opening tag. |
| IntelliSense | HTML Attribute Value Quotes | When enabled, which it is not by default, IntelliSense automatically supplies the quote marks around attribute values in HTML. |
| IntelliSense | XSLT Attribute Value Quotes | When enabled, which it is not by default, IntelliSense automatically supplies the quote marks around attribute values in XSLT (see Chapter 14). |

**TABLE 12-11**    Coding Features Enabled in Various Page Options Tabs *(continued)*

**Menu Options and Shortcut Keys**    The menu options and shortcut keys that you can use in entering code are in the Edit menu Code View, as shown in Figure 12-16. In addition, the IntelliSense option offers these additional choices:

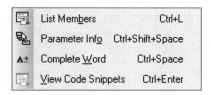

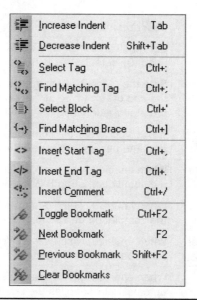

**FIGURE 12-16** Menu options and shortcut keys used in entering code

Try using the various menu options and shortcut keys in the following set of steps to see for yourself how they work:

1. In FrontPage, create a new page and open that page in Code view. Notice that even though there is nothing on the page in Design view, the basic tags described at the beginning of this chapter have already been added to the page, like this:

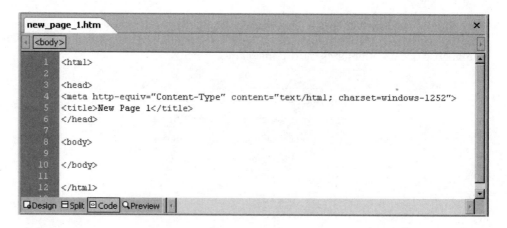

2. Place the insertion point on line 9 between the beginning and ending BODY tags, press ENTER twice, and then press UP ARROW.

3. Press TAB, type <, and the tag list automatically opens, as you can see here:

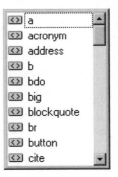

4. Scroll down until you see h1, double-click it, press SPACE, a list of attributes opens, double-click ALIGN, type =, a list of values opens, and, if you have HTML Value Quotes enable in Tools | Page Options | IntelliSense, a pair of double quotes appears. Double-click Center, press RIGHT ARROW (to move past the ending quote mark), type >, and the closing tag appears. Now, wasn't that really slick?

5. Type a main heading for the page, like **This is the Main Heading!**, press END, and then press ENTER. Notice that with Auto Indent enabled (Page Options | General tab), the insertion point automatically lines up with the previous line.

6. Type <, in the tag list, scroll down and double-click UL; type >, the closing tag appears, press ENTER twice, and then press UP ARROW.

7. Press TAB, type <, in the tag list double-click LI, type >, the closing tag appears, type **This is the first bulleted item.**, and press END. Press SHIFT-HOME and SHIFT-RIGHT ARROW twice to select the line you just entered, press CTRL-C to copy it, press END again, and press ENTER.

8. Press CTRL-V to paste the previous line, change the word "first" to "second," and save your page, which should look like Figure 12-17. Click Preview. Your page should look like this:

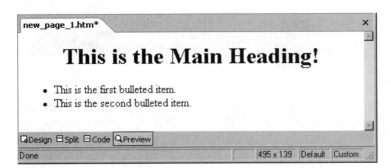

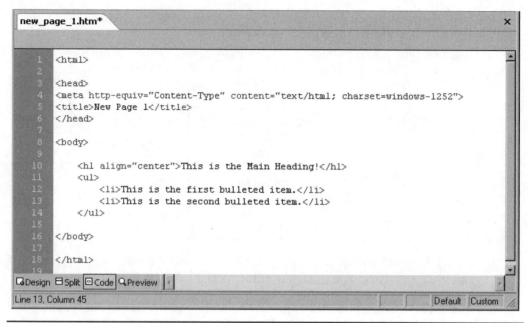

**FIGURE 12-17** HTML code created in this exercise

While it is obviously much easier to create this simple page in Design view, you have to agree that there are a lot of tools to make writing code easy.

### Saving and Using Code Snippets

One final tool that FrontPage 2003 has to help you with code is the ability to save and reuse small pieces of code. For example, say that you use a lot of bulleted lists. If you could reuse the four lines you entered for the bulleted list in the previous exercise, it would be helpful. Here is how to do that:

1. In the code page that you created in the previous exercise, select the code from the opening **<UL>** to the closing **</UL>**, like this:

```
10          <h1 align="center">This is the Main Heading!</h1>
11          <ul>
12              <li>This is the first bulleted item.</li>
13              <li>This is the second bulleted item.</li>
14          </ul>
15
```

2. Press CTRL-C to copy the code. Select Tools | Page Options | Code Snippets. Click Add. Type **blt** for the keyword, press TAB, type **Two item bulleted list.**, and press TAB again.

3. Press CTRL-V to paste the code into the snippet. Move the insertion point to immediately after the first **<LI>** and type a pipe character (" | " above the backslash). Move the

insertion point just to left of the first **</LI>** and again type a pipe character. Your snippet should look like this:

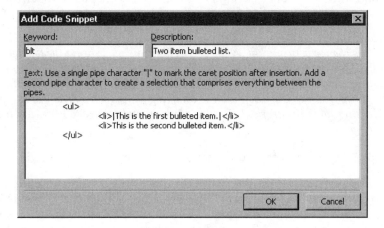

4. Click OK twice to close first the Add Code Snippet and then the Page Options dialog boxes.

5. Back in Code view, add some blank lines on the code page you have been using before the ending **</BODY>** tag and then press CTRL-ENTER. A list of code snippets will open from which you can select your snippet.

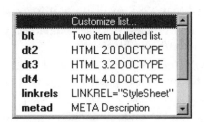

6. Double-click blt and the snippet will be placed on the page; the text between the first **<LI> </LI>** tags will be selected so you can easily change it. (If you added the pipes in the second bullet [as we did], they are ignored.)

7. Save your code page and close FrontPage.

If you work with code containing a lot of repetition, code snippets would be a substantial help.

## HTML Authoring Resources

There are a number of excellent resources on HTML authoring available on the Web. The following is a list of the ones that are most important. Some of these documents are ancient by Internet standards (several years old), but the basic information is still valid. It is important to understand that HTML has become a mature web language. HTML 4.0, the current version, is also probably the last version. The future of Web programming is in the languages such as DHTML and XML that will be covered in the following chapters. Nonetheless, a solid understanding of HTML, which these documents will provide, is still the first step.

---

**NOTE**    *URLs change very quickly. While every effort was made to get the following URLs correct when this book went to print, some probably will have changed by the time this book reaches the bookstores. If you are having trouble with a URL, drop off right-hand segments, delineated by slashes, until it works. Microsoft's site is changing faster than anybody's, so if one of their URLs isn't working, don't be surprised. The best work-around is to go to **http://www.microsoft.com/** and work forward.*

The following is a list of resources available online:

- *A Beginner's Guide to HTML* by NCSA (the National Center for Supercomputing Applications). NCSA is part of the University of Illinois at Urbana-Champaign, and is home to the original creators of Mosaic, the first of the web browsers from which Netscape Navigator, Microsoft Internet Explorer, and others have descended. Last updated January 24, 2001. The guide can be found at **http://www.ncsa.uiuc.edu/ General/Internet/WWW/HTMLPrimer.html**

- *Composing Good HTML* by James "Eric" Tilton (last updated July 13, 1998). Available at **http://www.ology.org/tilt/cgh/**

- *Style Guide for Online Hypertext* by Tim Berners-Lee (the originator of the World Wide Web). Last updated May 1995. Available at **http://www.w3.org/Provider/Style/**

- *Web Etiquette* by Tim Berners-Lee (last updated May 1995). Available at **http:// www.w3.org/Provider/Style/Etiquette**

- *A Basic HTML Style Guide* by Alan Richmond (NASA GSFC). Last updated July 11, 2001. Available at **http://heasarc.gsfc.nasa.gov/docs/heasarc/Style_Guide/ styleguide.html**

- Microsoft offers a number of documents that provide support of HTML authoring for the Internet Explorer. It is also one of the best sources for the latest developments in Web technologies. Both can be found at **http://msdn.microsoft.com/**; then do a search on "HTML Authoring." At the time this was written, several hundred documents came out of the search.

- Netscape's HTML resources for use with Navigator include a number of documents, some also referenced here, which are indexed at **http://developer.netscape.com/ docs/index.html**. Netscape's complete *HTML Tag Reference* (last updated January 26, 1998) is available at **http://devedge.netscape.com/library/manuals/1998/htmlguide/**

- For those with a technical inclination, there's no better source than the World Wide Web Consortium. A listing of Technical Reports and Publications can be found at **http://www.w3.org/TR/**

- World Wide Web Consortium's (W3C) *HTML 3.2 Specification* (dated January 14, 1997) is available at **http://www.w3.org/TR/REC-html32.html**

- World Wide Web Consortium's (W3C) *HTML 4.01 Specification* (last updated December 24, 1999) is available at **http://www.w3.org/TR/REC-html40**

- One of the most valuable HTML references on the Internet is *The HTML Reference Library* by Stephen Le Hunte. This is a very extensive Windows 95/98 Help System for HTML. It is a gold mine of information and is available for download from **http://www.htmlib.demon.co.uk/**

There are also a number of other good books on the Web and HTML authoring. Among them are

- *HTML: The Complete Reference, Second Edition* by Thomas A. Powell (McGraw-Hill/ Osborne, 1999).

- *Web Design: The Complete Reference* by Thomas A. Powell (McGraw-Hill/Osborne, 2000).

- The book that has become a standard for web design is *Designing Web Usability: The Practice of Simplicity* by Jakob Nielsen (New Riders Publishing, 2000).

# Using Dynamic HTML

I
n the previous chapter, you learned how HTML, the foundation language of the World
Wide Web, works with FrontPage. In this chapter, you will explore the first real advance
of web markup languages: Dynamic HTML (DHTML). DHTML, which, like HTML,
is dependent on support from browsers, was on the frontier of the Web until version 4
and later of Microsoft and Netscape browsers. Internet Explorer is now at version 6 and
Netscape is at version 7, making DHTML part of the mainstream of web development.

FrontPage simplifies using DHTML; in fact, many FrontPage features directly available
on the menus are actually DHTML based. However, you will need to actually write DHTML
code to take full advantage of its potential. This chapter presents an overview of DHTML
and looks at FrontPage's built-in support for DHTML.

## Dynamic HTML

Dynamic HTML is based on the Document Object Model (DOM), which moves HTML
to the next level of functionality by making every object on a web page dynamic and
interactive. It's hard to underestimate the impact this technology has on web design.
The Document Object Model concept makes each element of a web page an object with
properties that can be modified. For example, it allows content to be modified in real time,
without the user reloading the page in their browser from the server. Cascading style sheets
(CSS), which were introduced in Chapter 12, are also a part of the Document Object Model.
In addition to setting styles for text, CSS enables absolute positioning of elements on a
web page.

**NOTE** *The basic DHTML standard is defined in the HTML 4.01 Recommendation of the World
Wide Web Consortium (**http://www.w3.org/MarkUp/**). The Document Object Model is
covered in greater detail by the W3C at **http://www.w3.org/DOM/**.*

Unfortunately, as with most other developments on the Web, DHTML support varies
by manufacturer. Both Netscape and Microsoft support the W3C Recommendation to some
degree, but with some significant differences. Fortunately, DHTML degrades gracefully;
that is, pages that use it will appear normal to the user even if their browser doesn't fully
support DHTML. They will just lack the interactivity of full DHTML support.

At this time, it appears that Microsoft has developed the better implementation of DHTML. It adheres more closely to existing standards and provides more flexibility. For example, Microsoft's implementation supports both VBScript and JavaScript, while Netscape's supports only JavaScript. Part of this is probably based on Netscape's apparent desire to have as little to do with Microsoft technologies as possible. This is a business decision. As a web developer, you need to be concerned with functionality.

---

**Note**    *An area of possible confusion with DHTML is scriptlets—an idea that really didn't win acceptance. The basic concept of a scriptlet is a small, reusable piece of code that can be used throughout a web application. Internet Explorer 4 introduced the concept, but with the release of Internet Explorer 5, Microsoft recommended that DHTML behaviors be used instead.*

In this section, you will see how Microsoft has implemented DHTML. This is the version supported by FrontPage and Internet Explorer 5 and later. As a result, the examples you create may not function in Netscape Navigator. This doesn't mean that DHTML cannot be used with Netscape, only that you will need to check your specific DHTML code carefully in the browsers your intended audience uses. FrontPage's Browser Compatibility functions simplify this task.

---

**Note**    *Recent statistics show that Microsoft has all but won the browser wars with around 96 percent of global Web traffic using some version of Internet Explorer. While the argument can be made that this is not a good thing from the consumer's viewpoint (fewer choices), it does mean that the web developer's job is much easier. Designing for IE 5 or greater means that well over 90 percent of Web users will see your work as you intend and the number can be expected to increase.*

## Event Handling

In HTML, there is very limited support for handling events, such as moving the mouse pointer over an object. The only event that is really handled is clicking a hyperlink or form button. In DHTML, this has been greatly expanded. Table 13-1 lists mouse events Microsoft's flavor of DHTML supports and the actions that trigger them. Table 13-2 lists the keyboard events and actions.

---

**Note**    *The events listed in Tables 13-1 and 13-2 are by no means all the events that can be used with DHTML. To get the most from DHTML, study the documentation at **http:// msdn.microsoft.com/workshop/author/dhtml/dhtml.asp**.*

These events are used to trigger actions in the web page. For example, you could change the color or size of an object when the user points to it. FrontPage contains several ways to use DHTML without having to program the event and action, as you will see in the next section.

| Mouse Event | Action Triggered When |
|---|---|
| onmouseover | The mouse pointer is placed on an object. |
| onmouseout | The mouse pointer moves off an object. |
| onmousedown | Any mouse button is pressed. |
| onmouseup | Any mouse button is released. |
| onmousemove | The mouse pointer is moving over an object. |
| onclick | An object is clicked with the left mouse button. |
| ondblclick | The left mouse button is double-clicked on an object. |
| oncontextmenu | The right mouse button is clicked on an object (supported by IE 5 and later). |
| ondrag | An object is being dragged with the mouse (supported by IE 5 and later). |
| ondragend | The left mouse button is released after dragging an object (supported by IE 5 and later). |
| ondragstart | The dragging of an object starts (supported by IE 5 and later). |
| ondragenter | An object being dragged enters a specified target area (supported by IE 5 and later). |
| ondragover | An object being dragged is over a specified target area (supported by IE 5 and later). |
| ondragleave | An object being dragged leaves a specified target area (supported by IE 5 and later). |
| ondrop | The left mouse button is released while dragging an object over a specified target area (supported by IE 5 and later). |

**TABLE 13-1**    Microsoft Supported DHTML Mouse Events

| Keyboard Event | Action Triggered When |
|---|---|
| onkeypress | A key is pressed and released. Holding a key down will generate multiple onkeypress events. |
| onkeydown | A key is pressed. Holding the key down will not generate multiple events. |
| onkeyup | A key is released. |

**TABLE 13-2**    Microsoft Supported DHTML Keyboard Events

## Animating Text with DHTML

Animating text—making it move on a page—can be done a number of ways. Internet Explorer 4 supports the HTML Marquee tag (introduced in Chapter 12 and covered in Chapter 18), and this is a common use for a Java applet. DHTML does this also, and this is a good place to start your exploration of DHTML in FrontPage. Begin with these steps:

1. In FrontPage, create a new One Page Web Site named **AdvMarkup**.

2. Open the home page (Default.htm) in Design view and type **DHTML Moves Me**; then format it as Heading 2.

3. Select View | Toolbars | DHTML Effects. This displays the DHTML Effects toolbar, shown here:

   This toolbar allows you to apply DHTML effects to the selected object. In the On drop-down list, you select the event that will trigger the effect. The Apply drop-down list displays the available effects, and the third drop-down list allows you to set any available properties of the chosen effect. You can remove any effect by clicking Remove Effect, and the button at the far right of the toolbar toggles between whether or not the DHTML effect is highlighted in FrontPage.

4. With the cursor still on the same line as your text, click the down arrow in the On drop-down list in the DHTML Effects toolbar and choose Page Load.

5. Click the down arrow in the Apply drop-down list and choose Zoom.

6. Click the down arrow in the third drop-down list and choose Out. Your page should look similar to Figure 13-1.

7. Save your page.

   When you save the page, you should see a new file in your Folder List named Animate.js. This is a JavaScript file that actually controls the Zoom effect. This file is called by the DHTML code you added to your page. (JavaScript is covered in Chapter 15.) DHTML itself has the potential to implement this effect without JavaScript, but this method ensures the greatest compatibility with all browsers.

8. Open your page in Internet Explorer. When the page loads, your text will start out large and then decrease in size.

9. Repeat steps 5 through 7, choosing different types of animation from the Apply drop-down list and refreshing the page in your browser after each change.

10. In Design view, with the cursor still on the same line as your heading, select Mouse Over from the On drop-down list in the DHTML Effects toolbar.

PART III

**FIGURE 13-1**
AdvMarkup web
home page in
Design view

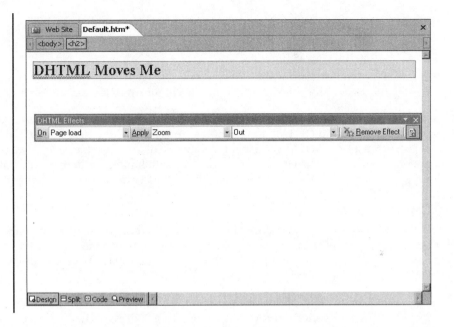

11. Select Formatting from the Apply drop-down list, and then select Choose Font from the third (Effects) drop-down list. The Font dialog box, shown here, is displayed:

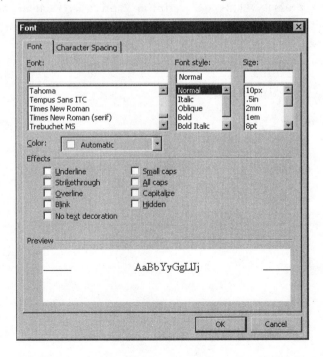

12. Select Arial Black from the Font scrolling list box and click OK.

13. Save your page and then load it in Internet Explorer. The Zoom Out effect runs when the page is first loaded.

14. Point to the heading and the font will change to Arial Black. When you move the mouse pointer off of the heading, it will return to the default font.

As you can see, FrontPage greatly simplifies using DHTML. You do not need to do any programming to add DHTML to your webs. You can also use these DHTML effects with any object, not just text. DHTML is also much more flexible than extended HTML tags, such as the Marquee tag, because it is a script, not a tag with limited predefined attributes. FrontPage support for other DHTML features is enabled in much the same way as animating objects.

## Collapsible Lists

*Collapsible* lists are any type of list (bulleted, numbered, and so on) where the list items below the top level of the hierarchy are not displayed until the user clicks a list item. This next exercise will show you how easy it is to create a collapsible list with FrontPage and DHTML. Begin now with these steps:

1. In Design view, place the cursor on the first line below your heading; then type **A Dynamic List** and format it as Heading 3. Press ENTER.

2. Click Bullets on the Formatting toolbar and type **Item 1**. Press ENTER, type **Description 1**, and press ENTER again.

3. Type **Item 2**, press ENTER, type **Description 2**, press ENTER again, and then type **Another Description**. Press ENTER twice to end the list. Your list should look similar to this:

> ### DHTML Moves Me
>
> **A Dynamic List**
>
> - Item 1
> - Description 1
> - Item 2
> - Description 2
> - Another Description

4. Place your cursor at the beginning of the Description 1 line and click Increase Indent on the Formatting toolbar twice.

5. Place the cursor at the beginning of the Description 2 line and click Increase Indent twice.

6. Place the cursor at the beginning of the Another Description line and press Increase Indent four times. Your list should now look similar to this:

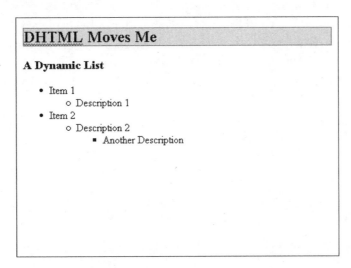

7. Right-click Item 1 in the list and select List Properties. In the List Properties dialog box, select Enable Collapsible Outlines and Initially Collapsed, as shown next. Click OK.

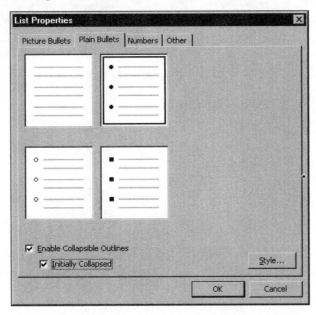

***TIP***   *The Enable Collapsible Outlines and Initially Collapsed check boxes are available on all the tabs of the List Properties dialog box.*

8. Save your page. FrontPage will create a file named Outline.js, which is a JavaScript file that controls the outline effect.

9. Reload your page in Internet Explorer. The list should appear with two list items: Item 1 and Item 2.

10. Click Item 1 in the list and Description 1 should now be displayed.

11. Click Item 2. When Description 2 is displayed, click it also. This displays the last item in the list, Another Description, as shown in Figure 13-2.

12. Click Item 2 to collapse the items below it in the list hierarchy—Description 2 and Another Description.

FrontPage and DHTML make adding advanced features, such as dynamically changing text and collapsible lists, extremely easy in your webs. In the next section, you'll see how DHTML can be used to "dress up" a form.

## Form Group Box

FrontPage provides a method of grouping form fields by creating a border with a label around the form fields. You will do this with these steps.

1. In FrontPage Design view, place the cursor on the first line after your collapsing list.

**FIGURE 13-2**
AdvMarkup web home page with collapsible list expanded in Internet Explorer

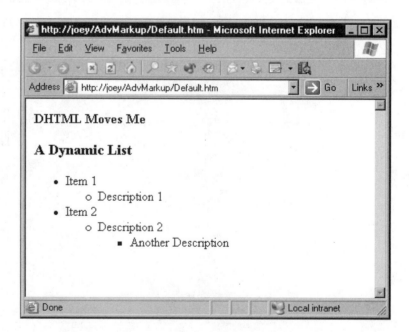

2. Select Insert | Form | Form. With the cursor to the left of the Submit button, press ENTER, then the up arrow once.

3. Select Insert | Form | Group Box. Your form should look like this:

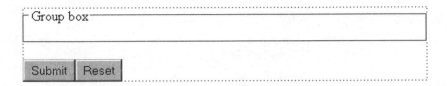

4. With the cursor placed within the Group Box outline, select Insert | Form | Option Button. Press SPACE and type **Red** followed by two spaces.

5. Repeat step 4 to create option buttons for **Green** and **Blue**.

6. Right-click the Group Box and select Group Box Properties to display the Group Box Properties dialog box.

7. In the Label text box type **Choose a Color**, as shown here, then click OK:

*TIP*   *You can also edit the label directly by selecting it as you would with any text in FrontPage.*

FrontPage, uses the DHTML FIELDSET tag to create the border around the form option buttons. This tag can actually do much more than what FrontPage uses. For example, with FrontPage, the FIELDSET tag is only used with forms. If you try to create a Group Box without a form, FrontPage will create the form. In the next section, you'll see how to edit your page code in the Code view to create a frame around a graphic using the FIELDSET tag.

## Adding a Border to a Graphic

While a single-cell table (one row and one column) can be easily used to draw a frame around a graphic, the task is more complicated if you want to have a label, such as a title, as part of the border. (This is not the same as the Table | Insert | Caption option, which adds a line above the table/cell.) At a minimum, a two-row, three-column table would have to be used. With these steps, you will use the FIELDSET tag to do this much more simply.

1. Place the cursor on the line below your form. Select Insert | Picture | Clip Art.

2. In the Clip Art task pane, select an image. It's not important which image you select. Insert the image you selected by double-clicking it.

3. Close the Clip Art task pane and save your AdvMarkup web home page. The Save Embedded Files dialog box will be displayed. Click OK.

4. Click your graphic in Design view to select it. The Pictures toolbar may be displayed. If so, close it, as you won't need it for this exercise.

5. Right-click your graphic and select Picture Properties. In the Picture Properties dialog box select Specify Size if not already selected. Click OK. This will add the Height and Width attributes to your <IMG> tag.

6. Switch to Code view. The IMG tag for your picture should be selected. Your code should be similar to this:

```
<p><img border="0" src="j00903861.gif" width="284" height="243"></p>
```

---

**NOTE**   *Your graphic path and filename, width, and height will be different if you used a different graphic.*

7. Place your cursor between the paragraph tag, <P>, and the image tag , <IMG...>, and press ENTER.

8. Type **<FIELDSET>**. FrontPage will create the closing FIELDSET tag.

9. Select the closing FIELDSET tag (</FIELDSET>), press CTRL-X to cut it, then place your cursor to the left of the closing paragraph tag, </P> .

10. Press CTRL-V to paste the closing FIELDSET tag before the closing paragraph tag.

11. Save your page and switch to Design view. There should be a line border that stretches across the page around the graphic.

12. Right-click in the Group Box surrounding the graphic and select Group Box Properties. The Group Box Properties dialog box, shown previously, is displayed.

13. In the Label text box, type **Home Sweet Home** (or a label suitable for your graphic), then click Style.

14. In the Modify Style dialog box, click Format, then select Border from the drop-down menu.

15. In the Borders And Shading dialog box Borders tab, select Box in the Setting list, select Solid in the Style list, type **1px** in the Width spinner, and then enter **8px** in each of the Padding spinners, as shown here, and click OK three times.

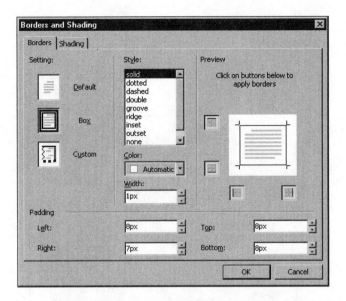

Your Group Box frame around the graphic is almost complete, but it still extends across the entire page. To fix this, you will need to add some code manually again.

16. Save your page and switch to Code view. Find your opening <FIELDSET> tag. It should look like this:

```
<FIELDSET STYLE="border-style: solid; border-width: 1px; padding: 8px">
```

17. Place your cursor after the 8px and type **;width=300px**. Your tag should look like this:

```
<FIELDSET STYLE="border-style: solid; border-width: 1px; padding: 8px;
width=300px">
```

---

**NOTE**  *If you have the HTML Attribute Value Quotes turned on (Tools | Page Options | IntelliSense | HTML Attribute Value Quotes), you may get an extra set of quotes in your code. If so, you should delete them. The entire Style attribute of the FIELDSET tag should be within one set of quotes.*

The semicolon separates the properties of the Style attribute. The value of 300 pixels for the width is determined by adding the padding (8 + 8) and the width of the graphic (284).

18. Save your page and switch to Design view. Your graphic with a Group Box should look similar to this:

This is actually a very simple use of the FIELDSET tag. For a more complete look at what it can do, refer to the documentation at **http://msdn.microsoft.com/library/ default.asp?url=/workshop/author/dhtml/reference/objects/fieldset.asp**.

In the preceding examples, DHTML was used to improve the appearance of the page, but it can also add a great deal of functionality. In the next section, you will use DHTML to add clickable form field labels, which make your web pages behave more like an actual Windows application.

## Clickable Form Field Labels

In Windows dialog boxes, you can select a check box or option button by clicking the label for the box or button. With web forms, you have to actually click the check box or option button to select it. You can use DHTML to make web form labels function in the same way as Windows dialog boxes. Do that now with these instructions:

1. On your AdvMarkup web home page in Design view, select the label Red and its option button in the Choose a Color form.

2. Select Insert | Form | Label.

3. Repeat steps 1 and 2 for the Green and Blue labels and option buttons.

4. Save your page and then open it in Internet Explorer.

5. Click a label and the corresponding option button is selected.

Another DHTML effect that adds a dynamic element to your work is page transitions, as you will see next.

## Page Transitions

*Page transitions* are effects that can be applied to a web page when the user enters or exits a page, or when the user enters or exits your site. You apply a page transition to the active page from the Page Transitions dialog box, shown next, which is opened by selecting Format | Page Transition:

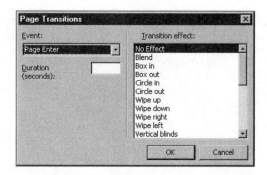

Page transitions can be triggered by four events, selected from the Event drop-down list in the Page Transitions dialog box:

- **Page Enter**   Invokes the transition when the page is loaded.
- **Page Exit**   Invokes the transition when the user leaves the page.
- **Site Enter**   Invokes the transition when the user enters your site by loading any page.
- **Site Exit**   Invokes the transition when the user leaves your site by loading a page that is not on your site.

You can specify the amount of time for the transition (in seconds) by entering a value in the Duration (Seconds) text box. The transition effect is selected from the Transition Effect scrolling list box.

A very useful DHTML effect that gives you greater control over your pages is the ability to position objects precisely on your page, as you will see next.

## Positioning

Tables are often used to position items in relation to each other, but there is little control of where the table is placed on the page. With HTML, tables can be positioned left, right, or center, and the size of the table can be defined, but that is about the limit of what you can do. DHTML extends this by allowing you to place an object, not just a table, at a specific offset from the top left corner of the page. You can also set how text will wrap around the object, much like text is wrapped around a graphic or table using the ALIGN attribute of the IMG or TABLE tags. The following exercise will show you how this works. Begin with these steps:

1. Create a new page in your AdvMarkup web and save it with the Page Title **DHTML Positioning** and the File Name **Position.htm**.

2. Type **This is a picture of a house** and format it as Heading 3.

3. Press ENTER, then select Insert | Picture | From File. Select the image you've used in the previous exercises and click Insert. The image is placed in the upper-left corner of your page, below your text.

4. Click the image to select it; then select Format | Position. The Position dialog box, shown next, is displayed:

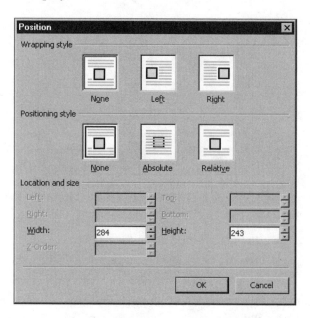

The Wrapping Style options set how text will wrap around the object (the house graphic in this case). The Positioning Style options allow you to choose no positioning (None), Absolute (an exact location on the page), or Relative (positioned relative to other objects on the page) positioning. When either Absolute or Relative positioning is selected, the Location And Size options become available. Left and Top are used to specify the position of the object from the upper-left corner of the page. Width and Height are the size of the object.

Z-Order sets the *layer* of the object. With style sheets, objects on a page can be placed in layers so that one object can be placed behind or on top of another object. Imagine that each object (text, graphics, and so on) is printed on clear plastic, like an overhead transparency. One sheet contains the text for the page, and another sheet contains the graphic. If the text is the top sheet and the graphic is on the bottom sheet, you will see the graphic behind the text. If you reverse the order, the graphic will cover part of the text. This concept is familiar if you have worked with page layout programs such as Adobe PageMaker, but was an unknown concept on the Web prior to style sheets and DHTML.

5. In the Position dialog box, select None for Wrapping Style and Absolute for Positioning Style; then type **75px** in the Left Location And Size spinner and **75px** in the Top Location And Size spinner. Click OK. Figure 13-3 shows the house graphic absolutely positioned in Design view.

**FIGURE 13-3**
Graphic absolutely positioned in Design view

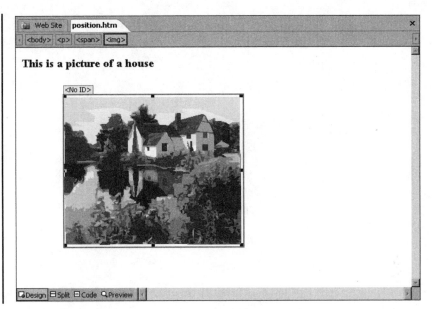

6. Place the cursor on the line you typed and select Format | Position. In the Position dialog box, select Absolute for Positioning Style. Notice that the text has both a width and height, as shown in the Width and Height Location And Size spinners. This is another new concept for a web page; the width displayed is the full width of the page, not just the width of the text. If you visualize the text as being on a separate piece of paper that is the width of the page and then placed on top of the web page, the concept is clearer.

7. Type **25px** in the Left Location And Size spinner and **80px** in the Top Location And Size spinner; then type **0** in the Z-Order spinner. Click OK, then click the page to deselect the text. Figure 13-4 shows what your page should now look like. The text has been absolutely positioned behind the graphic.

***

***TIP*** *When positioning has been applied to an object and it is selected, you can use the arrow keys to move it in one pixel increments.*

8. Select the graphic, then select Format | Position. In the Position dialog box, type **–1** in the Z-Order spinner. Click OK. Your page should look similar to Figure 13-5. The text is on the layer in front of the graphic. Click outside of the text and picture if necessary.

9. Click the graphic, then select View | Toolbars | Positioning. The Positioning toolbar, shown here, is displayed.

**FIGURE 13-4**
Text and graphic absolutely positioned in Design view with text behind the graphic

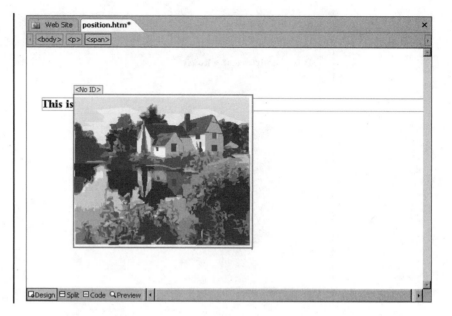

This toolbar duplicates most of the functions of the Position dialog box. The two buttons on the right end of the toolbar move the selected object forward one layer or back one layer.

10. With the graphic still selected, click Bring Forward on the Positioning toolbar. This changes the Z-Order of the layers and places the text behind the graphic.

**FIGURE 13-5**
Graphic positioned behind text in Design view

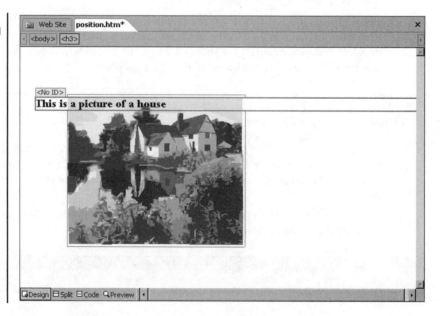

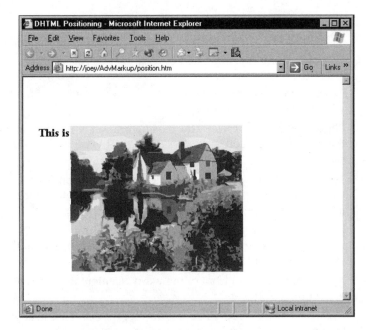

**FIGURE 13-6**
DHTML Positioning page in Internet Explorer

11. Save your work, including the embedded graphic, and then open your DHTML Positioning page in Internet Explorer, as shown in Figure 13-6, where you can see the layers effect.

## Extending DHTML in FrontPage

While FrontPage allows you to do quite a bit with DHTML, you can do even more by writing your own code in Code view. In this next exercise, you will learn how to extend DHTML in FrontPage using Code view. You will do this using these steps:

1. Create a new page in your AdvMarkup web and save it with the Page Title **Move Me** and the File Name **Moveme.htm**.

2. Type **Move Me**, format it as Heading 2, and press ENTER.

3. Type **Left | Center | Right** and click the Center alignment toolbar button. Press ENTER.

4. Select Insert | Picture | From File. Insert the graphic you used previously and save your page including the embedded graphic.

5. Switch to Code view and find the lines of HTML code for the graphic. It should look similar to this:

```
<p align="center"><img border="0" src="j0090386.gif"
  width="284" height="243"></p>
```

In the Document Object Model, both the paragraph and the image are objects that can be manipulated. You're going to manipulate the paragraph tag, so the first thing to do is give it an identifier that will simplify referencing it.

6. Place the cursor in the opening paragraph tag and select ALIGN="center", then type **ID="imgpara1"**. Make sure there's a space between the P and ID in the tag. Your modified paragraph tag should look like this:

```
<p id="imgpara1">
```

Next, you need to modify the Left | Center | Right text to control the paragraph tag which is wrapping the image.

7. Place your cursor between the closing bracket (>) of the opening paragraph tag and the first letter of "Left" and press ENTER. This is just to make the code easier to work with.

8. Type **<SPAN>**. FrontPage will create the matching closing tag. Select the closing SPAN tag, press CTRL-X to cut it, then place the cursor after the word "Left" and press CTRL-V.

9. In the opening SPAN tag, place the cursor between "span" and the closing bracket, press SPACE, then type **onClick="imgpara1.align='left'"**. Notice that the word left is enclosed in single quotes (') while the entire property of the onClick event is enclosed in double quotes ("").

10. Move your cursor in front of the word "Center" and press ENTER. Your code should look similar to this:

```
<SPAN onClick="imgpara1.align='left'">Left</SPAN> |
Center | Right</P>
```

11. With the cursor in front of the word "Center," type **<SPAN onClick= "imgpara1.align= 'center'">**. Select the closing SPAN tag FrontPage inserted and cut and paste it after the word Center.

12. Move your cursor to the start of the word "Right" and press ENTER. Type **<SPAN onClick="imgpara1.align='right'">**. Select the closing SPAN tag FrontPage inserted and cut and paste it after the word Right, and save your page. Your completed code should look similar to this:

```
<SPAN onClick="imgpara1.align='left'">Left</SPAN> |
<SPAN onClick="imgpara1.align='center'">Center</SPAN> |
<SPAN onClick="imgpara1.align='right'">Right</SPAN></P>
<P ID="imgpara1">
<IMG BORDER="0" SRC="j0090386.gif" WIDTH="284"
  HEIGHT="243"></P>
```

13. Open your Move Me page in Internet Explorer and click Right, then Center, then Left. Your image should move to the appropriate location. Figure 13-7 shows the page after Center has been clicked.

Left, Center, and Right are not hyperlinks, so they are not underlined and the cursor does not change appearance when placed on them. They are, under the DOM, objects, so they can have events attached to them; in this case, the onClick event.

The align attribute of the paragraph, which is what is being controlled in this example, is referenced in the form *object.property* where "imgpara1" is the object and "align" is the property. Each onClick statement changes the value of the paragraph's align property. Another important point is that the page is not reloaded from the server when the alignment is changed—everything is happening in the browser itself.

**FIGURE 13-7**
Move Me page in
Internet Explorer
after Center has
been clicked

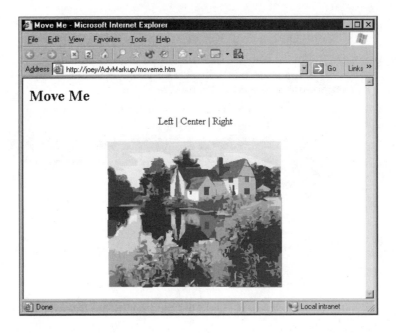

## Behaviors Task Pane

FrontPage has another way to work with DHTML—the Behaviors task pane, shown next. The Behaviors task pane allows you to select an object on the page, attach an event to it, and then build an action triggered by the event. In the next exercise, you will use the Behaviors task pane to display a message when you move the mouse over the graphic.

1. In FrontPage, select Design view, then open the Behaviors task pane by selecting Format | Behaviors.

2. Click your graphic to select it. In the Behaviors task pane, <img> will be displayed in the Scripts On Tag field. This field displays the page object that is currently selected.

3. Click the Insert button. This displays a list of available actions that can be used. This isn't a complete list of all the actions possible with DHTML—just the ones that have been pre-programmed in FrontPage.

4. Select Popup Message. The Popup Message dialog box, shown here, is displayed:

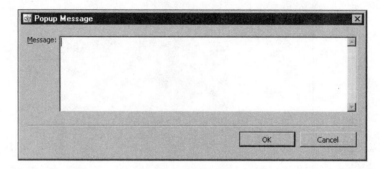

5. In the Message textbox, type **This can't be the Northwest—it isn't raining!**, then click OK.

6. In the Events list, an onclick event has been added for the popup message. You want this to be a mouseover action so you need to change this. Click the onclick event to select it. A small down-arrow is displayed.

7. Click the down-arrow, then select onmouseover from the displayed list.

**FIGURE 13-8**
Move Me page in Internet Explorer showing popup message.

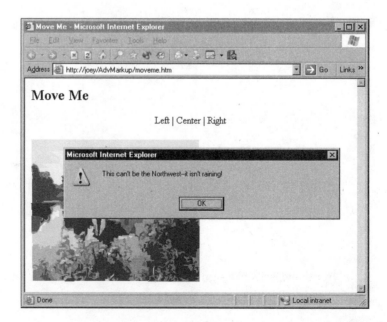

8. Save your page, then open it in Internet Explorer and move the mouse over the graphic. Figure 13-8 shows the page in Internet Explorer with the popup message displayed.

9. Click OK to close the message box, then close your AdvMarkup web in FrontPage.

Dynamic HTML greatly extends the power of HTML. You can use it without any hand coding with FrontPage's built-in support or you can expand the functionality with a little hands-on programming. In the past, differences in implementation by the various browsers have complicated its use, but that situation is greatly improved. As you will see in the following chapters, webs are becoming very active places, thanks to DHTML and the other advanced markup languages.

PART III

# Extensible Markup Language (XML)

Support for XML (Extensible Markup Language) in FrontPage 2003 is greatly enhanced from previous versions. In fact, FrontPage, along with the other Office 2003 applications, has fully integrated support for XML documents. This means that it has never been easier to share data between Office applications, or any other application that understands XML—a constantly growing list. This expanded support makes XML a subject that should be of interest to every web developer. It has survived its own hype and has become a popular and useful tool for the exchange of all kinds of data. XML has been described as "a golden hammer, for which every problem is quickly becoming a nail." This may be a slight exaggeration, but the world has certainly embraced XML as the solution to a variety of problems.

This chapter provides an overview of what XML is and the tools that FrontPage provides for working with it. It is in no way a "complete" XML reference or guide, but instead an introduction to XML and some of its uses. The next time someone asks you what XML is, you should be able to answer with confidence. This chapter will cover XML in enough detail to help you get started incorporating XML and related technologies like XSL (Extensible Style Language) and DTDs (Document Type Declarations) into your own work. If you decide that XML is your "golden hammer," there are a wide variety of dedicated books and online references available on the subject.

> **NOTE** *Microsoft's Internet Explorer has directly supported XML since version 4.01, while Netscape didn't add support until version 7.0. For this reason, all examples in this chapter that involve a web browser will only work with Internet Explorer version 4.01 or later and Netscape 7.0 or later.*

## What Is XML?

When trying to understand what XML is and what it's used for, it helps to drop the **X** and think of it in terms of another **M**arkup **L**anguage. By now, you should have a good grasp of what HTML (Hypertext Markup Language) is. In simple terms, it's just a set of structured identifiers (tags) that tell the browser how to format and display the content that resides within the tags. "<B>Hello</B>" is differentiated from "Hello" by the set of bold tags (<B></B>) that surround the text. That's what HTML is best at, *describing the format of how information should be displayed*.

But what is "Hello"? We know that it is a greeting in the English language. We know that when surrounded by HTML bold tags, it will display in a web browser as bold text, but what does it mean or refer to? That's what XML is used for, *describing the context and meaning of information (data) in a structured manner*. Like HTML, XML uses tags to mark up textual data. In XML, the tags might be <greeting>Hello</greeting>, which describes *what* the data is, not how it should be displayed. This is the fundamental difference between HTML and XML. The following example illustrates how XML could be used to mark up information about materials in a library. A library will have several types of materials, such as books, recordings, and movies.

```
<library>
  <book>
    <title>Peirce's Pragmatism, The Design For Thinking</title>
    <author>Phyllis Chiasson</author>
  </book>
  <recording>
    <title>What In The World</title>
    <performer>Richard Sinclair &amp; David Rees-Williams</performer>
  </recording>
  <book>
    <title>The King of Limbo and Other Stories</title>
    <author>Adrianne Harun</author>
  </book>
</library>
```

While this looks a little like HTML, it's doubtful you'll ever see a <book> or <recording> tag as part of an HTML standard. That's where the X in XML comes in—it's eXtensible, meaning that you create your own tags as needed, extending the language to describe and delimit (that is, clearly define the starting and ending points of) your data.

Applying common sense and your understanding of HTML, you can pretty well guess that we're talking about materials in a library and that everything that lies between the <library> and </library> tags has something to do with materials in a library. Taking a step down into the hierarchy, you can ascertain what information is about books, defined by the <book></book> tags, and a recording, with one set of <recording></recording> tags. Stepping further into the hierarchy, you also see that we have identified the title and author or performer of each item. This has nothing to do with how the library data is displayed, but instead gives you a standard by which the hierarchical data can be parsed (read and interpreted). Using your imagination, you can see how this could be useful when sharing information, not only between people, but also between different software applications.

Taking the library example, imagine that there are two libraries, not part of the same library system, that want to share information about their collections. Each is currently using a proprietary application to catalog their collection and the applications have incompatible file formats. This is the ideal situation to use XML as a "golden hammer." If both applications support XML, exchanging data between becomes very simple. The alternative is to write a custom application that would exchange the information, which is not always a simple task.

## XML Data Is Highly Structured

Like HTML, XML uses arrow-bracketed tags to separate markup from data. Start tags begin with the tag name and end tags begin with a forward slash, followed by the tag name (<performer>…</performer>). In HTML, there are also tags that do not require ending counterparts. The line break (<BR>) and horizontal rule (<HR>) tags are examples of this. Some HTML programmers also intentionally choose to leave out end tags on items like paragraphs (<P>) because they consider them logically unnecessary, and browsers really don't care if you use them or not. Unlike HTML, XML is said to be *well formed* because it *always* requires an end tag for every start tag. Miss an end tag in an HTML page, and the browser will likely be forgiving; miss an end tag in an XML document, and the entire document is broken and only an error message will be displayed.

Being well formed also means that tags must follow an ordered structure. While HTML lets you get away with miss-ordered tag placement such as <FONT><B>…</ FONT ></ B>, XML does not and will cause an XML parser (reader/interpreter program) to give an error if the first opened, last closed order is broken. While this might seem extreme from an HTML standpoint, think of it in terms of a database flat-file such as a comma-separated values (CSV) file to bring the reason for this restriction. For example, a CSV file, a file format used by Excel and other programs, stores data in columns and rows by using a comma to separate each column value and new lines to separate rows (records). Starting a new line means starting a new data record; if you then entered the last column of the previous record, no one would understand what you meant. Like the CSV file format, in XML structure conveys meaning. For an XML document to be understood, it must be structured with properly opened and closed identifiers.

## XML Data Describes Itself

Unlike CSV files, XML allows you to store data in a hierarchical form. Instead of columns and rows, XML uses nested tags to define relational data structures. Looking back at the previous XML example, you see that each book tag contains two sets of tags: title and author. Because these nested tags are placed within a book tag, you know that they contain information about the book. You also know that since the tags are different they do not contain the same type of data. The book tags are also nested within the library tag set, letting you know that each book tag set contains information about something in a library. Since the book tags are the same, you know that they contain the same type of data. Since the recording tag is different, you know that it contains information about a different type of material in the library.

```
<library>
  <book>
    <title>…</title>
    <author>…</author>
  </book>
  …
</library>
```

Whether or not you know what a library, book, recording, or title is, you can still see the relationships between the data. All book tag sets should contain the same type of information that relates in the same way to the library tag set, even though the title and author information contained within is different. All title tag sets should contain the same type of information that relates in the same way to all book tag sets. These inherent relationships, created by the structured placement of specific tags within the data, make XML self-describing. This self-describing nature of XML is further extended by DTDs (Document Type Declarations), which are covered in the section "Document Type Definitions (DTD)—Valid XML."

## XML Data Is Application Independent

You've probably run into the problem of file format incompatibility at least once. This often occurs when you try to use a file created by one software application with a different application. Software manufacturers have tried to ease your pain by offering various conversion programs, but file incompatibility still raises its ugly head now and then, usually at the worst possible time—when you're up against a deadline. XML may be the best solution yet to sharing data between different applications.

Instead of saving files in proprietary binary formats, software manufacturers are starting to allow users to save files in text-based formats, using XML to define special functionality and formatting. Save a Word document (Word 2000 or later) as an HTML file, then open that file in Notepad and look at the code. You'll see XML being used to store the document's properties and options.

```
<xml>
  <o:DocumentProperties>
  <o:Author>Erik Poulsen</o:Author>
  <o:Template>OMH.DOT</o:Template>
  <o:LastAuthor>Erik Poulsen</o:LastAuthor>
  <o:Revision>2</o:Revision>
  <o:TotalTime>1431</o:TotalTime>
  <o:Created>2003-01-21T17:08:00Z</o:Created>
  <o:LastSaved>2003-01-21T17:08:00Z</o:LastSaved>
  <o:Pages>29</o:Pages>
  <o:Words>7018</o:Words>
  <o:Characters>40007</o:Characters>
  <o:Company>Osborne/McGraw-Hill</o:Company>
  <o:Lines>333</o:Lines>
  <o:Paragraphs>80</o:Paragraphs>
  <o:CharactersWithSpaces>49131</o:CharactersWithSpaces>
  <o:Version>9.6926</o:Version>
 </o:DocumentProperties>
</xml>
```

Why would you care about this information when viewing the page in a browser? You probably wouldn't. But open the HTML file again in Word and you'll see that this information, which cannot be described in HTML, has been preserved.

Taking things a step further, what if the entire Word document were converted to and saved as XML? Since XML is used to describe data structures, not formatting, you would need to totally separate the content of the document from its presentation. Handling presentation is the work of languages like HTML, CSS, and XSL (covered in the section "Formatting XML"). This may seem strange at first, but looking deeper, it opens up a world of possibilities.

With a common, isolated source of data, it becomes very easy to change the way the data is displayed. It is also equally easy to change the data without having to worry about the presentation aspects. Most media companies, no matter what their primary domain (radio,

TV, newspapers, magazines, etc.), now offer information on the Internet. XML provides them with a method of reusing the same content in a variety of formats. The content stays the same—only the presentation method and formatting changes. You may have already experienced similar benefits to this type of separation through the use of linked cascading style sheets (CSS), changing a style and updating the look of an entire web site.

Understandably, businesses are very excited about XML as a method of reusing and exchanging data. In the ever-expanding world of e-commerce, both business to business (B2B) and business to consumer (B2C), information needs to be exchanged between online stores, payment services, fulfillment services, and manufacturers. These services are often provided by different companies that need a common way to communicate when exchanging data. XML provides a solution to this problem by providing a platform- and application-independent data format for this exchange.

# XML Data Structures

We've already discussed how XML is extensible, allowing you to create your own tags to define and structure your data. But there's much more to XML than basic tags. XML tags, which are known as *elements*, can contain *attributes* just like HTML tags. In fact, XML elements sometimes use only attributes, instead of placing data between start and end tags. Let's look at the various components that make up XML. (Some of this information has already been covered, but it is reprised here for completeness and reference.)

## Elements

Elements are used to define the type of data contained within the element. Once used, an element name should be reused for each occurrence of the same data type, but only for the same data type. An element is comprised of a start tag, an end tag, and any data that lies between. Both start tags and end tags are arrow bracketed, with end tags containing a forward slash (/) before the element name.

```
<element>some data</element>
```

If the element contains no data, or the data is specified as attributes (see the next section, "Attributes"), it can also be represented by adding a forward slash to the end of a start tag, eliminating the need for an end tag.

```
<element />
```

The scope of elements cannot overlap each other. All child elements must be closed before the parent element is closed. For example:

- <book><title></book></title> is not valid
- <book><title></title></book> is valid

The first element in every XML document must be a unique *root element*. This compares to the <HTML></HTML> tags that begin and end every HTML document. In the case of XML, it should be a name that meaningfully identifies the data contained within the document. In the example, <library></library> is the root element.

## Attributes

Unlike elements, which are used to define a type of data, attributes are used to provide additional or ancillary information about an element. This information sometimes takes the form of properties; known as *metadata* (which is essentially information about information), or in other cases can be used to store the element's data.

An attribute consists of a name/value pair in the form *attribute="value"* with values always enclosed in quotes. Attributes reside in element start tags and can only be used once within an element. They can, however, be used in any order within the element and can be used in different types of elements. If the element contains data, such as the <title> element in the Library example, the code would be written like this:

```
<element attribute="value">some data</element>
```

In the library example, a title element might be written as,

```
<title category="Philosophy">Peirce's Pragmatism, The Design For Thinking</title>
```

where the category attribute describes the type of book. The category attribute could also be an element:

```
<category>Philosophy</category>
```

Which method you use would depend on the data you are working with. You should choose a method that accurately reflects the structure of your data. The data for an element can also be included as attributes, like this:

```
<element attribute="value" attribute2="value" />
```

For example,

```
<price hardback="23.95" paperback="14.95" />
```

where the pricing information is contained as attributes. XML is extremely flexible, as you can see from these examples. Before deciding how to structure your data you should also think about the ability of your structure to deal with additional data that might be added in the future.

## Entity References

Entities serve two main purposes in XML: they allow you to use reserved characters, and they let you create shortcut references (abbreviations) to repeatedly used data, both internal and external. In each case, entities always begin with an ampersand (&) and end with a semicolon (;), just like entity references in HTML. The second case (abbreviations) is covered in the section "Entity Abbreviations."

Just like HTML, XML tags are surrounded with arrow brackets (<>) so these characters are reserved and cannot be used in data. Instead, you use the HTML encoded &lt; and &gt; equivalents. XML uses the same encoding to allow the use of these and other special characters.

| Reserved Character | Entity Reference |
|---|---|
| < | &lt; |
| > | &gt; |
| & | &amp; |
| " | &quot; |
| ' | &apos; |

## Processing Instructions, Comments, and CDATA Sections

In addition to the data defining structures within XML, there are also nondata-related structures that are used to add additional information to documents. This can take the form of information for the XML parser, human readable comments, or pass-through information that is used by an application other than the parser.

### Processing Instructions

Processing instructions (PI) are used to provide information to applications that interpret XML, known as parsers, and are not part of the XML data structure. They begin with a <? and end with a ?>. Unlike elements, processing instructions have no end tag. The *XML declaration* is an example of a processing instruction used in XML documents. It provides applications that process XML with important information about the document and, if included, must be the first line in the document.

```
<?xml version="1.0" encoding="UTF-8" standalone="yes"?>
```

This example tells the application reading the document that it contains XML as specified by the W3C standard 1.0 (**http://www.w3.org/XML**), that the characters in the document are encoded using the UTF-8 standard, and that the document does not contain any elements, attributes, or entities that are referenced by an external DTD (Document Type Declaration, covered in the section "Document Type Definitions (DTD)—Valid XML"). Minimally, you should always include "xml" and the version number (<?xml version="1.0" ?>). Currently, there's only one version of XML (1.0), but future releases will make version identification important.

### Comments

Just like HTML comments, XML comments begin with <!-- and end with -->. Comments can be placed anywhere in the XML document after the XML declaration, except within an element tag, and are used to improve human readability.

```
<!-- this is an XML comment -->
```

### CDATA Sections

CDATA (character data) sections are used to prevent an application from trying to interpret the markup contained within the section. They begin with <![CDATA[ and end with ]]>.

```
<![CDATA[
  This is an XML declaration:
  <?xml version="1.0" encoding="UTF-8" standalone="no" ?>
]]>
```

CDATA sections are primarily used to display code listings without that code being interpreted by the application parsing the data. The only set of characters that cannot be used within a CDATA section is the closing tag, ]]>.

## Syntax

Unlike HTML, XML's syntax is very important and strict. This is part of what makes XML well formed. Web browsers can make best guesses at how information should be displayed, but XML parsers depend on precise syntax to provide reliable data interpretation. After all, you wouldn't want a bank to guess at the amount you really meant to write on that check, would you?

### XML Is Case-Sensitive

XML treats upper- and lowercase letters differently. As a result, <book>, <Book>, and <BOOK> are completely different elements. To avoid case-related problems, it's usually a good idea to write all of your elements and attribute names in lowercase.

### XML Does Not Ignore Spaces

Unlike HTML, which ignores repeated spaces unless specifically written as nonbreaking spaces ( ), XML retains each space as it appears in the data. You may have noticed that there isn't a nonbreaking space entity. Because XML does not ignore repeated spaces, also known as *whitespace*, there is no need for a nonbreaking space entity.

### All Elements Must Be Closed

Being well-formed, each starting element tag in an XML document must have a corresponding end tag. This closing tag can be a matching end tag in the form <element></element>, or the shortcut version <element /> may be used when the element does not contain data. In XML terms, the element is then considered not to have a *value*, even though it may contain attributes that have values.

### All Element Attributes Must Be in Quotes

Unlike HTML, which allows you to not use quotes around numeric attributes (size=2), *all* XML attribute values must be enclosed in quotes (name="value"). Failure to do so will cause an XML parser to generate an error.

## Formatting XML

Since XML doesn't define the appearance of the data, you must use other technologies to actually format the displayed XML data. Starting with Internet Explorer 4, Microsoft has included an XML parser with their browsers. Included with IE 5 and above is the ability to display XML documents in a hierarchical tree view. Netscape added support for XML in version 7.0 of its browser. To see how this works, you'll create a web to work with XML files in the following steps:

1. In FrontPage, create a new One Page Web Site and name it **XML**.

2. Select Blank Page from the New task pane.

3. Select File | Save As. In the Save As dialog box, select XML from the Save As Type drop-down, type **Library.xml** in the File Name textbox, and then click Save. Since you saved the file with an .xml extension, the page is displayed in XML view. The

XML floating toolbar, shown here, may also be displayed. If not, select View | Toolbars | XML View to display it. This toolbar allows you to verify your XML and to reformat it.

4. Press CTRL-A to select all the HTML text on the Library.xml page, and then press DEL.

5. Enter the following text in your Library.xml page:

```
<library>
 <book>
  <title>Peirce's Pragmatism, The Design For Thinking</title>
  <author>Phyllis Chiasson</author>
 </book>
 <recording>
  <title>What In The World</title>
  <performer>Richard Sinclair &amp; David Rees-Williams </performer>
 </recording>
 <book>
  <title>The King of Limbo and Other Stories</title>
  <author>Adrianne Harun</author>
 </book>
</library>
```

6. Save your Library.xml page, then select File | Preview In Browser and choose Internet Explorer 4.1 or later, or Netscape 7 or later. Figure 14-1 shows the Library.xml page in Internet Explorer 6.0.

The first thing you'll notice is that IE's representation of the XML file looks surprisingly like the raw XML. There is a root <library> element that contains two instances of the <book> element, which each contain <title> and <author> elements, and one instance of the <recording> element, with <title> and <performer> elements. Color-coding has been added and there are minus (–) signs to the left of each element that contain children (lower-level elements). Clicking the minus sign next to the <library> element collapses the tree and leaves visible only the <library> element and a plus (+) sign to the left. Clicking the plus sign expands the tree, again showing all of the elements and their values. You should already be quite familiar with this interface after working with Windows Explorer and FrontPage Folders views. Internet Explorer is using its built-in XML parser to read and interpret the XML source in Library.xml. It then applies an internal (default) Extensible Style Language (XSL) style sheet to the data, transforming it into browser-readable HTML.

7. Click Verify Well-formed XML in the XML View toolbar. If your XML code is well formed and properly nested, the following dialog box is displayed:

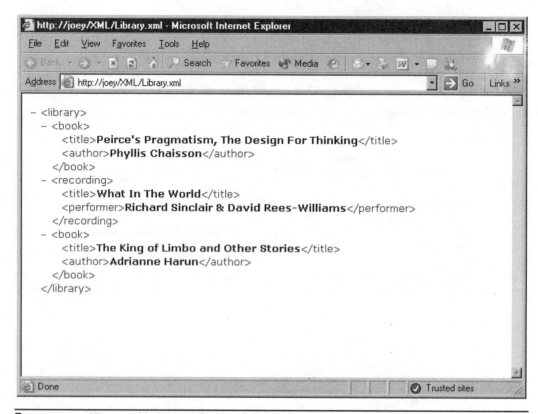

**FIGURE 14-1**    Library.xml in Internet Explorer 6.0 showing the hierarchical display

8. Find the closing </library> element in your XML and delete the leading forward slash (/). Click Verify Well-formed XML again. This time you should see an error message, like this:

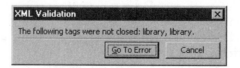

9. Click Go To Error and restore the leading forward slash in the closing </library> element.

10. Click Reformat XML in the XML View toolbar.

Clicking Reformat XML adds the processor instruction (PI) <?xml version="1.0" encoding="utf-8" ?> at the top of the page.

11. Save your work.

*TIP*   *You can also apply XML reformatting to files other than XML, such as HTML files. In Code view, right-click the page and select Apply XML Formatting Rules. Among other things, this will ensure that all tags are closed. For example, <HR> would be replaced by <HR />. This doesn't affect the display of the HTML code in a browser and helps ensures that the XML parser won't generate a syntax error.*

While IE's built-in parser and default XSL style sheet offers a great tool for viewing your XML and checking it for errors, its default display falls far short of how you'll want to display your XML data in real-world applications. To achieve the desired formatting results, you'll want to create and use your own style sheets.

## CSS

Cascading style sheets (CSS) were covered in Chapters 10 and 12 as a method of controlling the look of HTML. In the same way, CSS can also be used to control the display of XML. In CSS, you specify an element by name (such as H2) and then list properties (styles) of that element, setting their values as desired. Using CSS with XML works the same way. Instead of specifying HTML tags, you instead use XML element names. Here, title is the element name and color and font size are properties of this element for which you are specifying values:

```
title {color: #FF0000; font-size: 14pt;}
```

CSS style sheets can be *embedded*, that is, contained within the XML document; or *external*, a separate file that is linked to within the document. To embed a CSS style sheet within an XML document, you add an *xml-stylesheet* processor instruction to the top of the document specifying that the XML parser should use the styles specified within the document when displaying its output. The embedded style sheet processor instruction is as follows:

```
<?xml-stylesheet href="#style" type="text/css"?>
```

Anywhere after this instruction, you can place your style definitions as you would in an HTML file.

```
<?xml-stylesheet href="#style" type="text/css"?>
<style>
  library {background-color: #EEEEEE; width: 100%;}
  book {display: block; margin-bottom: 20pt; margin-left: 10;}
  recording { display: block; margin-bottom: 20pt; margin-left: 10;}
  title {color: #FF0000; font-size: 14pt;}
  ...
</style>
```

To use a linked CSS style sheet, you simply add a reference to the style sheet file to the processor instruction, listing the location of the style sheet that contains your style definitions:

```
<?xml-stylesheet href="library.css" type="text/css"?>
```

Linking has significant advantages over embedding. You can reuse the same linked style sheet with multiple documents. When you need to make a change, you change it a single time in the style sheet and it is automatically applied to all linking pages. You can also link to multiple style sheets within a single XML document. This is done by simply adding additional xml-stylesheet processor instructions for each additional style sheet you wish to use. This feature allows you to have one style sheet that specifies element layouts, another that specifies sizes, and a third that specifies colors. Using linked style sheets almost always is the best way to go. You will learn how to link in style sheet with these steps:

1. In FrontPage, add a Blank Page to your XML web.

2. In Code view, press CTRL-A to select all the text, then DEL to delete it.

3. Type the following text, pressing RETURN after each line:
   **library {background-color: #EEEEEE; width: 100%;}**
   **book, recording {display: block; margin-bottom: 20pt; margin-left: 10pt;}**
   **title {color: #FF0000; font-family: Verdana; font-size: 14pt;}**
   **author, performer {display: block; color: #0000FF; font-family: Arial; font-size: 12pt; margin-left: 20pt;}**

4. Save your page as **Library.css**.

5. Open your Library.xml, if it's not already open, place the cursor on the line below the opening processing statement, then type
   **<?xml-stylesheet type="text/css" href="library.css" ?>**

6. Save your work, then open Library.xml in your browser. Your page should look similar to Figure 14-2.

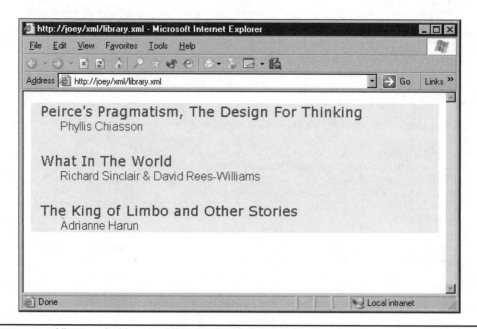

**FIGURE 14-2**    Library.xml with style sheet attached in Internet Explorer 6

By providing your own CSS style sheet and referencing it with the xml-stylesheet instruction in your XML document, you tell your browser that it should use your style sheet instead of its own. While CSS style sheets give you some control over how your XML data is displayed, they do not give you nearly the control and power of XSL.

## XSL

Providing all the functionality of CSS with greater power and control are XSL (Extensible Style Language) style sheets. XSL combines CSS with *templates* that define the format of the resulting code. It also includes powerful searching and filtering capabilities that give you much greater control over exactly how information is formatted. XSL is really made up of three parts:

- **XSLT (XSL Transformations)**    Used to transform XML into other types of documents including HTML; it can also be used to reshape one XML document into another.

- **XPath**    Used by XSLT to address specific parts and patterns of XML documents.

- **XSL Formatting Objects**    Used to define the display of XML elements.

**NOTE**    *Complete coverage of XSL is well beyond the scope of this chapter. Only a small portion of its abilities to format the display of information will be covered here.*

Unlike CSS, an XSL style sheet is actually an XML document itself. In the following instructions, you will create a XSL style sheet for your Library.xml file. The function of each section of style sheet is explained before the step to write the code.

1. In FrontPage, add a Blank Page to your XML web.

2. Press CTRL-A, then DEL to delete the default text.

   The XSL style sheet begins with a standard XML declaration. On the next line, an xsl:stylesheet tag identifies the start of the XSL style sheet. The beginning of the template is denoted on the third line by the xsl:template tag.

3. At the top of your page, type **<?xml version="1.0"?>** and press ENTER.

4. Type
   **<xsl: stylesheet xmlns:xsl="http://www.w3.org/TR/WD-xsl">**
   and press ENTER. As you enter each line with an XSL tag, FrontPage will offer to complete the XSL tag using AutoComplete. This helps to avoid spelling errors.

**NOTE**    *XML Namespaces (xmlns) are beyond the scope of this chapter. In this case, it identifies the standard to follow in the construction of the style sheet.*

5. Type **< xsl:template match="/">** and press ENTER. The match="/" attribute tells the XSL processor that the template will be associated with the root element of the XML data source.

   Once in the body of the template, you can enter any HTML you like, including CSS style declarations or links to CSS style sheets. When creating a template that generates an HTML page, you should always follow standard HTML structure. Begin the page with <HTML>, <HEAD>, and <BODY> tags, closing each when their section of the template is complete.

6. Start the HTML section of the file and define the styles for the table head and table rows by adding the following code:

```
<html>
<style>
  th {background-color: #000000; color: #FFFFFF; font-family: Verdana; font-size: 14pt;}
  td {background-color: #EEEEEE; color: #000000; font-family: Arial; font-size: 12pt;}
</style>
<body>
```

The next step is to define the HTML table and heading row that will display the data in your Library.xml file.

7. Type

```
<table border="1" cellpadding="5" cellspacing="0">
  <tr>
    <th>Title</th>
    <th>Author/Performer</th>
  </tr>
```

In the next section of code, you will see one aspect of XSL that offers much greater control over the display of information than either HTML or cascading style sheets by using an XML transformation. In this case, a For-Each loop.

8. Add this code to your Library.xsl document:

```
<xsl:for-each select="library/book">
  <tr>
    <td><xsl:value-of select="title" /></td>
    <td><xsl:value-of select="author" /></td>
  </tr>
</xsl:for-each>
```

The For-Each loop works by finding each instance of a book in the XML document and then placing the value of the title element in the first table cell and the value of the author element in the second table cell. This code, however, will only display the books in the Library.xml document, so you will add another For-Each loop to display the recording.

9. Type

```
<xsl:for-each select="library/recording">
  <tr>
    <td><xsl:value-of select="title" /></td>
    <td><xsl:value-of select="performer" /></td>
  </tr>
</xsl:for-each>
```

10. Close all your open tags with the following code:

```
</table>
</body>
</html>
</xsl:template>
</xsl:stylesheet>
```

11. Save your page as **Library.xsl**.

12. Click Verify Well-formed XML in the XML View toolbar to ensure your file is well formed, then resave your page if Verify Well-formed XML changed your code.

    Now you need to attach your XSL file to your Library.xml document by changing the xml-stylesheet processor instruction to point to the new file.

13. In your Library.xml file, change the xml-stylesheet processor instruction to
    **<?xml-stylesheet type="text/xsl" href="library.xsl" ?>**
    and save your work.

Figure 14-3 shows how Library.xml now looks in Internet Explorer 6.

The <xsl:for-each select="library/book"> tag tells the processor that it should run the code that follows repeatedly for each book element in the XML data source document (library.xml). When the </xsl:for-each> end tag is reached, the processor loops back and runs the code again, moving to the next book element and repeating the process until there are no book elements left. As the code runs each time, the processor reads the contents of the current book element and substitutes the value of the specified element in each of the <xsl:value-of select="[some element name]"/> tags. This is where the data contained in the XML file is inserted into the HTML code that is actually displayed in the browser. After all the books are displayed, the second for-each loop repeats the process for all the recordings.

You've just scratched the surface of the capabilities offered by XSL. Still, you can see that XSL provides much greater power and control over the display of XML compared to CSS. XSL is quickly gaining popularity and will likely become the accepted standard for manipulating and formatting the display of XML.

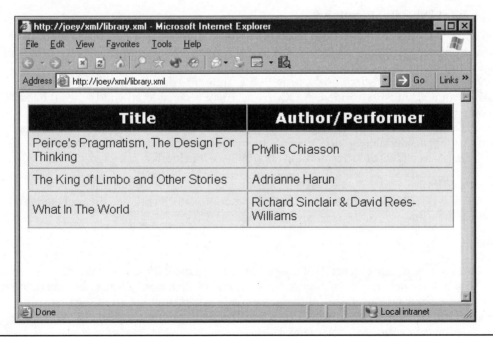

**FIGURE 14-3**   Linked XSL style sheet display of Library.xml in Internet Explorer 6

# Document Type Definitions (DTD)—Valid XML

Earlier in the chapter, you were introduced to XML's *self-describing* nature. You can look at an XML data structure and see obvious structures and relationships within the elements and data. This is fine when you are the only one working with your data, using XML as a data source to simply display information in a web page. But what if you were counting on someone else to provide your XML data source? Could you really trust them to always create the structure that you are expecting or fill it with the types of data you're counting on? Probably not... This is where DTDs are useful: *to define the logical structure and types of data, including attributes, within an XML document*. When XML is governed by a DTD, it is considered *valid XML*.

## Stand-Alone Documents

When no DTD or *schema* is associated with an XML document, it is considered to be a stand-alone document. You specify that a document is a stand-alone document by adding a *standalone="yes"* attribute to the XML declaration, as shown here:

```
<?xml version="1.0" encoding="UTF-8" standalone="yes" ?>
```

Stand-alone documents contain no method of validating their structure. As long as the document is well-formed, no errors will occur when it is processed by an XML parser. When starting out with XML, these are the types of documents you'll likely be creating. As long as you're not exchanging your XML documents with others (people or applications), you are in control of how your document is structured and the data it contains.

## Document Type Declarations

The real beauty of XML lies within its ability to be a universal, self-describing method of transferring data. To accomplish this effectively, you need a way to precisely tell others what is contained in your XML documents and a method of validating the contents. DTDs, sometimes referred to as *traffic cops*, provide a grammar to define constraints on how XML documents must be formed. An XML document is considered valid when it has an accompanying DTD to which it conforms.

DTDs can be contained within an XML document, externally in a referenced file, or both. Adding a standalone="no" attribute to an XML declaration specifies that the document uses a DTD but says nothing about where it is located.

### Internal DTDs

An internal DTD begins with a DOCTYPE declaration, which contains the root element name in the form:

```
<!DOCTYPE root_element_name [
```

The opening square bracket ([) at the end of this statement indicates that this is an *internal* DTD and that the definitions will follow. The DTD ends with a closing square bracket followed by a greater than symbol (]>). Within the square brackets, you list all of the markup declarations (elements, attributes, processor instructions, entities, and so on) that will be contained within your XML document.

## External DTDs

External DTDs come in two flavors, *private* and *public*, and are referenced within the XML document by a different type of DOCTYPE declaration. Private DTDs are those used by a single person or group of people. A private DTD lists the location (for example, /dtd/*filename*.dtd) of the external DTD document and is prefixed by the keyword SYSTEM, as follows:

```
<!DOCTYPE root_element_name SYSTEM "dtd_location">
```

Public DTDs are meant to be used by a larger group or groups of people. The public DTD declaration uses the word PUBLIC to identify this fact and provides both the name of the DTD and a public URL where it may be found. A common DTD declaration you've likely seen, possibly never knowing what it really meant, is

```
<!DOCTYPE HTML PUBLIC "-//W3C//DTD XHTML 1.0 Transitional//EN"
 "http://www.w3.org/TR/xhtml1/DTD/xhtml1-transitional.dtd">
```

The contents of an external DTD are the same element type declarations as are contained within the internal DTD's DOCTYPE declaration.

## Element Type Declarations

Whether within an internal DOCTYPE declaration or an external file, *element type declarations* are used to provide a strict guide to what items will be in an XML document, the order in which they will appear, and the number of times they will appear. These element type declarations take the form:

```
<!ELEMENT element_name allowable_contents>
```

The allowable_contents portion of this declaration lets you specify what will be contained within the element. This can be

- **EMPTY**   The element contains no data.
- **ANY**   The element can contain anything within the constraints of XML's rules.
- **(#PCDATA)**   The element contains data, but no child elements. PCDATA stands for *Parsed Character Data*.
- **(*Child elements*)**   The element contains only child elements. These elements are placed in a comma-delimited list within parentheses.
- **(*Mixed*)**   The element contains a mixture of data and child elements.

Putting this all together, the simplest XML document with an internal DTD might look like the following:

```
<?xml version="1.0" standalone="no"?>
<!DOCTYPE myxml [
  <!ELEMENT myxml (#PCDATA)>
]>
<myxml>my data here</myxml>
```

### Child Elements

To define the list of child elements contained within an element, you provide a comma-delimited list of the child elements within the element type declaration's allowable_contents section. You then follow that declaration with additional declarations for each of the child elements.

```
<!ELEMENT parent_element (child_element1, child_element2)>
<!ELEMENT child_element1 (#PCDATA)>
<!ELEMENT child_element2 (#PCDATA)>
```

In this example, each of the child elements must appear once and only once within the parent element. To further define the occurrence of variably appearing child elements, you use single character suffixes and separators, as shown in Table 14-1.

Going back to the original library.xml example, an internal document type declaration might look like the following:

```
<!DOCTYPE library [
  <!ELEMENT book (author)>
  <!ELEMENT author (#PCDATA)>
]>
```

## Entity Abbreviations

Entities serve two main purposes in XML: they allow you to use reserved characters, and they let you create shortcut references to repeatedly used data, both internal and external. In each case, entities always begin with an ampersand (&) and end with a semicolon (;). In addition to the default entities (covered in the section "Entity References"), you can create your own for frequently used data.

### Internal Entity Abbreviations

Internal entities allow you to create your own abbreviations for repeatedly used data. For instance, instead of repeatedly typing the company's name, Osborne/McGraw-Hill, in an

| Symbol | Use | Meaning |
|--------|-----|---------|
| ? | (*child_element*?) | **Optional**—The element may appear once or not at all. |
| * | (*child_element**) | **Optional Repeating**—The element may appear many times or not at all. |
| + | (*child_element*+) | **Forced**—The parent element must contain at least one child element of this type. |
| \| | (*child_element1* \| *child_element2* \| *child_element3*) | **Either Forced**—The parent element must contain at least one child element of the types separated by the pipe symbol. |

**TABLE 14-1**     Single-Character Suffixes and Separators

XML document's company element, you can create an internal entity within a DTD and abbreviate it thereafter. By adding the entity to the DTD, you can simply use the entity whenever you need to reference its value. The format of an internal entity declaration is as follows:

```
<!ENTITY name "entity_value">
```

The following example shows an XML document containing an internal DTD which includes an element definition for the company element and an entity definition for the internal entity abbreviation omh. This is followed by a short XML data structure that contains &omh; as data within the company element.

```
<?xml version="1.0" standalone="no"?>
<!DOCTYPE entity_example [
   <!ELEMENT publisher (#PCDATA)>
   <!ENTITY omh "Osborne/McGraw-Hill">
]>
<entity_example>
   <publisher>&omh;</publisher>
</entity_example>
```

### External Entity Abbreviations

External entities let you reference files that are outside the XML document. These files can be unparsed (non-XML) or parsed (XML). An image file is a good example of an unparsed entity. The XML parser doesn't need to actually read the binary data that makes up the image to validate its inclusion. A parsed file might contain commonly used XML data such as copyright information. In either case, using an external entity abbreviation to represent the actual data allows the data to be modified independently without affecting the XML data.

---

**NOTE**   *Adequate coverage of external entities goes beyond the scope of this chapter. They are referenced here only to make you aware of their existence and uses.*

---

## Additional XML Resources Online

This chapter provided a glimpse at the power and possibilities offered by XML. As you start implementing XML in your own web sites and applications, you'll likely discover that you need more in-depth and detailed information than can be covered in a single chapter. The following are a few online resources that you may find helpful:

- **http://www.w3.org/TR/REC-xml**   The World Wide Web Consortium (W3C) site offers the complete XML 1.0 Specification and links to a variety of book and online resources.

- **http://msdn.microsoft.com/XML**   The Microsoft XML Development Center offers information, examples, downloads, and tutorials on all of Microsoft's XML implementations.

PART III

- **http://www.w3schools.com** W3Schools.com offers free, web-based e-learning with a variety of tutorials on XML and HTML and related technologies.
- **http://www.zdnet.com/devhead** ZDNet's Developer offers news, articles, and tutorials on a variety of web-related topics including XML.
- **http://www.xml-zone.com** The DevX XML Zone site offers news, articles, tutorials, newsletters, and forums for the XML developer.

# Web Scripting Languages

The use of scripting languages on the Web is one of the reasons we now refer to web *applications,* rather than simply web pages or web sites. Scripting languages are the first stage in enabling true interactivity in web applications. A *scripting language* is a computer programming language in a simple text format. This is similar to HTML itself, which is technically a markup language. Both are written in plain text and interpreted at the time of execution (run time).

The general difference between scripting languages and other programming languages is in how they are treated when executed. Programming languages like Java, Visual Basic .NET, and C# (pronounced C sharp) create a *bytecode* file that is executed by the operating system. (Java is discussed in Chapter 18, and Visual Basic .NET and C# are discussed in Chapter 16.) A bytecode file is a binary (all 0's and 1's) file containing instructions that are directly used by the operating system. *Scripts* are text files that are interpreted at run time and converted into the bytecode the system needs. This explanation is a bit simplified. Java *applets,* for example, are bytecode files compiled from the text source file, but they are still interpreted at run time by the browser's Java interpreter (the Java Runtime Environment, or JRE), rather than directly by the computer's operating system. A good working definition is simply that scripts are text files that you can use directly, unlike Java applets or ActiveX controls, which must be compiled before they can be used.

JavaScript and VBScript (Visual Basic Script or Visual Basic Scripting Edition) are the two primary scripting languages used on the Web. Perl (Practical Extraction and Report Language) preceded them as the dominant web scripting language but is no longer as popular, for several reasons. Most importantly, it can only be executed on the server, requiring the data to make a round-trip over the Internet and using the server's processing time. This is because current web browsers do not include Perl interpreters. Both JavaScript and VBScript can run on the client (the user's computer), where the transit time and server overhead are eliminated, or on the server. This is an important consideration—client-side processing is much faster for the user. Perl is one of several scripting languages, which include newer languages such as Python, that are very good at what they do, but simply lack widespread support from the browser manufacturers. Unless you have a specific reason for choosing one of these other languages, sticking with JavaScript and VBScript makes the most sense.

---

**NOTE**    *Microsoft has developed its own variant of JavaScript called JScript. Information about JScript can be found at* ***http://msdn.microsoft.com/scripting/***. *An effort has been made to standardize JavaScript under the auspices of the European Computer Manufacturers Association (ECMA) as ECMAScript. Microsoft claims JScript fully conforms to the ECMAScript standard. The examples in this chapter use JavaScript as generated by FrontPage.*

Today, scripting languages primarily do relatively simple tasks on the client, such as validating form input (as you'll see in the next section). Active Server Pages (ASP) uses scripting (primarily VBScript) extensively on the server, but Active Server Pages .NET (covered in Chapter 16) uses primarily Visual Basic .NET or C# for server-side code. The speed benefits of compiled languages over scripting languages are very significant in server-side processing. What scripting languages offer is flexibility and ease of use. They accept information from the user, control the flow of data between objects, and prepare the output of the processing. Until recently, JavaScript had greater support than VBScript, due to the fact that Netscape's browsers have supported only JavaScript, while only Internet Explorer has supported both JavaScript and VBScript. Despite Internet Explorer's dominance in the browser market (in the Fall of 2002, Netscape's market share was only a little over 3 percent worldwide), JavaScript still has the advantage of being cross-platform, that is, it can be used on both Windows and UNIX (or Linux) servers, so that's where we'll start.

---

**NOTE**    *Active Server Pages (ASP) was the Microsoft technology that truly enabled interactive web applications. The introduction of ASP.NET and the other components of the .NET Framework has made ASP last year's technology. Legacy ASP applications are still functional, but the tools provided by ASP.NET ensure that fewer and fewer web applications will be written in ASP in the future. ASP.NET is covered in detail in Chapter 16.*

## JavaScript

JavaScript was developed by Sun Microsystems, Inc., with involvement from the early stages by Netscape. At the time (late 1995), Netscape was developing a prototype scripting language named LiveScript, but chose to abandon the name and combine their efforts with Sun. Support for JavaScript began with Netscape Navigator 3.0 and Internet Explorer 3.0. VBScript is still only supported by Internet Explorer.

The best way to understand JavaScript is to look at some code. FrontPage makes this easy to do, as it will generate either JavaScript or VBScript for you. In the next section, you will use FrontPage to generate a JavaScript script that will validate a form.

---

**TIP**    *JavaScript and VBScript are the subjects of entire books.* How To Do Everything with JavaScript *by Scott Duffy  (McGraw-Hill/Osborne, 2003) and* JavaScript, The Complete Reference *by Thomas Powell and Fritz Schneider (McGraw-Hill/Osborne, 2001) are excellent choices for more JavaScript information.*

### Form Validation with JavaScript

Before browsers supported JavaScript, *form validation*, the process of checking the data in each field of a form to be sure it is the correct type, was done on the server using a language such as Perl. This was done through the common gateway interface (CGI). You may be familiar with the term *CGI script* to describe this type of programming. This had the disadvantage of requiring a round-trip over the Internet and of using the server's processing time. With client-side form validation, the process is speeded up because the work is done on the user's computer, rather than on the server.

With FrontPage you use the Form Field Properties dialog boxes to define the criteria for validation, and the script is created for you—you don't need to know a thing about either scripting language. These steps will take you through the process:

1. In FrontPage, in the New task pane, select One Page Web Site.

2. In the Web Site Templates dialog box General tab, select One Page Web Site, name it **Scripting**, and click OK.

3. Open the home page (Default.htm) in Design view.

4. At the top of the page, type **Form Validation** and format it as Heading 1.

5. Move the cursor to the next line and click Textbox on the Form toolbar.

---

***TIP***   *You can make the Form menu a floating toolbar by dragging it from the Insert menu. Select Insert | Form, then point on the bar at the top of the Form menu and drag it.*

6. Press HOME to move the cursor to the beginning of the line and type **Enter some text:** (leave a space after the colon). Format the text as Formatted.

7. Press RIGHT ARROW one or more times to move the cursor to the end of the text box and before the Submit and Reset buttons. Press SHIFT-ENTER to move the buttons to the next line.

8. Click Textbox on the Form toolbar once more and then press HOME.

9. Type **Enter a number:** (leaving two spaces after the colon), press RIGHT ARROW, and then press SHIFT-ENTER.

10. Type **Select an option:**, click Option Button on the Form toolbar, type **Option 1**, press SPACE, click Option Button again, type **Option 2**, and then press SHIFT-ENTER.

11. Open the Page Properties dialog box and change the title of the page to **Form Validation**. Click OK and then save your work. Your page should look similar to Figure 15-1.

12. Right-click the first option button and select Form Field Properties. In the Option Button Properties dialog box, click Not Selected for the Initial State, then click OK.

    Next you will set the form validation criteria, which generates the validation script. First check which scripting language is set as the default.

13. Select Tools | Site Settings.

14. In the Site Settings dialog box, click the Advanced tab. JavaScript should be displayed in the Default Validation Script Language drop-down menu, as shown in Figure 15-2. (VBScript and None are the other choices.) All the pages in your web use the default scripting language selected here.

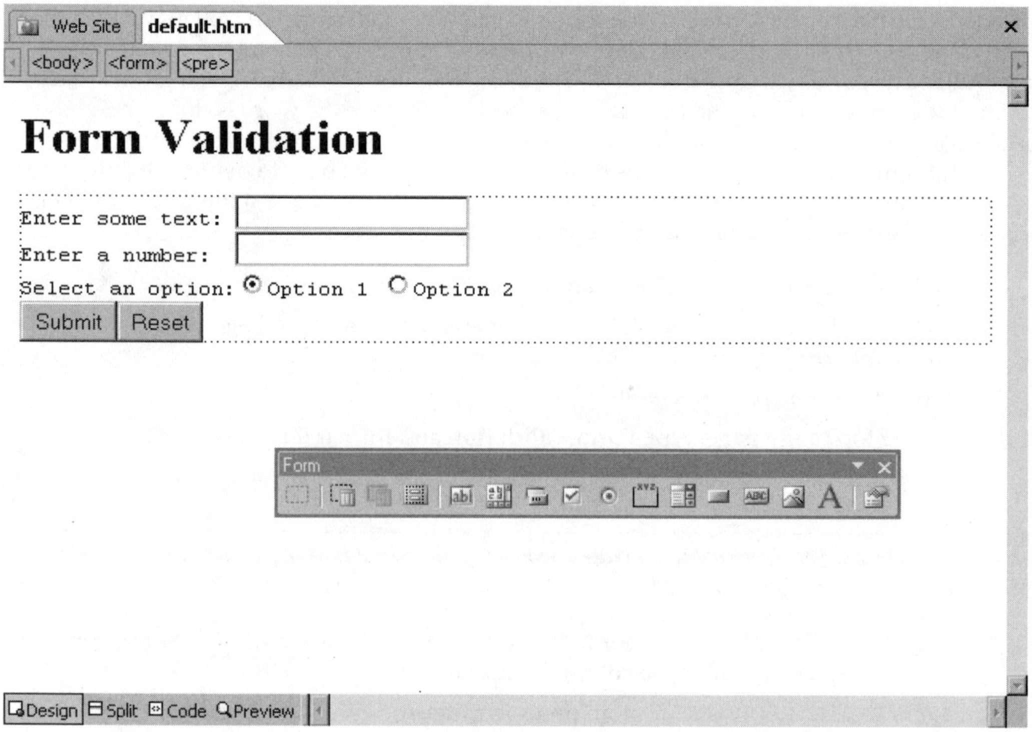

Web Site | default.htm | ✕

‹ | `<body>` | `<form>` | `<pre>` | ›

# Form Validation

Enter some text: [                    ]

Enter a number: [                    ]

Select an option: ⦿ Option 1    ○ Option 2

[ Submit ] [ Reset ]

Form ▼ ✕

☐ | 🔲 🔳 🗔 | ab 🔲 🔘 ☑ ⦿ ☐ 🔲 ▭ ABC 🖼 A 🔲

🔲Design ⊟Split 💻Code 🔍Preview ‹

**FIGURE 15-1** Form Validation Page

**FIGURE 15-2**
FrontPage Site
Settings dialog
box Advanced tab

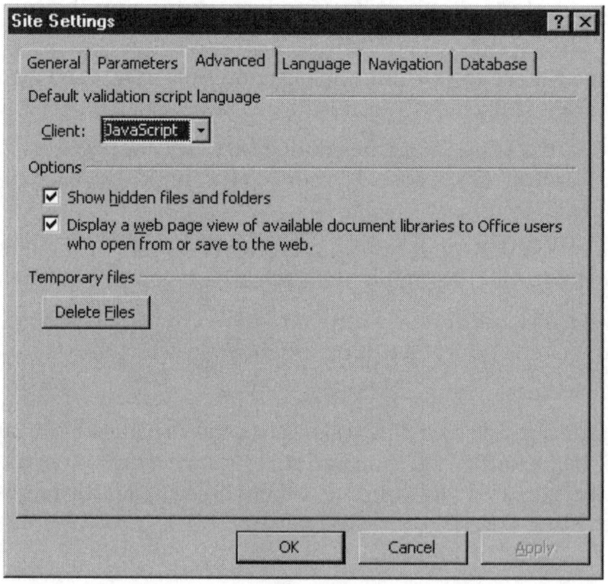

**Site Settings** ? ✕

General | Parameters | Advanced | Language | Navigation | Database |

Default validation script language

Client: [ JavaScript ▾ ]

Options

☑ Show hidden files and folders

☑ Display a web page view of available document libraries to Office users who open from or save to the web.

Temporary files

[ Delete Files ]

[ OK ] [ Cancel ] [ Apply ]

**NOTE**  *You can run one scripting language on the client (the browser) and another on the server itself. Since only Internet Explorer supports VBScript, JavaScript is the default for client-side scripting. Microsoft's Internet Information Services support both scripting languages, so you can choose either for server-side scripting.*

15. Click OK and then right-click the first one-line text box in the form. Select Form Field Properties from the context menu.

16. In the Text Box Properties dialog box, click Validate. In the Text Box Validation dialog box, select Text from the Data Type drop-down menu, and then click the Letters checkbox.

17. In the Display Name text box, type **Text Field**. This is the name for the field that will be used in the validation error messages. Click OK twice.

18. Right-click the second one-line text box, select Form Field Properties from the context menu, and then click Validate.

19. Select Integer from the Data Type drop-down menu and type **Numeric Field** in the Display Name text box.

20. Under Data Value, select the Field Must Be checkbox and type **5** in the Value text box.

21. Select the And Must Be checkbox and type **10** in the Value text box. Your Text Box Validation dialog box should look like Figure 15-3. Click OK twice.

22. Right-click the first option button, select Form Field Properties, and then click Validate.

23. In the Option Button Validation dialog box, select Data Required, type **Option Button** in the Display Name text box, click OK twice, and save your page.

**FIGURE 15-3**
Text Box Validation dialog box

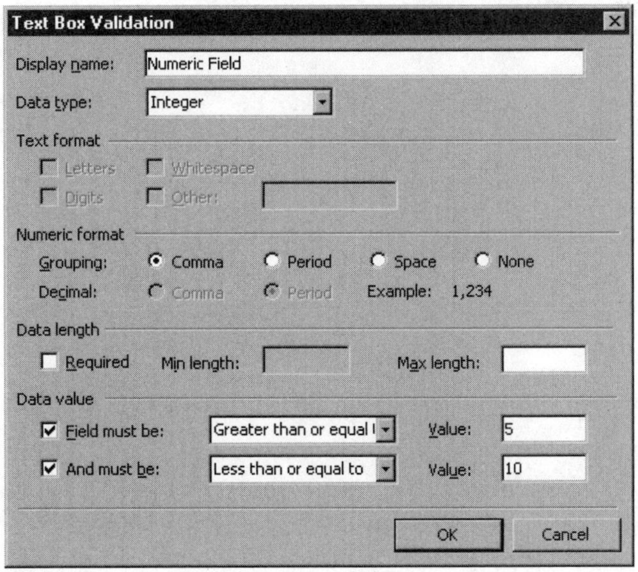

24. Open the page in your browser, type **11** in the Enter A Number text box, and click Submit. You should see an error message similar to this:

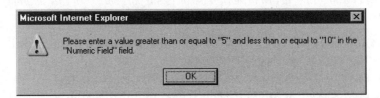

25. Click OK and then select Source from the View menu in Internet Explorer or Page Source from the View menu in Netscape Navigator. At the beginning of the HTML listing, you will see the JavaScript script that generated the error message. The JavaScript portion of the file is shown in Listing 15-1.

> **NOTE**  *Some of the characters may appear as small boxes in the source code listing. This is due to the character set supported by the text viewer displaying the code. If the supported character set doesn't include a character, it is replaced by a small box in the display. This doesn't affect the functionality of the script.*

**Listing 15-1:**
JavaScript
form
validation
script

```
<script Language="JavaScript" Type="text/javascript"><!--
function FrontPage_Form1_Validator(theForm)
{
  var checkOK = "ABCDEFGHIJKLMNOPQRSTUVWXYZabcdefghijklmnopqr
    stuvwxyzfŠŒ šœ ŸÀÁÂÃÄÅÆÇÈÉÊËÌÍÎÏÐÑÒÓÔÕÖØÙÚÛÜÝÞßàáâãäåæçèé
    êëìíîïðñòóôõöøùúûüýþÿ";
  var checkStr = theForm.T1.value;
  var allValid = true;
  var validGroups = true;
  for (i = 0;  i < checkStr.length;  i++)
  {
    ch = checkStr.charAt(i);
    for (j = 0;  j < checkOK.length;  j++)
      if (ch == checkOK.charAt(j))
        break;
    if (j == checkOK.length)
    {
      allValid = false;
      break;
    }
  }
  if (!allValid)
  {
    alert("Please enter only letter characters in the \"Text
      Field\" field.");
    theForm.T1.focus();
    return (false);
  }
  var checkOK = "0123456789-,";
  var checkStr = theForm.T2.value;
```

```
    var allValid = true;
    var validGroups = true;
    var decPoints = 0;
    var allNum = "";
    for (i = 0;  i < checkStr.length;  i++)
    {
      ch = checkStr.charAt(i);
      for (j = 0;  j < checkOK.length;  j++)
        if (ch == checkOK.charAt(j))
          break;
      if (j == checkOK.length)
      {
        allValid = false;
        break;
      }
      if (ch != ",")
        allNum += ch;
    }
    if (!allValid)
    {
      alert("Please enter only digit characters in the
        \"Numeric Field\" field.");
      theForm.T2.focus();
      return (false);
    }
    var chkVal = allNum;
    var prsVal = parseInt(allNum);
    if (chkVal != "" && !(prsVal >= "5" && prsVal <= "10"))
    {
      alert("Please enter a value greater than or equal to
        \"5\" and less than or equal to \"10\" in the
        \"Numeric Field\" field.");
      theForm.T2.focus();
      return (false);
    }
    var radioSelected = false;
    for (i = 0;  i < theForm.R1.length;  i++)
    {
      if (theForm.R1[i].checked)
          radioSelected = true;
    }
    if (!radioSelected)
    {
      alert("Please select one of the \"Option Button\" options.");
      return (false);
    }
    return (true);
}
//--></script>
```

If you've ever done any programming (particularly with any of the variations of C or Java), the JavaScript script in Listing 15-1 will look familiar to you. If you haven't, it may look very strange. The best way to understand what it does is to step through the script and look at each section, as follows.

> **NOTE** *Programming, like writing in any language, has a lot of room for style, and programmers tend to develop their own styles. There are rules for good programming, such as adding comments to explain each section, that make code easily understood. The JavaScript code in this section was generated by FrontPage using the rules defined by the team that programmed this feature of FrontPage. This is not the only way the script could have been written, but it is a good example of JavaScript scripting.*

## The JavaScript Form Validation Script

Don't worry if the JavaScript code looks indecipherable. The function of each section of a program is understandable once you begin to understand the type of shorthand it's written in. In this section, you will look at each piece of the code and see what it does and how it fits in with the other pieces to make a complete script. In the rest of this section, the script has been dissected to explain the purpose of each section of code. In doing so, the formatting has been changed somewhat. Listing 15-1 contains the correct syntax for the script.

> **NOTE** *JavaScript is case-sensitive, so form and field names must be exact, including upper- and lowercase letters, in both the form and the script itself.*

```
<script Language="JavaScript" Type="text/javascript"><!--
```

The script begins by declaring the programming language using the <SCRIPT> tag. The entire body of the script is within the opening and closing <SCRIPT> tags. If the browser doesn't support the scripting language, then the entire script is ignored. The Language property is required to inform the browser which language is being used (either JavaScript or VBScript). The Type property identifies the type of file, a text file that's a JavaScript script in this case. This property is optional, but it's a good idea to include it. There is also an additional optional property, SRC, which identifies the location of the script (as a URL) if it's not included on the HTML page. This allows you to create a library of scripts that can be used by many web pages without requiring you to include the script on each page. There is also a <NOSCRIPT> tag that is used to define the HTML that will be displayed if the script isn't supported. It is placed after the script in the HTML document.

> **NOTE** *You will notice a slight shift in terminology used to describe the components of scripting languages as compared to pure HTML. In Chapter 12, we used the terms "tags" and "attributes" to describe the basic HTML commands and their modifiers. Scripting languages approach the terminology of more conventional programming languages, so we use a hybrid set of terms. "Tag" is still used to describe a basic scripting language command, but the term "property" is used to describe how a certain tag can be modified (analogous to "attribute" in pure HTML-speak).*

After the <SCRIPT> tag is an opening HTML comment tag (<!--) matched by the closing comment tag (-->) at the end of the script. Without these tags, the entire text of the script would be displayed in browsers that don't support the <SCRIPT> tag. This is a holdover from the old days (pre-version 3 of Netscape's and Microsoft's browsers) and not strictly necessary.

```
function FrontPage_Form1_Validator(theForm)
```

This next line declares the function name and its arguments in the form `function functionName (arguments)`. Function is the JavaScript keyword, the `functionName` is `FrontPage_Form1_Validator`, and the single argument is `theForm`. A *function* is a series of JavaScript statements that performs a task and optionally returns a value. The function statements are enclosed within the { and } brackets. An *argument* is a value that is passed to the function. What this value can be will depend on the purpose of the function. For example, if the purpose of the function were to multiply two numbers, then the two numbers would be the arguments passed to the function. Since the arguments are represented by variables (which can be considered a container for the value), they could be passed from the web page through a form as variables, which is what is being done in this script. The argument `theForm` refers to the form that is calling the function. This is not the name of the form itself—that is passed with the values you enter in the form text boxes and then submit. The script intercepts the values before the form handler and checks them against the rules established by the function. If they meet the criteria, they are passed on to the form handler; if not, then an error message is generated, as you saw earlier, and the form handler never receives the data. Since the form handler will be on the server, this prevents unnecessary traffic and server time.

**NOTE** *Functions cannot be nested—that is, a function cannot be defined inside another function.*

```
{ var checkOK = "ABCDEF...";
  var checkStr = theForm.T1.value;
  var allValid = true;
  var validGroups = true;
```

These four lines define the variables that are used by the function to validate the first form field in the format `var variableName = variableValue`. Var is the JavaScript keyword followed by the variable name and the value of the variable. The first variable, checkOK, is a text string consisting of all the acceptable characters that can be returned by the first form field. (The list has been shortened here.) The second, checkStr, is the value entered in the first text box, `T1`. `T1` is the default name given to the form field when you created it in FrontPage. If you had given the field a different name, that name would be used in defining the variable. This variable illustrates a JavaScript naming convention—defining an object as a hierarchical string with each level of the hierarchy separated by a period. In this case, the hierarchy is the form itself, the field in the form, and the value contained in the field. Each level of the hierarchy is a property of the preceding level, so, in this example, `T1` is a property of `theForm`, which is a variable containing the name of the form that called the function.

**NOTE** *The hierarchical naming convention used by JavaScript is common to all object oriented programming (OOP) languages, which include Java, Visual Basic .NET, and C#. You will see this structure quite often if you choose to learn more about programming.*

This is one method by which data is passed between the HTML page and the script. To the script, the form is an object and so can have properties that can be processed. JavaScript can also recognize events, such as a mouse click or placing the mouse pointer over a defined area, and execute a function based on the event. The third and fourth variables, `allValid` and `validGroups`, are flags that will be used later in the script to determine if the data will be passed to the form handler. They are defined as TRUE, meaning that the script is interpreting the data entered in the first text box as valid. If the data fails to meet the criteria for the field, the value of the variable will be changed to FALSE, which will trigger the error message. (The variable `validGroups` is not actually used in this sample script.)

```
for (i = 0;  i < checkStr.length;  i++)
{
  ch = checkStr.charAt(i);
  for (j = 0;  j < checkOK.length;  j++)
    if (ch == checkOK.charAt(j))
      break;
  if (j == checkOK.length)
  {
    allValid = false;
    break;
  }
}
```

Before looking at this section of code in detail, the difference between = and == needs to be understood. In JavaScript, the equal sign (=) is the assignment operator. That is, it is used to assign a value to a variable. The double equal sign (==) is the equality operator. It compares the values on each side of it and returns TRUE if they are equal and FALSE if they are not.

This section of the script is the part that does most of the work. The first line is a For-Next loop. The variables i and j are counters that are used to determine which character in the text string is being evaluated. What's happening is that the text string entered in the text form field is being *parsed*; that is, the text string is being looked at one character at a time and compared with the legal characters defined in the `checkOK variable`. At each step, each counter is incremented by 1  (i++ and j++) until the last character in each string is reached (i < `checkStr.length;` and j < `checkOK.length;`). The variable `checkStr.charAt(i)` holds the character at position i  that has been entered in the text box. The variable `checkOK.charAt(j)` holds the character at position j in the string of legal characters. When the first loop is started, the character at position i in the input string is compared with the character at position j in the string of legal characters. For the first iteration, each of these is 0 (zero), since that is the first position as far as JavaScript is concerned. (If the input string were ten characters long, JavaScript would count them as zero to nine, not one to ten.)

The first character in the input string is loaded into the variable ch, and ch is compared with the first character in `checkOK`. If the characters don't match (if the character isn't A), j is incremented (j++) and the first character in the input string is compared with the second legal character (B). This continues, with j being incremented each time, until a match is found or the end of the string of legal characters is reached. If a match is found, the loop stops (break;) and i is incremented so that the next character in the input string can be checked. Then the process starts over, with j being reset to zero (j  = 0;) so that the entire string of legal characters will be checked.

If no match is found, meaning the character entered in the form field is invalid, the process stops and the value of the variable `allValid` is changed to FALSE. This happens if the end of the string of legal characters is reached without finding a match (`j ==` `checkOK.length`). If the character is determined to be invalid, the steps shown next are executed:

```
if (!allValid)
{
  alert("Please enter only letter characters in the \"Text
    Field\" field.");
  theForm.T1.focus();
  return (false);
}
```

The first line in the preceding code tests the value of the variable `allValid`. This line can be read as "If `allValid` is NOT TRUE, then…" (the exclamation mark is the JavaScript notation for the logical NOT operator). As you saw in the previous code, `allValid` is defined as TRUE at the beginning of the script, and the value is changed only if an illegal character is encountered. The "then" is defined by the next line, which causes an alert message box to be displayed, as you saw earlier when you entered the number **11** in the numeric text box and clicked Submit. This is a built-in function of JavaScript, so all you have to do is define the text that will appear in the alert ("`Please enter only letter…`"). In the alert text, the backslash (\) is an *escape* character. That is, the code needs to understand that the quotation mark (") following the backslash should be interpreted as a character to be displayed, rather than closing the string that is being defined. Text strings must be enclosed within quotes so a method is needed to include quotes as characters within the text string.

The next line contains a very useful JavaScript feature, the focus() method, written in the form *object*.`focus()`. What this does is make the form field where the error occurred in the selected object active (in this case, the cursor is placed in the text box). Once you click OK in the alert message box, your browser will return you to the first form field so you can fix the error. The form field (`theForm.T1`) is the object. Finally, the script returns the value FALSE (`return (false);`). This value can be used by the statement that called the function, or it can be ignored. In this case, it will prevent the data from being sent to the form handler.

If all the characters inputted pass the test, then the first loop ends when the last character in the `checkStr` variable has been checked. The script then begins the test for the data entered in the second text box.

```
var checkOK = "0123456789-,";
var checkStr = theForm.T2.value;
var allValid = true;
var validGroups = true;
var decPoints = 0;
var allNum = "";
```

Like the test for the first form field, this one also begins by defining the variables. There are two additional variables defined in this test, `decPoints` and `allNum`. `decPoints` is a flag that indicates that decimal points are not allowed in the input. It should be noted that this variable isn't actually used after it's defined. Since the validation rule allows only integers (a whole number, that is, a number without a fraction), the decimal point is an illegal character.

This is actually dealt with in the variable checkOK, which doesn't define the decimal point as a legal character. This redundancy is a result of the method FrontPage uses to generate the JavaScript code and does no harm. The other variable, allNum, is defined as an empty string. Its function will be explained in the next section of code, where similar loops and tests are started with the new variables:

```
for (i = 0; i < checkStr.length;  i++)
{
  ch = checkStr.charAt(i);
    for (j = 0;  j < checkOK.length;  j++)
      if (ch == checkOK.charAt(j))
        break;
    if (j == checkOK.length)
    {
      allValid = false;
      break;
    }
    if (ch != ",")
      allNum += ch;
}
if (!allValid)
{
  alert("Please enter only digit characters in the
    \"Numeric Field\" field.");
  theForm.T2.focus();
  return (false);
}
```

There's one significant difference between this section of code and the validation for the text string. This begins with the line if (ch != ","). This line and the next (allNum += ch;) are saying, "If the valid character is NOT a comma (it's a valid number), then add it to the variable allNum." The += operator means "place the value on the right side of the expression in the variable on the left." This is known as *concatenation*. This is not an addition operation; it simply places the character on the right side of the expression in the rightmost position of the string. For example, if allNum equals 12 and ch is 3, the resulting string is 123. It's important to realize that, at this point, the code is treating the values as characters, not numbers. The purpose of these two lines is to create a variable that can be treated as a number by the next section of code, which determines if the number entered is within the range specified:

```
var chkVal = allNum;
  var prsVal = parseInt(allNum);
  if (chkVal != "" && !(prsVal >= "5" && prsVal <= "10"))
  { alert("Please enter a value greater than or equal to
      \"5\" and less than or equal to \"10\" in the \"Numeric
      Field\" field.");
    theForm.T2.focus();
    return (false);
  }
```

This validation check differs from the previous two in that there is a single value to be checked, rather than parsing a string of multiple characters. The work in this section of code is done by the third line. After the second line converts the character string to an integer (var prsVal = parseInt (allNum) ;), three checks are performed: is it a null value (was a value entered), is it equal to or greater than five, and is it equal to or less than ten? The second line is necessary because the program can interpret a number in two ways: as a text string and as an actual number. This line converts the text to a number so that it can be used for the tests that follow. The != operator is the logical NOT EQUAL, so that the expression could be read as "is the value in the form field NOT EQUAL to null." The && operator is the logical AND. The third line could be read as "if the number is NOT equal to null AND it's not equal to or greater than five AND it's not equal to or less than ten, then display the alert error message." Focus would then be returned to the second form field box.

The next section of code validates the option buttons, one of which must be selected:

```
var radioSelected = false;
  for (i = 0;  i < theForm.R1.length;  i++)
  {
    if (theForm.R1[i].checked)
        radioSelected = true;
  }
  if (!radioSelected)
  {
    alert("Please select one of the \"Option Button\"
      options.");
    return (false);
  }
```

Unlike the first two validation tests, this begins by defining the status variable (radioSelected) as FALSE. This actually simplifies the remaining code since the validation rule is that one of the option buttons must be selected. This routine looks at every option button in the form field, and it needs to be understood that the form field is comprised of all the option buttons. In other words, option buttons are very similar to the choices in a drop-down list. The list itself is the form field, and the choices in the list are the possible values of that form field, as each option button is a possible value and all the option buttons together comprise the form field.

If the status were assumed to be TRUE, the value of radioSelected would have to be changed if an option button wasn't selected. This means that if the first option button were selected, then the loop would have to break since checking the second option button would change radioSelected to FALSE. This obviously can be done, but it would add a few lines of code to the routine. Simplicity can be a good thing in writing code, which this example illustrates. In the first two validation tests, it was easier (the code was less convoluted) to assume the status was TRUE until an illegal character was encountered. In checking the option buttons, the opposite creates less convoluted code.

```
return (true);
  }
  //--></script>
```

These last lines clean up and end the script. If all the values have passed all the tests, the value TRUE is returned, and the data is sent to the form handler. The last line contains three elements: the // is the JavaScript Comment tag, which is required at the end of the JavaScript script to comment out the HTML closing comment tag (-->); and finally, the HTML </ SCRIPT> tag ends the script.

Once a script has been created, there also has to be a method for calling the script. For the form validation script, the call is contained in the <FORM> HTML tag. This next line of code shows how the JavaScript validation script is called by the form:

```
<form method="POST" … name="FrontPage_Form1" …
onsubmit="return FrontPage_Form1_Validator(this)" … >
```

The HTML form code should look reasonably familiar to you (Chapter 12 contains an explanation of the HTML used for forms). The JavaScript validation script is called with the JavaScript event onsubmit, like this:

```
onsubmit="return FrontPage_Form1_Validator(this)"
```

The argument of the onsubmit attribute is the name of the JavaScript function, defined at the top of the JavaScript validation script. The argument being passed to the script (in the parentheses at the end of the function name) is this, which indicates the active form. In this manner, it's possible for multiple JavaScript forms on a single page to use the same validation script, provided the field names are identical.

You'll be using the Form Validation page again with VBScript, so leave your current FrontPage and browser windows open. You can close Notepad or your text viewer.

## VBScript

VBScript is similar to JavaScript. It is based on Microsoft's Visual Basic programming language, which gives Visual Basic programmers a bit of a head start. The problem with VBScript is lack of support among browsers. Currently, only Microsoft's Internet Explorer includes support for VBScript, and it's unlikely that Netscape will add support anytime soon, so even though Internet Explorer is currently the dominant browser, your client-side VBScript scripts will have a limited audience. VBScript could be your first choice if you are planning an intranet and can specify Internet Explorer as the browser everyone must use. Otherwise, it's hard to see why you shouldn't simply go with JavaScript for client-side scripting. There are enough differences in the languages to make learning both of them a burden.

For server-side scripting, VBScript offers advantages if your web server is Windows server-based. Visual Basic is more tightly integrated with Windows than Java and so could be a better choice for more advanced programming. That statement will bring howls from Java programmers, with good reason, as it ignores the fact that there are many criteria that should go into choosing a programming language. For the purpose of this chapter, which is an introduction to scripting languages, since VBScript is a subset of Visual Basic and VBScript is easier for the novice to understand, the learning curve is reduced. If you're using an operating system other than a Windows server, Java and JavaScript should be your choice for server-side programming, since VBScript and Visual Basic are not supported by other operating systems. (You can also use other languages like C++, but those languages are beyond the scope of this book.) As you can see, there are several factors that must be considered in choosing a scripting language, and the reality is that you need to have a basic knowledge of both.

You can see some of the differences in the two languages by changing the scripting language in the Advanced tab on the Site Settings dialog box. Do that now with these instructions:

1. In FrontPage, select Tools | Site Settings.

2. In the Site Settings dialog box, click the Advanced tab and select VBScript from the Default Validation Script Language Client drop-down menu. Click Apply. The FrontPage dialog box shown here will be displayed:

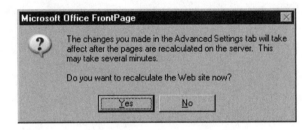

3. Click Yes. After the Scripting web is recalculated, click OK (the OK button will be inactive until the recalculation is done).

4. Load the Form Validation page in your web browser, and select Source or Page Source from the View menu, depending on which browser you are using.

Listing 15-2 shows the same form validation script as Listing 15-1, except that it is now written in VBScript. The flow of the script is pretty much the same, but the syntax has changed. You should still be able to follow what the script is doing.

**Listing 15-2:**
VBScript
form
validation
script

```
<script Language="VBScript" Type="text/vbscript"><!--
function FrontPage_Form1_onsubmit()
  Set theForm = document.FrontPage_Form1
  checkOK = ABCDEFGHIJKLMNOPQRSTUVWXYZabcdefghijklmnopqr
   stuvwxyzfšŒ šœ ŸÀÁÂÃÄÅÆÇÈÉÊËÌÍÎÏÐÑÒÓÔÕÖØÙÚÛÜÝÞßàáâãäå
   æçèéêëìíîïðñòóôõöøùúûüýþÿ"
  checkStr = theForm.T1.value
  allValid = True
  validGroups = True
  For i = 1 to len(checkStr)
    ch = Mid(checkStr, i, 1)
    If (InStr(checkOK, ch) = 0) Then
      allValid = False
      Exit For
    End If
  Next
  If (Not allValid) Then
    MsgBox "Please enter only letter characters in the
      ""Text Field"" field.", 0, "Validation Error"
    theForm.T1.focus()
    FrontPage_Form1_onsubmit = False
```

**PART III**

```
      Exit Function
    End If
    checkOK = "0123456789-,"
    checkStr = theForm.T2.value
    allValid = True
    validGroups = True
    decPoints = 0
    allNum = ""
    For i = 1 to len(checkStr)
      ch = Mid(checkStr, i, 1)
      If (InStr(checkOK, ch) = 0) Then
        allValid = False
        Exit For
      End If
      If (ch <> ",") Then
        allNum = allNum & ch
      End If
    Next
    If (Not allValid) Then
      MsgBox "Please enter only digit characters in the
        ""Numeric Field"" field.", 0, "Validation Error"
      theForm.T2.focus()
      FrontPage_Form1_onsubmit = False
      Exit Function
    End If
    If ((checkstr <> "" And Not IsNumeric(allNum)) Or
        (decPoints > 1) Or Not validGroups) Then
      MsgBox "Please enter a valid number in the ""T2"" field.", 0, "Validation Error"
      theForm.T2.focus()
      FrontPage_Form1_onsubmit = False
      Exit Function
    End If
    prsVal = allNum
    If ((prsVal <> "") And (Not (prsVal >= 5 And prsVal <= 10))) Then
      MsgBox "Please enter a value greater than or equal to ""5""
        and less than or equal to ""10"" in the ""Numeric Field""
        field.", 0, "Validation Error"
      theForm.T2.focus()
      FrontPage_Form1_onsubmit = False
      Exit Function
    End If
    radioSelected = False
    For i = 0 to theForm.R1.length - 1
      If (theForm.R1.item(i).checked) Then
        radioSelected = True
      End If
    Next
    If (Not radioSelected) Then
      MsgBox "Please select one of the ""Option Button""
        options.", 0, "Validation Error"
      FrontPage_Form1_onsubmit = False
      Exit Function
    End If
    FrontPage_Form1_onsubmit = True
End Function
--></script>
```

Some of the differences in the languages can be seen in how For-Next loops are constructed. In the JavaScript validation, the syntax is

```
for (i = 0;  i < checkStr.length;  i++)
```

With VBScript, the syntax is

```
For i = 1 to len(checkStr)
```

The first thing to notice is that VBScript starts counting at one (1) while JavaScript starts with zero (0). For nonprogrammers, starting at one may make sense, but most programming languages accept zero as the first number and the place where you start counting. If you use both JavaScript and VBScript, this can be a point of confusion. Another point of difference is that with VBScript it is assumed that the loop increments by one in each iteration, while JavaScript explicitly defines that value. These values can be specified in VBScript; it just isn't necessary if the default values are used. As you can also see, VBScript is easier to read if you don't know what the JavaScript operators mean (such as i++). On the other hand, JavaScript is more concise, which many programmers like. With JavaScript, for example, it is not necessary to explicitly close each If-Then statement or For-Next loop. This is handled by the structure of the code, while VBScript has End If and Next statements. Another example of the differences is JavaScript's use of single characters, such as the exclamation mark (!) as the logical NOT operator, while VBScript tends to use words, or at least parts of words (such as len for length).

Despite the differences, the overall structure and flow of both examples is very similar. Once the syntax differences are understood, you can work in either language without much difficulty.

## The Microsoft Script Editor

The examples in the previous sections used scripts created with the Text Field Validation dialog box and generated by the FrontPage Server Extensions. This is a good method if all you want the script to do is validate a form. Both languages are much more useful than that, as you will see in the following chapters.

There are two methods you can use to add scripts to your webs. The first is to use FrontPage to generate the script, as you did in the previous sections. The advantages of this method are that the script can be easily modified from within FrontPage, and you do not need to be a proficient JavaScript or VBScript programmer to create scripts. The second method is to create the script manually using either the Script Editor, shown in Figure 15-4, or by writing the script using FrontPage's Code view. The advantage with this method is that the page will use slightly less server resources when it is called, as the WebBot code doesn't need to be interpreted, and you will have more flexibility in creating your scripts.

Which method you use will depend on how comfortable you are with writing scripts manually and how often you expect the code to be modified. You can combine the benefits of each method by using FrontPage to generate the script, opening it using your browser's View | Source option, and then copying and pasting it into your page, overwriting the FrontPage WebBot code. The script will no longer be editable from within FrontPage (except by using Code view or with the Script Editor), but it will use slightly less server resources.

PART III

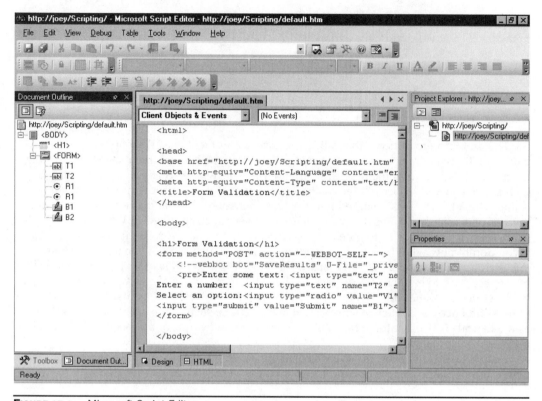

**FIGURE 15-4** Microsoft Script Editor

The Script Editor allows you to edit HTML files, much like the FrontPage Code view. In this section, only the script editing functions of the Script Editor will be covered. To see how the Script Editor works, follow these steps:

1. With your Form Validation page still open, open the Script Editor by selecting Tools | Macro | Microsoft Script Editor.

**NOTE**   *The Script Editor may not be installed on your system. In that case, a dialog box will be displayed stating that the Script Editor is not installed and asking if you want to install it now. Click Yes.*

In Figure 15-4, the leftmost pane of the Script Editor displays the Document Outline. (If the Document Outline isn't displayed, click the Document Outline tab at the bottom of the window.) The Document Outline window displays either an HTML outline, which shows the HTML elements on the page, or a script outline, which shows the scripting objects on the page. Which view is displayed is controlled by the buttons at the top of the Document window, in the upper-left corner. This pane can also display the Toolbox by selecting the Toolbox tab at the bottom of the window.

The center pane is the Text or Code Editing window. When the HTML button is selected at the bottom of the window, this displays the source code of your page. This view is similar to FrontPage when the Code button is selected. The upper-right pane is the Project Explorer window. This window displays the outline of the current project. Below it is the Properties window where the available properties and values of the selected object are displayed and can be edited.

2. In the Document Outline pane, click the Script Outline button, and then click the plus sign (+) to the left of the Client Objects & Events folder to expand the tree. In this view, shown in detail here, each object on the page is listed:

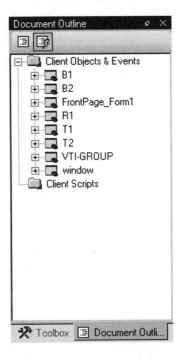

3. In the Script Outline window, click the plus sign (+) to the left of the FrontPage_ Form1 object to expand the tree. This displays a list of the available events for the object. Expanding the tree for an object will display a list of events available for that object.

---

**NOTE** *The Script Editor uses the default scripting language selected within FrontPage. In this case, that is VBScript. The events listed in the expanded tree are VBScript events. If JavaScript were set as the default scripting language, the available JavaScript events would be listed.*

4. If you double-click an event, the basic scripting code for the event is inserted into your page. Scripts are usually placed just before the closing </HEAD> tag. Double-click onsubmit in the event list for the FrontPage_Form1 object. The following code will be inserted in the page:

```
<SCRIPT ID=clientEventHandlersVBS LANGUAGE=vbscript>
<!--
```

```
Sub FrontPage_Form1_onsubmit
End Sub
-->
</SCRIPT>
```

This is the basic code for the event handler. It does not define the action to be taken when the event occurs; it only creates the skeleton code for your subroutine. The name of the VBScript subroutine is `FrontPage_Form1_onsubmit`. You must write the VBScript script that defines the action to be executed when the form is submitted. This code goes between the VBScript `Sub` (after the name of the subroutine) and `End Sub` statements.

5. Select Edit | Undo or press CTRL-Z to remove the onsubmit code from your page. In the Code Editing window, you can see that the VBScript validation script is not present (which you saw using your browser's View | Source option). What is on the page is the FrontPage WebBot code that the FrontPage Server Extensions use to generate the validation script when the page is requested.

---

**NOTE**    *The term Web Components is now used in FrontPage to describe what were formerly WebBots. However, the term WebBot still appears in the code generated by FrontPage. Usually, the only time you will encounter the term WebBot is when you are working with the FrontPage Code view or the Script Editor.*

6. Click the Form tag in the Code Editing pane (the center pane of the Script Editor). The Properties pane (in the lower-right corner of the Script Editor) will display the properties and their values for the form, as shown next:

You can edit any of the properties using the Properties window. For the Action property (shown selected in the preceding illustration), clicking the small box with the ellipsis (...) displays the Open dialog box so that you can select a file for the output of the form.

7. Select Method in the Properties window. A downward-pointing arrow appears in the value cell for the Method property. This opens a drop-down menu displaying the two choices for Method, either Get or Post.

8. Select Name in the Property window. Since this property is a user-defined value, there are no choices or dialog boxes presented. You simply enter the name of the form in the value cell for the property.

9. Close the Script Editor without saving any changes to your page.

To make the most of the Script Editor requires an advanced knowledge of the selected scripting language. If you do choose to write your own scripts, rather than having them generated by FrontPage, you will find it a valuable tool. For example, the Script Editor also contains extremely useful script debugging tools. You can insert *breakpoints* in your script that stop the execution of the script so that you can identify where errors are occurring. You can also view the values of your variables during execution. These features make debugging a script much easier.

Each of the technologies covered in this chapter could easily fill a book of its own, and, in fact, each does. The purpose here is to give you an overview of them so that you can make an informed decision about which technologies you want to add to your own webs. At a minimum, a working knowledge of JavaScript will be beneficial to web designers. If you plan to use server-side scripting on Windows servers, VBScript is also a must. If you want your webs to stand out in the crowd, these tools are part of your future.

PART III

# Active Server Pages (ASP) .NET

The functionality of the Web has grown with the introduction of new technologies such as DHTML and scripting languages, but without an overarching view of what would be done with the technologies. At each step, web programmers and designers have embraced the new tools and pushed the envelope of web functionality. As the Web matured, the capabilities and features that programmers and designers wanted became clearer. These included database connectivity, e-commerce, distributed data, and increased security. Technologies based on scripting languages, such as Active Server Pages (ASP), were the first step in meeting these needs. Active Server Pages is a server-side scripting environment—primarily using JavaScript and VBScript (Visual Basic Scripting Edition)—that includes built-in objects and components. These objects and components enable a degree of interactivity that was extremely difficult, if not impossible, to achieve previously.

As powerful as ASP is, it isn't a complete solution. Script-based solutions such as ASP have a serious limitation due to the fact that scripts have to be interpreted each time they are run on the server. ASP components can be built using other programming languages, but they are referenced through scripts. It has also become clear with the growth of the Web that the traditional client/server network model has limitations when applied to the Internet. To address these and other issues, Microsoft developed the .NET Framework, of which ASP.NET is a part. This chapter will provide an overview of ASP.NET and FrontPage support for it.

It needs to be emphasized that the .NET Framework is truly a revolutionary step forward, rather than the evolution of existing technologies. If you're familiar with "classic" ASP, for example, most of what you know is no longer applicable to ASP.NET, despite the similarity in names. It's also hard in 25 words or less to explain the totality of the .NET Framework. In some aspects, it is more similar to a new operating system than just another programming paradigm. Given the breadth and depth of ASP.NET, it's not possible to do more than cover the basic features here. A list of resources is included at the end of the chapter if you choose to explore the .NET Framework in depth.

> **NOTE**   While "classic" ASP has not disappeared from the face of the Earth, its functionality
> compared to ASP.NET is limited. ASP.NET and ASP webs can coexist on the same server
> without any difficulties, but it makes little sense to continue to develop in ASP when ASP.NET
> offers so much more functionality. For that reason, classic ASP will not be covered in this chapter.

## ASP.NET Overview

ASP.NET is part of Microsoft's .NET Framework, a computing platform optimized for creating
distributed applications. A *distributed application* consists of components (or modules), each
of which contains part of the functionality of the complete application. The modules may
reside in different locations on the network, rather than in a single software application.
When a user accesses the application, the modules and data "talk" to each other over the
network connections. The .NET Framework also fully integrates XML (see Chapter 14 for
an explanation of XML). This is a significant advantage because XML is the common data
language of distributed applications.

> **NOTE**   Distributed applications are also called n-tier applications, indicating that the application is
> constructed from a number of separate layers.

This system has a number of advantages. For example, a corporation has a number of
departments that generate reports on their activity. Managers need a system for reviewing
the reports for their departments as well as for the other departments. Imagine yourself as
the programmer responsible for making that happen. You're going to have to deal with
issues of data compatibility and application updates, among others. The .NET Framework
gives you the tools you need to actually pull off this task. Each department would store its
data in an XML format or in a database. Most current applications will generate XML files,
and database connectivity is also common, so this isn't as difficult as it may sound. These XML
or database files can reside anywhere on the network, such as each department's server, as
long as the other components of the distributed application have access to the files.

Next, you need to write your business logic—the rules for manipulating and displaying
the data. These may include functions that generate summary data, such as average production
over a period of time. These become *classes* in the application. A class is an encapsulated
function that performs some type of processing. This might be as simple as generating an
average from a data set, or as complex as you choose to make it, though in practice complex
classes should be built from smaller pieces. This brings us to object-oriented programming
(OOP), which is integral to the .NET Framework. OOP can be understood by using building
blocks as an analogy. Just as a large building is built from a number of smaller, standard
pieces, an extremely complex software application is also built from a number of smaller,
standard pieces—your custom classes and the prebuilt classes that are part of the .NET
Framework.

Finally, you need a user interface. Each department may want its own interface to reflect
its needs, rather than a standard "one size fits all" approach. At one time, you would have to
write a complete application for each department and integrate (and update) the data. Early
on, it became possible to separate the data from the application, which greatly simplified things,
but you still needed an application for each department and would have to install it on each

computer that needs it. When you upgraded the application, such as modifying the business logic, the application would need to be updated on each computer.

The distributed application solution provided by the .NET Framework solves most, if not all, of your problems. The only component that needs to be written for each department is the user interface. It calls the business logic and data as needed, which are, in effect, separate programs and are common to everyone using the application. When you modify the business logic, the changes are immediately available to the application without any installation on the client computer. The updated data is always available to the user and will reflect the most recent changes.

ASP.NET is the part of the .NET Framework that is optimized for the Web. The user interface is a web browser, and its appearance is controlled by HTML. The HTML may be static or generated by the ASP.NET application. The business logic is encapsulated as a dynamic link library (DLL), which can access the resources, such as databases, that it needs. Your data sources can be databases, XML files, or any other form of structured data. Another advantage to the .NET Framework is that there is very little difference between a web application and a Windows application running on a desktop. With the exception of the user interface, virtually all the programming code is the same for both applications. This obviously makes a programmer's life much easier.

---

**NOTE**  *DLLs have not always been greeted with pleasure, as the phrase "DLL Hell" indicates. With the .NET Framework, most, if not all, of the pain of using DLLs has been removed. This has been greeted with much enthusiasm.*

## ASP.NET Is Compiled, Not Interpreted

The largest performance bottleneck of classic ASP, as with all script-based solutions, is that each time a page is called, the server must interpret the page before it can perform the functions it contains. In contrast, ASP.NET is compiled, which means that the application is stored in machine code—the set of native instructions that the computer uses internally. Put another way, with interpreted languages the computer first has to figure out what it needs to do and then do it. With compiled applications, the computer just does it. This greatly increases the efficiency of the server. With the runaway growth of the Internet, server resources are a significant issue, so this is an important feature of the .NET Framework.

## ASP.NET Is Multilanguage

Classic ASP has two languages available—JavaScript and VBScript. There is no limit to the languages that can be used with ASP.NET (or the .NET Framework) because of the Common Language Runtime (CLR). The CLR sits between the machine code and the programming language that the application is written in. What this means is that any language for which a CLR interpreter exists can be used to program ASP.NET and .NET Framework applications. COBOL and FORTRAN are no longer "dead" languages. This allows developers to bring all their programming skills to a project.

The .NET Framework supports Visual Basic .NET, Visual C++ .NET, a new language named C# (pronounced "C sharp"), J# .NET (Microsoft's version of Java for the .NET Framework), and JScript (Microsoft's version of JavaScript). Support for VBScript is not provided since Visual Basic .NET is much more useful. Microsoft has also released the information that developers need to interface additional languages with the CLR.

---

**NOTE**    *This chapter uses C# in the examples. If you are already proficient in another programming language, such as Visual Basic, C# might not be the best choice for you because it's one more thing to learn. C# was written for the .NET Framework and is very flexible, which is why it was selected for the examples included here.*

---

## ASP.NET Is Browser and Device Independent

With the varying capabilities of web browsers, it has been a major headache for web developers to write for all the possibilities. Should the target browser be Internet Explorer 5.*x* or 6.*x*? Or Netscape 4.*x* or 7.*x*? What will work in each browser, and how will functionality be affected? What about the new generation of hand-held devices, such as personal digital assistants (PDAs)?

Again, the .NET Framework has effectively addressed this problem. Behind the scenes, the .NET Framework detects the target browser and device, and generates the appropriate code in HTML, DHTML, JavaScript, and so forth. This alone is reason enough to embrace the .NET Framework!

## ASP.NET Is Control Driven

Going back to the building block analogy used earlier, the .NET Framework provides a rich selection of prebuilt controls for constructing applications. The different types of controls are explained in the section "ASP.NET Server Controls" later in this chapter, and examples of most types will be used in the remainder of the chapter. You also have a great deal of flexibility in designing and building your own controls.

## ASP.NET Configuration and Security Models Are Portable

Another problem with conventional web development arises when the application is to be deployed from the development server to the production server—especially for secured (password protected) applications where user accounts and permissions must also be transferred from the development server to the production server. The .NET Framework deals with these problems by making the configuration an integral part of the application. This is done with several XML files that contain the configuration information for the application. These files are hierarchical so that settings in lower-level elements may override higher-level settings. This allows a great deal of control over the configuration of an application.

The machine.config file is the highest-level configuration file. This file controls the overall settings for the server. In effect, this file sets the defaults for all the applications on the server. The following code is a sample from a machine.config file, which sets the location of the security configuration files, which are also XML files:

```
<?xml version="1.0" encoding="UTF-8"?>
<configuration>
  <securityPolicy>
    <trustLevel name="Full" policyFile="internal"/>
    <trustLevel name="High" policyFile="web_hightrust.config"/>
```

```
        <trustLevel name="Low" policyFile="web_lowtrust.config"/>
        <trustLevel name="None" policyFile="web_notrust.config"/>
    </securityPolicy>
    ...
</configuration>
```

Each application may also have a global.asax file, which is similar to the global.asa file found in classic ASP applications. There is a single global.asax file for each ASP.NET application, and it is located in the root directory of the application. This file controls the settings for the entire application. The global.asax file is used primarily to control application and session events. *Application* events start when the web application is started, end when the application is shut down, and apply to all users. *Session* events are tied to individual users and start when the user accesses any page within the application. A session event ends when the user leaves the application or is inactive for a preset time (usually 20 minutes). In addition, each directory in the application can have its own web.config file, which controls the configuration of the files within that directory.

With the exception of the machine.config file, all these files are part of the application and are deployed with it. This greatly reduces the need to configure the server using tools outside of the ASP.NET application, which means much easier deployment from development to production server.

### The ASP.NET Application

In its simplest form, an ASP.NET application consists of a virtual directory and all its subdirectories and files. Along with the web pages and subdirectories, this includes the global.asax and any web.config files. In more detail, an application is a compiled assembly (a DLL) and the web pages (.aspx files), which are called *web forms* in ASP.NET.

Now that you've had a very fast lap around the .NET track, it's time to examine some of these features in more detail. First, you need to configure your computer to work with .NET Framework applications.

---

**NOTE**   *SharePoint 2 (Windows SharePoint Services or WSS) is incompatible with the server-side scripting used in this chapter. To complete the exercises in this chapter, you can use the FrontPage Server Extensions (FPSE) and SharePoint 1 (SharePoint Team Services or STS, which is compatible with FPSE) installed, but not SharePoint 2.*

---

## ASP.NET Prerequisites

If you want to write ASP.NET applications, you will need to download and install the .NET Framework Redistributable. In addition, if you want to learn about the .NET Framework in detail, you also need the .NET Framework Software Development Kit (SDK). The redistributable is a 24MB download, and the full SDK is a 109MB download. The SDK is available from Microsoft on a CD, so you may prefer to order the CD if you choose to install the full SDK. Either can be installed on Windows 98, NT 4.0, XP, ME, 2000, and 2003 (the redistributable is installed by default with Windows Server 2003), with Internet Explorer 5.01 or later installed and Microsoft Data Access Components (MDAC) 2.6 (MDAC 2.7 is recommended) installed. You will also need to download and install any Service Packs that are available.

The full SDK is recommended if you are serious about working with ASP.NET. It contains documentation and code samples that aren't included in the redistributable, which is the minimum set of files needed to work with and deploy ASP.NET. Whichever version you choose to install, the first steps are to check the versions of your database drivers and Internet Explorer. First, check your version of IE with these steps:

1. In Internet Explorer, select Help | About Internet Explorer. If the version number displayed in the About Internet Explorer window does not begin with 5.01 or later, you will need to update it.

2. If you need to update IE, type **http://www.microsoft.com/windows/ie/** in your browser's address bar and press ENTER. If you already have IE 5.01 or later, proceed to checking your database drivers, unless you choose to update your browser, which is recommended. The current version is Internet Explorer 6 Service Pack 1 (SP1).

3. On the Internet Explorer home page, find and click the link to download the latest version of IE and the current Service Pack.

4. Select your language in the drop-down list box and click Go. On the next page, follow the instructions for installing IE.

5. When the installation is complete, you will need to restart your computer. Save all your work, and then click Finish.

Checking your ODBC (Open Database Connectivity) drivers is a little more involved than updating Internet Explorer. The exact steps depend on your operating system, as explained in the next set of instructions.

1. In Windows 2000 Professional, select Start | Settings | Control Panel | Administrative Tools | Data Sources (ODBC).

2. In Windows 2000 Server or Server 2003, select Start | All Programs | Administrative Tools | Data Sources (ODBC).

3. In the ODBC Data Source Administrator dialog box, select the Drivers tab.

4. This displays all the ODBC drivers installed on your system and their version numbers. If you are using Access, the version number should be 4.00.6200.00 or greater. For SQL Server, it should be 2000.81.9030.14 or greater.

5. Click Cancel to close the ODBC Data Source Administrator dialog box.

Starting with MDAC 2.6, Microsoft is no longer including the Jet database engine components. This is the database engine used by Access. If you plan on using Access as your database, and your drivers need updating, you will need to install the updated Access ODBC driver separately. Access updates are now part of Microsoft's Office updates, rather than a separate download, and should be current if you've installed Access and updated Office recently. These next steps will install the MDAC 2.8 download and then the Jet 4.0 download:

1. In your browser, open Microsoft's Universal Data Access site at **http://www.microsoft.com/data/**.

2. In the Essential Info box, in the upper-right corner of your browser, click Data Access Downloads.

3. On the downloads page, find the latest MDAC release (MDAC 2.8 at the time this is written) and select it.

4. Follow the instructions on the download page. If you choose to save the file, locate the saved file and double-click it to start the installation when the download is complete.

   The following steps use Office Update to update your Access database drivers, if necessary:

5. Type **http://office.microsoft.com/ProductUpdates/** in your browser's address bar and press ENTER.

6. Click Scan My Computer To Find Office Updates I Need. You may see a dialog box requesting permission to install Windows Installer. If so, install it and then proceed with the update.

7. If your Access drivers aren't current, the update will appear in the list of Recommended Updates. Follow the instructions on the page to install it.

Now that the prerequisites are completed, you need to install the .NET Framework. These instructions are for the redistributable version, rather than for the full SDK. Begin using these steps:

1. In your browser, open the .NET Framework home page, **http://msdn.microsoft .com/netframework/**, shown in Figure 16-1.

2. In the Essential Info box on the right side of the page, select Microsoft .NET Framework Redistributable. This will open the .NET Framework Downloads page. If you're installing the SDK, select .NET Framework SDK Download instead of the redistributable. This will open the Microsoft .NET Framework Software Development Kit page.

3. Locate the link to the current version of the redistributable (1.1 at the time this was written) on the .NET Framework Downloads page and select it.

4. Follow the instructions on the Microsoft .NET Framework Redistributable page to download and install the file.

Your computer is now configured to explore ASP.NET. When you want to start using it with your production webs, you will have to be sure your ISP also has their web servers properly configured. This shouldn't be a problem as the .NET Framework is becoming increasingly popular.

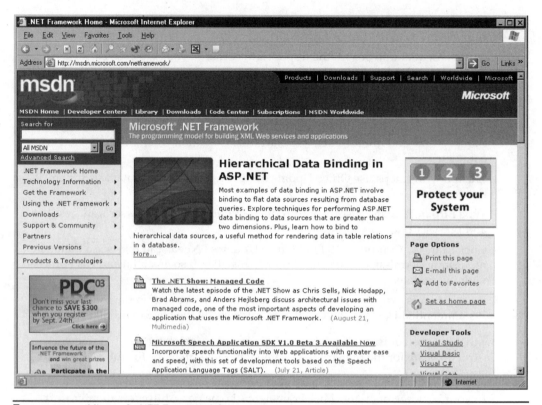

**FIGURE 16-1**   Microsoft .NET Framework home page

## ASP.NET Web Forms

As with every new technology, ASP.NET has its own jargon. What were once web pages are now *web forms* in an ASP.NET application. At the most basic level, a web form is a text file, just like ordinary HTML pages, with a filename extension of .aspx. There's much more, of course. This name change also signifies a fundamental change in the way a web page is processed. With HTML, the web page is simply a text file that is interpreted by your browser and displayed, meaning the only server processing is to send the requested file over the Internet. With ASP, a page is interpreted on the web server when a browser requests it, then sent to the browser. This means that the page is run through the script engine each time it is requested, which requires a certain amount of server resources. With ASP.NET, the web form is compiled to a .NET Framework class object the first time it is requested. Each additional request uses the existing class, saving resources and time. Since the class object is compiled, rather than interpreted for each call as a script is, the process is faster and uses less server resources.

The best way to learn about ASP.NET is to create an ASP.NET web form, which you will do with these next steps. The first step is to configure IIS to allow a page with an .aspx extension to be the default home page of your web.

1. Open the IIS Manager. In Win 2000 Professional, select Start | Settings | Control Panel, double-click Administrative Tools, and then double-click Internet Services

Manager. In Win 2000 Server and Win Server 2003, select Start | All Programs | Administrative Tools | Internet Information Services (IIS) Manager.

2. In the Win Server 2003 IIS Manager, expand the server tree, right-click the Web Sites folder, and select Properties.

3. In the Web Sites Properties dialog box, select the Documents tab. In Win 2000, right-click the name of your server and select Properties. In the *computer_name* Properties dialog box, click Edit in the WWW Service Master Properties box and select the Documents tab.

4. If necessary, click Add, then type **Default.aspx** in the Add Content Page dialog box, as shown here:

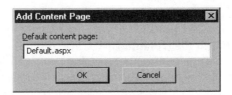

5. Click OK. Default.aspx is added to the list of default content pages as shown next. When a web is requested without a page being specified, as in http://localhost/ AspNet/, IIS uses these settings to determine which page to display. The first match it finds is the page that it uses. If a page isn't found in the web that matches one of the pages listed, then an HTTP 403 – Forbidden error is displayed in the browser. You can set the order the pages will be searched for by selecting one of the pages and using the Move Up and Move Down buttons to change the order.

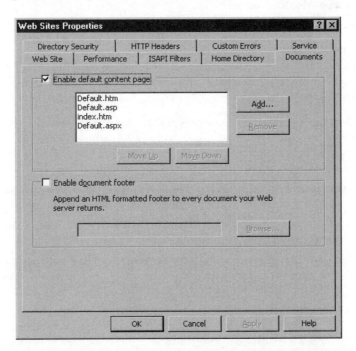

PART III

6. Click Apply and then OK to close the Web Sites Properties dialog box; then close the IIS Manager.

7. In FrontPage, create a One Page Web Site and name it **AspNet**. The location of the AspNet web should be in the default web created with the installation of IIS. This will normally be C:\Inetpub\Wwwroot and the URL is http://*computer_name*/. The URL to access this web will be http://*computer_name*/AspNet/. The default web is a virtual directory, so it meets the requirement that the root of an ASP.NET web be a virtual directory.

---

***Tip*** *You can use* localhost *rather than your computer name when creating the web. In that case, the URL would be http://localhost/AspNet.*

8. In the Folder List, right-click Default.htm and select Rename.

9. Rename the Default.htm file **Default.aspx**. Click Yes in the Confirm Rename dialog box, and then click Yes again if you get a dialog box warning that changing the extension of a filename may cause the file to become unusable.

10. Double-click Default.aspx to open it for editing. In Design view, type **It's An ASP.NET World** at the top of the page and format it as Heading 2.

11. Save your page and then open it in your browser. At this point, since you haven't actually added any ASP.NET functionality, the page behaves the same as any HTML web page.

With your web server and FrontPage configuration complete, you're ready to venture into the brave new world of ASP.NET. You will use this web to learn how to use FrontPage to create and manage ASP.NET webs.

## ASP.NET Server Controls

ASP.NET provides different types of controls, all of which run on the server rather than the browser (the client). You will work with examples of most of these controls in this chapter. The types of controls are

- **HTML Server Controls**   The familiar HTML tags that run on the server. This is accomplished by adding the `runat="server"` attribute to the tag. Any existing HTML tag can be converted to an HTML server control by adding the `runat="server"` attribute.

- **Web Server controls**   Duplicate the functionality of the more familiar HTML tags, but have a more consistent and expanded set of properties and methods.

- **List controls**   Can be bound to data sources, such as databases, XML files, arrays, and so forth. This makes these controls extremely useful.

- **Templated controls**   Repeat a template for each item in a data source. Some of these controls allow you to use different formatting to display the data, edit the data, provide support for pagination, and so forth.

- **Rich controls**   Are advanced controls that generate quite a bit of HTML and JavaScript code with only a couple of lines of ASP.NET code. This is one of the great advantages of ASP.NET, making it very easy to add a great deal of functionality to your webs with very little actual coding.

- **Validation controls**   Enable you to validate user input. In Chapter 15, you learned how to use JavaScript and VBScript to validate a form. ASP.Net Validation controls make this process even easier.

- **Mobile controls**   Duplicate the functionality of the Web Server, List, and Rich controls for mobile devices, such as personal digital assistants (PDA), smart-phones, and so on. Though you won't work with them in this chapter, these controls are increasingly important as these devices become more widespread. They allow you to migrate existing web applications to mobile devices with a minimum of pain.

In addition, you can create user controls, which are very similar to Include files in classic ASP. These might be as simple as a few lines of HTML such as a footer that contains copyright and contact information. They can also be much more complex—virtually any ASP.NET code can be used as a user control.

In this next set of instructions, you will convert the HTML Heading 2 to an ASP.NET HTML server control. Begin with these steps:

1. In FrontPage, switch your Default.aspx page to Code view.

2. Place your cursor at the top of the page, before the opening <HTML> tag, and type

   **<%@ Page Language="C#" %>**

   then press ENTER.

3. Place your cursor before the closing </HEAD> tag and type **<script runat="server">**. If you are using IntelliSense, the closing script tag will be inserted. Make sure the code in the following steps is placed between the script tags.

---

**NOTE**   *C#, unlike VBScript, is case-sensitive. This means that "heading01" is not the same as "Heading01". When typing the code in this chapter, be sure to use exactly the same case.*

4. Press ENTER, type **void Page_Load()**, and press ENTER. Type

   ```
   {
   heading01.InnerHtml="It's An ASP.NET World";
   }
   ```

5. If IntelliSense did not insert the closing script tag, type **</script>**.

6. Select your Heading 2 tag and type **<h2 id="heading01" runat="server" />**. Your Default.aspx page should look similar to Figure 16-2.

7. Save your work and open the page in Internet Explorer. It should look exactly the same as the plain HTML page you originally created.

FIGURE 16-2    Default.aspx with ASP.NET code added

**NOTE**    *The first time the page is loaded it may take longer than you expect. After the first load, the contents are cached so that subsequent loads are faster.*

8. In your IE, select View | Source. The code for the page should look similar to this:

```
<html>
<head>
<meta http-equiv="Content-Language" content="en-us">
<meta http-equiv="Content-Type" content="text/html;
charset=windows-1252">
</head>
<body>
<h2 id="heading01">It's An ASP.NET World</h2>
</body>
</html>
```

As you can see, ASP.NET has generated a page with only static HTML from the web form you created in the previous steps.

There are a number of things to understand about the page you just created, starting with the first line on the page. The line <%@ Page Language="C#" %> is a *page directive*. Page directives are used to set attributes for the page and are usually located at the top of the page, though they can be located anywhere on the page. All page directives begin with the At symbol (@) and are enclosed by <% %>, which are *delimiters*. Delimiters set the boundaries of code and distinguish it from the HTML code on the page. Table 16-1 lists the page directives that are available in ASP.NET.

---

**NOTE**   *A complete description of all the ASP.NET classes, objects, and controls is well beyond the scope of this introductory chapter. The Help files that are included with the .NET Framework SDK are a good place to start understanding the potential. (The Help files are not included with the .NET Framework redistributable.) The "ASP.NET Programmer's Reference" (Charles C. Caison, Osborne/McGraw-Hill, 2002) is also an excellent resource.*

Each page directive has one or more properties that can be set. The @Page page directive is one of the most flexible, with 26 properties that can be set. These properties are as follows:

- **ASPCompat**   Is set to either TRUE or FALSE (the default value), and is used to provide compatibility with older COM+ objects and Active Server Pages objects. This type of backwards compatibility also brings with it the performance bottlenecks of classic ASP and is not recommended.

- **AutoEventWireup**   Indicates if the events on the page (such as onClick) are enabled when the page is loaded. It is set to TRUE (the default value) or FALSE. In classic ASP and with client-side scripting languages such as JavaScript, an event is raised and processed on the client. An example of this is JavaScript form validation—the event is usually onClick, which is attached to the submit button. With ASP.NET, the event is raised on the client, but generally handled on the server. When the event is raised (for example, when the mouse is clicked on an object), a message is sent to the server, which triggers the processing. When AutoEventWireup is set to TRUE, any code required to process events is initialized, usually through the Page_Init and Page_Load methods.

- **Buffer**   Enables HTTP response buffering. The default value is TRUE.

- **ClassName**   Is the name of a class that will be dynamically compiled with the page. This allows the functionality of the specified class to be part of the page without any additional coding.

- **ClientTarget**   Sets the client (browser) compatibility level. ASP.NET can render the page for an advanced browser, such as Internet Explorer 6, or limit the functionality to match an older browser.

- **CodePage**   Is a numeric value that sets the character set that will be used by the page. Code pages are used for internationalizing an application and usually enable different platforms and languages.

- **CompilerOptions**   Is used to set the parameters used by the compiler.

- **ContentType**   Sets the HTTP content type of the page as a standard Multipurpose Internet Mail Extension (MIME) type. This can be text, audio, image, and so forth.

- **Culture**   Sets the culture for which the page is targeted. The culture includes the language, writing system, calendar, and the format of dates, time, and money.

| Name | Function |
|------|----------|
| @Assembly | Links assemblies to the page. Assemblies are compiled code (classes) that performs specific tasks. This allows you to reuse code for common tasks rather than creating the code on each page. |
| @Control | Sets the attributes used to include and compile user controls. |
| @Implements | Includes another .NET interface in the current page. This allows you to include all the functionality in the implemented interface with a single line of code. |
| @Import | Includes a .NET namespace from the .NET Framework class library or a user-defined namespace. A basic set of System namespaces is included by default. |
| @OutputCache | Sets a time limit to cache the ASP.NET web form. At the end of the time, the page will be recompiled. |
| @Page | Defines attributes specific to a page. |
| @Reference | Sets a user control or web form to be included and compiled with the page. |
| @Register | Adds a custom server control to a page. |

- **Debug**   Sets whether or not debugging symbols will be compiled into the page code. Inserting the debugging symbols helps when you're developing an application, but should be removed before the application is deployed.

- **Description**   Is a text description of the page. The ASP.NET parser ignores this information, so its main use is for documenting the page.

- **EnableSessionState**   Sets how the page will be able to access session information. A session begins when users first request a page from an application and ends when the users abandon the session by requesting a page outside the application. Session state is used to "remember" things such as a user's login or preferences. The default value is TRUE, which means that the session information is available to the page. The other values are FALSE and READONLY, which allows the information to be read but not changed.

- **EnableViewState**   Sets whether view information will be maintained across page requests. The values are TRUE (the default) and FALSE. View state is maintained as a hidden form field on the page and is used to maintain user information and selections during multiple reloads of the same page. Since much of the processing in ASP.NET is done on the server, this allows the information to be maintained over each trip to the server.

- **EnableViewStateMac**   Is similar to EnableViewState with implementation of the Machine Authentication Check (MAC). This encrypts the view information that is contained in the hidden form field. When set to TRUE, the encrypted value is checked to ensure that it hasn't been changed on the client. The default value is FALSE.

- **ErrorPage**  Sets the URL of the page that will be displayed if an unhandled exception occurs on the page. An unhandled exception is an error that is not dealt with by the error handling procedures on the page.

- **Explicit**  Applies only to pages where the language is Visual Basic and implements Visual Basic's Option Explicit mode. This requires all variables to be declared before the page can access them.

- **Inherits**  Defines another page that will be included with the current page. This is another method for reusing existing code modules.

- **Language**  Sets the programming language that is used on the page, such as C# or VB (Visual Basic).

- **LCID**  Sets the geographic location of the page, using a numeric Locale ID (LCID). By default, this is the LCID setting of the web server itself, unless you change it with this attribute. The LCID for U.S. English is 1033.

- **ResponseEncoding**  Sets the response character set encoding for the page content. By default, this would be the same as the web server setting. Some typical values are 1252 for the Windows operating system and 20127 for ASCII.

- **Src**  Is the filename of a code module that will be used by the page.

- **Strict**  Applies only to a page using Visual Basic and indicates the Strict mode will be used.

- **Trace**  Is used to enable tracing, which is used to follow the flow of the program during execution for debugging. The default value is FALSE.

- **TraceMode**  Controls how tracing messages will be displayed if tracing is enabled. Settings include SortByTime (the default value) and SortByCategory.

- **Transaction**  Sets the way transactions will be supported on the page. Possible values are NotSupported (the default value), Supported, Required, and RequiredNew.

- **WarningLevel**  Sets the error level at which the compiler will abort page compilation. Possible values are 0, 1, 2, 3, and 4.

The next line to look at is the script that is used to set the content of the H2 tag, shown here:

```
<script runat="server">
void Page_Load()
{
  heading01.InnerHtml="It's An ASP.NET World";
}
</script>
```

Like the H2 tag, the script is set to run on the server, rather than the browser. The only function of the script is to set the value of the text for the H2 tag, using the InnerHtml attribute of the H2 tag. This is not an attribute of only the H2 tag—it is available to any HTML tag that has an opening and closing tag, such as <TABLE></TABLE>, <DIV></DIV>, and so forth, but not tags such as <BR>.

The second line, `void Page_Load()`, uses the C# method `void` to indicate that a value is not returned by the function. If the function were designed to return a value, such as the product of multiplication or retrieving a value from a data source, you would not use the `void` method. You would use the keyword that described the data type to be returned, such as `int` for an integer. `Page_Load()` is a C# event that causes the following code to run when the page is loaded. The one line of code that is executed is to assign the value "It's An ASP.NET World" to the InnerHtml attribute of the HTML tag with the ID of "heading01." The code itself doesn't care what the actual HTML tag is—it could be an H1 or Span tag, for instance—it only looks at the ID attribute of the tag. This means that to implement ASP.NET, you need to assign IDs to all tags for which you want to programmatically control the attributes.

In this example, the advantage of programmatically assigning the value of an attribute may not seem to be much of a benefit, but this method gives you a great deal of flexibility. The value of the attribute does not have to be statically defined, as it is here. It could be drawn from an XML file, a database, or another data source. For example, if the page required a login, you could add the user's name to the InnerHtml attribute to personalize the heading.

The last line to look at is the H2 tag, which doesn't look much like the standard H2 tag after it's been converted to ASP.NET. The tag is now *self-closing*, meaning that the forward slash (/) before the closing greater-than bracket (>) closes the tag, and there is no need for the usual closing tag (</H2>), though you could use that method if you choose. The `runat="server"` attribute instructs ASP.NET to execute the code on the server and return the static HTML, as you saw in the browser source code. The ID identifies the tag for ASP.NET.

This example showed an ASP.NET HTML Server control, which isn't as useful as a Web Server control. Web Server controls duplicate the functionality of the more familiar HTML tags, but have a more consistent and expanded set of properties and methods, as you will see in the next section.

## Web Server Controls

Web Server controls duplicate the functionality of traditional HTML tags, but offer a more consistent set of attributes. They are not identical in name to HTML tags, but compile to browser-appropriate HTML before being delivered to the client. In other words, the same control will generate different HTML for an older browser with limited capabilities such as Netscape 4.*x* than it will for a feature-rich browser such as Internet Explorer 6.*x*.

The easiest way to see the differences between an HTML control (used in the previous section) and a Web Server control is to duplicate the functionality of the previous example using a Web Server control. There isn't a direct equivalent of the H2 tag, so you will use the ASP.NET Label tag in this exercise. Begin with these steps:

1. In FrontPage, with your Default.aspx page in Code view, place the cursor at the end of heading01.InnerHtml line in your script at the top of the page. Press ENTER.

2. Type **label01.Text="An ASP.NET Label";**. Don't forget the semicolon at the end of the line—this is a required delimiter that sets the end of the line of code.

3. Place your cursor at the end of your H2 tag in the body of the page and press ENTER.

4. Type **<form>** and the closing </form> tag should be inserted. Place the cursor between the Form tags and press ENTER twice; then press UP ARROW once.

5. Type **\<asp:Label ID="label01" Font-Bold=True Font-Size=18pt Runat=server/\>**. Save your page, which should look like Figure 16-3. If you are using IntelliSense, your capitalization might appear different.

6. Open your page in your browser. It should look similar to Figure 16-4.

The most important item to notice in this code is the Form tags. Web Server controls must be placed within a form, and there can only be one form on an ASP.NET web form. Other than that, using a Web Server control is very similar to using an HTML control, as you did in the previous exercise. In this exercise, you used the Font-Bold and Font-Size properties of the ASP:Label tag, but you also could have referenced a style sheet using the CssClass property.

In your browser, view the source of the code. In Internet Explorer 6, ASP.NET generates a Span tag to format and display the ASP.NET Label, like this:

```
<span id="label01" style="font-size:18pt;font-weight:bold;">An ASP.NET Label</span>
```

This code will vary depending on the browser viewing the page, as ASP.NET will tailor it to the capabilities of the browser.

The preceding exercises give you a general understanding of the nature of ASP.NET. You should study the documentation included in the SDK to learn the full range of controls

```
 1 <%@ Page Language="C#" %>
 2 <html>
 3
 4 <head>
 5 <meta http-equiv="Content-Language" content="en-us">
 6 <meta http-equiv="Content-Type" content="text/html; charset=windows-1252">
 7 <script runat="server">
 8 void Page_Load()
 9 {
10     heading01.InnerHtml="It's An ASP.NET World";
11     label01.Text="An ASP.NET Label";
12 }
13 </script>
14 </head>
15
16 <body>
17 <h2 id="heading01" runat="server" />
18 <form runat=server>
19 <asp:Label ID="label01" Font-Bold=True Font-Size=18pt Runat=server/>
20 </form>
21
22 </body>
23
24 </html>
25
```

**FIGURE 16-3** Default.aspx with ASP.NET Label added

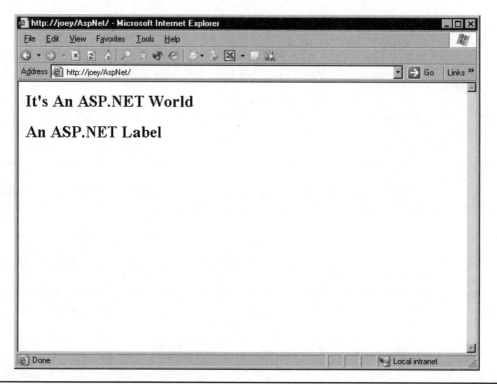

**FIGURE 16-4**    Default.aspx in Internet Explorer

and their properties. In the next section, you will learn about Rich controls, which offer features that had only been available with a great deal of custom programming prior to ASP.NET.

## Rich Controls

Rich controls incorporate a great deal of functionality with a few lines of code. Table 16-2 lists the available ASP.NET Rich controls.

As you can see, the Rich controls fall into two categories: form validation and added functionality. The Calendar control offers the user a simple, graphical means to select a date. The AdRotator control helps the web developer easily control the display of ad banners on a site. The remaining controls are used for form validation. Traditionally, JavaScript is used for client-side validation because it is supported by virtually all browsers. With scripting technologies such as classic ASP, server-side validation is often needed, because client-side validation can be bypassed by a knowledgeable user. Particularly when the form input is written to a database, it's very important that it be properly validated. Since JavaScript isn't always used on the server, this has required the validation code to be written in two languages (with classic ASP, generally JavaScript on the client and VBScript on the server). The ASP.NET Rich controls automatically generate both client-side and server-side validation code using the appropriate languages—JavaScript on the client and the specified language on the server.

| | Control | Function |
|---|---|---|
| **TABLE 16-2**<br>ASP.NET Rich<br>Controls | AdRotator | Creates a control that displays a randomly selected ad banner. This function is also available in classic ASP. |
| | Calendar | Creates a control that displays one month and allows the user to select days of the week, weeks of the month, or months of the year. |
| | RequiredFieldValidator | Generates both client-side and server-side required field validation. The associated input field must contain data—it cannot be empty. |
| | CompareValidator | Generates client-side and server-side validation comparing the values in two input fields. |
| | RangeValidator | Generates client-side and server-side validation that requires the input to be within the specified range. |
| | RegularExpressionValidator | Generates client-side and server-side validation that compares the input to a specified range of characters. This is especially useful for validating e-mail addresses. |
| | CustomValidator | Generates client-side and/or server-side validation using custom code. This is used when the validation function can't be accomplished with one of the other validation controls. |
| | ValidationSummary | Displays a summary of the validation errors generated by the other validation controls. |

The exercises in this chapter use C#, so this is the language the server-side code would be written in. This greatly simplifies the programmer's job. The prebuilt validators cover the most common validation functions, and the CustomValidator allows you to write custom code to cover any other situations.

In this next exercise, you will use the Calendar control to insert a calendar on your web form and select a date from it. Begin with these steps:

1. In FrontPage, with your Default.aspx in Code view, add the **runat=server** property to the opening Form tag so the tag reads <form runat=server>. This is required for the Calendar control to work properly.

2. Place your cursor at the start of the closing Form tag (</form>) and press ENTER twice; then press UP ARROW once.

3. Type **<asp:Calendar ID=calendar01 Runat=server/>**. Save the page and then open it in your browser. It should look similar to Figure 16-5.

This is the basic calendar control without any formatting. As you enter the properties for the Calendar control, IntelliSense will display the available properties and methods, as shown here. In the next steps, you will format the Calendar control.

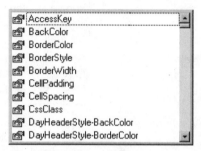

4. In FrontPage, place your cursor immediately after ID=calendar01 and press SPACEBAR. Type **DayStyle-BackColor** (or select it from the IntelliSense list), and then type = and double-click Pick Color in the IntelliSense list.

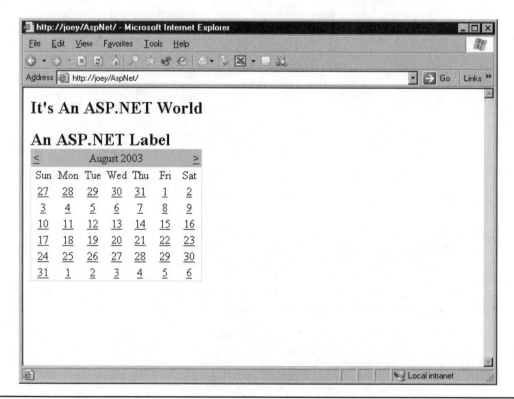

**FIGURE 16-5**   Calendar control in Internet Explorer

5. In the More Colors palette that opens, select Yellow, as shown here. Click OK.

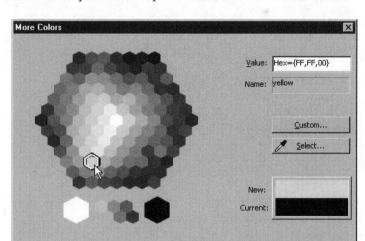

6. Press SPACEBAR, then type **TodayDayStyle-BackColor=** and select Blue from the More Colors palette. Click OK.

7. Press SPACEBAR, then type **SelectedDayStyle-BackColor=** and select Red from the More Colors palette. Click OK.

8. Save your page and then open it in your browser. It should look similar to Figure 16-6. The Background color for the days of the month is now yellow, today's date is in blue, and a day you select by clicking it will be red. Scroll through the list of properties for the Calendar control, and try different properties to see the many formatting options that are available.

The preceding steps have shown you how to format the Calendar control, but to be useful, the control needs to return a date that you can use in your web application. These next steps show you how to use the input the Calendar control provides.

1. In FrontPage, your cursor should still be in the Calendar control line of code, immediately after SelectedDayStyle-BackColor=#FF0000. Press SPACEBAR and type **OnSelectionChanged=**, or select it from the IntelliSense list, as shown here:

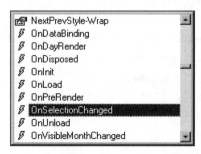

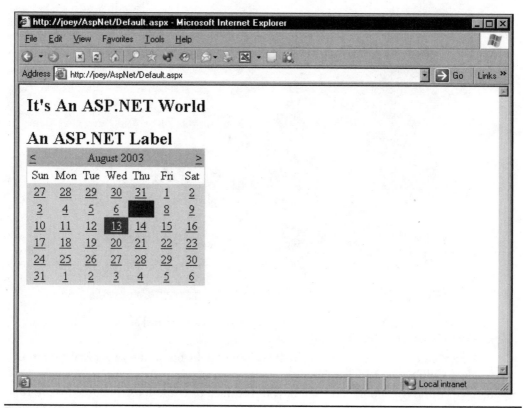

**FIGURE 16-6** Calendar control with formatting in Internet Explorer

Notice that there is a lightning bolt icon next to OnSelectionChanged. This indicates that it is a *method* of the Calendar control, rather than a property. This method fires when the selected date is changed in the control. You need to specify the action that will be called by the OnSelectionChanged method, which you will do in the next steps.

2. With the cursor still immediately after the equal sign in OnSelectionChanged, type **Date_Changed**. This is the name of the routine you will write to display the selected date.

3. Place your cursor in front of the closing Script tag (</script>), press ENTER, and then press UP ARROW.

4. Type **void Date_Changed(Object sender, EventArgs e)** and press ENTER.

5. Type {, then press ENTER, and press TAB.

6. Type **lblCalendarDate.Text="<br>You selected " + calendar01.SelectedDate;**, press ENTER, and type }. Your finished script should look like this:

```
void Date_Changed(Object sender, EventArgs e)
{
```

```
    lblCalendarDate.Text="<br>You selected " + calendar01.SelectedDate;
}
```

Next you need to add a label to display the selected date. The label text was created in the preceding steps, and the label itself will be added with these steps.

7. Place your cursor immediately before the closing Form tag (</form>), press ENTER, and then press UP ARROW.

8. Type **<asp:Label ID=lblCalendarDate Runat=server/>**. In Code view, your page should look similar to Figure 16-7.

9. Save your work, and then open the page in your browser. Click a date and the date you selected will be displayed in the label underneath the Calendar control, as shown in Figure 16-8.

The example with the Calendar control barely scratches the surface of what's possible with ASP.NET controls. The next section, "ASP.NET Resources," lists additional resources to help you learn more about the full functionality of ASP.NET. It is a steep learning curve, but the results will be worth the time invested if you want to create interactive web applications.

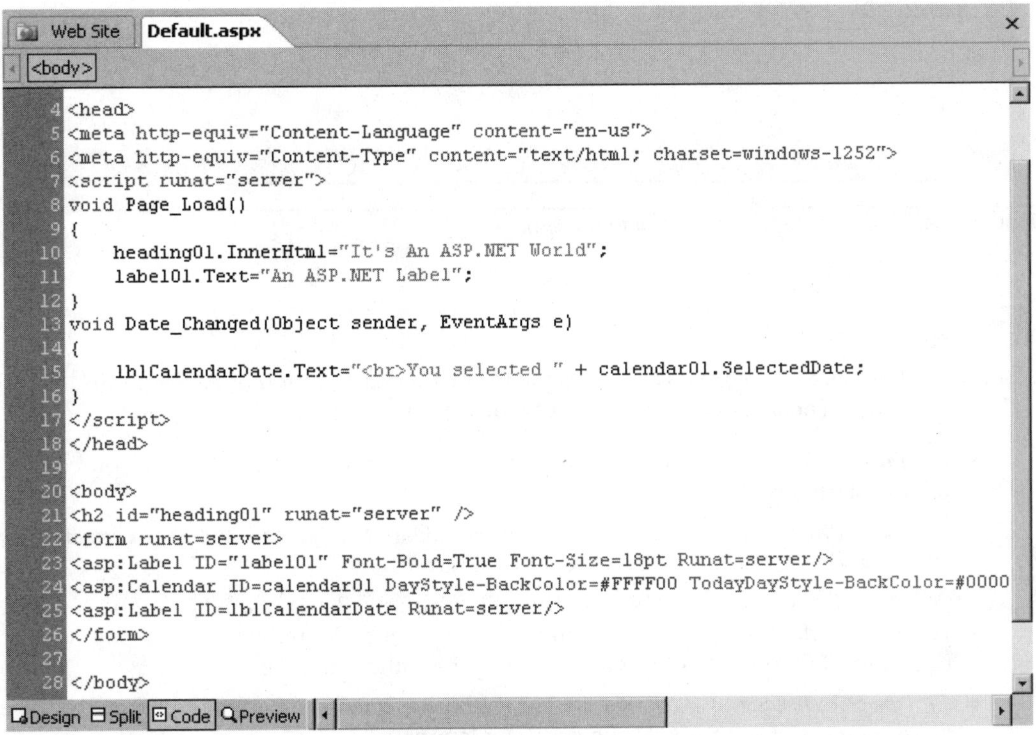

PART III

```
  4 <head>
  5 <meta http-equiv="Content-Language" content="en-us">
  6 <meta http-equiv="Content-Type" content="text/html; charset=windows-1252">
  7 <script runat="server">
  8 void Page_Load()
  9 {
 10     heading01.InnerHtml="It's An ASP.NET World";
 11     label01.Text="An ASP.NET Label";
 12 }
 13 void Date_Changed(Object sender, EventArgs e)
 14 {
 15     lblCalendarDate.Text="<br>You selected " + calendar01.SelectedDate;
 16 }
 17 </script>
 18 </head>
 19
 20 <body>
 21 <h2 id="heading01" runat="server" />
 22 <form runat=server>
 23 <asp:Label ID="label01" Font-Bold=True Font-Size=18pt Runat=server/>
 24 <asp:Calendar ID=calendar01 DayStyle-BackColor=#FFFF00 TodayDayStyle-BackColor=#0000
 25 <asp:Label ID=lblCalendarDate Runat=server/>
 26 </form>
 27
 28 </body>
```

**Design   Split   Code   Preview**

**Figure 16-7**   Finished Default.aspx in Code view

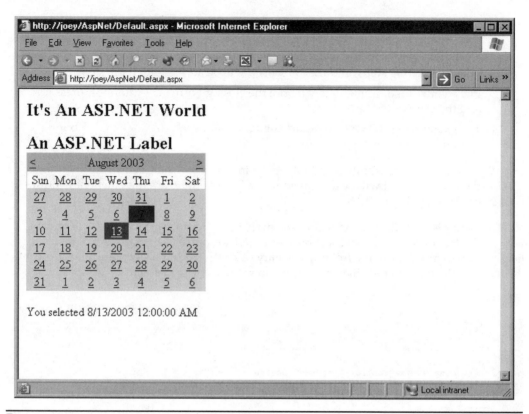

**FIGURE 16-8** Finished Default.aspx in Internet Explorer

## ASP.NET Resources

A number of books and web sites are available for further exploration of ASP.NET and the .NET Framework. The following list includes many of the most useful resources:

- *Instant ASP.NET Applications* by Greg Buczek (Osborne, 2001) is a good resource for getting started with ASP.NET.

- *ASP.NET Programmer's Reference* by Charles C. Caison (Osborne, 2002) covers all the classes and controls, and is an excellent resource.

- *ASP.NET Tips & Techniques* by Greg Buczek (Osborne, 2002) will help you by giving you real-world examples. The examples are written in Visual Basic .NET, so it won't be as useful if you are programming in C# or another language.

- *C# Tips & Techniques* by Charles Wright (Osborne, 2002) is a very good book for learning more about the C# programming language.

The following is a list of sites that are particularly useful:

- **http://asp.net/**   The best site on the Web for ASP.NET information. The site includes tutorials and starter applications so that you can immediately create ASP.NET applications.

- **http://msdn.microsoft.com/netframework/**   Microsoft's .NET Framework site. Along with ASP.NET, information on the entire .NET Framework and their new C# programming language is available, including code samples.

- **http://www.aspfree.com/**   A comprehensive ASP.NET resource, this site also has the ASP.NET Quickstart samples (included with the .NET Framework SDK) online, which means you don't have to download the SDK and install them to see how ASP.NET works.

- **http://www.aspng.com/**   ASP Next Generation offers a number of tutorials and an excellent e-mail discussion group.

- **http://www.asp101.com/**   ASP 101 offers a growing collection of information related to ASP.NET.

- **http://www.4guysfromrolla.com/**   4GuysFromRolla.com has a number of articles on web technologies including ASP.NET.

- **http://www.devx.com/**   Another source for a variety of technical information relating to web technologies, DevX covers just about everything.

This chapter has barely scratched the surface of the potential of ASP.NET. With FrontPage, you will need to use the Code view to gain its benefits, as is the case with ASP, but the potential for integrating ASP.NET into FrontPage is greater than with ASP. If you choose to embrace ASP.NET, you can expect future releases of FrontPage to offer a great deal of support.

PART III

# Working with Databases

U p to this point, you have learned how to create webs containing information that is basically static. In the previous chapters, you learned how to integrate the capabilities of ASP.NET to greatly expand the interactivity of your webs, but the content was still mainly static. In this chapter, you will see how to take your webs to the next level—using databases to provide the information displayed on your web pages. This is a tremendous advantage over traditional webs.

Webs that are database driven, where the content is coming from a database rather than static pages, allow for a great deal of user interactivity while simplifying the task of the web administrator. For example, an e-commerce site needs to display information about products and prices. If the web is static, a price change requires you to manually find all the pages that contain the old price and change it to the new one. If the web is database driven, the price is updated in the database, and all pages will show the new price the next time the page is loaded. Using a database to provide content also reduces the number of pages in a web. If a company's product line contains 100 items, and each one is displayed on a single page, there would be 100 pages to maintain. With the content being drawn from a database, there would only be a single page, which would be a template for displaying the information about the selected product.

The focus of this chapter is to provide you with an understanding of databases and how to add them to your webs using FrontPage and ASP.NET. Each of these subjects really requires a book of its own. The information here, however, will give you an overview of how the pieces fit together and show you how to get started using databases with your webs. The first step is to understand what a database is.

---

**NOTE** *In FrontPage, you can have database-driven webs that use the FrontPage Server Extensions (FPSE) or Windows SharePoint Services (WSS or SharePoint 2). These are not compatible, so you have to choose one or the other. In this chapter, you will first use FPSE to create a database-driven web and then use SharePoint 2. See Chapter 22 and Appendix A for more information about SharePoint.*

## Understanding Databases on the Web

A *database* is an organized collection of information. This can be a simple list of names and telephone numbers, or a complete collection of all the information about a company—its products, salespeople, sales, and inventory. In a database, all the information about one item, such as the name and telephone number for one person, is a *record*. Each record is made up of a number of *fields* or *columns*. In a list of names and telephone numbers, each name is one field, and the telephone number associated with the name is another field in the record. A collection of records is a *table*. A simple *flat-file* database is made up of one table, while a *relational* database has two or more tables with one or more relationships, or *links,* between fields in the tables. In the database table shown here, there are four records, each consisting of five fields. Each row in the table is a record; each column is a field. At the top of each column is the field name for that column. The CustomerID field provides a unique number to identify each record. You may have customers with the same name, or in the same city and state, so you need a way to uniquely identify each customer. There should be at least one field in each record that contains a unique value to identify that record. This field is the *primary key* for the table.

| | CustomerID | CustomerName | CustomerAddr | CustomerCity | CustomerState |
|---|---|---|---|---|---|
| + | 1 | Honeymoon Island Hardware | 1010 County Road 1 | Palm Harbor | FL |
| + | 2 | Tom's Tools | 1313 East Oak St. | Ojai | CA |
| + | 3 | Bulldog Hardware | 3609 Bulldog Lane | Athens | GA |
| + | 4 | Bloomfield Tools | 3787 Meadow Road | West Caldwell | NJ |
| ▶ | (AutoNumber) | | | | |

Customers : Table — Record: 14 ◀ | 5 | ▶ ▶I ▶* of 5

***Tip***   *With many databases, the names displayed at the top of the column, as shown above, do not have to match the actual field name. This can cause confusion if the displayed name and the actual field name are different. Your database queries must use the actual field name, not the displayed name if it is different. In Access, you can also find the actual field names by looking at the table in Design view.*

Simple flat-file databases are of limited use. Relational databases, on the other hand, can contain millions of records that can be sorted and organized by use of complex criteria. Relational databases get their name from the fact that relationships are created between fields in two or more tables. Figure 17-1 shows the relationships between the tables in the North Beach Tools database that will be used in this chapter. This is a very simple relational database whose purpose is to introduce you both to relational databases and to integrating a relational database into a web.

The North Beach Tools database contains four tables, as described in Table 17-1. The Orders table has a relationship with fields in each of the other three tables. These are one-to-many relationships, which means that the contents of a field must be unique in one table, but can appear many times in the other table. In Figure 17-1, this is shown by a *1* next to the field with the unique value and by the symbol for infinity (∞) next to the field that can have many occurrences of the same values. For example, the Customers table contains a unique

**FIGURE 17-1**
Relationships in the North Beach Tools database

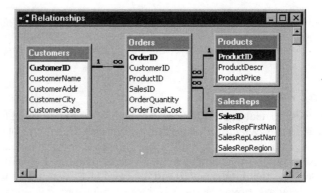

CustomerID to identify each customer. This is the "one" side of the relationship. The Orders table contains a record for each order the customer places, so there can be a number of records for each customer. This is the "many" side of the relationship. There can also be one-to-one relationships, but these are less common.

The benefit of a relational database is that by linking a unique field in one table to a field in another table, all the information in the first table is made available to the second table without having to be entered each time. The North Beach Tools database illustrates this. The database has tables for customers, products, sales representatives, and orders. In a simple flat-file database, each record in the Orders table would have to contain all the information about the customer, the product, and the salesperson, as well as the information about the order itself. In a relational database, each record in the Orders table would contain only the information unique to the order. The information about the customer, product, and salesperson is collected from the appropriate table as needed. This greatly reduces the size and complexity of the database. For example, to record a price change for a product, only one field in one table (the ProductPrice field in the Products table) needs to be changed. From that point on, every new record in the Orders table will reflect the new price. Relational databases also reduce the total size of the database by avoiding the duplication of information, an important consideration when the database contains thousands or millions of records.

There are two primary database programs that you would use with FrontPage in creating webs. These are Microsoft Access and Microsoft SQL Server. Access (included with Office 2003 Professional Edition) is an excellent database for applications where the number of queries is limited. If the database will be queried often (more than a few hundred times a day), or will contain thousands of records, Access is not up to the task. SQL Server, on the other hand, is a robust, full-featured client/server database application that can handle millions of records.

**TABLE 17-1**
Tables in the North Beach Tools Database

| Table | Description |
|---|---|
| Customers | Contains the information relating to individual customers |
| Products | Contains the information describing each product |
| SalesReps | Contains the information relating to each salesperson |
| Orders | Contains the information for each order |

PART III

**NOTE** *You can use any Open Database Connectivity (ODBC)–compliant database with your webs. These include Microsoft's Visual FoxPro and Oracle Corporation's (**http://www.oracle.com**) Oracle databases. ODBC is covered in the section "Open Database Connectivity (ODBC)" later in this chapter.*

## Microsoft Access

If you are new to relational databases, Access is an excellent place to start. It contains a number of features, such as wizards, that guide you through the process of creating relational databases. Access is a good choice for a small office intranet. You can also use Access to develop your databases and then upsize them to SQL Server using its Upsizing Wizard. Access 2003 was used to develop the database that will be used in the examples in this chapter. Access is still a desktop database, however, designed for single users. It is not a real client/server database, like SQL Server, so it is of limited use for web applications.

**TIP** *A few excellent resources for learning more about Access are* Access 2002: The Complete Reference *and* How to Do Everything with Access 2002, *both by Virginia Andersen (McGraw-Hill/Osborne, 2001).*

## Microsoft SQL Server

SQL Server is a *Structured Query Language (SQL)* database. SQL (pronounced "sequel") is a programming language for creating, managing, and querying large relational databases. SQL Server can easily handle millions of records and tens of thousands of queries per day. For large corporations, this is a common scenario. It lacks Access' interface and is not so user-friendly. However, you can use Access as a front end to SQL Server tables (the back end). This gives you the best of both worlds.

**NOTE** *A good example of SQL Server in action can be found at **http://terraserver.microsoft.com/**, an online database of aerial photographs and maps of the United States. On an average day, about 40,000 people visit the site, and more than 4.4 million database queries are generated. The current peak day had over 277,000 visitors and 12 million database queries.*

A detailed discussion of SQL Server is beyond the scope of this book, nor is it necessary in order to understand how to integrate databases into your webs. You should understand, though, that any serious database work requires a serious database programmer. Large databases, such as SQL Server, are complex applications, and while the basic concepts of relational databases are easy to understand, in actual use the design of the database structure can be quite complex. This is an important point. Poor relational database design will haunt you, and, as more records are added to the database, the problems will become harder to resolve. Just as a building has to have a properly constructed foundation, so must your database.

**TIP** *You can learn more about SQL Server and other large relational databases, as well as ways to gain a better understanding of how to design relational databases, from* SQL: The Complete Reference, *by James R. Groff and Paul N. Weinberg (McGraw-Hill/Osborne, 2002).*

## Open Database Connectivity (ODBC)

The Open Database Connectivity standard was developed as a way to allow databases to be accessed by different programs—not just the database program that created the data. For example, by using ODBC, you can access a database file using Microsoft Word. This is an important feature for organizations that have data in a number of different database formats, as well as for using databases on the Web. In effect, the ODBC driver is an interpreter between the data stored in the database and the program that is querying the data.

To use an ODBC-compliant database on the Web or with a database program other than the one that created the database itself, the proper ODBC driver must be installed. In the case of web-based databases, the ODBC driver for the database being used must be installed on the web server. To run the examples you will create in this chapter, you will need the Access ODBC driver installed on your computer. This driver, along with ODBC drivers for other popular database programs, can be found on the Windows CD, and on Microsoft's web site at **http://www.microsoft.com/data/download.htm**.

---

***TIP*** *It's important to use the latest ODBC drivers and to make sure you test your application with the same versions as are on the server. Patches and security updates should also be installed when released.*

You can check what ODBC drivers you have installed and the versions with these steps:

1. Open Start | Administrative Tools | Data Sources (ODBC). For Windows 2000 and XP, open Start | Control Panel | Administrative Tools | Data Sources (ODBC).

2. In the ODBC Data Source Administrator dialog box, click the Drivers tab, shown here:

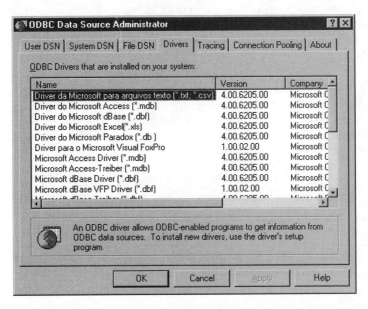

3. Click Cancel to close the ODBC Data Source Administrator dialog box.

As you can see, a number of ODBC drivers are installed by default with Windows. The Access driver is also updated through Windows Update, so you shouldn't have any problems with it.

## How the Web Server Handles a Request

When a web browser makes a database request (by requesting a page with a database call), a number of things happen before the data is returned and displayed by the browser:

1. The request for a database page is sent by the browser to the web server.
2. The web server reads the requested page and passes the name of the data source and the SQL statement to the ODBC driver.
3. The ODBC driver executes the SQL statement on the specified data source.
4. The data source returns the results of the SQL statement to the ODBC driver.
5. The ODBC driver passes the query results to the web server.
6. The web server formats the query results and sends the file to the web browser.

With a properly configured server with adequate resources, the delay introduced by this process is unnoticeable to the user. This is one reason Microsoft's Access database and other desktop databases are unsuitable for large-volume web sites—they cannot process multiple database queries fast enough. Another bottleneck is the server's hard drive. Database work involves numerous database file reads. Slow hard drives will also be unable to process requests quickly enough for the process to remain transparent to the user when the server is experiencing high traffic volumes. If at all possible, use a client/server database, such as SQL Server, and fast hard drives, such as Fast-Wide SCSI drives. This doesn't mean Access can't be used, only that you should be aware of its limitations and be prepared to upsize it if traffic warrants.

## Data Source Name (DSN)

A *Data Source Name (DSN)* allows a user with the correct permissions to use a database over a network. This can be an intranet, extranet, or the Internet. The DSN contains the location and type of database, the time-out and other system values, and the username and password. There are three types of data source names:

- **User**   Allows a single user on the local computer to access a data source
- **File**   Allows all users with the same ODBC drivers installed to access a data source
- **System**   Allows all users to access a data source

---

**TIP**   *The File DSN is a plain text file, which is easily transported between computers. This makes it useful while you're developing applications.*

There are several ways you can define a DSN to use a database with FrontPage. When you import a database file into a FrontPage web (in the section "The FrontPage Database Interface Wizard") and add it to a web, you will be prompted for the database location as part of that process. FrontPage will then create the DSN in the Global.asa file. You can also set a System DSN, using the Windows Control Panel. You will use FrontPage's DSN in the following sections.

---

**NOTE**    *In FrontPage, a DSN is also called a* database connection. *These terms are used interchangeably in this chapter, but in general use, DSN is preferred.*

A web application does not care where the database is physically located or what type of database it is, as long as it has a valid DSN and the correct ODBC drivers are installed. Depending on the database program you are using, you may not be able to import the file into your FrontPage web. Access databases can be easily moved around, but this is much harder to do, if not impossible, with a database program such as SQL Server. With Access, a database is a single file that can be copied and moved like any other file. With SQL Server, a database is a collection of files that cannot be moved easily, similar to an application. With larger web sites, the database program may be running on its own server, creating a situation where it's physically impossible to have the database itself as part of the FrontPage web.

There's also the question of accessing the database for updates and maintenance. For a small web with a few hundred visitors a day, an Access database that is part of the FrontPage web is a viable solution. The database can be maintained on a local computer and uploaded to the server as needed. As the web grows, and traffic increases, this solution may start to provide unacceptable results. It may then be necessary to upsize the database to a more robust database program. This creates its own problems since it may require access to the server that your web presence provider, for valid security reasons, is unwilling to provide. This could add a step between you and your database, requiring you to go through your provider for certain database tasks. These issues will have to be resolved with your web presence provider.

One of the benefits of the DSN system is that these changes will not necessarily mean major changes to your web application. Since the database is referenced through the DSN, not its physical location or type, only the DSN properties would need to be updated.

## The FrontPage Database Interface Wizard

Now that you've learned the basics of how databases are integrated into webs, it's time to put theory into practice. In this section, you will first import an Access database and then create a web using the Database Interface Wizard. You will need to download the North Beach Tools database (NorthBeachTools.mdb) from the Osborne FTP site with these steps:

1. In your web browser, open Osborne's web site at **http://osborne.com**.

2. On the Osborne home page, click the Free Code link.

3. On the Free Downloads page, find the title of this book, *Microsoft Office FrontPage 2003: The Complete Reference*.

4. Download either the Access 2000 or 2003 version of the file NorthBeachTools.mdb to your desktop.

Now you are ready to create your database web with these steps:

1. In the FrontPage New task pane, select More Web Site Templates.

2. In the Web Site Templates dialog box General tab, select Database Interface Wizard.

3. In the Specify The Location Of The New Web Site text box, type **http://localhost/ NorthBeach**. This cannot be a disk-based web and must be opened using the URL. The URL should be http://localhost/NorthBeach or http://*computer_name*/ NorthBeach. By default, the path is C:\Inetpub\wwwroot\NorthBeach. (In the figures in this chapter, a computer named Joey is being used, so the URL is http:// joey/NorthBeach.)

4. Click OK. FrontPage creates the web and then displays the Database Interface Wizard, shown in Figure 17-2. Before you can use the Database Interface Wizard, you need to add the NorthBeachTools database to your web and create the data connection.

5. Click Cancel to close the Database Interface Wizard.

6. Select File | Import. In the Import dialog box, select Add File.

7. In the Add File To Import List dialog box, navigate to where you saved the database you downloaded from the Osborne web site and select **NorthBeachTools.mdb**. Click Open and then OK. The Add Database Connection dialog box, shown next, is displayed.

**FIGURE 17-2**
Database
Interface Wizard

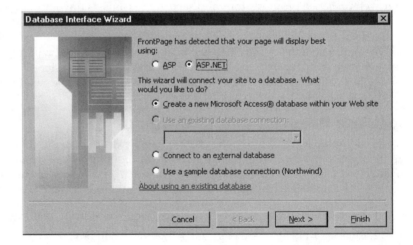

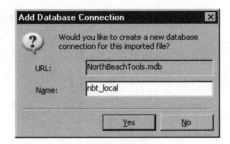

8. Type **nbt_local** in the Name text box and then click Yes.

   The function of the Add Database Connection dialog box is to create a DSN (or database connection) for the database. FrontPage does this by adding the DSN properties to the Global.asa file. (If you open your Global.asa file, you will see the changes made.) This method has the advantage of being very simple for the user to implement. The disadvantage is that the DSN is only valid for the web application that uses that Global.asa file. This can create a problem if you need to access the database using a DSN from outside the web application. This situation may arise in a network environment where the database may be accessed from several workstations. A System DSN is a better choice in that case.

9. A message box is displayed recommending that your database be stored in the folder "fpdb", which FrontPage creates automatically (if it doesn't already exist) when you import a database file. Click Yes.

   The fpdb folder is the preferred location for file databases (such as Access—SQL Server cannot be stored in a single file) in a FrontPage web. The only difference between this folder and any other folder you might create is the default permissions assigned to it. When you create a new folder, the default permissions allow scripts to be run and allow the contents of the folder to be browsed. You can see this by checking the properties of the folder.

10. Right-click the root folder (http://*computer_name*/NorthBeach) and choose Properties.

11. In the NorthBeach Properties dialog box, shown in Figure 17-3, the Allow Scripts To Be Run and Allow Files To Be Browsed check boxes are selected. New folders inherit the permissions of their root folder. In this case, the root folder has both script and browsing permissions. This dialog box allows you to change the permissions for a folder.

---

***T***IP   *On your local computer, the Allow Files To Be Browsed check box can be selected, but your production web should not allow file browsing. File browsing permits Internet users to read the file structure of your web server. It's a significant security issue, and one you should be aware of.*

**FIGURE 17-3**
The NorthBeach web properties dialog box

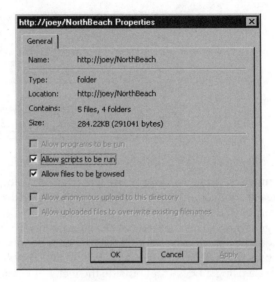

Your database folder, however, should not allow either of these permissions. You want to keep your database itself as far from the public as you can. This is one reason you may not want your database to be included in your FrontPage web if at all possible. When FrontPage creates the fpdb folder, by default it will not allow either script or browsing permissions. You can check this by looking at the properties of the fpdb folder.

12. Click Cancel to close the dialog box.

    Next, you need to reopen the Database Interface Wizard and finish the configuration of your database web.

13. In the New task pane, click More Web Site Templates. In the Web Site Templates dialog box General tab, select Database Interface Wizard.

14. Select the Add To Current Web Site check box and click OK.

15. In the Database Interface Wizard, select the ASP.NET and Use An Existing Database Connection option buttons. Click Next.

16. In the Select The Table Or View You Would Like To Use For This Database Connection drop-down list, select Products. Accept the default in the Specify A Location For The New Files and click Next.

    The next step in the Database Interface Wizard displays the fields or columns that are in the database table you selected previously. You may need to define a primary key (the unique identifier for each record) for the table. The database itself has a primary key defined, but this piece of information isn't always recognized by FrontPage, so you may need to also set it here.

17. Suppose you get an error message stating, "There is no primary key defined." If so, click Yes, then select ProductID and click Modify. In the Database Interface Wizard dialog box displayed, shown here, select the Primary Key check box and click OK.

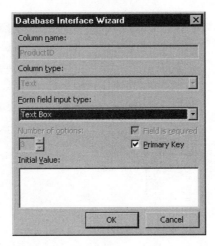

18. Click Next. In the next step of the Database Interface Wizard, select all three check boxes: Results Page, Submission Form, and Database Editor. Click Next.

    The next step in the Database Interface Wizard allows you to set a username and password to access the database for editing. To keep things simple, select the Don't Protect My Submission Page Or My Database Editor With A Username And Password check box. Click Next; then click Finish. Figure 17-4 shows the competed Database Editor page in FrontPage.

19. Select File | Preview In Browser. Figure 17-5 shows the Database Editor page in Internet Explorer.

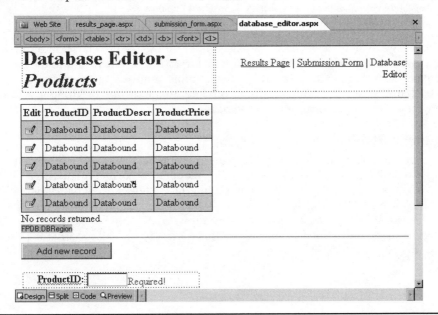

**FIGURE 17-4**    Database Editor page in FrontPage Design view

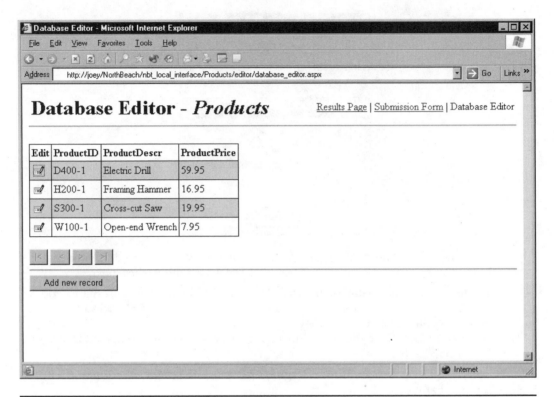

**FIGURE 17-5**     FrontPage Database Editor page in Internet Explorer

In FrontPage Design view, you see a placeholder for the recordset. If you scroll down the page, you will also see the fields and buttons for adding a new record to the database. These are not displayed on the page in Internet Explorer unless you select the Add New Record button. You will be adding a new record later in the section "Writing to a Database," but first you will do some formatting of the pages.

## Formatting a Database Interface Page

When you are working with plain HTML pages in FrontPage, formatting is as simple as selecting text and applying formatting from the menu bar or Format menu. It's a bit different when you are working with Database Interface pages since what is displayed is actually an ASP.NET DataGrid. To change the formatting, you must modify the properties of the DataGrid. When the page is loaded into a browser, ASP.NET generates the HTML on the server, using the defined properties. In this exercise, you will modify the properties of the Results page with these steps:

1. In FrontPage, open the Results page (results_page.aspx) in Design view. The page should already be open so you can select the results_page.aspx tab.

2. Right-click the Database Results Region (the table), shown here, and select Format Results Region. This opens the Format Results Region dialog box, shown in Figure 17-6. This dialog box allows you to format the Database Results Region by setting the table, header, and footer settings:

| ProductID | ProductDescr | ProductPrice |
|-----------|--------------|--------------|
| Databound | Databound | Databound |
| Databound | Databound | Databound |
| Databound | Databound | Databound |
| Databound | Databound | Databound |
| Databound | Databound | Databound |

No records returned. FPDB:DBRegion

3. In the Format Results Region dialog box, click Edit Columns.

4. In the Edit Columns dialog box, shown next, select ProductID in the Columns list box; then change the title for the first column by typing **Product Number** in the Header Text text box. Change the second column heading to **Description** and the third column heading to **Price**. Click OK twice. The appearance of the DataGrid in Design view will change after these modifications. All that will be displayed is a

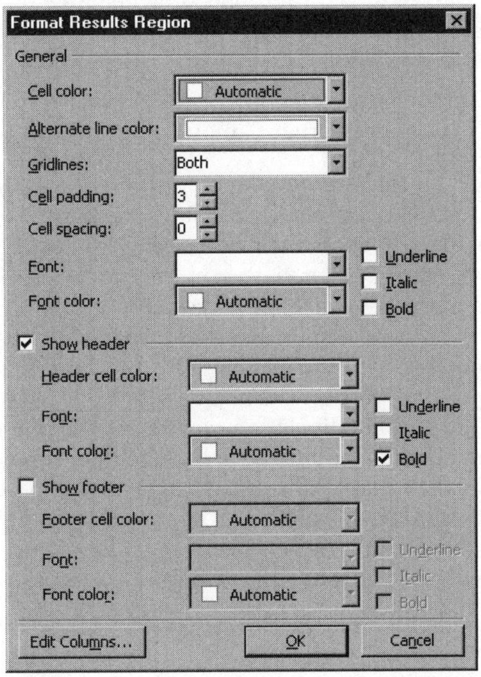

PART III

**FIGURE 17-6**
Format Results
Region dialog box

placeholder with the text "ASP.NET Control: DataGrid." The page will still be displayed properly in your browser.

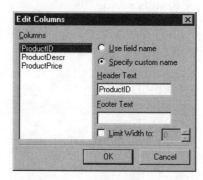

5. Switch to Code view and find this line on the page (it should be line 40 or close to it):

```
<asp:BoundColumn DataField="ProductPrice" HeaderText="Price"/>
```

6. Place the cursor between the closing quote for the HeaderText and the forward slash (/), and then press SPACEBAR. Select ItemStyle-HorizontalAlign from the IntelliSense list, type an = sign, and double-click Right from the IntelliSense list. Your line of code should now look like this:

```
<asp:BoundColumn DataField="ProductPrice" HeaderText="Price"
ItemStyle-HorizontalAlign=Right/>
```

7. Switch to Design view and select the heading "Results Page." Type **All Products**. If you select more than the text itself, you will lose the formatting. If that happens, press CTRL-Z to undo your edit and reselect only the text.

8. Save your work and then open File | Preview In Browser. Figure 17-7 shows the All Products page in Internet Explorer.

In FrontPage, you saw placeholders for the selected fields. In your browser, the actual data in the database table is displayed. Since the page is a mixture of both HTML and ASP.NET, some items, such as the text heading, can be directly edited in Design view. To format the DataGrid in Design view, you use the Format Results Region dialog box. In Code view, you can edit the code directly, as you did by changing the horizontal alignment in the Price cells. Many more options are available in Code view than are exposed by the Format Results Region dialog box. The Database Results region will automatically create as many rows as are required to display the results set.

What you had to do to display the contents of the Products table on a web page was relatively simple. If you want to take a look behind the scenes, open the _fpclass folder and look at its files. ASP.NET is a powerful programming paradigm, but it's not the simplest to work with in its raw form. FrontPage's user interface greatly simplifies the amount of work required to get the benefits of the technology.

Next you will learn how to write to a database using a web browser interface.

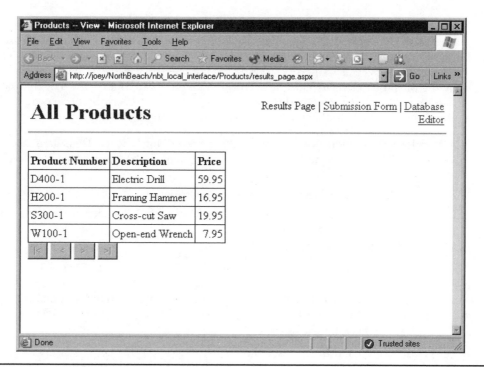

**FIGURE 17-7**    All Products page in Internet Explorer

## Writing to a Database

There are a number of scenarios in which you would want the user to be able to write to a database on your web server—for example, a user survey where the user answers a series of questions. If users write their responses directly to a database, you can easily compile and analyze the results. An organization may have a number of remote staff people who need to access and update a database. This might be a business where salespeople need to record sales data from remote locations, such as the customer's place of business. You also need a means for database administrators to update information in the database. Administrators will have much greater access than a regular user.

---

*NOTE    Allowing a user to write to a database on your web server raises some serious security concerns. Authorized users, such as employees, can be given this type of access with methods that are more secure than using a web interface. One simple method using the Web is to have the database that is written to located separately, with its own DSN, rather than in the main database. At regular intervals, the two databases could be synchronized. How to do this will depend on the database application. If no public access to the database is required, there are network methods that use the Internet without a web interface, such as a Virtual Private Network (VPN). These techniques are beyond the scope of this book, however. In this chapter, security is being left open to simplify the exercises. In a production scenario, security should be much tighter. Database security is a complex issue, and you will need the services of a good database administrator (DBA) to configure it properly.*

In this next exercise, you will use the two pages FrontPage created—the Submission Form page and the Database Editor—to add a product to the North Beach Tools database. The Submission page allows you to add a product record, while the Database Editor allows you to add records as well as to modify existing records. Security issues will be kept to a minimum; the purpose here is to learn how FrontPage's database tools work. The Internet user account, IUSR_*computername* by default, must be given write permission in order for a web user to be able to write to the database. Do that now with these steps:

1. In Windows Explorer or My Computer, locate your North Beach Tools database. The location will be C:\Inetpub\wwwroot\NorthBeach\fpdb\NorthBeachTools.mdb, unless you installed it elsewhere.

2. Right-click NorthBeachTools.mdb and choose Properties.

3. In the NorthBeachTools.mdb Properties dialog box, select the Security tab, shown in Figure 17-8. The server Administrators group has full control of the file.

> **NOTE** *The permission settings explained here are for Windows Server 2003 (Windows 2000 Professional and Windows 2000 Server are very similar) with NTFS-formatted drives (rather than FAT32) and without Active Directory configured. The permissions on Active Directory servers are configured differently, though the results are similar. If your drives are not formatted with NTFS, there won't be a Security tab.*

4. Select Users in the Group Or User Names list. This should appear as Users (*computer_name*\Users). This group has much less permission than the Administrators group.

**FIGURE 17-8**
NorthBeachTools.
mdb Properties
dialog box
Security tab

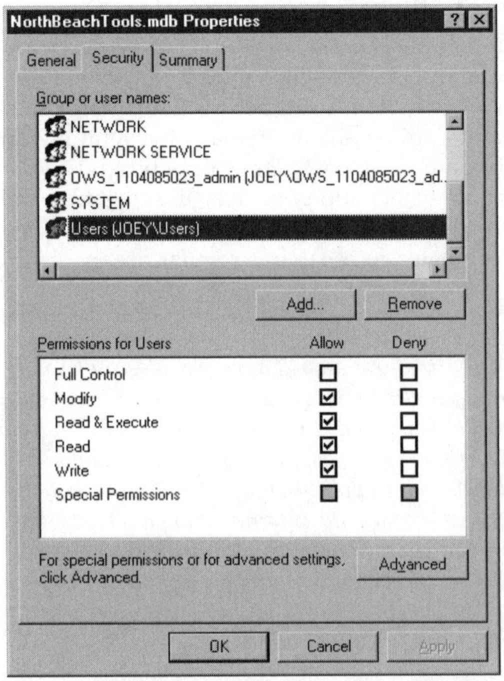

For the purpose of this exercise, you will give this account permission to write to the database file. In real life, it will be up to your ISP to correctly configure database permissions, as configuring permissions requires Administrator permission on the web server.

5. Select the Modify check box under Allow. This will also select the Write check box. Click Apply and then OK.

   With your permission issues taken care of, you are ready to add a record to the Products table in your North Beach Tools database.

6. In FrontPage, open the Submission Form page (submission_form.aspx) in Design view. It should appear similar to Figure 17-9.

   FrontPage has created a very complete page that requires little or no modification on your part, with the exception of any formatting you wish to add. Notice the text "Required!" after the ProductID text box and the text "Invalid!" after the ProductPrice text box. These are the error messages that will be displayed if the data entered in either text box is invalid—FrontPage has already created the form validation. Below the form, the text "[Place holder for page error messages]" indicates where other error messages (such as database errors) will be displayed using an ASP:Label control.

7. Select the Required! text and switch to Code view. A line of code beginning with "<asp:RequiredFieldValidator…" should be selected (at or close to line 92). When the page is loaded, the JavaScript code for client-side validation will be generated from this ASP.NET server control.

8. Open the Submission Form page in Internet Explorer, as shown in Figure 17-10. Notice that the error messages are not displayed in the browser.

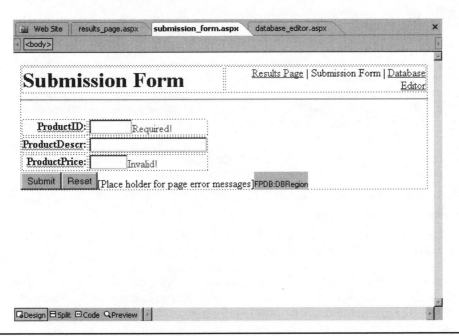

**FIGURE 17-9**    Submission Form in Design view

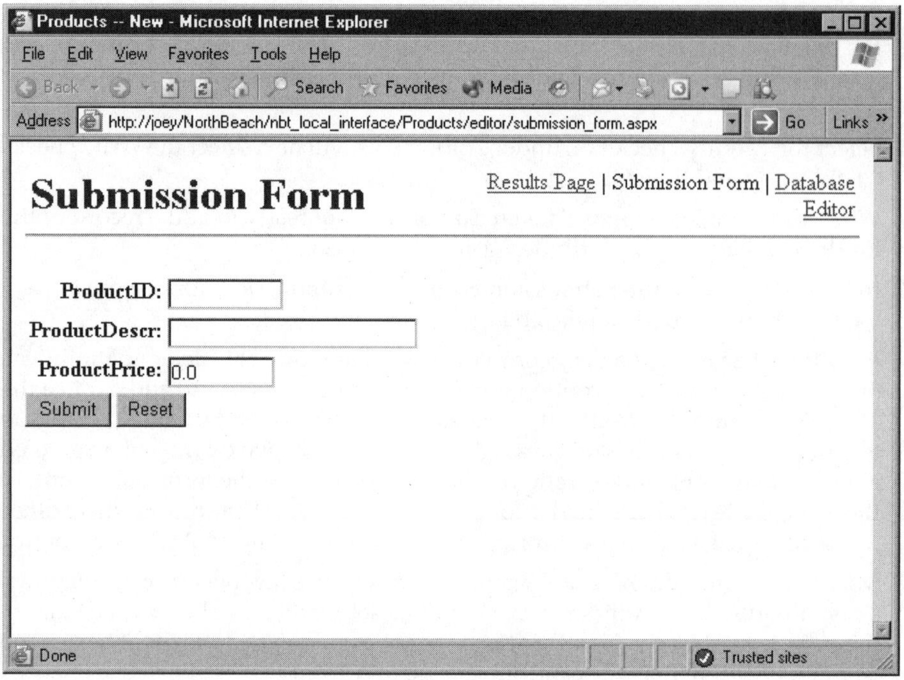

**FIGURE 17-10** Submission Form in Internet Explorer

9. In Internet Explorer, click the Submit button.

   The Required! error message is now displayed. The Invalid! message is not displayed because the field validation is only checking for numbers separated by a decimal point, so 0.0 (the default value) doesn't generate an error. If you needed all the products in the database to have a price greater than 0.0, you would need to change this. You do need more validation on the ProductID, however, as the database field is only eight characters long, and the page will allow you to submit much more than that. This will generate a database error, which is not as easily handled as a form validation error.

10. In FrontPage, open the Submission Form page in Design view. Select the ProductID text box and switch to Code view. The line of code

    ```
    <asp:TextBox ID="txtProductID" Columns="8" Runat="server" />
    ```

    should be selected (at or close to line 91).

11. Place your cursor after the closing quote in Columns="8" and press SPACEBAR. Type **MaxLength="8"**. Save your work.

**TIP** *This is an easy way to limit the input to a specified number of characters. You could also do this, with much greater control, using RegularExpressionValidator, as is used on the ProductPrice text box. The .NET Framework documentation (see Chapter 16) contains complete information on using the RegularExpressionValidator.*

12. Select File | Preview In Browser.

13. In your browser, type **S400-1** in the ProductID text box and press TAB.

14. Type **Radial-arm Saw** in the ProductDescr text box and press TAB.

15. Type **129.75** in the ProductPrice text box and click Submit. The All Products page, shown in Figure 17-11, will open in your browser.

This illustrates one of the prime advantages of a database-driven web—a change made to information in the database will appear on your web pages the next time they are loaded, without any further human intervention. In the next exercise, you will modify a record using the Database Editor page. Begin with these steps:

1. In FrontPage, open the Database Editor page (database_editor.aspx) in Design view.

2. Select File | Preview In Browser. The Database Editor should be similar to Figure 17-12. The DataGrid appears similar to the product listing in your All Products page with the addition of a column on the left labeled "Edit." The column headers and cell alignment are also the defaults, as you only modified the All Products page.

3. Click the icon in the Edit column for the Cross-cut Saw record. At the bottom of the page (you may have to scroll down to see them), text boxes for the ProductDescr and ProductPrice fields are now displayed.

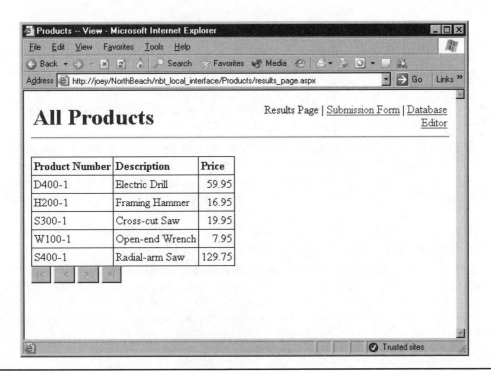

**FIGURE 17-11**    All Products page in Internet Explorer with the Radial-arm Saw added to the database

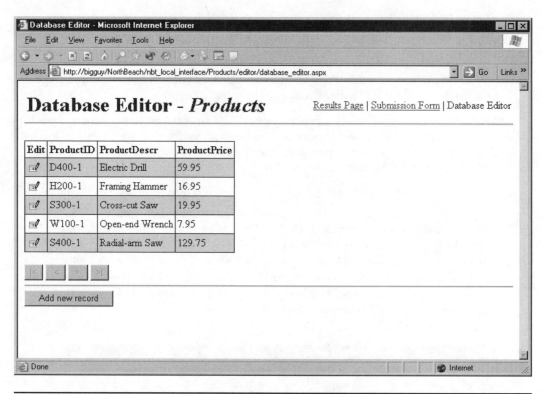

**FIGURE 17-12**    Database Editor in Internet Explorer

4. Change the ProductPrice to **21.95** and click Apply Changes. The Database Editor page is reloaded with the new price for the Cross-cut Saw.

5. Open the All Products page in your browser. Your price update will be displayed. Refresh your browser if necessary.

6. Open the Database Editor in your browser and click Add New Record. Text boxes for the ProductID, ProductDescr, and ProductPrice are displayed at the bottom of the page.

7. In the ProductID text box, type **H300-1**. In the ProductDescr text box, type **Tack Hammer**. In the ProductPrice text box, type **14.95**. Click Apply Changes.

The Database Editor will reload, but the new record is not visible. This is because, by default, only five records per page are being displayed. If you open the All Products page, you will see the same thing. The only indication that this is what's happening is the fact that the two rightmost buttons underneath the DataGrid are no longer grayed out, as shown here. Click either button—the arrow pointing to the right displays the next record, and the arrow with the vertical bar displays the last record, which in this case are the same. Unfortunately, there isn't an easy way to make the fact that the recordset is being paged (broken into segments) visible to the user. The code that controls the buttons is buried in the _fpclass folder. However, there is a way to change the number of records that will be displayed on each page.

1. Open the All Products page in Design view, right-click the DataGrid, and then select Database Results Properties.

2. Without changing any of the settings displayed, click Next four times. This brings up the paging page of the Database Results Wizard, shown here:

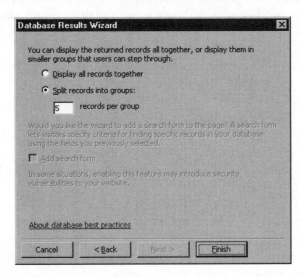

3. Select the Display All Records Together option and click Finish.

4. Save your work and then select File | Preview In Browser. All the records now appear in the DataGrid. If you have the All Products page already open in a browser, clicking Refresh may not show the change, as the recordset is being cached.

As you can see, quite a bit of functionality has been created with relatively few steps using the Database Interface Wizard.

Before moving on to building a database-driven web with SharePoint 2, you need to create a home page for your North Beach Tools web and add some navigation links. Do that with these steps:

1. In FrontPage, create a new normal page in Design view. Save the page with the title **North Beach Tools** and the filename **Default.htm** in the NorthBeach web root directory.

2. At the top of the page, type **North Beach Tools** and format it as Heading 1. Press ENTER.

3. Type **Products** and format it as Heading 2. Move the cursor to the next line and click Bullets on the toolbar.

4. Type **View All Products** and press ENTER.

5. Type **Add a Product** and press ENTER.

6. Type **Modify or Delete a Product** and press ENTER.

7. Click Bullets to end the bulleted list.

8. Select View All Products and click Insert Hyperlink.

9. In the Insert Hyperlink dialog box, select nbt_local_interface/Products/results_page.aspx and click OK.

10. Select "Add a Product" and click Insert Hyperlink. In the Insert Hyperlink dialog box, select nbt_local_interface/Products/editor/submission_form.aspx and click OK.

11. Select "Modify or Delete a Product" and click Insert Hyperlink. In the Insert Hyperlink dialog box, select nbt_local_interface/Products/editor/database_editor.aspx and click OK.

12. Save your page and then open your All Products page (results_page.aspx) in Design view, if it's not already open.

13. Place your cursor immediately before the text "Results Page" in the upper-right corner of the page.

14. Type **Home** | leaving a space before and after the pipe symbol ( | ). Select Home and click Insert Hyperlink.

15. In the Insert Hyperlink dialog box, click the Up One Folder button, select Default.htm in the root directory, and click OK. Save your work.

16. Repeat steps 13 through 15 for the Submission Form and Database Editor pages. You can also use Copy and Paste to add all the links to the Submission Form and Database Editor pages.

17. Open the home page in your browser and check that your navigation links work.

Your North Beach Tools web using FrontPage and FP Server Extensions is now complete. In the next section, you will learn how to build a database-driven web using SharePoint 2.

## Working with SharePoint Web Parts

SharePoint 2 is the latest iteration of SharePoint from Microsoft. The original SharePoint Team Services (STS or SharePoint 1) was compatible with Front Page Server Extensions (FPSE), but this is not the case with Windows SharePoint Services (WSS or SharePoint2). In giving up the FPSE, you actually gain functionality in some areas. SharePoint 2 is built upon the .NET Framework—which is the source of the improved functionality. Unfortunately, FPSE and SharePoint 2 don't play well together, so you can only have one active on your server. Appendix A covers installing SharePoint 2, which you will need to complete the rest of this chapter.

### The OLEDB Connection

The first change in working with SharePoint 2 is that you will use an OLEDB connection to the database. OLEDB is designed to be used with a variety of data sources—not just databases. These other data sources include XML files, spreadsheets, and so forth. OLEDB is also a more direct path to the data source, which means that it is faster in operation. An OLEDB connection string has four keywords, shown in Table 17-2.

**TABLE 17-2**
OLEDB Connection
String Keywords

| Keyword | Description |
|---------|-------------|
| Provider | The name of the OLEDB provider |
| Data Source | The filename and path of the data source |
| User ID | The username that will access the data source |
| Password | The password for the username that will access the data source |

In the following sections, you will work with the North Beach Tools database using SharePoint 2 rather than FPSE. This will show you some of the practical differences between the technologies. Again, the first step is to import the database you will use. Begin with these steps:

1. In Windows Explorer or My Computer, create a new folder named **data** in your default web directory. The default path is C:\Inetpub\wwwroot\, so the full path would be C:\Inetpub\wwroot\data. The database for this exercise will be placed here, so, in production, this folder should be secured. For these exercises, it will be left with the default settings.

2. In your web browser, open Osborne's web site at **http://osborne.com**.

3. On the Osborne home page, click the Free Code link.

4. On the Free Downloads page, find the title of this book, *Microsoft Office FrontPage 2003: The Complete Reference*.

5. Download either the Access 2000 or 2003 version of the file NorthBeachTools.mdb to your data folder created in step 1.

6. Right-click NorthBeachTools.mdb and select Properties.

7. In the NorthBeachTools.mdb Properties dialog box, select the Security tab.

8. Select Users in the Group Or User Names list. This should appear as Users (*computer_name*\Users). If you don't have a Users group in your Security tab, you can add it by clicking Add, typing **Users** in the Enter The Object Names To Select text box, clicking Check Names, and then click OK.

   For the purpose of this exercise, you will give this account permission to write to the database file. In real life, it will be up to your ISP to correctly configure database permissions, as configuring permissions requires Administrator permission on the web server.

9. Select the Modify check box under Allow. This will also select the Write check box. Click Apply and then OK.

Your database is now properly configured for you to add it to the SharePoint Data Source Catalog.

## The SharePoint Data Source Catalog

The OLEDB connection, which you will create in this section, allows more than just databases to be used as a data source. XML files, spreadsheets, and so forth, can all be used. To manage these data sources, FrontPage has the Data Source Catalog, shown in Figure 17-13. For this exercise you will create a Database Connection using OLEDB, but the steps are similar for the other data sources. Create your SharePoint database connection with these steps:

1. In FrontPage, create a new One Page Web Site named **NorthBeach_SP**.

2. Open View | Task Pane if the Task Pane isn't visible, and select Data Source Catalog from the list of task panes. (Click the down arrow next to the task pane title to see the list).

3. Expand the Database Connections list, as shown in Figure 17-13, to the right, and click Add To Catalog.

4. In the Data Source Properties dialog box, click Configure Database Connection. The Configure Database Connection dialog box, shown below, is displayed:

**FIGURE 17-13**
Data Source Catalog task pane

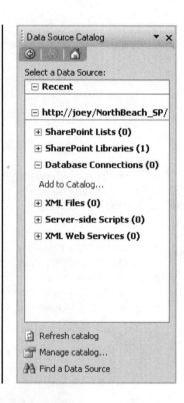

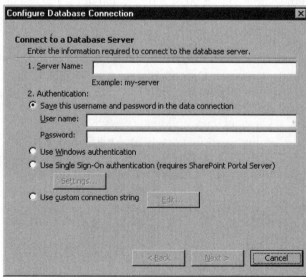

This dialog box allows you to create a connection to a database. If you are using a server-based database, such as SQL Server, you would enter the name of the server in the Server Name text box. You have several options for authentication—storing the username/password combination in the connection string, using Windows authentication, and (if SharePoint Portal Server is installed) using a single username/password for server authentication. However, this exercise is using a file-based database, Access, so you will create the connection string manually.

5. Select the Use Custom Connection String option; then click Edit.

6. In the Edit Connection String dialog box, type

   **Provider=Microsoft.Jet.OLEDB.4.0;Data**
   **Source=c:\Inetpub\wwwroot\data\NorthBeachTools.mdb;**

   as shown here, and click OK. To keep things simple, the database isn't protected by a password. In a production environment, you would have a username/password combination for the database.

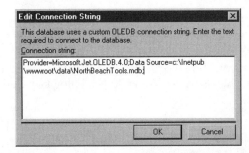

7. Click Next. A warning that the custom connection string stores the username and password as clear text is displayed. Click OK.

8. In the next page of the Configure Database Connection Wizard, select Products in the Table, View Or Stored Procedure list, and then click Finish.

9. In the Data Source Properties dialog box Source tab, click Fields. In the Displayed Fields dialog box, shown here, select ProductDescr in the Displayed Fields list, and click Move Up:

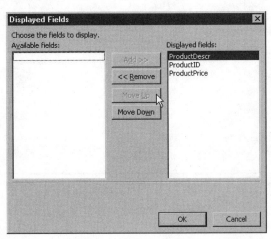

10. Click OK twice to close the Data Source Properties dialog box.

## Adding and Formatting a Data View

Now that you have a valid database connection, you will add it to your SharePoint web with these steps:

1. Rename the home page (default.htm) to **default.aspx**. Click Yes in the Confirm Rename dialog box that's displayed.

2. Open your home page in Design view, then type **North Beach Tools** at the top of the page, and format it as Heading 2. Press ENTER.

3. From the Data Source Catalog task pane, drag Products On Root to your new page. Your page should look similar to Figure 17-14.

4. Save your work and select File | Preview In Browser. You may need to supply a password to see the page.

   The database information is displayed in a very basic format, as shown in Figure 17-15. Using the Data View Details task pane, you can modify the style of the Data view, filter the output, and sort and group the results.

5. In FrontPage, with your home page in Design view, click Style in the Data View Details task pane. This opens the View Styles dialog box General tab, shown in Figure 17-16.

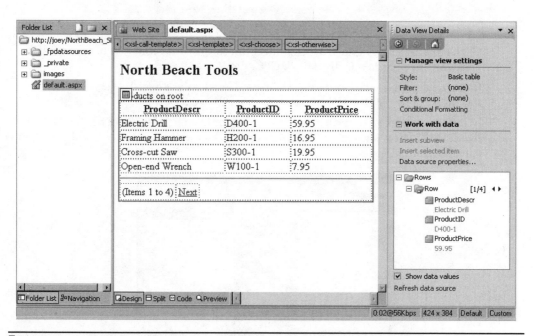

**FIGURE 17-14**   North Beach Tools home page in Design view with Data View added

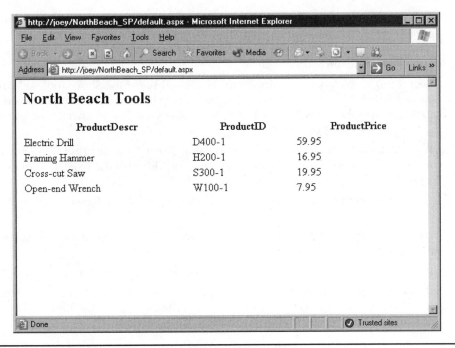

**FIGURE 17-15**    North Beach Tools home page in Internet Explorer

**FIGURE 17-16**
View Styles dialog
box General tab

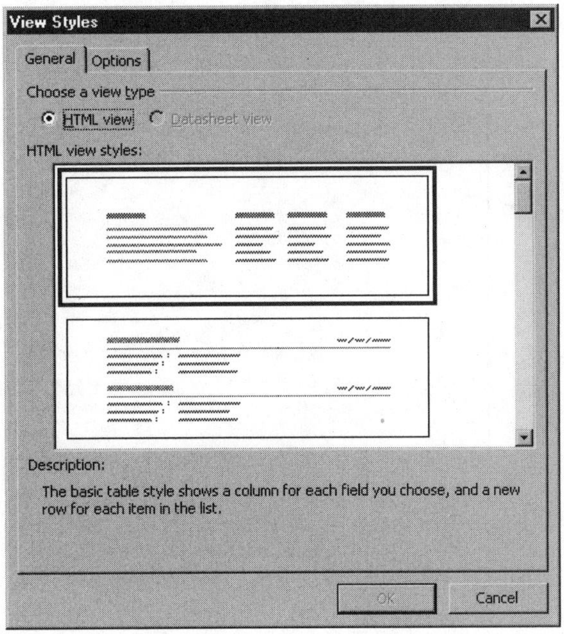

6. Scroll through the list of HTML View Styles to get an idea of the prebuilt formatting options. When you select an option, the description of the option appears below the HTML View Styles list. Scroll back to the top of the list and select the second option—the repeating form style.

7. Select the Options tab, shown in Figure 17-17, and select the Show Toolbar With Options For check box. The Filter, Sort, and Group check boxes should also be selected. Select the Show View Header and Show View Footer check boxes, and the Display All Items option button.

8. Click OK, then Yes to acknowledge any custom formatting or provider Web Part connections will be removed, and save your page. Refresh the page in your browser—it should appear similar to Figure 17-18.

9. In the Sort By drop-down, select ProductPrice. The listing will be reorganized by price.

10. In the Group By drop-down, select ProductDescr. The listing will be reorganized by the product description.

11. Click Filter to show the Filter Choices drop-down lists, as shown in Figure 17-19.

12. Select different values in the drop-downs to see the effect on the display. After each change, you will need to select Change Filter to expose the Filter Choices drop-down lists.

**FIGURE 17-17**
View Styles dialog
box Options tab

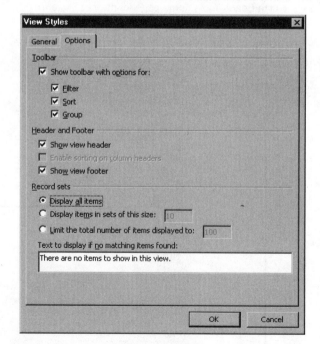

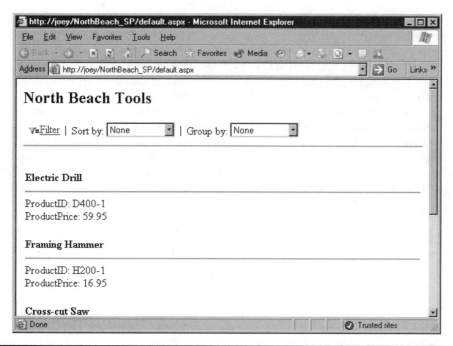

**FIGURE 17-18**    North Beach Tools home page in Internet Explorer in a repeating form style

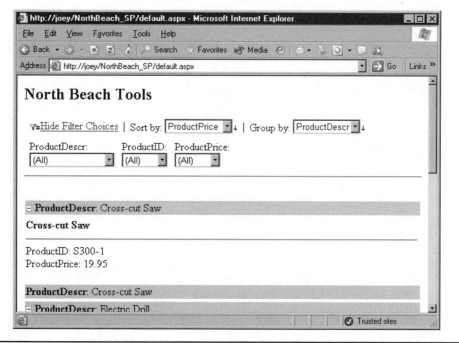

**FIGURE 17-19**    Filter Choices drop-down lists on North Beach Tools home page

You're using a very small database, so the sorting features don't have a lot of records to reorganize. However, the functionality that you've created for this database will work just as well with a database with thousands of records.

Now that you've seen how easy it is to add database functionality using ASP.NET technologies, the next step in exploiting the power of SharePoint 2 would be to incorporate the database in a SharePoint Team Site or workspace for use on a corporate intranet. In Chapter 22, you will see how to add a link to a Team Site. (In this case you would just create a link to http://localhost/NorthBeach_SP to see the North Beach Tools database.)

The examples in this chapter have barely scratched the surface of what you can do with FrontPage, ASP.NET, SharePoint 2, and the Web. It has been an introduction designed to give you some ideas about the possibilities of integrating databases into your webs. FrontPage streamlines the task of creating database pages, but a thorough knowledge of a scripting language, SQL programming, and relational database theory are still essential. These subjects are beyond the scope of this book, however. If you don't have these skills yourself, consider finding a good relational database programmer who can help make your ideas a reality. More and more, the creation of world-class web sites is becoming a team effort.

CHAPTER

# 18

# Activating Your Webs

The World Wide Web has come a long way since the ability to create hyperlinks between documents was a revolutionary technology. Today's web browsers support animation, video, and audio files integrated into webs, but even these advances have been overshadowed. You've seen how JavaScript, VBScript, and ASP.NET produce true interactivity on the Web. Java and ActiveX further expand your horizons. Java applets and ActiveX controls are computer programs that can be downloaded to and then executed on your computer by your web browser, or can be run on the server in the same manner as server-side scripting. These technologies are truly revolutionary and are the future of world-class web sites.

In this chapter, you will first learn how current web browsers support HTML features such as *marquees* (text that scrolls across a web page) that do more than statically display information, and how these are different from Java applets and ActiveX controls. Then you will learn how to use these newest web technologies in your own webs. This is the frontier of the World Wide Web.

## Active Browser Features

As you've learned in the previous chapters, a web page is a text file containing HTML instructions. Your web browser loads the HTML file and creates the web page displayed in the browser by interpreting the HTML instructions. In Chapter 19, you will see how to add multimedia to your web pages by using some of the newest HTML tags. However, these features only work with web browsers that support these HTML tags. This means that there often needs to be a cycle of browser upgrades before the features are widely supported. Even after browser support is available, not everyone downloads the latest version of his or her favorite browser promptly (particularly as browser downloads have become quite large). This all means that you use these features at your own risk—in other words, only a small portion of your audience may see your webs the way you intended.

Java, ActiveX, JavaScript, and VBScript are fundamentally different from HTML. If a browser supports these programming languages, as both Netscape Navigator and Microsoft Internet Explorer do to some extent, what you can do on a web page is limited only by your imagination. This frees the web designer from waiting for browser upgrades to begin using the latest web features. The resulting stability is essential as the Web grows. One of the biggest problems in creating webs is the dependence on the user's web browser. Almost

545

every current browser can support the standard HTML features, such as displaying tables, to one degree or another, but support of multimedia varies greatly. Since Netscape and Microsoft offer HTML tags that conflict with each other, the situation will not resolve itself soon.

With Java and ActiveX, the problem is simply sidestepped. You can either write your own applets and controls (which requires a good knowledge of computer programming), or download them from a number of sources on the Web.

---

**NOTE**    *Support for these technologies in current browsers is better than ever. You can expect that most web users will be able to see your activated webs exactly as you intended.*

## Adding a Scrolling Marquee

A good example of how an HTML tag (interpreted by a browser) differs from a Java applet (a stand-alone executable computer program) can be seen by adding a marquee to a web page. Microsoft's Internet Explorer and Netscape's Navigator (verson 6 and later) both support this HTML tag, but do so differently, as you will see. By creating the same effect with a Java applet, you can make it possible for more of the people visiting your web site to see your pages as you intended. To understand the differences, first create a web page with a marquee in FrontPage using the Marquee HTML tag with these instructions:

1. Open FrontPage if it's not already open, and then create a new One Page Web Site and name it **Active**.

2. At the top of the home page, type **Welcome To the World of Active Web Pages** and format it as Heading 2.

3. Select the text and select Insert | Web Component. In the Insert Web Component dialog box, select Dynamic Effects in the Component Type list and Marquee in the Choose An Effect list, and then click Finish. The Marquee Properties dialog box, shown next, will be displayed. The selected text is shown in the Text text box.

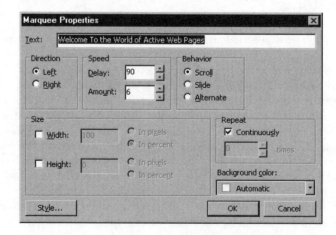

4. In the Marquee Properties dialog box, specify the text to be displayed; the direction, speed, and type of movement of the text; the number of times it repeats; the width and height of the marquee box; and the background color of the marquee.

5. Accept the defaults and click OK.

6. Save your page with the Page Title **Active Web Home Page** and the File Name **Default.htm**.

7. Open your Active Web Home Page in Internet Explorer. The text you entered previously will scroll from the right side of the page to the left and repeat continuously.

8. Open Netscape Navigator and load the Active Web Home Page into it. The behavior will be the same in newer versions of Navigator (version 6 or later). In older versions, the text will simply sit there, because the Marquee tag isn't supported. There is still a difference between the browsers in how the tag is supported, though.

9. In FrontPage, right-click the marquee text and select Marquee Properties.

10. In the Marquee Properties dialog box, select the Alternate Behavior option and click OK. Save the page again.

11. In Internet Explorer, click Refresh on the toolbar. The marquee will now travel back and forth between the left and right margins of the page.

12. In Netscape Navigator, click Reload Current Page. The marquee will travel back and forth as it does in Internet Explorer, except that in IE the leading edge of the text (the W when it's traveling right to left and the s when it's traveling left to right) "bounces" off the edge of the browser. With Navigator, the text travels completely off the screen before reversing direction.

As you can see, the Marquee tag can add a little life to a web page, but support can vary. In the next section, you will find other ways to activate your webs that have better cross-platform support.

## Java

The Java programming language was developed by Sun Microsystems, Inc., and initially released in fall 1995. Netscape was an early licenser of Java, and Microsoft soon followed. With the release of Microsoft's Internet Explorer 4.0, the uneasy alliance between Sun and Microsoft came to an end. Sun sued Microsoft for alleged violations of their licensing agreement, which Microsoft denied. Sun claimed that Microsoft changed certain core interface components in violation of the agreement. Microsoft did make the changes, but maintains that the licensing agreement allowed them to. In 2001, Sun and Microsoft reached an agreement giving Microsoft the license to continue distributing their existing versions of Java with current products, provided all future product versions "conform to and pass Sun's compatibility tests." The meaning of this is that Microsoft has chosen to discontinue their virtual machine (Microsoft VM) by January 2004. This means that Internet Explorer does not natively support Java, since the VM was the component that supported it. To support Java in IE, it's now best to use Sun's Java Run-time Environment (JRE).

---

**NOTE**   *In the examples in this chapter, Netscape's Navigator will be used as the default browser since its support for Java is a little more straightforward. You can learn more about Microsoft's position on Java at **http://www.microsoft.com/mscorp/java/**. Microsoft's latest iteration of Java is called J# (J "sharp"), released with the .NET Framework.*

---

Java's proponents see it as a replacement for the Windows operating system, which is a bit of wishful thinking. Microsoft probably wishes Java would go away so everyone would use ActiveX and the .NET Framework. In all probability, neither side will get what it wants. Regardless of the bombast, it is and will continue to be an important language for many network and web applications.

## Object-Oriented Programming

Java is an *object-oriented* programming language very similar to C++, one of today's standard programming languages. An object-oriented programming language defines an *object* as a process that accepts information, processes it, and then outputs the result of the processing. The format of the input is always clearly defined, as is the output. One object may receive its input from the output of another object. For example, an object may be a simple program that accepts a text string and then converts the text to all capitals. The input is the text string, regardless of case, and the output is the same text string converted to all uppercase. The object is the code that performs the conversion. Java applets are built by combining a number of objects (each performing a relatively simple task) into a computer program that can carry out complex operations. This concept is very powerful, as you will learn in the following sections.

---

**NOTE**   *Programming your own Java applets is a complex subject, well beyond the scope of this book. Two excellent resources for learning more about object-oriented programming and Java are* The Art of Java *by Herbert Schildt and James Holmes (McGraw-Hill/Osborne, 2003) and* Java 2: A Beginner's Guide *by Herbert Schildt (McGraw-Hill/Osborne, 2002). There are many preprogrammed Java applets available on the Web, so programming your own applet is not necessary for you to add Java applets to your web. The examples in this chapter will use readily available Java applets.*

---

By its very nature, Java offers several features besides object orientation that make it suitable for programming on the Web. It's safe, robust, interactive, platform-independent, and offers high performance.

### Safe

Since Java applets are computer programs downloaded and executed on the user's computer, what's to stop the unscrupulous programmer from sending a destructive applet over the Web to wreak havoc on thousands of computers? With the rapid growth of the Internet, this has become a leading concern for many, including the creators of Java. Their solution was to strictly limit what a Java applet can do. Java applets cannot access or misuse operating system resources, which leaves little room for vandalism. It is possible, for example, to write an applet that will slow down your computer by monopolizing resources, but this does not cause permanent damage.

### Robust

With millions of users around the world connected to the Internet, any program written for use there must be able to function flawlessly on many different computers with unique configurations. By Java's very nature, these problems are kept to a minimum. Provided the browser includes support for the Java language, properly coded applets can usually be depended on to function properly.

### Interactive

Many web sites today display information passively; that is, the content is defined by the web author and displayed by a browser in much the same way as a page in a magazine is produced. In Chapter 17, you saw how databases could be integrated in webs so that information could be presented dynamically. Java and the other technologies covered in this chapter take the process a step further. As you will see in the examples in this section, Java applets, because they are computer programs running on the user's computer, can accept input from the user, process it, and display the output on a web page. All this can be done locally (on the user's computer), leaving the web server free to handle other tasks.

### Platform Independent

On the Internet (and intranets), computers running Windows, Apple's Macintosh operating system, and UNIX (and its variants such as Linux) can coexist along with a few other minor operating systems. One of the beauties of HTML and the Web is that all these systems can access and display the same web pages. Java extends this platform independence by creating code that does not rely on a specific operating system. Each browser that supports Java applets contains a Java interpreter that handles the interaction between the applet itself and the computer operating system. In this way, a single Java applet will function properly on a Windows PC, a Mac, or a Unix computer. This is a capability with far-reaching implications. Up to this point, computer programs were written to run on only a single –operating system. With Java, it is now possible to write complex applications that can run on any operating system for which an appropriate browser is available.

---

**NOTE**    *Though Sun's "write once, run anywhere" Java motto has often been rephrased to "write once, debug everywhere," it is still a quantum leap forward in platform independence.*

---

### High Performance

All the features of Java applets mentioned so far would be of limited use if the applets were not high performance. Almost every computer user has experienced the frustration of slow response times when running some applications. Java's creators made sure the Java code would work efficiently even on older, slower computers. Also, both Netscape and Microsoft have worked to make the Java interpreters in their web browsers as fast as possible.

The features just described combine to make Java the first of a new generation of programming languages created to work efficiently and flawlessly across the Internet or across a company intranet. Now that you have some understanding of just what Java is and can do, it's time to add an applet to your web.

## Banner Ad Manager Component

You need look no further than FrontPage's Insert menu to find your first Java applet. The Banner Ad Manager is a Java applet at heart. The FrontPage Banner Ad Manager rotates two or more ad banners (or any images) on a page. The first step is to make sure that the Banner Ad Manager is displayed on your Insert menu. Do that with the following steps:

1. Select Tools | Customize.

2. In the Customize dialog box, click the Commands tab.

3. In the Categories list, select Insert. In the Commands list, drag Banner Ad Manager to the Insert menu. The Insert menu will open, and you can place the Ad Banner Manager on the menu. Release the mouse button when the Banner Ad Manager is where you want it.

4. Click Close to close the Customize dialog box.

   Next, you need to import the images to use the Banner Ad Manager. You will use three of the images included with Office with it. The images need to be the same size.

5. In your Folder list, select the images directory, the open File | Import. In the Import dialog box, click Add File.

6. In the Add File To Import List dialog box, navigate to C:\Program Files\ Microsoft Office\Templates\BUTTONS\.

7. Locate the file named BRDRB1A.GIF and select it. Press CTRL and select the files named BRDRB1B.GIF and BRDRB1C.GIF.

8. Release CTRL, click Open, and then click OK.

9. In Design view, place your cursor on the first line below your Marquee text, and then open Insert | Banner Ad Manager. The Banner Ad Manager Properties dialog box, shown here, is displayed:

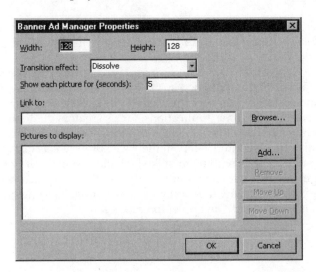

In the Banner Ad Manager dialog box, you set the size of the graphics to display, the transition effect to be used to change the graphic displayed, the length of time to display each graphic, a hyperlink for the graphics, and you select the graphics to be used.

10. Type **400** in the Width text box and **80** in the Height text box.

11. Select Dissolve in the Transition Effect drop-down list and type **1** in the Show Each Picture For (Seconds) text box.

12. In the Link To text box, type **Default.htm**. (Do not include the ending period.)

13. Click Add to add the graphics to display in the Pictures To Display list box.

14. In the Add Picture For Banner Ad dialog box, open your Images folder. Select BRDRB1A.GIF and click Open.

15. Click Add, then select BRDRB1B.GIF and click Open.

16. Click Add, then select BRDRB1C.GIF and click Open, then OK.

17. Save your work and then open your Active Web Home Page in your browser. Figure 18-1 shows the page in Netscape Navigator.

18. In FrontPage, right-click the graphic and select Banner Ad Manager Properties.

19. Select Blinds Horizontal from the Transition Effect drop-down list and click OK.

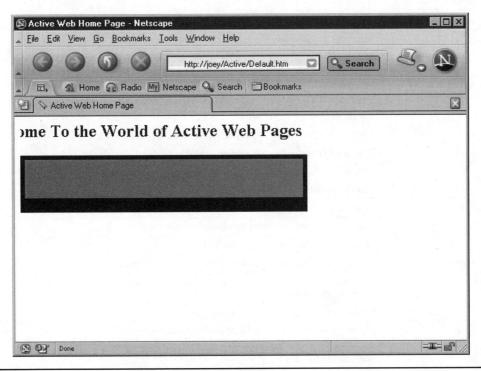

**FIGURE 18-1**  Active Web Home Page in Netscape Navigator

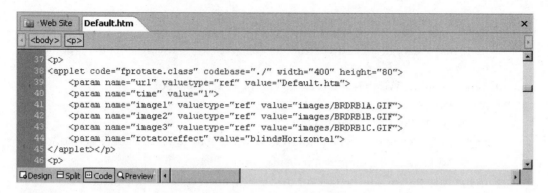

**FIGURE 18-2**    Default.htm in FrontPage Code view

20. Save your page and then reload it in your browser to see the effect.

21. In FrontPage, select Code view. Here you see the HTML that displays the Banner Ad Manager applet, as shown in Figure 18-2.

The <APPLET> tag is used to identify the Java applet using the parameters listed in Table 18-1. There will usually be a series of <PARAM> tags between the opening and

| Property | Description |
|---|---|
| Align | Specifies the alignment of the applet. The values are the same as for the <IMG> tag. |
| Alt | The alternative text displayed for the applet. It's used in the same manner as the Alt property for the <IMG> tag. |
| Archive | The location of a compressed file containing the applet and any other files it needs, such as multimedia files. This property is Netscape-specific. |
| Class | Identifies a style sheet to use with the applet. |
| Code | The name of the applet. The location is relative to the Codebase. |
| Codebase | The URL of the directory that contains the applet. |
| Datafld | The column name from a data source that the applet is bound to. |
| Datasrc | The data source that the applet is bound to. |
| Height and Width | The height and width in pixels of the applet's display area. |
| Hspace and Vspace | The horizontal and vertical space around the applet in pixels. |
| ID | A unique identifier used with a style sheet or to reference it in a script. |
| MayScript | A flag that indicates if the applet can be scripted using JavaScript functions. |
| Name | A unique name for the applet that can be used by other applets on the same page to interact with the applet. |
| Src | A URL that can point to resources used by the applet. |
| Style | Identifies any inline styles to be applied to the applet. |
| Title | A title for the applet. This is Internet Explorer–specific and is displayed as a Screen Tip when the applet is pointed to. |

**TABLE 18-1**    Applet Tag Properties

closing <APPLET> tags. These are name/value pairs that contain the values passed to the applet. The correct names and the types of values are determined at the time the applet is written, so there are no standard names. The values that can be passed to the applet should be explained in the applet's documentation. In this case, using the FrontPage Banner Ad Manager, the parameters are exposed in the Banner Ad Manager Properties dialog box.

Java is not the only way to add motions to your page, however. JavaScript is also very useful, as you will see with the interactive button, which you will use in the next section.

## Creating an Interactive Button

An *interactive* button is one that changes in some way or that controls an action triggered when the user moves the mouse pointer over it. The easiest way to understand how it works is to create one. Do that now with these steps:

1. In Design view, place the insertion point on the third line (under the banner image).
2. Open Insert | Web Component.
3. In the Insert Web Component dialog box displayed, select Dynamic Effects in the Component Type list and then Interactive Button in the Choose An Effect list.
4. Click Finish and the Interactive Buttons properties dialog box shown next is displayed:

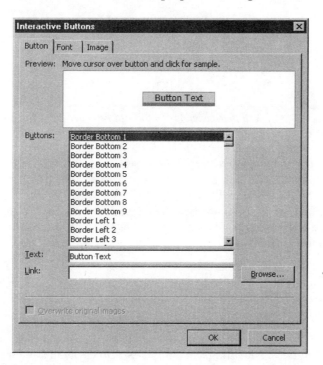

In this dialog box, you can select a button, set the button's text, and create its hyperlink. The Font tab allows you to select the font, style, size, colors for normal, hover, and pressed states, and the horizontal and vertical alignment. The Image tab allows you to set the size of the button, if hover and pressed versions will be created, if the button images should be preloaded with the page, and if the images should be created as GIF or JPEG images.

5. Accept the defaults in the Hover Button Properties dialog box by clicking OK.

6. Click Save on the menu bar, and the Save Embedded Files dialog box is displayed. Click Change Folder and select Images in the Change Folder dialog box. Click OK twice.

7. Refresh the page in your browser, and move your mouse pointer over the Button Text graphic to see the interactive button effects.

These examples show how easily a Java applet and JavaScript can be used in FrontPage. The next step is learning how to find applets available for downloading. Then you will add a java applet to your Active web and modify its parameters.

## Finding Java Applets

Unless you're an experienced C++ programmer, your first Java applets will probably be ones you download from the Web. A growing number of web sites have applets available for downloading. The first step, then, is to get onto the Web and find some Java applets. A good place to start is Sun Microsystems' Java home page. The following steps will take you there.

---

**NOTE**    *Web sites that offer Java applets change often as new applets are added. The descriptions of the web sites in this book reflect their status in the third quarter of 2003 (when this book was written).*

---

**TIP**    *The current versions of both Netscape Navigator and Internet Explorer support Java, but there are differences. The ongoing turf war between Sun and Microsoft has made it even more important to have the latest versions of Netscape's Navigator and Microsoft's Internet Explorer browsers and to test your applets with both the newest and older browser versions.*

1. Make sure your Internet connection is functioning, and open your browser.

2. In the Location or Address text box, type **java.sun.com/applets/** and press ENTER. In a few moments, the web page shown in Figure 18-3 should be displayed in your browser.

---

**TIP**    *Web sites change often, and URLs sometimes become outdated. If the URLs used in this chapter no longer work when you try them, start from the home page and follow the hyperlinks to the resources described.*

3. Scroll down the page until you see the heading "Freebie Applets." In the first paragraph under the heading, click the "free applets available for use" hyperlink.

4. When the Freebie Applets You Can Use web page is displayed, scroll down to the Clock hyperlink and then click it. This takes you to the page (**http://java.sun.com/ openstudio/applets/clock.html**) where you can download the applet's files, as

shown in Figure 18-4. This page also contains sample HTML code for using the applet and lists the applet's parameters.

---

**NOTE**   *The file you will download will be compressed, and you will need to extract the individual files using a Zip utility such as WinZip from WinZip Computing, Inc.,* **http://www.winzip.com/**.

5. Click Download Now. If your browser prompts you to open the file or save it, choose to save it to disk. Select a work folder on your hard drive to save the file. You will have to unzip the download in this folder and then place the necessary files in your Active web. The compressed file actually contains several sample applets you can use, but this exercise will focus exclusively on the Clock applet.

6. When you have finished downloading the compressed applet file, you will need to unzip it. Do this in the work folder where you saved the download. When the compressed file is unzipped, it will create a folder named Demo that will contain subfolders for the Clock applet as well as the other sample applets.

7. In FrontPage, import the Clock applet to your Active web by opening File | Import.

8. In the Import dialog box, click Add Folder. In the File Open dialog box, locate the folder that contains the Demo folder created when you unzipped the file.

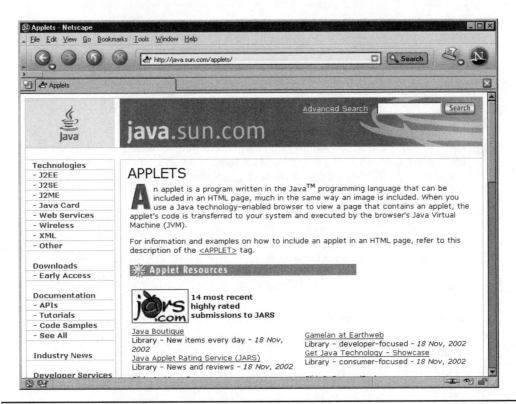

**FIGURE 18-3**   Sun's Java home page

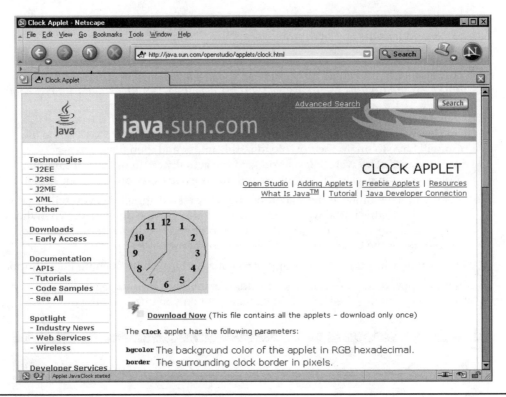

**FIGURE 18-4**     Sun's Clock applet home page

9. Open the Demo folder, then select the Clock folder and click Open and then OK. This will import more files than you absolutely need for this exercise, but it is easier at this point than selecting the individual files. When the folder is imported, your Active web should have a folder named Clock that contains two subfolders, Classes and Src, as shown in Figure 18-5.

The Classes folder contains the compiled Java applet files that have a .class file extension. These are the files you will use when you add the applet to your page. The Src folder contains the source code for the applets, and these have a .java file extension. You will learn more about the source files and how to use them in the section "Compiling Java Applets" later in this chapter. Two other files were also imported in the Clock folder. GNUmakefile is a batch file used to create the .class files. You will not use this file. The other file is a web page (Index.html) that displays the Clock applet. Figure 18-6 shows this page in Netscape Navigator.

10. In your Folder List, select the file GNUmakefile and press DEL. In the Confirm Delete dialog box, click Yes.

11. In Design view, place your cursor on the line below your interactive button.

12. Open Insert | Web Component.

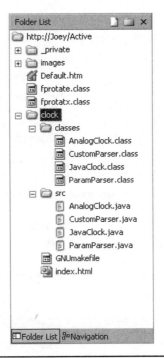

**FIGURE 18-5**    FrontPage Folder List with Clock applet imported

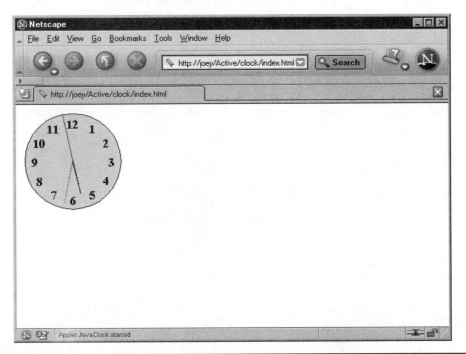

**FIGURE 18-6**    The Clock applet default home page in Netscape Navigator

13. In the Insert Web Component dialog box, select Advanced Controls in the Component Type list, and then select Java Applet in the Choose A Control list.

14. Click Finish, and the Java Applet Properties dialog box (shown in Figure 18-7) appears.

15. Type **JavaClock.class** in the Applet Source text box; then type **Clock/Classes** in the Applet Base URL text box. Click OK. This is the minimum information FrontPage needs to properly display the Clock applet. Figure 18-8 shows the page in FrontPage Design view. FrontPage displays a graphic placeholder for the applet.

16. Save your page and then open it in your browser. Figure 18-9 shows the page in Netscape Navigator.

    Most applets accept additional parameters that control their appearance and/or functionality. The parameters the Clock applet accepts are listed in Table 18-2. In the remainder of this exercise, you will use the Java Applet Properties dialog box to set some of these parameters. The applet will use default values for any parameters that are not specifically set.

17. In Design view, right-click the Clock applet and choose Java Applet Properties.

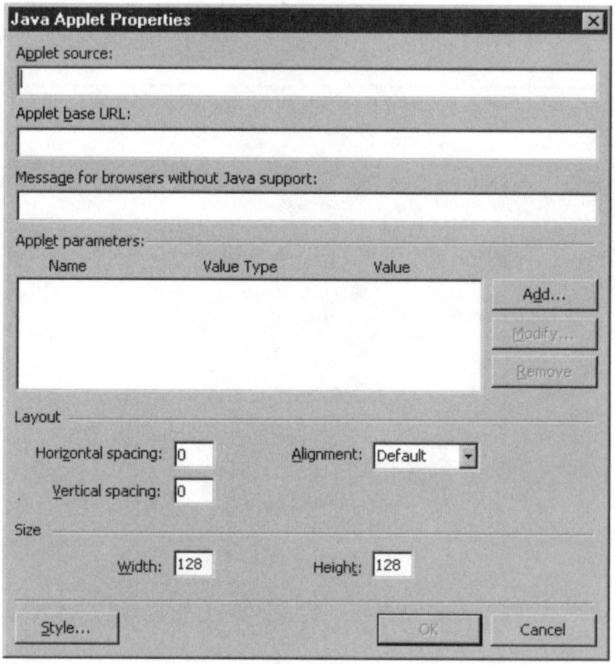

**FIGURE 18-7**
The Java Applet
Properties
dialog box

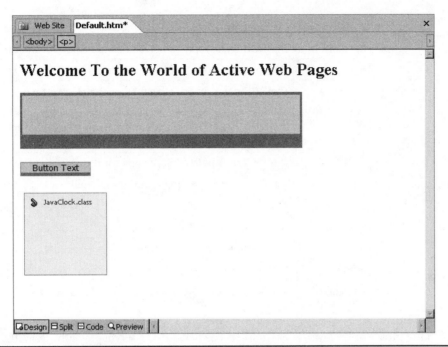

**FIGURE 18-8** The Active Web Home Page with Clock applet in Design view

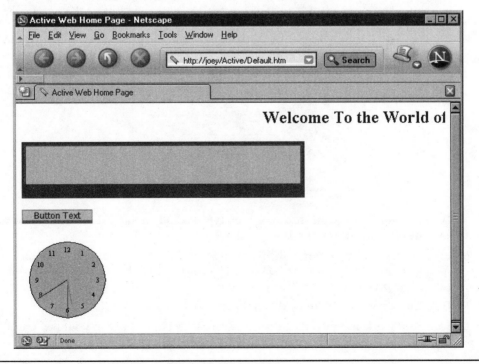

**FIGURE 18-9** The Active Web Home Page with Clock applet

**TABLE 18-2**
Clock Applet
Parameters

| Parameter | Description |
|-----------|-------------|
| bgcolor | The RGB background color, in hexadecimal, for the applet. |
| border | The width in pixels of the space around the clock's face. |
| ccolor | The RGB color, in hexadecimal, of the clock's face. |
| cfont | The text string containing the font, style, and point size of the numbers on the clock's face. Each element is separated by the I ("pipe") character. |
| delay | The refresh rate in milliseconds for the applet. |
| hhcolor | The hour hand RGB color, in hexadecimal. |
| link | The optional URL if the clock is to be a hyperlink. |
| mhcolor | The minute hand RGB color, in hexadecimal. |
| ncolor | The RGB color of the numbers, in hexadecimal. |
| nradius | The radius, in pixels, where the numbers will be drawn. |
| shcolor | The second hand RGB color, in hexadecimal. |

18. In the Java Applet Properties dialog box, click Add. This displays the Set Attribute Value dialog box shown next. You will enter the name of the parameter in the Name text box and a value for the parameter in the Data text box. The Specify Value check box should be checked and the Data option selected when setting the parameters in the following steps.

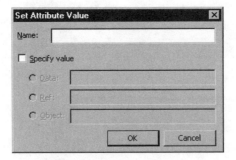

19. Type **bgcolor** in the Name text box, then type **0000FF** in the Data text box. This will give the clock a blue background. Click OK.

20. Click Add, then type **cfont** in the Name text box and **Arial I Bold I 18** (there are no spaces in this text) in the Data text box. The vertical bar (the "pipe" character) is entered by pressing SHIFT-\. Click OK.

21. Type **150** in both the Width and Height text boxes and click OK.

22. Save your work and then reload your Active Web Home Page in your browser. Figure 18-10 shows the page in Netscape Navigator.

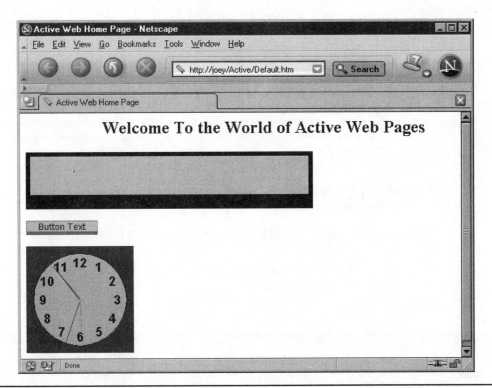

**FIGURE 18-10**    The Active Web Home Page with Clock applet and added parameters

For any applets you have that are compiled (you have a file with a .class extension), this is basically all you need to do to add a Java applet to your FrontPage webs. The next step is understanding how Java applets are created. First, you need to download and install some Java development tools.

## The Sun Java Development Kit

Java applets are often distributed as source code that must be compiled before it can be used in your webs. This provides an additional measure of security. Rather than downloading an executable applet that may or may not perform as advertised, you download a text file that is compiled into the executable. This helps ensure the applet will do what it's advertised to do and nothing more. There are several sources for Java toolkits. Formerly known as the JDK, the Java 2 Software Development Kit, Standard Edition (J2SE™ SDK), available from Sun Microsystems' web site (**http://java.sun.com/j2se/**), is the one you will use in the following sections. It contains the source code for a number of sample applets as well as a Java compiler for converting the Java source code into Java applets that can be included in your webs. Microsoft would like everyone to transition to J# (J sharp) and the .NET Framework. More information and downloads can be found on the Microsoft Visual J# .NET home page, **http://msdn.microsoft.com/vjsharp/**.

**NOTE**    *A number of other Java tools simplify the process of creating Java applets. If you decide to write your own applets, you should investigate these products. Probably the best place to start looking is Sun's Java Solutions Guide at* **http://solutions.sun.com/catalog.html**.

All the basic tools you need for working with Java code are included with Sun's J2SE SDK. The J2SE includes example Java applets, both as source code and compiled applets, one of which you will use in the exercises in the following sections. The documentation files are in HTML format, and the demos also include HTML pages. Begin your exploration of Java by downloading the J2SE package.

**NOTE**    *The J2SE package is a hefty download—45MB for the current SDK—but the tools provided are necessary if you really want to work with Java.*

1. In your web browser, go to Sun's J2SE home page at **http://java.sun.com/j2se/**, shown in Figure 18-11.

2. Under Hot Downloads, find the link for the J2SE 1.4.2. At the time this was written, 1.4.2 is the current version, but version 1.5 (codenamed Tiger) should be released in the first quarter of 2004. Click the link to the latest version.

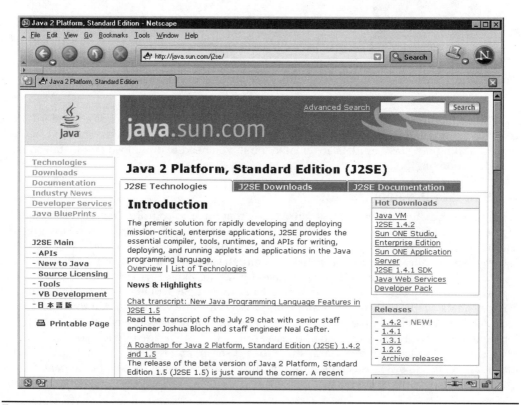

**FIGURE 18-11**    Sun's J2SE home page

3. On the page that opens, find the Microsoft Windows link. Figure 18-12 shows the current location for version 1.4.2. The Windows Installation link will download and install only the options you select during setup. The Windows Offline Installation downloads all the files for installation, allowing you to install the SDK offline. Click either link, depending on whether you want to download all the files or not. The remaining steps in this example assume the full SDK is downloaded, but this isn't strictly necessary. In either case, be sure you download the SDK and not the JRE.

4. The Sun License Agreement will be displayed. Scroll to the bottom of the page and click Accept if you accept the terms of the agreement. This will load the download page. Click the download link to start downloading the file.

5. You will be prompted for a location to save the J2SE SDK to. This should be your Temp or work folder. Select the location to save the file and click OK.

6. After the files are downloaded, open the folder in Windows Explorer where you saved the J2SE SDK program file (j2sdk1_4_2-windows-i586.exe at the time this is written) and double-click it. A dialog box will be displayed indicating the files are being unpacked; then the installation program will start.

7. When the setup Welcome dialog box is displayed, click Next. The next dialog box will display the license agreement.

8. After reading the license agreement (use the vertical scroll bar or PAGE DOWN to see more of it), select I Accept The Terms In The License Agreement option if you agree to the terms, and then click Next. (If you do not agree, the software will not be installed.)

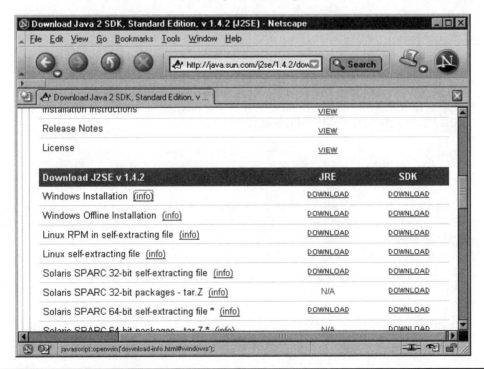

**FIGURE 18-12**    Sun's J2SE Download page

9. In the next window, you can select which components to install and the folder in which to install the J2SE SDK. Accept the default installation and location (C:\ j2sdk1.4.2\) by clicking Next. (You may change the location by clicking Change if you prefer to install the J2SE SDK in another location.)

10. Next you are asked which of the browsers that you have installed you want to register with the Java Plug-In. Select at least one of your installed browsers and click Install. The J2SE SDK installation on your system will begin.

11. When the files are installed, the Setup Complete dialog box will be displayed. Click Finish.

You now have the tools needed to compile Java applets from the source code files. In the next section, you will use these tools to compile a sample applet included with the J2SE SDK.

## Compiling Java Applets

While the Java 2 Software Development Kit contains some precompiled applets as well as the complete HTML pages that demonstrate them, knowing how to compile a Java applet from source code is a necessary skill for web designers who intend to use Java in their webs. Even if you never intend to write your own applets, you will probably still need to compile the applets you download from the Web, many of which are available only as Java source code. The process is relatively straightforward, but it does require using the Command Prompt interface included in Windows and a basic knowledge of using MS-DOS command syntax. The following steps will take you through the process:

1. Create a temporary folder on your hard drive for the source code file. Name the folder **Javawork**.

2. Copy the TicTacToe.java file (C:\j2sdk1.4.2\Demo\Applets\TicTacToe\ TicTacToe.java if you used the default folder structure) to the Javawork folder.

3. Open WordPad (Start | All Programs | Accessories | WordPad), and then select Open from the File menu. In the Open dialog box, select All Documents (*.*) from the Files Of Type drop-down menu.

---

**NOTE**   *Notepad is not suitable for opening or editing the Java source code files included with the J2SE SDK. These files contain characters that do not display properly in Notepad.*

---

4. Open your Javawork folder from the Look In drop-down menu, then open the file and folder list, and double-click TicTacToe.java. The TicTacToe.java source code file will be displayed.

The source code includes a number of comments that describe the function of each Java statement in the file. Comments are all the text between the /* (or /**) and */ markers. For example, in the lines

```
/**
 * White's current position. The computer is white.
 */
int white;
```

the comment ("White's current position...") explains that the Java statement `int white;` is an integer that represents the current grid position of white's move. The variable name, white, contains the integer value. This variable is used to pass the current position of white to other functions in the applet. It is an axiom of programming that one of the best ways to learn a new programming language is to study other people's code. This is equally true of Java. If you are familiar with programming languages such as C++, the Java code will look familiar to you.

5. Close WordPad without changing the file.

6. Open a Command Prompt by selecting Start | All Programs | Accessories | Command Prompt.

7. At the C:\> prompt in the Command Prompt window, type **cd \javawork** (or use the path where you created the Javawork directory), as shown here, then press ENTER. CD is the DOS command for Change Directory. This will make the Javawork directory the current directory, and the prompt will read "C:\Javawork>."

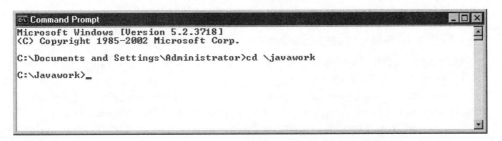

**NOTE**  *If you created the Javawork directory on another drive, such as drive D:, you will first need to change to that drive before issuing the CD command. To change drives, enter the drive letter, followed by a colon (that is, **D:**), and press ENTER.*

8. Type **dir** and press ENTER. This is the command to display the contents of the current directory. Your Command Prompt window should display a listing similar to this:

```
Command Prompt                                                      _ □ X
Microsoft Windows [Version 5.2.3718]
(C) Copyright 1985-2002 Microsoft Corp.

C:\Documents and Settings\Administrator>cd \javawork

C:\Javawork>dir
 Volume in drive C has no label.
 Volume Serial Number is 5C7C-5E78

 Directory of C:\Javawork

08/13/2003  08:26 PM    <DIR>          .
08/13/2003  08:26 PM    <DIR>          ..
08/13/2003  08:17 PM             8,247 TicTacToe.java
               1 File(s)          8,247 bytes
               2 Dir(s)   1,326,084,096 bytes free

C:\Javawork>
```

9. Compile the TicTacToe.java source file by typing

   **C:\j2sdk1.4.2\bin\javac TicTacToe.java**

   at the C:\Javawork> prompt and pressing ENTER. The name of Sun's Java compiler is javac. The command you entered instructed it to convert the source file TicTacToe.java into the executable applet TicTacToe.class.

10. When the C:\Javawork> prompt reappears in the Command Prompt window, type **dir** and press ENTER. In the listing that is displayed, you will see there are now two files in the Javawork directory—the original source file and TicTacToe.class, the executable applet.

    In the preceding steps, you used the simplest form of the javac command to generate the applet. You can also use a number of options with javac to control the compiling or to generate messages. In the next step, you will use the -verbose option to generate a list of all the steps the compiler is taking to generate the applet. This will overwrite the applet you just created.

11. At the C:\Javawork> prompt, type

    **C:\j2sdk1.4.2\bin\javac -verbose TicTacToe.java**

    and press ENTER. As each step is executed, the compile event and the time it takes to compile are displayed.

    A complete listing of the options for the javac compiler can be found in the documentation web pages at **http://java.sun.com/j2se/1.4.2/docs/tooldocs/windows/javac.html**. You can open this page and find information about the other tools included with the J2SE SDK. You can open the documentation home page (**http://java.sun.com/j2se/1.4.2/docs/**) and click the Tool Documentation hyperlink. This takes you to the Java 2 SDK Tools and Utilities documentation index. Scroll down the page to the Basic Tools section, shown in Figure 18-13, which contains a brief description of each tool and a hyperlink to the page where the tool is explained in detail.

12. Close the Command Prompt window by typing **exit** at the C:\Javawork> prompt and pressing ENTER.

The final step in compiling a Java applet is to test it on a web page. Do that now with these instructions:

1. In FrontPage, open your Active Web Home Page in Design view (if it isn't already open).

2. Create a new folder in your Active web with the name **TicTacToe**. Make sure the folder is selected.

3. Open File | Import. In the Import dialog box, click Add File.

4. In the Add File To Import List dialog box, select your Javawork folder in the Look In drop-down list. Select TicTacToe.class and click Open.

5. With the Import dialog box still open, click Add Folder.

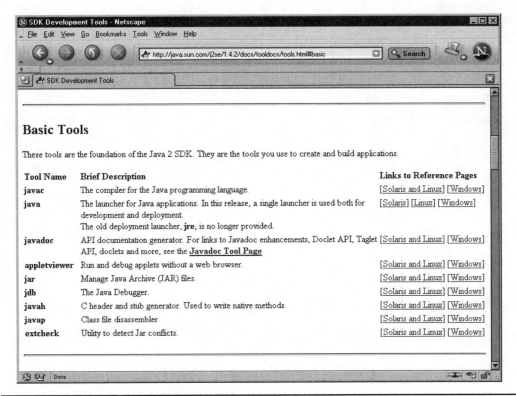

**FIGURE 18-13**   Java 2 SDK Basic Tools index in Netscape Navigator

6. In the File Open dialog box, select the folder in the J2SE SDK that contains the sound files the applet uses. The default path is C:\j2sdk1.4.2\ Demo\Applets\ TicTacToe\Audio. Click Open to add this folder to the import list.

7. Repeat step 6 to select the folder containing the graphic files the applet uses. The default path is C:\ j2sdk1.4.2\Demo\Applets\TicTacToe\Images.

8. Click OK in the Import dialog box to add the selected files and folders to your web.

9. In Design view, place the cursor on the line below your Clock applet.

10. Open Insert | Web Component.

11. In the Insert Web Component dialog box that is displayed, select Advanced Controls in the Component Type list and then Java Applet in the Choose A Control list. Click Finish to display the Java Applet Properties dialog box.

12. In the Java Applet Properties dialog box, type **TicTacToe.class** in the Applet Source text box and **TicTacToe** in the Applet Base URL text box.

13. Type **150** in both the Width and Height text boxes, and then click OK.

14. Save your work. In Design view, your Active Web Home Page should look similar to Figure 18-14.

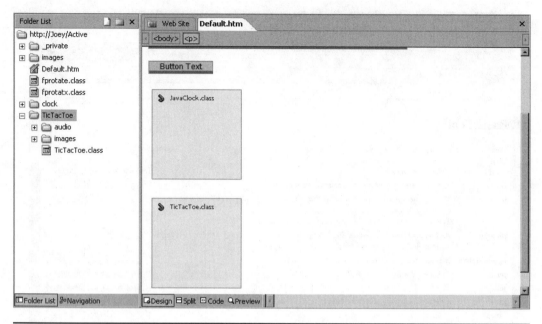

**FIGURE 18-14**    The Active Web Home Page in Design view with the TicTacToe applet added

15. Open the page in your browser. Figure 18-15 shows the TicTacToe applet in Netscape.

16. Start the game by clicking in any empty cell. An *X* will be placed in that cell, and the applet will counter by placing an *O* in a cell that will block you, as shown here:

This has been only a brief trip through the world of Java. It is a powerful programming language that opens new doors for the web designer. Because Java is a true programming language, it also requires a comprehensive knowledge of the language and its capabilities to be used effectively. If you are a C++ programmer, the transition will be smooth. If Java is your first real programming language, you will have to devote a significant amount of time and energy to learning it. It is a language that is playing a significant role in web design, so your time may be well spent. If you don't want to learn a programming language, you can find a great number of precompiled Java applets on the Web. The information in this section has presented the basics you need to download and use applets you find on the Web.

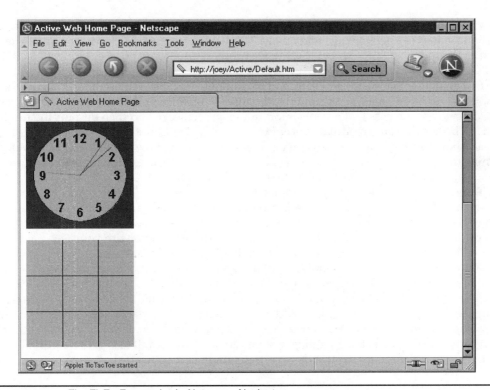

**FIGURE 18-15**    The TicTacToe applet in Netscape Navigator

In the next section, you will learn about ActiveX, Microsoft's technology that is designed to offer even more advantages to the web designer than Java.

## ActiveX

Java is a new technology. In a sense, its designers began with a clean sheet of paper. (An interesting personal history of Java is included in *The Java Handbook* [Osborne/McGraw-Hill, 1996] by Patrick Naughton, one of the original team members at Sun who created the language. This book is currently out of print, but you can find copies in used book stores and online.) ActiveX is more evolutionary, having its roots in Microsoft's OLE (object linking and embedding) technology.

OLE was developed as a method of sharing text and graphics, generally called *objects*, between applications on a computer. If an object was linked between documents, a pointer was created in the receiving document pointing to the object in the original document. When the original object was updated, the linked object was also updated. For example, you could link a spreadsheet to a word processing document. When the data in the spreadsheet changed, it would be reflected in the word processing document. When an object was linked, it actually existed only in the original document. The receiving document only contained a pointer to the original. When an object was embedded, an actual copy was placed in the receiving document.

While this method worked fine when both documents were on a single computer, it had its shortcomings in a networked environment. This led Microsoft to develop new technologies, such as Component Object Model (COM), Distributed Component Object Model (DCOM), and OLE Control Extensions (OCX).

Essentially, ActiveX is object-oriented programming for the Web. In the section of this chapter on object-oriented programming, the concept of objects was introduced. An object was defined as a process that accepts information, processes it, and then outputs the result. ActiveX brings the same modular concept to a web page, with the addition that an object can also be a data file. This is a greatly simplified explanation of the technology, but it avoids turning this chapter into a programming handbook, rather than a guide for web designers who want to add the latest features to their FrontPage webs.

The ActiveX equivalent of a Java applet is an ActiveX control. Because ActiveX has evolved from OLE, ActiveX controls can be used with many different programming languages, including all the Microsoft programming and database languages. This means you can use the same control with your Access database as you do with your web page. This is also an area where ActiveX differs from Java.

ActiveX is a very useful technology, but it does have its drawbacks. In particular, it is a Windows-based technology. This leaves Mac and UNIX users out of the picture, at least for the present. If and when support is added for these platforms, the code will need to be compiled separately for each. This would lead to maintaining separate web pages for each operating system. Of course, Windows computers make up the majority of the market, and with corporate intranets, the operating system can be controlled. It also is less secure than Java, which is balanced by the fact that it is potentially more powerful.

---

**NOTE**    *Neither Java nor ActiveX is totally secure. Creative programmers can almost always find a way to get around security safeguards. When implementing any web technology, you must use caution and pay attention to what is happening on your web site.*

---

These issues are not new to computing. At every stage of growth in the industry, the question of features vs. compatibility has arisen. Often, as with ActiveX, compatibility has suffered in order to increase the usefulness of software. These are simply issues you need to consider before using ActiveX with your webs.

Since ActiveX controls are commonly written in Visual Basic, this section will not go into writing your own controls. Instead, you will use ActiveX controls included with FrontPage and readily available on the Web. Additional information about ActiveX can be found on the MSDN Online Web Workshop (**http://msdn.microsoft.com/workshop/ components/activex/intro.asp**).

The next section will show you how to use ActiveX with your FrontPage webs.

## ActiveX and FrontPage

FrontPage comes with a number of ActiveX controls you can add to your webs, as you will see next. Your Active Web Home Page should still be open in FrontPage.

1. In Design view, move the cursor to the line below your TicTacToe Java applet.

2. Open Insert | Web Component.

3. In the Insert Web Component dialog box that is displayed, select Advanced Controls in the Component Type list and then ActiveX Control in the Choose A Control list. Click Next to display a list of available ActiveX controls, as shown here:

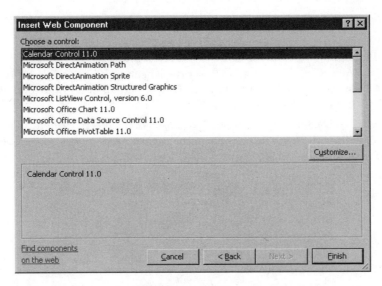

4. This looks like quite a collection of ActiveX controls, but there are actually more.

5. Click Customize in the Insert Web Component dialog box. The Customize ActiveX Control List dialog box shown next is opened:

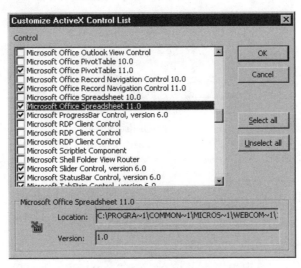

6. In the Customize ActiveX Control List dialog box, scroll down until you find the Microsoft Office Spreadsheet 11.0 check box. Select the check box if it's not selected and click OK.

7. In the Choose A Control list of the Insert Web Component dialog box, select Microsoft Office Spreadsheet 11.0 and click Finish. A functioning spreadsheet is placed on your page, as shown in Figure 18-16.

8. Save your page and then open it in Internet Explorer.

9. In Internet Explorer, scroll down until the ActiveX spreadsheet is visible. In cell A1, type **2** and then press DOWN ARROW.

10. In cell A2, type **2** and press ENTER. Cell A3 should now be selected.

11. Click the AutoSum ($\Sigma$) button on the spreadsheet's toolbar and then press ENTER. Cell A3 now contains the formula =Sum(A1:A2) and displays the total of the numbers in those cells, as shown in Figure 18-17.

12. In FrontPage Design view, right-click the spreadsheet ActiveX control in an area outside of the cell matrix and select ActiveX Control Properties. This opens the ActiveX Control Properties dialog box, shown here:

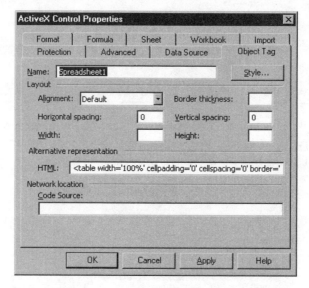

The options available in the ActiveX Control Properties dialog box will depend on the specific ActiveX control. As you can see, the Microsoft Office Spreadsheet 11.0 ActiveX control has quite a few options. The choices shown here in the Object Tag tab will be available for most controls.

1. In the HTML Alternative Representation text box, select the existing text and type

   **<h1>This browser doesn't support ActiveX.</h1>**

   then click OK.

2. Save your page and then open it in Netscape Navigator, as shown in Figure 18-18.

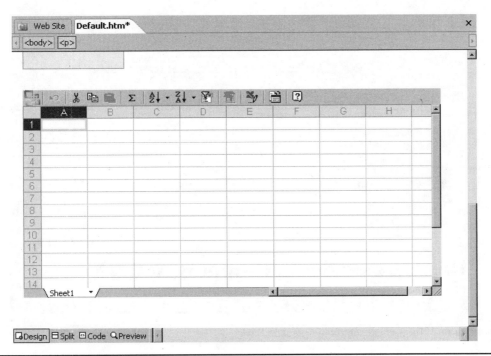

**FIGURE 18-16**   The Microsoft Office Spreadsheet 11.0 ActiveX control in Design view

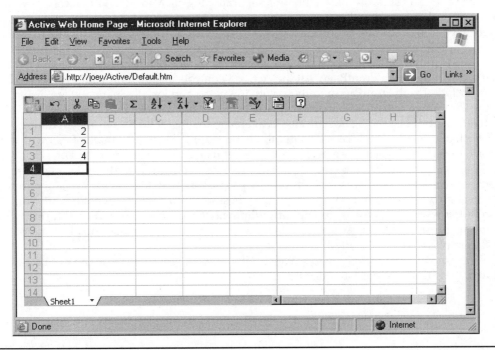

**FIGURE 18-17**   The Spreadsheet ActiveX control in Internet Explorer

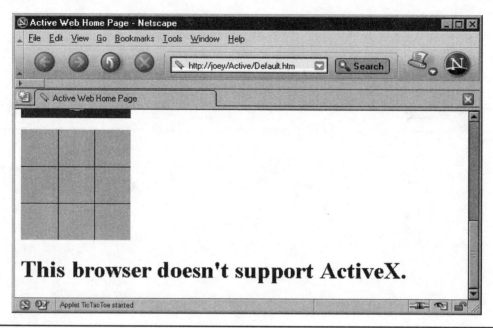

**FIGURE 18-18**    The ActiveX control in Netscape Navigator

The preceding example illustrates one of the problems with ActiveX controls—Netscape Navigator doesn't support them without a separate plug-in. Microsoft still doesn't own the browser market, so using ActiveX controls may limit some people from getting the full effect of your web site. On an intranet, if you can control the browsers used, this limitation doesn't apply.

The Microsoft Office Spreadsheet ActiveX control is one of a number of ActiveX controls that are included with FrontPage. All the ActiveX controls installed on your system (both those included with FrontPage and those you download and install separately) are displayed in the Customize ActiveX Control List dialog box. The controls selected in the Customize ActiveX Control List dialog box are also available in the Insert Web Component dialog box.

Each of the technologies covered in this chapter could easily fill a book of its own, and in fact, each does. The purpose here was to give you an overview of them so you could make an informed decision about which technologies you want to add to your own webs. Both Java applets and ActiveX controls require programming that is not for the faint of heart. If you already program in C++, the step up to these new languages will not be difficult. The Sun (**http://www.sun.com**), Netscape (**http://home.netscape.com**), and Microsoft (**http://www.microsoft.com**) web sites all have a variety of programming tools, documentation, and examples to get you started.

These technologies continue to advance—if you want your webs to stand out in the crowd, these tools are part of your future.

# Extending Your Web Site

I n earlier sections, you learned how to do a large number of things with your webs, some simple and some very sophisticated. In Part IV, you'll learn how to add some frosting to your web cake. In Chapter 19, you'll see how to add multimedia, especially sound, to a web. Chapter 20 looks at how to manage the security of your webs, while Chapter 21 discusses how to set up an e-commerce site. Chapter 22 describes how to set up an intranet, including the SharePoint Team Web Site, and Chapter 23 looks at publishing and promoting web sites.

# Adding Multimedia to Your Web Site

The World Wide Web started off silent and motionless. Those days are over. Audio is commonplace, and video and sophisticated animation are establishing a strong foothold. In webs you'll see links to WAV audio files, MPEG4, AVI, and QuickTime (MOV) video files, and even DVDs. There are also links to audio and video files like RealNetworks' (**http://www.real.com**) RealOne Player and Microsoft's (**http://www.microsoft.com**) Window3's Media Player. Animation has also moved beyond the capabilities of animated GIFs with the introduction of Macromedia's (**http://www.macromedia.com**) Flash technology, as well as dynamic HTML. The possibilities are exploding for web developers. Audio, video, and animation capabilities are changing very quickly. RealNetworks, Microsoft, and Macromedia are the major players, but a lot of others are fighting for a piece of this pie.

Audio and video files used to have to be completely downloaded before they could be played and, because they are very large files, the download time is much longer than the playing time. This put audio and video in the category of cool but not very useful. RealNetworks changed that when they released the first streaming audio player. With *streaming* audio, you don't have to download the entire file to listen to it—about ten seconds of the file downloads and then it starts playing. This broke the time barrier, and now there is no limit to the length of the file being played.

Streaming audio not only allows longer pieces to be put up on the Web, but it also allows live webcasting. Soon after the introduction of streaming audio, radio stations began broadcasting on the Web 24 hours a day. Now live concerts appear on the Web. And in early 1997, RealNetworks launched RealVideo, which brought streaming video to the Web on a large scale. Microsoft was not far behind with streaming audio and video using their NetShow product.

Video still has its limitations on the Web because of insufficient bandwidth. Streaming video over a 56K modem is pretty limited because the image is small and it's not full-motion video. Although it is amazing how good it actually is over slower modems, streaming video is still in the cool but not very useful category. The availability of larger bandwidth connections is changing this. As ISDN (Integrated Services Digital Network), cable modems, and DSL (Digital Subscriber Line) technology become more widely used, there is an explosion in the use of streaming video. Intranets generally are not as bandwidth limited and can make good use of this technology today.

Creating video content is not for the faint of heart or those with small pocketbooks. The equipment is more expensive than the equipment for recording sound. The software to edit video is also more expensive, and there are many more elements to consider in editing and creating video. You have all the elements of audio to deal with plus the more complex visuals. There is more to video than can be covered in a chapter, so this chapter will focus on audio.

Technology like Macromedia's Flash can provide some very sophisticated animations, but animation is also a very specialized field, so it will not be covered in this chapter. If you want to do simple animations, look at using GIF Construction Set Professional from Alchemy Mindworks (**http://www.mindworkshop.com/alchemy/alchemy.html**) to produce animated GIFs or dynamic HTML, as described in Chapter 13.

Audio can be included in a web site using equipment that most people already have. A computer with a sound card, a CD player, a tape recorder, and/or a microphone allows you to put audio files on your web: streaming and nonstreaming, live, or on-demand. Whether it is a baby's first cry or a live musical performance from your living room, you can put those sounds on the Web for your friends, family, and the world to hear.

The rest of this chapter will tell you how to capture sound and use both nonstreaming and streaming files to deliver that sound in your web applications.

## Capturing the Sound

The first step is to capture the sound in a digital format on your computer—to record it digitally through your sound card and create a WAV file that can be edited and saved. This includes identifying the source, connecting the source to your computer, and actually doing the recording.

---

**NOTE**    *The RealAudio encoder Helix Producer has the capability to encode a RealAudio file directly from a sound source without first producing a WAV file. Producing the WAV file first, though, allows you to edit the WAV file to delete any silent spots in the beginning and end of the selection, as well as to make any other desired changes to the file.*

### The Sound Source

The source can be any playback device such as a CD player, tape recorder, MIDI player, or phonograph. The source can also be live from a microphone or several microphones using a mixing device. If you can get an audio signal to your sound card, you can digitally record it on your computer.

### Connect the Sound Source to the Sound Card

You've got the sound source and a sound card. The question is, how do you connect them? There are two things to consider: the connectors and where to put them.

#### Connectors

Anyone who has set up a stereo has dealt with this. Numerous wires come out of the back and go to speakers and to the tape deck or CD player. At the end of the wires are the connectors.

Life would be simple if there were only one connector, but life is not simple. The wires coming out of your stereo generally do not have the connector that will fit into your sound card.

There are two types of connectors you are dealing with: the 1/8-inch miniplug and the RCA plug, which are shown next:

**NOTE**    Jacks *are female and are in the hardware being connected.* Plugs *are male and are on the ends of the cables being plugged in.*

A stereo commonly has RCA jacks, which need the corresponding RCA plug for connecting, and your sound card uses a 1/8-inch minijack, which needs a 1/8-inch miniplug. If you have a source that uses an RCA jack, you will need to get an adapter. Radio Shack is an excellent place to get these adapters, or you can get a cable with a pair of RCA plugs on one end and a 1/8-inch stereo miniplug on the other end.

Sometimes you may run into another type of connector. If you do, go back to Radio Shack, because they have adapters and combinations that will fit most requirements.

### Where to Put the Connectors

Where you plug in the sound source connector is very important. You always want to connect a line-out to a line-in. Generally, you should not use a speaker output or the headphone output. These are amplified signals that are difficult to control and that may overpower your sound card. The line-out is not amplified. You connect the line-out on your sound source (tape deck, CD player, or mixer) to a line-in on your sound card.

It helps to visualize where the signal is going. Let's use the stereo receiver/amplifier connected to a tape deck as an example. When you put a tape into the tape deck and play it, the signal is going from the tape deck to the receiver/amplifier. It is going from the line-out on the tape deck to the Tape line-in on the receiver/amplifier. When you record something, it is going from the Tape line-out on the receiver/amplifier back to the line-in on the tape deck.

**NOTE**    *Some stereo manufacturers confuse the issue by using Play and Record designations where you plug Play to Play and Record to Record. In these cases, the Play on the tape deck is the line-out, and the Play on the receiver/amplifier is the line-in. This gets confusing. Fortunately, if you connect them wrong, nothing will be hurt. You just won't get any sound. If this happens, just switch them around.*

Similarly, if you are recording from a tape recorder or stereo, you go from the line-out on the source to the line-in on your sound card. This may be the most difficult part of this process because you will have to crawl behind your computer, find the jacks on your sound card, and decipher the miniscule hieroglyphics to tell where to plug in the cable from your sound source.

---

*TIP*    *Check the documentation that came with your sound card for a schematic showing the positions of the jacks. This little bit of research may save you a lot of frustration connecting to your machine.*

## Record the Sound Digitally

Now that your source is attached to the sound card, you are ready to create a digital recording. There are two elements used in recording: a mixer and a digital audio editor. A *mixer* adjusts the incoming audio levels from several sources, and a *digital audio editor* edits and then creates the digital file. These elements are usually programs, which come with your sound card. How much capability they have can vary. The more expensive sound cards have programs with quite a few controls; the less expensive cards have fewer controls. There are also some very good digital audio editors available having free demos with a reasonable registration. One such editor is GoldWave, available from GoldWave, Inc. at **http://www.goldwave.com**. Several other digital audio editors are available for download on the Web, including Cool Edit, which is available from Syntrillium Software Corporation at **http://www.syntrillium.com**.

### Mixer

A mixer adjusts the level of the sound going into the sound card—the input volume. If the sound level is too high, it will be distorted. If it is too low, it will be hard to hear. A mixer lets you adjust it to the right level. A mixer can be an external hardware soundboard or a software program that comes with your sound card. Here you can see the Volume Control mixer controls that come with Windows XP:

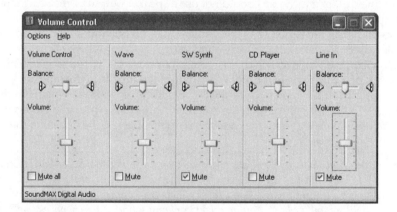

The vertical slider bars control the volume of the sound. Moving the slider bar up increases the volume of the audio signal, and moving it down decreases the volume. At the top of each section is a balance control that adjusts the sound between left and right.

### Digital Audio Editor

A digital audio editor edits and records sound. The examples shown in this book use both GoldWave 5 and Cool Edit 2000 digital audio editors. Different digital audio editors work fundamentally the same. The steps to get a finished audio (WAV) file are as follows:

1. Set the recording levels where you set controls for volume and balance that will be in place when you actually record the file.

2. Select the recording settings which control the size and type of sound file, and its resolution or number of sound snapshots per wave.

3. Record the sound where you capture and save the audio file.

4. Edit the sound, which allows you to edit out sections of the sound, or combine audio files, or move sections around.

5. Save the sound.

**Set the Recording Levels**    The first step is to view the recording levels using the digital audio editor and to use the mixer (Volume Control) to set the levels. Figure 19-1 shows the GoldWave 5 digital audio editor ready to record with the mixer also showing. Start playing what you are going to record. The Control dialog box shows the sound device controls and a visual display of the volume and the balance between the left and right channels. The left

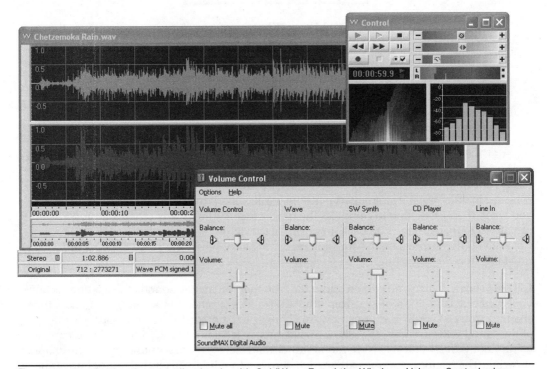

**FIGURE 19-1**    Setting the recording levels with GoldWave 5 and the Windows Volume Control mixer

and right channel bars show the recording level. You want to check it with a loud section of what you are recording. The bars move from left to right indicating the level. When the bar is all the way to the right, you are starting to get distortion or clipping. You want it to just fill up the bar at the loudest sections of the piece you are recording. Slide the appropriate slider up and down until the levels look the way you want them. Other digital audio editors may look a little different, but they use the same principles.

**Select the Recording Settings and Record the Sound**    Several recording settings need to be set. Here are the common settings that are available (this dialog box is from Cool Edit 2000):

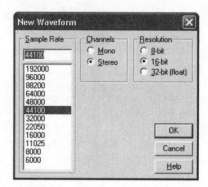

- **Mono or stereo (channels)**    Mono will give you smaller files, but you lose the stereo effect.

- **Sampling rate**    A *sample* is a digital snapshot. When these samples are close together in time, they produce a smooth sound. CD quality is 44,100 Hz (hertz or cycles per second). The higher the sampling rate, the bigger the file.

- **Sampling size (resolution)**    Available sizes are 8-bit, 16-bit, or 32-bit. The bigger the sampling size, the bigger the file, but also the higher the quality.

A 44,100-Hz sampling rate at 8 bits for a mono recording will give you the same sound quality as a 44,100-Hz sampling rate at 16 bits for stereo.

If your final product is going to be a WAV file that the user will download, you might consider making the file as small as possible while still giving you the minimum quality you want. If you are going to compress the file for RealAudio, or any other compression, you can afford to increase the size some to improve the quality.

With all the settings made, start the recording and, when the piece to be recorded is finished, stop the recording.

**Edit the Sound**    When you edit an audio file, you manipulate the sounds by deleting sections you want out, combine sections from other audio files, or change the levels, or make other changes. You can control where you want changes to be made by using a visual display of the sound waves. Figure 19-2 shows what a recorded sound looks like in both channels using Cool Edit 2000. If this were mono rather than stereo, there would only be one channel showing. The beginning at the extreme left shows a thin line. This indicates that no audio was recorded. The line expands as the audio begins. The thickness of the line indicates how

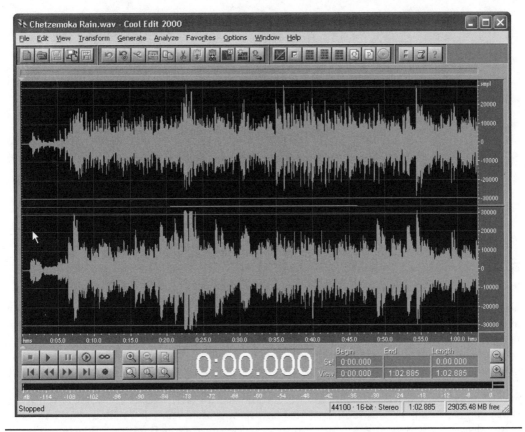

**FIGURE 19-2**    A recorded sound in Cool Edit 2000

loud it is. When the thickness fills the frame, there is maximum volume. If the sound crosses the threshold lines at the top and bottom, it is distorting or *clipping*. A little bit of clipping might be all right, but listen to those sections carefully. You may have to record again with the recording levels turned down a little. You can play the digital recording and listen to it with the controls in the digital audio editor.

Most editors provide a lot of functions for editing an audio file. You select a point of time or a section of time visually. To select a point of time, place the mouse pointer where you want and click. A vertical line appears that shows the point of time selected. This is useful if you want to insert something at that point.

To select a section of time or a sound segment, drag the mouse across it to indicate the section you want. In Figure 19-3, a section is selected for deletion using GoldWave 4.21. Use the Delete or Cut command to delete the section that is selected.

Copying and pasting is very similar. To copy and paste, you select the section of the audio you want to copy, press CTRL-C to copy, select a point where you want to insert it, and press CTRL-V to paste. In more elaborate digital audio editors, you have a lot of control over the sound. This example shows only the basic steps to edit your audio file.

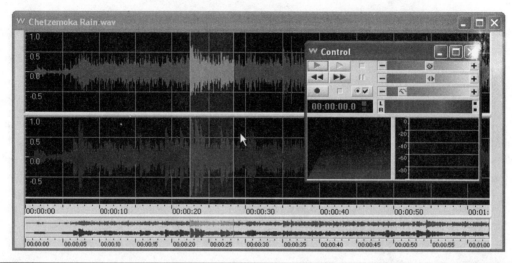

**FIGURE 19-3**     Selecting a section of sound to delete

**Save the Sound**     When you have the audio file the way you want it, you need to save it either as a WAV file or in one of the compressed formats, the most popular of which is Motion Picture Experts Group (MPEG) Layer-3 (MP3). WAV files are the most common and the easiest for your users to play, since all recent browsers can open WAV files. At the same time, WAV files can be very large. A one-minute WAV file recorded at 44,100-Hz, 16-bit stereo, is over 10MB. If you are going to put a WAV file in a web, try to keep the size down by making it very short or by using lower-quality recording settings. *MPEG 3 (MP3)* is an audio compression that will give you near-CD quality while compressing the WAV file to about one-tenth its original size. (A 10,835KB WAV file compresses down to 1,095KB with MP3.) The same 10MB WAV file, if it is recorded in 8-bit mono at 22,500 Hz, will only take 1,293KB.

## Using Nonstreaming Audio Files

Nonstreaming audio files are simpler to handle than streaming files and don't require special software. Let's look at using both standard WAV files and compressed MP3 nonstreaming files.

### Using Standard WAV Files

A nonstreaming audio file is one that you listen to on your computer or other listening device. You turn it on, it loads on your computer, you listen to it, and then turn it off. It is stored on your computer or on a CD. When you want to link to a WAV file, you import the file into your web and create a hyperlink to it on your web page. This is done in the same way you would create a hyperlink to any other object. Here are the steps to do that:

1. With FrontPage loaded and the page on which you want the audio file open in Design view, select File | Import. The Import dialog box will open.

2. Click Add File and in the Add File to Import List dialog box, supply the path to your WAV file. Click Open. The file will appear in the Import dialog box. Click OK. The WAV file will be imported into your web.

3. On your web page, select the word, phrase, or picture to which you want to attach a hyperlink to the WAV file and click Hyperlink on the toolbar.

4. On the dialog box, double-click the WAV file. Save your web page.

5. To test your link, view the page in FrontPage's Preview mode and select the link to the WAV file. Your default audio player will load and play the audio clip, as shown in the bottom of the media pane in Figure 19-4.

---

**NOTE**    *Our sample WAV file, "Chetzemoka Rain," is composed and copyrighted 1993 by David Michael and is played by David Michael and Randy Mead. It is taken from their CD Keystone Passage. You can reach David Michael through Purnima Productions, P.O. Box 317, Port Townsend, WA 98368, (360) 379-9732, or on his web site at **www.David@acousticdogma.com**. The piece is used with his permission.*

---

**TIP**    *By importing the WAV file, it becomes part of the web and will be uploaded when you publish the web. If you use an FTP program to upload your files, remember to upload the WAV file, too.*

## Compressing the WAV File with MP3

For the audio file to be used on a web site from a server, the file needs to be compressed so that it can be transmitted on the Internet quickly. MP3 is the most popular format, and its

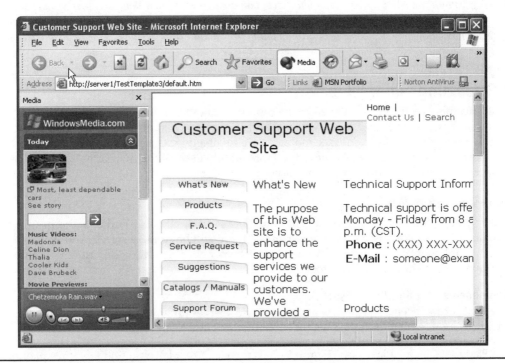

**FIGURE 19-4**    Playing an audio selection on a web page

usage far exceeds other formats because of the quality and small size of its compression. Listening to an MP3 file requires an MP3 player. The Windows Media Player handles MP3 files. RealOne from RealNetworks, Inc. (**http://www.real.com**) is an alternative that can be downloaded for free but starts charging you for it if you do not cancel within 14 days. Also, the web site **http://www.mp3.com** has links to several MP3 players. The costs vary from several thousand dollars to under $10. Two popular packages are Windows Media Player and Winamp from Nullsoft, Inc. (**http://www.winamp.com**). Many bands are using MP3 files for promotional purposes because they can provide a CD-quality song with a relatively small file size. These files are still relatively large. The Band released a three-minute and 56-second song as an MP3 file that came out to 3.61MB. While a number of the bands using MP3 are unknown, many larger recording labels are also now using the MP3 format. MP3.com is an excellent site from which to download copies of many of the songs that have been saved in MP3 format. A required feature is as encoder within the player. If the player you choose doesn't include an encoder, you will need to get one separately.

---

**NOTE**   *It is also easy to copy music from CDs that are copyrighted. This is illegal. Always be sure the material doesn't belong to someone else, or that you have the owner's permission to use or copy it.*

---

When you have an MP3 file you want in a web, you need to import it and create a hyperlink to it on your page as you did with a WAV file.

---

**TIP**   *If you put an MP3 audio file on your web, you are assuming that your web's users have an MP3 player. Although most will have a player, some may not, depending on your audience. Older systems may not. As a precaution, you might include a link to MP3.com or Real.com where users can download a player if they don't have one.*

---

# Using Streaming Audio Files

With streaming audio, you don't need to be concerned about the length of the audio clip. The user will click your link, the player will load, and after a short period, the clip will start to play. The two major streaming audio technologies are RealNetworks RealAudio and Microsoft's Windows Media Player. RealAudio is the more widely used of the two. Consequently, this chapter focuses on creating streaming audio with RealOne Player.

## How RealAudio Works

Before you get into the nuts and bolts of doing RealAudio, it helps to understand how the system works. Following a system description, there will be step-by-step instructions on how to implement streaming RealAudio in your own web. This section describes the primary components and how they work together.

### Components of a RealAudio System

The RealAudio system is a client/server system. RealServer provides the content, the RealAudio file; sends it over a network (the Internet or an intranet); and RealPlayer then plays it.

**RealPlayer**    RealOne Player (see Figure 19-5) is the client that lets you find, organize playing lists, and download or listen to RealAudio files and watch RealVideo files. You can download

**FIGURE 19-5**    RealOne Player Plus for playing RealAudio and RealVideo files streamed over the Internet or an intranet

RealOne Player Plus for a monthly fee (after a free evaluation period of 14 days) from the RealNetworks web site (**http://www.real.com/player/**). As you play an audio file, the area immediately under the menu bar displays information about the RealAudio or RealVideo being played. Below it are the controls that let you play, pause, stop, and move to any spot in the RealAudio file. (When viewing a video, the play controls are beneath the video screen.) The information and control bars are shown here:

**RealAudio Encoder**    The encoder is the program that creates a RealAudio or RealVideo file from a digitized audio or video file or a live audio or video signal. Encoding takes in the source audio files or live recordings of audio or video, and creates packets using an algorithm (or a codec) to compress the data. The data packets are then streamed over a network to the user. The codec at the user's site then translates the packets back into the audio or video file for playing. RealNetworks most current product is Helix Producer. There are two versions of the encoder, Helix Producer Basic and Helix Producer Plus with additional features. They are available from the RealNetworks web site (**http://www.realnetworks.com/products/producer/**).

---

**N**OTE    *Codecs (short for compressor/decompressors) are listed by the type of sound being encoded; they control the degree of compression used in the RealAudio file created.*

**Helix Universal Server**    Helix Universal Server is the program that delivers the RealAudio and RealVideo files over a network. One Helix Universal Server can deliver many RealAudio files to many RealPlayers at the same time. Each file being delivered is referred to as a *stream*. RealNetworks has several Helix Servers with different prices and capabilities:

- **Helix Universal Server Basic**    Free. Can serve a small number of on-demand or live audio or video streams.

- **Helix Universal Server Standard**    Costs around $2,000 at this writing. Includes extra tools and can serve more streams than Basic.

- **Helix Universal Server Enterprise**    For business applications, it costs around $6,000 at this writing. Includes extra tools and can serve more streams than Standard.

- **Helix Universal Server Internet**    Aimed at Internet service providers. Currently starts at about $8,500 for a 100-stream server and goes up from there.

These servers are available from the RealNetworks web site (**http://www.realnetworks.com/products/server**). The prices and capabilities change regularly as the technology advances, and there are many variables, especially at the upper end, so check the RealNetworks web site for the latest information.

---

**N**OTE    *While Helix Universal Server Basic is free, and Helix Universal Server Plus is reasonably priced, the limitation will be the bandwidth available to you. Even a 256K DSL line will only support around ten streams. If you will only need limited streaming, this may work, or you may need to go to an Internet service provider with a Helix Universal Server Internet and large available bandwidth.*

### RealAudio Files and Metafiles

Two file types are commonly used in the RealAudio system: the RealAudio file (.ra) and the RealAudio metafile (.ram). RealMedia technology has added the capability to include pictures and animation with audio to create synchronized multimedia presentations using the RealMedia file format (.rm). Here, though, we will focus on the older and more common RA and RAM files.

**RealAudio Clip (.ra)**    The RealAudio Clip is an audio file encoded in the RealAudio format. The file is created with the RealProducer encoder and delivered by the RealSystem Server.

**RealAudio Metafile (.ram)**    If you linked directly to the RealAudio file, it would download like a WAV file. The RealAudio system uses a metafile that contains the location of the RealAudio file and is the file that is linked to from the web page.

### How the RealAudio File Is Delivered

Figure 19-6 shows the RealAudio components and how they deliver the RealAudio file. The numbers in the figure match the following steps:

1. At the request of a web browser, the web server delivers a page to the browser that has a link to a RealAudio metafile.

2. If the user clicks the link, the web browser requests the metafile from the web server.

3. The web server delivers the metafile to the web browser. Based on the .ram file extension, the web server sets the MIME type (defined later under "Creating a RealAudio Metafile") of the file to *audio/x-pn-realaudio*.

4. Based on the MIME type, the web browser starts RealOne as a helper application and passes it the metafile.

5. RealOne reads the URL from the metafile and requests the RealAudio file from the RealServer.

6. RealServer begins streaming the requested RealAudio file to RealOne.

**NOTE**   *RealOne does not require a web browser to function. The user can enter the URL of a RA or RM file directly into RealOne or use the Preset or Scan buttons on RealOne Plus.*

## Creating a RealAudio File

The first step in using RealAudio is to create an on-demand RealAudio file (that is, not a live stream, which is covered shortly). RealAudio files are created with the Helix Producer encoder that is shown in Figure 19-7. The following sections will focus on the different parts of the encoder and how they are used to produce a RealAudio file for on-demand streaming.

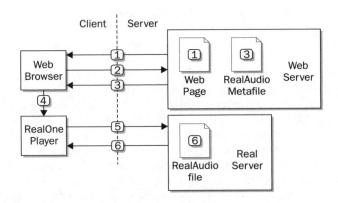

**FIGURE 19-6**    How a RealAudio file is delivered

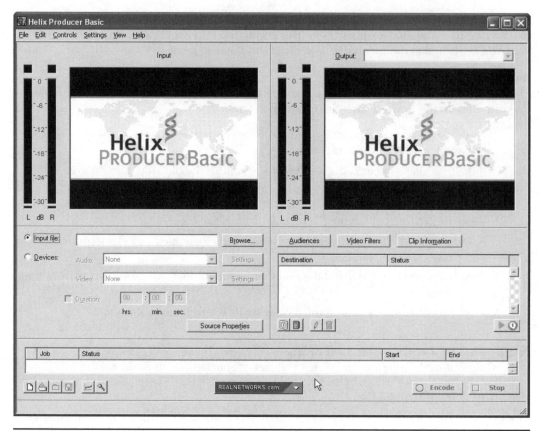

**FIGURE 19-7**   Helix Producer used to encode RealAudio files

### Set Up Helix Producer Input

Begin setting up Helix Producer by loading it. The program loads with a New Job window. But if you are starting with another job and want to begin again, select File | New Job. The New Job window will open, allowing you to select the recording characteristics that you want to use, as shown in Figure 19-8.

On the left pane of the window, you specify the Input characteristics; on the right, the Output. On the left of each pane is an audiometer that displays the volume of the input and output. Below the volume display on the Input side, you define the source of the input. Your choices are Input File or Devices (for recording live broadcasts). If you select Input File, you can Browse to establish the path of the file. In this case, you will create a RealMedia file with an .rm extension from an existing file in another format, such as a WAV file. When you enter the input file path, you will see the default filename in the Output Destination pane.

If you choose Devices, you can choose Audio or Video. In this case, you can take a live audio and/or video stream coming into your computer and feed it to a RealServer. You can specify devices such as microphones, VCR, video camera, a CD player, a radio or television

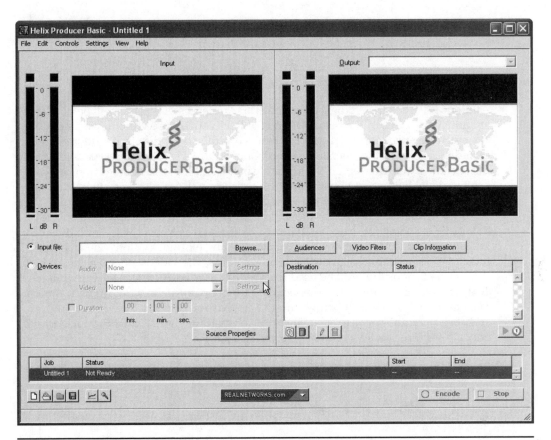

**FIGURE 19-8**    New Job window to begin encoding

in or connected to your computer, or a digital camera. Select the device from the pull-down list. Live broadcasts will be covered in the section on live RealAudio. When an input device or file is specified, the Source Properties can be displayed.

---

***NOTE*** *For your input files, you can use compressed AVI, WAV, uncompressed QuickTime 3, 4, and 5 file formats under any circumstances. On a Windows operating system, you can also use AIFF (.aif, .aifc, .aiff), MPG, MPEG, MLV, MP2, MP3, MPA, MPE, MPV2, and M3U file formats; and Digital Video Files (.dv); and Windows Meta Files (.wma, .wmf). With some of these formats, you may also need DirectX 8 to be installed, which is available from either Microsoft or RealNetworks. Some other formats also are available with other operating systems.*

### Entering the Audio Output Information

The destination and characteristics of a RealMedia file are defined on the right of the window. You can save the output as an RM file to be used later as on-demand streaming, or in a live broadcast on a Helix Universal Server. You can enter more than one output destination, and it will be encoded correctly. Enter the following information:

---

**NOTE**    *The file will be saved with an .rmvb extension if you are encoding a Variable Bit Rate (VBR) file.*

---

- **Audiences**    Click the Audiences button. The Audiences dialog box will be displayed, as shown next. One of the better features of RealNetwork's technology is that you can create an encoded RealAudio file that is optimized for different modem speeds, or audiences. When this encoded file is streamed from a server, the server determines the encoding to use based on the available bandwidth. If a fast connection becomes bogged down because of network traffic, the server will seamlessly switch to a lower bandwidth encoding until the network clears. In this dialog box, you select the type of encoding and bandwidth or audience. The Encoding Settings specify the type of data to be encoded, for example, type of Audio, such as Music, Voice, or No Audio. The type of Video Mode allows you to select among Normal Motion Video, Sharpest Image, Smoothest Motion, Slide Show, or No Video. The Video Codec specifies which compression algorithm will be used to encode the video. The Audience Selection Templates setting allows you to select the number of audiences the job will contain. The audience is the size of bandwidth to be used. You click the audience on the left and click the right arrow to select it and place it on the right. (Helix Producer Basic only allows three audiences to be selected in a job.)

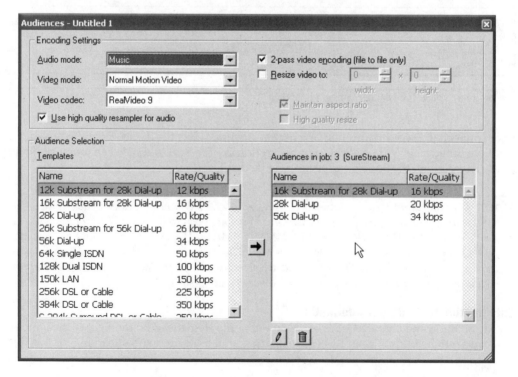

- **Clip Information**   Clicking the Clip Information button allows you to enter the title, author, copyright, description, and keywords that are displayed in RealOne when the RealMedia file is played. This is how ownership and copyright information is recorded in a RealMedia file.

- **Destination icons**   Below the Destination box in the Output side are four icons used to Add File Destination, Add Server Destination, Edit Destination, and Remove Destination. You can click the Edit Destination icon to find out or change the folder in which the file will be stored.

### Select Preferences

There are a few additional options to set for encoding. Select Edit | Preferences to open the Preferences dialog box, as shown here:

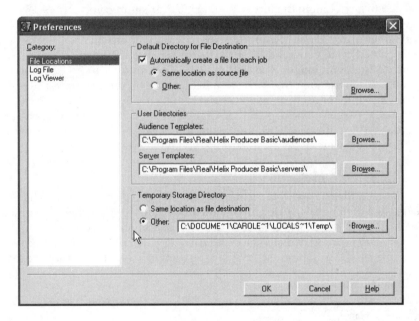

If you click the items under Category, you will find the options that apply to them. For File Locations, you can establish whether a file will be created for each job and where it will be stored. Under User Directories, you can select where the Audience Templates, the Server Templates, and the Temporary Storage Directory are stored.

If you click Log File under Category, you can set options to control where the log file is stored and some characteristics about the content. The Log Viewer sets the Log Viewer Cache size. It defaults to 1,000 messages in Helix Producer Basic.

### Encode the WAV File

The final step after selecting the Input and Output options is to click Encode. The encoding will begin. The status bar in the lower left shows the percentage of encoding as the job is done. As the encoding progresses, you can check the audio levels from the Audio Level bars on the Input and Output panes.

PART IV

If you are encoding a WAV or other file, the end of the file will automatically stop the encoding. If you are encoding either a live stream or some other continuous source, you'll need to click Stop to conclude the encoding. When the encoding concludes, the status bar contains the Start and End times.

## HTTP Streaming vs. Network Streaming

Two types of streaming are available for RealAudio files. Although you have seen that you need a RealServer to stream RealAudio files, you actually can stream files without RealServer. This is called *HTTP streaming*; streaming from a RealServer is called *network streaming*.

Many Internet service providers don't have a RealServer, and HTTP streaming is useful if you are being hosted with one that doesn't. The downside is that, while it will deliver multiple streams, HTTP streaming is not as robust or efficient. With network streaming, you can move ahead to any point in the file, but with HTTP streaming, you cannot—you can only move backward to a point in the file that has already played. The downside of streaming using a RealServer is that, since the Internet service provider has paid for RealServer, that cost could be passed on to you in additional fees for use of RealServer.

If you are dealing with longer RealAudio files—15 minutes or more—or plan to have a lot of usage, it is recommended that you use a RealServer. If you use shorter files that will not be streamed by a lot of users at once, use the HTTP streaming.

The RealAudio file has to be copied to a server either locally for an intranet or remotely at your Internet service provider. If you are using HTTP streaming, you will copy it to the web server. If you are using network streaming, you will copy it to RealServer.

## Creating a RealAudio Metafile

The RealAudio metafile is a one-line text file to which a web page is linked. The metafile starts RealOne and then passes the location of the RealAudio file to RealOne. The RealAudio metafile is usually automatically created when Helix Producer encodes a RealAudio or RealMedia file. The metafile can also be created using a text editor like Notepad. A word processor can be used, but you must save the file as a pure text file without formatting.

### An HTTP Streaming Metafile

Before you can stream RealAudio files through HTTP, you need to define the following MIME type for your web server:

```
Audio/x-pn-realaudio (files with .ra, and .rm file extensions)
```

---

**NOTE**    *Multipurpose Internet Mail Extensions (MIME) is the standard for attaching nontext files to standard Internet mail messages. Nontext files include graphics, spreadsheets, formatted word processor documents, sound files, and so on. In addition to e-mail software, the MIME standard is used by web servers to identify the files they are sending to web clients; in this way, new file formats can be accommodated simply by updating the browser's list of pairs of MIME types and appropriate software for handling each type.*

---

Some web servers are preconfigured with the RealAudio MIME type. There are three ways to find out if your web server is one of these. The first is to create a link to an HTTP streaming file and see if it works. If the server is not configured, it won't work. The second way is to call your local network administrator or Internet service provider and ask if the server is preconfigured. If it isn't, request that the RealAudio MIME type be set up.

If you are administering your own IIS server on Windows 2000, or Windows Server 2003, or XP Professional, you can check this for yourself as a third way. To do that on the Windows 2000 Server, open the Start menu and choose Programs | Administrative Tools | Internet Services Manager. For Windows Server 2003, open the Start menu and choose All Programs | Administrative Tools | Internet Information Services (IIS) Manager. In the case of Windows Server 2003, right-click your server and choose Properties. At the bottom of the Internet Information Services tab in the area Computer MIME Types, click MIME Types. Scroll down the list of Registered MIME Types and look for the RealAudio's RA and RM file types. If they are not there, installing either RealOne or Helix Producer will put them there. On Windows XP Professional, open Start and choose Control Panel | Administrative Tools | Internet Information Services. There is no Properties option for XP's web server.

You should have already copied the RealAudio file to the web server because you need to use the path and the filename of the RealAudio file in the metafile. The metafile will have a single line with the following form:

```
http://hostname/path/file.ra
```

*Hostname* is the name of your web server. Here is a listing of a typical metafile, which you would save with a .ram file extension:

```
http://www.whidbey.net/rafiles/matthews/media/summertime.ra
```

### Network Streaming Metafile

If you copied your RealAudio file to RealServer for network streaming, you will use the pathname and the filename of the RealAudio file in the metafile. The metafile will take one of two forms depending on if it is a RealSystem Server or an older version of RealServer, or if you are targeting RealPlayer 3.0 to 5.0 or RealPlayer 8. The older RealServers and RealPlayers use the PNM protocol as shown here:

```
pnm://hostname/path/file.ra
```

*Hostname* is the name of your RealServer. Again, the file is saved with a .ram extension.

The primary protocol for RealServer is RealTime Streaming Protocol (RTSP), so the metafile would appear like this:

```
rtsp://hostname/path/file.ra
```

RAM files for network streaming are identical to RAM files for HTTP streaming with the exception that they use PNM or RTSP as the protocol instead of HTTP.

## Linking to the Metafile

Use FrontPage to import the RealAudio metafile to your web, and then create a hyperlink to it the same way you imported and created a hyperlink to an audio segment earlier in this chapter. When you do that, your web page will stream your RealAudio file when a user clicks the link to the metafile.

## Live RealAudio

All the audio in the previous sections has been on-demand. Anyone can select the audio file at any time and listen to it from the beginning of the file. But RealAudio also can play in real time, such as a radio broadcast or a live show. While a radio broadcast may be playing prerecorded material, it is still going out in real time, so if someone selected the link after the show had started, they would join it somewhere in the middle in real time.

Producing live RealAudio is very similar to on-demand streaming. One difference is that live RealAudio requires the use of a RealServer because HTTP streaming only works with on-demand material. Another difference is that with on-demand RealAudio, you create a WAV file from an audio signal and then encode the WAV file into a RealAudio file. With live RealAudio, you bypass the WAV file step and encode the audio signal on-the-fly.

### Start with a Live Audio Signal

The first step is having a live audio signal. This signal is delivered to the sound card the same way you delivered a signal to record a WAV file. The signal can be prerecorded material from a CD or tape recorder, or it can be live going from a microphone to the sound card. If you are using multiple microphones, you will need a mixing device, such as a soundboard or mixer-amplifier, to combine the different microphone signals into one signal for the sound card.

### Set Up the RealAudio Encoder for Live Streaming

The Helix Producer encoder is uniquely set up for live streaming. In the initial New Job dialog box, you select Devices, and from the Audio drop-down list, select the input device for the live audio, such as a sound card. Click Settings to select the Recording Mixer for the Helix Producer Recording control dialog box or Vendor-Provided Controls for your own. From this you can control the Balance and Volume of the input stream and indicate whether the input is from a CD Player, Microphone, or Line In to your computer. At this point, you can enter the Output characteristics, such as the Audience and Clip Information, which supply the file type, target audience, and audio format as you did for an on-demand stream.

To enter the Media Server information that you want to use, click the Add Server Destination beneath the Destination box. The Server Destination dialog box will be displayed, as shown in Figure 19-9. This will establish the RealServer from which you will be broadcasting your live stream. Enter this information:

- **Destination Name**   This will be the name in the Output section of the Helix Producer window. If you are planning to use the server for other jobs, click Templates and set up the server as a template that can be used in the future.

- **Stream Name**   This will become the filename of the encoded output.

- **Broadcast Method**   Select from the drop-down list. You can choose among several methods of push and pull technology: Push, Account-Based Login; Push, Password-Only Login; Push, Multicast (encoder broadcasts to multiple servers at the same time or to a one-way satellite network); Pull; and Legacy Push (prior to version 9 of Helix Universal Server). *Push* is when a user brings up your web page and the streaming audio is immediately available to them; *Pull* is when a user brings up your web page and asks for the streaming audio they want to hear. Push will be the easiest to implement. The rest of the options may differ depending on the Broadcast Method chosen. The following describes a Push, Account-Based Login choice.

- **Server Address**    This is the IP address or name of the Helix Universal Server that has been set up as the physical server for your job.

- **Path (Optional)**    You may enter one to the server.

- **Port/Port Range**    Port 80 is the RealAudio default. This port will receive the encoded packets.

- **Transport**    Choose between UDP and TCP for the Internet protocol to be used. This determines how the packets will be sent to the server from the encoder. UDP sends with minimum communication between the server and the encoder. It will be the more efficient technique and is recommended for broadcast jobs. However, TCP is required if network devices such as firewalls are used. Such devices interfere with the control between the server and the encoder, increasing the risk of lost packets.

- **Username and Password**    These are needed to use the RealServer. Select Remember Password if you want to bypass the password request.

- **Advanced Options**    If you are an advanced user, you can click this button to handle some broadcast aspects, such as how often to reconnect if the connection is broken, how to protect against lost data, and so on.

### Encode the Audio Signal for a Live Stream

After completing the settings necessary for the media server, select the job to be encoded. Make sure your recording equipment is ready and click Encode. You will see the audiometer

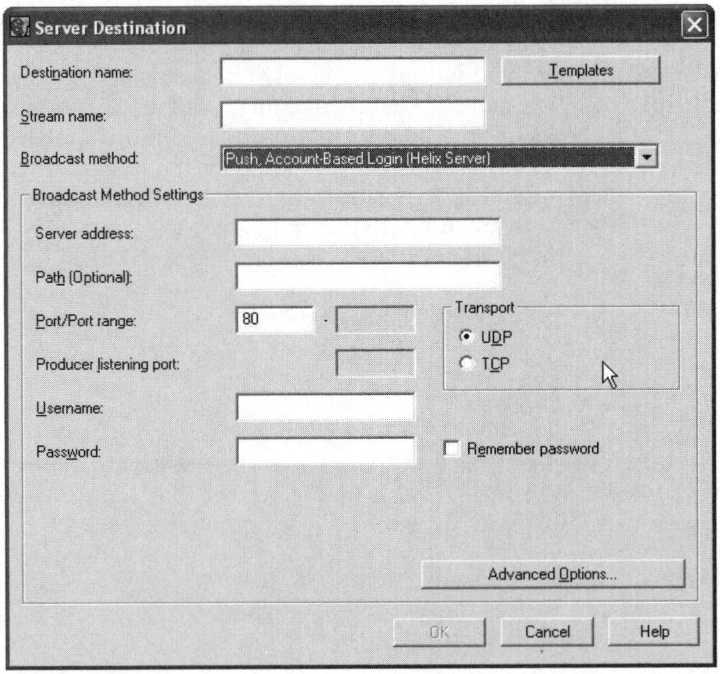

**FIGURE 19-9**    The Server Destination dialog box is used to establish the live broadcast server.

monitor the volume and quality of the sound. Use the Recording Control mixer to control the sound level as you did for recording a WAV file, and you can see the statistics reflected in the status bar. When you are finished with the broadcast, click Stop.

### Live Webcasts

There is a lot of live streaming audio and video on the Web today, including concerts, sports events, and radio programs. These are called *webcasts* and range from large-budget professional productions to small-budget shows done in a living room, basement, or garage. Many of the large-budget events treat web broadcasting as they do radio and TV broadcasting, with lots of equipment and people and traditional formats. Some of the smaller ones, though, are experimenting with the technology and the format to produce something different.

One such low-budget experimental show is *TestingTesting* (**http://www.electricedge.com/ testingtesting/**), which is a live 30-minute performance of interactive improvisational Internet music done in the producer's living room. The show has two regular musicians and a special guest musician, or musicians, each week. Because of the living room atmosphere, the performers are relaxed, and it becomes much more fun than a more formal performing space. One of the differences between this show and radio or TV is that they use a guest book on their web site in which the Internet audience can enter comments during the show. Those comments are read to the performers during breaks in the music. This changes the direction of the show, making the Internet audience a part of it. The show is advertised as being 60 minutes or so long, but it often runs shorter or longer. There are no rules. Each show is saved and is available for those who were not able to be there live. The guest book comments are saved along with digital pictures taken during the show.

The audience for a show like this isn't measured in millions, it is measured in dozens— dozens who become personally involved with those on the show. *TestingTesting* uses a music format because the people involved with it are mostly musicians and there are a lot of talented players where they live. But webcasting like this could use any number of formats. It could be used for talk shows or other live programs like old radio shows but with an interactive element from the Internet audience. Or someone could play music from their record collection that others might like to hear but can't on commercial radio. This is niche webcasting on a low budget with an audience that talks back. Use your imagination in this new medium. Participate with the *TestingTesting* crew on their web site in figuring out what it can do.

# Security on the Web

As the use of the Web has grown to permeate most aspects of our society, especially the economic side, so have the criminal aspects. As important, and maybe more important than the outright criminal activity, is the malicious mischief that hackers inflict on the Web with viruses and other programs that cause damage to information or interrupt Web service. Add to this the number of transactions that users would like to keep private for business or personal reasons and the needs for security measures becomes very significant.

## Security Needs

The Internet, which, grossly simplified, looks something like Figure 20-1, has hundreds of millions of users connected to millions of interconnected computers. Added to this are a growing number of intranets connected to the Internet. As information is transferred between two users on the Internet, it is routed through a large number of intermediary computers under the independent control of many different entities. There is no way to control where the information may be routed or limit who controls the computers it is routed through. Also, for the modest price of an Internet account, anyone can get on the Internet and do what they wish. Consider what is happening on the Internet:

- E-mail is being sent, routed, and received. It can contain anything from "Hi, how are you?" to very sensitive trade secrets or large monetary transactions.

- Web sites are being accessed to read, print, or download their information. On the majority of sites, access is unlimited and free, but on others, access is limited (by a password or other means) for various reasons.

- In an already large and growing number of web sites, goods and services are being sold, purchased by way of credit card or other payment forms.

- Newsgroups are being read and contributed to, again generally with unlimited access, although occasionally access is password controlled.

- Direct real-time audio and video communications, which today are a moderate part of the Internet traffic, will grow as the bandwidth of the Internet expands. For the most part, the communications are not sensitive in nature, but there may be charges for its receipt.

- Telnet, Gopher, and other classical Internet services have all but disappeared.

- Web servers are being maintained; web pages are being added, revised, and removed; user IDs and passwords are being changed; and scripts are being worked on.

- Increasingly, people on intranets are gaining access to the Internet.

- Increasingly, people on the Internet are gaining limited access to intranets through the use of extranets that allow businesses and corporations to conduct much of their work with off-site business partners.

- A large portion of the computer population, especially its younger members, are sharing music and other files using a peer-to-peer file sharing system first developed by Napster where you can go through a directory computer to reach and copy files that are on another individual's computer.

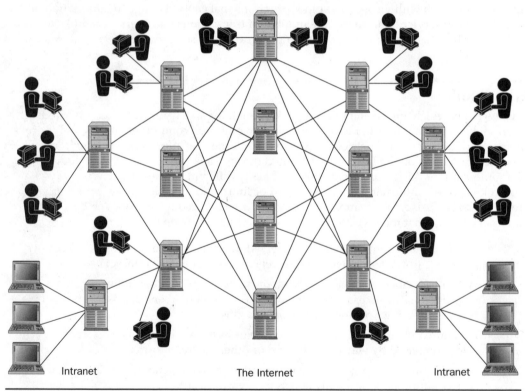

**FIGURE 20-1**   The Internet

Where are the risks in this Internet activity? There are, of course, many, but among them are

- Interception and misuse or misdirection of e-mail
- Creation and transmission of e-mail from a misrepresented source
- Accessing a controlled-access web site without the appropriate permission
- Interception and misuse of credit card or other financial information during an Internet business transaction
- Misrepresentation on the part of a buyer or seller in an Internet business transaction
- Gaining unauthorized access to the administrative functions of a web server to misuse the user IDs and passwords, or to otherwise upset the operation of the server
- Gaining unauthorized access to a web server and changing web pages or scripts
- Gaining unauthorized access to an intranet for whatever reason

The primary security goals, then, are just these three:

- Limiting access to web pages, web servers, and intranets to only those with proper authorization
- Securing the transmission of information, whether sensitive e-mail, credit card data, or financial information
- Authenticating the sender, the receiver, and the data transferred

# Controlling Access

"Controlling access" has at least two different connotations:

- Limiting access to all or part of a web site to only a certain group, such as subscribers to an electronic publication or administrators on the web site
- Securing an intranet site from access via the Internet by setting up a computer, software, or other device called a *firewall,* which controls entry to and possibly exit from the intranet

## Limiting Access to a Web Site

Limiting access to a web site means that you have a specific list of people or groups of people to whom you have granted some type of permission to access your site. When you install FrontPage on your computer, you (really your computer) are automatically given permission to access the web pages you create. Also, a default *root web* (containing your home page) is automatically created (by IIS), and, depending on your web server, varying levels of permission are by default granted to access it. Also, in most instances, by default, all the web pages you create are given the same permission as the root web, meaning that if the server administrator has done nothing to limit permission, it could be that everyone will be able to access all the pages you've built—and maybe that is what you want.

If you publish your web to IIS 6, running on Windows Server 2003 (which is assumed here), the default permissions are more limited and have probably been further limited by a network administrator. You still have some latitude in setting permissions for those who visit your web site, however.

---

**NOTE**  *You cannot establish permissions in FrontPage if you are working with a web you have not published (that exists only on your hard disk). However, if you are using the New Technology File System (NTFS), you can control permissions at the file and folder level. See the next Note below.*

As a default, you set the level of permission for the root web (home page), and all subwebs under it will automatically have the same level of permission. If you are directly working on your server, this is http://localhost, or the server name, like http://www.myserver.com. If you want, though, you can separately set the level of permission for any or all of the subwebs, such as http://localhost/winesnthings or http://www.myserver.com/winesnthings.

---

**NOTE**  *To use permissions with Windows and IIS, the webs must be stored in an NTFS partition and not a FAT (file allocation table) partition. This is because the permissions depend on Access Control Lists (ACLs) that are implemented with NTFS. Also, your Web Presence Provider (WPP) must create a user account on the web server you will use to access your files.*

### Creating Subwebs

On your local computer or server, a web like Wines 'n Things has been formally set up in its own folder. In this case, it is easy to open that web and establish permissions. But what if you wanted to establish a subweb within Wines 'n Things, so, for example, you could let everyone (anonymous users) browse many of the pages in the web, but have some pages in a subweb that only subscription members could access. To do this, you must create a folder, move the pages you want into it, and then make that folder a separate web. To do this, follow these steps:

1. Load FrontPage and then open the Wines 'n Things web you created earlier in this book. This must be a copy of the Wines 'n Things web that has been published to IIS, not just a local copy on the hard disk (see Chapter 23 for more on publishing).

2. In the Folder List, click the primary folder for the Wines 'n Things web (on our server, this is http://server1/ winesnthings, as you can see here).

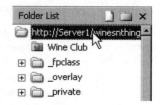

3. Click New Folder in the Folder List toolbar. Type **Wine Club** for the folder name. Drag Wines.htm, the table of selected wines that you created in Chapter 7, into this new folder.

4. Right-click the new folder and choose Convert To Web. A message is displayed telling you the penalties of converting the folder to a new subweb. You need to determine if these penalties are worth having a separate set of permissions. In most cases, the warning is worse than the actual consequence. Note how it works here.

5. Click Yes. The Wine Club folder gets a new icon showing it is a subweb and in the contents pane, you are told you can no longer view the files without opening the subweb. This allows you to set separate permissions for it.

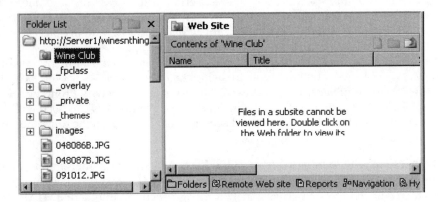

6. Double-click the Wine Club folder. Another instance of FrontPage is opened with the Wine Club subweb, like this:

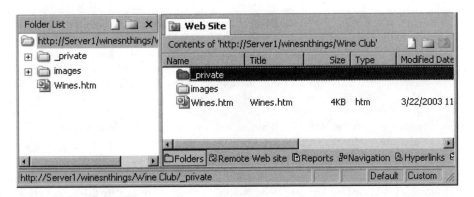

7. Double-click Wines.htm to open it in Design view. Look at the page; it should look pretty much the same as the original page.

8. Close the copy of FrontPage displaying the Wine Club subweb. The original instance of FrontPage, with the Wines 'n Things web, should remain open.

With your Wine Club pages separated into a subweb, you can now set the permissions you want for both the parent web Wines 'n Things and the subweb Wine Club.

## Setting Permissions

In Windows NT, 2000, and 2003 using NTFS, permissions are set for users and groups in terms of the roles assigned to each. In many situations, people come to a web site as anonymous users. In other words, they don't sign on to the site with a username and password, so you don't know who they are. Your first task in setting permissions, then, is to set the permissions you want to give an anonymous user, or really to the group of all people who are anonymous users. You can also identify specific users with a username and password and determine the permissions or roles you want these users to have. Finally, you can establish the roles, and the permissions inherent in those roles, you want available to assign to people, anonymous or otherwise.

How permissions are set in FrontPage depends on the server environment on which the webs have been published—whether you are using the latest Windows Server 2003, IIS 6, and Windows SharePoint Services; Windows 2000 Server and IIS 5 with FrontPage Server Extensions (FPSE) 2002 and SharePoint Team Services; or Windows NT or 2000 with IIS and FPSE 2000, but without SharePoint. (See the discussion in Chapter 2 on the difference in these server environments.)

### Setting Permissions with Windows Server 2003, IIS 6, and Windows SharePoint Services

With Windows Server 2003, IIS 6, and Windows SharePoint Services (WSS) hosting the web page for which you want to set permissions, FrontPage opens an interactive HTML page in a browser that allows you to perform the necessary administrative tasks. Use the following steps to see how this is done with the Wines 'n Things web:

---

**NOTE**   *In Windows Server 2003 and available for download from Microsoft is Internet Explorer Enhanced Security Configuration component, which provides an added layer of security for Internet Explorer that is not only important to the user of Internet Explorer, but also for the web site developer who will want to know to work with clients using the Enhanced Security Configuration component. For further information, go to http://www.microsoft.com and do a search on Internet Explorer Enhanced Security Configuration.*

---

1. In FrontPage with the Wines 'n Things web open, select Tools | Server | Administration Home. The Site Settings page will open. Under Administration, click Go to Site Administration. The Site Administration page opens.

2. Under Users And Permissions, click Manage Permission Inheritance. Under Permissions, click Use Unique Permissions, as shown in Figure 20-2, and click OK. You are returned to the Site Settings page.

**Anonymous Access Settings**   The first step in granting permission to your web site is to determine if you want to allow anonymous users to the site, and what roles or permissions you want to give them. Do that now and see how you begin the process of permission setting.

1. Click Go To Site Administration again, and then click Manage Anonymous Access. The Change Anonymous Access Settings page opens and allows you to turn anonymous access on (in Windows Server 2003 and IIS 6 it is turned off by default) for the Entire Web Site, for Lists And Libraries, or for Nothing, as shown in Figure 20-3.

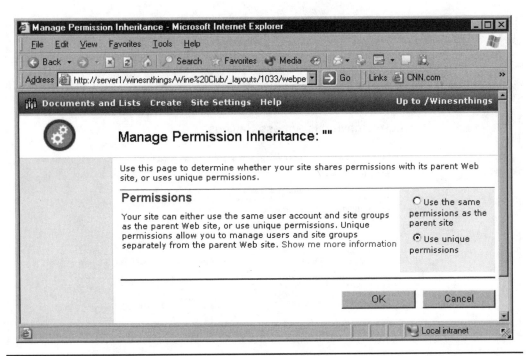

**FIGURE 20-2**    Managing Permission Inheritance in Windows Server 2003, IIS 6, and Windows SharePoint Services

***TIP***    *If the Anonymous Access options are disabled ("grayed"), anonymous access has not been enabled for the default web site in IIS. Do that by selecting Start | Administrative Tools | IIS Manager. In the IIS Manager, open Server | Web Sites. Right-click Default Web Site and choose Properties. In the Directory Security tab, click Edit under Authentication And Access Control. Click Enable Anonymous Access and click OK twice and close the IIS Manager. Refresh the Change Anonymous Access Settings page.*

2. Click Entire Web Site, given that is what you want, and click OK. You are returned to Site Administration where you can set users and roles as well as a number of other web administration functions both for the root web and subwebs.

3. Close the Internet Explorer with the Site Administration page and return to FrontPage.

**Changing Subweb Permissions**    Changing subweb permissions is what you did initially, where you had a choice between using the same permissions as the parent web or not. In that case, we were talking of Wines 'n Things as a subweb of http://servername. What we want to do now is change the subweb permissions for Wines 'n Things own subweb, Wine Club. The overall scenario we are discussing is one where the parent site has anonymous access permission, but has a subweb with only specific user access permission. In the previous section,

PART IV

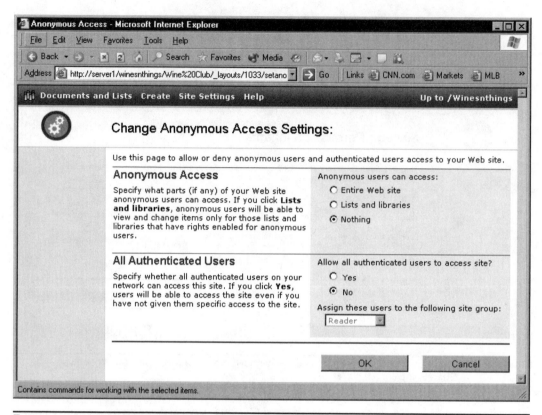

**FIGURE 20-3** Determining how to handle anonymous access

we turned on anonymous access. Here, and in the next couple of sections, we will turn it off (because it is inherited in this subweb) and set specific user permissions. Use these steps for that purpose:

1. With Wines 'n Things still open in FrontPage, double-click the Wine Club folder. A new instance of FrontPage will open, displaying the Wine Club subweb.

2. Select Tools | Server | Administrative Home. In the Site Settings page under Administration, click Go To Site Administration.

3. In the Site Administration page under Users And Permissions, click Manage Permission Inheritance. Under Permissions, click Use Unique Permissions. You are returned to the Site Settings page.

4. Click Go To Site Administration and then click Manage Anonymous Access. If you selected Entire Web Site for the parent web site, click Nothing here and click OK. You are returned to Site Administration.

You have successfully changed the permissions for a subweb. Now add access permission to this subweb for individual users.

**Adding and Managing Users** The Manage Users option allows you to add named users already defined on the system, and assign them roles. Here are the steps to do that:

1. In Site Administration, under Users And Permissions, click Manage Users. The Manage Users page will open like this:

2. Click Add Users. Enter a user and select a Site Group (role) for the user, as shown in Figure 20-4. When you are done, click Next.

3. Confirm the new user and complete any information not originally entered. If you want to send this person an e-mail message telling them they are a new user of the subweb, click that option, change the subject and body as you wish, and click Finish.

4. Click the new user you just added. The Edit Site Group Membership page opens. Here you can change the Site Group or role of a user, but not the username, which requires that you delete the name and re-add it. Click Cancel to return to the Manage Users page.

5. Click the check box next to your new user and then click Remove Selected Users. Click OK when told you are about to remove this user.

6. Click Site Settings at the top of the page to return to that page.

**Managing Site Groups or Roles** You manage the Site Groups or roles that are assigned to users which in turn give them permission to perform various functions on or in a web site. The Manage Roles option on the Permissions or Web Site Administration pages allows you to add, change, and delete roles and the permissions that are attached to them. Look at how this is done next:

1. From the Site Settings page, click Go To Site Administration; from there, click Manage Site Groups. The page shown in Figure 20-5 opens, displaying the five default Site Groups or roles and their description.

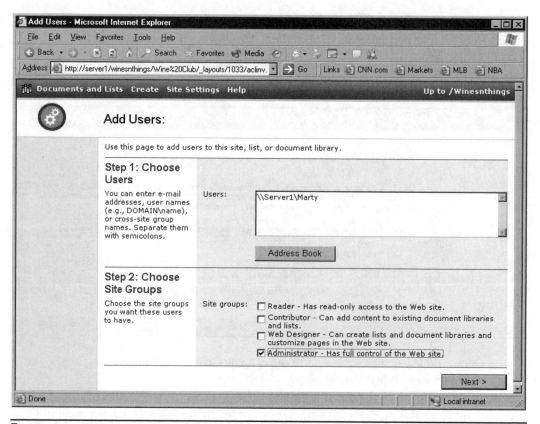

**FIGURE 20-4**    Adding a new user with permission to access the subweb

**FIGURE 20-5**    Managing the Site Groups or roles that can be assigned to users

2. Click Add A Site Group. Type **Manager** as the Site Group Name, **Manage Contributions** as the Description, and click Manage List Permissions and Manage Site Groups. A number of additional permissions are automatically selected. When you are done, the top of your page should look like Figure 20-6.

3. Scroll down to the bottom of the page and click Create Site Group. You will see Manager appear in the list of Site Groups in the Manage Site Groups page.

4. Click the check box opposite Manager, click Delete Selected Site Groups, and click OK that you are sure you want to delete a site group.

5. Click Up To /Winesnthings to open the Home Page of the web. Here, you can try out any changes you made in users, roles, and permissions. When you are done, close your browser, the Wine Club subweb, the Wines 'n Things web, and FrontPage.

## Add a Site Group

Use this page to create a site group.

| **Site Group Name and Description**<br>Enter a name and description for this site group. | Site group name:<br>Manager<br><br>Description:<br>Manage Contributions |
|---|---|
| **Rights**<br>Choose which rights to include in this site group. Use the **Select All** check box to select or clear all rights. | Select the rights to include in this site group.<br>☐ **Select All**<br><br>**List Rights**<br>☑ Manage List Permissions  -  Grant, deny, or change user permissions to a list.<br>☑ Manage Lists  -  Approve content in lists, add or remove columns in a list, and add or remove public views of a list.<br>☐ Cancel Check-Out  -  Check in a document without saving the current changes.<br>☐ Add Items  -  Add items to lists, add documents to document libraries, add Web discussion comments.<br>☐ Edit Items  -  Edit items in lists, edit documents in document libraries, edit Web discussion comments in documents, and customize Web Part Pages in document libraries.<br>☐ Delete Items  -  Delete items from a list, documents from a document library, and Web discussion comments in documents.<br>☑ View Items  -  View items in lists, documents in document libraries, view Web discussion comments, and set up e-mail alerts for list.<br><br>**Site Rights**<br>☑ Manage Site Groups  -  Create, change, and delete site groups, including adding users to the site groups and specifying which rights are assigned to a site group.<br>☐ View Usage Data  -  View reports on Web site usage. |

PART IV

**FIGURE 20-6**    Creating the Site Group of Manager

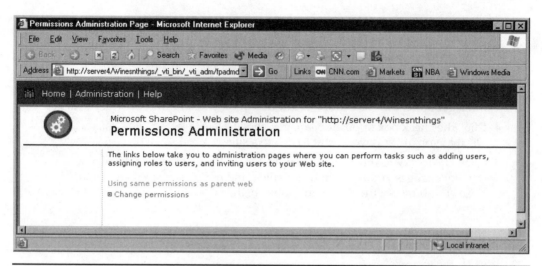

**FIGURE 20-7** Permission Administration with Windows 2000, IIS 5, and SharePoint Team Services

### Setting Permissions with Windows 2000 Server, IIS 5, and SharePoint Team Services

With Windows 2000 Server, IIS 5, and SharePoint Team Services (STS) hosting the web page for which you want to set permissions, FrontPage opens a different interactive HTML page in a browser that allows you to perform the necessary administrative tasks. To see how this is done with the home page of the Wines 'n Things web displayed, open the Tools menu and choose Server | Permissions. The Permissions Administration page will open, as shown in Figure 20-7.

**NOTE** *Your Permissions Administration page may look different than the one in Figure 20-7 due to what users, roles, and permissions have already been set for the server and web you are looking at.*

Initially, it is assumed that the Wines 'n Things web is using the same permissions as the parent web—in this case, the server. If you click Change Permissions, select Use Unique Permissions For This Web Site, click Submit, wait a minute, and click Cancel, you get a new set of permissions that allow you to

- Set or change anonymous access
- Set or change subweb permissions
- Set up and manage named users
- Set up and manage the roles that are available for both anonymous and named users
- Invite people to join a SharePoint web

**Anonymous Access Settings**   The first step in granting permission to your web site is to determine if you want to allow anonymous users to the site, and what roles or permissions you want to give them. Do that now and see how you begin the process of permission setting.

1. Click Change Anonymous Access Settings. The page of that name opens and allows you to turn anonymous access on or off and to assign a role to those users, as shown in Figure 20-8. It is turned on by default in Windows 2000 and IIS 5, which is what we want in this scenario.

2. Open the drop-down list of roles, as shown here. These roles, which you can change as you'll see in a moment, have the following default definitions:

   - **Administrator** can view, add, and change all server content, and manage server settings and accounts.

   - **Advanced Author** can view, add, and change pages, documents, themes, and borders, and recalculate hyperlinks.

   - **Author** can view, add, and change pages, as well as documents.

   - **Contributor** can view pages and documents, and view and contribute to discussions.

   - **Browser** can view pages and documents.

3. Make the anonymous access settings that are correct for you and click Submit. You are asked if you are sure you want to change the security of your site.

4. Click OK and you'll be sent to a Web Site Administration page where you can set users and roles as well as a number of other web administration functions for the root web.

5. Close the Internet Explorer with the Web Site Administration page and return to FrontPage.

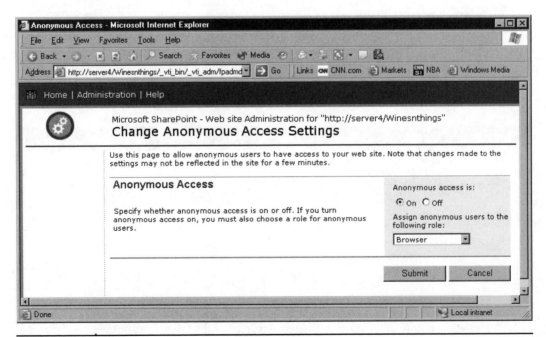

**FIGURE 20-8**  Determining how to handle anonymous access

> **NOTE** *The roles you will see in the Anonymous Access page will depend on how the network administrator has configured your web on the web server she or he manages. If you get an error message in the Change Anonymous Access Settings page saying you can't change roles for this web because it inherits the access control of the parent web, open Tools | Server | Administration Home and change the permissions for the Wines 'n Things subweb from inherit to unique permissions from its parent.*

**Changing Subweb Permissions**    Changing subweb permissions is what you did initially, where you have a choice between using the same permissions as the parent web or not. In that case, we were talking of Wines 'n Things as a subweb of http://servername. The Change Subweb Permissions we want to talk about now is for Wines 'n Things' own subweb, Wine Club. The overall scenario we are discussing is one where the parent site has anonymous access permission, but has a subweb with only specific user access permission. In the previous section, we made sure anonymous access was set. Here, and in the next couple of sections, we will turn it off (because it is inherited in this subweb), and set specific user permissions. Here is how to do that:

1. With Wines 'n Things still open in FrontPage, double-click the Wine Club folder. A new instance of FrontPage will open, displaying the Wine Club subweb.

2. Select Tools | Server | Permissions. In Permissions Administration, click Change Permissions.

3. In Change Subweb Permissions, click Use Unique Permissions For This Web Site, click Submit, and then click Cancel. You are returned to the Web Site Administration page.

You have successfully changed the permissions for a subweb. Now add access permission to this subweb for individual users.

**Adding and Managing Users**    The Manage Users option allows you to add named users, give them usernames and passwords, and assign them roles. Here are the steps to do that:

1. Click Manage Users. The Manage Users page will open like this:

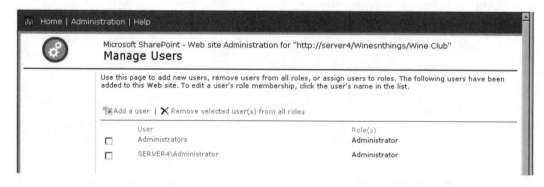

2. Click Add A User. Enter a username, password, and select a role for the user, as shown in Figure 20-9. When you are done, click Add User. Another user will be added to the list.

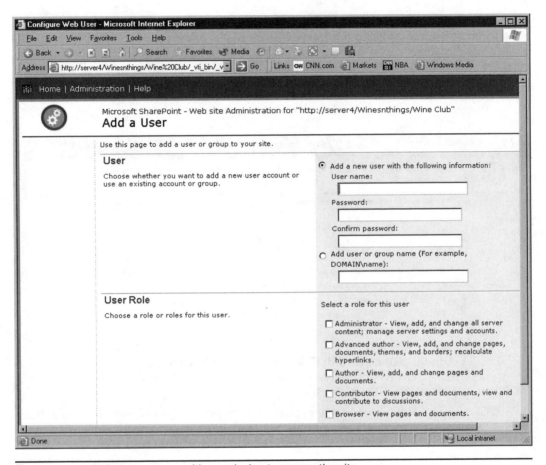

**FIGURE 20-9**    Adding a new user with permission to access the site

3. Click the new user you just added. The Edit User Role Membership page opens. Here you can change the role of a user, but not the username or password; those require that you delete the name and re-add it. Click Cancel to return to the Manage Users page.

4. Click the check box next to your new user and then click Remove Selected User(s) From All Roles. Click OK when asked if you are sure you want to delete this user.

5. Click Administration at the top of the page to return to the Web Site Administration page.

**NOTE**    *The Send An Invitation option invites a person who you have just added in Manage Users to use a SharePoint team collaboration web site and communicates to them their username and password. SharePoint is discussed further in Chapter 22.*

**Adding and Managing Roles**  With both anonymous and named users, you give them permissions by assigning them predefined roles. The Manage Roles option on the Permissions or Web Site Administration pages allows you to add, change, and delete roles and the permissions that are attached to them. Look at how this is done next:

1. On the Web Site Administration page, click Manage Roles. The page shown next opens, displaying the five default roles and their permissions:

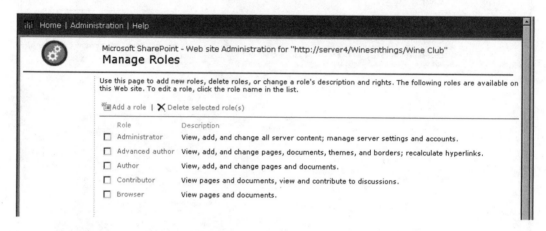

2. Click Administrator. The Edit Role Administrator page opens. Here is a detailed list of rights or permissions that can be assigned to a role. Scroll down this list to see all that are available. Click Cancel.

3. Click Add A Role. Type **Manager** as the Role Name, **Manage Contributions** as the Description, and click Author Pages and Manage Lists (a number of others are automatically selected). When you are done, the top of your page should look like Figure 20-10.

4. Scroll down to the bottom of the page and click Create Role. You will see Manager appear in the list of roles in the Manage Roles page.

5. Click the check box opposite Manager, click Delete Selected Role(s), and click OK that you are sure you want to delete a role.

6. Click Home to open the Home page of your web. Here, you can try out any changes you made in users, roles, and permissions. When you are done, close your browser, the Wine Club subweb, the Wines 'n Things web, and FrontPage.

## Setting Permissions with Windows NT or 2000, IIS, prior to SharePoint

If the server hosting the web for which you want to set permissions does not have SharePoint and the FrontPage 2002 Server Extensions, then the process of setting permissions has a third look. If you open that web in FrontPage, you can establish three levels of permissions:

- **Browse**  Allows the user to look at, read, and navigate the web site
- **Author**  Allows the user to change as well as browse the site
- **Administer**  Allows the user to set permissions as well as to author the web site

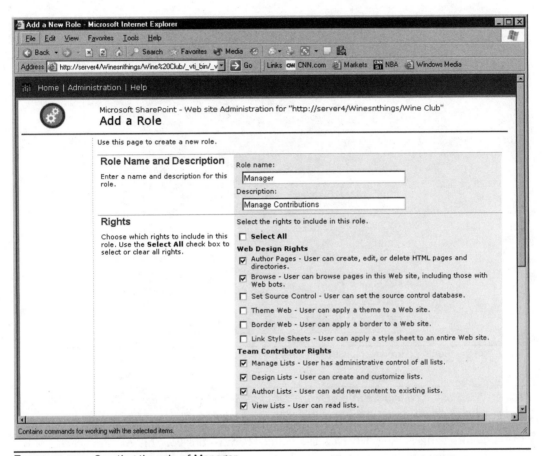

**FIGURE 20-10**    Creating the role of Manager

Like the newer server software, you can set the permissions for the root web and all subwebs under it will automatically have the same set of permissions, or you can separately set the permissions for any or all of the subwebs.

To change the permissions on a web you have published to a server with older software, you must load that web into FrontPage, then use the Server | Permissions option in the Tools menu, as you did with the newer software. Do that now and see how permissions are set.

1. With a web displayed, and Tools | Server | Permissions chosen, the Permissions dialog box will appear, as shown in Figure 20-11.

2. The default is Use Same Permissions As Parent Web, which means that to change the permissions, you must change them for the parent web.

3. Click the Groups tab, and you'll see that Everyone has been granted Browse permission, and the Administrators group has full control, like this:

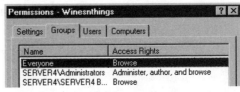

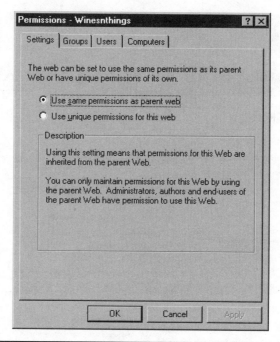

**NOTE**     *The groups you will see in the Groups tab of the Permissions dialog box will depend on how the network administrator has configured your web on the server.*

4. Return to the Settings tab, click Use Unique Permissions For This Web, and click Apply (if you don't click Apply, you won't be able to open the Users and Groups tabs).

5. Click the Users tab and then your account name in the user list, then click Edit. (If Edit is dimmed, click OK to close the dialog box and then reopen it.) In the Edit Users dialog box (shown here), click Browse This Web.

6. Click OK to return to the Users tab of the Permissions dialog box.

7. Click Add to open the Add Users dialog box. If you have a list of names on the left (this is the list of User accounts on the network of which the web server is a member), double-click one that you want to have some level of permission with this web.

8. Click the permission level you want for this person, as shown in Figure 20-12. (Given that Everyone has Browse permission, the person you're adding should have a higher-level permission.)

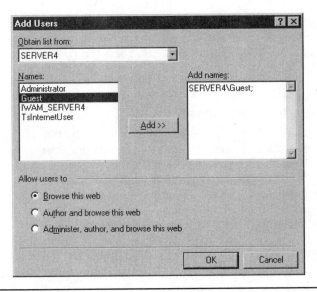

**FIGURE 20-12**    Assigning a role to a new user

9. Click OK. Your Users tab should now resemble this:

10. Click Groups and then click Add. Again, you can double-click an entry on the list on the left or type a new group on the right. Select the permission level desired, and then click OK to close the Add Group dialog box. Then click OK again to close the Permissions dialog box. You can also close your web and FrontPage.

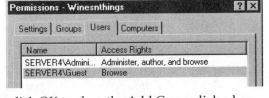

**NOTE**    *In addition to users and groups, you may also be able to set permissions for computers, so anyone using that computer can access your web. Permissions can be set for a single computer by giving it a complete IP address, or for groups of computers based on an IP mask, as shown here. This is particularly useful for limiting access to just those people in a particular company.*

**Setting up Users, Groups, and Computers**    The users, computers, groups, and members of groups to whom you grant permission to access your web are established within the server outside of FrontPage and are maintained in *Access Control Lists (ACLs)*, which are referenced by FrontPage. The individual users are assigned IDs and passwords that they must use to gain

PART IV

access, while computers are assigned IP addresses. The users and computers may also be assigned to one or more groups. FrontPage can then reference the users and computers either individually or by group. The process of setting up users and computers and establishing groups is handled by the network or server administrator and is a function of the operating system.

## Controlling Access to a Web Server

The permissions you set for the web pages you create are used by the web server to implement the access controls you want. If your server or that of your Internet service provider (ISP) is not Windows NT 4.0, 2000, or Server 2003 with IIS, then you must work with your network administrator or ISP to set up the access controls you want by using the services available on the web server. Most web servers have a multiple-level permission scheme set up by user, group, and/or computer that allow you to implement an access scheme similar to Windows's older Browser, Author, Administrator scheme. In fact, most servers go beyond this.

Windows NT 4.0, 2000, or Server 2003 with IIS provide at least four security mechanisms, each of which give you one or more levels of access, as you can see in Figure 20-13. These four mechanisms, which can be implemented in any combination by IIS, are

- Internet Protocol (IP) address control
- User account control
- Virtual directory control
- Windows NT File System (NTFS) control

### IP Address Control

The IP address control checks the *source* IP address (where the data is from) on every packet of data received by the server and compares it against a list of IP addresses that contains predefined actions to be applied to packets with that address. The packet is then handled in accordance with the predefined actions. IP address control is useful for either blocking or accepting major groups of users, like everyone from a particular company or organization within a company. This is the principal mechanism used by firewalls (discussed later in this chapter). The major limitation in IP address control is that you cannot identify particular directories that can be accessed by a given IP address.

### User Account Control

A standard part of Windows NT/2000/2003 security is user account control, which requests a user ID and password when accessing the server or specially designated directories. Such access can be over a LAN or over the Internet, so part of the IIS security that is implemented can include user account control. To make user account control simpler, define an anonymous account allowing access to nonsensitive directories with limited privileges—normally read-only—for anyone who makes it through the IP address control. For additional access and privileges, users are asked to enter their user ID and password. These are checked for validity by use of either *Basic* or *Challenge/Response* user authentication. The difference between these two authentication schemes is in the way that the ID and password are returned to the server. In the Basic scheme, the user ID and password are simply encoded in a manner that is not

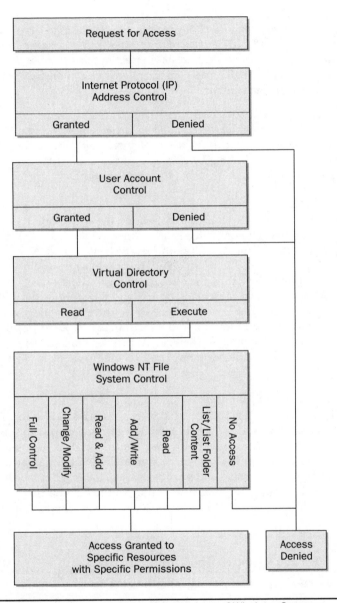

**FIGURE 20-13**    Levels of access control with recent versions of Windows Server

terribly hard to decode by someone intercepting it on the Internet. The Challenge/Response scheme never requires that the password be transmitted, but rather uses a cryptographic challenge sequence to authenticate it. The Challenge/Response scheme only works on Microsoft Internet Explorer 2.0 and above.

---

**NOTE**    *In Windows Server 2003 and IIS 6, there are four Authentication Access methods available: Integrated, Digest, Basic, and .NET Password. Integrated is what we are calling the Challenge/ Response scheme, Digest is only available when Active Directory is in use, Basic is the same as the Basic discussed above, and .NET Password is a full-featured authentication process that can include fingerprint and retina scanning.*

---

**TIP**    *User account control discussed in this section and virtual directory control described in the next section are both handled in the IIS Manager by opening the local server in the left pane, right-clicking Web Sites, and choosing Directory Security | Authentication And Access Control | Edit for the current section, and Web Site Properties | Home Directory for the next section.*

---

### Virtual Directory Control

With IIS, you can define an alias for a directory path on the server and then use that path in a URL (the uniform resource locator, which is an address on the Internet). This alias is called a *virtual directory*. For example, the default path for a web site called Wines 'n Things on a server named Server1 could be C:\Inetpub\Wwwroot\Winesnthings. If you define the alias for this path to be /winesnthings, then the URL for the web site would be **http://server1/ winesnthings**, which you have seen on many figures and illustrations throughout this book.

When you define an alias, you can give it one of two access privileges, Read or Execute, used for the defined path and all files and folders within it. The Read privilege allows the user to read and download the contents. The Execute privilege only allows the user to execute the contents—not to read or download them. The Execute privilege is used for scripts and applications.

### Windows NT File System (NTFS) Control

The Windows NT File System (NTFS) control in Windows NT 4.0, Windows 2000, and Windows 2003 is what associates a user account (name and password) with specific directories, files, and folders, as well as other server resources. This association is accomplished through the Access Control List (ACL) for each server resource. The ACL for a particular resource— say, a folder—will have a list of users and groups of users and a set of permissions, which, for Windows Server 2003 using NTFS, are shown in Figure 20-14. The permissions for Windows NT 4.0, Windows 2000, and Windows 2003 are described in Table 20-1.

| Permission Level Windows NT / 2000 or 2003 | Description |
| --- | --- |
| No Access / No Access | Prevents any access to the directory and its files. |
| List / List Folder Contents | Allows the listing of filenames and subdirectory names and the changing of the subdirectories. Prevents access to file contents. |
| Read / Read | Allows listing filenames and subdirectory names, changing subdirectories, viewing data files, and running applications. |
| Add / Write | Allows adding files and subdirectories to directories, but does not allow viewing data files or running applications. |

**TABLE 20-1**    Descriptions of ACL Levels of Permissions

| Permission Level Windows NT / 2000 or 2003 | Description |
| --- | --- |
| Add & Read / Read & Execute | Allows listing filenames and subdirectory names, changing subdirectories, viewing data files, and running applications, as well as adding files and subdirectories to directories. |
| Change / Modify | Allows add and read permission, as well as changing data in files, and deleting the directory and its files. |
| Full Control / Full Control | Allows change permission for the directory and its files, and takes ownership of the directory and its files. |
| – / Special Permissions | In Windows Server 2003, there is a seventh permission, Special Permissions. To use this, you must click Advanced to open the Advanced Security Settings dialog box, which was also available through an Advanced button in Windows 2000 Server. Editing entries in this dialog box gives you 14 levels of permissions in place of the 6 or 7 in the Properties dialog box. |

**TABLE 20-1**    Descriptions of ACL Levels of Permissions *(continued)*

**NOTE**    *Windows 2000 and Windows 2003 have slightly different names for their levels of permission than does Windows NT.*

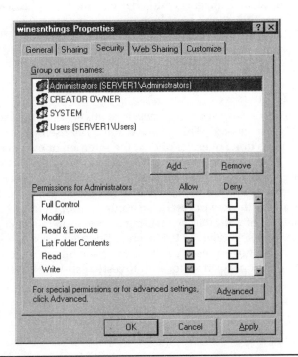

**FIGURE 20-14**    Windows Server 2003 Access Control List for a folder

## Limiting Access to an Intranet Site

One type of access control that is not handled by FrontPage is limiting access to an intranet web site. This is the situation in which you have an intranet that you want to connect to the Internet. It may be that you want to just allow your intranet users access to the Internet. Alternatively, you may want to allow people on the Internet—for example, your own employees who are traveling—to get onto your intranet. This is done with several schemes, but the most common is a firewall, which is a separate computer through which all traffic to and from the Internet must pass, as shown in Figure 20-15. At the simplest level, a firewall works by *packet filtering,* which checks each packet of information that is transferred, either outbound or inbound, through the firewall and makes sure that its IP address is acceptable.

To add a further level of protection and in some cases speed up this process, the firewall computer may be set up as a *proxy server.* A proxy server, which is simply software running in a computer acting as a firewall, acts as a relay station between your intranet and the Internet. It acts like an "air lock" between the two. Requests to servers on either side of the firewall are made to the proxy server, which examines them, and if they are appropriate, sends a proxy on to the addressed server to fulfill the request.

# Securing Transmission

Transmission security means the *encryption* or concealment of the information being transmitted so it cannot be read and misused without the ability to *decrypt* or reveal it. Encrypting of information is probably as old as the human race and has really blossomed with the advent of computers. Data encryption has become so sophisticated that the U.S. government, worried that they won't be able to decrypt the data (can you imagine that!), wouldn't for some time allow the technology to be exported (although this has changed). Several encryption schemes for securing Internet transmissions are in use. They are private key encryption, public key encryption, and combinations of the two.

## Private Key Encryption

*Private key* encryption, or *symmetric cryptography,* is relatively old and uses a single key to both encrypt and decrypt a message. This means that the key itself must be transferred from sender to receiver. If this is done over the phone, the Internet, or even a courier service, all someone needs to do is get hold of the key, and he or she can decrypt the message. Private key encryption, though, has a major benefit in that it is much faster (as much as 1,000 times faster) than the alternatives. Private key schemes are therefore valuable in situations where you do not have to transfer the key or can do so securely—for example, personal use such as encrypting the contents of your disk or sending information to someone that you first meet face to face. There are several private key encryption schemes being used with the Internet, including the U.S. government's Data Encryption Standard (DES) and the private RC2 ("Rivest Cipher" or "Ron's Code" [for Ron Rivest] 2) and RC4 from RSA Laboratories.

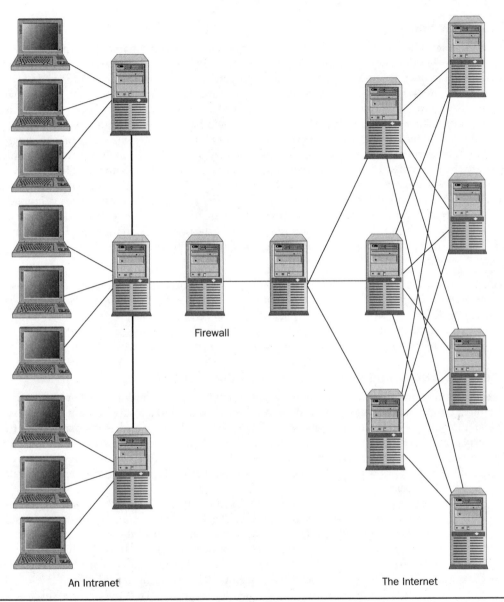

An Intranet                                                    The Internet

**FIGURE 20-15** A firewall between an intranet and the Internet

## Public Key Encryption

*Public key* encryption, or *asymmetric cryptography,* was developed in the mid-1970s and uses a pair of keys—a public key and a private key. The public key is publicly known and transferred, and is used to encrypt a message. The private key never leaves its creator and is used to decrypt the message. For two people to use this technique, each generates both a public and a private key, and then they openly exchange public keys, not caring who gets a copy of it. They encrypt their messages to each other using the other person's public key, and then send the message. The message can only be decrypted and read by using the private key held by the recipient. The public and private keys use a mathematical algorithm that relates them to the encrypted message. By use of other mathematical algorithms, it is fairly easy to generate key pairs, but with only the public key, it is extremely difficult to generate the private key. The process of public key encryption is relatively slow compared to private key encryption. Public key encryption is best in open environments where the sender and recipient do not know each other. Most public key encryption uses the Rivest-Shamir-Aldman (RSA) Public Key Cryptosystem, called "RSA" for short, developed and supported by RSA Laboratories.

---

**NOTE** *You can encrypt your e-mail in newer versions of Outlook, Outlook Express, and other e-mail programs using features built into the programs, or in any e-mail program using the Pretty Good Privacy (PGP) software that uses RSA public key encryption and is available from PGP Corporation at their web site **http://www.pgp.com/** (select PGP Freeware under their Products heading). See their freeware PGP Mail at **http://www.pgp.com/products/freeware.html**.*

## Combined Public and Private Key Encryption with SSL

Most encryption on the Internet is actually a combination of public and private key encryption. The most common combination was developed by Netscape to go between the Hypertext Transfer Protocol (HTTP) used in servers and browsers on the Web and Transmission Control Protocol/Internet Protocol (TCP/IP) used in both local and wide area networks (including the Internet) and is called Secure Sockets Layer (SSL). It provides a fast and highly secure means of both encryption and authentication (see "Authenticating People, Servers, and Data" later in this chapter).

Recall that private key encryption is very fast, but has the problem of transferring the key. And public key encryption is very secure but slow. If you were to begin a secure transmission by using a public key to encrypt and send a private key, you could then securely use the private key to quickly send any amount of data you wanted. This is how SSL works. It uses an RSA public key to send a randomly chosen private key for either a DES or RC4 encryption, and in so doing sets up a "secure socket" through which any amount of data can be quickly encrypted, sent, and decrypted. After the SSL header has transferred the private key, all information transferred in both directions during a given session—including the URL, any request for a user ID and password, all HTTP web information, and any data entered on a form—is automatically encrypted by the sender and automatically decrypted by the recipient.

There are several versions of SSL, with SSL version 3 being the most commonly used as of this writing (Summer 2003). Compared to earlier versions, SSL 3 is more secure and offers improved authentication. Microsoft also has its own improvement of SSL called Personal

Communications Technology (PCT). Both SSL 3 and PCT have been proposed to the World Wide Web standards committee (W3C) as security standards.

---

**NOTE**  *Internet Explorer 5 added (and IE 6 has continued the use) another encryption standard called TLS 1 for "Transport Layer Security," which is an open security standard similar to SSL 3.*

## Implementing SSL

You may be thinking that SSL sounds great, but it also sounds complex to use. In fact, it's easy to use. All that's required is a web server that supports SSL and has it enabled, such as the Netscape Commerce Server or the Microsoft IIS, plus a supporting web browser such as Netscape Navigator 3.0 or Microsoft Internet Explorer 3.0, and their respective later releases. From the browser, simply begin the URL you want with "https://" in place of "http://." SSL will then kick in, and without you even being aware that it's happening, the browser and server will decide whether to use DES or RC4, use RSA to transfer a private key, and then use that key and the chosen private key encryption scheme to encrypt and decrypt all the rest of the data during that session. The only thing you see is a message saying you are about to use a secure connection, similar to this:

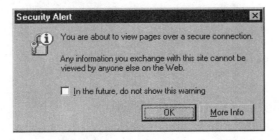

  Once you are connected using SSL, your browser will indicate that a secure connection is established. Netscape and Microsoft display an icon of a padlock in the browser's status bar.

---

**NOTE**  *Even though the combination of public and private encryption is relatively fast, it is still significantly slower than no encryption. For that reason, it is recommended you only use SSL when you send sensitive information such as financial or credit card data.*

## FrontPage and SSL

FrontPage implements SSL in several ways. You can specify whether a new web is to use SSL by selecting Encrypted Connection Required (SSL) in the Web Site Templates dialog box, as you can see in Figure 20-16. Also, FrontPage automatically (without you doing anything) uses SSL for all communications between the FrontPage client and the server. This provides protection when you are transferring a web page to the server and when you are doing remote web authoring. To use SSL, you must publish the web on a server that supports SSL, such as Windows NT 4.0, 2000, or 2003 with IIS.

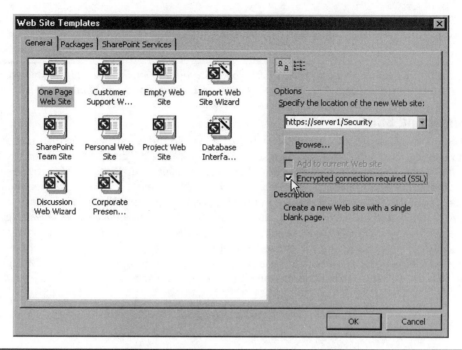

**FIGURE 20-16**    Selecting SSL for a new web site

## Authenticating People, Servers, and Data

SSL is designed to do double duty. Not only does it provide a secure method of data transmission, but it also provides the authentication of the data and the server, and with SSL 3, it provides authentication of the user. Authentication is important for three reasons:

- To make sure that senders are who they say they are, and to prevent them from denying that they are the sender. This is authentication of the client or sender.

- To make sure that recipients are who they say they are, and to assure that they received the information. This is authentication of the server or recipient.

- To make sure that the data being sent has not been modified before it was received. This is authentication of the data.

SSL addresses each of these areas of authentication with the following steps:

1. A *message digest* is generated for the data being sent through use of a sophisticated algorithm that is very sensitive to changes in the data. This is equivalent to computing a checksum or a cyclical redundancy check (CRC) for a large number.

2. The message digest is encrypted with the sender's private RSA key to produce a *digital signature*.

3. The recipient uses the sender's public key to decrypt the digital signature that came with the data exposing the message digest. If the public key works, then the sender is who she said she was and in fact sent the data.

4. The recipient then recomputes a new message digest using the data that was received. If the two message digests are the same, then the data has not been altered in transit.

5. The recipient next encrypts the new message digest using the recipient's private RSA key to create a new digital signature and sends it to the original sender.

6. The original sender uses the recipient's public key to decrypt the second digital signature. If the public key works, then the recipient is as claimed, and if the two message digests are the same, then the original data was received by the recipient.

This sounds complicated, but if you are using SSL, it is all done automatically, and you only know if there is a problem. There is one flaw in this security scheme—how can either the sender or the recipient be sure they have the public key of the other and not of someone masquerading as the other person? In this situation, the false person would be able to use the private key that went with the false public key to decrypt and misuse the data. To counter this flaw, a public key can be enclosed in a *certificate*. A certificate uses the private key of a *certifying authority* to encrypt both a message digest of the human-readable name of the sender and the sender's public key. Then, by using the public key of the certifying authority, you can get the public key along with the name of the owner. Of course, you must trust that the public key of the certifying authority is legitimate! A prominent certifying authority, where you can obtain a certificate for yourself, is VeriSign, Inc., at **http://www.verisign.com/**.

## What's Coming for Internet Security

Recognizing the reluctance of the public to use the Internet as a trusted medium for transferring financial and other confidential data, Microsoft and other software leaders have developed, or are developing, several features to ease security concerns. These range from *security zones*—where you can adjust the level at which you allow active content to be run on your computer and data to be copied to your computer—to *safe houses*, where you can securely store data on your computer or removable media.

In Internet Explorer 4.0 and later, you have four zones, as shown in Figure 20-17. In each of the zones, you can select the level of security from among four defined levels (three levels in IE 4.0) and one custom level. You can then assign web sites to the zones. The zones and levels are shown in Table 22-2 (note that all levels apply to all zones).

**NOTE** *Due to the potential to allow damaging content in the Internet and Restricted Sites zones, you are given a warning, such as the one shown here, when you select a security level that may be too low:*

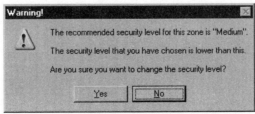

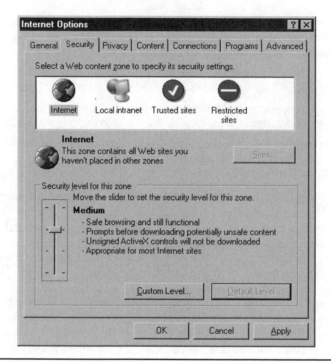

**FIGURE 20-17** Assigning security levels to web content zones

| Security Zones | Levels of Security |
|---|---|
| *Internet* is a catch-all of those sites that haven't been placed in other zones.<br><br>*Local Intranet* includes fully trusted sites behind a corporate firewall.<br><br>*Trusted Sites* are frequently visited web sites, such as the web site of a business partner that you trust will not adversely affect your computer.<br><br>*Restricted Sites* are those that could adversely affect your computer. | *High* provides the most predefined security measures. It prevents damaging content from being downloaded.<br><br>*Medium* provides a warning message for content that may damage and won't download unsigned ActiveX controls.<br><br>*Medium-low* doesn't provide warning messages, but won't download unsigned ActiveX controls (not in IE 4).<br><br>*Low* provides no warning for content that has the potential for damage.<br><br>*Custom* allows you to select specific security settings. |

**TABLE 20-2** Security Zones and Levels of Security

In Internet Explorer 4.0 and on, the security zone features are available from the Security tab of the Internet Options dialog box (opened from the Tools menu). The security zone you are currently using is displayed in the browser's status bar.

Today you can use certificates and the Microsoft Profile Assistant options available in the Content tab of the Internet Explorer 5.0 and later Internet Options dialog box, to provide safe and easily retrievable access (for those you want to have access) to personal verification and data. On the horizon is support for conducting business using smart cards and Internet cash, where you electronically move "money" from one silicon repository to another.

Like it or not, much of how we conduct our daily lives in the future will be through the Internet in some capacity. As with other technologies that we may have initially approached reluctantly but now fully embrace, the security on the Internet will be refined and improved because too much will depend on it to do otherwise.

## Bibliography

There are mountains of information on Internet and intranet security issues. Listed here is a sampling of documents, as well as two books on the subject. Most of the Internet sites mentioned have many more related documents.

- Computer Security Institute, publishers of the *Computer Security Journal*, and other publications on Computer security, **http://www.gocsi.com/**

- Microsoft Corporation, *Microsoft Privacy and Security Fundamentals*, **http://www.microsoft.com/security/**

- National Security Institute, *Connecting to the Internet: Security Considerations*, CSL Bulletin, July 1993, **http://www.nsi.org/Library/Compsec/intersec.txt**

- National Security Institute, *Security Issues in WWW*, **http://www.nsi.org/Library/Internet/security.htm**

- Netscape Communications Corporation, *Netscape Security Center*, **http://home.netscape.com/products/security/index.html**

- NT Bug Traq (**http://www.ntbugtraq.com**) offers a mailing list to keep you informed of the latest security issues regarding Windows NT and 2000 Server (and in the near future, Windows Server 2003), as well as Windows XP and a web site where you can locate the latest fixes.

- Redmond, Frank III, *Making Sure Your Server's Secure*, Microsoft Developer Network (MSDN), 11/96, **http://www.microsoft.com/mind/1196/iissecurity.htm**

- RSA Laboratories, Inc., *Frequently Asked Questions about Today's Cryptography*, Version 4.1, 2000, **http://www.rsasecurity.com/rsalabs/faq/**

- RSA Laboratories, Inc., *Public-Key Cryptography Standards (PKCS)*, **http://www.rsasecurity.com/rsalabs/pkcs/**

- Stein, Lincoln D., *The World Web Security FAQ*, Version 3.1.2, 2/4/2002, **http://www.w3.org/security/faq/**

- Rutstein, Charles B., *Windows NT Security*, 1997, Computing McGraw-Hill

- Cox, Philip and Sheldon, Tom, *Windows 2000 Security Handbook*, 2001, McGraw-Hill/Osborne

# Doing E-Commerce

W hat is electronic commerce? There are many different answers to this question. E-commerce is buying a book, an airplane ticket, or a computer online. E-commerce is also an airline ordering aircraft parts for a Boeing 767 electronically, and it is a bank sending a financial transaction to another bank electronically. It can also be any aspect of buying and selling online, which could include marketing, order taking, or customer service.

*E-commerce*, in this chapter, is when someone offers a product for sale on the Web and someone else buys it. This sounds simple, but a lot of different things must be considered to make that sale over the Web. Many of those considerations are similar to what the traditional physical storefront deals with. You are offering products for sale, and they must be marketed, sold, paid for, and delivered. The details are different for e-commerce, but, whether the store is a physical or electronic storefront, you are still running a store, and your web storefront must meet many of the same requirements of a physical storefront to be successful.

The e-commerce market is also growing rapidly. Predictions of how big the e-commerce market will be are many, but all agree it is growing rapidly and is already enormous. A University of Texas study released in January 2001 reports that revenue from e-commerce grew 11 percent between the first and second quarters of 2000, generating over $127 billion in revenue in the first half of 2000. This was growth of 66.7 percent over the first quarter of 1999 and a 57.8 percent increase over the second quarter of 1999 (**http://www.internetindicators.com**).

More and more companies are jumping into this market. These include Internet-only companies like Amazon.com, Priceline.com, and eBay, traditional bricks-and-mortar retailers like Kmart, Barnes & Noble, and JCPenney, and offline electronic retailers like the Home Shopping Network and QVC. Large companies with physical storefronts and catalog sales are on the Web. But the move to the Web is not just with large companies. In 1995, Amazon.com opened an Internet book-selling storefront that was created and run with software they developed themselves. Today the potential web storeowner has many off-the-shelf options that can be used to create an e-commerce store. Some of these options do everything from creating the pages to handling all the ordering and payment; others rely on tools like FrontPage to create the pages, while depending on software running on the server to add features for ordering and payment. The prices for various software options also vary quite a lot, but they all provide a much less expensive solution than starting from scratch like Amazon.com.

While putting a store on the Web is easier than ever, putting a successful store on the Web is not easy. It is no easier, in fact, than establishing a successful physical store. After all, long before your grand opening, there is plenty to do in the way of setting up a retail store. Thankfully, a wealth of advice for such ventures is available on the Web. The Microsoft bCentral site (**http://www.bcentral.com**) offers tips and advice to e-business entrepreneurs, along with service offerings ranging from marketing tools to site hosting, to shopping cart systems and advertising services. Internet.com's E-commerce Guide (**http://ecommerce .internet.com**) is another site devoted to e-commerce. Even software companies that want to sell you e-commerce software will often have sections of their site devoted to general information on e-commerce and doing business on the Web.

## Factors Important to E-Commerce

While the primary focus of this chapter is the creation of a web store, before that discussion begins, it is useful to talk about other factors important to e-commerce: security, payment options, and designing for success.

### Security

In e-commerce, security is a major issue, as it is in any transfer of money. Since Chapter 20 discusses security on the Web, you might want to review the sections on encryption, private and public keys, Secure Sockets Layer (SSL), and authenticating servers. These subjects are essential to creating and maintaining a secure e-commerce site. This section will go into more detail describing how security is implemented and some options you have regarding digital certificates.

The perception of security by your customer is critical to your success. When customers give out personal or credit card data at a physical store, or through a mail-order catalog, those customers are basing their trust on a variety of visual clues as to the professionalism with which their data will be handled. A customer at a high-end store like Nordstrom does not question the security of their credit card data when they hand it over to a sales clerk. That same customer may think twice about handing it over to someone on the Internet he or she knows nothing about. You need to show you are taking care of the customer's data as it crosses over the Internet and that you will be handling it responsibly once you receive it.

The key to secure transactions (both actual and perceived) is the *digital certificate*. VeriSign (**http://www.verisign.com**) is the leading issuer of digital certificates. Before issuing a digital certificate, VeriSign reviews the applicant's credentials, such as the Dun & Bradstreet number, articles of incorporation, or business license, and takes several other steps to ensure that the organization is what it claims to be and not an imposter. VeriSign then issues the digital certificate, which is your electronic credential. VeriSign's price for this service is quite reasonable, but an even lower-cost alternative is another VeriSign company, Thawte Certification (**http://www.thawte.com**), which also offers SSL certificates.

Not only does the digital certificate identify the owner of the web store, but it also enables Secure Sockets Layer (SSL) to establish secure communications between your server and the customer's browser. SSL provides the following components for online commerce:

- **Authentication**   By checking the digital certificate, your customer can verify that the web site belongs to you and not an imposter.

- **Message privacy** SSL encrypts all traffic between your web server and the customer's computer using a unique session private key. To securely transmit the session key to the customer, the server encrypts it with the customer's public key, automatically sent to the server by the customer's computer. Each session key is used only once, during a single session with a single customer.

- **Message integrity** When a message is sent, the sending and receiving computers each generate a code based on the message content. If even a single character in the message is altered, the receiving computer will generate a different code and alert the recipient that the message is not legitimate. If not alerted, both parties will know that what they are seeing is exactly what the other party sent.

When you open a web page that is secure, you will get a Security Alert box like this:

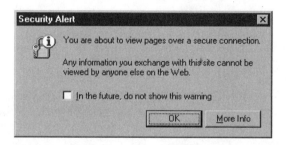

When SSL has been enabled, and the secure web page loaded, Internet Explorer shows a small, closed padlock at the bottom of the browser. The padlock does more than tell you that the connection is now secure. It also gives you access to information about the digital certificate. When you double-click the padlock, the Certificate box appears, as in Figure 21-1. The General tab has the name of the owner of the digital certificate and the period of its validity. Selecting the Details tab gives you the details about the digital certificate, such as the serial number and dates between which it is valid. Selecting the Certification Path tab then tells you who issued the digital certificate and its current status.

You have a couple of options for getting digital certificates. The first is to get one from a certificate issuer (VeriSign, Thawte, and so on) in the name of your company. The second is to use the digital certificate of the web presence provider (WPP) who is hosting your site, if they offer that service. If you are using a simple form that is on one page, you can use the second option if your Internet service provider (ISP) who is acting as the WPP has a secure server with a digital certificate. The secure page would be on a secure server, and you would access it with the HTTPS protocol.

The problem with the second option is that the customer may receive notification that a name other than the one they expect is on the digital certificate. This will cause many to hesitate, and they may not go on. One way around this is to use the ISP's domain for secure pages, but the best long-term solution is to get your own digital certificate. If you do get you own certificate, it is important to keep it renewed. Otherwise, your potential customers will get a Security Alert saying the certificate has expired, as shown in Figure 21-2.

Some e-commerce programs process orders and then use a form-mail program to e-mail the information to you. If your WPP is also your ISP and handles your e-mail as well as your secure server, the information is probably going from the secure server to the mail

**FIGURE 21-1**
Checking a
certificate by
clicking the
padlock

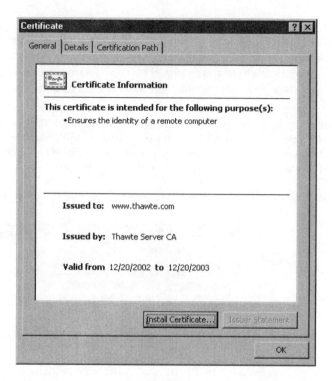

server to you via their network and not over the Internet. If the secure server you are using and your mail server are in different locations, and the information is being passed on via the Internet, you need to explore securing the e-mail data, too. Some e-commerce packages recognize this and provide ways to secure that data. Some e-mail programs can use SSL, and there are other encryption schemes available such as PGP (Pretty Good Privacy—see

**FIGURE 21-2**
Security Alert for a
certificate that has
expired

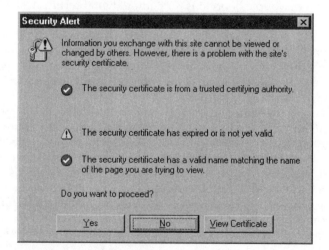

Chapter 20). Contact your WPP to see what they have to secure your e-mail data if it is going over the Internet. Another low-cost alternative is to store the customer and order information in an online database, accessible to the business owner using their browser over a secure connection. FrontPage provides you with the tools required to do this, and we'll further investigate this low-cost alternative later in this chapter.

When you receive sensitive data, you should also have a way to keep it secure in your offline environment. Only trusted people should have access to your customers' credit card information, so it needs to be password-protected on your server, and you need to control access to any paper copies you might make. Leaving other people's credit card information lying around is like leaving their money lying around. It may get picked up.

## Payment

Cash is not an option for paying online, but there are a number of other ways to transfer funds. Some are familiar and others are specific to the Internet. They include

- Credit cards
- Checks
- Electronic cash
- Smart cards

### Credit Cards

Credit cards are the preferred method of payment for online customers. They are easy to use, and consumers are familiar with them. Credit cards also have an advantage for the customer since they limit the customer's liability. Customers can cancel the transaction if they wish, and if credit card fraud is involved, they are only liable for $50 if they meet the card company's requirements for reporting the incident.

In any sale, you are trying to make it as easy as possible for customers to buy. Credit cards are the easiest method for them. All they have to do is fill out the credit card information and submit the order. What makes it easy isn't just that credit is involved. Debit or check cards are included here, too, because they act just like credit cards, but the funds are deducted from the customer's checking account. What makes it easy is the existing card company and banking infrastructure that processes the credit or debit card.

**The Credit Card Process**   The basic process for using a credit or debit card is that the customer submits the credit card number to the merchant, and the merchant sends the merchandise to the customer. The merchant also sends the credit card number and amount to a *merchant processor*. The merchant processor transfers the money into the merchant's account, usually within 48 hours, and begins the process of billing the customer. The merchant's account is a bank account set up to automatically receive these funds. An easy way to sign up with a merchant processor is to go to your bank and ask for a merchant account. Not all banks offer this service, but many do. Their rates vary for this service, so shop around. Costco (**http://www.costco.com**, click Services and see "Services For Your Business") also sets up merchant accounts through NOVA Information Systems (**http://www.novainfo.com**), a leading merchant processor, for very reasonable fees.

In the preceding scenario, the question is, how does the e-commerce merchant get the credit card transaction to the merchant processor? The answer is that you can either automate the process with online processing or use traditional manual processing.

**Online Processing**    To do online processing, you can use a service like PayPal (**http://www.paypal.com**) that handles the acceptance of the customer payment. You simply place a customized link on your site, which takes customers to PayPal, returning them to your site after they have submitted the payment. The downside to this type of online processing is that you have no automated way of telling whether the customer completed the payment transaction other then e-mail verification from PayPal or checking your account's transaction history. To do truly automated online processing, you need both an e-commerce package that will submit an online order to a merchant processor and a merchant processor that will receive it. The middleman between you and the merchant processor can be VeriSign Payment Services, originally "CyberCash" (go to **http://www.verisign.com/** and under Security And Payment Services, select Payment Processing), which offers online credit card processing for merchant processors. Many of the e-commerce software packages are set up to tie into VeriSign Payment Services, and many merchant processors use it. One of the things that online processing can do is quickly verify that the credit card is valid and provide authorization in real time during the purchase.

Online processing with VeriSign Payment Services does add another step in the process, which also adds to the cost of the transaction over manual processing. If you have a small web store with a small number of transactions, you might do better to use a payment service like PayPal or manual processing. Manual processing has its costs also, so you will have to figure out what is best for you. But be sure to look at manual processing.

**Manual Processing**    Manual processing is done with the Point-of-Sale (POS) terminal. When a credit card is swiped at a store, it is at a POS terminal. Taking credit card numbers over the Internet means you can't swipe the card, but you can key in the number. This is how mail-order companies process the credit card numbers they receive. You may find that there is a higher processing charge for key-in over swiping. Terminals can be reasonably leased or purchased from the merchant processor. There are also software programs that allow you to process the numbers with your PC. NOVA provides this service with Windows-based software. Again, shop around with different merchant processors, because you need to add in the cost of the POS terminal or software along with the service charges.

### Checks

Not everyone has a credit card, and though most can get a debit card with their checking account, many people aren't able to, or choose not to. Most small businesses can't afford to turn away paying customers, so you need to decide if you want to handle check orders.

There are several ways to handle check orders. The first is to have the customer print the order form and mail it in with the check. If the customer fills out the online form and prints it, the entries may or may not print, so it may be easier on the check customers to create a separate snail-mail form to print and fill in with pen or pencil, or to provide them with a plain-text printable version once they have filled out the form. The second way is for the customer to fill out the online form and submit it electronically with "Check" being selected as the method of payment. Then, hold the order until the check arrives, at which time you can process it. The customer has to do less this way. A third method of accepting check payments is to use a check acceptance service like E Commerce Group's Speedpay (**http://www.ecommercegroup.com**). Speedpay allows customers to make payments by debiting their checking account, similar to the way a check card works. Whichever method makes sense for your business, always make it as easy as possible for the customer, and accept as many methods of payment as you can.

### Electronic Cash

Some items are too inexpensive to purchase with a credit card. Nobody uses a credit card to buy a newspaper, which is why a number of companies are working to find a way to charge customers for items costing $5 or less. These inexpensive things are not worth the service charges with credit cards. Attempts to promote *micropayment* methods are not doing well, with several players abandoning their efforts. They require the customer to install and learn new software. With few merchants participating, acceptance has been very low. Services like PayPal, which allows individuals to make these minute payments using prefunded accounts, seem to be gaining greater acceptance, however.

### Smart Cards

Smart cards are plastic cards onto which consumers can digitally download money. They are popular in Europe, but haven't caught on in the United States yet. Smart cards are efficient, secure, and easy to use in both real and virtual stores. Many banks and tech firms, including Microsoft, are working on smart card systems for the United States. InfoSpace, Inc. (**http://www.infospaceinc.com/wwd/merchant/**) has gained a level of acceptance by partnering with several larger sites. Still, this is a technology whose time has yet to come.

## Web Design Tips for a Web Store

Chapter 1 goes into detail on designing a web application, but there are some additional considerations with web stores:

- **Make first-time buyers comfortable.**   Give them tips on shopping at your site and possibly offer incentives for their first purchase. First-time buyers are reluctant to order online, so make sure your phone, fax, and e-mail information are listed prominently at strategic locations throughout the site. If buyers don't have a positive experience the first time, they probably won't be back.

- **Make the process fast.**   Not only make it fast to load by reducing heavy graphics, but make the buying process simple from start to finish. Don't put any barriers in the way, like making them download plug-ins or fill out forms so they can shop in your web store.

- **Make it easy to find the products.**   Pay attention to navigation and searching so customers can easily find what you have to sell.

- **Make all your products available.**   Provide a good selection, particularly if it is a web store that has a real-store counterpart. Customers expect to see everything online that they see in the physical store or catalog.

- **Make it easy for customers to give you their money.**   Don't hide the cash register. Make it clear how to get to the checkout stand, and make it easy to go there.

- **Make it clear what the customer is paying.** Don't hide shipping, handling, or any other extra charges. The order summary should show exactly what the customer is paying.

- **Make communication important.** Send e-mails letting your customers know their order has been received, shipped, and where it is in transit.

- **Encourage your customers to stay.** Don't put links to nonshopping pages on your product pages.

# E-Commerce Sites Using a Form

E-commerce sites can range from a one-page web store to major outlets like Amazon.com. These extremes use very different software packages. It doesn't take complex software to offer four or five items on a single page, but it does to offer millions of books, CDs, videos, and many other products. We will look at the range of options available based on the size and budget of the web store.

There are two basic approaches: a simple form for web stores with just a few items, and the shopping cart site for web stores with more items than can fit on a single page. The shopping cart site uses a shopping cart metaphor to collect all the customer's choices. Then it adds up all the subtotals and extra charges, such as shipping and taxes, and sends the information to the merchant. Shopping cart sites will be discussed further later in this chapter.

A form can be used in a simple e-commerce site when there are just a few items because the form limits it to one page. In that page, you have to put all the items for sale as well as all the fields necessary to identify the customer. If the page starts getting long and requires a lot of scrolling, or there are too many items to put on a single form, consider using a shopping cart site, covered later in this chapter.

Here, we'll look at a simple, yet fully functional form-based store. Customers will enter their order on a single-page form. When they submit the form, the information will be stored in a database within the site, and a reporting system will be developed for looking at and tracking the orders. While a real sales transaction might require more information, this example in the spirit of the Wines 'n Things site, illustrates a simple order entry form web store system and all the steps to create it.

A form-based store can be built in two different ways, depending on whether the server on which you are developing and running this is using FrontPage Server Extensions (FPSE) 2002 or Windows SharePoint Services ("SharePoint 2"). We'll look at both of these cases.

## Building a Form-Based Store with FPSE

Using FrontPage Server Extensions means that the server on which you develop and host this web site is running FPSE 2002 (you don't want to use an older version due to the many enhancements in 2002). This is a commitment to the future for as long as you want to run this web site. FPSE 2002 is the last of the line of FPSEs, so if this site is to be used for any length of time, you need to get a commitment from the web presence provider (WPP) that they will provide FPSE 2002 for the period you foresee using the site.

With FPSE 2002, you start by creating a form in any way you wish, including using the Form Wizard. Here we'll take the table of wines that was developed in Chapter 7 and add some form fields to it. Then, using a copy of the same table, we'll create a confirmation page. Next, the form will be used to build a database and then will be attached to it. A JavaScript will be added to the form to perform the needed calculations, and code will be added to the form to call the JavaScript. Finally, the Database Interface Wizard will be used to extract information from the database. To recap, the necessary steps with FPSE are

1. Create an order entry form.

2. Create a confirmation page.

3. Attach that form to a database.

4. Attach a JavaScript routine for totaling.

5. Create a database retrieval page.

### Creating the Form

Use the following steps to build a form that will be used as a simple web store within the Wines 'n Things Wine Club subweb site:

1. Open the Wines 'n Things web site and the Wine Club subweb. Open the Wines.htm page. (If you did not build the security subweb in Chapter 20 and don't have a subweb, just open Wines.htm or your equivalent web page.) Select the table and its heading, and click Copy on the Standard toolbar or press CTRL-C. Close the Wines.htm page.

2. Click New Page, enter a blank line, and click Paste or press CTRL-V.

3. Select the Description column, select Table | Delete Columns, select the Varietal column, select Table | Insert | Rows Or Columns, increase Number Of Columns to **3**, leave Right Of Selection chosen, and click OK.

4. To simplify this exercise, select four rows (not counting the header row, we selected the second, fifth, seventh, and ninth rows) and select Table | Delete Rows.

5. In the top cell of the leftmost new column, type **Price**. In the top cell of the middle new column, type **Qty**. At the top of the right new column, type **Total $**. Select all three new columns and click Right-Align.

6. In the Price column, enter the prices shown in Figure 21-3 and save the page as **WineShop.htm**.

7. Click in the first cell under the Qty heading. Select Insert | Form | Textbox. Press SHIFT and then press RIGHT ARROW twice to select Submit and Reset.

8. Select Cut from the Standard toolbar or press CTRL-X. Click immediately below the table and select Paste or press CTRL-V.

9. Right-click in the new text box and choose Form Field Properties. In the dialog box that opens, type **Qty1** for the name, **0** for the Initial Value, **3** for the Width, **1** for the Tab Order, and then click Validate.

10. In the Text Box Validation dialog box, select Integer for the Data Type, enter **Qty 1** for the Display Name, click Field Must Be, select Greater Than Or Equal To, enter **0** for the value, click And Must Be, select Less Than Or Equal To, and enter **99** for the value, as you can see in Figure 21-4.

**FIGURE 21-3**
Getting a table
ready for a
shopping form

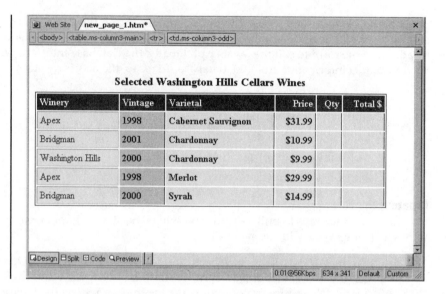

11. Click OK twice. Right-click the text box and choose Copy. Right-click in the cell immediately below the text box and choose Paste. Repeat this for the remaining three cells in the Qty column.

12. Right-click in the second text box from the top, the first one you pasted, and choose Form Field Properties. Notice that the name was automatically incremented. Change

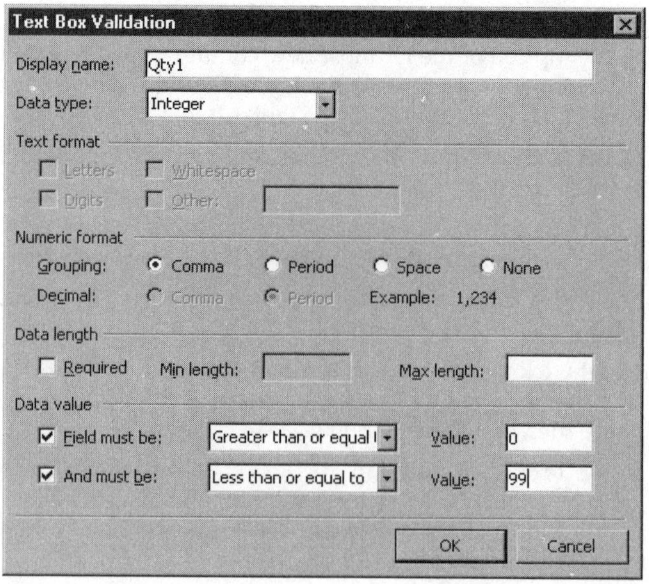

**FIGURE 21-4**
Setting the criteria
for validating the
entry in a form
field

the Tab Order to **2** and click Validate. Change the Display Name to **Qty 2** and click OK twice. Repeat this for the three remaining Qty cells.

13. Right-click the top cell in the Total $ column and choose Paste. Press LEFT ARROW and type **$**. Right-click that same cell again and choose Form Field Properties. Change the Name to **Total1**, change the Width to **8**, delete the Tab Order to leave it blank, and click Validate.

14. Change the Display Name to **Total 1**, the Data Type to **Number**, deselect the two Data Value check boxes, and click OK twice. Point the mouse just to the left of the **$** in the text box you just created, press SHIFT-END, right-click, and choose Copy.

15. Right-click in the next cell down and choose Paste. Repeat this in the next three cells down. Right-click the text box in the second cell in the Total $ column, choose Form Field Properties, click Validate, change the Display Name to **Total 2**, and click OK twice. Repeat this for the remaining cells.

---

**NOTE**   *If you get an extra line when you paste a form field, simply press* BACKSPACE *to remove it.*

16. Select the entire bottom row, of the table, select Table | Insert | Rows Or Columns, and leave the default entries Rows, 1, and Below Selection. Click OK.

17. In the new bottom row select the left two cells, right-click in one of these cells, and choose Merge Cells. Select the next two cells, right-click in one of these cells, and choose Merge Cells. Select the right two cells, right-click in one of these cells, and choose Merge Cells.

18. In the left cell of the new row, type **Enter I.D.**, select Insert | Form | Textbox, select the Submit and Reset buttons, and press DEL. Right-click the new text box and choose Form Field Properties. Type **ID** for the Name, make the Width **12**, enter **6** for the Tab Order, and click Validate. Click Required under Data Length, enter a Display Name of **ID**, and click OK twice.

---

**NOTE**   *The concept of the ID is that this is a wine buying club. To get to this area in the web site, customers had to enter a username and password, so at this point all they need to do is enter an ID to confirm the purchase. Their name, address, and method of paying either by credit card or a bill are on file and do not need to be entered here. (Besides, it makes the exercise shorter!)*

19. In the middle new cell, type **ORDER TOTAL**, make it bold, and center it. Select the bottom $ and form field in the Total $ column, press CTRL-C to copy it, right-click the bottom-right cell, and choose Paste.

20. Right-click the form field you just pasted and choose Form Field Properties. Change the Name to **TotalAll**, change the width to **10**, click Validate, change the Display Name to **Total All**, and click OK twice.

21. If any of the new form fields is encircled by a dotted line representing a form, right-click that field, press CTRL-X to cut the field, press DEL to remove the form, and then press CTRL-V to paste the field back. The top quantity and the ID fields probably have the form in them.

22. Select all of your table, including its heading and the Submit and Reset buttons, and select Insert | Form | Form. The dotted line of a form will surround the table and buttons. In the blank line above the form, type **Please enter the quantity you wish to purchase:**, and format it as Heading 3. Your final product should look like Figure 21-5.

Customers will select the quantity of wine that they want by entering a number in the Qty field. When they move off a quantity field, the page will automatically calculate the totals. We'll accomplish this by adding some JavaScript and several hidden form fields to the page.

---

**NOTE** *For more information on creating forms, refer to Chapter 8.*

The validation and constraints were added to define the information that a customer may enter. For example: the Qty fields only accept integers and are not required; the ID field is required. By setting these rules for each field, you help ensure that the customer will give you the information you need, reducing expensive customer service calls. You also help FrontPage create a well-designed database by telling it what kind of data will be stored.

---

**NOTE** *Special form-field naming conventions were also used, which will be covered later as we discuss their use in "Setting Up the Form Fields."*

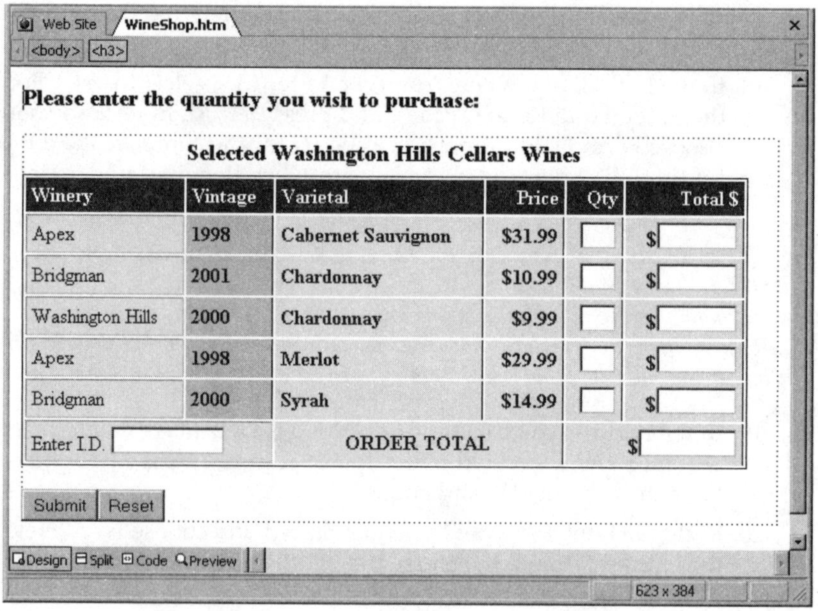
Web Site
WineShop.htm
<body> <h3>
Please enter the quantity you wish to purchase:
Selected Washington Hills Cellars Wines
Winery Vintage Varietal Price Qty Total $
Apex 1998 Cabernet Sauvignon $31.99 $
Bridgman 2001 Chardonnay $10.99 $
Washington Hills 2000 Chardonnay $9.99 $
Apex 1998 Merlot $29.99 $
Bridgman 2000 Syrah $14.99 $
Enter I.D. ORDER TOTAL $
Submit Reset
Design Split Code Preview
623 x 384

**FIGURE 21-5** Form ready to be used in a web store

### Adding a Custom Confirmation Page

With the form completed to your satisfaction, it can be used to create a custom confirmation page. See how this is done as well as add some hidden fields with the next set of steps:

1. In FrontPage, with the Wine Club subweb open, click New Page, name the new page **Confirmation.htm**, and click Yes if asked to confirm the renaming of the page. In WineShop.htm, click in the table, select Table | Select | Table, and press CTRL-C.

2. Open Confirmation.htm in Design view, and on the first line, type **Thank you for your order shown below. Print this page for your records.** Press ENTER and then press CTRL-V to paste the table onto the page. Format the top line you just typed as Heading 3.

3. In the copy of the WineShop table, select the top price (31.99, not the dollar sign), and then select Insert | Web Component | Advanced Controls | Confirmation Field | Finish. Type **Price1** for the Name Of Form Field To Confirm and click OK.

4. Select the new confirmation field, click Copy, select the second price, and click Paste. Right-click the second confirmation field and choose Confirmation Field Properties. Change the name to **Price2** and click OK. Repeat this for all the prices, quantities, totals, the overall total, and the ID field, appropriately renaming each confirmation field. When you are done, save the confirmation page. It should look like this:

**Thank you for your order shown below. Print this page for your records.**

**Selected Washington Hills Cellars Wines**

| Winery | Vintage | Varietal | Price | Qty | Total $ |
|---|---|---|---|---|---|
| Apex | 1998 | Cabernet Sauvignon | $[Price1] | [Qty1] | $[Total1] |
| Bridgman | 2001 | Chardonnay | $[Price2] | [Qty2] | $[Total2] |
| Washington Hills | 2000 | Chardonnay | $[Price3] | [Qty3] | $[Total3] |
| Apex | 1998 | Merlot | $[Price4] | [Qty4] | $[Total4] |
| Bridgman | 2000 | Syrah | $[Price5] | [Qty5] | $[Total5] |
| Enter I.D. [ID] | | ORDER TOTAL | | | $[TotalAll] |

5. Open the WineShop form page, right-click in the form area (inside the dotted line), and choose Form Properties. Click Advanced to open the Advanced Form Properties dialog box, and then click Add. Type **Price1** in the Name field, **31.99** in the Value field, and click OK.

6. Similarly, add the remaining four prices as follows, clicking OK after each:

   **Price2**  10.99
   **Price3**  9.99
   **Price4**  29.99
   **Price5**  14.99

At this point, your Advanced Form Properties dialog box should look like this:

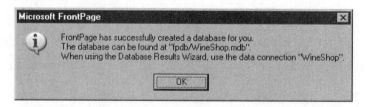

7. Click OK to return to the Form Properties dialog box, but leave that open.

### Attaching a Database

The next step is to attach the form to a database that will be used to hold the information entered into the form. With FPSE, all of the work setting up the database is done in the Form Properties dialog box. Here you configure the form to save its results to an Access database within the site and to actually create the database based on the fields in the form. See Chapter 17 for more information on working with databases. FrontPage puts the database connection information in ASP code that runs in the server and is not available to client browsers. (ASP is the primary reason that this does not work with SharePoint 2.)

In the next set of instructions, you'll set up the database. It is important to have completed the form, its confirmation page, and the hidden price fields before the database because all the fields are used in the creation of the database.

1. In the Form Properties dialog box, click Send To Database, and then click Options. In the Options For Saving Results To Database dialog box, click Create Database. When the database is created, you are told where the database can be found and what the data connection is, as you can see here:

2. Click OK. Click the Saved Fields tab, and note that all the form fields are in the database. Click the Additional Fields tab, and note the additional fields that are also stored in the database.

3. Return to the Database Results tab, click in the text box under URL Of Confirmation Page, and type **Confirmation.htm**. Click OK to close the Options dialog box, and click it again to close the Form Properties dialog box.

4. You will be told that the page now contains components that require the .asp file extension. Click OK. In the Folder List, right-click the WineShop.htm file, choose Rename, change the extension to **.asp**, press ENTER, and then save the file. Change the extension of the confirmation page to **.asp** for the same reason. When you change the name of the confirmation page, you are told that one page has a link to this file, and you are asked if you want to update that link. Click OK.

5. To test your form and its confirmation page, open WineShop.asp in a browser. Enter amounts in all fields. (In a bit, you will automatically calculate the totals, but now you are just making sure all the fields are working in both the order form and in the confirmation page.)

6. When you are done, click Submit. Your confirmation page should be completely filled in as shown in Figure 21-6, except with your numbers. Close your browser.

7. If you see any problems, go back to the form and the confirmation page, look at the field names in both, and make sure they are spelled the same for the same field. For example, on our confirmation page we had the Qty fields spelled "Qry." Make any necessary changes, resave the pages, and try them again.

### Attaching JavaScript for Totaling

To make the form do the totaling, you need to enter a JavaScript routine to perform the calculations. Here is how to do this:

1. In FrontPage, open WineShop.asp in Code view. As you can see, there's lots of server-side script (it should be a lighter color) that FrontPage has added to handle

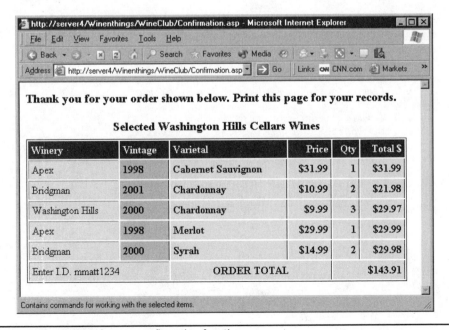

**FIGURE 21-6**   Testing the form-to-confirmation function

saving the form results to the database. Scroll down the page until you find the
<body> tag.

2. Place the cursor at the end of your <body> tag line, press ENTER twice to leave a
   blank line, and enter the following script. Remember to let FrontPage help you by,
   for example, entering a less-than symbol, selecting "script," pressing SPACEBAR,
   selecting "language," entering an equal sign, selecting "javascript," pressing RIGHT
   ARROW, and entering a greater-than symbol. The ending </script> will appear. This
   helps eliminate misspellings. Press ENTER twice and then enter the second line and
   subsequent lines. Remember to indent the lines and add the extra lines to separate
   blocks of code to make it easier to read.

```
<script language="JavaScript">

    function getSubTotal(itemNum) {

        var frm = document.FrontPage_Form1.elements;
        var qty = parseInt(frm['Qty' + itemNum].value,10);
        var price = parseFloat(frm['Price' + itemNum].value);

        if (!isNaN(qty))
          frm['Total' + itemNum].value =
             formatDollar(parseFloat(qty * price));
        else
          frm['Total' + itemNum].value = '';

        getTotal(5);

    }

    function getTotal(itemCount){
      var i;
      var sub = 0;
      var count = 0;
      var frm = document.FrontPage_Form1.elements;

      for (i=1;i<=itemCount;i++) {
        sub = parseFloat(frm['Total' + i].value);
        if (!isNaN(sub))
          count = parseFloat(count + sub);
      }
      frm['TotalAll'].value = formatDollar(count);
    }

    function formatDollar(Val) {

      Val=''+Val
      if (Val.indexOf(".", 0)!=-1) {
        Dollars = Val.substring(0, Val.indexOf(".", 0));
        Cents = Val.substring(Val.indexOf(".", 0)+1,
          Val.indexOf(".", 0)+3);
        if (Cents.length==0)
          Cents="00";
```

```
      if (Cents.length==1)
        Cents=Cents+"0";
    }
    else {
      Dollars = Val;
      Cents = "00";
    }
    return (Dollars+"."+Cents);
  }
</script>
```

**Script Functions**   Take a quick look at the three script functions and what they do:

- **getSubTotal(itemNum)**   Takes a single argument, the item number, and concatenates that number with static field names to resolve the proper field names used in the form. For example, if itemNum is "1," then "Price" + itemNum = "Price1." (Here # is used to represent the item number for the sake of discussion.) It then multiplies the contents of the Qty# field with the Price# field to get the Total# field's contents, provided that the Qty# field contains a number. After calculating the Total for the specified item, the function then calls the getTotal() function.

- **getTotal(itemCount)**   Takes a single argument, the number of items on the form. It then loops through all of the Total fields in the form and adds their values to get the order's total. Since we want to maintain an accurate order total at all times, this function is called getSubTotal each time an item quantity is changed.

- **formatDollar(Val)**   Takes the value passed to it (for the item totals and the order total), turning it into the standard U.S. currency form with two numbers to the right of the decimal. This conversion is strictly for cosmetic purposes and adds a touch of professionalism that customers expect.

**Implementing the Script**   Implementing this script is quite easy; just call the getSubTotal() function when the customer changes any of the Qty fields. It does, however, require some manual source code editing:

1. Switch to Design view, click the first field in the Qty column, and then switch back to the Code view. On the far right of the highlighted line should be the following code:

   ```
   <input type="text" name="Qty1" size="3" value="0" tabindex="1">
   ```

2. At the end of this tag, before the greater-than symbol, add an **onchange** event handler, providing the corresponding item number as the argument of the getSubTotal() function call:

   ```
   <input type="text" name="Qty1" size="3" tabindex="1" onchange="getSubTotal(1);">
   ```

3. Locate the "Qty2" field lower in the page, and add another **onchange** event handler, passing it the number of this Qty# field. (You can copy what you type above and change the *1* to a *2*.)

   ```
   <input type="text" name="Qty2" size="3" tabindex="2" onchange="getSubTotal(2);">
   ```

4. A total of five Qty# fields are in the form. Locate each of the other three and add the **onchange** event as you did in the previous step, incrementing the number passed to the getSubTotal() function to match the item number.

5. Save WineShop.asp.

**Testing the Form**   To test the auto-totaling form, open it in a browser, enter a number in the first Qty text box, and press TAB. The total of the number you entered times the corresponding price should be displayed in the Total field. As you enter numbers in other boxes within the Qty column and tab to the next field, you should see the Total of the current item update as well as the total for the entire order. Pretty cool, huh? Figure 21-7 is proof that it does work (except for a $0.01 rounding error in the Order Total).

If your form is not calculating correctly, take heart, ours didn't either the first time we tried it. The problem is almost always either a spelling error or the mixing of words (our problem was entering "total" when we meant "subtotal"). Carefully compare your script to the script shown earlier, and you will find your error.

---

**TIP**   *The very best way to debug a program is to explain it line by line to a very patient friend (wife or husband). Often in doing the explanation, the programmer will see his or her error.*

---

There's really only one problem with this form in its current state. To see for yourself, move to a Total field and change its contents. Oops, our form's information is now invalid. To prevent users from making a similar change, you need to keep anyone from manually changing the Total fields. This can be done with one of two methods: adding a read-only attribute to the Total <input> tags or calling the JavaScript blur() function whenever the cursor enters one of the fields. While adding the read-only attribute is the cleanest and

**FIGURE 21-7**
Proof that the totaling works

**Please enter the quantity you wish to purchase:**

### Selected Washington Hills Cellars Wines

| Winery | Vintage | Varietal | Price | Qty | Total $ |
|--------|---------|----------|-------|-----|---------|
| Apex | 1998 | Cabernet Sauvignon | $31.99 | 2 | $ 63.98 |
| Bridgman | 2001 | Chardonnay | $10.99 | 6 | $ 65.94 |
| Washington Hills | 2000 | Chardonnay | $9.99 | 8 | $ 79.92 |
| Apex | 1998 | Merlot | $29.99 | 3 | $ 89.97 |
| Bridgman | 2000 | Syrah | $14.99 | 5 | $ 74.95 |
| Enter I.D. | | ORDER TOTAL | | | $ 374.75 |

Submit   Reset

easiest way, earlier versions (prior to version 6) of Netscape Navigator ignored this attribute. See how to add both of these next:

1. Switch to the Design view and click the first Total field.

2. Switch to the Code view and add the readonly attribute or an onfocus event handler as follows. (The *onfocus* event is triggered each time the cursor is placed in the corresponding field.)

```
<input type="text" name="Total1" size="8" value="0" readonly>
<input type="text" name="Total1" size="8" onfocus="blur();">
```

---

**NOTE**   *You only need to add one or the other of the* readonly *attribute or the* onfocus *event handler.*

---

3. Repeat steps 1 and 2 for the remaining four Total# fields and for the TotalAll field to add the readonly attribute or the onfocus event handler to each. Figure 21-8 shows both methods applied to different totals.

4. Save the page and open it in a browser. You can no longer directly alter the contents of the Total or TotalAll fields, and more importantly, neither can your customers.

### Retrieving Orders with the Database Interface Wizard

Now that customers are able to enter orders that are saved to a database and a confirmation page is displayed, the next step is to build a system that allows Wines 'n Things to retrieve

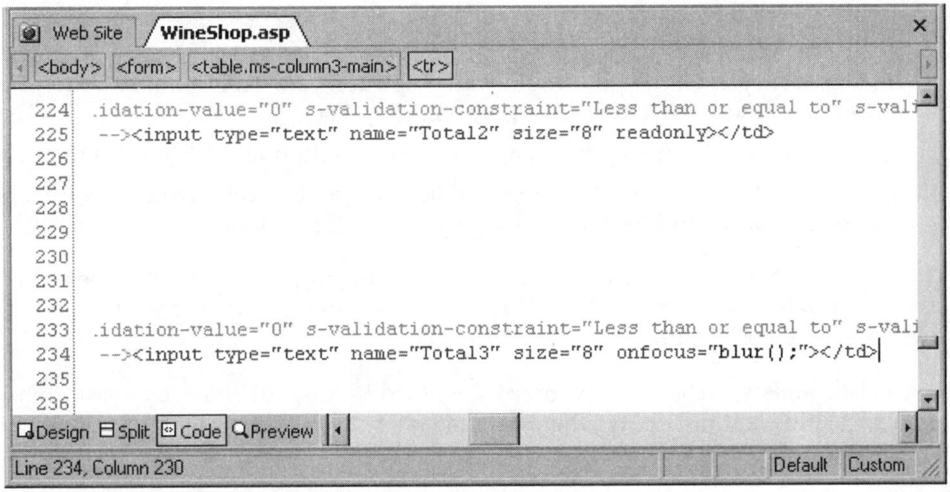

**FIGURE 21-8**   Protecting the totals from being overwritten

and maintain those orders. With the Database Interface Wizard, this can be done without programming.

---

**NOTE**   *For detailed coverage of this wizard, see Chapter 17.*

---

1. In FrontPage, select File | New. In the New task pane, select One Page Web Site.

2. Select the Database Interface Wizard in the Web Site Templates dialog box and check the Add To Current Web Site check box.

3. Click OK to open the wizard.

4. The first step is to determine if you should use ASP or ASP.NET. Since throughout this section we are using FPSE 2002, ASP must be used. (If you were using SharePoint 2, you would need to use ASP.NET.)

5. Next, the wizard lets you create a new database or use a variety of existing data sources. You have already created a database and therefore select the Use An Existing Database Connection option. The existing database connection, WineShop, is selected by default.

6. Click Next and select the table to use. The database only has one table, Results, so that table is automatically selected.

7. Click Next and select which table columns (fields) to use in the wizard-generated pages.

8. Keep all of the information the customer sent and proceed to the next step without changing the field list by clicking Next to continue.

9. The Database Editor portion of the wizard is what is needed for this example. Check that check box, uncheck the others, and click Next.

10. In normal circumstances, you would want to protect your order information and use a Username and Password for that purpose. Here, click Don't Protect and click Next.

11. Click Finish to start the wizard's page generation, building the Database Interface.

12. The files created by the wizard are placed in a new folder called WineShop_interface/results/editor. Expand the Folders view to display these files.

The Database Interface Wizard produces a number of pages. Many will not be used in this example, but two, List.asp and Detail.asp, will be modified here to create two reports, one a list of orders and the other a copy of the order.

**Creating a List of Orders**   The built-in order list, named List.asp, includes more information than you probably want to display when selecting an order. Modify it with the following steps to create a more usable report:

1. Close the Database_editor.asp page and, from the Folder List, open \WineShop_Interface\Results\Editor\List.asp. As you can see in Figure 21-9, this is a table that contains a heading for a list and then one example line of the listing that will be produced beneath the heading. If you want to add, remove, or change a field, you must do it for both the heading and the detail line.

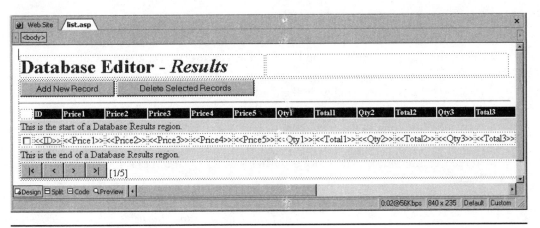

**FIGURE 21-9** Initial layout for the order list

2. Since we're primarily interested in a quick index of orders here, delete all of the table columns except ID, ID1, TotalAll, Remote_Computer_Name, and TimeStamp, by right-clicking the individual cells and choosing Delete Cells. Delete both the heading cells and the Database Results Region cells, but be very careful not to delete the two yellow bars indicating the start and the end of the Database Results Region.

---

***TIP*** *You can select multiple cells at a time by holding down* SHIFT *as you click in the cells, and then right-click in these cells to choose Delete Cells. If you should happen to delete one or both of the Database Results Region markers, press* CTRL-Z *(Undo) until they return.*

3. When finished, save this page and close it. You'll look at it in a moment.

**Using the Form for Order Display** The second page to edit is the actual order display page named Detail.asp. Open this page in FrontPage. While the wizard-generated page displays the complete order information, the default formatting looks nothing like the order form. Customize this page's look using the confirmation page form and changing all of the confirmation fields to column value fields.

1. Click anywhere within the Comments code at the top of the page. Press DOWN ARROW and then RIGHT ARROW. Your cursor should now be at the end of the top yellow bar of the Database Results Region.

2. Press ENTER a few times to add some space between this bar and the table below.

3. Select all but the last row of the table listing the database fields, making sure not to select either of the yellow bars or the final table row containing the Edit and Delete buttons.

4. Delete these table cells by opening the Table menu and selecting Delete Rows.

5. Open Confirmation.asp, click in the table, select Table | Select | Table, and press CTRL-C to copy the table.

6. Reopen Detail.asp, click on the first blank line following the top yellow bar, and press CTRL-V to paste the copied table.

7. Select the [Price1] Confirmation Field and select Insert | Database | Column Value.

8. Open the Column To Display drop-down list. Select Price1 and click OK to replace the existing field. Note the change in the field's display, indicating a column value field.

9. Repeat steps 7 and 8 until you have replaced each confirmation field with the corresponding column value field. In the bottom-left cell, change the label from "Enter I.D." to **Customer I.D.** so it fits the reporting situation. Also, use the ID1 field there.

10. In the bottom middle cell, remove "ORDER TOTAL" and replace it with the User_name field.

---

**NOTE**   *Be sure to replace all of the confirmation fields with column value fields, or your order retrieval page may not function properly.*

11. Select the bottom row of the table, select Table | Insert | Rows Or Columns, leave the defaults of Rows, 1, Below Selection, and click OK.

12. Click in the left new cell, type **Order #**, leave a space, select Insert | Database | Column Value, choose ID, and click OK.

13. Click in the middle new cell, type **IP:**, leave a space, select Insert | Database | Column Value, choose Remote_Computer_Name, and click OK.

14. Click in the right new cell, click Left Align, type **Time:**, leave a space, select Insert | Database | Column Value, choose Timestamp, and click OK.

15. Select all but the top row of the table and press CTRL-B to turn off bold characters. Delete any blank lines between the bottom of the table and the Edit/Delete buttons, and then save the page.

After changing the form as described, your page should look like Figure 21-10.

To open the new order retrieval system in your browser, load the page database_editor.asp in the WineShop_interface/Results/editor folder. You are presented with the Results - Home frameset page. Orders are displayed by clicking an order ID hyperlink, as shown in Figure 21-11. When you are done looking at your order retrieval system, close your browser, the Chapter 21 web, and FrontPage.

This exercise has shown how Wines 'n Things can set up a simple form-based order system to take order information over the Internet. Before putting this example into production, we would also need to obtain and install a digital certificate, enable SSL, and use the HTTPS protocol when sending customers to the order page or accessing the order retrieval system. Even with password protection preventing unauthorized access to the Database Interface, we still owe it to our customers to protect their information when sending it across the Internet. Our example system shows that creating a form-based order system in FrontPage is relatively simple to do. This system might work for you if you only need to offer a few

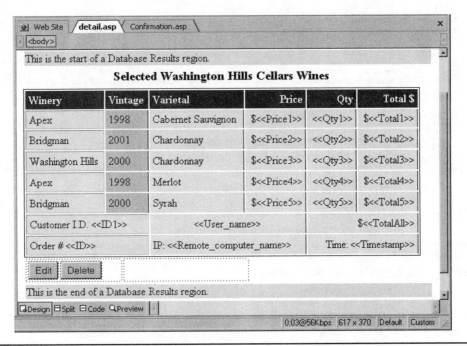

This is the start of a Database Results region.

### Selected Washington Hills Cellars Wines

| Winery | Vintage | Varietal | Price | Qty | Total $ |
|---|---|---|---|---|---|
| Apex | 1998 | Cabernet Sauvignon | $<<Price1>> | <<Qty1>> | $<<Total1>> |
| Bridgman | 2001 | Chardonnay | $<<Price2>> | <<Qty2>> | $<<Total2>> |
| Washington Hills | 2000 | Chardonnay | $<<Price3>> | <<Qty3>> | $<<Total3>> |
| Apex | 1998 | Merlot | $<<Price4>> | <<Qty4>> | $<<Total4>> |
| Bridgman | 2000 | Syrah | $<<Price5>> | <<Qty5>> | $<<Total5>> |
| Customer I.D. <<ID1>> | | <<User_name>> | | | $<<TotalAll>> |
| Order # <<ID>> | | IP: <<Remote_computer_name>> | | Time: <<Timestamp>> | |

Edit    Delete

This is the end of a Database Results region.

Design  Split  Code  Preview

0:03@56Kbps   617 x 370   Default   Custom

**FIGURE 21-10**   Completed order display form

items. If the number of items grows and the page starts getting very long, it becomes time to consider going to a shopping cart-based web store.

## Building a Form-Based Store with SharePoint 2

Using Windows SharePoint Services (WSS) or SharePoint 2 means that the server on which you develop and host this web site is running Windows Server 2003 with SharePoint 2. (SharePoint 2 runs only on Windows Server 2003.) This is a commitment to the future for as long as you want to run this web site. WSS, while it is the second version, is significantly changed from SharePoint 1. It is aimed at organizational intranets, and it is possible that most web presence providers (WPPs) will not have it, at least in the near term. On the other side, WSS offers a lot of capabilities, and if you have a host that has it installed, it will benefit you.

With WSS, all of the work setting up the form, the database, the calculations, and the reporting is done in Data view through setting up a SharePoint List. It is primarily a process of identifying the fields in the form used for purchasing. The only task remaining when you are done is to customize the form and report.

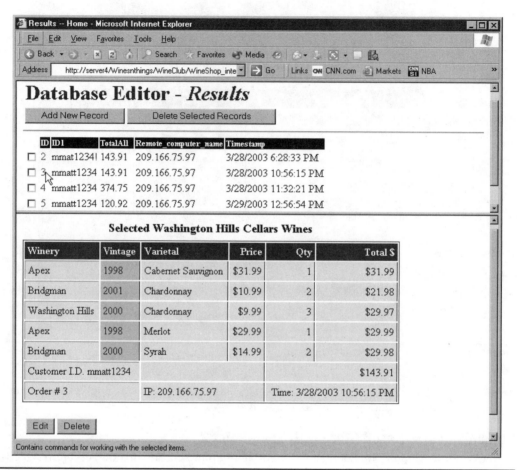

**FIGURE 21-11** Selecting and viewing an order

## Setting Up the Form Fields

In the next set of instructions, you'll identify the form fields and their properties. This will be used to automatically build the form, the database, and a preliminary report. You don't need anything but a web site open in FrontPage.

1. Open the Wines 'n Things web site and the Wine Club subweb. Select Data | Insert Data View. The Data Source Catalog task pane opens like this:

2. In Select A Data Source, open your current site and then open SharePoint Lists, if they are not already open. Click Create New SharePoint List. Accept the default of the New List Wizard and click OK. The New List Wizard will open. Click Next.

3. Name the new list **WineShop** and click Next. You next need to define the list contents one field at a time.

4. Enter the first wine in the list, like this:

   a. Click Add, type **Wine1**, click Next, type **1998 Apex Cabernet**, and click Finish.

   b. Click Add, type **Price1**, select Currency for the Information Type, click Next, type **31.99**, uncheck Allow Blank Values, and click Finish.

   c. Click Add, type **Qty1**, select Number for the Information Type, and click Next. In the Number Of Decimal Places select None, select Minimum Value Allowed, type **0**, select Maximum Value Allowed, type **99,** and click Finish.

   d. Click Add, type **Total1**, select Calculated for the Information Type, and click Next. With the insertion point in the Formula field, double-click Price1, click in the Formula field after [Price1], type *, double-click Qty1, select Currency as the Data Type Returned, and click Finish.

5. Repeat step 4 for each of the following wines (we dropped one from the previous exercise to reduce typing here). Remember to add the Qty and Total fields for each of these wines and their price, as you did earlier, giving you a total of 16 entries for the four wines:

| Wine2 | 2001 Bridgman Chardonnay | 10.99 |
| Wine3 | 1998 Apex Merlot | 9.99 |
| Wine4 | 2000 Bridgman Syrah | 14.99 |

6. Enter two additional fields:

   a. Click Add, type **TotalAll**, select Calculated for the Information Type, and click Next. With the insertion point in the Formula field, double-click Total1, type **+**, double-click Total2, type **+**, double-click Total3, type **+**, double-click Total4, select Currency for the Data Type Returned, and click Finish.

   b. Click Add, type **Customer**, select User for the Information Type, click Next, select ID for the Field, uncheck Allow Blank Values, and click Finish.

7. When you have entered all the fields, click Next. Allow readers to read All Items, but to edit Only Their Own. Click Finish. After a fair amount of processing, a SharePoint page named AllItems will open in Design view. It should look like Figure 21-12.

8. If you open the Folder List and then open your new SharePoint list, you should see four files: AllItems.aspx (primary page for looking at the site), DispForm.aspx (used for displaying the database content), EditForm.aspx (used to edit a database record), and NewForm (used to enter a new record into the database).

9. With AllItems.aspx open in FrontPage, click Preview In Browser. Click New Item. The form that was automatically generated appears, as you can see Figure 21-13.

10. Enter several orders so there are some entries in the database. After each entry, click Save And Close.

   As you are making the entries, analyze the form and determine what you want to change. For example, the Title field, which is built into the SharePoint list and is required, needs to be removed, and the Wine fields need to be shortened.

11. When you have entered a few orders (we entered four), stop and take a look at the list you are building. Note that to see it all, you have to do a fair amount of horizontal scrolling, that the wine name requires each entry to take three lines, and that the title, which isn't even a field we wanted, also pushes the entry into multiple lines.

12. Move the mouse pointer over one of the Title fields; you see it is a link that if you click, you get a vertical list of that particular record. Return to the full database list if you left, and again hover over a Title field and click the drop-down arrow. This

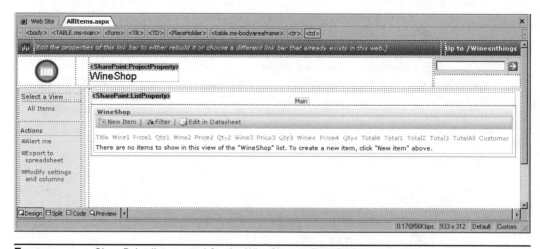

**FIGURE 21-12**    SharePoint list created for the WineShop in FrontPage

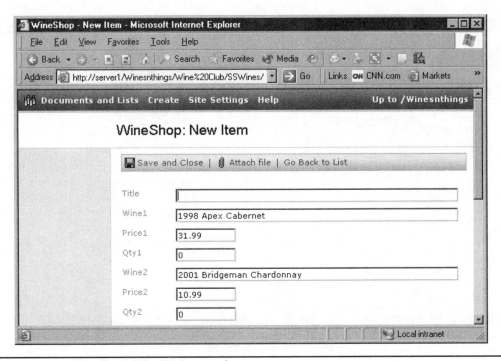

**FIGURE 21-13**    SharePoint default data entry form

produces the context menu shown in Figure 21-14 where you view the record (same as clicking the item), open the record in an editing form, delete the record, and establish an alert when the record is changed.

13. Click Filter in the menu at the top of the list. A series of drop-down list boxes appears, one for each field containing the different contents of that field. Using the list boxes, you can create a filter to select just some of the records. Click Edit In Datasheet. Here you get a view similar to Excel. By opening the task pane, you can export the database to either Excel or Access; cut, copy, and paste within the current view; and add a total line of all the selected records.

14. When you are ready, close your browser and return to FrontPage.

### Customizing SharePoint Objects

What you were able to create using the SharePoint list is really terrific, considering the number of steps that it took. At the same time, there are a number changes you may want to make; among these are

- Remove the Title field.
- Reduce the field length of the wine fields.
- Change the layout of the data entry form to be more like a table.
- Remove the ability to attach files, which is not necessary.

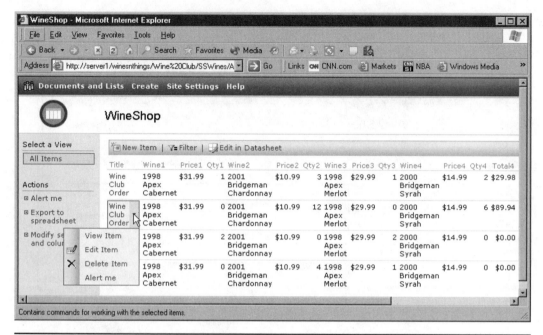

**FIGURE 21-14**    The WineShop database in the full list format

- Limit entry to just the Qty fields.
- Generate a confirmation form upon receiving an order.
- Make the listing easier to read by pulling the wines and pricing up to a separate table.

Some changes are trivial and some more difficult. There are several places to implement these changes, including

- The List Properties dialog box
- The Web Part Properties dialog box
- The Web Part Zone Properties dialog box
- The Data View Details task pane
- The Web Part Connections dialog box
- The SharePoint list form

Look at each of these areas and see what can be accomplished.

**Changing List Properties**    The List Properties dialog box, shown next, provides the primary place for changing the fields, the name of the list, and additional settings, including whether attachments are accepted. Use the following steps to see what is available in the List Properties dialog box, to turn off the use of attachments, and to change the field length.

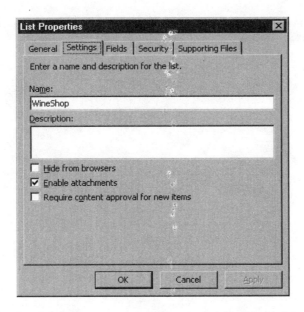

1. In FrontPage with the Wines 'n Things web and the Wine Club subweb open, right-click the Wine Shop list in the Folder List and click Properties. In the List Properties dialog box that opens, click the Settings tab. Here you can change the name of the list if you want.

2. Click Enable Attachments to turn off that selection. This means that the user cannot attach a file to the order record. Click the Fields tab. Here you'll see the list of fields, both built-in and the ones you entered.

3. Select the Title field. Notice that the Remove button is dim, meaning that field cannot be deleted, but Modify is enabled. If you click Modify, you see you can change the name, but the Information Type is fixed at a Single Line Of Text. Leave the field unchanged and click Cancel; you'll see in a bit how to simply not display it, which serves our purpose.

4. Click the Wine1 field, click Modify, and click Next. Select the value 255 for the Maximum Number Of Characters Allowed, change it to **26**, and click Finish.

5. Repeat step 4 for the other three wines. Make any other changes to the fields that you want. When you are done, click OK to close the List Properties dialog box. You are told that disabling attachments will result in the deletion of any attachments that have been sent. Click OK.

6. Double-click NewForm.aspx to open it, and then click Preview In Browser. You'll see that Attach File is removed, and that the field lengths are shortened, as shown in Figure 21-15.

7. When you are ready, close your browser, but leave the NewForm.aspx page open in FrontPage.

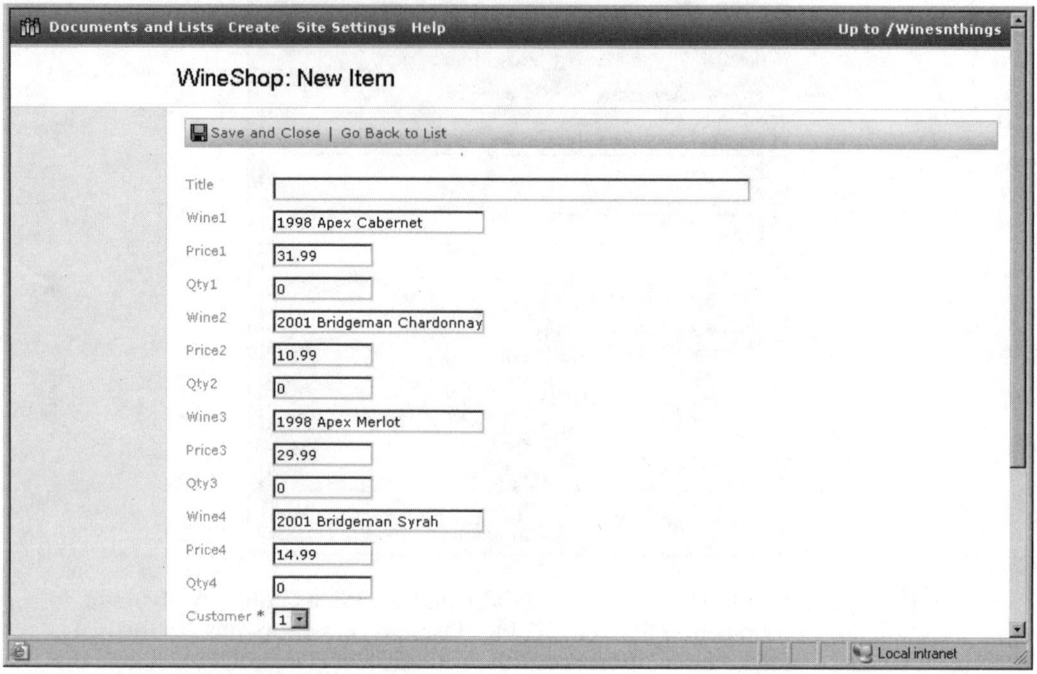

**FIGURE 21-15**    Revised data entry form

**Changing Web Part Properties**    Web Part properties are those that relate to how a form or list (the "web parts") relate to the SharePoint list. They allow you to change the title on the web part, determine how the web part is displayed, and whether several features and links are enabled, as you can see in Figure 21-16. None of the items that we want to change is here, but quickly look at what you can do in this dialog box:

1. Right-click in the Main area of the NewForm.aspx order entry form and click Web Part Properties.

2. In the Title field, type **Order Entry**. Scroll down the dialog box and look at the settings and options that are available.

3. Open both the Layout and Advanced expansion areas to look at the settings there.

4. Close the Web Part Properties dialog box.

**Reviewing Web Part Zone Properties**    A web part zone sets up a Dynamic Web Template's editable area with both formatting conventions and controls on what a user can do with and to the area in a browser, as shown next. There are no items on the list of changes desired that can be accomplished here, but it is instructive to see what you might do in a different situation.

**FIGURE 21-16**
Web Part
Properties dialog
box

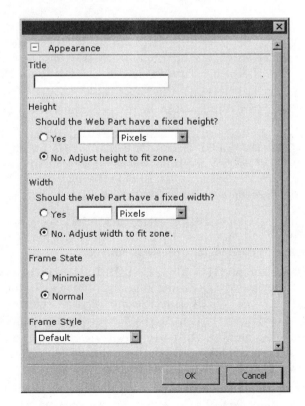

PART IV

**Changing the Data View Details Task Pane** The Data View Details task pane lets you create a new data view or, in our case, manage an existing one. Here we want to turn off the display of the Title field, make some other field changes, and consider different layouts of the data:

1. Close NewForm.aspx and double-click AllItems.aspx. Right-click within the Main area and choose List View Properties. The Data View Details task pane will open.

2. Click Fields. Here in the Displayed Fields dialog box, you can add or remove the fields that are displayed. In the right column, click Title, and then click Remove.

---

**NOTE** *The Title field that was included by default has a link to the menu that you saw open in Figure 21-14. If this field is deleted, your access to the menu is also deleted. A better solution might be to rename the field in the List Properties dialog box. (Changing the name of the Title field also changes the name of the Title fields linked to the record or the menu.)*

3. In the left column, click Created, click Add, select Created at the bottom of the right column, and click Move Up a number of times until Created is at the top of the list. This adds the date the order was entered.

4. Select Total1 and click Move Up until Total1 is immediately below Qty1. Repeat this so Total2 is below Qty2, and Total 3 is below Qty3. (Total4 should already be just beneath Qty4.) Click OK to close the Displayed Fields dialog box.

5. Click Style in the Data View Details task pane to open the View Styles dialog box shown in Figure 21-17. Here you can select alternative layouts (HTML View Styles) for the primary listing to which you return after entering a record. The first layout is the default, which you have been looking at.

6. Select an alternative layout and click OK to look at the results. When ready, click Style again. Do that to look at as many layouts as you want to. When you are done checking the alternatives, select the fourth layout, entitled "Repeating Form With Border," and click OK.

**FIGURE 21-17**
Looking at alternative layouts for the primary listing

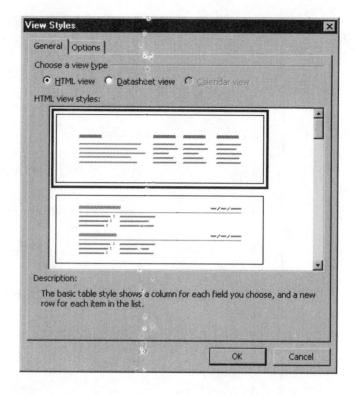

7. Click Filter in the Data View Details task pane. Click Click Here To Add A New Clause. Open the drop-down list under Field Name, select Created, and by default, "Equals" and "Current Date" are filled in for the Comparison and Value fields. Click OK.

8. Click Sort & Group. Select ID in the right column and click Remove. Select Created in the left column and click Add. Click Descending to show the most recent orders first. Click OK.

9. Save the page. Click Preview In Browser. What you should see is a list of today's orders sorted in descending order using the new layout, as shown in Figure 21-18. (The Title field is back because it is a built-in part of the layout used.)

10. When you are ready, close the browser and close the Data View Details task pane.

**Reviewing the Web Part Connections Dialog Box** The Web Part Connections dialog box, which is opened by right-clicking in the Main area of AllItems.aspx, allows you to create a new connection between the current web part and another. You can choose to provide the current row or the current view to the other web part or to use another web part to specify the sort/filter criteria to be used in the current web part. Depending on your choices, subsequent dialog boxes lead you through the necessary steps to set this up.

**FIGURE 21-18**
Revised listing
layout with filtered
and sorted
records

**Customizing the SharePoint List Form**    SharePoint provides a built-in capability to customize its forms. See how this can be used to tailor the data entry form being used with the Wine Shop example.

1. Close the AllItems.aspx page, right-click NewForm.aspx, and choose Copy. Right-click in the web site right pane and choose Paste. Right-click the copy of NewForm.aspx, choose Rename, and type **EntryForm.aspx**.

2. Open EntryForm.aspx. Right-click in the Main area and choose Customize SharePoint List Form.

3. Select the right column in the table that appears, select Table | Insert | Rows Or Columns, enter **2** for the number of columns, accept the default of Right Of Selection, and click OK to add two new columns to the table.

4. Right-click in the top new cell next to Title and choose Insert List Field. Select Customer, click Show The Field Name, and click OK.

5. Right-click in the cell next to the one just entered and choose Insert List Field. Select Customer, leave Show The Field Data selected, and click OK.

6. Right-click in the new cell next to Wine1 and choose Insert List Field. Select Price1, leave Show The Field Data selected, and click OK.

7. Right-click in the new cell next to the Price1 you entered in step 6 and choose Insert List Field. Select Qty1, leave Show The Field Data selected, and click OK.

8. Repeat steps 6 and 7 for Wine2, Wine3, and Wine4. Select the rows with the labels Price1 and Qty1, right-click in the selected rows, and choose Delete Rows. Repeat this for the rows with the labels Price2, Qty2, Price3, Qty3, Price4, Qty4, Customer, and Attachments.

9. Save EntryForm.aspx and click Preview In Browser. Your new entry form will appear similar to the one shown in Figure 21-19. If you want to make the form more compact, open the List Properties dialog box Fields tab and change the maximum characters allowed in the Title field to **26**.

### Conclusions about Using SharePoint 2 for a Shopping Form

SharePoint 2 was able to provide a basic data entry and data reporting capability very quickly without having to write JavaScript or worry about its implementation. But after a fair amount of customization work, the resulting site only partially satisfied our wish list. Here are the results:

- **Remove the Title field.** The Title field can be renamed or not displayed, but it can't be removed.

- **Reduce the field length of the wine fields.** This was easily accomplished in List Properties.

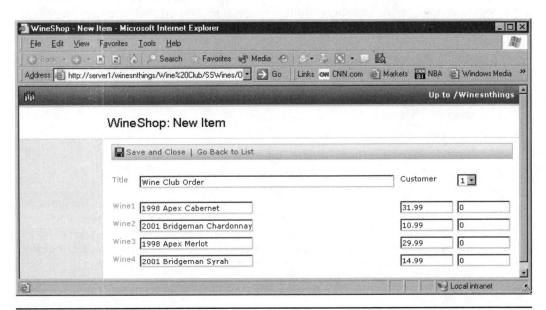

**FIGURE 21-19** Modified order entry form

- **Change the layout of the data entry form to be more like a table.**    This was accomplished.

- **Remove the ability to attach files, which is not necessary.**    This was easily removed.

- **Limit entry to just the Qty fields.**    This cannot be done in SharePoint 2, but see following paragraph.

- **Generate a confirmation form upon receiving an order.**    This cannot be done in SharePoint 2.

- **Make the listing easier to read by pulling the wines and pricing up to a separate table to reduce scrolling.**    This was accomplished by changing the style or layout of the listing.

Making the wine name and its price into a label for the Qty field, for example, changing the label for Qty1 to "1998 Apex Cabernet  $31.99," would have eliminated the need to limit entry to just the Qty field and simplified the resulting listing. This is an example of visualizing this solution in terms of the FPSE one, when a different concept is required. We needed to think outside the box of the original solution.

## Shopping Cart Stores

One hundred years ago, stores were very different from what they are now. Clerks brought the merchandise from the product display to you and then added up the totals. Over the last century that all changed, with customers now going through the product displays and getting their own merchandise, loading it into their shopping cart, and then going to the checkout stand for the total to be added up. The early successful e-commerce sites took the shopping cart metaphor and successfully brought it into cyberspace. This has served e-commerce sites well in providing a familiar way for customers to select and purchase products.

Although the shopping cart metaphor rules in the online stores, a number of different shopping cart programs are available that do things a little differently. All of them, though, provide these four elements to a shopping cart store:

1. Getting the shopping cart

2. Viewing the product displays

3. Putting the items into the shopping cart

4. Buying the products at the checkout stand

This section will look at these four different elements and then explore some of the options available to you with software packages for putting that shopping cart into your web store.

To see how it works, we'll enter the fictional Wines 'n Things Store site, a store set up to sell wines and accessories. The Home Page is the front door to the web store. After entering, the first thing a customer needs to do is get a shopping cart.

### Getting the Shopping Cart

The shopping cart is the metaphor for the parts of the e-commerce program that keep track of who you are and what you have decided to purchase. Computers are very good at keeping track of items. That is not the tricky part of the online shopping cart. The tricky part is keeping track of who you are.

Keeping track of who you are involves the concept of *state*. Maintaining state means a constant connection is maintained, like with a telephone. Even if there is no conversation, the line is still open and the connection is maintained. That doesn't happen with the Web and HTTP. When you click a link and your browser requests a page, a connection is made with the web server. The web server passes the page back to the browser, and the connection is broken. When you click another link that asks for a page from the same web server, the web server has no clue that it has ever sent you anything in the past.

When you are in a web store, and you put something in your shopping cart, how does the web server know it is still you when you go to another page and select something else? There are a lot of ways of doing that, but one of the most common ways is by use of cookies. A *cookie* is a file the e-commerce program puts on your local machine. When you are in the web store, it looks for the cookie to see who you are, so it knows which shopping cart is yours.

---

**NOTE**  *Cookies are pieces of information that a web application leaves on your computer and that are interrogated by that application to determine who you are and what you are doing.*

There are other ways to do the same thing. Some systems embed a unique identifier into all the links and forms when it sends a page back to the browser. That way, when a page is requested from a link, or the contents of a form are sent, the identifier is returned to the e-commerce program. The program knows who it came from and re-embeds that identifier into the page it sends back to the browser.

### Viewing the Store's Wares

From the home page of our store, you click the link to the featured wine or region, and you are in the online store. From here, you can view the product displays. Only after you add a product to your basket are you actually given a shopping cart. Then the system starts tracking who you are.

Organizing and presenting the products are web design issues discussed in Chapter 1. You might want to review Chapter 1 and make sure all your products are easy to find, and that it's easy to move around in your site. At this point, your customer is being sold on the product, so do your best. On an actual Wine store site, you would likely have the opportunity to view detailed information about the wine and see reviews and ratings of it.

### Putting the Products into the Shopping Cart

Look at any shopping cart site, and you'll see that it contains a text box and an Add To Cart button, along with an automated bookmark and e-mail forwarding options. The customer simply puts a quantity in the text box and clicks Add To Cart to add the product to the shopping cart.

It is also important to be able to handle options. When selling clothing, you may want to let the customer specify size and color. For wine, you might want to specify a vintage (year). There might be a drop-down list that displays the options for the customers to choose from and add to the shopping cart.

Depending on what is being sold, there may be many items on a page or only one item on a page, unlike our form-based web store discussed earlier. We don't have to list all of our products on the same page, because you can go to any page in the store and add items to the same shopping cart. In fact, if you don't want to purchase an item at that moment, but would like to leave it in your cart for later, you can save your cart.

At the top of every page in most shopping cart stores is a Cart button that lets you look in the shopping cart. When you click Cart, you are shown a web page with all the items you have selected.

Sometimes, in a physical store, you change your mind and take something out of the cart, putting it back on the shelf. Your e-commerce program should allow you to do the same thing. Not only does the shopping cart show you what you've selected, but it also allows you to change the quantity, delete items, or save the cart for a later visit. A Recalculate Order button usually updates your cart after you have changed the quantity. Different e-commerce programs may have different ways of doing this, but they should allow the same basic functionality.

### Buying the Products at the Checkout Stand

When you have selected all the items and adjusted the quantities, it is time to go to the checkout stand. At the bottom of the cart page is usually a Checkout button. Selecting it opens a web page that requests your payment, billing, and shipping information.

Since you want to encourage repeat customers, most programs make it easy for them to check out by allowing them to log in, retrieving all of their billing and shipping information. New shoppers fill in this information once and never have to again, provided their information hasn't changed. Normally there is a Verify button at the bottom that lets customers review all of their information one final time before sending the order to the e-commerce program, which then responds with either or both a web page confirming the order and an e-mail confirmation and then sends an e-mail to the store owner with the order information.

## E-Commerce Packages

While it would be possible to program your own shopping cart system, a number of excellent, thoroughly tested systems are available to you. The look-and-feel as well as the functionality of the site are often determined by the e-commerce package you choose. Some of the packages offer a lot of flexibility in how you build your site, while others take you down a narrower path with fewer options for laying out and organizing your site. A lot depends on your budget and how much effort you want to put into your web store.

A number of companies offer e-commerce solutions that integrate with FrontPage. The following examples are only to illustrate what is available in each category. Each package offers different features, of which we only have space here to scratch the surface. The e-commerce field is changing fast, so it is important to do your research before committing to an e-commerce package. Check out the manufacturers' web sites for a complete list of features and, in many cases, comparisons with competing products.

### Low-Mid Priced E-Commerce Software

AddSoft's StoreBot 2002/2003 (**http://www.addsoft.net/storebot**) is a FrontPage Web Component–driven product that generates ASP code by simply inserting a web component (bot) into your page. This means that once created, your pages can use standard FrontPage themes and navigation controls. StoreBot uses an Access or SQL database to store site configuration, as well as product and order information, allowing you to configure and maintain the site from any browser. StoreBot comes in a number of editions and prices ranging from $49.95 for the 2002 Standard Edition, to $299 for the 2003 Professional Edition, and $1,853 for the 2000 Enterprise Complete Package. The professional package provides additional reporting and configuration options, and is probably the minimum version you'll want to use in this product, although you can also arrange with a web hosting site for their services and get the StoreBot Standard Edition for free.

Some places on the Web let you build your site from a browser with online-only solutions. These sites do not integrate with FrontPage, but are pretty easy to set up. One of the larger ones is Yahoo!Store (**http://store.yahoo.com**). Yahoo!Store uses predefined templates that you choose. You upload your information and pictures, which are plugged into the templates, and you are online in minutes. Yahoo!Store provides online malls to which you can link your store. There are no web developers or WPPs to deal with. Pricing is complex— charging a monthly fee, a product fee, a transaction fee, and a network fee. (Yahoo calls their pricing, "Simple, reasonable pricing.") Check this out carefully to see just what you have to pay.

LaGarde Inc. offers a full-featured, FrontPage integrated e-commerce system called StoreFront (**http://www.storefront.net**). StoreFront integrates with either FrontPage or Dreamweaver as an add-in, inserting a new toolbar that provides access to their Web Creation Wizard, site configuration utility, reports site maintenance, and a well-written online help system. Clicking the Web Creation Wizard, you answer a few questions, and StoreFront creates an entire store, including Access database and DSN. Site customization and setup of the database-driven site is primarily handled through dialog boxes, although the full ASP code is available for editing as well. StoreFront fully integrates with a long list of payment processing systems or can be set to send orders via e-mail. StoreFront is available in several versions for $99 to $499 up front and $39 to $129 per month thereafter.

Rounding out the list is ComCity's SalesCart (**http://www.salescart.com**). Like the other low- to medium-priced packages, SalesCart comes in three flavors: SalesCart, SalesCart Pro, and SalesCart SQL. SalesCart offers a wizard-driven interface for creating completely ASP-driven stores, integrates with most payment processing systems, and offers both customer and merchant e-mail verifications. SalesCart sells for $250 if you download it, and the Pro version, which offers additional configuration and management features, sells for $400 if you download it. SalesCart SQL supports a SQL Server order database back-end and sells for $800 if you download it. All versions are available on a CD with a manual for an additional $27.

## Higher-Priced E-Commerce Software

The mid- to high-end packages start at around $7,000 and can support the most demanding web store. Microsoft's Commerce Server 2002 (**http://www.microsoft.com/commerceserver**) and IBM's WebSphere Commerce Suite (**http://www.ibm.com/software/webservers/commerce/**) are in this category. These provide robust capabilities for database integration and multiserver hosting, and can link to enterprise order and fulfillment systems. They require experienced programming support to use their functionality, and they require substantial hardware, including multiple processors and lots of memory. They also require other software. For example, Microsoft's Commerce Server, which starts at $6,999, requires SQL Server, which starts at $4,999. Both numbers are *per processor*, so for a four-processor machine, you are talking about almost $50,000.

# Marketing Your Web Store

Once your web store is up and running, you need to market it. The types of promotion mentioned in Chapter 23 are essential for your web store, but many business sites are using an additional type. It is often the case that a business going onto the Web already has a customer base and a customer snail-mail list. Take advantage of this. Do a snail-mailing using a postcard to invite your customers to check out your new web site. On the front of the card, have your business logo and your web site address. On the back of the postcard, you can have any additional message. Check out your local printer to see if they do postcards. Five hundred four-color postcards should cost between $95 and $100 to print and another $115 for postage. This is an effective way to let people who are already familiar with your business find out about your web store.

## Keep Them Coming Back

Once customers have come to your web store, you want them to return. A very effective way to remind customers that you are still there and let them know about ongoing sales and specials in your web store is through an e-mail list. Set up a form on your web store to gather e-mail addresses, and then send periodic announcements of web store activities to keep your customers coming back.

Don't forget your e-mail manners. Let your customers know how you plan to use their address. You will be more successful in getting addresses if you tell them that the addresses are to be used only for your store's communications and will not be sold. You are also asking your customers to give you something of value: their address. Offer them something in return. It could be a simple gift or a discount on future purchases.

## The E-Commerce Future

The e-commerce revolution is just reaching adolescence. The large companies have already staked out their claims on the Internet, huffing and puffing about how great they are on every web page they turn out. Still, the Internet lets the creative small business be heard, too, and may benefit them the most. After all, the entry costs are very low to have access to a market the size of the Internet. No doubt, as more people turn to the Internet for their shopping, it will be the creative and the nimble who profit on the Web. Join the fun (and hopefully profit).

# Setting Up an Intranet Web Site

L ike the Internet with its World Wide Web, LANs and intranets are an exploding phenomenon. As this growth increases, many expect the use of intranets to exceed that of the Internet. The competitive success of a company often depends on internal communication and the ability to quickly share information—two major benefits of intranets. As with any new technology, however, there are and will be many opportunities to stumble. How a company implements an intranet may be even more important than the decision to do so.

This chapter will look at intranets—what they are, why they are needed, and how to set them up—both in terms of the hardware and software needed to make them function, and the content they should provide. You will see how intranets can help your business or organization, and how to create an intranet by using FrontPage. Finally, this chapter will discuss how to set up a SharePoint web site on an intranet.

## What Is an Intranet?

An *intranet* site is a web site that is viewable only to those within an organization's network. Although based on the same protocols as the World Wide Web, an intranet is protected from the outside world either by not being connected to the outside or through a series of hardware and software obstacles known as a firewall.

Focusing on the World Wide Web and on connecting to the world over the Internet (a wide area network, or WAN), some people overlook the fact that the same protocols and technology can be used over a local area network (LAN). With a LAN, Windows 2000/XP Professional and Microsoft Internet Information Server (IIS), you can create your own web to link computers in an office. With Windows 2000 Server/Server 2003, IIS, and a LAN or private WAN, you can set up an intranet within a large office, between buildings, or even among company sites around the world.

An intranet may be as simple as two computers networked in a home office, or as complex as a network linking the offices of a global corporation. In the latter case, an intranet could link the computers within regional segments of the organization, while the Internet could be used to connect the various intranets—this is referred to as an *extranet.*

Networking computers to share information is, of course, not a new concept. Networked computers can be found in virtually every medium-to-large business and in many smaller ones. When networked, the resources on any computer can be shared by any other computer on the network. With Windows, the addition of a network interface card can turn any PC into either a network server or a workstation. For larger networks, specialized software, such as Novell's NetWare, or Windows NT/2000/2003 Server, is required to effectively allow computers to share information.

Classical networking involves the sharing of files and some hardware devices such as printers. More recently, it has included the use of e-mail. An intranet that uses the technology of the Web significantly enhances the functionality of a LAN or a corporate WAN by adding the ability to read and interact with a large set of documents that are easily created and kept up to date. Almost as important, many of these documents already exist as word processing, spreadsheet, and database files. With FrontPage, they can be easily converted to interactive web pages.

---

***TIP***   *Existing word processing, spreadsheet, and database files can be easily converted for use on an intranet by importing them into FrontPage. In the classic example of the company procedures manuals, the web's ready availability, search tools, and easy maintenance and updating are powerful incentives to having an intranet.*

---

As was explained in Chapter 1, the Internet and the World Wide Web are built upon three software technologies:

- **TCP/IP (Transmission Control Protocol/Internet Protocol)**   The underlying technology of the Internet for the exchange of information and the identification of parts of the network

- **HTTP (Hypertext Transfer Protocol)**   Handles the actual transmission of web documents

- **HTML (Hypertext Markup Language)**   The programming language of the Web

These same technologies are used to implement an intranet, and they must be added to the networking software that is already in place. HTTP and HTML are used only by the web server and the browser, and do not affect the classical networking software. TCP/IP, on the other hand, directly competes with classical networking protocols such as IPX/SPX or NetBEUI on Intel-based computers. TCP/IP can be used instead of or in addition to other protocols, and setting it up is straightforward. The objective, of course, is to have the protocols operate in harmony to perform all of the necessary networking functions.

One of the problem areas with classical networking was linking different types of computers, such as PCs, Macintoshes, Sun, and various UNIX- and Linux-based computers. Each operating system (or platform) requires its own specialized software, which isn't always compatible between systems. An intranet built with TCP/IP, HTTP, and HTML doesn't have the compatibility problems of other networking systems. The early support of the U.S. government ensured the widespread adoption of TCP/IP as a network protocol, and HTTP servers and HTML browsers are available for virtually every platform. For organizations that have acquired a variety of computer hardware, creating an intranet is not difficult. While a simple file-sharing network allows files to be accessed between computers, the three Internet technologies allow much greater interactivity by use of hypertext links, searches, forms, and discussion boards. Some of these features are available with products such as NetWare, but at greater cost and complexity, and without the hardware flexibility. A FrontPage-created intranet, especially with SharePoint, presents a much superior solution for sharing and collaboration within an organization.

# Why Have an Intranet?

The reasons for having an intranet are as varied as the organizations creating it, but the common purposes are to communicate among the members of the organization and to involve them in improving their effectiveness and collaboration. An intranet that is carefully planned and implemented can significantly improve overall productivity in the organization, and reduce costs involved with communication, such as costs for phone calls, faxes, and paper, not to mention the costs of missed opportunities, missed meetings, or misunderstandings.

## Communication

The intranet can replace newsletters, reports, lists of job openings, manuals, procedures, employee guidelines, meeting schedules, details of benefit plans, and lunch menus. Almost anything that is written or graphic and has an audience of more than a few people is a candidate for the intranet. The benefits of using the intranet are substantial:

- An intranet document can be put up when convenient for the creator, and read when convenient for the reader.

- Readers can keep and conveniently file an intranet document, or they can just read it and discard it, knowing the source document will be there for some time.

- The documents can be simple text or full multimedia. By including multimedia, you can make documents more inviting to open and read.

- The communication can be one-way, from the creator to the reader, or it can include forms and discussion boards to let the reader communicate back to the creator or to other fellow readers.

- The documents can be easily indexed and searched, making the information they contain easier to find and use.

- The cost of printing, distributing, and maintaining manuals, procedures, and guidelines is reduced, as are some fax and delivery expenses.

- Information can be shared over many different computers and workstations, not just PCs. The Internet protocols and technology have been implemented on most computers, giving them the ability to attach to an intranet.

One of the biggest benefits, though, and the second major reason for using an intranet, is that it facilitates the involvement of more members of the organization in the organization's activities. The reasoning is that if you make it easier to locate, read, excerpt, file, and dispose of documents, more people will use them and acquire the knowledge they contain. If you make it easier to comment on and participate in the creation of something that can be put on an intranet, more people will. If you provide easy access and easy use of indexing and search capabilities, end users will directly seek more archival information. If you add multimedia and color graphics and thereby make a document more fun and interesting, more people will read it. If you allow many different types of computers and workstations to connect to an intranet, more people will be able to participate.

Simply stated, an intranet greatly facilitates the dissemination of information within an organization, as well as the communication and involvement of its members.

## Productivity

An intranet can greatly increase productivity. When critical documents are located in a central place, people can find them easily. Historically, many hours are lost in just trying to locate information within a company. Often one of the first applications built for intranets is a central repository of forms, in electronic format, so that users can find the form they need quickly, and print it at their convenience.

## Cost Reduction

Several significant cost reduction studies have been performed on organizations using intranets. With intranets, you can easily track the change in copy and fax paper used per month and in telephone costs. If you communicate to users that the intranet can be used in place of the telephone (for discussion or collaborative-based communication) and in place of the printer (for on-demand information such as employee phone lists, chart of accounts information, and forms), you can begin to monitor other uses of communication within the company.

## Employee Involvement

But the most important reason to have an intranet is that it enables greater employee involvement in the company. If the intranet is perceived as a team effort, and everyone is given the chance to participate, they will use it often and take pride in its growth.

# What Do You Put on an Intranet?

The decision regarding what to put on an intranet is one of the most difficult; much depends on the character and philosophy of the organization. How open does your organization want to be, and how much security do you need? What does the company want to do with their intranet? Disseminating relatively simple information, such as newsletters, administrative manuals and procedures, and lunch menus, is not a problem; doing so with financial information, marketing reports, and corporate plans may well be more difficult.

## Conducting a Needs Analysis

A *needs analysis* is by definition an analysis of what users need on the intranet in order to meet the intranet's objectives. If those objectives are to increase communication across the company and boost productivity, an analysis of how that might be accomplished must take place. There are many strategies you can take, depending on the overall objective of your company. First, of course, you must talk with the members of your organization who will authorize your intranet project.

Before you begin collecting information, a policy needs to be set on how open the company wants to be with its employees. This broad policy then needs to be translated into specific examples of documents in each of the major areas of the company (marketing, production, finance, and so on) that are allowed on the intranet and those that are not. It is very easy to gloss over this issue in the crush of all the other issues, but unless this is clearly thought through and then delineated, problems can occur.

Once the policy is established, specific documents and their priority have to be identified. This is best done by a committee of users and providers. A *user* is, obviously, a person or persons who will be using the intranet. The *providers* are the people who will be providing the content for the intranet. In an intranet scenario, the providers can be either a small group set up for this purpose or a number of independent people, depending on the kind of intranet structure you are building. There are two kinds of intranet structures: a decentralized model and a centralized model, both of which are discussed in the next section.

The users can set out their needs and desires, and the providers can respond with their ability and willingness to satisfy the requests. Either group alone is liable to create an intranet that is not as effective as it might be.

### Questions to Be Answered

With the committee constituted, it should look at all the documents the company produces that fit within the policy guidelines. For each document, the following questions should be answered:

- How wide an audience does it have?
- How often is it produced, and is that schedule supportable on the intranet?
- Do the layout and graphics lend themselves to the document being easily placed on the intranet?
- Does the addition of intranet features such as searching, forms, and hyperlinks make it a particularly attractive candidate?
- Are there any pressing needs to get the document up on the intranet?
- Is the document going to be revised soon?

Based on the answers to these questions, a prioritized list of documents to go on the intranet should be drawn up, and the documents created and placed on the intranet in their designated order. The review process should be repeated periodically to confirm that the documents on the intranet should stay there and to determine what new documents should be added.

## Types of Intranets

There are both decentralized and centralized intranets, and they each have pros and cons that you should consider.

## Decentralized Intranets

An intranet is *decentralized* when more than one group within an organization creates and services a web site. Very large corporations tend to have decentralized intranets, especially if the corporation does not have a department that is responsible for organizing and maintaining an intranet. There are many good reasons for having a decentralized intranet:

- It allows a "grass-roots" approach to intranet development, so departments and groups have control over what content they want to put up in their area.
- Since many groups are involved in the development of their area of the intranet, they have bought in to it and are more inclined to use the entire intranet.
- The content of the intranet tends to change more quickly because more groups are involved with its upkeep.

However, there are some cons in having a decentralized intranet—the most significant of which are the strengths of a centralized intranet: consistent design, consistent frequency of update, and consistent quality of information. There is also the possibility that there may be several dispersed intranet servers (one per department, for example), and these servers will eventually need maintenance. This could put an extra load on the Information Services (IS) department if they are expected to maintain these servers.

## Centralized Intranets

A *centralized* intranet is an intranet that has one central group (or person) who is responsible for developing the structure (both technical and informational) and maintaining the intranet. The benefits of having a centralized intranet are the following:

- A consistent interface design, which helps usability and navigability
- A consistent quality of information and frequency of updating that information
- Easier maintenance from a technical perspective, because usually there is only one server or server farm

However, there are also some cons to having a centralized intranet:

- Usage levels can be low due to lack of involvement in the development process
- Site content can get out of date more easily if one group is trying to keep many different groups' content up to date
- Growth of the intranet can be slow

Whichever model you choose, it is important to consider the pros and cons of your decision and strategize ways to maximize the pros and minimize the cons. One very important task that can make or break the success of an intranet is getting buy-in from end users.

## Getting Buy-In from Users

In both types of intranets, probably the most important thing you can do before you begin building or even planning your intranet is to get buy-in from your end users. *Buy-in* is the understanding from the people you want to use the intranet of how important the intranet will be for them. Depending on who your end users are, you may need to develop a campaign for the intranet, promoting its virtues as a method of communication that your organization will understand and appreciate. It is very important that your end users are aware of the project, that they are asked to participate in its development, and that they are adequately trained to use it.

# Building Your Infrastructure

This section broadly discusses building an intranet—covering the technical aspects of setting up your network infrastructure and providing appropriate security.

## Setting Up and Configuring Your Environment

The first requirement in setting up your intranet environment is that you have a local area network (LAN) that supports the TCP/IP protocol. One highly recommended source of information on setting up LANs and networking is Tom Sheldon's *McGraw-Hill's Encyclopedia of Networking & Telecommunications* (published by Osborne/McGraw-Hill, 2001).

Once your LAN is functioning, you can use FrontPage as the basis for creating an intranet as small as two computers in the same office, or one that links many computers in a number of remote locations. The limits on growth for your intranet will be determined by the number of users and the amount of traffic on the LAN. For several computers in an office, you do not need a dedicated server. In other words, a Windows 2000 or XP Professional computer running IIS can also be used for other tasks. As the number of users and the network traffic grow, a computer will need to be dedicated to running IIS.

For larger intranets, you should consider using a dedicated server running Windows NT or 2000 Server, or Server 2003 and IIS as your HTTP server software. IIS is an integral part of Windows 2000 Server and Server 2003. FrontPage and IIS are completely compatible.

## Installing TCP/IP on Your Network

The first step in building an intranet on your local area network is to install the TCP/IP protocol if it is not already used. If you have a connection to the Internet, through either a dial-up or network connection, TCP/IP will already be installed and configured on your computer. If you need to install TCP/IP, follow these steps:

> **NOTE** *If you are using a dial-up connection for the Internet, you may still need to install TCP/IP for your LAN, so you should go through the next set of steps just to check it out.*

1. Click Start | Settings | Control Panel in Windows 2000 or Start | Control Panel in Windows XP or Server 2003.

2. When the Control Panel opens, double-click Network and Dial-up Connections in Windows 2000 or just Network Connections in Windows XP or Server 2003. In Windows 2000, XP, and Server 2003, you then need to double-click (single-click in Server 2003) Local Area Connection and click Properties.

3. In Windows 2000, XP, and Server 2003, the Local Area Connection Properties dialog box will open; select the General tab if it isn't already selected. Your Network or Local Area Connection Properties dialog box should appear, similar to Figure 22-1 (you may have to scroll down to see the Internet Protocol).

**FIGURE 22-1**
Looking for the
TCP/IP protocol

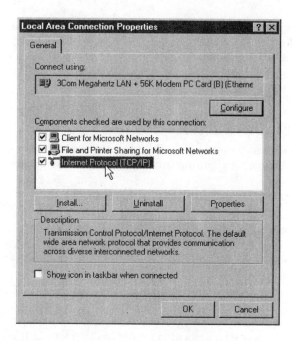

4. Figure 22-1 shows the TCP/IP protocol being used by the network interface card (NIC) for our LAN connection. If some other protocol such as NetBEUI (NetBIOS Enhanced User Interface) or IPX/SPX (Internetwork Packet Exchange/Sequenced Packet Exchange) is bound to the NIC, then TCP/IP will have to be added. Multiple protocols can be bound to these cards, so TCP/IP can be added to the network interface card without removing any existing protocols.

5. Click Install in Windows 2000, XP, or Server 2003. In the Select Network Component Type dialog box, select Protocol and click Add.

6. In Windows 2000, XP and Server 2003, select Internet Protocol (TCP/IP) from the Network Protocol list. In either case, click OK.

In a moment, the Network or Local Area Connection Properties dialog box will be redisplayed, showing that the TCP/IP protocol has been installed.

## Configuring TCP/IP

If you are just installing TCP/IP, you need to configure the protocol for the device it is being used with. For an intranet, the device is your network interface card. Configure your network card with these instructions:

1. In the Network or Local Area connection Properties dialog box, select the TCP/IP component for your network card and click Properties. Your TCP/IP Properties dialog box will open, as shown in Figure 22-2, for Windows Server 2003.

2. In the TCP/IP Properties dialog box, select the IP Address or General tab if it's not already selected.

3. The IP (Internet Protocol) address is a group of four numbers that uniquely identify your computer on a TCP/IP network. For a dial-up connection to the Internet, your IP address will usually be assigned automatically by the server, as might be the case with large intranets using dedicated web servers. For smaller intranets, you need to specify an IP address. You should consult your network administrator to learn what IP address you should use. However, on a small TCP/IP network, you can basically make up your own number—10.0.0.1, for example. You could then increment the number for each computer—10.0.0.2 for the next machine, and so on. As long as your computer does not try to use your IP addresses on the Internet (which it won't, if you use the dial-up adapter to connect to the Internet), you will not have a problem. The IP addresses you use for your network card will not affect your settings for your dial-up adapter.

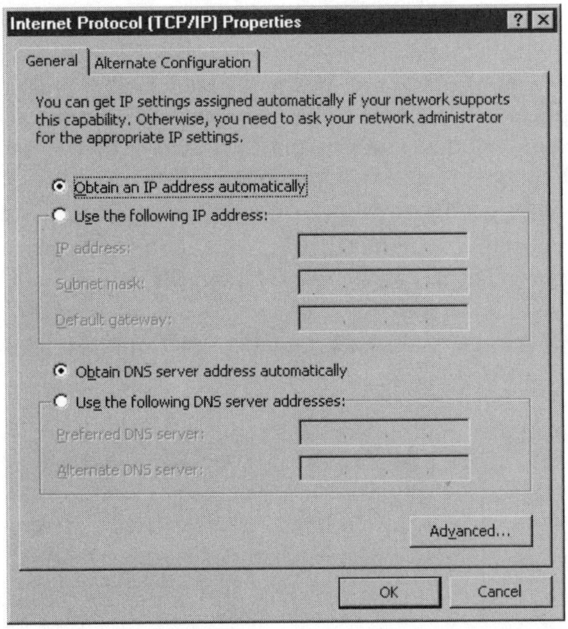

**FIGURE 22-2**
Configuring TCP/IP

An IP address is like a phone number. If you set up your own small phone system, you can use any phone numbers you want. But if you then connect your phone system to the outside world, you may have to use the phone numbers assign d by an outside authority. (Three series of IP addresses, 10.0.0.0 through 10.255.255.255, 172.16.0.0 through 172.31.255.255, and 192.168.0.1 through 192.168.255.255, have been set aside and are not currently assigned as Internet addresses. These are therefore available for you to use internally in your organization.)

---

**NOTE** *Do not use an IP address beginning with 127 (for example, 127.0.0.1), as this is reserved as a localhost, or loopback, address.*

---

4. If your server does not automatically supply an IP address, click Specify An IP Address or Use The Following IP Address, click in the left IP Address text box, and type your IP address. If any number is fewer than three digits, you'll need to type a period or press the RIGHT ARROW to move to the next block of numbers. If you don't have an assigned IP address, use the 10.0.0.*n* (*n* is a number between 1 and 255) set of numbers with 10.0.0.1 being the first. (Type **10**, press the RIGHT ARROW, type **0**, press the RIGHT ARROW, type **0**, press the RIGHT ARROW, and type **1** to get the address shown next.)

5. Click the left end of the Subnet Mask text box and type **255255255.0** (with three-digit numbers, you don't need to type the periods). This is the default subnet mask, applicable in almost all circumstances; in most instances, it is automatically entered for you. We're suggesting that you enter it here to cover the few instances where it will hang you up if it is missing.

6. In Windows 2000, XP, and Server 2003, click OK to return to the Local Area Connection Properties dialog box. Client For Microsoft Networks and File And Printer Sharing For Microsoft Networks should both be selected. Click them if they are not selected.

7. Click OK or Close as necessary to close all open dialog boxes, then click Close to shut any open windows.

After changing your network settings, you may have to restart your computer for the changes to take effect. Make sure you save any open documents before restarting.

***

*CAUTION* *For TCP/IP on your dial-up adapter, you do not want to have File And Printer Sharing selected. This is for security. If you are connected to the Internet by use of your dial-up connection, it is possible (though unlikely) for others on the Internet to access your shared resources over the TCP/IP connection. You can still share resources with others on your network by using File And Printer Sharing on your LAN adapter.*

## Using Your FrontPage-Created Intranet

Once TCP/IP is configured properly on your network, accessing your FrontPage-created webs from any computer on the network is a simple process. First, make sure IIS is running on the computer that will be the server. Then, start your web browser on one of the other computers on the network. To access a web, use the URL http://*computername*/*webname* where *computername* is the computer's name running the server, and *webname* is the name of the web you want to open.

For example, we have two networked computers named "Marty" and "Server1." Marty runs Windows XP and Server1 runs Windows Server 2003 with IIS 6.0. The Wines 'n Things web is on Server1. Here are the steps we needed to open the Wines 'n Things web across the intranet on Marty:

1. Made sure to set up the TCP/IP protocol on both computers, as described earlier.

2. Restarted both computers.

3. Made sure IIS was running on the server. (This is done in different ways dependent on the operating system running on the server; see Appendix A for instructions on installing IIS.)

    a. In Windows 2000 Server, click Start | Programs | Administrative Tools | Internet Services Manager. In the left pane, double-click the local server. In the right pane, the second column, State, should say "Running" for all services. If not, right-click the desired service, such as the Default Web Site in either the left or right pane, and select Start.

    b. In Windows Server 2003, open Start | Administrative Tools | Internet Information Services (IIS) Manager. In the left pane, open the local server and click Web Sites. In the right pane, the third column, State, will tell you if a service is running or not, as you can see in Figure 22-3. If a service is not running, right-click it in either pane and select Start.

4. Start a browser on your workstation (Marty here), enter the address **http://server1/winesnthings/**, and press ENTER. The Wines 'n Things home page that was created earlier in this book appears as shown in Figure 22-4.

***

*NOTE* *About the only way you know you're looking at an intranet page vs. an Internet page is the icon in the right of the status bar that tells you the zone you're in, as mentioned in Chapter 20.*

If your intranet doesn't immediately come up the first time you try, take heart, ours didn't either. Next is a list of troubleshooting questions.

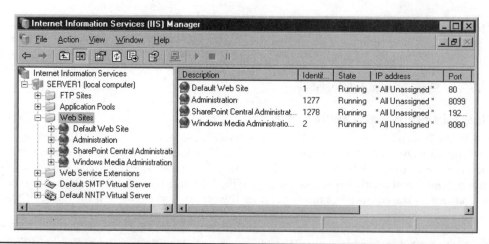

**FIGURE 22-3**    Determining whether IIS is running on Windows Server 2003

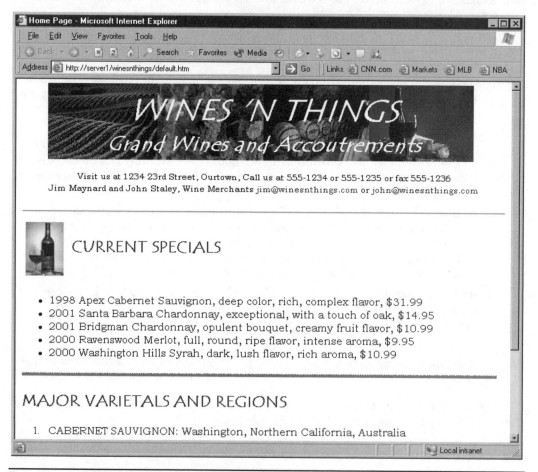

**FIGURE 22-4**    Wines 'n Things web site received over an intranet

- Does your network otherwise function normally between the two computers you are trying to use with an intranet? If not, you must solve your networking problems before trying to use an intranet. See your network administrator or other technical network reference.

- Has TCP/IP been successfully installed for your LAN adapter (not just to your dial-up adapter)? On *both* machines? Reopen your Network or Network And Dial-Up Connections control panel to check this.

- Did you restart both computers after installing TCP/IP?

- Is IIS started and running on the computer where the webs are located? When you address this machine from the second machine, your hard disk light should blink.

- Have you entered the correct server name and web name in your browser?

- Does the web you are trying to open have a Default.htm file? If not, you must specify the filename to open as well as the server and web name. For example, http://servername/webname/ will open if there is a Default.htm file. If not, you must enter http://servername/webname/filename.htm.

If you take a couple of minutes to make sure that each of the preceding questions is answered in the affirmative, your intranet will almost surely work. Errors we have made include forgetting to restart one of the computers and not spelling the web name correctly.

## Security and Firewalls

Anytime you share resources over a network, the possibility exists that someone may access your files without your permission. The risk is greater when one or more computers on an intranet are also connected to the Internet. There are several things you can do to protect yourself and your files. One of the simplest, as mentioned previously, is to disable file and printer sharing for TCP/IP on your dial-up adapter. You can still share files over your LAN, but you have closed access to everyone on the Internet coming in through TCP/IP and your dial-up adapter.

Greater security can be achieved through the use of a firewall and possibly a proxy server, as was discussed in Chapter 20. A firewall is a computer that controls the flow of data between an intranet and the Internet by packet filtering.

*Packet filtering* passes or rejects IP packets based on the IP address that sent the packet. This allows you to configure your firewall to allow access from specific computers outside your intranet that you trust. This method isn't as secure as a proxy server because it's possible for someone to duplicate a trusted IP address.

Use of a proxy server means that every request and response must be examined by the proxy server. This can slow the response of your network, but the proxy server can also cache frequently requested information, thus speeding some responses. If the source of a request is a computer without permission to access your intranet, the proxy server will reject it.

## Building Your Intranet

Once your network environment is complete, you can begin creating content. The needs analysis that you perform in the early stages of intranet development is a critical piece of information now. This section focuses on the "front end" of your intranet: the design and the information that make up your intranet. In the first topic in this section, you will get an overview of how to quickly put up documents on your intranet. Read this first if you are raring to go. Following this overview are more in-depth discussions of how FrontPage can help you create your intranet.

## Overview

In Chapter 11, you read about importing existing, or legacy, files into FrontPage to create webs both on the Internet and on your intranet with examples of word processing, spreadsheet, and presentation files being used. In Chapter 17, you saw how to access database files in a FrontPage-created web. With the techniques in these chapters, just about all organizational information can be accessed through an intranet. Once you have imported the raw material from existing files, you can add any of the interactive features available with FrontPage. Among these are

- **Table of Contents Component**   To quickly build an index of the material that is brought in
- **Web Search Component**   To add the capability to search the material
- **Dynamic Web Templates or Shared Borders**   To place headers and footers on each page with link bars, time stamps, and mailto addresses
- **Forms**   To solicit responses from the reader
- **Discussion Board or Discussion Web**   Associated with the legacy-derived web to promote a discussion about the contents of the legacy material
- **Interactive Spreadsheets and Charts**   To allow users to interactively work with data that has been placed on the intranet

Most legacy material does not contain a lot of graphics or multimedia. Consider augmenting your legacy-derived webs with additional graphics and multimedia to make them more interesting to read and/or use.

One obvious question is: All the components, graphics, and multimedia are great, but I don't have time for all that. Can I quickly put my legacy documents on the company intranet and have them usable? The answer is yes—most definitely yes—if they have a consistently applied style in the documents. Look at the few steps it takes to put a single directory of titles on a web, and the neat results:

1. Load FrontPage, click File | New. In the New task pane, click One Page Web Site. In the Web Site Templates dialog box, name the folder **ImportTest** and click OK. The new site will open. Select the Default.htm page, press DELETE, and click Yes you are sure you want to delete the home page.

2. Click File | Import. Click Add Folder, browse your hard drive or network, and select the source directory containing the files you want to import. Click Open. (Make sure some Word files are in there!) Select the files in the directory that you *don't* want and click Remove. When you have just the subfolders and files you want, click OK to bring the folder and its contents into your site. Open the folder you brought in and select a Word document.

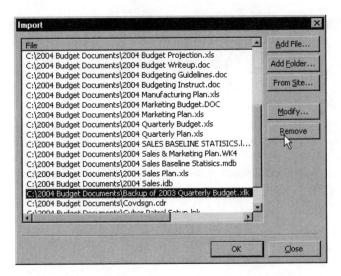

3. Select File | Preview In Browser and choose a Browser. If you are asked if you would like to open the file, click Open and voilà! your document appears, as shown in Figure 22-5. (If your document has headings formatted as a headings style and you don't have the index on the side, open the View menu and choose Document Map, if you are using Microsoft Word and Internet Explorer.)

4. After you have had a chance to look at your imported document, close the web site.

If you have headings formatted as such, all of your headings are automatically made into a table of contents with hyperlinks to the actual headings in the document, so you have a built-in navigation system without doing anything. You can, of course, do much more to improve this document in FrontPage, but the point is that almost without doing anything, you have a web complete with navigation around a document.

## Creating an Intranet

With the needs analysis and other information collected in the planning stage of your intranet project, you can begin the process of creating an intranet. The first step of this is to organize the information you want to provide on your intranet. You can then bring the tools in FrontPage—including wizards, templates, and themes—to bear on your creation task.

### Organizing Information

Earlier in the chapter, you read how planning and collecting information and conducting a needs analysis was critical to the success of your intranet. When you have completed assessing what the end users need to have on the intranet in order to meet its overall objective, and you have collected the necessary documents and other media, then you are ready to begin organizing this information.

Looking at what you have assembled, you will see that certain groups need certain information, and there is some information that all groups need—such as access to Human Resources information, the cafeteria menu, and how much vacation time they have left. Look for information people will want to have immediately at their fingertips. Take a large

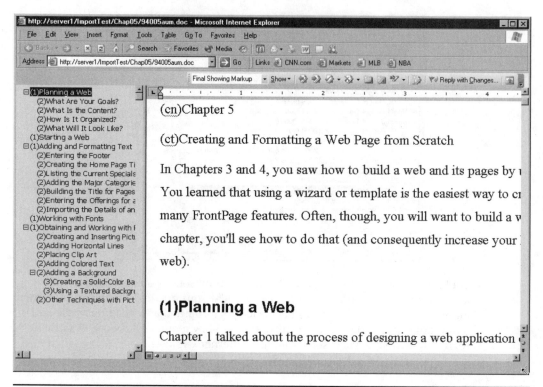

**FIGURE 22-5**   Word document on an intranet with an automatically created table of contents

piece of poster board or butcher paper and write the word "Home" on it. This is your intranet home page, also known as the top-level page. What would people want to see at this level? Try to mimic the terms and structures that are in place and working within your organization—for example, if your Library, Office Supplies, and Imaging departments are known as Resource Services within your organization, then you will want to logically group these together under that same heading on your intranet. When you have arrived at a structure you think will work, go back to your committee and present your ideas. Be prepared to do this at least twice before you hit upon a structure that makes sense to the majority of your end users.

Once you have a structure that is approved by your committee of users, you are ready to begin physically building your intranet.

### Using Wizards to Create an Intranet

As you saw in Chapter 3, FrontPage comes with wizards that walk you through the process of creating certain kinds of web sites, as well as wizards that help you import web sites from other locations. There are two wizards that are especially relevant to intranet development: the Import Web Site Wizard and the Discussion Web Site Wizard.

**The Import Web Site Wizard**   If any piece of your intranet already exists on any computer on your network, you can import this set of folders by using the Import Web Site Wizard. You

can also import folders from your own hard drive, or from any computer on your LA
You saw the process for doing this in the "Overview" section earlier in this chapter.

**The Discussion Web Site Wizard**    Another wizard that can be used in an intranet is the
Discussion Web Site Wizard if you are NOT using Windows SharePoint Services (WSS
or SharePoint 2). The Discussion Web Site Wizard creates a FrontPage web that enables
bulletin-board communication among users. Users submit topics by entering text in a
form, they can search previous messages using a search form, and they access articles
using a table of contents.

### Using the Microsoft Intranet Tools

Microsoft has provided a web site exclusively for intranet building. You can visit the Microsoft
TechNet Intranet site at **http://www.microsoft.com/technet/intranet/** (see Figure 22-6). Here
you will find many tools to plan, create, and work with intranet sites.

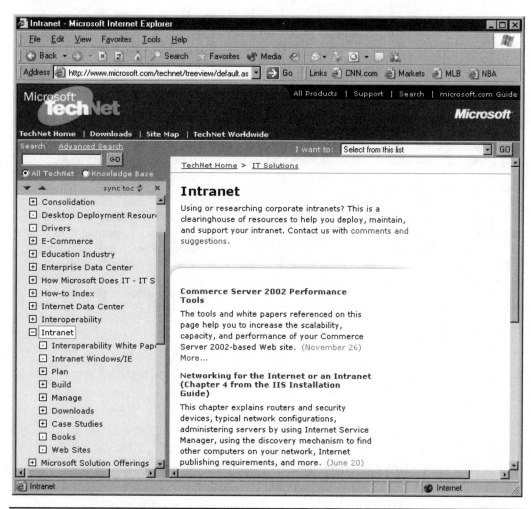

**FIGURE 22-6**    Microsoft's TechNet Intranet site

### Using Themes

Themes are a feature of FrontPage that can be particularly useful when you're creating an intranet—for a number of reasons:

- Themes provide consistent graphical interfaces throughout the site.
- Themes can be easily changed, so if you use one theme and later decide you don't like it, you can easily switch to another theme and change all of the parts of a web that use the theme.
- The themes that come with FrontPage are well designed and provide a built-in hierarchy to aid in creating graphical user interfaces that work.

You can either initially create your web with a theme, or add it after you have created a new web by clicking Theme on the Format menu. Chapter 3 shows how to use themes and Chapter 10 shows how to customize them.

One obvious use of themes within an intranet would be to differentiate between departments. If each individual department did not have a graphic designer to create a unique look for their department, they could use themes as a quick way to get an interface up. Remember, though, to include a link back to the home page of the intranet—ideally a graphical link that is used throughout the site—so that users begin to associate that image with the home page.

## Adding Content to Your Intranet

There are many ways to add content to a FrontPage web. This section discusses using page templates, dragging Office documents, and importing text into your FrontPage web.

### Page Templates

Page templates are part of FrontPage's stock collection of content. The kinds of templates that are available to you are either content templates or formatting templates. Page templates are excellent starting points for creating intranet web pages. *Formatting* page templates enable you to easily create pages with complex layouts. *Content* templates (such as a bibliography or photo gallery template) help you create common types of web pages often found on an intranet web site.

Content templates are on the General tab of the Page Templates dialog box and include:

- Bibliography
- Confirmation Form
- Feedback Form
- Frequently Asked Questions
- Guest Book
- Photo Gallery
- Search Page

Formatting templates are on the Web Part Pages tab and include the following:

- Header, Footer, 2 Columns, 4 Rows

- Header, Footer, 4 Columns, Top Row

- Header, Right Column, Body

There are many other formatting templates for you to choose from. To access these page templates, open the drop-down list on the right of the New icon in the Standard toolbar and choose Page. The Page Templates dialog box will open listing all the templates from which to choose, as shown in Figure 22-7.

To read more about page templates, see Chapter 4.

### Dragging and Dropping Office Documents

Much of the content you will want to have on your intranet site will be in the form of Office documents. Most of the critical documents produced in an organization are created in either Word or Excel, and in some cases, it's ideal to keep these documents in their native form. For example, an Excel spreadsheet produced by the Finance department that includes interactive pivot tables might be of greater value in its native file format than if it was converted into HTML, because HTML is static. If you are using Internet Explorer as your intranet browser, you will want to take advantage of its ability to display Office documents over an intranet or Internet site in their native formats. Also with FrontPage, you can have the best of both a static HTML document and a fully interactive Excel spreadsheet and not run the risk of having your original spreadsheet changed by using the FrontPage Spreadsheet, PivotTable, or Chart components in an HTML page.

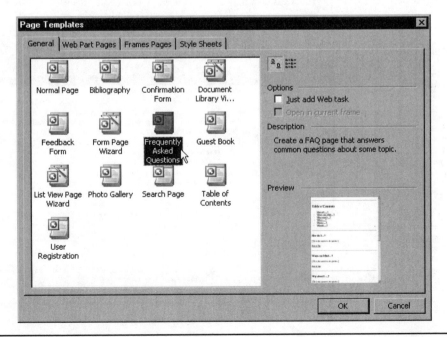

**FIGURE 22-7** Page templates available in FrontPage

When you are creating your intranet, you will have many documents you want to get into your FrontPage web quickly, and with FrontPage, you can easily drag and drop files and folders from your hard drive or network directly into your FrontPage window. See Chapter 11 for more information on importing files.

## Managing Content on Your Intranet

Managing an intranet is a challenging task. To manage a large site effectively, you need to have flexible tools that integrate with both your production process and your system infrastructure. This is where FrontPage really shines as a site management tool. FrontPage provides tools that check the quality of your site, allow you to perform sitewide managerial tasks, and provide flexibility in working with both large and small intranets. The tasks involved with managing an intranet site include link verification, task management, sitewide spelling, and when necessary, some level of overall site design and quality assurance.

If you have created subwebs for your departments or groups, then someone will need to become "webmaster" to each of these subwebs. These people will be responsible for managing the content of their respective webs. Web administrators can use FrontPage's management tools to perform management tasks on their web. The best place to start is in Reports view.

### Using Reports View

FrontPage's Reports view, shown in Figure 22-8, provides the means to look at your web site and determine if you have problems, or if something needs attention. Reports view starts with a Site Summary, which gives you an overview of your site, including the number

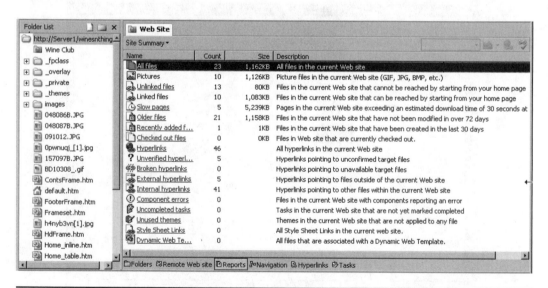

**FIGURE 22-8**   Reports view provides site management tools

and size of your files, the pages that may be slow in loading, broken hyperlinks, and component errors among a number of other statistics and facts.

---

***Note***    *As a default, files in hidden folders, such as the _Private folder, are included in the file counts. You can change that by opening the Tools menu, choosing Site Settings, Advanced tab, and clicking Show Hidden Files And Folders.*

If you click many of the summary lines in the Site Summary, a new page is displayed showing the individual web pages that have a certain characteristic. In some cases, you can also set (in the Reporting toolbar) the criteria for determining if a page fits into a particular category. For example, for slow pages you can set the number of seconds that defines the threshold of "slow," like this:

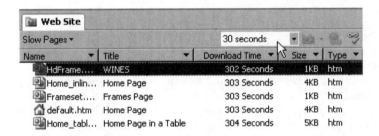

When you open a detail report, you can return to the Site Summary by selecting it in the Reports list on the left of the Reporting toolbar, or by opening the View menu and choosing Reports | Site Summary. Take time familiarizing yourself with the detail reports in Reports view. They can provide a lot of valuable information with which to manage a site.

## Task Management

One of the most powerful tools in FrontPage for managing a site is the Tasks list. This allows you to establish tasks for creating and maintaining the site, attach those tasks to particular pages, assign the task to individuals, and then track the status of the tasks. Starting the task opens the associated page, and saving the page opens a dialog box asking if you want to change the task status. See how this is done with the following steps:

---

***Tip***    *To have an associated task, you need to have a page opened when you create the task. If you create a task without a page open, you can still do it, but it won't be associated with a page.*

1. To add a new task to the Tasks list, open the Edit menu, possibly extend the menu, and choose Tasks | Add Task. The New Task dialog box will open. Fill out the dialog box and click OK.

2. To begin working on a task, open Tasks view, right-click the task, and choose Start Task. The associated page will be opened in Design view for you to edit.

3. When you save the page that was opened from Tasks view, you will be asked if you want to mark the page as completed. If you choose No, the status will be changed from "Not Started" to "In Progress." If you choose Yes, the status will be marked "Completed." You can see the three possible statuses here:

| | Web Site | default.htm | Home_table.htm | third_page.htm | MainFrame.htm | | |
|---|---|---|---|---|---|---|---|

| Tasks | | | | | | |
|---|---|---|---|---|---|---|
| Status | Task | Assigned To | Priority | Associated With | Modified Date | Description |
| Not Started | Upsate Home Page | George | High | Home Page | 7/9/2003 11... | Update the selection of wines displa |
| In Progress | Update main frame ... | Eric | Medium | Visit us at 123... | 7/10/2003 1... | Update the list of wines displayed |
| Not Started | Replace Background | Susan | Medium | Second Page | 7/10/2003 1... | Replace the page background with |
| Completed | Replace photo | Bill | Low | Third Page | 7/10/2003 1... | Replace the photo on this page |

While it will take some effort to create and maintain the Tasks list, it will pay significant dividends in helping you manage a dynamic site.

### Facilitating Site Design and Maintaining Quality

One of the more difficult tasks of managing an intranet's content is providing consistent global navigational tools that can be used throughout the various content areas and subwebs. One common strategy is to provide a single, global navigation bar or link bar with certain visual conventions, such as Home and Search buttons or other sitewide elements. This global link bar enables the different web authors working on the site to provide a way to get to the central areas of the site from within their subweb or content area. Providing this kind of tool ensures smooth navigation, because end users become accustomed to seeing this global link bar and will quickly learn how to navigate swiftly between content areas.

---

**NOTE** *Providing a global link bar may sound like common sense; however, in very large intranets that are decentralized and maintained by many different web authors, it is common to see almost no consistent navigational convention. These intranets are true "web" experiences in that when you click around, you are definitely entering cyberspace. In an efficient intranet, though, it is critically important that users find the information they need quickly and easily, which demands a standardized set of navigational tools.*

---

### Creating Subwebs for Departmental Web Sites

It's a very good idea—in fact, it is highly recommended—that you break up your intranet into subwebs in order to manage the growing content areas. In the beginning, it might seem like overkill to assign each department its own subweb, but as the web grows, and more people take on the responsibility of creating content for it, having a separate subweb for areas that have a significant amount of content in them will end up being much more manageable.

When FrontPage webs get very large, the time it takes to open, edit, and save a page can be very irritating. If your web site gets to be more than about 50 pages, it's time to think about breaking sections of it into subwebs.

## Using Permissions for Subwebs

When you partition your FrontPage intranet into subwebs that correspond to departments or groups within your organization, you can use your existing user/group permissions to grant access to the different subwebs. This means that any user in the Human Resources group can be granted author and browse access to the Human Resources subweb, but users outside of HR may only be able to browse, or they may be locked out all together. See Chapter 20 for more on and how to set permissions.

## Verifying Hyperlinks Within an Intranet Site

One of the biggest maintenance problems in large, decentralized (or even centralized) intranet sites is ensuring that all of the links point to the correct files. In large web sites, this can be a full-time task without tools to help. FrontPage provides tools for verifying the hyperlinks in your web site. To verify that all your hyperlinks are valid in FrontPage, select Reports view and select Tools | Recalculate Hyperlinks. The Recalculate Hyperlinks dialog box appears. Note that the process may take several minutes, and then click Yes. When you click the Broken Hyperlinks report, you get both broken internal hyperlinks and external hyperlinks that need to be checked, and a dialog box asking if you want to check these, as shown in Figure 22-9.

---

**NOTE**   *The hyperlink verification process can be very slow. It is the kind of task that you want to start and then go to lunch. Hopefully, it will be done when you return. The status bar will tell you the progress.*

To fix the broken hyperlinks, double-click the hyperlink entry in the Broken Hyperlinks report. An Edit Hyperlink dialog box appears, as shown next, which allows you to replace the hyperlink with a new one for which you can browse, or you can edit the page containing the hyperlink and change it.

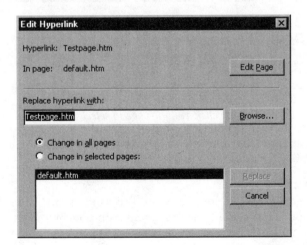

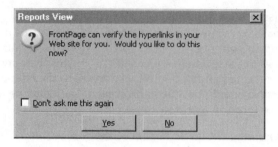

## Sitewide Spelling

FrontPage has two tools to check spelling within web pages:

- In Design view, the Tools | Spelling command or the Spelling button on the toolbar checks the spelling within the active page.
- In all other views, the same Spelling command or toolbar button opens the Spelling dialog box, where you can choose to check the spelling in just the selected pages or throughout the entire web, as shown next:

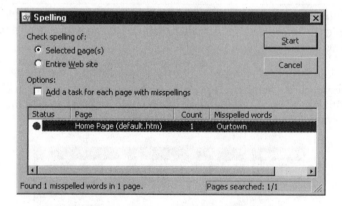

---

***TIP***   *Multiple pages can be selected in most of the Views for checking spelling or other purposes using* CTRL-*click, or you can just click a single page to select it alone.*

The Spelling dialog box also allows you to have pages with misspellings automatically added to the task list.

## Using Web Components

Several web components are commonly used in successful intranet sites. Among these are the Web Search component and the Table of Contents component to make finding information easy and intuitive, and the Included Page component to place consistent elements on every page. See Chapter 9 for a more detailed description of these components.

**NOTE**   *As has been mentioned elsewhere in this book, the web components that are available to you differ depending on the version of SharePoint that you have installed. SharePoint Team Services (STS or SharePoint 1) gives you web components that are frequently dependent on the FrontPage Server Extensions (FPSE). WSS gives you newer components that do not require FPSE.*

**The Web Search Component**   The Web Search component contains two different types of searches, one for each version of SharePoint. The Current Web search component is available only with STS and provides a keyword search through all documents in a web. The Full Text Search component is available only with WSS and provides a full text search of all documents in a web including lists and document libraries. Both search components create a form in which users type the text to locate, after which the components display a list of hyperlinks to pages containing the search text. The STS search form is shown here above the WSS search form:

Enter the text you want to find, and then clink Start Search.

Search for: [                    ]

[ Start Search ]   [ Reset ]

Enter the text you want to find, and then clink the arrow to start the search.

[                    ][→]

**TIP**   *To protect pages from being found by users searching your web site with the Search form, move the pages into the _Private folder in the current FrontPage web. The Search form does not search in this folder.*

**Table of Contents Component**   The Table of Contents component allows you to produce up to two types of tables depending on the version of SharePoint you are using. STS allows you to create a table of contents called "For This Web Site" that lists all the page titles in the site based on the links from the home page. Both STS and WSS allow you to create a table of contents called "Based on Page Category" that lists all the page titles on the site based on the categories that have been established.

**NOTE**   *You will not be able to see the detail within a table of contents until you look at it in a browser. The table of contents is a dynamic feature that is rebuilt and displayed when someone accesses the page. When pages are added or deleted, they will automatically be added to or deleted from the table of contents when the table of contents is accessed.*

**Included Page Component**   The Included Page component allows you to include the contents of one web page on another web page when you load the second web page in a browser. Included pages are good to use when you have content that can change and that appears on many pages in a web site. An *included page* references another file, so when the content of the included page changes, you do not have to modify the page in which it loads.

Included pages can be used to add a consistent title or banner and link bar to every page in a web, or just as easily to add the contact, update, and copyright information at the bottom of every page.

There are five different types of content that can be included if you are using STS, as shown next. If you are using WSS, the two contents based on a schedule are not available.

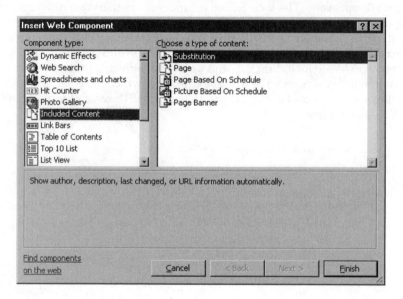

## Using a SharePoint Team Site

The SharePoint Team Site is an intranet site set up to facilitate the communication and sharing of information among a team of people who work together. With a SharePoint Team Web Site, people can be invited to be team members, and once members, they need only a browser to add or access such group-common items as calendar events, phone numbers, names and addresses, to-do lists, and Office documents, as well as hold discussions and take polls. SharePoint does not require FrontPage, but FrontPage can be used to customize the site using themes, style sheets, and Web Components. SharePoint is a major resource and in many ways is a web-centric equivalent to Lotus Notes.

In Appendix A, there is a discussion of installing SharePoint on a local server, and Chapter 4 discusses using the SharePoint Team Web Site template with both STS and WSS to create a team collaboration web site. If you did not do that before, go first to Appendix A and then to Chapter 4 and follow the instructions to first install and then build a SharePoint site. Then open that site in FrontPage. If you are using STS, your site should look like the one shown in Figure 22-10; if you are using WSS, it should look like Figure 22-11.

Using the Team Web Site, the next several sections will look at adding and managing team members and adding and managing content, as well as customizing. All work except customization will be done in a browser.

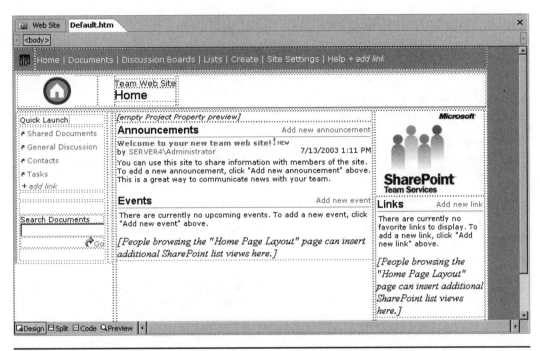

**FIGURE 22-10**    SharePoint Team Services (SharePoint 1) site in FrontPage

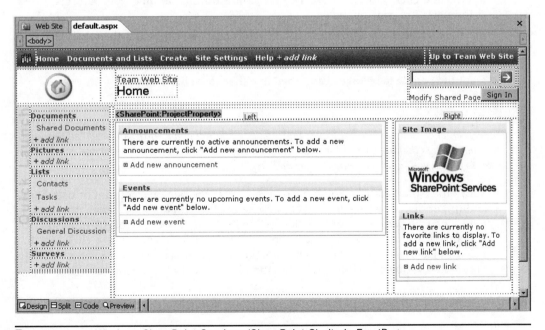

**FIGURE 22-11**    Windows SharePoint Services (SharePoint 2) site in FrontPage

## Adding and Managing Members

Team members join the site through an invitation that includes the member's username and password. Once a member is on board, you can change the roles for which they have permission, delete them and make other modifications to their membership.

### Inviting Members to the Team Site

Invite several members to your Team web with these steps:

1. With the Team Web Site displayed in FrontPage (as mentioned above, it is assumed here that you have gone to Chapter 4 ), click Preview In Browser. The Team site should appear in your browser.

---

*TIP    The SharePoint Team site discussed here uses the SharePoint Team site template in the General tab of the Web Site Templates dialog box. If you are using WSS, there are additionally eight other SharePoint templates in the SharePoint tab and three more in the Packages tab that you might want to explore.*

---

2. Click Site Settings in the link bar at the top of the page. The Site Settings page will appear. In STS, scroll down until you can see all of the Web Administration section, as shown in Figure 22-12. If you see Send An Invitation, skip to step 4. Otherwise click Change Permissions. In WSS, click Go To Site Administration and then click Manage Permission Inheritance.

3. Select Use Unique Permissions For This Web Site in STS or Use Unique Permissions in WSS and click Submit or OK. The Web Site Administration or Site Settings Administration page opens.

4. In STS, click Send An Invitation. In WSS click Manage Users and then Add Users. Type the e-mail addresses, (for example bill@microsoft.com) each on a separate line, of the people you want to invite to be team members. In WSS enter the group you want the people to belong to and then in either case click Next.

---

*NOTE    In STS, if you get a message that you can't send e-mail because the service is not set up on your server, click Change Configuration Settings Page. Scroll down until you see Mail Settings, enter the settings that are correct for you, and then click Submit. You must enter the actual mail server to which you go to send and receive mail.*

---

5. Verify the e-mail address you have entered, enter the person's account or user name and full or display name. In STS, click Next. In either SharePoint enter a personal message to the person you are inviting to the site. In STS select the role (Administrator, Advanced Author, Author, Contributor, or Browser) and in either case click Finish. A confirmation is displayed of the information you entered and your invitation is sent. Figure 22-13 shows what the STS invitation looks like to the person receiving it.

---

*NOTE    In WSS, the person you are adding must already have an account on the server with a user name.*

---

6. Click Home to return to the Team Web Site.

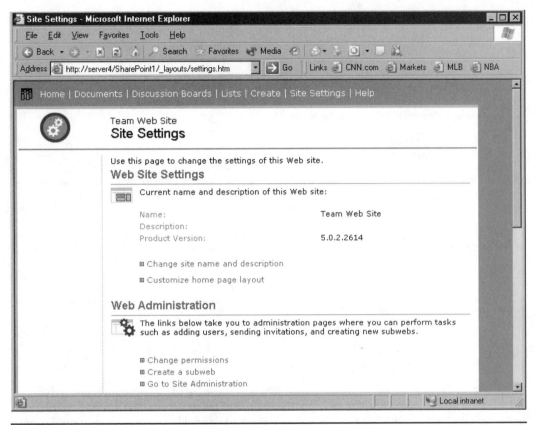

**FIGURE 22-12**    Administering a team collaboration site in STS

If the person to whom you are sending an invitation is not already set up as a user on the server hosting the SharePoint Team Web Site (they must be with WSS), then a new password is generated for that person and sent to them in the invitation, as you can see in Figure 22-13. If the person is already set up on the server, the invitation is silent about the password with the assumption that the person will use their existing password.

### Managing Team Member Accounts

Change the role of a team member or make other changes to their account next.

1. In both STS and WSS, from the Team site Home page, click Site Settings, scroll down beneath either Web Administration or Administration, and click Manage Users.

2. Click the user you want to manage. Click the new role you want assigned to the user and click Submit or OK.

3. Add a user by clicking Add A User or Add Users, entering the e-mail address, username and in STS a password, selecting a role, and clicking Add User or Finish.

4. Delete a user by clicking in the check box opposite the user and then clicking Remove Selected Users. Click OK to confirm that you are sure you want to delete the user.

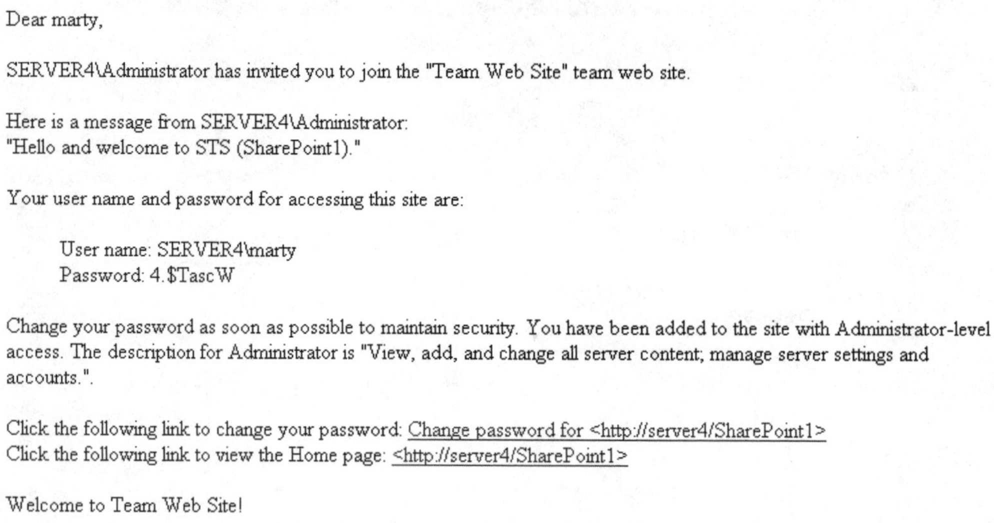

Dear marty,

SERVER4\Administrator has invited you to join the "Team Web Site" team web site.

Here is a message from SERVER4\Administrator:
"Hello and welcome to STS (SharePoint1)."

Your user name and password for accessing this site are:

> User name: SERVER4\marty
> Password: 4.$TascW

Change your password as soon as possible to maintain security. You have been added to the site with Administrator-level access. The description for Administrator is "View, add, and change all server content; manage server settings and accounts.".

Click the following link to change your password: <u>Change password for <http://server4/SharePoint1></u>
Click the following link to view the Home page: <u><http://server4/SharePoint1></u>

Welcome to Team Web Site!

---

**FIGURE 22-13** An STS invitation received by a new team member

5. When you are done with managing users, click Home at the top of the page to return to the team site's home page.

In STS, there is not a clear distinction of when you use Send An Invitation and when Add A User is the appropriate way to go. Send An Invitation can generate a password and notify the new user. Add A User allows you to enter a password but doesn't do any notification. You choose which fits your needs the best.

You can manage your own membership record by opening Site Settings, scrolling down to (in STS) User Information, and clicking Edit My Information, or (in WSS) Manage My Information, and clicking Update My Information. Your User Information page will open. Here you change your password (in STS), edit your user information, and manage personal subscriptions, like this:

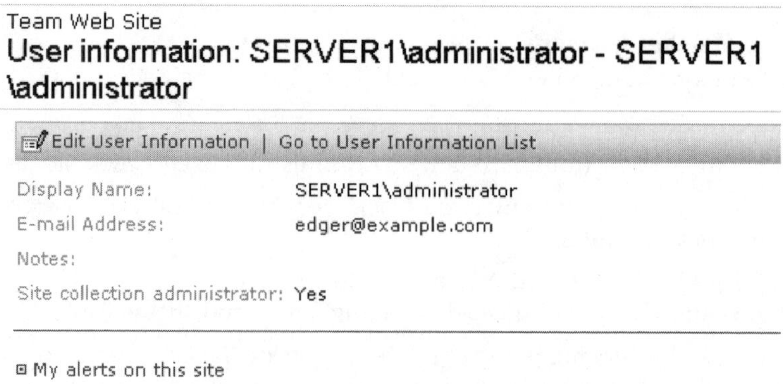

Team Web Site
## User information: SERVER1\administrator - SERVER1 \administrator

✏️ Edit User Information  |  Go to User Information List

| | |
|---|---|
| Display Name: | SERVER1\administrator |
| E-mail Address: | edger@example.com |
| Notes: | |
| Site collection administrator: | Yes |

⊡ My alerts on this site

## Adding and Managing Content

There are many ways to add a number of different types of content to a team site created with either STS or WSS. From the Home page, you can directly add a new announcement, a new event, or a new link. Then, through Shared Documents, you can add a new document or upload an existing one, through General Discussion you can start a new discussion group, and through Contacts and Tasks you can add and manage those types of items. All of these items use capabilities built into the default SharePoint Team Web Site. If these don't satisfy you, you can use the options at the top of the page to add additional document libraries, discussion boards (in STS), new lists, or create a new custom page. In the sections that follow, you'll look at a number of ways to add content.

### Adding and Managing Content Directly

The default Home page allows you to directly add announcements, events, and links. Follow these steps to see how:

1. On the Home page of the Team Web Site in either STS or WSS, click Add New Announcement. Enter a title, body and expiration date, as shown in Figure 22-14. When you are done, click Save And Close. Your new announcement will appear on the Home page.

2. Click Add New Event. Enter the Title, the Event or Begin Date, the End Date (the date to remove the event), the Description, and the location of the event. In WSS, you can also select the period on which the event reoccurs and whether a meeting workspace is needed for the event. Click Save And Close. Also, in WSS, if you say that a workspace is required, you will be asked to select where that is and how to set up a SharePoint web page for this event. The event will appear on the Home page.

3. Click Add New Link. Enter the URL, a description, and comments, then click Save And Close.

4. Change or delete an announcement or event by clicking its title to open a page for that item where you can click Edit Item or Delete Item, to go, for example, to the editing page, as you can see next:

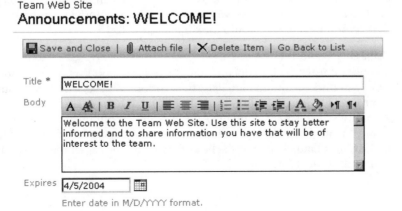

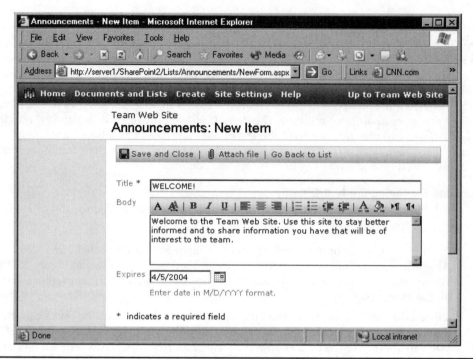

**FIGURE 22-14** Entering a new announcement in a SharePoint site

    5. Clicking Edit Item opens the page where you originally entered the item. Click Go Back To List and you will be returned to the Home page.

    You cannot change or delete a link in the same way you can announcements and events, because a link references the URL to which it points. To change a link, you must open the Lists or Documents And Lists option at the top of the page, click Links, and click the Edit icon next to the link you want to change. This opens a page similar to where you originally enter the link. Here, you can edit or delete it. Announcements and events, as well as tasks and contacts can be entered in the same way. When you have entered an announcement, event, and a link, your Home page should look like Figure 22-15.

### Adding and Managing Content Indirectly

SharePoint classifies information into documents, discussions, and lists. The announcements, events, and links you directly entered are lists. In addition to these, there are contacts and tasks, which you access indirectly either through the Quick Launch area on the left of the Home page or through the Lists/Documents And Lists link or option at the top of the page where you can also create new lists. Documents and discussions are only accessed indirectly, either through the Quick Launch area or the links that are on the top of the page, where again you can create new document folders.

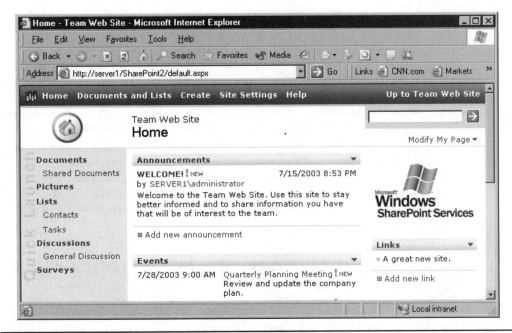

**FIGURE 22-15**   An announcement, event, and link in a WSS Team Web Site

**Working with Lists**   You have seen how to directly enter items on the announcement, event, and link lists. See how this is done first through the Quick Launch area, and then through the option at the top of the page.

1. Click Contacts to open the Contacts page. Click New Item. Type in the information requested and click Save And Close. The new entry will appear in the list. You can click the last name to see a detailed listing of the item, as well as to edit, delete, or export it (in WSS, you can export with both Edit In Datasheet in the list of contacts and Export Contact in the detail record of a contact). You can also click the e-mail address to open a preaddressed e-mail message.

2. On the Contacts page, click Filter. Here, in each field or column, you can select an entry that has been made and display only items that contain that entry. The column you filter will have a funnel by its title and you can remove or change the filter by clicking Change Filter.

3. Click Import Contacts. You will be asked to choose a profile, or, if you don't have one, that you need to first create one, and click OK. If you have an Outlook contacts list, you will be asked to select the names to import. When you are done, click OK. You'll be told that a program is trying to access your Outlook e-mail addresses. Click Yes to allow this. The Outlook contacts will be brought in and added to the Team Web Site's list of contacts.

PART IV

**NOTE** *If you have not installed Outlook or set up a profile for it, you may be asked to insert your Office CD, go through the process of setting up an e-mail account, and adding a user before the importing can take place.*

4. Click Home to return there and click Tasks. You'll see a very comparable list structure with similar commands above the list. Click New Item. Enter a title and select a status, priority, percentage complete, who it is assigned to, and finally, start and due dates. When you are done, click Save And Close. The task will appear in the list.

5. Click Home and click Lists (or Documents And Lists in WSS) at the top of the page. The Lists (or Document And Lists) page will open showing all the lists currently in the Team Web Site. Click New List (Create in WSS) to do that. Create Page will open. Click Custom List (scroll way down to see Custom List in WSS). In the New List page, enter the list name, description, and whether you want it on the Quick Launch bar, as shown in Figure 22-16.

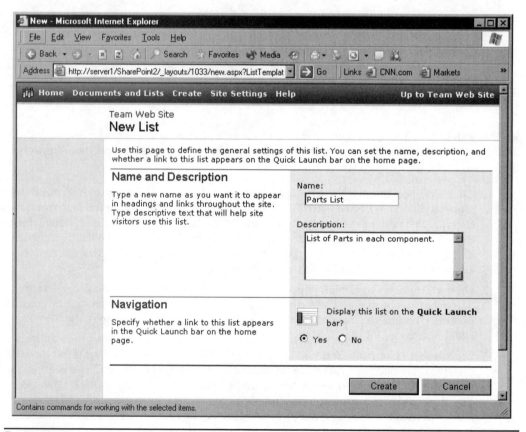

**FIGURE 22-16** Creating a custom list

6. Click Create. The new list will open with only a Title column. Click Modify Settings And Columns (in WSS, it is in the Quick Launch bar). Scroll down until you see Columns and click Add A New Column. Enter a column name, select the type of information you want the column to contain, a description, and other information. Click OK. When you have entered the columns you want, click Go Back To and the name of your new list.

7. Enter several items in your new list. After entering three or more items, click one of the column headings to sort the list by that field.

8. Return to the Home page. If you chose to include your new list in the Quick Launch area, you should see it there, like this:

**Working with Documents**    Documents in SharePoint not only appear on a list of documents, as you saw in the various lists, but electronic copies of the documents are stored in the Document Library. Look at how this is handled with the following set of steps:

1. If you are not on the SharePoint Home page, return there now. Click Shared Documents. Here you can create a new document in Word, upload an existing document from anywhere on the network, filter the list, and modify the settings and columns. The last two items are as you saw with lists. Click New Document. Microsoft Word opens, given that you have it.

2. Type a short paragraph (it really doesn't need to say anything). Save the document in the default Shared Documents folder and close Word. The document will appear in the list on the Shared Documents page.

3. Click Upload Document, enter the document path and name or browse to the name and double-click it. Click Save And Close. Again the document will appear in the list on the Shared Documents page, as you can see in Figure 22-17.

4. Click a document filename in the list. You may be asked if you want to download it to your hard disk or open it. If you download it, you will be asked for the folder in which you want it saved, the file will be saved there, and you can then open it in its associated program or return to the list. When you are ready, return to the Shared Document list.

PART IV

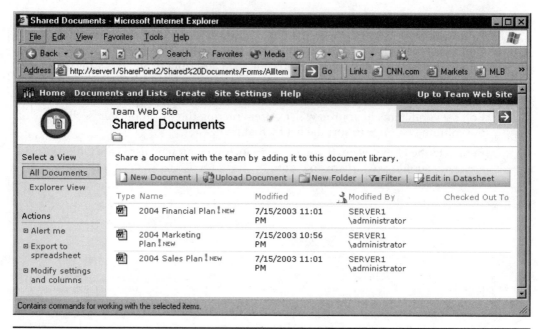

**FIGURE 22-17** A list of shared documents

5. In STS, click Edit next to a document in the list. The filename and title will appear in a new page where you can delete the document, send it to someone for review (since this implies you are sending it to someone who is not on the Team Web Site because they already have access to it, you are asked if you really want to do that), open a discussion thread about the document, or open it in the program it is associated with.

6. Click Home, click Documents (Documents And Lists in WSS) in the menu at the top of the page, and click New Document Library (Create | Document Library in WSS). Enter the name of the library, a description, the template type (Word, Excel, FrontPage, PowerPoint, Basic, Web Part, or none; pick Excel Document or Microsoft Office Excel Spreadsheet for this exercise) and whether it is to be in the Quick Launch bar. When you are done, click Create. A document list will open, as you saw with Shared Documents.

7. Click New Document, and if you chose Excel Document or Microsoft Office Excel Spreadsheet in the previous step, Excel will open and you can create a spreadsheet. Like Shared Documents, you can download documents and edit documents. As you saw with lists, you can filter the list of documents and modify the settings and columns.

8. In STS, click Subscribe. Select the document library, list, or discussion group you want to subscribe to (meaning you will be notified if a change occurs), the type of change you want to be notified about, your e-mail address, and the time to notify you. When you are done, click OK and click Home.

In WSS, you can accomplish this by first selecting the document library, list, or discussion group you want to be notified about changes, and then clicking Alert Me in the Quick Launch bar. You can then change your e-mail address, identify the type of change you want to be notified about, and the frequency of your notifications. When you are done, click OK and click Home.

**Working with Discussions or Discussion Boards**    Discussions (in WSS) or discussion boards (in STS) are threaded messages where anyone on the Team Web Site can enter a new message, someone else can reply or comment on the message, and a third person can reply or comment on the second message creating the thread. A fourth person can create a whole new thread by entering a new message unrelated to the first three. Discussions or discussion boards can be general in nature or on a specific topic. Here is how discussion boards are implemented in the Team Web Site:

1. From the Team Web Site Home page, click General Discussion in the Quick Launch area. The General Discussion page opens looking very much like the list and document library pages.

2. Click New Discussion. Enter a subject, the text of your message, and then click Save And Close.

3. Reply to an existing message by clicking it and then clicking Reply (Post Reply in WSS), entering the reply, clicking Save And Close, and then clicking Go Back To Discussion Board. Figure 22-18 shows what two discussion threads look like.

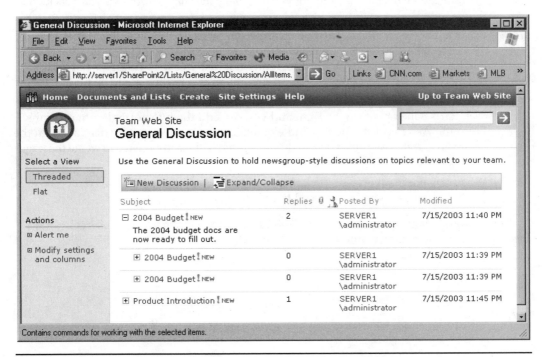

**FIGURE 22-18**    Two ongoing discussions

4. Click Home. In STS, click Discussion Boards on the top link bar, and click New Discussion Board. In WSS, click Discussions in the Quick Launch bar, then click Create Discussion Board, and then click Discussion Board. In either version of SharePoint, enter the name of the discussion board, a description, whether it is to be in the Quick Launch area, and click Create. The new discussion board will open.

5. Click Home.

## Customizing a Team Web Site

There are a number of ways to customize a SharePoint Team Web Site. You've seen how to add lists, document libraries, and discussion boards. You've also seen how you can add and change columns in a list. So here you'll look at other types of customizing, including modifying the Home page and adding a different type of document: surveys.

### Customizing the Home Page

While there are a few items you can change in FrontPage, like the names "Quick Launch" and "Home" and the pictures, the majority of the page is generated and can only be changed by the mechanisms that have been built into the Team Web Site.

1. In your web browser displaying the Home page, click Site Settings and, in STS, under Web Site Settings, click Change Site Name And Description. In WSS in Site Settings, scroll down until you can click Change Site Title And Description under Customization. In either SharePoint version, make the changes you wish and click OK.

2. In STS, in Site Settings under Web Site Settings, click Customize Home Page Layout. A block diagram appears. The two columns on the right, shown in light blue, present the components currently displayed on the page, while the gray column on the left contains the components that are currently not displayed. To change what and where components are displayed, you drag them where they are to be placed.

3. In WSS in Site Settings under Customization, click Customize Home Page. The Add Web Parts pane opens on the right and you can edit the two normal right columns. From the Web Part list, you can add elements that are not currently displayed. In the normal two right columns, you can delete and move the components to create the page you want.

4. When you are ready in STS, click Save and in WSS, close the Web Part dialog box. In both cases, you will be returned to the Home page.

If you were to remove the Microsoft logon image, move Links up, and insert General Discussion, the home page would look like Figure 22-19.

**FIGURE 22-19**    A customized home page

### Adding Surveys

There is one type of document that the Team Web Site can work with but it is not in the
default STS site (it is in the default WSS Quick Launch bar). This is a survey of team
members. See how to create a survey here:

1. In STS in the Home page, click Create, then scroll down and click Survey. In WSS,
   click Surveys in the Quick Launch bar and then click Create Survey | Survey. In
   either version, enter the survey name, description, whether the survey is in the
   Quick Launch area, the survey options (for this exercise, leave Allow Multiple
   Responses set to No), and then click Next.

2. Enter the question you are asking, the type of answer, the choices for the answer,
   and the default value. When you are done, click OK or Finish. This opens a page
   where you can modify the survey that includes deleting it or putting an additional
   question on it.

3. Click Go Back To and the name of your survey. Click Respond To This Survey, answer the question and click Save And Close. Click Home to return there. You should see the survey in the Quick Launch area.

4. Click the Quick Launch entry and click Respond To This Survey. You will be told you are not allowed to respond to this survey because only one vote is allowed per person. You can look at a list of all responses, look at a graphical summary, or an overview, which for our survey looks like Figure 22-20.

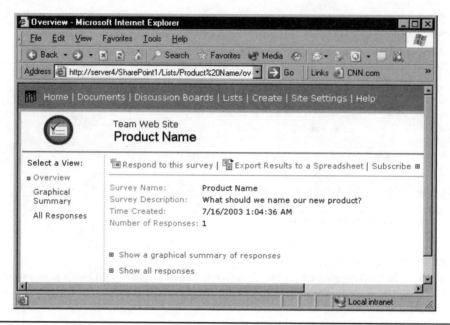

**FIGURE 22-20**    Overview of survey being taken

# Publishing and Promoting Webs on the Internet

With the help of this book and FrontPage, by now you have created your own webs and possibly put them on your intranet or tested them on a local server. In this chapter, you will see how to make your efforts available to the millions of people worldwide who have access to the Internet. You'll do this by first publishing your web on a web server, a computer that is connected to the Internet. Then you'll promote your web site using web-based and traditional advertising.

## Publishing Your Web Pages

Publishing a web means copying the files that contain the web's pages and graphics to a web server connected to the Internet. Unless you have your own such server, you will need to find a web presence provider (WPP) who will rent you space on their web server for your site. Also, depending on the FrontPage Web Components used in your site, your WPP should support either FrontPage Server Extensions (FPSE) or Windows SharePoint Services (SharePoint 2 or WSS).

Providing access to the Web has become a very competitive field, and you should be able to find several WPPs in your area to choose from. You can find a local WPP by asking others, by looking in your regional newspapers and other periodicals, and even by checking a current phone book. You can also use the Internet. Begin by using one of the many search engines available, such as Google (**http://www.google.com**). Simply enter a search criterion such as **"Internet hosting [*your city*]"** (include the quotes). For example, Figure 23-1 shows the results of entering "Internet hosting - Seattle." Another Internet site with a list of providers is Yahoo (**http://www.yahoo.com**). Microsoft also provides the ability to search for WPPs with FrontPage Server Extensions through the options at **http://www.microsoftwpp.com/wppsearch/**. With a little searching, you should be able to locate several WPPs in your area. It is not necessary that your WPP be located close to you. Most of your transactions will occur over the Internet, and there are a number of national providers, such as EarthLink (**http://www.earthlink.net/**) and AT&T's WorldNet Service (**http://www.att.com**), that offer FPSE as part of their service.

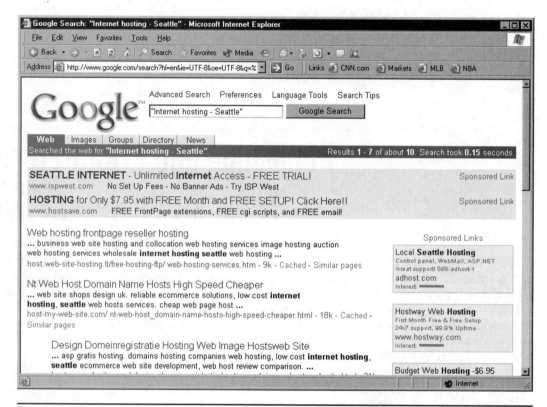

**FIGURE 23-1** Finding a hosting service in a city

Generally, a WPP will provide dial-up access to the Internet, as well as hard disk storage for webs. Many offer space for a personal (noncommercial) web as part of their basic Internet access package. The amount of hard disk space allowed for a personal web site varies. In many areas, this basic service costs $10 to $30 a month with unlimited Internet access. (These rates are for 28.8- to 56.6-Kbps modems; rates for ISDN, DSL, and cable modems may be higher.)

Rates for commercial web sites can vary greatly—from under $20 to several thousand dollars a month—depending on the WPP, the amount of hard disk storage, and the bandwidth used. *Bandwidth* is the amount of data that is transferred from your web site over the WPP's Internet connection. For example, if your web is 1 megabyte (MB) in size and it was accessed 100 times in the course of a month, you used 100MB of bandwidth (or transfer bandwidth) that month.

Another point to consider is whether you want to have your own domain name. Without your own domain name, your web's URL would begin with the WPP's domain name, such as *http://www.WPPname.com/yourname*. With your own domain, your URL would be *http://www.yourname.com*. Your own domain is unnecessary for a personal web site, but it should be seriously considered for a commercial web. Your WPP can help you set up a domain name for your web site. Alternatively, you can contact InterNIC at **http://www.internic.net/**

to get a list of accredited registrars. You then can go to one of those registrars and, with some information from your WPP and for a fee (ranging from around $10 to over $50 per year; sometimes there is a minimum of two years), you can register your own domain name. Each registrar has complete instructions at their site. Also, at both the InterNIC and registrar's sites, you can search for existing domain names using InterNIC's Whois facility to make sure the one you want is unique.

In deciding upon a WPP, you should be more concerned about the quality of the service than the price. The Internet is a little chaotic—new technologies (particularly in data transmission) are coming into play, and finding people who truly understand and can use these technologies is not always easy. Software doesn't always work as advertised, and keeping everything flowing smoothly sometimes requires a little "spit and baling wire." When evaluating a WPP, look at the design and features of their web site, and contact others who have their webs on the WPP's server. Choosing the cheapest WPP could be an expensive decision in the long run if they don't provide the services you need, such as FPSE or WSS.

## FrontPage Server Extensions

HTML used to be written by hand using text editors such as Windows Notepad. When you wanted to include a form for the user to fill out, you had to make sure there was a script available on the server that would implement it. There were (and are) a number of scripts to do this, so you needed to know the syntax required by the particular script on your server. If your web page was transferred to another server with different scripts, your HTML probably had to be modified.

A great deal of the functionality and usefulness of previous versions of FrontPage came from the fact that it included a standard set of server extensions that can run on virtually any HTTP server platform with any major server software. This means your FrontPage-created web could be placed on any web server running FPSE or WSS and would function correctly. FrontPage 2003 can still use FPSE, the most recent version of which is FPSE 2002, but Microsoft has added a number of features to FrontPage 2003 that make it unnecessary to use FPSE. As a result, Microsoft will not update FPSE 2002. Finally, some of the Web components that are in FPSE are now also in WSS.

As a web content creator, you need to be aware of the components and services that require FPSE or WSS. You can then decide if their use is worth requiring that FPSE or WSS are installed on your WPP's web server. (On your local computer, FPSE or WSS were installed as a part of the FrontPage or SharePoint installation; see Appendix A.) If FPSE or WSS are installed by your WPP, you are assured that any Web Components, forms, or discussion groups you've included in your web will function in your site on the WPP's server.

---

**NOTE**   *You might also want to check with your WPP to make sure their version of FrontPage Server Extensions is the same version (or later) as the FrontPage version you used to create your web application, although many of the FrontPage 2002 components are handled by the FrontPage 2000 Server Extensions.*

### Features that Require FPSE or WSS

A number of FrontPage features and Web Components use FPSE, SharePoint Team Services (SharePoint 1 or STS), or WSS. Since not all ISPs immediately install the latest products, the following lists are broken out by the oldest version of FrontPage Server Extensions that will support the feature. (The newer versions of FPSE will handle all the features of the earlier versions.)

- Features Requiring WSS (SharePoint 2)
  - Web Search Full-Text Search
  - Dynamic Web Template
  - Data View
  - Web Parts
- Features Not Available in WSS
  - Web Search Current Web
  - Included Content Scheduled Content
  - Table Of Contents For This Web Site
  - List View And Document Library View
  - Additional Components Visual InterDev Navigation Bar

---

**NOTE**   *The Document Library View Page Wizard and the List View Page Wizard are available in WSS, just not the two Web Components.*

- Features Requiring STS (SharePoint 1)
  - Top 10 Lists (requires either STS or WSS, but not FPSE)
  - Lists and List View Web Component
  - Document Libraries and Document Library View Web Component (see earlier Note)
- Features Requiring at Least FrontPage 2002 Server Extensions
  - Custom link bars
  - Multiple navigation structures
  - Role-based security
  - Shared border background properties
  - Single-page publishing
  - Top 10 lists
  - Usage analysis reports
- Features Requiring at Least FrontPage 2000 Server Extensions
  - Categories Web Component
  - Database Results Wizard
  - More than one level of subwebs
  - Send To Database form

- Source Control, document check-in/check-out
- Style sheet links to multiple files
- Features Requiring at Least FrontPage 98 Server Extensions
  - Confirmation field
  - Discussion form
  - Image maps
  - Hit counter
  - Registration form
  - Save results form
  - Search form

## Identifying Which Pages to Publish

When you create a new page, it is automatically identified as a page to be published. If you want, though, you can change this so that the page will not be copied to the web server. You might do this if you are not finished building a page, but have other pages in the web you want published. When you are ready to publish a page, you simply have to identify the page as "Publish." It is also useful to mark certain files as "Don't Publish" if you don't want them recopied to the web server, such as pages with a hit counter or with a guest book, which would be zeroed out if they were republished. Use the following steps to identify the pages that you do and do not want published:

1. With FrontPage running and your local copy of the web that you want to publish open, click View | Reports | Workflow | Publish Status. The Publish Status report will appear in the FrontPage window.

2. To change the status of a particular page, click the right side of the Publish field for that page to open the drop-down list of choices, as shown in Figure 23-2.

---

*TIP*    *If you click the down arrow next to the Publish column header, you can publish or not based on criteria. Also, if you right-click a listed page, there's a toggle on the context menu.*

3. Click Publish or Don't Publish as desired. Your page will be so marked, and when you publish your web, your Publish setting will be followed.

## Publishing to a Server with FPSE or WSS

Once your FrontPage web is completed and tested on your local computer, it's ready for the big time: the World Wide Web. With any luck, your WPP has either the FPSE or WSS installed and has created a folder for your web on the web server. (Publishing your web to a server without the FPSE or WSS is covered in the next section.)

To publish a FrontPage web to a server with FPSE or WSS, you must first have permission to write files to the server. Your webmaster or server administrator will be able to assign the proper permission to your account. As an additional security measure, your webmaster or administrator may have you publish your web to a temporary folder. Once

PART IV

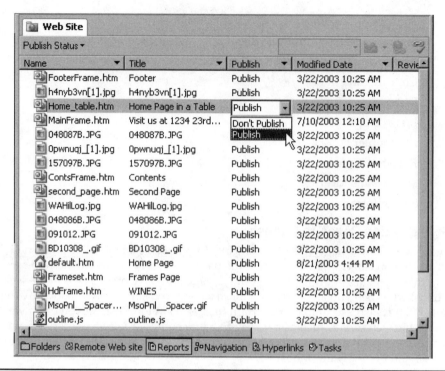

**FIGURE 23-2** Identifying whether to publish an individual page

you have the proper permissions and location on the server for your web, use the next steps to publish your web.

**NOTE** *If you do not have your own domain name and virtual or real server, your WPP may not let you create a new web or delete a web that is your primary folder, and FrontPage will not let you publish to a subsidiary folder. That means that you must create your web on your computer and publish it to your server. Then you can edit it, publish a new version of the web replacing the original version, add pages to it, and import other webs to it, but you can only delete individual folders and pages—you cannot delete the web itself.*

1. Start FrontPage if necessary. If you use a dial-up account to access the Internet, activate your Internet connection.

2. In FrontPage, open the web you will place on the web server.

3. Open the File menu and select Publish Site. When the window refreshes and if the Remote Web Site Properties dialog box does not automatically open, click Remote Web Site Properties. Select the type of server, with FrontPage Or SharePoint Services being the default and what is assumed here. Enter or click Browse so the URL or path to the Remote Site on which you want to publish appears in the text box, and click OK. If asked, log onto your server by entering your username and password,

and clicking OK. Click OK again to create a new web if one does not already exist. The Remote Web Site publishing window will be displayed, as shown in Figure 23-3.

If you click Publish Web Site, the default is for all of the files on the left marked with arrows to be published to the remote web site. You can also select individual files and folders and click the right-pointing arrow in the middle.

---

**NOTE**    *A question mark (?) next to filenames means they have been changed on both the local and remote site, and FrontPage does not know what to do to resolve this conflict. When you try to publish the site, you'll get a Conflicts dialog box where you can Ignore And Continue, Overwrite Remote Files, or Overwrite Local Files.*

4. Click Publish Web Site. You'll see a message telling you how the publishing is going and a thermometer bar showing you how far along you are. When it is done, your files will also appear on the right of the window.

5. Test your web by clicking View Your Remote Web Site. Your web should appear in a browser. When you are done looking at your web, close your browser and click Done.

In most cases, publishing your web to a server with FPSE or WSS will be this simple. The biggest hang-up is often that your URL, user ID, and password have been garbled in

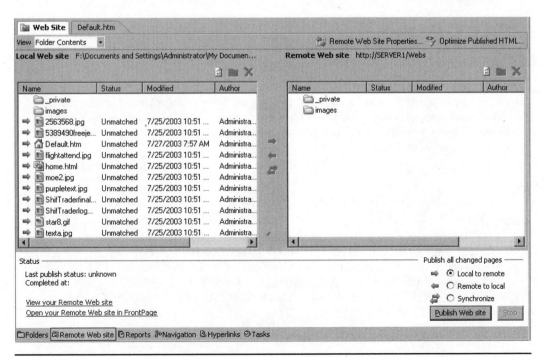

**FIGURE 23-3**    Getting ready to publish a web to a server with FPSE or WSS

getting the information from your WPP, and the correct ones were not used in the preceding steps. If you are having problems, this is the first thing you should check with your WPP.

### Editing a Web on a Server

One of the great beauties of putting your webs up on a server with FPSE or WSS is that you can directly edit your web on the server just as you would on your computer. To do this, follow these steps:

1. Make sure you can connect to the server by being connected to either the Internet or an intranet.

2. Click File | Open Site to open the dialog box of the same name. If it is not already selected, click My Network Places or Web Folders, depending on your operating system. You should see both the original local version and the one on the WPP's server.

3. Double-click the web and click Open to open it in FrontPage. Except for the fact that you are doing it long distance, this is no different from editing on your own computer.

4. When you are done, save and close the web as you would on your local server.

---

*NOTE   If you can't edit online because of policies your WPP has instituted or for any other reason, you can still edit the web on your computer and publish it again on the server (either the entire web or just the pages that have changed). It is also a wiser policy to make changes locally, test them there, and then republish the site.*

### Deleting a Web on a Server

Another approach to correcting or changing a web on a server is to delete it from the server and copy it again.

---

*NOTE   As explained earlier in this chapter, depending on how you are set up on your server, your WPP may not allow you to delete your entire web because it would be the same as deleting your primary folder on the server. You can instead delete all of the contents and republish the entire web to replace the contents.*

To delete your web:

1. In FrontPage, with your Internet connection active, open the web as just described to edit it.

2. When the web has opened in FrontPage, select Delete Web from the File menu. You may be asked for your username and password. In the Confirm Delete dialog box, you are asked to choose Remove FrontPage Information From This Web Site Only, Preserving All Other Files And Folders, or Delete This Web Site Entirely. To fully remove a web, you need to choose Delete This Web Site Entirely. Make your choice and click OK.

*NOTE*   *If you don't have Delete Web on the File menu, you can add it by opening the Tools menu and choosing Customize to open the Customize dialog box. Select the Commands tab, click File in Categories, and scroll through the commands until Delete Web is visible. Then drag Delete Web to the File menu in your FrontPage window. The File menu will open and allow you to put the command where you want it in the menu (we put it just below Close Site).*

*TIP*   *To delete single or multiple pages in a web, simply delete them on your local computer and then republish your web. FrontPage will compare your local web with the one you published and ask if you want a particular page deleted.*

Once the web is deleted, repeat the steps given previously to again copy the web to the web server. If you continue to have problems doing this, contact the webmaster or server administrator. It may be possible to delete individual files from the web server outside of FrontPage (provided you have the correct permissions), but this can confuse FrontPage. FrontPage keeps track of all the components of your web; if you change any of them outside of FrontPage, it may end up looking for files that no longer exist or are in a different place.

If you successfully copy your web to the server but find that some elements don't function correctly, first make sure that the web works correctly on your local server. Then contact your webmaster or server administrator and explain the problem. If other webs using the same feature work correctly on the web server, the odds are that the problem is in your web. If the problem is common to other webs on the web server, then FPSE or WSS might not be installed correctly.

## Publishing to a Server Without FPSE or WSS

You can also publish a web created in FrontPage to a web server that isn't running FPSE or WSS. While any features relying on the server extensions (forms, Web Components, and so on) will not function, all the standard HTML functions, such as hyperlinks, will be unaffected.

Using FrontPage's Publish Site option to publish to a web server without FPSE or WSS is very similar to publishing with FPSE or WSS. The Publish Site option publishes your web pages to your choice of an FTP (File Transfer Protocol) server, a WebDAV (Web Distributed Authoring and Versioning) server, or a local network computer. The FTP or WebDAV server usually provides access to the same directories as the WPP's web server, so a web browser can immediately open your web pages. In some cases, the webmaster or server administrator will have to activate your pages once they are uploaded to the FTP server. You will need permission to write to the destination FTP server. Your webmaster or server administrator will be able to assign the proper permission to your account.

The following instructions show you how to publish a FrontPage web to a server without FPSE or WSS using the Publish Site option. (The first several steps are exactly like those given earlier for publishing to a server with FPSE or WSS.)

1. Start FrontPage if necessary. If you use dial-up networking to access the Internet, activate your Internet connection.

2. In FrontPage, open the local copy of the web you want to place on the web server.

3. Click File | Publish Site. If the Remote Site Properties dialog box does not automatically open, click Remote Web Site Properties. Select the type of server; select FTP. Enter or Browse to the URL or path to the Remote Site as you would if you used FPSE or WSS, except precede it with **ftp://** (similar to Figure 23-4), and click OK. If asked, log onto your server by entering your username and password, and clicking OK.

---

**NOTE**   *Your folder path for an FTP transfer is probably different from the URL used in a web browser. Be sure to clearly understand from your WPP the path to use for each.*

4. If you are told that web does not exist, click OK to create a web at that location.

5. When the Publishing window opens and a connection has been established, click Publish Web Site. You'll see a message about how the publishing is going and how much of the process has been completed. When the web is published, you'll see a completion message similar to the one you saw when publishing to a server with FPSE or WSS, except that you may not be able to immediately go and view your web.

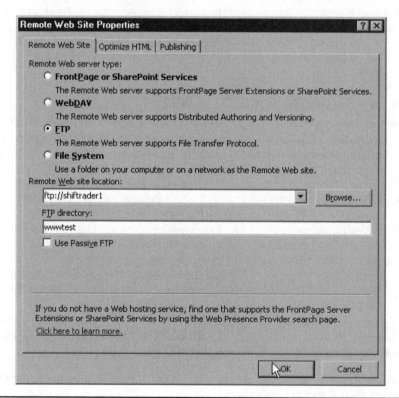

**FIGURE 23-4**   Publishing to an FTP server

6. To test your web, start your favorite browser and enter the URL that you have been told to use (it may not be the same server name and path that you used in step 3). Your web should appear.

Entering the correct information in these steps is crucial. If anything is wrong, the publishing process won't work. Be very clear with your WPP about the server name to which you will publish through FTP your web (step 3); the path to your web site on that server (step 3); the user ID and password to use (step 3); and the URL, user ID, and password to access the Internet and view your site with a browser (step 6). Carefully look for typos and spurious characters. Do not assume that any of the example information used in these steps is correct for you; it probably isn't. Keep trying. If you are using a correct server name, path and folder, and user ID and password, this will work.

---

*TIP    The specific information that you should enter for the FTP server name and path is unique to a WPP or network installation. If after several attempts the copying is not working, you need to contact your WPP or network/server administrator and work out the problems.*

Even if the web server that will host your web pages does not have FPSE or WSS, you may still be able to have the same functionality. For example, most servers will have an application or script for handling form input. You will need to ask your webmaster or server administrator how to access the application and then incorporate it into your web page by editing the HTML. Of course, it would be much easier if the server hosting your web supported FPSE or WSS.

## Promoting Your Web Site

Once your web site is published to a web server, you need to let people know that it is there. If your web site is business related, the first step is to tell your existing customers about it. You might include an announcement with your regular invoicing, for example. You should also include your URL in all your conventional advertising, including your business cards, invoices, statements, purchase orders, drawings, reports, and any other document you produce. It's not uncommon to see URLs on everything from television commercials to billboards.

---

*TIP    A good reason to get your own domain name is that the address is usually easier to remember and easier to include on other literature than if your web were hosted on another domain. For example, consider **http://www.yourserver.com/yourweb/** compared to **http:// www.yourdomain.com**.*

### Being Found by a Search Engine

You also need to make sure you can be found on the Web by anyone looking for the products and services you offer. A number of search engines for the Web have been developed. Some, like Google, actively search the Web for information. Others, like Yahoo, which also searches the Web, allow web sites to suggest their sites to them. Figure 23-5 shows Yahoo's How To Suggest Your Site page (**http://docs.yahoo.com/info/suggest**).

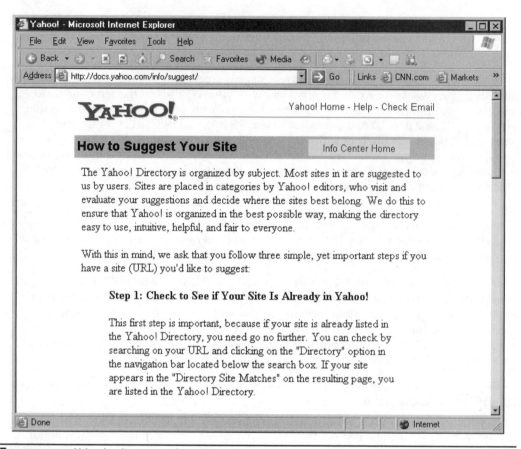

**FIGURE 23-5**   Yahoo's site suggestion page

You can also suggest your web site to virtually all the search engines. A simple way to reach a number of search engines is to use the Submit It! web site (**http://www.submit-it.com/**), where for a fee (currently $79 for one URL), your single entry is submitted to a number of search engines and directories that you select, as shown in Figure 23-6.

Table 23-1 gives names and addresses of a few of the search engines that you should make sure you are correctly listed on.

## Making Your Web Search-Engine–Friendly

Since many search engines are actively searching the Web for sites, it helps to have an introductory paragraph on your home page that gives a concise description of your site. The introductory paragraph should include the keywords that apply to your site. You can also enter a page title (as distinct from the title at the top of the page) and keywords or *meta tags* on your home page; some search engines will reference your page title and index your web based on the keywords. The page title and keywords can be entered in the Page

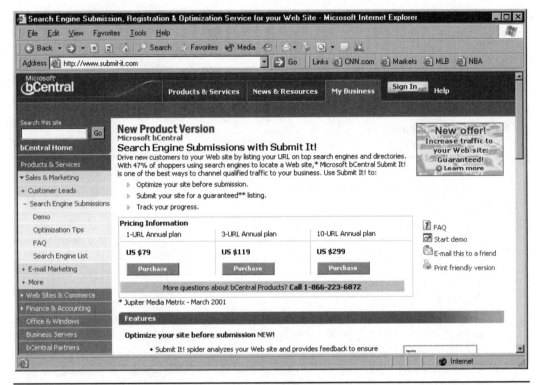

**FIGURE 23-6** Submitting your URL to a number of search engines at once

**TABLE 23-1**
Search Engines

| Search Engine | Web Address |
|---|---|
| 800Go | http://www.800go.com/ |
| AltaVista | http://www.altavista.com/ |
| AOL Search | http://search.aol.com/ |
| Ask Jeeves | http://www.ask.com/ |
| Excite | http://www.excite.com/ |
| Google | http://www.google.com/ |
| Hot Bot | http://www.hotbot.com/ |
| Infoseek | http://www.go.com/ |
| Lycos | http://www.lycos.com/ |
| MSN Web Search | http://search.msn.com/ |
| Overture | http://www.content.overture.com/ |
| Switchboard | http://www.switchboard.com/ |

**TABLE 23-1** Search Engines *(continued)*

| Search Engine | Web Address |
|---|---|
| Web Crawler | http://www.webcrawler.com/ |
| Yahoo! | http://www.yahoo.com/ |

Properties dialog box or directly in the HTML view of your page. Here are the steps to use the Page Properties dialog box:

1. Open FrontPage, open the home page in Design view, open the File menu, and choose Properties (you may have to expand the menu). The Page Properties dialog box will open, as shown in Figure 23-7.

**NOTE** *The automatic page titles that get generated during page creation are often not useful for purposes of searching, such as theShifTrader Home title shown in Figure 23-7. It is therefore important that you look at this and set the page title to something more appropriate.*

2. Replace the page title with one that is more descriptive of the web and open the Custom tab.
3. In the User Variables section, click Add to open the User Meta Variable dialog box. In the Name text box, type **keywords**. In the Value text box, type the words you want indexed, separated by commas.
4. When you have entered all the keywords you can think of, click OK twice to close both the User Meta Variable dialog box and the Page Properties dialog box.

**FIGURE 23-7** Setting the page title and keywords

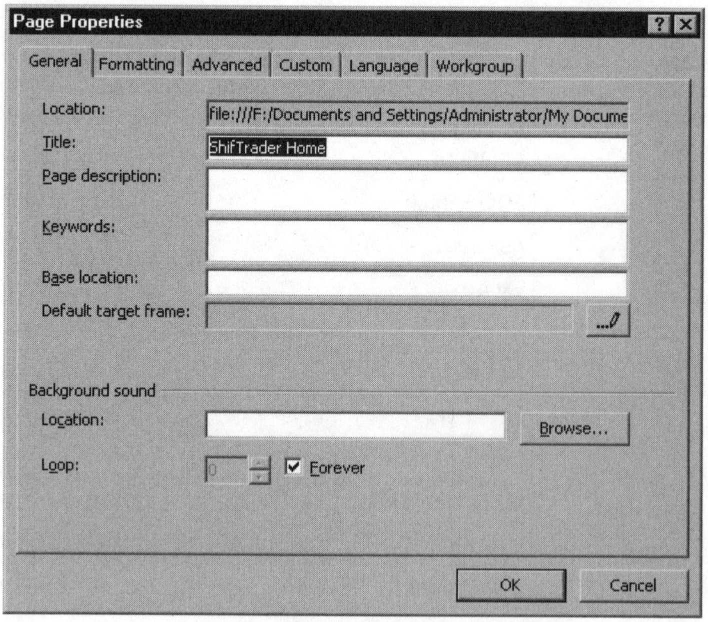

5. In FrontPage, click Code view on the views bar. In the Head section at the top of the listing, you should see the page title and keywords that you entered.

You can also go into Code or Split view and directly enter or change a title and keywords.

## Other Promotional Steps You Can Take

A useful tool for promoting your web site is *reciprocal links*. These are simply hyperlinks on your web page that point to someone who has a link to your site. Say you sell mountain climbing equipment. You could search the Web for climbing clubs and other groups with web sites relating to climbing. You then contact the owners of the sites, offering to put a link from your site to theirs if they will return the favor. This way, anyone who finds any of the sites you're linked to has a direct link to your site. If you gather enough links on your site, it may become a starting point for people who are surfing the Net.

You shouldn't overlook a press release, either. When your web site goes online or you make a major addition to your site, let the press and publications related to your business know about it. What you should *not* do is advertise your web site or business in newsgroups, unless the newsgroup is specifically run for that purpose. Say you decide to have a sale on climbing equipment. In your zeal to let the world know, you post a message on a recreational climbing newsgroup. The one result you can count on is that you will be flooded with "flames" (rather unpleasant, pointed e-mail messages), and frankly, you will deserve them.

A surefire way to get your web site widely known is to produce an outstanding web site. Today there are over 100 million web sites on the World Wide Web. Aim to be in the top 5 percent for your particular type of organization. In the era of conventional marketing, that goal would have been virtually impossible for a small business, but the Web is a new paradigm. Creativity and content count more than advertising budgets. Give people a reason to visit your site by providing content that is unique and useful to them. Then package it in an effective, pleasing design. Review the section on rich content toward the end of Chapter 1. Take the time to explore the Web and gather ideas for your own site. (Gathering ideas is fine; however, gathering graphics or other actual content, no matter how easy it is, is a violation of copyright laws.)

The World Wide Web, whether you use it for business or pleasure, is having an effect on society as fundamental as the invention of the printing press. With FrontPage, you have the tools to participate in this new world.

## Case Study: Promoting the BookBay

The BookBay is a small rural bookstore located on Whidbey Island in Puget Sound in Washington State. Its owner, Brad Bixby, is also the innovative creator of its web site, **http://www.bookbay.com/**, which you can see in Figure 23-8. Since the BookBay is a small independent bookstore, the problem of trying to promote its site loomed quite large. As a result, we asked him what his secrets were. Here are his answers.

"I advertise my web site address in everything my customers see, from yellow page ads to fliers, bag stuffers, bookmarks, and business cards.

"It is important to know how each of the search engines (or directories—since they work a bit differently) operate. Do they use page titles, meta tags (company name, description, and

**FIGURE 23-8**   BookBay's home page

keywords), first paragraph text, keyword frequency, or submitted site descriptions, or all of them in their search? These are the things that put your page on top of everyone else's."

---

**TIP**   *As an example of how meta tags are used, the BookBay's meta tags are shown here:*

```
<html>
<head>
  <meta http-equiv="Content-Type" content="text/html; charset=iso-8859-1">
  <meta name="description" content="BookBay.com and The BookBay on Whidbey Island">
  <meta name="keywords" content="BookBay, Book Bay, whidbey Island, whidbey, washington,
Bookstore, Book Clubs, Northwest, Freeland, Gay, Lesbian, Bestsellers, Brad Bixby, Seattle,
Langley, Coupeville, Clinton, Oak Harbor, Puget Sound ">
  <title>The BookBay - whidbey Island's Premiere Independent Bookstore </title>
</head>
```

"Also, think like someone surfing the web and tailor your keywords, titles, meta tags, etc., accordingly. What are they looking for? What keyword queries would they use in a search engine? The statistics I gather on my web site include information on referring links. Especially helpful are links from search engines, which often detail the keywords entered by the visitor.

"Develop a 'hook' to bring people to your page. It may not be a direct income source, but the first thing you need to do is get them to your site. Not one sale has ever been made on the Internet from someone who doesn't know you exist. One hook on my page is book clubs. Another is local authors. A hook not only gives people a reason to come to my page, it gives them a reason to come back. I also have Whidbey Island and Freeland (the town where I'm located) history pages to attract people interested in the area. If someone is just looking for a bookstore or books, they are probably not going to find me, but if they are looking for the Oprah Winfrey Book Club, Whidbey Island, or Freeland, they are very likely to see my site in the top of the list.

"After I have submitted my site to the major search engines, I check the top ones to see how I compare to other sites that have similar information, and in the book industry, that's a lot. If I am listed 30th, chances are people are not going to get to me. My objective is to be in the top ten listings when people go searching for any of my hooks.

"You may hear about promoting your web site using reciprocal links. For a personal or informational site I think that is a good idea. The problem with using links to other sites from a commercial site is that if someone uses the link, there is a good chance you have lost them before they have seen everything you have to offer. It's kind of like having a store that has all the popular items right next to the front door. The customers never get to the back of the store to see what else is offered. You may get some people linking to your site from elsewhere, but is that more important than keeping the ones you have in your site? I have seen very few commercial sites that use reciprocal links.

"If I find it necessary to link to another site, I do so in frames. Visitors are able to link to another site, but my logo and a link back to my site is always present."

—*Brad Bixby, the BookBay* ***http://www.bookbay.com/*** (The name "BookBay" and the quotations from Brad Bixby are used with the permission of the BookBay.)

Probably the two most important tips that Brad mentioned were to use every means possible to promote your web and to repeatedly test to see how your web is coming out on searches. By testing your ranking and then changing your title, meta tags, and keywords, you can fine-tune how people will find you. Brad has certainly done this successfully and provides a good example.

# Appendixes

# FrontPage 2003 Installation

Installing FrontPage 2003 is an easy task, as you'll discover in this appendix. The onscreen instructions are clear, the steps are few, and with the information in this appendix, you will soon have FrontPage ready to use.

FrontPage 2003 is available both as a component of Microsoft Office 2003, and as a stand-alone product. In both cases, the software comes in a separate CD package. In addition to FrontPage, this appendix will discuss the installation of SharePoint Team Services (STS or SharePoint1), Windows SharePoint Services (WSS or SharePoint 2), and FrontPage 2002 Server Extensions (FPSE).

## What You Need to Install FrontPage 2003

To install FrontPage 2003, you'll need the following minimum software and hardware:

- Windows 2000 with Service Pack 3 or later, Windows XP, or Windows Server 2003 (Windows 95, 98, ME, or NT do not support FrontPage 2003)

- A PC with a Pentium 133 MHz or higher (Pentium III 800 MHz or higher recommended, especially with WSS)

- 128MB of memory (256MB or higher recommended, required with WSS)

- 245MB of free disk space for the default installation of Office 2003 (FrontPage alone will require approximately 160MB, STS with FPSE 2002 will require another 14MB, while FPSE 2002 alone will require 10MB, and 550MB are required with WSS)

- Super VGA (800×600) or higher with 256 or more colors from your video adapter and monitor

- Microsoft Mouse or compatible pointing device

- CD-ROM or DVD drive (unless you do a network install)

- Connection to the Internet

To access the Internet or an intranet network in which FrontPage will be used, you also must have installed the TCP/IP network protocols (see Chapter 1 for a discussion of the protocols and Chapter 22 for the installation of TCP/IP) on a dial-up network using a modem and/or on a local area network (LAN) with its adapter card. If you are using an

Internet browser, you have already installed and correctly configured TCP/IP. If you are just now coming up on the Internet or a network, you need to install TCP/IP. The easiest way to do so is to use the Internet Connection Wizard discussed in the "Connecting to the Internet" section later in this appendix.

NOTE   *If you are upgrading from an earlier version of FrontPage (2000 or 2002), you need to have one of those versions installed on your computer, or have the CD available.*

# Installing FrontPage 2003

The only difference between the stand-alone version of FrontPage 2003 and one included with Office 2003 is the other components included in Office. FrontPage itself is exactly the same in both versions. In terms of installation, in either case FrontPage is installed from its own CD with a separate installer and a separate product key. For that reason, we will discuss only one approach to the installation.

You may use the defaults set up in the installer to determine which components of FrontPage to install, or use either the complete or custom installation procedure. In the custom installation, you determine what to install. If you use the defaults, recommended for most users, all FrontPage components will be installed except the additional themes, which will automatically be installed the first time you try to use them (given you put the FrontPage CD in its drive). The default installation is the choice assumed in this book and reflected in its examples and illustrations. If you choose Complete, all facets of FrontPage are installed (including the additional themes), whereas if you choose Custom, you can choose which components to install.

NOTE   *In FrontPage 2003, the folder or directory path for installation will be chosen for you. You no longer have a choice of where to install the applications. The Setup program creates the default directories in which Office and/or FrontPage will be installed.*

## Using the Default Installation

Follow these steps for the default installation of FrontPage:

1. Insert the FrontPage CD into your drive. You will see several messages to the effect that the installer is being set up. Then a dialog box will appear, requesting the CD key (located on the back of the CD case or sleeve). Enter this and press Next. Enter your name, initials, organization name, and press Next. The End User License Agreement (EULA) will appear.

2. Accept the license agreement and click Next. The dialog box shown in Figure A-1 appears (as seen in Windows XP)—here you can choose between a typical installation, a complete version, a minimal installation, and a custom one.

3. In most instances, you want to use the Typical Install and then click Next. You are shown the list of applications that will be installed—this list will normally only show FrontPage. If it doesn't, click Back, choose Custom, and go to the "Performing a Custom Installation" section to see if FrontPage is on the CD (it is not on the general Office one).

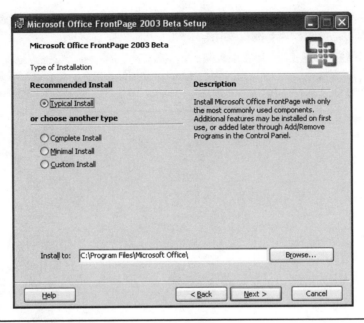

**FIGURE A-1**   Making the choice on the type of installation

4. Click Install. If you are upgrading from an earlier version of FrontPage, Setup will tell you that it will examine your system to confirm the existence of the previous version. Click Continue. If Setup can't find a qualifying product, a dialog box will appear telling you so. If you have FrontPage on another drive, or if you have already removed it but have the original disk, put it in its drive and tell Setup which drive to search. Click Locate. A Locate Directory dialog box will appear. Identify the correct directory and click OK.

5. You will see a dialog box that says Now Installing FrontPage, with a display of the installation's progress. When the installer has finished, you will be told the installation was completed successfully. Click Finish.

6. Start FrontPage by opening the Start menu and choosing (All) Programs | Microsoft Office | Microsoft Office FrontPage 2003. If you are asked whether you want to activate your copy of FrontPage or Office, decide and click Yes or No and, if Yes, follow the instructions. To do so, you will either need to be connected to the Internet or call in the information on the telephone using an 800 number. When activation is completed, the FrontPage window will open with a new page in Page view, as shown in Figure A-2. You have proven that the installation was completed successfully. Close FrontPage.

If your installation did not complete successfully, look carefully at the error messages you have received. Correct any anomalies that are mentioned, like exiting from all programs that are running except Windows, or providing more disk space, and then rerun Setup.

PART V

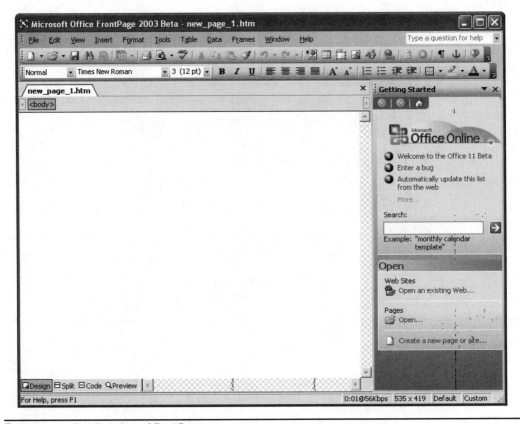

**FIGURE A-2** The first view of FrontPage

## Performing a Custom Installation

Use the Custom installation when you want to install only some of the FrontPage component programs—for instance, if you are reinstalling FrontPage 2003. If you are installing FrontPage over a previous copy, you will want to use the same directory structure you used originally, in order to preserve access to your webs. If you want to use a different directory, you will have to uninstall the first copy, and then reinstall the program to the desired directory.

To perform a Custom installation, follow these steps:

1. Complete the first two steps in the default installation until you arrive at the window where you choose the type of installation you want. Click Custom Install.

2. Click Next and then click the plus sign (+) next to Microsoft FrontPage For Windows. The FrontPage options will appear, as shown in Figure A-3. A gray container means only some of the options will be installed. A white container means all the options will be installed, and the numeral one in a container means the option will be installed on first use (at which time the CD will be needed).

**NOTE** *When you select a choice, its description is shown in the lower part of the dialog box.*

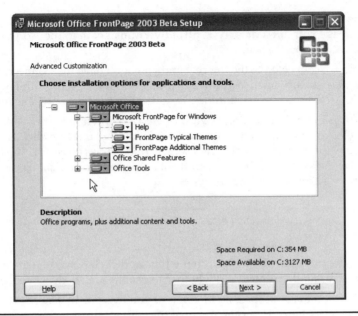

**FIGURE A-3**    The FrontPage installation options

3. Click FrontPage Additional Themes and choose Run From My Computer and you'll see the FrontPage parent container change from gray to white, meaning that all FrontPage options will be installed, unless you are installing FrontPage on Windows Server 2003 where you will have an additional option, .NET Programmability Support, which would also have to be selected. Make any other selections appropriate for you. Click Next. You will be shown the list of applications to be installed.

4. Click Install. The Now Installing Office dialog box will appear as in step 5 of the default installation and will continue as described in the previous section.

## Connecting to the Internet

If you are not connected to the Internet and wish to be, this section will help you. It is not necessary to be connected to the Internet to use FrontPage, but if you wish to put your webs on an Internet server and your company does not have an Internet server to which you have a LAN connection, then you need to be connected to the Internet. Use these steps to do so:

1. Click the Internet Connection Wizard if it is on your desktop. (Windows 2000 has the Internet Connection Wizard on the desktop by default, labeled "Connect to the Internet," if the connection has not been made. Windows XP and Server 2003 connect you to the Internet by default if that is possible.)

2. If the Internet Connection Wizard is not on the desktop, it is highly likely you are already connected to the Internet or have the ability to be (Windows XP in many circumstances automatically sets up the connection). To test this, double-click the Internet Explorer on the desktop or open the Start menu and select it. It should open

with the default web page or the home page chosen for this computer. If you see an Internet page without a date, type **http://www.msn.com** in the Address field at the top and MSN should open.

3. If you are not connected to the Internet and you don't have the Connect To The Internet icon on the desktop, open Windows Explorer and the C:\Program Files\Internet Explorer\Connection Wizard folder. Double-click the Icwconn1.exe file.

4. When the Internet Connection Wizard opens (as shown in Figure A-4 in Windows 2000), select if you want a new or use an existing account and click Next. Then select how you want to connect to the Internet, via phone lines or your LAN. If you choose LAN, click Next, select whether you want automatic or manual configuration of your proxy settings, and skip to step 8.

---

**NOTE**    *The figures here show the dialog boxes in Windows 2000. Those in Windows XP are slightly different.*

5. If you choose Connect Using My Phone Line and click Next, you are asked to enter the phone number, country, and whether to use the area code. Click Next again.

6. Enter the username and password given to you by your Internet Service Provider (ISP), then click Next. Enter the name of the connection and click Next again. When asked if you want to set up an Internet Mail Account, for now choose No, click Next, and then Finish. A Dial-Up Connection dialog box should open.

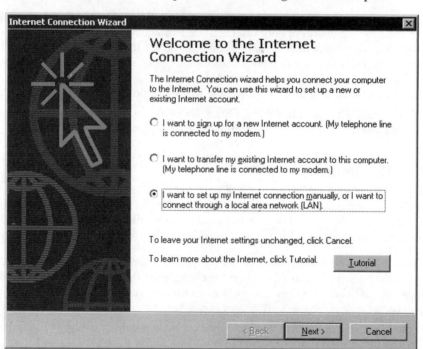

**FIGURE A-4**    Setting up an Internet connection

7. Click Connect. If you are trying to connect and your modem is not set up, you are told that will be done next. Follow the instructions to do this, and finally click OK to restart your computer. If necessary, double-click the Internet Explorer to try and connect again. This time you should connect. An icon should appear in the system tray on the right of the taskbar.

8. If you are told that file and printer sharing is turned on for your Internet connection, and that it should be turned off to protect you from someone on the Internet accessing your files, click OK.

9. Close Internet Explorer and, if it exists, double-click the connection icon in the system tray, and click Disconnect or Disconnect Now to shut down your Internet connection.

If you are having trouble with your Internet connection, the problem is probably related to one of several things: your modem; the ID and password; or settings associated with your Internet account. To check your account, call your network administrator or Internet service provider (ISP) and go over what you are using. If that is not the problem, look into the modem by opening the Control Panel and double-clicking Phone And Modem Options, open the Modems tab, select your modem, and click Properties. In the dialog box that opens, click the Diagnostics tab and then click either Query Modem or More Info. You should get a list of commands and responses, as shown next. If not, click Troubleshot in the Modems control panel General tab (Windows XP or Server 2003) or click Help in the Control Panel window itself and utilize the Modem Troubleshooter Troubleshooting Modems.

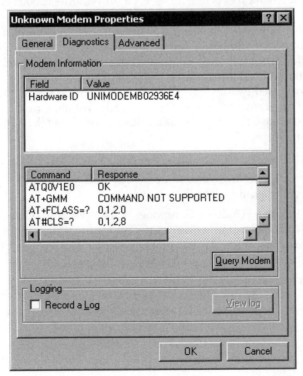

# Installing a Local Web Server

A local web server allows you to publish your webs on your computer and lets others on your network view your webs. It is not necessary to have a local web server to create FrontPage webs; you can keep your files on your computer as disk-based webs while you are creating them and then publish them to a remote server when you are ready for others to see them. FrontPage 2003 does not come with a web server, but depending on your operating system, you may have one available. If you are using Windows 2000 (either Server or Professional), Windows XP Professional, or Windows Server 2003, you have Internet Information Services (IIS) available to you. This book recommends and assumes you have installed and are using IIS on a local computer. The installation of IIS will be described next.

**NOTE**    *XP Home Edition doesn't have IIS, and any mention of XP in the book assumes XP Professional.*

**NOTE**    *If you are installing across a network—the installation files are located on a network server instead of a CD—use the Windows Explorer to open the appropriate folder on that server instead of using the CD in the following sections.*

## Installing Internet Information Services

Microsoft Internet Information Services included with Windows 2000 Server and Windows Server 2003 is a powerful, full-featured commercial web server and is the web server you need to run either a full World Wide Web site or a major intranet. Most importantly, IIS allows you to create and support a number of complex webs. The version of IIS in Windows 2000 Professional and Windows XP Professional does not allow subwebs (webs within webs). It also has some limitations on the number of simultaneous connections, and you cannot control the bandwidth used by any one user. Other than this, it has all the capabilities of the server version. To determine if you have IIS already installed, or to install IIS, you must have the operating system CD available, either directly or across the network, and then perform the following steps:

1. Open the Start menu, choose Settings | Control Panel (in Server 2003 or XP, you don't have to click Settings) and double-click Add (Or) Remove Programs. The Add/Remove Programs dialog box will open.

2. Click Add/Remove Windows Components. The Windows Components dialog box will open. Scroll down until you see Internet Information Services (IIS) (in Server 2003, you must first select Application Server and click Details). If it is checked, as shown in Figure A-5, then IIS is already installed and you can use it.

3. If IIS is not checked, insert the Windows CD in its drive or connect to the Windows CD files over the network, click the IIS check box, and click Next. Dialog boxes will appear telling you how the installation is progressing. When you are told you have successfully completed installation, click Finish.

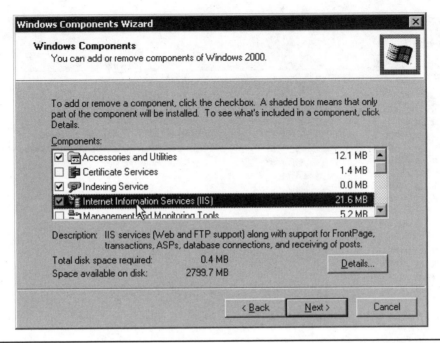

**FIGURE A-5**  Checking to see if IIS is installed

4. To check to see if IIS is installed in either Windows 2000 or XP Professional, double-click Control Panel | Administrative Tools and then double-click Internet Services Manager in Windows 2000 Professional or Internet Information Services in Windows XP Professional. In either Windows 2000 Server or Server 2003, open the Start Menu and choose (All) Programs | Administrative Tools | Internet Services Manager or Internet Information Services Manager.

5. Open your local server, possibly Web Sites, and click Default Web Site. In the toolbar, the three buttons on the right allow you to Start, Stop, and Pause IIS. The Start button should be dimmed, as shown in Figure A-6, meaning that IIS is running and ready to start delivering your webs over your network. You can see the same thing by right-clicking Default Web Site. In the context menu that opens, Start will be dimmed, while Stop and Pause will be black (active).

6. Close the IIS Manager and the Control Panel windows.

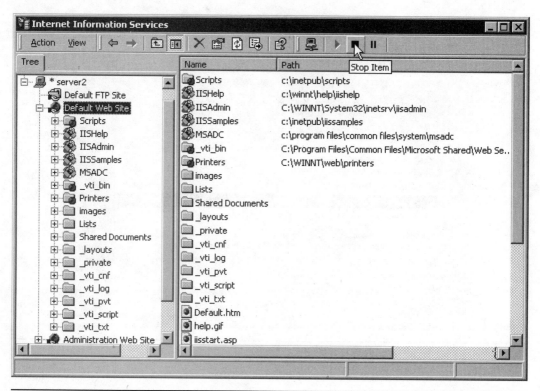

**FIGURE A-6**   Controls for starting, stopping, and pausing IIS

# Installing STS and FPSE

STS or SharePoint 1 is a set of server tools for creating and running an extensive team collaboration web site on an intranet. STS, which is a superset of the FPSE 2002 Server Extensions, is described in detail in Chapter 22. STS only runs under the Windows 2000, either Professional or Server, Windows XP, and Windows Server 2003 operating systems and requires either the FrontPage 2002 CD or that you download it from Microsoft. Use these steps to install it:

1. With the FrontPage 2002 disk in its drive, open Windows Explorer, open the CD drive, open the Sharept folder, and double-click Setupse.exe, as shown in Figure A-7. Microsoft SharePoint Setup will start.

---

**NOTE**   *If you are using Windows 2000, or Windows XP, and are still using FAT or FAT32, it is recommended you upgrade to NTFS (the NT File System). If you are using FAT or FAT32, you will get a message that you should upgrade, although you don't have to.*

2. Enter your username, initials, organization, and product key as you did earlier in the chapter when installing FrontPage. When you are ready, click Next.

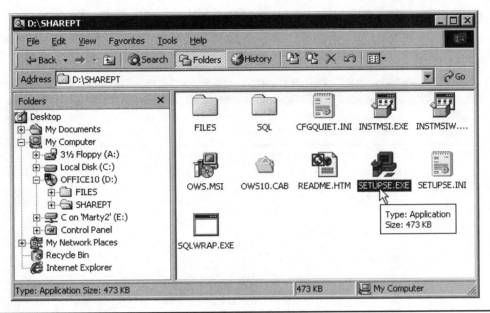

**FIGURE A-7**    Initiating the installation of SharePoint Team Services

3. Accept the End User License Agreement and click Next. You are shown you are about to install SharePoint, FrontPage Server Extensions, and other components. Click Install. If you are using FAT or FAT32 and Windows 2000, or XP, you will get two messages recommending you upgrade to NTFS. If you don't want to, simply click OK twice; otherwise, quit the SharePoint installation, insert your Windows CD, and follow the instructions to upgrade to NTFS. If you continue with the SharePoint installation, it will begin. You will then be told how the installation is progressing, including when it is completed.

4. Remove the checkmark for "Take Me To My SharePoint Home Page" and click OK. Restart your computer (you may be asked to do this, but if not, do it manually). When your system restarts, you should see a new icon in the system tray of the taskbar that looks like a stack of books with a green arrow. This shows that SQL is running (SQL is a Microsoft database application that is used with SharePoint).

5. In Windows 2000 Server, open Start | Programs | Administrative Tools | Microsoft SharePoint Administrator. In Windows Server 2003, open Start | Administrative Tools | Microsoft SharePoint Administrator. Internet Explorer will open with the Server Administration page, as shown in Figure A-8. Here you can select the settings necessary to make SharePoint operate the way you want.

6. Click Administration under Virtual Servers (not the Administration in the menu bar). Here is where you do the primary administration of SharePoint. Click Go To Site Administration For Http://servername. This provides the administration of your particular server. Click Close and then click Go To Http://servername. The

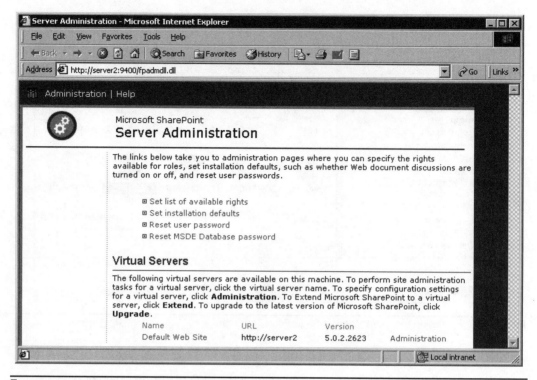

**FIGURE A-8** Initial SharePoint Server Administration page

SharePoint Home page should open, as shown in Figure A-9, showing you it is fully installed.

7. Familiarize yourself with the various administrative pages available. When you are ready, close both instances of your browser.

## Installing FrontPage Server Extensions by Themselves

If you do not want to install SharePoint, but do want to install the FrontPage 2002 Server Extensions (FPSE), you must be using Windows Server 2003, which includes them (although they much be specifically installed) or you must download the FPSE from Microsoft (they're free) and then install them. Here's how to do it:

1. Open your browser and the Microsoft web site **http://www.microsoftwpp.com/info**. Select the version of FPSE you want to download (for FPSE 2002, click the line Try Out The New FrontPage "10" Server Extensions [Beta2]), along with the supported platform you want to use.

2. Click OK to save the program to disk, then click OK to begin the download. The file is about 90MB, so it will take a fair amount of time depending on the speed of your Internet connection.

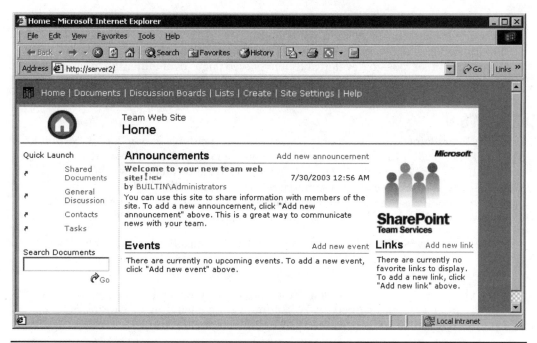

**FIGURE A-9** SharePoint Team Services Home page

3. When the download is complete, double-click the file to unpack it. Select the folder where the FPSE will reside and click Unzip. When you are told the files were unzipped successfully, click OK and Close.

4. Double-click Setupse.exe, enter your username, initials, and organization, then click Next. Accept the End-User License Agreement and click Next. You are shown a list of what you will be installing—just the FrontPage Server Extensions.

5. Click Next. Installation will begin. You will be shown how far along you are and then told when the FPSE have been successfully installed. Click OK.

6. Restart your computer. To check the presence of the FPSE, open FrontPage. In the New task pane on the right (choose File | New), click More Web Site Templates and double-click One Page Web Site.

7. Double-click the Default.htm file to open it in Design view, then open the Insert menu and choose Web Component.

If in steps 6 and 7 you did not get any error messages about not having FrontPage Server Extensions installed, and if the only dimmed components in the Insert Web Component dialog box are List View and Document Library View (which are dependent on SharePoint), then you have successfully installed FPSE. If this is not the case, the first question to ask is did you restart your computer as requested in step 6. If you did restart, then the installation did not go correctly. Did you get the successful completion message?

PART V

Were there any error messages during installation? If so, these may point to a problem. The best solution is to try the installation again.

FrontPage, IIS, and SharePoint 1 or FPSE should now all be installed. They represent a very powerful set of tools to develop and deliver web pages over either the Internet or an intranet. Turn to Chapter 1 to begin using them.

## Installing WSS

Windows SharePoint Services can only be installed on Windows Server 2003. WSS replaces STS and FPSE. It still provides a Team Web Site with a large number of features, as well as several other SharePoint site templates. WSS requires IIS and can only be installed with Windows 2003 or later operating systems (it does not work with Windows 9x, Me, NT, 2000, or XP). SharePoint 2 is not installed by default, nor are you given an option to install it when you install Windows or Office 11. Use these instructions to install WSS:

1. Place the WSS CD in its drive. If it doesn't automatically load, open Windows Explorer, select your CD drive, and double-click Setupsts.exe. WSS Setup will begin. Follow the instructions on the screen.

2. When WSS Setup has completed, the WSS Home page will appear, as shown in Figure A-10. You can open the WSS administrative window by clicking Start | Administrative Tools | SharePoint Central Administration.

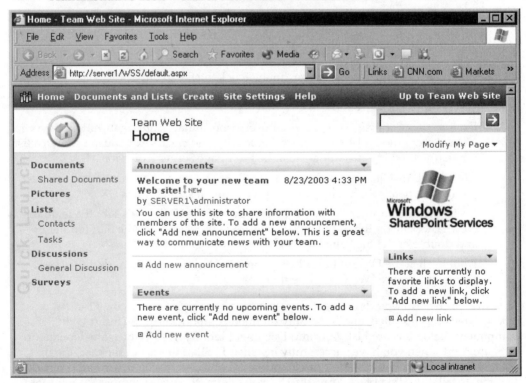

**FIGURE A-10**    Home page for WSS

# FrontPage's Shortcut Keystrokes

When carrying out various FrontPage tasks, it is often easier to use a quick set of keystrokes instead of tedious mouse manipulations. In fact, many people prefer using the keyboard solely, rather than switching back and forth between mouse and keyboard. In light of this, a large number of shortcut keystrokes have been defined in FrontPage. This appendix lists these keystrokes according to the specific functions they perform, categorizing them so they loosely correspond to their related FrontPage menus (though not every keystroke listed is on the menu under which it is shown). They are as follows:

- File Menu Keystrokes
- Edit Menu Keystrokes
- View Menu Keystrokes
- Insert Menu Keystrokes
- Format Menu Keystrokes
- Tools Menu Keystrokes
- Table Menu Keystrokes
- Help Menu Keystrokes
- Other Keystrokes

Many of FrontPage's shortcut keystrokes are common to other Office 2003 applications, especially Word.

---

**TIP**    *You can show shortcut keys in ScreenTips by selecting Tools | Customize | Options tab | Show Shortcut Keys In ScreenTips.*

## File Menu Keystrokes

| | |
|---|---|
| Create A New Normal Page | CTRL-N |
| Open page | CTRL-O |
| Close page | CTRL-F4 |
| Save page | CTRL-S |
| Preview page in browser | CTRL-SHIFT-B OR F12 |
| Print page | CTRL-P |
| Exit FrontPage | ALT-F4 |

## Edit Menu Keystrokes

| | |
|---|---|
| Undo action | CTRL-Z or ALT-BACKSPACE |
| Redo/repeat action | CTRL-Y or SHIFT-ALT-BACKSPACE |
| Cut selected text or graphics to clipboard | CTRL-X or SHIFT-DELETE |
| Copy selected text or graphics | CTRL-C or CTRL-INSERT |
| Paste clipboard contents | CTRL-V or SHIFT-INSERT |
| Delete one character to the left | BACKSPACE |
| Delete one character to the right | DELETE |
| Delete one word to the left | CTRL-BACKSPACE |
| Delete one word to the right | CTRL-DELETE |
| Select all objects on a page | CTRL-A |
| Find text | CTRL-F |
| Replace text | CTRL-H |
| Check out a file from source control | CTRL-J |
| Check in a file to source control | CTRL-SHIFT-J |
| Create a bookmark | CTRL-G |
| Quick Tag Editor | CTRL-Q |

## View Menu Keystrokes

| | |
|---|---|
| Toggle Folder List | ALT-F1 |
| Toggle Task Pane | CTRL - F1 |
| Reveal HTML tags | CTRL-/ |
| Refresh a page | F5 |

| Switch between open pages | CTRL-TAB or CTRL-SHIFT-TAB |
| Switch between Views bar views | CTRL-PAGEUP, CTRL-PAGEDOWN |
| Switch between Code and Design in Split view | ALT-PAGEUP, ALT-PAGEDOWN |

## Insert Menu Keystrokes

| Insert a line break | SHIFT-ENTER |
| Insert a nonbreaking space | CTRL-SHIFT-SPACEBAR |
| Create a bookmark | CTRL-G |
| Create a hyperlink | CTRL-K |

## Format Menu Keystrokes

| Display nonprinting characters | CTRL-SHIFT-8 |
| Change the font | CTRL-SHIFT-F |
| Change the font size | CTRL-SHIFT-P |
| Apply bold formatting | CTRL-B |
| Apply an underline | CTRL-U |
| Apply italic formatting | CTRL-I |
| Apply superscript formatting | CTRL-SHIFT-EQUAL SIGN |
| Apply subscript formatting | CTRL-MINUS SIGN |
| Copy formatting | CTRL-SHIFT-C |
| Paste formatting | CTRL-SHIFT-V |
| Remove manual formatting | CTRL-SHIFT-Z or CTRL-SPACEBAR |
| Center a paragraph | CTRL-E |
| Left align a paragraph | CTRL-L |
| Right align a paragraph | CTRL-R |
| Indent a paragraph from the left | CTRL-M |
| Indent a paragraph from the right | CTRL-SHIFT-M |
| Apply a style | CTRL-SHIFT-S |
| Apply the Normal style | CTRL-SHIFT-N |
| Apply the Heading 1 style | CTRL-ALT-1 |
| Apply the Heading 2 style | CTRL-ALT-2 |
| Apply the Heading 3 style | CTRL-ALT-3 |

PART V

| | |
|---|---|
| Apply the Heading 4 style | CTRL-ALT-4 |
| Apply the Heading 5 style | CTRL-ALT-5 |
| Apply the Heading 6 style | CTRL-ALT-6 |
| Apply the List style | CTRL-SHIFT-L |

## Tools Menu Keystrokes

| | |
|---|---|
| Accessibility check | F8 |
| Check spelling on a page | F7 |
| Look up a word in the Thesaurus | SHIFT-F7 |
| Display, edit, or run macros | ALT-F8 |
| Display the Microsoft Script Editor | SHIFT-ALT-F11 |
| Display the Microsoft Visual Basic Editor | ALT-F11 |
| Create an Auto Thumbnail of a selected picture | CTRL-T |

## Table Menu Keystrokes

| | |
|---|---|
| Insert a table | SHIFT-CTRL-ALT-T |
| Select the next cell's contents | TAB |
| Select the preceding cell's contents | SHIFT-TAB |
| Extend a selection to adjacent cells | Hold down SHIFT and press an arrow key repeatedly |
| Select a column | Click in the column's top or bottom cell then hold down SHIFT and press the UP ARROW or DOWN ARROW key repeatedly |

## Help Menu Keystrokes

| | |
|---|---|
| Display the online Help | F1 |
| Display context-sensitive Help | SHIFT-F1 |

## Other Keystrokes

| | |
|---|---|
| Go to the beginning of the line | CTRL-SHIFT-LEFT ARROW |
| Select one character to the right | SHIFT-RIGHT ARROW |
| Select one character to the left | SHIFT-LEFT ARROW |

| | |
|---|---|
| Select to the end of a word | CTRL-SHIFT-RIGHT ARROW |
| Select to the end of a line | SHIFT-END |
| Select to the beginning of a line | SHIFT-HOME |
| Select one line down | SHIFT-DOWN ARROW |
| Select one line up | SHIFT-UP ARROW |
| Select to the end of a paragraph | CTRL-SHIFT-DOWN ARROW |
| Select to the beginning of a paragraph | CTRL-SHIFT-UP ARROW |
| Select one screen down | SHIFT-PAGE DOWN |
| Select one screen up | SHIFT-PAGE UP |
| Display the properties of a selection | ALT-ENTER |
| Cancel an action | ESC |
| Show the shortcut menu | SHIFT-F10 |
| Activate menu bar | F10 |
| Once active, select menu | RIGHT ARROW or LEFT ARROW |
| Once selected, open menu | DOWN ARROW |
| Select the next or previous command on the menu or submenu | UP ARROW or DOWN ARROW |
| Close the visible menu and submenu at the same time | ALT |
| Close the visible menu; or, with a submenu visible, close the submenu only | ESC |
| Open the program menu | ALT-SPACEBAR |

## Code View Keystrokes

| | |
|---|---|
| Go to line | CTRL - G |
| Autocomplete | CTRL - L |
| Insert code snippet | CTRL-ENTER |
| Insert start tag | CTRL-< |
| Insert end tag | CTRL-> |
| Insert HTML comment | CTRL-/ |
| Complete word | CTRL-SPACEBAR |
| Quick tab editor | CTRL-Q |
| Next bookmark | F2 |
| Last bookmark | SHIFT-F2 |

# Constructing Web Templates

In Chapter 4, you saw how to create a page template. You even created a web template (although it was stored with the page templates). Here you will see how to create and properly store a full web template. A web template is just a web (simply a group of pages) stored in a special folder on your hard disk. The next exercise will show you how to create and save a web to use as a template.

1. Open FrontPage and create a new web using the Empty Web template. Name the web (and the folder in which it will be stored) **Budget**.

---

**NOTE** *Dependent on which version of SharePoint (1 or 2) or just FrontPage Server Extensions (FPSE) you are using, where this folder and file are stored can vary. The general storage location is http://local server/Budget, but that does not tell you where to look for the files with Windows Explorer. With FPSE and/or SharePoint 1 (STS), the default physical location is C:\Inetpub\ wwwroot\. With SharePoint 2 (WSS), you need to look in either \My Documents\My Webs\ or C:\Document and Settings\user\NetHood\server\.*

---

2. In Navigation view, click New Page on the Navigation toolbar to create a page automatically named Home Page.

3. Right-click the Home Page in Navigation view and select Rename from the context menu. Type the new name, **Annual**, and press ENTER.

4. Click New Page again to add another page to your site. Click New Page three more times to create a total of five pages (the Home Page plus four more).

5. Click slowly twice (don't double-click) on each of the four pages in the Navigation pane and rename them **Q1**, **Q2**, **Q3**, and **Q4**, respectively.

---

**TIP** *Press TAB to accept the first new page name change. This simultaneously moves you to the next new page.*

---

6. Slowly click twice on the page names in the left Folder List pane, one at a time. (If you do not see the files, press F5 to refresh; if your Folder List is not displayed, choose Folder List from the View menu.) Rename them so the page with the title "Q1" has a filename of **qtr1.htm**, "Q2" has a filename of **qtr2.htm**, and so on. The file with the title "Annual" should be renamed **Default.htm**. When you have renamed and retitled your pages, your Folder List and Navigation view should look like Figure C-1.

7. After you have completed the Budget web that will be used as a template, edit the content and structure of each page in the template, just as you would if building a normal web.

**NOTE** *Depending on the content you create, your files and folders may not match the examples precisely.*

8. When you are happy with the web, save the Annual page (Default.htm) as a template (File | Save As, change the Save As Type to FrontPage Template, then click Save). In the Save As Template dialog box, change the Title to **Annual Budget**, change the Name to **Annual_Budget**, type **Create a quarterly budgeting model.** as the Description, click Save Template In Current Web Site, and click OK.

If you look at the FrontPage title bar, you will see that your template was saved to the C:\Documents and Settings\*username*\Application Data\Microsoft\FrontPage\Pages\Annual_Budget.tem (.t in Server 2003) folder in Windows 2000 XP, or Windows Server 2003. At this point, you have a normal web (not a template) of your full (five pages) Budget web that you want to be a template, and a single *page* template with the Annual page. To complete your web template, you need to import the special template pages into the original web, copy the web to the template Webs folder, and clean up several miscellaneous files.

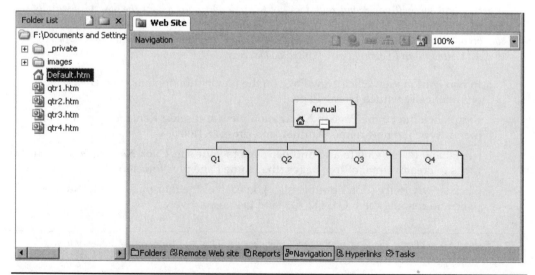

**FIGURE C-1**    Framework for budgeting macro

## Importing the Template Files

The easiest way to get the template files back into the original web is to import them. Do that now.

1. From the File menu, choose Close to close the newly created template page.

2. Open the File menu again and choose Import (expand the menu if necessary). The Import dialog box will open. Click Add File. The Add File To Import List dialog box will open.

3. Click the down arrow opposite Look In, select the C:\Documents and Settings\ *username*\Application Data\Microsoft\FrontPage\Pages\ Annual_Budget.tem folder, click Annual_Budget.dib, press CTRL, click Annual_Budget.inf, click Open, and then click OK. The two template files will be imported, and your Folders view will look like this:

| Name | Title | Size | Type | Modified Date | Modified By |
|------|-------|------|------|---------------|-------------|
| _private | | | | | |
| images | | | | | |
| Default.htm | Annual | 1KB | htm | 8/4/2003 8:12 AM | Administrator |
| qtr1.htm | Q1 | 1KB | htm | 8/4/2003 8:10 AM | Administrator |
| qtr2.htm | Q2 | 1KB | htm | 8/4/2003 8:10 AM | Administrator |
| qtr3.htm | Q3 | 1KB | htm | 8/4/2003 8:10 AM | Administrator |
| qtr4.htm | Q4 | 1KB | htm | 8/4/2003 8:11 AM | Administrator |
| _sharedtemplates | | | | | |
| annual budget.inf | annual budget.inf | 1KB | inf | 8/4/2003 9:07 AM | Administrator |
| annual budget.dib | annual budget.dib | 15KB | dib | 8/4/2003 9:07 AM | Administrator |

## Copying Files to Create a Web Template

Once you have created a web structure, you can transform it into a web template by copying all the files from the original folder to the web template folder, and modifying the special template files necessary for FrontPage to recognize the web as a template. You will copy and modify these files in Windows Explorer.

1. Locate the folder that holds all the files for the Budget web you just created. As was explained in an earlier note, this can be in several places. When you locate and open the folder, you'll see the five HTML files you created, as well as other folders that contain additional files used in FrontPage webs, as you see in Figure C-2. The FrontPage folders (not all of which are in the current web or all webs) are described in Table C-1.

2. Right-click the Budget web folder in the left pane of Windows Explorer, and select Copy from the context menu.

3. Click the folder where FrontPage web templates are stored to open it. If you used the default installation for FrontPage, this folder is C:\Documents and Settings\ *username*\Application Data\Microsoft\ FrontPage\Webs in Windows 2000 or XP.

PART V

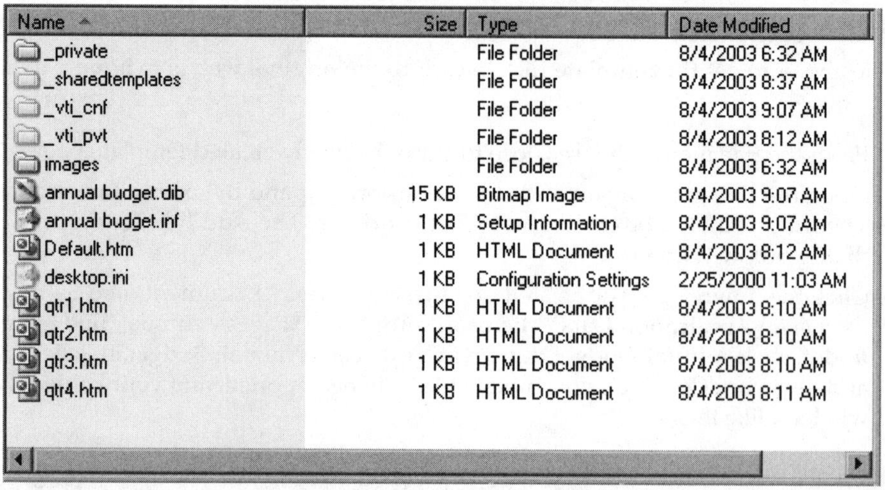

| Name ▲ | Size | Type | Date Modified |
|---|---|---|---|
| _private | | File Folder | 8/4/2003 6:32 AM |
| _sharedtemplates | | File Folder | 8/4/2003 8:37 AM |
| _vti_cnf | | File Folder | 8/4/2003 9:07 AM |
| _vti_pvt | | File Folder | 8/4/2003 8:12 AM |
| images | | File Folder | 8/4/2003 6:32 AM |
| annual budget.dib | 15 KB | Bitmap Image | 8/4/2003 9:07 AM |
| annual budget.inf | 1 KB | Setup Information | 8/4/2003 9:07 AM |
| Default.htm | 1 KB | HTML Document | 8/4/2003 8:12 AM |
| desktop.ini | 1 KB | Configuration Settings | 2/25/2000 11:03 AM |
| qtr1.htm | 1 KB | HTML Document | 8/4/2003 8:10 AM |
| qtr2.htm | 1 KB | HTML Document | 8/4/2003 8:10 AM |
| qtr3.htm | 1 KB | HTML Document | 8/4/2003 8:10 AM |
| qtr4.htm | 1 KB | HTML Document | 8/4/2003 8:11 AM |

**FIGURE C-2**    The Budget web with the files and folders it contains

4. With the Webs folder open in the right pane of Windows Explorer, right-click the right pane and select Paste from the context menu. You have now copied most of the files required for a template.

5. Right-click the new copy of the Budget folder, choose Rename, and change the name to Budget.tem.

| Folder | Contents |
|---|---|
| _borders | Includes up to four .HTM files that are embedded in each page with the content of top, bottom, right, or left Shared Borders |
| _private | Pages that you don't want available to a browser or to searches; for example, Included pages |
| _sharedtemplates | Templates used in the web |
| _vti_bin | FrontPage-created common gateway interface (CGI) programs for controlling browse-time behavior, administrator, and author operations on the server |
| _vti_cnf | A configuration page for every page in the web, containing the name of the page, the created-by and modified-by names, and the creation and modification dates, among other variables |
| _vti_pvt | Several subfolders with both the current and historical To Do List files, meta-information for the web, and the dependency database |
| _vti_script | Visual Basic and Java scripts used in the web |
| _vti_txt | Text indexes for use by the Search boxes |
| Images | All images associated with a web |

**TABLE C-1**    FrontPage Web Folder Structure

## Working with the INF and MAP Files

In addition to the files you already copied, you will need to add one file and modify another in order for FrontPage to detect and use your template web. You need to add the MAP file, which stores the navigational links that the web may contain, and modify the INF file, which stores the information used to list your template in the Web Site Templates dialog box.

1. Open the folder for a web template that comes with FrontPage: the Personal template. The path to the Personal folder is C:\Program Files\Microsoft Office\Templates\1033\Webs\Personal.tem.

2. With the Personal.tem folder open, click Personal.map, as shown next. Press CTRL-C to copy the file.

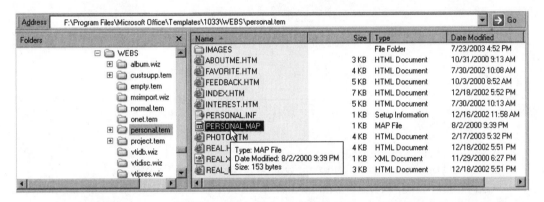

3. Open the new C:\Documents and Settings\\*username*\Application Data\Microsoft\ FrontPage\Webs\Budget.tem folder you just created, right-click the right pane, and choose Paste to paste the MAP file into this folder.

4. Right-click the Personal.map file and rename it **Budget.map**.

5. Right-click the Annual_Budget.inf file, rename it Budget.inf, double-click that file, and edit the contents using Notepad. The new contents of the file should look like this:

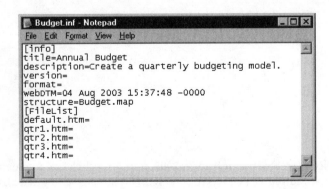

---

***Tip***   *The webDTM line is your current date/time stamp and doesn't have to match what is shown here.*

6. Save and close the Budget.inf file. Right-click the Annual_Budget.dib file and rename it Budget.dib.

7. Double-click the file Budget.map. If Windows does not recognize this file type, select Notepad as the application to open with MAP files.

8. Edit the file Budget.map so it looks like this (type the first line and then copy and change it for the other three lines):

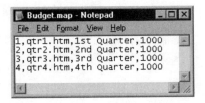

---

***Note***   *The MAP file changes the title of the page files from Q1, Q2, and so on, to 1st Quarter, 2nd Quarter, and so on.*

9. Save and close the Budget.map file. Now that you have finished the INF and MAP files in your folder, your template will be recognized by FrontPage.

10. In FrontPage, open the File menu and choose Close Site to close the original Budget web. Then click the down arrow next to the New button in the toolbar and choose Web Site to open the Web Site Templates dialog box. Click the My Templates tab, click Annual Budget, and your description will appear, as shown here:

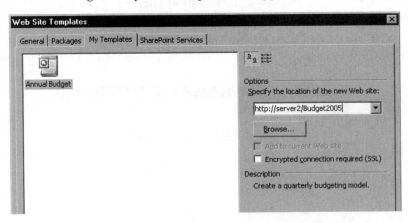

11. Enter a folder/web name of **Budget2005**, and then click OK to create a new web based on the template. The web opens with an already-designed structure and navigation links, all ready for you to customize the individual pages, as shown in Figure C-3 (your view might be different depending on the pages in your template).

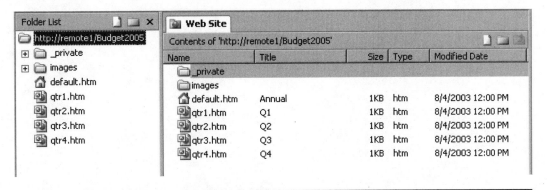

**FIGURE C-3**   A budget web created from the template

12. Delete the new web you just created and close FrontPage.

If your new web does not work as expected, look at the files in the template. Make sure all your files are placed where they should be and that the INF and MAP files look like those shown earlier. Since you have to edit the content of those files by hand, it's easy to make a typing mistake.

# Index

*References to figures and illustrations are in italics.*

# INTERNATIONAL CONTACT INFORMATION

**AUSTRALIA**
McGraw-Hill Book Company
Australia Pty. Ltd.
TEL +61-2-9900-1800
FAX +61-2-9878-8881
http://www.mcgraw-hill.com.au
books-it_sydney@mcgraw-hill.com

**CANADA**
McGraw-Hill Ryerson Ltd.
TEL +905-430-5000
FAX +905-430-5020
http://www.mcgraw-hill.ca

**GREECE, MIDDLE EAST, & AFRICA
(Excluding South Africa)**
McGraw-Hill Hellas
TEL +30-210-6560-990
TEL +30-210-6560-993
TEL +30-210-6560-994
FAX +30-210-6545-525

**MEXICO (Also serving Latin America)**
McGraw-Hill Interamericana Editores
S.A. de C.V.
TEL +525-1500-5108
FAX +525-117-1589
http://www.mcgraw-hill.com.mx
carlos_ruiz@mcgraw-hill.com

**SINGAPORE (Serving Asia)**
McGraw-Hill Book Company
TEL +65-6863-1580
FAX +65-6862-3354
http://www.mcgraw-hill.com.sg
mghasia@mcgraw-hill.com

**SOUTH AFRICA**
McGraw-Hill South Africa
TEL +27-11-622-7512
FAX +27-11-622-9045
robyn_swanepoel@mcgraw-hill.com

**SPAIN**
McGraw-Hill/
Interamericana de España, S.A.U.
TEL +34-91-180-3000
FAX +34-91-372-8513
http://www.mcgraw-hill.es
professional@mcgraw-hill.es

**UNITED KINGDOM, NORTHERN,
EASTERN, & CENTRAL EUROPE**
McGraw-Hill Education Europe
TEL +44-1-628-502500
FAX +44-1-628-770224
http://www.mcgraw-hill.co.uk
emea_queries@mcgraw-hill.com

**ALL OTHER INQUIRIES Contact:**
McGraw-Hill/Osborne
TEL +1-510-420-7700
FAX +1-510-420-7703
http://www.osborne.com
omg_international@mcgraw-hill.com

# Sound Off!

Visit us at **www.osborne.com/bookregistration** and let us know what you thought of this book. While you're online you'll have the opportunity to register for newsletters and special offers from McGraw-Hill/Osborne.

## We want to hear from you!

# Sneak Peek

Visit us today at **www.betabooks.com** and see what's coming from McGraw-Hill/Osborne tomorrow!

Based on the successful software paradigm, Bet@Books™ allows computing professionals to view partial and sometimes complete text versions of selected titles online. Bet@Books™ viewing is free, invites comments and feedback, and allows you to "test drive" books in progress on the subjects that interest you the most.

# Microsoft
# Office 2003
## *Answers for Everyone*

**Make the most of the entire Office system with help from these other books from Osborne**

How to Do Everything *with* **Microsoft Office PowerPoint 2003**

Create professional-quality presentations

Learn from real-world examples

Deliver your show on-screen or on the Web

Ellen Finkelstein

**How to Do Everything with Microsoft Office PowerPoint 2003**
0-07-222972-1

The Complete Reference

Microsoft Office 2003

Get expert advice and thorough coverage of Microsoft Office 2003 applications

Use words, figures, and graphics for more persuasive documents, spreadsheets, and presentations

Customize the Microsoft Office application settings to streamline your work

**Microsoft Office 2003: The Complete Reference**
0-07-222995-0

How to Do Everything *with* **Microsoft Office FrontPage 2003**

Design and publish your own Web site

Add graphics, sound, links, and movies to your site

Create interactive forms, guest books, and databases

David Plotkin

**How to Do Everything with Microsoft Office FrontPage 2003**
0-07-222973-X

Microsoft Office **Access 2003**

**Professional Results**

Perform enterprise-level database development and management

Learn to program .NET applications with Access 2003

Explore XML support and advanced query development

Download ready-to-use solutions

Noel Jerke, *author and consultant*

**Microsoft Access 2003 Professional Results**
0-07-222965-9

**Available at Bookstores everywhere**

OSBORNE DELIVERS RESULTS!

Mc Graw Hill **Osborne**